10-29-03

FB

KOOKS

KOOKS

Donna Kossy

FERAL HOUSE

ACKNOWLEDGEMENTS

I AM MOST INDEBTED TO THE FOLLOWING people, whose contributions were integral to this project: Ken DeVries and Nenslo for their encouragement, insight, inspiration, art, leads and constructive criticism; Adam Parfrey for the opportunity to write this book and for providing excellent source material and leads; Walter Minkel for generously lending crucial source material as well as critical comments on portions of the manuscript; Trevor Blake for support, leads and comments on portions of the manuscript; Barron for comments, discussions, sources, information and fun; and Dr. Ahmed Fishmonger for his vital contributions to *Kooks* Magazine, and whose unequalled fervor for kooks carried over into this book.

Thanks are also due to those who contributed articles and/or source material to *Kooks* Magazine, and to those who provided source material, information or leads specifically for the book: Dr. Agon, Walter Alter, Greg Bishop, John Bridgman, Bonnie Jo Campbell, Ed Castello, Rob Chalfen, T.S. Child, Tim Cridland, Richard Dengrove, Yael Dragwyla, Alex Eisenstein, Jason Fairchild, Tony Fitzgerald, Thomas Frick, R. Seth Friedman, Sally Frye, Andrew Gaze, Tom Gengler, Mike Gunderloy, David Hauptshein, Wayne Henderson, J-Hova-10, Janor Hypercleets, Matt & Melissa Jasper, John F. Kelly, Pagan Kennedy, Larry King (not the radio/TV personality), Jay Kinney, Lee Knutson, John Kohut, Barbara Kossy, John Kuhlman, Everett Long, Tom Lyttle, Chris Magson, Tim Maloney, John Marr, Paul Mavrides, Scott Murphy, David Nestle, Steve Ross, Woody Russell, Paul Rydeen, Joe Schwind, Billy Sol, Rev. Ivan Stang, Skippy Stone, and Kerry Wendell Thornley. There are also many people who generously provided flyers, books, addresses and letters over the past ten years, whose names I may have missed, or who sent them anonymously.

Special thanks to Bernie Bane, Richard Kieninger, Les U. Knight, Paul Laffoley, Kathy Marquis and Tim Wilhelm for interviews.

The author may be contacted at:
PO Box 13067
Los Angeles, CA 90013

Feral House
PO Box 13067
Los Angeles, CA 90013

8 7 6 5 4 3 2 1

Feral House is distributed by
Publishers Group West

Copyediting provided by
Stephen J. Beard

CONTENTS

INTRODUCTION

RESEARCH FOR THIS BOOK BEGAN TEN YEARS ago when, living in San Francisco, I became the recipient of countless home-made flyers handed to me and other passers-by on the street. If they were advertisements for bands or announcements of a grand opening I would have thrown them away immediately, but these dense tracts were desperate pleas from the victims of mind control, or mad saints who detailed a theory that would solve all the world's problems, or obsessed litigants who described their legal quandaries with the aid of inexplicable numerical equations. Handwritten or typed, their authors usually covered every inch of space on the paper, no matter its size. These flyers were so intriguing that I couldn't throw them away, even though I didn't really know what to do with them.

When in 1984 I began to publish a little xeroxed magazine called *False Positive* I finally found a home for the tracts. I reprinted them, either whole or in part, and called this section of the magazine the "Kooks Pages." I realized that my collection was too small to sustain an on-going kooks section, and suggested that those with similar material could send it to me. Soon, readers were mailing literally boxes full of books, pamphlets and flyers, and my apartment became Kooks Central.

After the eleventh issue of *False Positive,* I finally realized that my readers were more interested in kooks than anything else. So was I. I laid the old typed and xeroxed rag to rest, and in 1989 started *The Original Donna Kossy's Kooks Magazine* (later renamed *Kooks Magazine).* By this time, my "kooks files" were bulging and my brain was reeling, but I was having fun. The new magazine, now devoted exclusively to kooks, contained not only reproductions of found kook material but fully researched articles on the subject. It occurred to me that I had the makings of a book.

I envisioned my *magnum opus* as the result of thirty years of scholarly research. I pictured myself hunched over crumbling manuscripts and antiquarian books in the life-long pursuit of solving the mystery of kooks. My office would be in the corner of a "Kooks Museum," located in a crumbling industrial area, accessed by climbing a rickety stairway. The museum would be one large room crowded with ancient perpetual motion devices, glass cases containing diagrams and manuscripts providing solutions to the World Riddle, bookcases overstuffed with self-published tomes, and filing cabinets bursting with the ephemera of fevered visionaries. My thirty years of solitary research would result in a book which would definitively explain the causes and nature of belief, and might even contain a new theory of reality.

Well, this isn't that book. I haven't even the faintest idea of what "reality" is.

But kooks do — or at least they say they do — and that is why I am consulting them on the matter. Before looking at the kooks themselves, it may be useful to define what I mean by the term "kook," and my reason for a kook's inclusion or exclusion.

The word "kook" was coined by the beatniks as a pared-down version of "cuckoo," as in "going cuckoo." A kook is a person stigmatized by virtue of outlandish, extreme or socially unacceptable beliefs that underpin their entire existence. Kooks usually don't keep their beliefs to themselves; they either air them constantly or create lasting monuments to them.

Though I have great affection for kooks, the term is usually used by others on a pejorative basis; the word is often invoked but rarely aimed at oneself. Granted, there are people, self-styled or corporate-styled bohemians, who by virtue of their desire to belong to a particular in-crowd, call themselves kooks as easily as saying, "I'm weird" or "I'm crazy." I am not concerned here with a trendy or self-conscious usage of the term.

Being assigned kook status is inherently a matter of perspective, relative to history and culture. A kook of the 19th century might become a scientific hero in the 20th. Take the example of geologist Alfred Wegener (1880-1930), who hypothesized continental drift. In his day, Wegener's theory was dismissed as a "fairy tale." More recently he is honored for originating the theory of plate tectonics. More frequently, a person presumed to be a genius in a previous century is regarded a kook in today's. In the 19th century, phrenologists were as respectable as psychiatrists are today.

Similarly, the beliefs and mores of one culture are mocked as kooky or even sinister by another. On a large scale, the projection of these attitudes can mobilize millions into warfare or cause governments to deploy military assaults against "cults."

What distinguishes "kook" from other dismissive and stigmatizing terms? The various words denoting insanity — "crazy," "psychotic," "schizophrenic," etc. — are not, for my purposes, interchangeable with "kook." An obsessed murderer may be considered psychopathic or crazy, but more often than not these words categorize action, not belief. The obsessed serial killer is not necessarily a kook.

We must also distinguish kooks from quacks, frauds and hoaxers, for kooks are invariably sincere. Their main intent is not to deceive or defraud; to the contrary, they are trying to impart an essential truth. A kook's thoughts rarely turn to profit; some squander personal fortunes to investigate or spread The Word. A New Age personality who channels a wise entity from the Pleiades is not a kook if his channeled voice is designed to attract funds.

Finally, it is important to differentiate a kook from an eccentric. An eccentric is defined as someone with an unorthodox lifestyle, which may or may not include unorthodox beliefs. Is a hermit a kook? Can we call a scatological fetishist a kook? Not necessarily, especially if they haven't codified their own preferences as an eternal truth.

Outside of their value as a kind of intellectual side-show, why should we care what kooks have to say? They are kooks, after all.

There is a tendency common to those who define the boundaries of reality — scientists, religious figures and politicians — to dismiss countervaling beliefs as a delusion or hallucination. A kook's desperation becomes more vivid as he or she is nudged into a psychic Siberia, their ideas ridiculed, shunned, or, worse, ignored. By writing kooks off, the experts ignore the role that they themselves are playing as enforcers of the status quo, completely missing the social implications of the existence of kooks.

Martin Gardner has written many books on what he calls "pseudoscience." Therein he presents prosecutorial briefs on those he claims are not legitimate scientists. As science's representative, Gardner is explaining — but primarily reinforcing — its rules for entry. Gardner, in addition to the Committee for the Scientific Investigation of Claims of the Paramormal (CSICOP) have contributed a significant body of research on purveyors of fringe and unorthodox ideas. I appreciate their work enormously. However, their main motive is to suppress the possible contagion of a contrary notion.

In contrast, my purpose in putting together *Kooks* is neither to debunk nor to proselytize. My intent is similar to those who study folklore and mythology.

By documenting lives and ideas that might otherwise be lost in the onrushing tide of the dominant paradigm, we may be able to examine the process by which an idea comes to marshal its forces. Perhaps we will come to appreciate the subtleties and gradations of human inspiration. In addition, we may be able to overcome an ingrained xenophobia of the mind.

For this book I've included raw material, reproductions of flyers and handouts. I have also re-typeset and excerpted texts that were too unwieldy or difficult to read in their virgin form. I also found it important to provide historical context to kooks and notable kook themes, integrating the original material in lengthier articles.

Kooks is structured thematically, and it was a struggle to decide in which category to place several personalities. For example, most people who believe in the hollow earth also believe in some kind of UFO conspiracy as well. The ideology may also include anti-Semitism, the coming Apocalypse and general obsession with biblical themes. Is this "Science," "Religion," or "Conspiracy?" The article on Norma Cox, for example, could have easily gone into any of these sections. So, I asked myself, "What makes Norma Cox unique?" and realized that it was her Universal Conspiracy theory that set her apart from the other hollow earth believers; thus, I put the article in the "Conspiracy" section.

In my early study of kooks, the many ideas seemed so outlandish that I read great originality into pieces that liberally borrowed from other kook literature. Over the years, as I saw more and more kook literature I noticed a great deal of repetition, borrowing and overlap. It became obvious that in the early days I took the ideas to be different only because I hadn't seen them before. Now it has become almost impossible to find anyone whose beliefs really are different. All belief systems — no matter how unorthodox — follow definite patterns and exhibit recurrent themes.

There are certain themes and concepts which circulate more than others. Sadly, it seems that the most unattractive ones are the most popular. Anti-Semitism, I think wins the prize as the most pervasive kook belief. Even those whose overriding passion has nothing to do with anti-Semitism — such as the Space Brothers or the Hollow Earth — end up explaining it all as an International, or even Intergalactic Jewish Conspiracy. The second prize goes to belief in the biblical Book of Revelation, interpreted in any number of different ways. Even New Agers who claim to adhere to a completely new religion show their true colors when they start talking about Jesus and the Battle of Armageddon.

What all this proves is that kooks are not as isolated as we might think. Ideas discredited by powerful institutions are often driven underground to the realm of kookdom. Many kooky ideas have a long history. Some of the articles here trace this history ("The Flat Earth," "The Anglo-Israelites") and others contain episodes from that history ("The End of the World"), and still others only hint at it.

Those who read this book with even a passing familiarity with the subject will feel that I've left someone out. I am forced to be selective, and the selections won't please everyone. I've excluded Jack T. Chick, Lyndon LaRouche, Nikola Tesla, Roky Erikson, Richard Shaver and Charles Manson. There are no sections on Free Energy, the occult roots of Nazism, or Dianetics. As much as I would have liked to cover something like Free Energy, for example, my understanding of physics is limited. More famous subjects, L. Ron Hubbard for example, are covered adequately elsewhere. A book that covered every important kook or even every important kook area, would be an encyclopedia.

Finding current kook literature is almost effortless. As Rev. Ivan Stang puts it in *High Weirdness by Mail,* "Simply by writing for information ... you can embark on a never-ending tour of the zoo of beliefs, the circus of gullibility, the freak show of faith, the arena of the utter strangeness of true genius, of that which is all-too-literally ahead of its time." To find current addresses, simply browse the classified ad sections of magazines that kooks might read (I've found some good ones in *Fate, Gnosis* and *Biblical Archeology Review).* Addresses may also be found on books and on posted flyers. *High Weirdness* was once a good source, but now most of the addresses listed there are obsolete. In any case, once you get on a few mailing lists, or order some literature, it will be difficult not to receive large amounts of kook mail.

Kooks are everywhere. Keep alert to their presence, or their products, in thrift stores, used book stores, libraries and even new book stores. Don't shun the odd-looking character passing out fistfuls of paper. Search promising lamp-posts for messages from God. Listen to the street preachers and collect their tracts.

This nebulous sort of research can take on a life of its own. For example, shortly after beginning work on this book I was rummaging in a small thrift store and came upon an old volume called *Lawsonomy,* by Alfred Lawson. I thought it was very promising, but I lacked further information. Just a week after that, a correspondent sent me a leaflet from the people who currently publish Lawson's works. And soon after I noticed an old newspaper article on Lawson in one of the magazines I had recently ordered. Then, also within this very short period of time, a friend sent me a copy of an article on Lawson. All the information I needed to get me started on Lawson literally flew towards me, as if I were a magnet. This kind of thing has happened repeatedly. My conclusion is that the greater forces, whatever they are, wanted me to write this book.

I hope that *Kooks* will entertain you, but more importantly, I hope it will cause you to become more aware of your own beliefs, where they came from, how you acquired them, why you keep them.

Because potentially we are all kooks.

— Donna Kossy
January, 1994

PART I

RELIGION

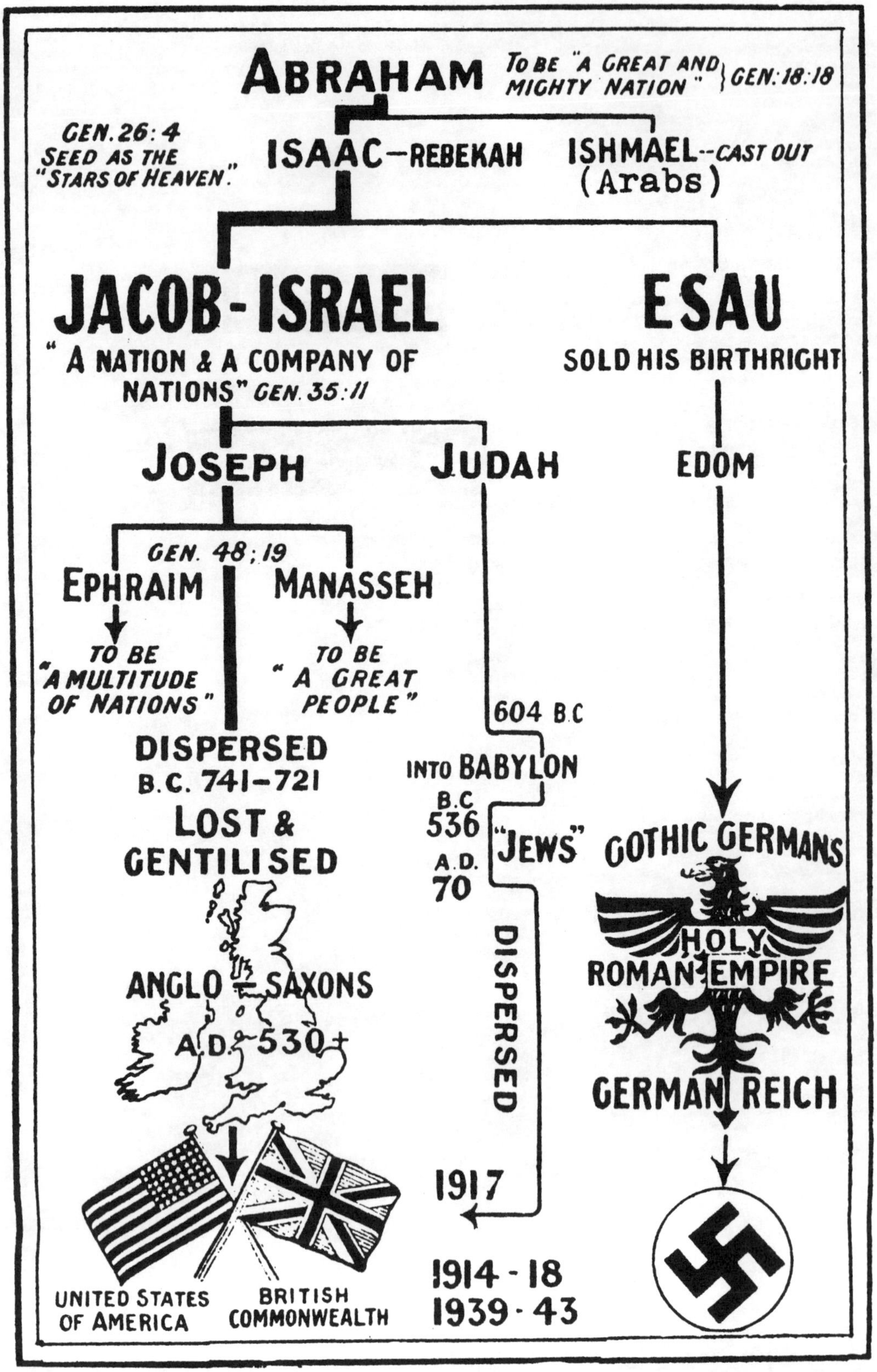

The Anglo-Israelite bloodline; from Joseph Jeffers' tract, "Yahweh -- Yesterday, Today and Tomorrow."

THE ANGLO-ISRAELITES

ANGLO-ISRAELISM BEGAN AS THE RAVINGS of a "harmless madman" but today has thousands of adherents, including Idahoan **Randy Weaver,** who shot it out with agents of the "Zionist Occupation Government" in 1992, resulting in the death of a U.S. Marshall and Weaver's son and wife.[1] The Anglo-Israelites of various persuasions, both in England and the United States, believe that the modern Anglo-Saxons are the direct descendents of the Ten Lost Tribes of Israel, and are therefore "God's Chosen People." The variations on this belief, for the most part, concern the "true" origins of Anglo-Israelites' apparent competition, the present-day Jews.

The above-mentioned harmless madman, **Richard Brothers** (1757-1824), born in Newfoundland, joined the British Navy, and while at sea discovered that his wife had been living with another man; devastated, he retired at half-pay at the age of 30 and moved to London. Styling himself "Prince of the Hebrews and Nephew of the Almighty," in 1794 Brothers published a two-volume work, *A Revealed Knowledge of the Prophecies and Times,* predicting the millennium would begin on November 19, 1795, and that he would personally lead the Ten Lost Tribes of Israel back to Jerusalem. The book was popular, stimulating debate throughout England, and, for Brothers, a following among its readers. Brothers announced that as a descendent of King David he was the rightful heir to the British Throne, but King George II was not amused. Six months before his announced apocalypse was to take place Brothers was committed to a lunatic asylum. His incarceration, however, didn't prevent his ideas from spreading to more respectable citizens.

Anglo-Israelism might well have developed without Brothers, for the idea that England and Israel are intimately connected goes back at least to the 17th century. The more extreme English Puritans of that time believed they were God's Chosen People, the Old Testament Hebrews reincarnated, and chose appropriate biblical names for their children. In 1653, "Praisegod Barebone" and other members of Cromwell's "Little Parliament" replaced the English constitution with the Old Testament Laws of Moses. Cromwell told his parliament that God's message to Israel in the 68th Psalm was addressed to them; they were chosen by God to preside over the establishment of His rule on earth.

The Anglo-Israelites go much further than the Puritans, believing their link with Israel to be historical as well as spiritual. They regard the scholar **John Wilson,** who in 1840 published *Our Israelitish Origin,* as the true "Father of the Rediscovery of Israel," since he provided the Israel-obsessed Britains with a "scientific" foundation. His theory was that the modern Europeans, particularly the Anglo-Saxons, are the progeny of Scythian tribes, who could presumably be traced to the Ten Lost Tribes of Israel. Several scholars of his day embraced Wilson's theories; he was not generally thought of as a crank. But it wasn't until a certain **Edward Hine** discovered Wilson that his theories became the basis for a religious crusade.

At the age of fifteen, Edward Hine had attended one of Wilson's lectures, and forever after became a crusader for British Israel. Hine's own version of Wilson's theory, which he eventually came to call "Identity," was that the British, but not the other Europeans, were the true children of Israel. The Germans had the distinction of their own biblical identity, descending from the Assyrians.

Wilson, Hine, and other Anglo-Israelites of their time were not anti-Semites. They viewed Jews as their brethren under the same almighty God. In fact, Hine believed that as soon as the rest of the British discovered their true identity as the Ten Lost Tribes of Israel, they would join the tribes of Judah and Levi (the Jews) in the Holy Land; the reunion of the 12 tribes was a precondition for the second coming of Jesus, which would soon follow.

Later, those who hated Jews rationalized their feelings in modified versions of the orig-

The Anglo-Israelites of John Wilson and Edward Hine's time were not anti-Semites. They viewed Jews as their brethren under the same almighty God.

1. Anglo-Israelism is also known as "British-Israelism," "Christian Identity," and, in the U.S., "Destiny of America."

inal theory. Hine paved the way for this bigotry with his extremely liberal interpretations of the bible. In time, virtually any bigotry could be justified by identifying the hated group with the various biblical enemies of Israel, such as Canaanites, Amorites, Assyrians and Jebusites.

Howard B. Rand

Hine's *Forty-Seven Identifications of the British Nation with the Lost Ten Tribes of Israel,* published in 1874, correlates biblical Israel with the British Empire of his day. He singles out Jeremiah's vision, in which The God of Israel tells His children that He would save their remnant and "bring them from the north country, and gather them from the coasts of the earth ..." (Jeremiah 31:8). "Hear the word of the Lord, O ye nations, and declare it in the isles afar off ..." (Jeremiah 31:10). These vague references, most likely included in the bible to prophesy that the seed of Israel would be scattered far and wide, told a different story to Hine. His novel interpretation was that latter-day Israel must be a nation that resides on *islands* located to the *north* of Palestine. Reading deeply into other biblical passages, he concluded that this nation would be in possession of a declining international empire whose peoples are physically and culturally distinct from the Jews. This nation, of course, was Britain.

Hine was not enamored of the non-Anglo tenants of the British Empire. He was convinced that not only the Australian Aborigines, the Maoris and the American Indians, but particularly the Irish were on their way to extinction. The Irish, Hine reasoned, are really the Canaanites, described in the Book of Numbers, who "dwell by the sea" (Numbers 13:29), the arch-enemies of the Israelites. They, of course will be struck down, along with the rest of British-Israel's enemies.

Hine's movement was confined to the U.K. until he embarked in 1884 on the world's first Anglo-Israelite mission, to North America. The purpose of Hine's tour was to convince North Americans they were the descendants of the tribe of Manasseh. Hine gained several disciples, including **General Winfield Scott Hancock,** who had been the 1880 Democratic candidate for President, losing against James A. Garfield. He visited **Charles Latimer,** a practitioner of dowsing, who published the magazine *International Standard,* which contained rants against the metric system based on his studies of the Great Pyramid of Giza. Attempts to convince Latimer to publish a British-Israelite magazine did not succeed.

Hine's mission, particularly among non-English speaking German and Polish immigrants in Buffalo, met with failure. The Baltic immigrants who understood Hine were unmoved by the news that the Anglo-Saxons were God's Chosen People. Hine became destitute, returned home, and died three years later.

But the Anglo-Israelite seeds had been planted. One of the earliest American Anglo-Israelite treatises was *Two Sticks, or the Lost Tribes of Israel Discovered,* by an anonymous minister in the Church of the Brethren. But it was **J.H. Allen's** *Judah's Sceptre and Joseph's Birthright,* published in 1902, that introduced Anglo-Israel to Adventists and Independent bible students, among them **Herbert W. Armstrong,** who would later spread the doctrine through his Worldwide Church of God. Not until the 1920s would Anglo-Israelism capture a large audience in the U.S.

In 1928, **Howard B. Rand** (1889-1991) — who would become Anglo-Israelism's foremost crusader on this side of the Atlantic — founded the Anglo-Saxon Federation of America, and appointed himself its National Commissioner.

Prior to his involvement in Anglo-Israelism, Rand had been a lawyer, inventor and small businessman in his home town of Haverhill, Massachusetts. A solid citizen, Rand lent a veneer of respectability to the Anglo-Israelite cause. His contribution to the literature was considerable; after a stint as crusader and lecturer on behalf of Anglo-Israelism during the 1930's, Rand settled into his role as publisher and writer for the movement. Destiny Publishers, which he started in 1937, is still printing the newsletter *Special Alert,* as well as hundreds of books and pamphlets. Apparently, Rand made some effort to enter public service; in 1944, 1946, 1950 and 1952, Rand was the Prohibition Party candidate for Attorney General of Massachusetts.

One of Rand's accomplishments was to smoothly integate anti-Judaism with Anglo-Israelite ideology. His account of the history of the Jews, based on the Old Testament, begins with the separation of the tribe of Judah, who resided in the Southern Kingdom, from the rest of Israel. The Northern Kingdom, or House of Israel, was overthrown and the Israelites were carried away into captivity by the Assyrians. Meanwhile, the House of Judah was kept intact for 130 years, until decadence and rebellion compelled God to send the Babylonians to attack them. They were conquered and taken into captivity, remaining in Babylonia for 70 years. "It was at the time of the captivity of the Southern Kingdom that the term 'Jew' began to be used and it applied only to the remnant of Judah (II Kings 18:26; Jer. 41:3)." This "remnant" returned to Jerusalem and "the Nation of the Jews came into being." Therefore, Rand claims, the Jews are descended only from the Southern Kingdom of Judah and do not constitute the whole of Israel. Furthermore, "the remnant who returned to Palestine ... intermarried with the Hittites and other Gentile people ..." When the Temple in Jerusalem was destroyed in 70 A.D. the "Nation of the Jews" ceased to exist, but various individual Jews scattered and intermarried with tribes such as the Khazars. Reasoned Rand, the people referred to as Jews today are basically frauds, if they claim to be the Israelites, God's Chosen People of the bible.

Meanwhile, according to Rand in Destiny Publishers' "Statement of Belief," the rest of the Israelites who had been captured by the Assyrians began to migrate to the west, ending up in Europe, Scandinavia and the British Isles. They were now known as the Scutai, Sak-Geloths, Massagetae, Khumri, Cimmerians, Goths, Ostrogoths and Visigoths. It is implicit in various Destiny publications that these tribes, as opposed to the Judeans, managed to remain "intact." It never occurred to Rand to ask why the pure tribes changed their names, while impure Jews kept theirs. Be that as it may, the tribes lived in ignorance of their true identity for 2000 years. It wasn't until the End Times, which began in 1821 and will end in 2001, that "God's Kingdom people began to be identified with the Anglo-Saxon-Celtic and kindred peoples." In these latter days, the old "Gentile" order is in the process of disintegration, and "will be replaced by the restoration of the Kingdom of God on the earth," with the Anglo-Israelites at the helm.

A lawyer, inventor, and small businessman, Howard Rand lent a veneer of respectability to the Anglo-Israelite cause.

Most Anglo-Israelite literature takes the form of biblical interpretation; the slim evidence for identification between Britain and Israel is taken straight from the bible. Anglo-Israelites claim, however, that evidence comes not only from the bible, but also from archaeology, heraldry, ethnology and philology. You might be surprised to find out that the word "SAXON" is actually derived from "SAAC'S SONS" which was derived from "ISAAC'S SONS." And "BRITISH" is from "BERITH-ISH" because in Hebrew, "BERITH" means "covenant," and "ISH" means "man," and therefore, "BRITISH" really means "MEN OF THE COVENANT." Try as you may, you'll never find these root-meanings in the *Oxford English Dictionary*.

Rand's Destiny publications repeatedly claim that they do not disparage other races and that the Anglo-Saxons' status as the Chosen People is not a claim of superiority, but rather a "burden" and a "responsibility," and that the Anglo-Saxons were chosen for "special service," phrases uncannily similar to "White Man's Burden." Despite protestations to the contrary, the literature is pervaded with sentiment against the Jews as well as arguments for racial segregation.

Rand's post-war booklet, *Palestine: Center of World Intrigue,* predicts the Jews' days are numbered. "God has declared that He will visit upon [the Jews] the type of suffering they have been instrumental in bringing upon others ... They will be numbered for the sword and will bow down to slaughter." He had calculated, based on General Allenby's capture of Jerusalem in 1917, that Armageddon was to take place in 1953, in

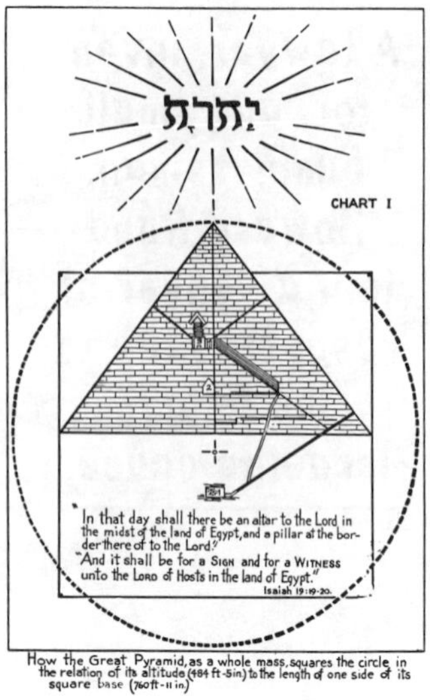

Anglo-Israelite Pyramidology, From *Miracle of the Ages*

Jerusalem. Rand thought that the post-war migration of Jews to Israel was God's round-up for execution.

Rand is mild compared to those who see the Jews not as remnants of Judah, but as the offspring of various "wild tribes," most often the "Mongol Chazars." **R.H. Sawyer** declares, in the booklet, *The Jewish Question,* that those who did descend from Judah disobeyed God and intermarried with Canaanites, Hittites, and other "inferior races."

A 1985 Destiny Publications booklet authored by **"Wm. Norman Saxon"** entitled *The Mask of Edom,* describes the International Conspiracy to hide the false identity of the Jews and the true identity of the Israelites. The Jews are actually the progeny of Esau, the bad brother of Jacob — not Judah. Furthermore, these descendants of Esau intermarried with Hittites, and were joined by converts from the Edomites, Amalekites and Canaanites. "...these Shelanite-Jebusite Canaanites who returned to Jerusalem with the remnant of real Judaites from Babylon, and who took over and corrupted the nation of the Jews, were but a small part of the Babylonian conspirators who had palmed themselves off as the Diaspora or 'Dispersion of the Jews.'"

Eventually, "Babylon became the real headquarters of Judaism. The Jews' masquerade as the LORD's chosen people is undoubtedly the greatest hoax in history. This is the basis of the anti-God conspiracy ... If [the Jews] could foist themselves off on the world as Israel, their grandiose ambitions for world dominion would be greatly enhanced ..." Saxon goes on to emphasize the inferior pedigree of the Jews, quoting from **Lothrop Stoddard,** author of the 1926 treatise, *The Pedigree of Judah.* Professor Stoddard's choice of words suggest vermin, as did the 1938 Nazi propaganda film, *Der Ewige Jude,* which intersplices footage of Jews with swarming rats.

> Lured to the Khazaria as to the Promised Land, Jewry pushed northward from Asia into southeastern Europe — swarming in by the hundred thousand, by sea, by river, and by mountain trail ... This migration involved sweeping racial changes. In the first place, Jewry's slow progress through the Armenian and Caucasian highlands implied a further admixture and strengthening of the Armenoid at the expense of the Semitic element. Then, once in Khazaria, the extensive inter-marriage with the converted Khazars resulted in a further influx of Turkish and Mongoloid blood ...

Saxon's obsession with racial impurity goes further than Rand, but nowhere near as far as **Jonathan Ellsworth Perkins,** who claims in *Jesus Was Not a Jew* that the Son of God is Anglo-Saxon.

In yet another variation, the Anglo-Saxons are shown to be direct descendants of the "Hyksos," or the "Shepherd Kings." According to **Worth Smith,** the author of a 1934 book on the Great Pyramid of Egypt, the Hyksos were the first believers in the One True God, the builders of the Egyptian Pyramids, and, later, the twelve tribes of Israel. Smith presents measurements within the Great Pyramid that correspond to biblical references and constitute "overwhelming proof" of the relationship between the Hyksos and Israel. Later in the book Smith reveals that the Great Pyramid foretold (among other things) the outbreak of World War One, specifically England's entry into it. Smith's imaginative readings of the links between pyramidology and English history lead to his breathless conclusion that, "... it is a definitely established truth to informed and discerning minds that the Anglo-Saxon (the people of the British Empire and the United States of America) *is the direct blood-descendant of the mighty Hyksos!"* And furthermore, this truth is encoded within the Great Seal of these fair United States of America, which depicts an *unfinished* pyramid — missing its apex stone. All this leads to Smith's rapturous conclusion:

> But of far greater importance to all men is another discovery of kindred nature, a gem of supernal wisdom which gleams forth from the exhibit cited like a lone planet thru a small rift in the storm-clouds that obscure all else on a dismal night. It is this: both the Great Pyramid and the Great Seal of the United States of America emblazon in the understanding mind the sublime allegory of the builders' error in that mystical "house not built with hands, eternal in the heavens," as featured very prominently in the Holy Bible, the Great Light, in numerous places, Jesus

the Christ being the "Stone that the builders rejected".

Despite their belief that they were God's Chosen, Rand and his successors did not secede from society at large. Instead, they sought to make their views acceptable to mainstream Christianity.

On the other hand, **Dr. Joseph Jeffers** (1898-1988) and his flock, variously named "Kingdom Temple," "Kingdom of Yahweh," and "Yahweh's New Kingdom," have never shied away from cultish practices, and on several occasions courted infamy. They subscribe to Anglo-Israelism, but also to "Yahwism," which holds that The Lord, God of Israel is not just plain "God," that He has a name, "Yahweh," that his son also had a name, "Yahoshua," and that Yahweh and his son are very particular that you address them by their names.

Jeffers, who began preaching Yahwism in the 1930's, claims to have been the first minister in America to do so. He points out, however, in his pamphlet *Yahweh, Yesterday, Today and Tomorrow,* that:

The Kingdom of Yahweh is not a new organization. It is the continuation of Yahweh's original Kingdom, which was covenanted with Abraham, Isaac and Jacob; later continued by David and Solomon. After becoming disorganized under the reign of Solomon's sons, Jereboam and Rheaboam, it was re-established when the Master of Justice, or Messiah, was born. Toward the end of his lifetime, Yahweh then promised that in the "end of the Age" or aeon, or approximately 2068 years, His Kingdom would be re-established again. I believe that the 20th Century is the END OF THE AGE.

This is what Jeffers calls "The Aquarian Age"; indeed, his *Kingdom Voice* newsletters reflect a New Age flavor, containing channeled messages from Yahweh along with an obsession with naturopathic health cures that still seems to enchant the Identity crowd.

Jeffers fancied himself a prophet, a distinction that he alone deserved because of his first-name intimacy with the Creator.

The preachers today have lost the art of prophecy because they have lost contact with YAHWEH. They preach in the names of Baal. How can the blind lead the blind? In the Old Testament alone, the translators were guilty 6,823 times of forgery, whey they substituted "The Lord" and "God" for the proper and sacred Name of YAHWEH. In Genesis alone, the personal Name YAHWEH occurs 156 times. (Kingdom of Yahweh, "The True Name.")

Jeffers boasted of a 98% accuracy rate on his predictions; in July of 1962, he prophesied the assassination of President Kennedy, only one of many dire predictions.

Nearly four years before it took place, we predicted the day and hour that Hitler would come into power ... For years we have given the weather-conditions all over the country. We have told of droughts, floods, famine, hurricanes and earthquakes, and we have told where they would take place ... The late Dr. Helene Jeffers announced the coming assassination of Mahatma Gandhi six months before it happened. (Quoted in the November 25, 1963 *Phoenix News-Gazette.)*

In July, 1962, Joseph Jeffers prophesied the assassination of President Kennedy.

As with his fellow Anglo-Israelites, Jeffers taught that various odd groups — including Native Americans — are direct descendents of the Hebrews. His tract, *The Indians worshipped Yahweh,* based on a 1775 British book by **James Adair** entitled *The History of the American Indians,* contains very good examples of the kind of logic involved in arguing the Anglo-Israelite case:

We know from what Yahweh has told us that the Ten Lost Tribes of Israel actually did not disappear, but became the Anglo-Saxon, Celtic, Scandinavian and kindred peoples. The Tribe of Dan, for instance, left its mark wherever it went. For example, DANmark, DarDANelles, DANube, LonDAN, SweDAN, etc. were all named by the people of the tribe of Dan.

Many other peoples descended from the Hebrews ... The Japanese and Chinese, Yahweh says, actually came from the sons and daughters of Lot ...When Eve seduced Adam, she gave birth to a white child who took a wife from neighboring people. They, in turn, had offspring who left the tribes of Yahweh because they knew they were different and they started out for another land. They journeyed and settled where the Americas are today.

Adair had lived with American Indians and, like many in his day, interpreted their practices in the only manner he knew. Biblically.

While His Devoted Followers Mourned, the Ex-Potentate of Kingdom Temple Abandoned His Trip to Paradise and, Instead, Rode Straight Into Jail in the Hotly Fought-Over "Golden Chariot of Kingdom Come."

Jail For Mr. Jeffers Via His Golden Chariot

The Romantic Prophet and His Pretty Blond Goddess Started Out for "Kingdom Come" in a Gasless Buggy, but the Celestial Journey Ended When His Ex-Wife Dug Up a Four-Year Legal Detour

THE Golden Chariot of Kingdom Come, which burns non-rationed butane gas instead of gasoline, is back where it belongs. Joe Jeffers, who founded the Kingdom Temple in Los Angeles because he believes he is a reincarnated deity, is where the government says he belongs—in Punta Gorda prison, Florida, for a four-year stretch.

And all because Joe, who has a penchant for pretty young women, proposed to take a beautiful platinum blonde out into the desert to become the mother of his "sacred child."

When Joe and the blonde and three other followers set out from Los Angeles in the golden chariot, everybody thought the desert goal would be in Arizona or New Mexico. But they landed in Florida. And when Joe was sentenced the other day in Miami for theft of the chariot, he explained the switch by predicting that a drought would make at least a part of Florida fit the desert specifications.

Joe, who looks only a little more than half of his 47 years, has been a notable figure in his field for a long time. Since he was ordained a minister in 1918, he has been shot at in many places, but never hit. He has coughed his way out of tear gas-filled tents and watched another go up in flames. He led a jail delivery to free a follower in Arkansas and left town just before a killing which police attributed to an emotional upset that followed some of his meetings.

Then he went on a European honeymoon with his wife, Joy, and, after being entertained for some time in Berlin, went along in a taxi as a spectator when the Nazi legions invaded Czechoslovakia.

After he had founded the Kingdom Temple in Los Angeles, he was accused of pro-Nazi "prophecies." He and his wife were also accused of appearing at ritualistic ceremonies in the temple draped in American Flags, which is strictly out of form.

But Joe's fondness for his younger female followers — particularly the slim, blond Helen Veborg—eventually annoyed Joy Jeffers. She sued for divorce and got one. She was also awarded the family car, a raky eight-cylinder job which had been converted to butane and was referred to by the papers as the Golden Chariot of Kingdom Come.

Other members of the cult thought the car should belong to the temple and not to their leader's ex-wife. At the Miami trial, one of them, Sam King, told the court that he heard a voice from Orion—their name for Heaven—and another, Mildred Whitmore, said she saw pictures in the air telling them to take the car for the work of the cult.

Joe wasn't convinced at first, but finally he put his finger at random in a Bible which he had rewritten for his followers and oddly enough the finger pointed to a passage which said: "Then the spirit said unto Philip 'Go near, and join thyself to this chariot.'"

That was the clincher. The temple flock found the car at the home of Joy's sister and, because the butane wasn't burning properly, pushed it through the streets to the temple, singing at their labor. Then Joe and the receptive Helen and Leota Mulkins, a priestess, and a couple of male cohorts of the cult, started on the hegira into the desert.

Joy Jeffers Who Thought It Was Quite Unheavenly for Her Ex-Husband to Elope With a "Goddess" in HER Chariot.

But Joy, who followed them to Florida and had Joe arrested, had no illusions about the purpose of the trip. At the trial she shouted:

"You wanted to use the car to take Helen Veborg into the desert. You claimed you were a reincarnation of a deity and said I wasn't holy enough for you."

Joe, who went to court for a month to study procedure, conducted his own case. Addressing the jury, he chanted a prayer in a rich baritone voice and recited quotations from the Scriptures, but the jurors refused to be swayed.

Outstanding sensation of the trial was Helen's dramatic announcement that she had married Joe last June in Miami. Mrs. Ida Garrett, a backsliding member of the flock, said Joe and Helen merely joined hands, read long passages purportedly from a Bible and then declared themselves wed.

The "ceremony," she said, was not conducted by any recognized clergyman but by Miss Mulkins, the priestess who accompanied Joseph and his girl friend on the transcontinental tour.

Joe scoffed at that. Mrs. Garrett, he said, had been kicked out of the cult because she insisted on bringing her small dog to the dinner table in her handbag.

In the end, Joe outsmarted himself as his own counsel. He was convicted, but it was taken for granted that he would be freed for several months on bail pending appeal. He exhibited a diamond-studded gold watch that Helen had given him to raise money for his defense.

He even informed the court that every one of his followers would spend every last dollar to clear his name, even if they had to take the case to the United States Supreme Court.

But Joe hadn't realized that his appeal papers must be ready when sentence is pronounced. So instead of being released, he was rushed off to prison, where all he'll have to worry about for the next four years is how to raise the $1,000 fine that was added to his jail term.

International

Helen Veborg (Left), and Joe Jeffers, the Self-Styled Deity, Outside the Florida Court.

As the Israelites were divided into TRIBES, and had chiefs over them, so the Indians divided themselves: each tribe forms a little community within the nation — and as the nation hath its particular symbol, so hath each tribe the badge from which it is denominated ...

By a strict, permanent, divine precept, the Hebrew nation were ordered to worship at Jerusalem, the true and living God, and who by the Indians is styled "Yohewah' ...

If Jeffers' teachings are bizarre, his life and career are even more so. Jeffers was the sixth of 15 children born to a poor railroad worker in Roanoke, Alabama. He was ordained as a Baptist minister in 1918, but began his career as a "pulpit clown," with a natural flair for theatrics. He later became a charismatic evangelist, travelling widely and always attracting attention; he was shot at on one tour, on another his evangelical tents were set afire. As if this wasn't enough, police blamed a murder on the emotional upset caused by one of his meetings. Jeffers no doubt had intimations that he was destined for higher things.

Breaking with the Baptists in 1935, Jeffers formed Kingdom Temple, Inc. in California, to jump-start his career as a prophet. During the rise of National Socialism Jeffers was accused of pro-Nazi sentiments. He and his wife Joy honeymooned in Europe and were entertained "for some time" in Berlin. "[Jeffers] went along in a taxi as a spectator when the Nazi legions invaded Czechoslovakia," reported *The American Weekly.*

In 1943 Jeffers announced that he was, in effect, Christ. Though married, he sought to fulfill prophecy by taking a pretty young acolyte named Helen Veborg to the desert to become the mother of his "sacred child." Strangely, Jeffers chose Florida as the destination of his desert pilgrimage. Jeffers explained later in court that a drought was soon to transform Florida into a desert. Joy, his unhappy wife, followed them to Florida, where she sued and won her divorce from Christ. According to the June, 1945 story in *The American Weekly,* she was awarded the family car, "a raky eight-cylinder job which had been converted to butane and was referred to by the papers as the Golden Chariot of Kingdom Come." Nonetheless, Jeffers and his followers were directed from heaven, to "join with the chariot." Following heavenly advice they stole the car. Heaven did not intervene when Jeffers was convicted of the theft and handed a four-year prison sentence.

While Jeffers was imprisoned, his 5,000 followers paid $60,000 for a 32-room mansion with five chauffeur-driven cars and a house full of servants, preparing for the Son of the Creator's release from prison. Soon after his release, however, Jeffers violated his parole, and, despite his divinity, was forced to serve more time in prison.

The flock eventually settled in a *bona fide* desert, Arizona; today they reside there under the name "Yahweh's New Kingdom," despite Jeffers' earthly demise in 1988. The October, 1992 issue of *Kingdom Voice* contains health advice, messages from Yahweh, documentation on Yahweh's name, as well as the requisite items about End Times. If nothing else, the Yahwists are true survivors; they roll with the times.

Anglo-Israelite and Yahwist teachings are now supplemented by "Secrets About Yahweh's Spaceships" and "Secrets About Lost Civilizations." Channeled messages from Yahweh continue to exhort people to "GET OFF THE COASTS." Yahweh warns that "New York City will be completely destroyed, as well as Miami, Los Angeles and San Francisco!"

Although Anglo-Israelism, Christian Identity, and Yahwism aren't exactly household words, they were thrust into public consciousness when Anglo-Israelite **Randy Weaver** was caught in a shootout with Federal Agents over firearms violations. With his son and wife killed by snipers, and his young daughters armed with sidearms, Weaver held the federal agents and their "New World Order" at bay for over a week. In the meantime, his belief that he was fighting off evil "Zionist Occupational Government" (ZOG) robots was fueled by the agents' murderous tactics.

Weaver's supporters see the siege of his cabin near Sandpoint, Idaho, as the escalation of a holy war between God's Chosen (white separatists) and the dreaded Zionist

Jeffers sought to fulfill prophecy by taking a pretty young acolyte to the desert to have his "sacred child."

Occupational Government. Soon Federal troops will be back to attempt to force them to accept the Mark of the Beast, a computer chip planted in the brain or on the hand. But through their faith in Great White Yahweh, they will resist the Mark of the Beast, and will be saved by Yahoshua (Jesus) when he returns in a fury.

6.00

GIVE US A KING

an expose' of HUMANISM

Give Us A King painstakingly reveals HOW the Religion of HUMANISM has crept into our Churches and is the cause of America's degeneracy. HUMANISM has destroyed:

(1) Virtue and Traditional Values
(2) Freedoms and Individual Rights
(3) Productivity and Land
(4) Goodness and Charity
(5) Families and Marriages
(6) Constitutional Form of Government
(7) Justice - Equity - Fairness

Never before have you read such convincingly detailed "Cause and Effect" sequences that control our daily lives from the Cradle to the Grave.

Give Us A King is simple, yet thought-provoking. It deals with philosophy while touching reality. It exposes the deeply buried FOUNDATIONS of Humanism - the religion of despair and despotism - yet offers so much hope.

Find out WHY Give Us A King has become a religeous "Hot Potatoe." WHY "Christian" book stores are afraid to touch it. WHY Religious leaders want it "swept under a rug."

If you have been looking for just the RIGHT book to give to a Pastor, Church leader or other influential individual this is it. Order yours today.

An example of contemporary Anglo-Israelism
An advertisement in the *Christian Patriot Association Review*

BLACK MESSIAHS

WHEN HE WAS PROVIDING REEFER TO HEP cats and jazz men in Harlem, **Malcolm Little** was known as "Detroit Red." In prison, the quick-witted cynic was nicknamed "Satan." Finally, directed to the teachings of **Elijah Muhammad** by his brother and sister, Malcolm was soon to embrace the clean life, release from prison, and yet another name. Elijah Muhammad, Messenger of Allah, decreed that "X" would replace Malcolm's "slave name," "Little."

Messianic religions almost universally offer new names and new diets to the downtrodden and displaced. The pantheon of North American Black Messiahs, including Noble Drew Ali of Moorish Science, Elijah Muhammad of Nation of Islam and Yahweh Ben Yahweh of The Nation of Yahweh, provide all this and more. A convert begins his or her new life with not only a new name and different eating habits, but also a genealogy, exotic rituals and colorful clothing: in short, a new identity.

Religious groups providing a radical break for "the so-called Negro" in America emerged as early as the 1920s. They espoused a complete rejection of Christianity, white domination and the history that supported it. All of them cast off the word "Negro" and replaced it instead with terms such as "Moorish-American," "Asiatic," "Hebrew" and "Nubian."

They attacked Christianity because it provided salvation in the next life, but not in this one; it favored "Pie in the Sky" over Justice and Progress. The lure of the bible was so strong that some black messiahs included it in their teachings. Be that as it may, "The White Man's Religion," had to be replaced with "The natural religion of the Black Man." For some, this was Islam, and for others it was Judaism, both altered almost beyond recognition, to fit the special circumstances of African Americans in the 20th century.

MOORISH SCIENCE

The Moorish Science Organization of **Noble Drew Ali** (1886-1929) was the first Black Islamic group in North America. How Islam, completely foreign to most Americans at that time, inserted itself into the black imagination, is still somewhat of a mystery, though several authors provide clues.

Clifton E. Marsh, historian of Black Islam, dates the black discovery of Islam at 1851, when a West Indian scholar, **Edward Wilmont Blyden** emigrated to Monrovia, advocating Islam as a "qualitative change from Christianity."

Islamic expert Peter Lamborn Wilson suggests that it all began with Black Freemasonry. Black Masonic lodges had existed clandestinely at least since the Revolution as *Chapter of the Eastern Star, Order of the Golden Circle* and *Knights of the Invisible Colored Kingdom.* Early in their history, the white Masons had borrowed some ideas and symbols from Islam, though their connection with the mainstream of this eastern religion is undoubtedly tenuous. This, however, didn't stop the Shriners, the "Ancient Arabic Order Nobles of the Mystic Shrine," founded in 1877 by Scottish Rite Masons, from parading publicly in exotic headgear; the fez was to become their trademark. In his article, "Shoot-Out at the Circle 7 Koran," Wilson elaborates on the Oriental veneer of the Shriners, some of which was later borrowed by Moorish Science: "They concocted a legend claiming initiations from a Grand Shaykh of Mecca, honors from the Ottoman sultan Selim III, a charter from Adam Weishaupt of the Bavarian Illuminati, and links with the Bektashi Sufi Order. They bestowed the title 'Noble' on themselves, wore fezzes, displayed a crescent moon and star with Egyptian ornaments (including the Great Pyramid), and founded lodges called 'Mecca,' 'Medina,' 'Al Koran,' etc."

Wilson also introduces evidence which strengthens the connection between Freemasonry and Black Islam, and may point to the real origin of the ideas of Noble Drew Ali: "During the Great Columbian Exhibition in Chicago (1893) … American blacks claiming

Noble Drew Ali

Noble Drew Ali taught that American "Negroes" are descended from the biblical Moabites and from Ham, father of the Canaanites.

initiation from visiting Moslem dignitaries founded the Ancient Egyptian Arabic Order of Nobles of the Shrine ('Black Shriners') ... Certain photographs exist of Noble Drew Ali in Egyptian Shriner gear; even his famous Napoleonic pose is Masonic, as are his title, headgear, and other favorite symbols. ..."

The various legends of Noble Drew Ali's origins tell us much about the followers of Moorish Science, as well as the mind of Noble Drew Ali. Derived from Ali's own claims, these legends explain how B. Timothy Drew, born in North Carolina to ex-slaves in 1886, was transformed into the religious prophet Noble Drew Ali, founder of Moorish Science. The story goes that Drew was raised by Cherokee Indians and later ran away with gypsies. One day, after he heard a voice say repeatedly, "If you go I will follow," he ran away to Egypt. Sources disagree, however, on whether he went there as a merchant seaman, a railway expressman, or a magician in a traveling circus.

According to Wilson's account of the legend, while in Egypt, Drew met "the last priest of an ancient cult of High Magic who led him in [to the great Pyramid] blindfolded, and abandoned him. When Drew found his way out unaided, the magus recognized him as a potential adept and offered him initiation. ... He received the name Sharif ('Noble') Abdul Ali." Apparently the religious scripture, *The Circle 7 Koran,* was written while he was in Egypt. Then in 1913, back in Newark, New Jersey, Ali had a dream in which he was ordered to found a religion "for the uplifting of fallen mankind." Wilson cites another source who places Noble Drew Ali's pilgrimage in Mecca rather than Egypt, though Marsh says he went to Morocco, where he received a commission from the King to teach Islam to North American Blacks.

One point that all sources agree on is that 1913 was the year that Noble Drew Ali first appeared in Newark, New Jersey, armed with his homespun, 64-page holy scripture, *The Circle 7 Koran.* There, he would establish the Moorish National and Divine Movement — soon renamed the Moorish Science Temple — claiming to be a prophet ordained by Allah Himself. *Circle 7 Koran* in hand, Ali began teaching that American "Negroes" are really descended from the biblical Moabites who later inhabited Morocco, and also from Ham, the father of the Canaanites. Thus Negroes would more accurately be designated "Moorish-Americans," descended from the ancient Moors. He didn't stop with Negroes, however. He also taught that the ancient Moors' territory extended to Atlantis, and even America, so that Native Americans are also "Asiatics" or "Moors."

Allah's prophet preached that the once-illustrious but sinful Moors were stripped of their nationality by our white founding fathers:

> Through sin and disobedience every nation has suffered slavery, due to the fact that they honored not the creed and principles of their forefathers. That is why the nationality of the Moors was taken away from them in 1774 and the word negro, black and colored, was given to the Asiatics of America who were of Moorish descent, because they honored not the principles of their mother and father, and strayed after the gods of Europe of whom they knew nothing. [from *The Circle 7 Koran.*]

The ancient Moors' modern-day children can find true emancipation only by attaining the forgotten knowledge of their true heritage, and by converting to Islam. Christianity is for Europeans, but Islam is for "Asiatics." Ali taught that one day soon, a star and crescent moon will appear in the sky. "This betoken[s] the arrival of the day of the Asiatics and the destruction of the Europeans."

Membership in the Moorish Science Temple was restricted to "Asiatics," which for some reason included those of Celtic descent. These white members, undoubtedly few in number, were known as "Persians." (Wilson is the only author to state that some whites were allowed membership.) New members were required to affirm their desire to follow Noble Drew Ali, and pay an initiation fee of $1. All were given a "Free National Name," either "El" or "Bey" and a "Nationality Card," which they believed would impress the "Europeans," i.e. their white neighbors.

This pocket sized card contained the symbols of the Star and Crescent, clasped hands and the number "7" enclosed in a circle. It proclaimed that its bearer honored "all the Divine Prophets, Jesus, Mohammed, Buddha and Confucius" and pronounced upon him "the blessings of the God of our Father, Allah." The bearer was identified as "a Moslem under the Divine Laws of the Holy Koran of Mecca, Love, Truth, Peace, Freedom, and Justice," and concluded, "I AM A CITIZEN OF THE UNITED STATES."

The new "Asiatic" identity consisted of more than just an identification card and new name. The convert was actually now a member of a *nation,* and along with this went responsibilities and a way of life. Though their current citizenship was in the United States, Morocco was seen as the original homeland. They honored the Moroccan flag, red with a five-pointed green star in the center, which they claimed was at least 10,000 years old.

The dress requirements were strict. Men were to wear a red fez with a black tassel at all times, because the "fez is the first head dress worn by man and the turban the first head dress worn by woman. The fez and turban symbolize that knowledge is embedded within them and these wraps protect the wearer." The turbans were optional, though women were required to wear long pants or long dresses to their shoe tops.

The Asiatic food regimen was also strict. Diet was vegetarian; smoking, drinking, straightening of hair and cosmetics were forbidden. As for recreation, that too was contrary to Moorish-American religious life. Sports, games, movies and secular dancing were all discouraged.

Though they were ostensibly Islamic, the Moorish-Americans' understanding of Islam was limited to their garments, their food and their prophet's teachings through *The Circle 7 Koran*. It teaches that: Jesus is a prophet of Allah who was sent to earth to save the Israelites "from the iron-hand oppression of the pale-skin nations of Europe"; Jesus was reincarnated into the Prophet Mohammed; angels are thoughts of Allah manifested in human flesh, who carry messages to all nations — Noble Drew Ali is one of them; the Garden of Eden is in Mecca, and Adam and Eve went to Asia; angels (Asiatics) guard the Holy City of Mecca from unbelievers; the parents of the angels are also the parents of Moorish-Americans.

This new belief system and way of life brought new confidence, and then over-confidence to the zealous Moorish-Americans. In Chicago, members, conspicuous in their fezzes, began accosting "the white enemy" in public, displaying their nationality cards and proclaiming that in the name of their prophet, Noble Drew Ali, they were now free of European domination. This did not exactly endear them to the police, and some disturbances developed. Ali ordered his followers to stop flashing their cards at "Europeans."

The Moorish Science Temple continues to this day, but it is mostly forgotten now, eclipsed by Nation of Islam and the like. But during its heyday in the 1920s, it is estimated to have had up to 30,000 members in Chicago, Detroit, Harlem, Pittsburgh, Philadelphia, Kansas City, West Virginia, Brooklyn, Richmond, South Carolina and Georgia. It was most successful in Chicago, where many Moorish-American businesses thrived, including grocery stores, restaurants and variety stores. The Moorish-Americans had taken Noble Drew Ali's maxim — "A beggar people cannot develop the highest in them, nor can they attain a genuine enjoyment of the spiritualities of life" — to heart.

Shortly before his death in 1929, the prophet began to designate power to underlings and some of them began to exploit their new-found power. Their greed led them to the practice of selling herbs, magic amulets and literature to the unwary membership, at high prices. They were successful in these enterprises and became wealthy.

While Noble Drew Ali attempted to put an end to this practice, **Sheik Claude Greene,** described as "a small-time politician and former butler of the philanthropist Julius Rosenwald," subsequently challenged his leadership. Greene removed all the furniture from Ali's office and declared himself Grand Sheikh of the Moorish Science Temple. This caused a split in the movement, culminating

"A beggar people cannot develop the highest in them, nor can they attain a genuine enjoyment of the spiritualities of life."
— Noble Drew Ali

in a violent conflict at the Unity Club in Chicago, where Greene was stabbed and shot to death. Even though Noble Drew Ali was reported to be somewhere other than Chicago at the time, the police arrested him and charged him with murder. He was released on bond, and died a few weeks later under suspicious circumstances.

> **Those who believed the chauffeur remained Moorish-Americans; those who believed Wali Fard Muhammad became part of the Nation of Islam.**

Some say Ali died from injuries inflicted by the police during imprisonment. Others that he was killed by followers of Sheik Claude Greene. Still others maintain that he died of "natural causes."

Just a year later, both **Wali Fard Muhammad** and **John Givens El,** Noble Drew Ali's chauffeur, claimed to be Noble Drew Ali, reincarnated. The chauffeur claimed that sometime after the prophet's death, he was working on his car. He fainted, and his eyes were examined. "He had the sign of the star and crescent in his eyes and they knew right then he was the prophet reincarnated into his chauffeur."

At least two factions developed based on these claims: those who believed the chauffeur remained Moorish-Americans; those who believed Fard became part of the Nation of Islam.

NATION OF ISLAM

Nation of Islam began much like Moorish Science, as an obscure cult known only to its members. It was suddenly thrust into the national consciousness in the late 50s and early 60s, when **Malcolm X** became its chief spokesman. Much has been written about Nation of Islam, and even more about Malcolm X. But it's evident that very few outside the group have ever seen the writings of Elijah Muhammad, or examined the group's belief system in detail. There has been more emphasis on the group's "black nationalism" than their religious beliefs, which may be too zany for the average social scientist to take seriously.

Nation of Islam is Moorish Science with bite; there is much more emphasis on explaining, denouncing and separating from the white "devils." Moorish Science membership cards had proclaimed "I AM A CITIZEN OF THE UNITED STATES," but Nation of Islam advocates establishment of a separate black nation.

If Noble Drew Ali was a mysterious character, W. D. Fard, also known as Wali Fard Muhammad, was even more so. Fard, a light-colored, oriental-looking man, appeared in Detroit's black ghetto in 1930, identifying himself as the reincarnation of Noble Drew Ali. Working as a peddler selling exotic silks and clothing door-to-door, he claimed that his silks were similar to the garb worn by people in his "home country." This piqued the curiosity of his ghetto consumers, who became a captive audience to his preaching of Islam, the "natural religion for the black man."

One source reports that Fard had taken over a Detroit Moorish-Science Temple and renamed it the Lost-Found People of Islam. This story, for some reason, is denied vociferously by the Nation of Islam.

Fard's claims, as well as the legends surrounding him, rival those of his predecessor. He reported that he was born in Mecca of royal ancestry, from the same tribe as the prophet Mohammed. Light skinned as he was, the people believed him. Others believed that he had studied at the University of California and in England, training for a diplomatic career in the "Kingdom of Hejaz." Still others believed that Fard was a Jamaican whose father was a Syrian Moslem. Another story had it that Fard had been a Palestinian racial agitator. A reporter for *The New Crusader,* a Chicago paper, once described Fard as "a Turkish-born Nazi agent [who] worked for Hitler in World War II."

The official Nation of Islam story is that Fard was born in Mecca in 1877, the offspring of a black father and white mother. This enabled him "to go among both black and white without being discovered or recognized." He could speak 16 languages and write in 10 of them, knew 150,000 years of world history and "knew the beginning and end of all things." He arrived in the "Wilderness of North America" in 1910, and was the teacher, not the follower, of not only Noble Drew Ali, but also black religious leaders Father Divine and Daddy Grace.

Only a few years after establishing his temple, Fard's sect, like Moorish Science before him, was subject to internal strife, ending in murder. One of Fard's followers was arrested and the Detroit police dubbed it a case of "human sacrifice" and "voodoo murder." The media picked up on this and labeled Fard's fledgling group a "Voodoo Cult" with Fard as "Chief of the Voodoos." The murder suspect was declared insane and committed to an asylum. But police pursued the elusive Fard for some seven months. When they finally caught up with him, he was ordered to leave Detroit, only to be arrested again shortly after his arrival in Chicago, for "disorderly conduct." This is the last official document on Fard.

Until his final disappearance in 1933 or 1934, Fard taught his heritage-starved audience about their own "glorious history," utilizing various history texts, the bible and the Koran, as well as his own *Secret Ritual of the Nation of Islam,* and *Teachings for the Lost-Found Nation in a Mathematical Way* written in his own symbolic language. Fard's formidable mission was to "wake the Dead Nation in the West, to teach them the truth about the white man, and to prepare them for Armageddon." His version of the Battle of Armageddon had the war between the good (black) Muslims and the evil (white) Christians, taking place in "Har-Magedon," "the wilderness of North America."

Fard left as mysteriously as he had appeared. The official Nation of Islam story is that he was "ordered out of the country" and flew to Mecca. Rumors circulated that he was last seen aboard a ship bound for Europe, where he met with foul play at the hands of either the police or dissident followers. But it may well be, as quoted in a recent issue of an orthodox Muslim newspaper, that Fard is alive and living in California as an orthodox Muslim.

Fard's disappearance caused two factions to develop. One group, which remained in obscurity, asserted that Fard, though a prophet, was mortal. The other, led by **Elijah Muhammad,** held that Fard was actually "Allah in Person."

Elijah Muhammad — born Elijah Poole, one of 13 children of a Baptist minister/sharecropper in Georgia — had been one of Fard's first ministers. As part of the massive emigration of southern blacks to northern industrial cities, Elijah ended up in Detroit as an auto worker. Some time after losing his job, he attended one of Fard's sermons. Muhammad circulated the story that he told Fard, "I know who you are, you're God himself." Fard answered, "That's right, but don't tell it now. It is not yet time for me to be known."

As Fard's successor, Elijah Muhammad moved to Chicago to establish Temple #2, the new headquarters. He began teaching that Fard was "God in person" to be worshipped as a deity, with prayer and sacrifice. Elijah Muhammad emphasized that Christianity, the white man's religion, teaches that God is a "spook," while Islam, the natural religion for the black man, teaches that God is a man; evidently, this teaching had great appeal. In no time Elijah Muhammad was leading the Nation of Islam with a firm hand, calling himself Allah's "Prophet" and "Messenger."

If W.D. Fard's teachings have bite, then Elijah Muhammad's have fangs. Muhammad developed Fard's ideas in astounding detail, accounting for the state of the world as the product of the evil white race and its hold on world power. He taught that "the Original Man is the Black Man," that white people are the result of a genetic plot, and have only been around for six thousand years. The "so-called Negro" came from "The Tribe of Shabazz" within the Asiatic Nation, who originated in Africa when a great explosion divided the earth from the moon 60 trillion years ago. Members of this eminent tribe were the first explorers of Earth, and the first inhabitants of the Nile Valley. Furthermore, they authored not only the bible but the Koran.

Elijah Muhammad's main text for the dissemination of his teachings, *Message to the Blackman in America,* tells the story of the "grafting" of the evil white race. The woeful story begins 6800 years ago, when Yacub, an evil scientist from Mecca, angered the Meccan authorities and was exiled, along with 59,999 of his followers, to an island in the

While in exile, Yacub, an evil scientist from Mecca, plotted his revenge. He would enslave the Tribe of Shabazz by breeding an evil white race that would rule over them for 6,000 years.

Aegean Sea. While in exile, he plotted his revenge. He would enslave the Tribe of Shabazz by breeding an evil white race that would rule over them for 6,000 years. He created the Brown Race from the Black using the old biblical method of infanticide. "... He ordered the nurses to kill all black babies... by pricking the brains with a sharp needle as soon as the black child's head is out of its mother. ... When there was a birth of a brown baby, the nurse would come and make much ado over it, and, would tell the mother that she had given birth to a holy child and that she would nurse it for the next six weeks, for her child was going to be a great man..." Using the same method, 200 years later, he created the Red Race from the Brown, and 200 years after that the Yellow Race from the Red. Finally, after 600 years, his work was completed; he had created the White Devils.

> The Yakub-made devils were really pale white, with really blue eyes; which we think are the ugliest of colors for a human eye."

These hateful creatures were exiled in "West Asia" (Europe), and became savages, remaining in that condition for 2000 years.

> They lost all knowledge of civilization. The Lord, God of Islam, taught me that some of them tried to graft themselves back into the black nation, but they had nothing to go by. A few were lucky enough to make a start, and got as far as what you call the gorilla. In fact, all of the monkey family are from this 2,000 year history of the white race in Europe.

After 2000 years Allah raised Moses to civilize the white race, who found his job quite difficult. After the process of civilization, the White Devils fulfilled Yakub's vengeance by enslaving the tribe of Shabazz. Fortunately, the end of this sad chapter of history is now in sight. The six thousand year white rule ended in 1914. We are now living in the post-1914 "Years of Grace," which will last until the chosen of Allah will be resurrected from the mental death imposed upon them by the white man. Achieving this resurrection was the holy mission of Elijah Muhammad, Messenger of Allah and Spiritual Leader of the Lost-Found Nation in the West. The Messenger of Allah left this earth in 1975, but he may yet accomplish his mission.

Elijah Muhammad had chosen his son, W. D. Muhammad, to take over the leadership following his death. Soon after, Nation of Islam was officially disbanded and W.D. Muhammad and his followers embraced a more orthodox version of Islam, much as Malcolm X did after his break with Elijah Muhammad. But **Louis Farrakhan,** who had succeeded Malcolm X as the group's spokesman, soon resurrected the old Nation of Islam.

Elijah Muhammad is alive and well in the hearts of the followers of Louis Farrakhan. And not just in their hearts; he flies to earth from time to time aboard a giant flying saucer, occasionally summoning Farrakhan to receive his instructions. So claims the notorious Minister Louis Farrakhan.

Louis Farrakhan didn't become a household word in America until 1984, when he was accused of making anti-Semitic remarks. But he had been the charismatic leader of the new Nation of Islam for years, leading 50,000 followers. Born Louis Eugene Walcott in 1933, Farrakhan had been a trained musician and calypso singer nicknamed "The Charmer." He "took his X" — becoming Louis X — when he joined Nation of Islam in his home town of Boston, and soon became a close associate of Malcolm X. Later renamed Farrakhan by Elijah Muhammad, Louis X became a leader in the sect, though he didn't graduate to chief spokesman until the assassination of Malcolm X.

Farrakhan's current Chicago-based group continues the legacy of the old Nation of Islam. He advocates black separatism, as his predecessor did, although the new black homeland is no longer America, but Africa; his newspaper, *The Final Call,* implores the resurrection of the spirit of Marcus Garvey.

Farrakhan's devotion to even the the most obscure teachings of Elijah Muhammad is reflected in his belief in flying saucers as Ezekiel's vision:

> The Great Wheel which many of us see in the sky today is not so much a wheel as one may think in such terms, but rather a place made like

a wheel. The like of this wheel-like plane was never seen before. You cannot build one like it and get the same results. ... His vision of the wheel ... reveals just where and how the decisive battle would take place (in the sky).

... Today, we see the white race preparing for the sky battle to determine who shall remain and rule this earth, black or white.

... The present wheel-shaped plane known as the Mother of Planes, is one-half mile by a half mile and is the largest mechanical man-made object in the sky. It is a small human planet made for the purpose of destroying the present world of the enemies of Allah. ...

The small circular-made planes called flying saucers, which are so much talked of being seen, could be from this Mother Plane. This is only one of the things in store for the white man's evil world. Believe it or not! This is to warn you and me to fly to our own God and people.

Elijah Muhammad has evidently taken residence on that Mother Ship in order to direct the proceedings that will end the 6,000 year rule of white devils.

On October 24, 1989 Louis Farrakhan held a press conference in which he detailed his September, 1985 vision that he was carried to a mountain in Tepotzlan, Mexico, and then to Elijah Muhammad's mother ship:

As we reached the top of the mountain, a Wheel, or what you call an unidentified flying object, appeared at the side of the mountain and called to me to come up into the Wheel ...

A beam of light came from the Wheel and I was carried up on this beam of light into the Wheel ...

As the Wheel lifted off from the side of the mountain, moving at a terrific speed, I know I was being transported to the Mother Wheel, which is a human-built planet—a half-mile by a half-mile that the Honorable Elijah Muhammad had taught us of for nearly 60 years. ... I was escorted by the pilot to a door and admitted into a room ...

At the center of the ceiling was a speaker and through the speaker I heard the voice of the Honorable Elijah Muhammad speaking to me as clearly as you are hearing my voice this morning.

... [Mr. Muhammad] began to speak to me. He said, *"President Reagan has met with the Joint Chiefs of Staff to plan a war. I want you to hold a press conference in Washington, D.C., and annou their plan and say to the world that you got the information from me on the Wheel."*

Minister Farrakhan realized that Elijah Muhammad was referring to a war planned against Moammar Qaddafi. And so he traveled to Libya to warn Qaddafi of his vision. But this was only the beginning. The real war was to be against the black people of America, and himself, Louis Farrakhan. "The vision that the Honorable Elijah Muhammad gave me from the Wheel in 1985, is now manifested fully in that President Bush has met with his Joint Chiefs of Staff, the chairman of which is a Black man, General Colin Powell, and again, they too have planned a war. ... most importantly, against the rise of Black youth and Black people in America." Later, Farrakhan stated that "As [Qaddafi] was to Reagan, Farrakhan is to Bush."

The Final Call
UFOs AND THE NEW WORLD ORDER
IS THERE A CONNECTION?
Requiem for a Heavyweight
Minister Abdul Wali Muhammad honored

The September 8, 1992 issue of *The Final Call* could be mistaken for a supermarket tabloid with its headline, "UFOs and the NEW WORLD ORDER" emblazoned on its cover. The accompanying story reveals a government plot to institute a New World Order which may involve alien beings and so-called UFO's, that are, in fact, created by the government. An interview with Nario Hayakawa, a "UFO researcher," reveals the high order conspiracy:

The U.S. government, behind a veil of secrecy, is testing these aerial devices or select pilots may be receiving instructions (from alien beings) on how to fly these disk shaped crafts developed by the government for the purpose of staging a fake extraterrestrial event in the very near future, perhaps around 1995. ... Secret international banking groups and other global secret groups are going to forcefully eliminate international borders and create some kind of controlled society. ... The most amazing weapon they will use to do this will be the extraterrestrial threat ...

ANSAARU ALLAH COMMUNITY

Outfitted in white gowns and skull caps, the members of Ansaaru Allah Community look like nice, religious people with concrete links to Islam and Africa. The bespectacled man sitting outside of a neighborhood transit station proffering literature and incense to Boston's black community is cordial to curi-

A depiction of Michael the Archangel who has come to earth to defeat the demonic paleman. From an Ansaaru Allah Community publication.

ous passers-by, both black and white. He gives every appearance of representing a wholesome alternative to ghetto life. A closer look however, reveals that the literature — all penned by leader and founder **Isa Muhammad** — isn't just about Islam or black pride: it is also about denouncing the subhuman, pale, blue-eyed Amorite devils who are descended from lepers and mate with dogs, and, more importantly, about the coming apocalypse in the year 2000.

Isa Muhammad, who has begun to call himself **As Sayyid Al Imaam Issa Al Haadi Al Mahdi,** founded the group in 1970. He claims to be the great-grandson of Sudanese leader **Muhammad Ahmed Ibn Abdullah** (1845-1885), whom the Ansaars believe to be a true "Successor" or "Mahdi" in the line of Prophet Muhammad. In no uncertain terms they oppose the line of successorship accepted by Orthodox Sunni Muslims.

Isa likes to keep his origins shrouded in mystery, but his followers say that he was born in 1945 — exactly 100 years after his "great-grandfather" — in Omdurman, Sudan and was given the name Isa at birth; his full Sudanese name is Isa al Haadi al-Mahdi. They concede that he also has an American birth certificate under the name "Dwight York," explaining that Dwight was his nickname and that York was his mother's family name. The official story continues that Isa emigrated from the Sudan to Massachusetts, where he lived until he was seven, was then taken by a guardian to Aswan, Egypt and then back to the Sudan where his "grandfather" **As Sayyid Abdur Rahman al-Mahdi** recognized him as the one possessing "the light." He returned to the U.S. and attended high school in Teaneck, New Jersey. Isa claims that after high school he attended universities in Egypt and the Sudan, but detractors say that he was in prison, not Africa.

During the 1960s and 70s, Isa became aware of both Moorish Science and the Nation of Islam, and his mentor was Shaikh Daoud of the State Street Mosque in Brooklyn. In 1967 he organized his first Muslim group, the "Ansaar Pure Sufi," whose symbol was a crescent containing a Star of David with an Egyptian ankh inside. Though critics say that the Star of David was used to attract members of Black Jewish sects, Isa's explanation is that its six points represent the six prophets — Adam, Noah, Abraham, Ismael, Moses and Jesus, all of whom were black. In contrast, he says, the five-pointed star of the orthodox Muslims is an inverted symbol of Satan.

Isa soon changed the name of the group to the "Nubians." The members had originally been asked to wear green and black, but now they were to wear long African robes. In 1969, in line with his fast changing theology, Isa changed the group's name again, to the "Nubian Islamic Hebrews" and added the mahdist crescent and spear to their symbol. The costume became more elaborate as well; they were now asked to wear a dashiki, a black fez, and a small bone in the left ear.

The Nubian Islamic Hebrew costume became more elaborate; members were asked to wear a dashiki, a black fez, and a small bone in the left ear.

The Nubian Islamic Hebrews were officially founded as a sect in 1970. Communal living was established, males and females living separately from each other and from their children. During the early 70s Isa purchased the building on Bushwick Avenue in Brooklyn which would become their headquarters. He also began publishing their now massive supply of tracts, pamphlets, books, posters, newspapers and journals.

In 1973 Isa traveled to Egypt and the Sudan. By the banks of the Nile he met a teacher — the teacher of Moses no less — known by Islamic mystics as al-Khidr, or "The Green One." The teachings of al-Khidr have since guided Isa in his understanding of the Koran.

When Isa returned from his journey abroad, he changed the sect's name to the "Ansaaru Allah Community," which translates as "helpers of Allah." It was at this time that he began to say that he was the great-grandson of **Muhammad Ahmad,** the mahdi of Sudan. He had forged links with the Sudan, his new homeland, and the Sudanese, his new ancestors. During the late 70s, grandsons of the mahdis of Sudan did, in fact, visit the Ansaars' Brooklyn mosque; Sudanese students came as well, to assist the Ansaars with Arabic and the Koran. The official garb worn by Ansaar males was changed again, to white pants, robe and cap, with the maḥdist symbol of spear and crescent between two pyramids on the cap. It was also in the late 70s that Isa, going by the name "Dr. York," was lead singer in a band called "Passion."

In 1981 Isa returned to Egypt to study the ancient monuments and temples. When he returned he announced that he had discovered the truth about the ancient Egyptians, which has been cleverly concealed by the devil for thousands of years. The Egyptians were, in fact, not only black, but they were also Muslims, the direct ancestors of the Nubians. "We refer to ourselves as Nubians," he writes, "knowing our origin comes from across the pyramids. ... The ancient Mizraimites [Egyptians] did not worship many gods — they were Muslims! The devil has also interpreted the hieroglyphics to be a language. Hieroglyphics is an art form, not a spoken language. They are the means by which we are able to understand the customs of this great Muslim society."

An ex-member of the Ansaar organization charges that married couples are allowed to engage in sex only in the "green room," and must sign up for it in advance.

Isa's genealogical claims were becoming increasingly grandiose. By 1988 he had traced his descent via **Husayn,** Muhammad's grandson, to Muhammad himself. Isa now felt that he was in a position to criticize Moorish Science and Nation of Islam as inauthentic versions of Islam. He pointed out that Noble Drew Ali's *Circle 7 Koran* is a motley blend of plagiarized material, and that neither Noble Drew Ali nor Elijah Muhammad are true prophets of Allah. Isa however, is the divinely inspired, one true Koranic oracle. His hundreds of books, pamphlets and recordings are not his own doing, but the result of Allah speaking through him.

Isa also began to see himself as the savior of all Muslims: "It is my job as the reformer," he wrote, "to reform Islam and re-institute it in its pristine purity; not only here in the West but also in the East, where it is needed. Despite the fact that the people of the East were raised speaking Arabic, and were thus able to read the Koran, they still do not understand it, nor its relationship to the Old and New Testaments." In fact, the "so-called Arabs," sent to the West to confuse Nubians, deliberately mistranslated some verses of the Qur'an in order to conceal the damnation of all blue-eyed criminals to Hell. Islam as practiced by pale Arabs — agents of Satan — he says, is racist. Furthermore, the Muslim World League is a communist organization.

Isa's inflammatory literature, as well the Ansaar lifestyle did not go unnoticed by the Muslim world. In 1988, a Jamaican convert to Sunni Islam, **Abu Ameenah Bilal Philips,** published an exposé entitled *The Ansaar Cult,* denouncing Isa Muhammad's sect as a perversion of orthodox Islam. In response, Isa published *The Ansaar Cult: Rebuttal to the Slanderers,* which denounces Sunni Islam and defends the Ansaaru Allah Community as living out the one true interpretation of Islam.

Philips and former members charge that the Ansaars live in isolation, not as true Muslims, but as a cult. Men are required to bring in money through begging, and those who fail to bring in the required amount are punished. Isa's reply is that "to beg donations for the upliftment of Islaam" is in accord with Islamic law. Former members have also revealed some strange practices with regard to sex. Married couples, who live separately, are allowed to engage in sex only in "the green room," and must sign up for it in advance. Those whom Isa chooses to punish, for any reason, are denied access altogether. Isa's defense is that "The green room was the only alternative that we had to keep certain people who didn't have sexual control from going totally berserk and that was their doing, not mine."

The role of women in the Ansaaru Allah Community is characteristically Muslim. Though men and women are "equal," Isa says that according to the Koran, women do not have their own spirits. Women are expected to fulfill their traditional roles as wives and mothers, avoiding appearance in public, except for business. When they do go out, they are required to wear loose clothing which covers every inch of their bodies, except hands and feet; a full face veil must also be worn, with only a slit for the eyes; their gaze should be lowered, and they must walk "decently." A woman should neither

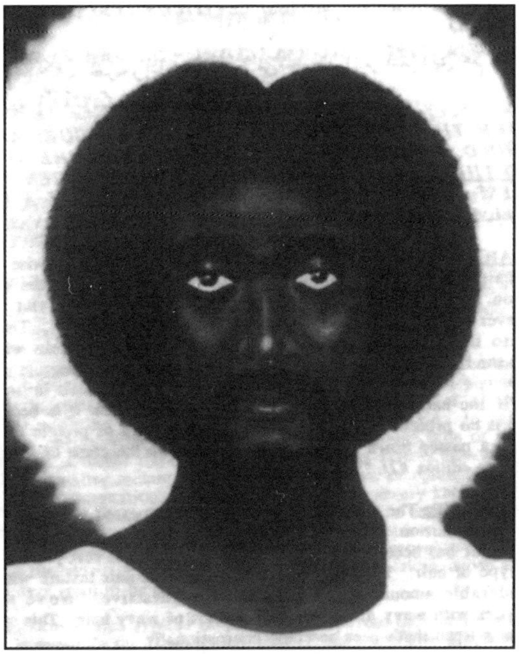

The world according to As Sayyid Isa Al Haadi Al Mahdi.

Traditional white bigotry (upper left) is turned on its head in the publication *The Paleman,* in which hirsute paleman Isaac Asimov is compared to a gorilla.

"The Messiah Jesus at the age of 33. His wooly hair and Nubian Features speak for themselves," reads the caption to illustration (upper right) in *Paleman.*

The Revelation of the Paleman Beast 666 in the 465 page "pamphlet," *Leviathan 666.*

"Because Canaan was an albino, he lacked normal eye coloring which caused his eyes to weaken and become sensitive to direct and indirect sunlight."

enjoy herself, laugh, talk loudly, nor eat in public; in short, she should be invisible.

Most of the Ansaar publications look as Middle Eastern as their clothing, but on closer scrutiny reveal adherence to Judeo-Christian and Western symbols as well. The Seven-Headed Beast of the Apocalypse, for example, bursts from the cover of a 400-page "pamphlet" entitled *Leviathan 666*. Pop culture icons illustrate a 300-page diatribe, *The Paleman,* which details the inferiority and evil rapacity of the white devils.

It is only by reading these rants that one can truly appreciate the mind of the man who describes himself as "The Son of Man who raised us up from the 'Mentally Dead' to 'Life Everlasting.'" His works show that he has incorporated not only the works of Elijah Muhammad and Noble Drew Ali in his writings, but also the classic conspiracy books authored by white supremacists.

Isa apparently believes in the literal truth of fiction, movies and even tabloid articles, such as "Woman Gives Birth to 14-lb. Dog Baby." These are presented as evidence that the International Bankers, Freemasons, Jews, the Pope and the Media are all part of The Conspiracy to cover up the superiority of Allah's chosen, the Nubians. Even the UFO and Hollow Earth literature, including the Shaver Mystery, are presented as fact.

Isa's conspiratorial potpourri is juxtaposed with sermons about building a Nubian nation. "Our land is Sudan," he writes, "which is the original name for what is called Africa today. We are Nubians. We are the Israelites, the Ishmaelites and the Midianites..." In order for this nation to materialize, Isa must clear the way for the Messiah by converting 144,000 Nubian souls:

> We call ourselves Ansaarullah because we consider ourselves the Nasrullah or the Ansaarullah mentioned in Al Qur'aan 61:14 when they use the word as Jesus' disciples. We consider ourselves the HAWAARIYUWNA, those gowned in white robes who will raise the 144,000 and we will be with the Messiah Jesus on the final day. WE ARE MUSLIMS FOR CHRIST.

The real Black-Skinned Christ however, should not be confused with the Pale Jew Jebusite Christ worshipped by Christians, specifically, THE DEVIL, who, along with a race of fallen angels have incarnated on Earth in human form. This pale-skinned race is the cursed seed of Canaan, THE CAUCASIANS. "They have spread all over the planet Earth," Isa writes, "and are in contact with Evil U.F.O.'S they call God. They worship the image of the beast, a pale Jew, the picture of your pale Jesus Christ."

Though the true story of how the White Race came to be can be found in many of Isa's books, *The Paleman* is devoted exclusively to this topic. Elijah Muhammad's version of the white devil story, Isa points out, is incorrect.

Now, Isa's version, which begins with a story from the Old Testament:

In the beginning ... everybody was Black, or rather, Nubian. Until one day Noah accidentally got drunk on the wine from his vineyards, undressed and retired to his tent, naked. His son Ham walked by, in a rather weak state, after an argument with his wife. The Devil then took the opportunity to possess Ham's body, causing Ham to mock Noah's nakedness, and then look at him with the thought of sodomy. Sodomy, even the thought of Sodomy was a sin, so Allah cursed Ham's yet-to-be-born fourth son Canaan. This curse on Canaan was the curse of Leprosy. Isa continues:

> Because Canaan was an albino, he lacked the normal eye coloring which caused his eyes to weaken and become sensitive to direct and indirect sunlight. So Canaan ... sought refuge in the mountains where the light was dim. The cold climate of the mountains was also conducive to [his] leprous condition because it stopped the leprosy from spreading. Canaan's descendents were the original cavemen.
>
> When they fled to the mountains, Canaan and his wife began reproducing and remained there for 309 years, with their progeny ... After that time, ALLAH sent the Prophet Abraham to clean them up. This is why the so-called Jews (cursed Jebusites of Canaan) called the Prophet Abraham their father.
>
> ... In time, they descended to the level of animals, eating raw carcasses, walking on all fours and mingling freely with the animals, mainly dog-like animals.

Once the salts in their bodies reached a dangerous low, they lost their ability to reproduce. It was at this point that the lepers went down from the mountains, kidnapped and raped clean Nubian women. The mixture produced an offspring with black skin and straight, black hair. ...

The lepers that did not mix (predominately the women) were pushed further back up the mountains and fell so low as to mate with the dog-like animals. The result of this mixture were ape-like animals. They had sexual intercourse with the jackal (the original dog) and through this intercourse the offspring that was brought forth was an ape-like man. They loved the dog so much that they turned his name around to worship it, DOG = GOD. The phrase "A Dog is Man's Best Friend," came out of this situation. The dog would lick the festered sores of the leper and clean the sores for them.

It is only the cursed Paleman who is descended from apes:

Today, the Paleman would admit proudly, in firm agreement with Darwin's 'Theory of Evolution' that man, meaning himself, mankind, emerged by a process called evolution from the ape when in reality, the ape is an alien. Correctly, if he was to go back in time a couple of thousand years, he would indeed encounter these ape-like animals that are partly responsible for his emergence as far as race.

If you're Asian or Native American, don't think you're off the hook. Your race is also the result a curse: the "Curse of Esau."

The dragon represents the Edomites, the people of the "rising sun," the curse placed on Esau (father of the Edomites) can be seen through their slanted eyes. When ALLAH places a curse on someone (the Edomite race), it appears in the genes of man. ...

One clear example of the curse placed on Esau by ALLAH is the disease known as "Mongolism" (Down Syndrome). Now ask yourself why it is that any mongoloid or retarded child born to any race always has the same appearance, they look Asian. They are always born with slanted eyes, broad heads, large tongues, no matter what race their parents are from. How can this be possible? The answer is very simple. As we previously stated, when ALLAH places a curse on people, HE places the curse in their genes.

The Paleman is inferior and evil, and perhaps, the "Edomites" are merely inferior. But, the Jews and the Jesuits are worst of all. Isa identifies the Jews as the cursed "Jebusites," and "Khazars." The Jews are responsible for everything from Christianity to the Bolshevik Revolution. The Jesuits, on the other hand, are responsible for both world wars and wrote *Mein Kampf* for Hitler.

The conspiracy involves not only the International Bankers, the Pope, the Zionists, and Communists, but also Geraldo Rivera:

Many of you do not know, there are Jews in the entertainment world who are disguising themselves as being other than Jews. For example; the well-known newscaster Geraldo Rivera is in reality a Jew (Jebusite). Recently, his Jewish identity was revealed to the public in a popular magazine. He had a six-pointed star tattooed on his left hand when he was a child and is now being denied the right to be buried in a Jewish cemetery ground. According to the Jewish faith, tattoos are forbidden.

Yet, he did not think of this as he passed himself off as an Hispanic. I have been telling you he was a Jew for years. Geraldo Rivera is his stage name, his real name is Jerry Rivers. ...

Isa delivers the big news that movie stars such as Tony Curtis, Woody Allen and Shelley Winters are Jewish, listed alongside Pope John Paul II as hiding their true identities.

Some of Isa's ideas are borrowed from such publications as *America's Promise*, an Anglo-Israelite periodical, portions of which are reprinted in *Leviathan 666*, Isa's compendium of the coming apocalypse. His accounts of our checkless cashless computerized society run by Mark of the Beast hand-scan machines and barcodes closely resembles the literature of millennialists such as Mary Stuart Relfe and Ron J. Steele. Isa reveals a plot, however, far more insidious than those uncovered by his pale colleagues.

According to Isa, Satan was born on earth as a human being in the year 1966. The Devil gave birth at that time to 13 children all over the world, one of them in New York City. This fact was "camouflaged" in a series of movies, the first of which was *Rosemary's Baby*. Everything that happens in this movie is, according to Isa, historical truth. "Rosemary was not a fictitious character," Isa writes. "She was a real Amorite. The name Rosemary (Satan's mother) was chosen

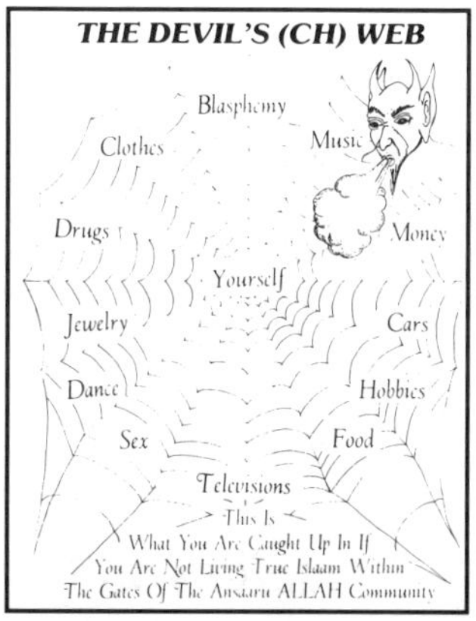

From *Leviathan 666*

America the Beast will crumble to the ground. Isa will then open the seventh seal, and the 144,000 Nubians will ascend Mount Zion.

because it symbolizes the ancestral background of the physical Devil, the Amorites."

But Satan will be defeated in the end, as prophesied in the Book of Revelation. According to Isa's interpretation, the Four Horsemen of the Apocalypse represent the Babylonian, Persian, Roman and European/US empires respectively, who all oppose Allah.

> The Amorite, on account of his leprosy is pale and deteriorating with blue eyes and blond hair. ... The International Trade Center, Wall Street and the Empire State Building are going to be the first to be overturned. They are the heart, capital and economy of NEW BABYLON. ... America. All are located in New York City: THE EMPIRE STATE.

In the year 1998, World War III and the reign of the Anti-Christ will begin.

> The Anti-Christ will rise in the Arab World. He will not come out of the Christian world. Politically, in the early 1990's A.D., Arab supremacy will dominate the world. It will be achieved by the final Anti-Christ, the one to come out of the Arab World. He will be of Moorish/Mongolian extraction and will come to power in 1994 A.D. His victories will begin with the conquest of Europe, beginning with Italy. Europe will be attacked by land, air and sea. Rome the seat of Christianity, will be among the first places to be destroyed and Christianity will be wiped out by a universal brotherhood of Muslim nations.
>
> This will be the beginning of the Third World War, which will last for almost twenty-seven years. ...As the Arab world launches three set of six missiles, three will be intercepted and three will penetrate. As a result, New York and the entire Eastern Seaboard of the United States will be completely destroyed. ...

America the Beast will crumble to the ground, "broken into pieces by the GREATEST KINGDOM, THE KINGDOM of ALLAH." Isa will then open the seventh seal, and the 144,000 Nubians will ascend Mount Zion.

RASTAFARIANS

Some Black Jewish sects believe that blacks are descended from the Hebrews, and others that **Haile Selassie** was secretly a Jew, but Rastafarians go even further. They believe that Selassie, a.k.a. Ras Tafari, a.k.a. His Imperial Majesty Haile Selassie I, King of Kings, Lord of Lords, Conquering Lion of the Tribe of Judah, Elect of God, Emperor of Ethiopia, is the Black Man's Messiah.

Haile Selassie (1892-1975), born **Tafari Makonnen,** claimed, in the Ethiopian royal tradition, a descent from King Solomon and the Queen of Sheba, and that his eventual position as Emperor was divinely sanctioned. He did not, however, see himself as any kind of Messiah, despite his Jamaican fans' contention that he is God, or Jah.

Given that Haile Selassie was a devout member of the Ethiopian Orthodox Church, Emperor and spiritual figurehead of a Christian nation, it is hard to imagine why he would be selected as the Messiah of this group which views Christianity as a tool of the white oppressor. Consistency and rationality, are not, however, necessary to religion, least of all, messianic religion.

But prophecy is. During the 1920s, **Marcus Garvey,** the Jamaican "Back to Africa" leader, declared, "Look to Africa, where a black king shall be crowned, for the day of deliverance is here." Haile Selassie was crowned emperor in 1930, and soon after, in Jamaica, the Rastafarians were born. The fulfillment of Garvey's prophecy, supplemented by the usual panoply of biblical quotes, became the basis for this new Jamaican messianic movement.

In the early days of the movement, while Ras Tafari was still in this world, the Rastafarians believed that he would literally rescue them from their oppression, and take them "back" to Ethiopia. **Reverend Howell,** one of the movement's founders urged his followers to sell 5000 photographs of the Emperor as passports to Ethiopia. This dubious enterprise landed Howell in jail.

Apparently, the lesson was lost, for in 1959, **Rev. Claudius Henry,** calling himself a modern Moses, told the Rastafarians that he'd lead them back to the promised land with "Repatriation Cards," upon which were printed: "Pioneering Israel's scattered children of African origin 'Back home to Africa.' This year, 1959, deadline date October 5th: This new government is God's righteous kingdom of peace on Earth. 'Creation's second birth'... Please reserve this certificate for removal. No passport will be necessary for those returning to Africa."

On the appointed day, thousands of believers showed up for their repatriation, having sold their homes and material possessions. Suffice to say, the Jamaicans were not shuttled back to Africa as promised. But the unfulfilled prophecy only served to strengthen the faith of the believers. What would it matter if repatriation was delayed? One day soon, Blacks will rule the world, after Babylon destroys itself in a nuclear holocaust.

Yet another disappointment, or what you might think was a disappointment, occurred in 1966 when Haile Selassie, Jah himself, visited Jamaica. Upon his arrival, thousands of Rastafarians fell before him as he attempted to exit his airplane. Alarmed by his devotees, Selassie stepped back into the plane, shut the door and refused to come out for an hour. He finally indulged his worshippers with a speech urging the prostrate horde not to seek repatriation in Ethiopia until liberating the people of Jamaica. The Rastafarians made Selassie's directive the basis of their new ideology.

The Rastafarians have shown themselves flexible when confronted with various disappointed hopes, changing ideology to fit the new situation. Their biggest test, the death of their Messiah in 1975, preceded the sect's international impact with reggae, dreadlocks and the sacred herb. They are very much alive, and, to them, Ras Tafari is very much alive too. He is in the "Spiritual Body" now.

HEBREW ISRAELITES

Certain Black Jewish sects have talked about returning to the Promised Land, be it Ethiopia or Palestine. The Hebrew Israelites actually made it there. The Promised Land for this group, members of the Abeta Israel Hebrew Center, is the more traditional chosen land of Israel. Thirty-nine of them emigrated there in 1969 from the South Side of Chicago, by way of Liberia, and more were soon to follow. This was a fulfillment of divine prophecy, which also scheduled Armageddon for 1977.

The Hebrew Israelites were admitted to Israel under the "Law of Return" which allows the emigration of all officially approved Jews back to the homeland. The Hebrew Israelites don't really think of themselves as "Jews" however, for Judaism is only a *religion,* while Hebrew Israelite is a *nationality.*

After settling in Dimona, the Hebrew Israelites began to assert that only they were the authentic Hebrew people, and that the Jews were frauds, part of the International Conspiracy to conceal the true identity of the Hebrew Israelites as God's Chosen People. Hebrew Israelite eschatology holds that the Jews, along with the remainder of the sect's enemies, will be destroyed in the battle of Armageddon. This didn't sit too well with Israeli authorities, who determined that the Hebrew Israelites were not Jews, and could legally be expelled from Israel. However, as of May, 1992, they had not yet been deported; the group, which grew to one thousand, is reported to be currently enjoying cordial relations with the Israeli government.

The group had first come together in the early 1960s when Gerson Parker, a.k.a. **Nasi Hashalom,** and Louis Bryant, a.k.a. **Nasi Shaliach Ben Yehuda** had been separately preaching Black Judaism. They met in 1964, and soon developed a partnership based on their mutual belief in Black Zionism, which distinguished them from the other Black Jewish cults at that time. Fluent in Hebrew, Nasi Hashalom became spokesman as well as the "Prince of Peace" (Messiah). He answers to a number of different names, corresponding with his various divine incarnations.

The question remains, as always, Who exactly are the Chosen People? In the case of the various groups of black Jews, the answer could be just the members of a particular group of believers, or all African-Americans, or all those of black African descent. The Hebrew Israelites have solved the quandary by singling out those descended from American slaves, whether they know their special status or not:

> We said that the children of Israel came through Jacob. We got the Edomites that came

Alarmed by the thousands of prostrate Rastafarians, Haile Selassie, Jah himself, stepped back into his plane, shut the door, and refused to come out for an hour.

After settling in Dimona, the Hebrew Israelites began to assert that they were the authentic Hebrew people, and that Jews were impostors.

through Essau, the Hittites, the Jebusites, all those people were Canaanites from Canaan. There were many tribes that made up Canaan's people. Israelites were another distinct group of people. All of these [other] people were black people, are people of color. But the Israelites were a distinct group from within the world of color...

The slaves that reached the final form of physical slavery in America were truly the Hebrew Israelites. The others were dropped in the isles of the Sea: Haiti, Cuba, Jamaica... The true Israelites were brought on to America to fulfill a prophetic utterance of the sages of old so that it would be beyond a shadow of a doubt that they were the people. ... The prophecy... is in [Deut. 28],... when he alludes to the cursings and blessings that would befall the nation of Israel if they did not adhere to the divine laws of our Father. ... [Moses said]: 'thy sons and daughters would be taken to a far land, and again you shall go into Egypt but this time by ships and there you will be sold as bondsmen and bondswomen and now man shall buy you.'

Nasi Hashalom explains European domination and American slavery as God's curse upon the Hebrews:

Ancient Israel fell because of nonadherence to written law... As a nation the preachment has always been here. But we couldn't come together as a nation because the curse was upon us. At the end of the final chastisement in 1863, but the bondage really stopped in 1845, that was the end of the 400-year period...1445... In order for the chosen people never to be duped, taken in by idolatry or follow false doctrines or gods again, they had to be in the place where every imaginable form of idolatry would be practiced and the highest technological society would be practiced, the highest intelligence would be produced so that they would know all things. You see our brothers on the continent of Africa are still being duped by the Europeans; they are still convinced that modern technology is the salvation for their people, where we know that cigarette smoking, whiskey drinking, still-producing plants, plastics, "corning ware," all these so-called modern trinkets are the things that are killing man. We know that, but they don't know that yet. That's why we had to be placed in America so that we could never be taken in again by the trinkets that once deceived us...

Justice will prevail in the end, however:

So when the great battle comes it will be that the devil manifests himself through his wicked interventions, airplanes, tanks and what-nots, and the almighty God fighting back the devil through his power, divine power. This is going to happen in the very near future. What is happening is that the great battle, sometimes called Armageddon is shaping up. After this great battle, finally Gentiles are going to see that we are the people of the almighty God...

NATION OF YAHWEH

Ideologically almost identical to the Hebrew Israelites, though much more successful in terms of numbers and wealth, are the Nation of Yahweh. The "Yahwehs" were founded in the late 1970s by Hulon Mitchell, Jr., a.k.a. **Yahweh Ben Yahweh,** or The Son of God. Mitchell had been a leader in Nation of Islam before creating his own sect and becoming the Son of God, deliverer of the Black Race. The Yahwehs, like the Hebrew Israelites, believe that Blacks are the Lost Tribes of Israel, and will soon be returning to Israel. They are meanwhile biding their time in Miami, sending their children to "Yahweh University" and making money for their "Temple of Love" to fill up those long days before deliverance.

Their beliefs are summed up in a flyer entitled, "Who are the Followers of Yahweh?":

The followers of OUR GREAT GOOD AND TERRIBLE BLACK GOD **YAHWEH** are HEBREW ISRAELITES of the NATION OF ISRAEL. The so-called black people of America are the true FOLLOWERS of **YAHWEH,** of THE TRIBE OF JUDAH, chosen to be the chief ruler for ever (I Chronicles 28:4; 5:2). The so-called black people of America are a Holy people unto **YAHWEH** your God: your God **YAHWEH** has chosen you to be a special people unto himself, above all people that are upon the face of the earth (Deuteronomy 7:6). ...

YAHWEH BEN YAHWEH is here among us doing the work necessary to save and preserve us from destruction along with the white man. ...

A FOLLOWER OF **YAHWEH** serves the so-called black people of America, who are HEIRS to NEW JERUSALEM. He is always busy taking the necessary legal steps for putting the so-called black people of America in possession of their rightful property, THE PROMISED HOLY LAND, ISRAEL. ...

Our people are beginning to follow **YAHWEH** all across America. As you begin to follow

YAHWEH BEN YAHWEH

THE SON OF GOD IS WORLD FAMOUS

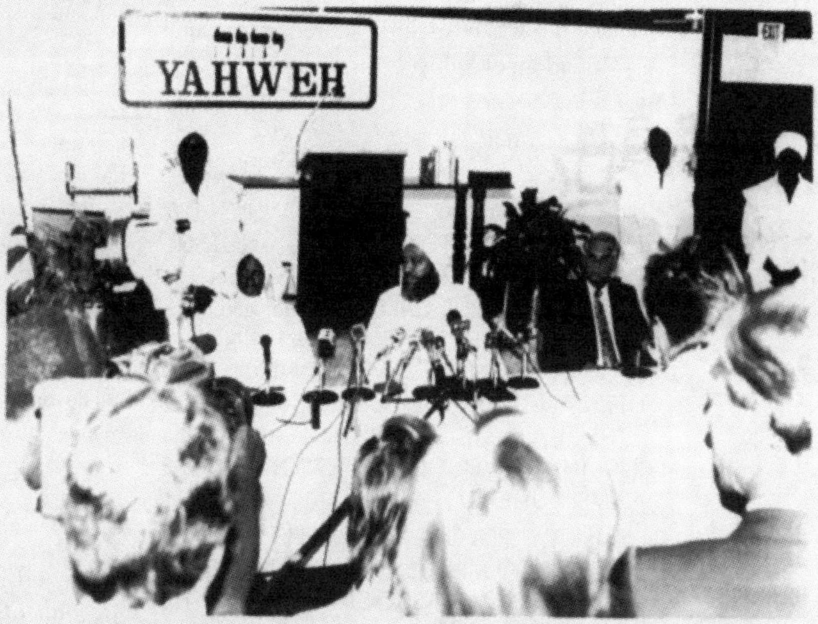

EXCLUSIVE INTERVIEWS WITH YAHWEH BEN YAHWEH ARE

THE WORLD'S BEST KEPT SECRETS

MEDIA FROM AROUND THE WORLD HAVE COME TO SPEAK WITH YAHWEH BEN YAHWEH, AND THEY SPEND HOURS RECORDING HIM & HIS MESSAGE, YET 99% IS NEVER TOLD..WHY?

READ, SEE, & HEAR THE 99% NOT TOLD!

Available Soon!

BOOKS, CASSETTES, & VIDEO TAPES

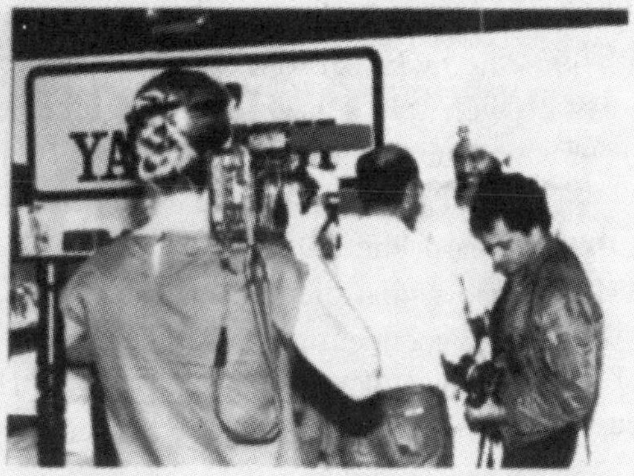

SYGNA NEWS AGENCY
(ITALY & FRANCE)

YAHWEH & CBS WEST 57TH STREET
YAHWEH & UNITED PRESS INTERNATIONAL
YAHWEH & ASSOCIATED PRESS
YAHWEH & TIME MAGAZINE
YAHWEH & USA TODAY
YAHWEH & EUROPE'S NEWSPAPER/TV MEDIA
YAHWEH & PALM BEACH POST NEWSPAPER
YAHWEH & THE MIAMI TIMES
YAHWEH & THE MIAMI HERALD
YAHWEH & THE MIAMI NEWS
YAHWEH & PUBLIC TV OF SO. FLA.
YAHWEH & CH 4 (CBS)
YAHWEH & CH 7 (NBC)
YAHWEH & CH 10 (ABC)
YAHWEH & CH 17 (MIAMI TV)
YAHWEH & CH 51 (SPANISH-TV)
YAHWEH & HOUSTON,TX RADIO
YAHWEH & WIOD RADIO (MIAMI)
YAHWEH & WPBR RADIO (PALM BEACH)

"In order to join the Brotherhood," the indictment states, "an individual had to murder a 'white devil' and bring a severed body part to Mitchell as proof of the killing."

OUR GREAT GOOD AND TERRIBLE BLACK GOD YAHWEH you will discover how good and pleasant it is for BRETHREN TO DWELL TOGETHER IN UNITY (Psalm 133:1).

HURRY TO YAHWEH NOW ! ! ! !

OUR MOTTO IS: ONE GOD! ONE MIND! ONE LOVE! ONE ACTION!

Like the white Anglo-Israelite groups such as "Kingdom of Yahweh," the Yahwehs place great importance on correctly identifying the creator's name:

NAME IS ALL IMPORTANT! THE NAME IS MORE THAN AN ARTIFICIAL TAG WHICH DISTINGUISHES ONE PERSON FROM ANOTHER. THE NAME HAS A MYSTERIOUS IDENTITY WITH ITS BEARER; IT CAN BE CONSIDERED AS A SUBSTITUTE FOR THE PERSON. KNOWLEDGE OF THE NAME GIVES CONTROL, AND UTTERANCE OF THE NAME IS EFFECTIVE EITHER UPON ITS BEARER OR AS CONTAINING THE POWER OF THE PERSON WHOSE NAME IS UTTERED...

STRICTLY SPEAKING, YAHWEH IS THE ONLY NAME OF GOD. IN GENESIS, WHENEVER THE WORD NAME IS ASSOCIATED WITH THE DIVINE BEING, THAT NAME IS YAHWEH.

"Staying with us is 'A Cultural Experience.' In ancient times, there was a prayer for the stranger within our gates. Because this motel is a human institution to serve people, and not solely a money-making organization, we hope that YAHWEH will grant you peace and rest while you are under our roof." The three motels run by the Yahwehs, Yahweh Economy Inn, Yahweh Sun City Motel and Yahweh Resort Mote, advertise such luxuries as color TV, kitchenettes and swimming pools. One of the Yahwehs' latest hotel purchases is called, weirdly enough, the "Saxon Hotel." The group also owns beauty salons, food markets, real estate and boutiques. In "The Exciting World of Yahweh," we find Yahweh businesses named "Celestial Landscaping," "Gabriel Upholstery" and "Yahweh Creative Printing." They have branched out from Miami, as well and own Chicken King Supreme in Atlanta, despite the fact that the Yahwehs themselves are vegetarians.

The Yahwehs project wealth and prosperity. Yahweh Ben Yahweh won praise from various public officials, including the mayor of Miami, for transforming decaying black slums into successful business districts. But on November 7, 1990, Yahweh Ben Yahweh, Son of God, was arrested by FBI agents, along with 15 of his followers. He was accused of sacrificial slayings in addition to racketeering charges. According to the Boston Globe:

The grand jury charged Yahweh, 55, and the codefendants with operating a continuing racketeering enterprise dealing in extortion and murder while masquerading as religious people.

The indictment describes a series of ritualistic murders that Yahweh allegedly ordered. Five of the accused were identified as members of "the Brotherhood."

"In order to join the Brotherhood," the indictment states, "an individual had to murder a 'white devil' and bring a severed body part to Mitchell as proof of the killing."

The full charges included racketeering, conspiracy in 14 murders of white vagrants and disobedient disciples, two cases of attempted murder, as well as the burning of an entire block in Delray Beach, 50 miles north of Miami. This crisis prompted communiqués from dutiful Yahwehs, calling themselves "The People For Truth," informing the Yahweh brethren on the persecution of their messiah. One flyer proclaimed that "U.S. Government Systematically Starves Yahweh Followers: Malnutrition Drives One Member Insane."

The Yahweh 16 went on trial in January, 1992. After a long and confusing trial, the jury spent five days deliberating, finding Yahweh ben Yahweh and six of his followers guilty of conspiracy; they failed to reach a verdict on the racketeering charge. Yahweh ben Yahweh was sentenced to eighteen years in prison and was fined $20,000. The judge in the trial commented, "From the evidence I heard, the crimes were so horrendous, so gross, that the 20-year maximum is simply not commensurate with the crimes." The son of the GREAT GOOD AND TERRIBLE BLACK GOD YAHWEH will soon face trial for the actual murders.

THE EXCITING
WORLD OF
יהוה
(Psalm 149:2)
YAHWEH
GROCERIES
OPEN TO THE PUBLIC
יהוה
RESORT HOTELS
II Chron. 17:13
(Psalm 150:3)

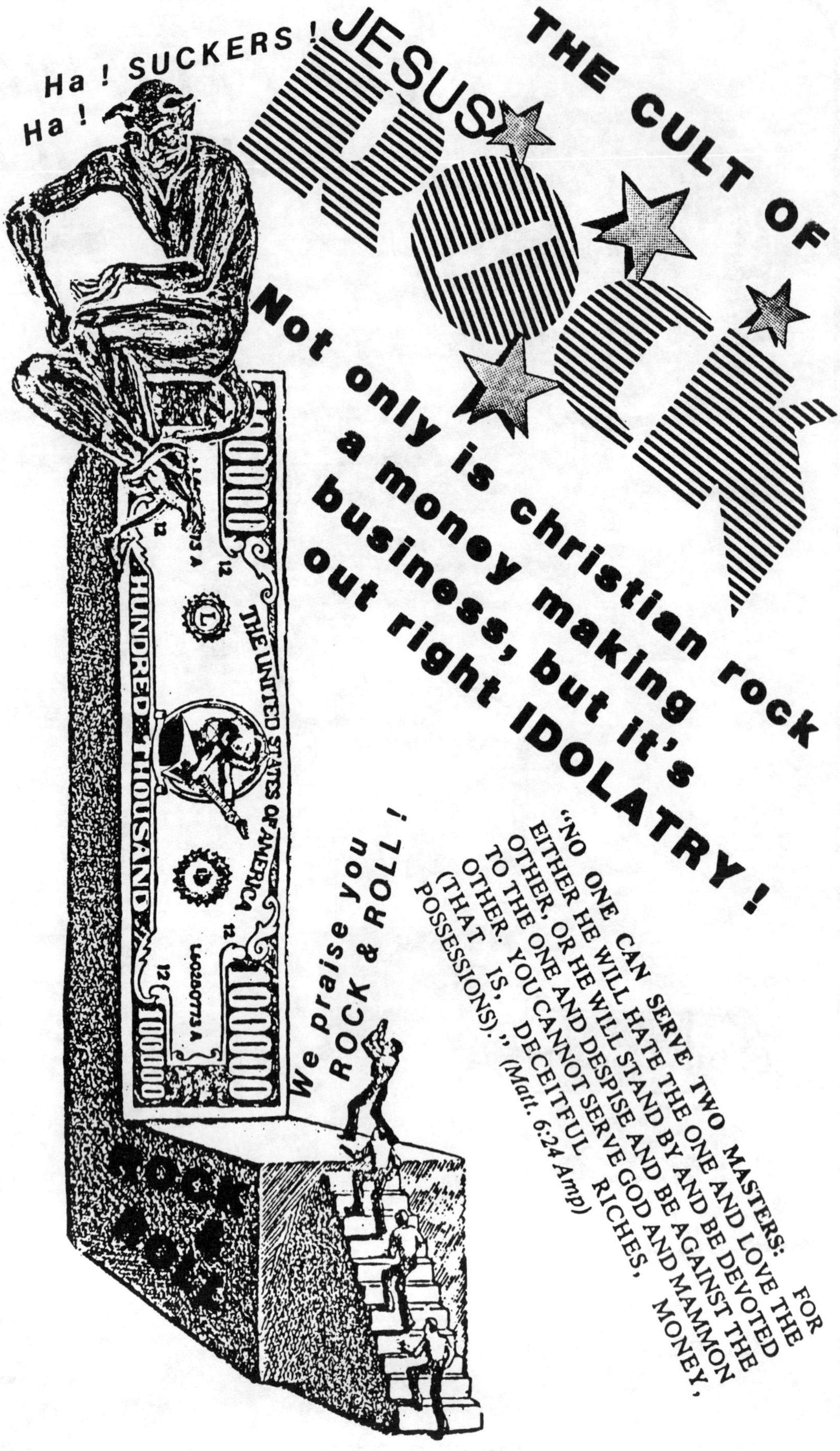

A cautionary graphic from Free Love Ministries' pamphlet, "Jesus Loves to Rock and Roll ... Or Does He?"

AGGRESSIVE CHRISTIANITY MISSIONS TRAINING CORPS

The camera focuses on brightly colored statues of the well-loved Hindu deities Ganesha and Hanuman, cuts to blue-skinned Krishna smiling down from a billboard, then to orange-clad Indians kneeling before incense soaked shrines. We ride with the droning narrator through typical Indian streets, brimming over with humanity and their enticingly attractive religious paraphernalia.

As soon as the viewer is drawn into this colorful, lurid scene, the camera cuts to a bleak, grey camp, inhabited by an orderly group of Indians dressed in khaki military fatigues. Both the Indians and the camera focus on Brigadier General **Lila Green** of Free Love Ministries, a.k.a. Aggressive Christianity Missions Training Corps (ACMTC), who is delivering a sermon.

Lila Green is sickened by the idolatrous world that surrounds her little camp. Hers is a mission of mercy and love for poor heathens unaware they were slaves of the devil until Jesus Christ came to save them, courtesy of ACMTC. Her shiny black hair is pulled tightly back in a bun. Her dark complexion and fine features are such that, dressed in *sari* rather than army fatigues, she would appear to be in her native land. But her accent gives her away; faint southern emphasis comes through whenever she talks of "Jesus." She and husband **Jim Green** are "taking Jesus to the world," and recording their work for posterity in a video-travelogue, *Operation Mobilization*.

Lila Green doesn't smile even once while delivering her sermon to these new recruits for God's End-time Army. After repeating the phrase "fishers of men" a half dozen times, she pauses for emphasis; the crease in her brow becomes so deep that it looks like it's stabbing her skull.

ACMTC, an updated, ferocious version of the Salvation Army, brings Fightin' Jesus to the demon-possessed heathen around the globe, with missions in India, the Philippines, Nepal, Nigeria, Zimbabwe and Malawi. The Greens served in Miami's Salvation Army in 1978, and credit them for ACMTC's military structure. Like the Salvation Army, ACMTC emphasizes spiritual warfare. Unlike the Salvation Army, which ministers to the drunk and vagrant, ACMTC ministers to modern teens possessed by drugs, rock 'n' roll, occultism, Dungeons & Dragons, Video Games, and sex.

With just a handful of recruits, ACMTC fights Satan on all fronts, targeting drug-crazed teens in particular, but also such groups as Native Americans. The ACMTC tract, "Indian Idolatry," is illustrated with Native American symbols and gets right to the point:

> The root of the Indian Religion is demons, and these forces of evil give power unto various animals through the mythology of the power of such demons, people are held in captivity for generations. In these modern times, one would think it hard to believe that men and women are resorting to a belief system which is so shallow and superstitious. However, as men are not presented with the truth, their hearts cry out and the devil, the master of deceit that he is, is willing to offer a belief system which offers power to the believers or adherents to it. Such a solution to man's quest for God is the "Indian Religion." ...
>
> The problem with such belief systems is that they are based primarily on fear and also ignorance. The believers in such religions are held captive by demons and are unable to act or think without consulting the familiar spirit or demon which lights upon the object of worship. Many in this hour are "returning" to Indian religion which actually means they are being possessed of devils. ...

"Indian Idolatry" observes that the degradation on Indian reservations today is testament to the devil's influence, without noting that this degradation didn't occur until Christians defeated the Indians and confiscated their land.

Aggressive Christianity Missions Training Corps, an updated, ferocious version of the Salvation Army, brings Fightin' Jesus to the demon-possessed heathen around the globe.

Jim was "as green as the Kentucky countryside" when he arrived on the West Coast, but it wasn't long before he was wired on crank, throwing his hunting knife and screaming, "KILL, KILL, KILL!"

But the majority of ACMTC's printed matter, in the form of offset printed booklets boldly illustrated with clip art, or comic books drawn by Jim Green, is directed at troubled teenagers and young adults. The publications give the appearance of punk rock or heavy metal fanzines, but the accompanying text gives them away:

> The end of the age has come, and the devil's disciples are hard at work. They are mean, they are ugly, surly, and perverted. They sing a message of destruction, decay, and debauchery. They glorify death, drug addiction and sexual perversion. Their message is one that is aimed at taking as many to hell as possible, for the end has come and the devil has commissioned his disciples!!!!
>
> The master magician, satan, continues with his cheap tricks, and unsuspecting listeners become caught in his spell. Soon, their bodies become the vehicles for demons, and they are saying and doing the thoughts of demons. They become part of the demonic scheme, while they think that they are having fun, they are actually selling their souls to the devil.
>
> Sensory bombardments, is the medium of rock music, for it is sounded everywhere and everyone is rocking. While the world is yielding itself to the rock, the devil continues to mock, thinking smugly of all those he has persuaded to follow him to hell. Through the blasting of the continual degradation, people are taught to behave as animals, to act as vampires, and to eat the flesh of others. All the acts of paganism are glorified and personified as desirable, and the actions of men and women become more VILE than words can express and the workings of EVIL are allowed to manifest through their lives and satan is delighted because he desires to reduce man who was made into the image of God into a state of utter depravity. The repetition of his brainwashing tactics is evident as morality and decency continue to erode and youth are swept away to the sea of death. More and more youth are dying of Aids having fallen to the trap of homosexuality, brainwashed by rock.
>
> Human sacrifice will be the next step taken by these demons incarnate. With all of the glorification of satanic ritual, the offering of children is the next in the sequence of events. The land is already being polluted with blood.

Teenagers who listen to Rock Music aren't just influenced by it, but actually controlled by Satan's agents via the music:

> With the sounds being produced today, there is quite commonly a coven of witches who place a spell on everyone who listens to the recording. Satan is very serious about his work for the witches hold a special mass, invoking the spirits of evil to come through the recording. The music of Satan is sensual, arousing the sensual side of man. Often times, people say, "I love the music, it turns me on." But, what does it turn on? It turns on the demons who have found domain in the heretofore innocent listener who thinks that it is him or her that the "music is turning on." But, the truth of the matter is that from experience in working in deliverance, I have found many, many demons in people that came in through Rock Music.

The Greens were once themselves possessed of demons; each had gone off the deep end as flower children in the 60s and 70s. Former ACMTC member Maura Schmierer, who later sued the group for maltreatment, met Lila in 1970. They became friends, joined the hippies, and sought to "find God through nature." Jim Green entered the picture when they joined a "radical, back-to-nature" group in Montana called the Bear Tribe. Jim, then known as "Buffalo Sun," was experimenting with "blood ceremonies" where he found "pleasure inside of pain." "We used to run around the mountains and live in teepees," Schmierer told a reporter for the Sacramento News & Review. "Jim used to run around in a loin cloth and howl at the moon."

The Greens don't deny their past. Like many a preacher, they use their histories of spiritual confusion to gain the trust of young people, and as an object lesson in demon possession.

Long before he donned a loin cloth, Jim Green left a good Christian home in Kentucky to seek worldly pleasures in California. He was "as green as the Kentucky countryside" when he arrived on the West Coast, but it wasn't long before he was wired on crank, throwing his hunting knife and screaming, "KILL, KILL, KILL!" He confesses, "the blaring HARD ROCK MUSIC provided inspiration to my insane frenzy."

> Many times, I would withdraw into myself listening to the moody, depressing music of the ROCK STARS of that day. Little did I realize that

the helpless depression that was to grip my soul then and for years after was planted in me through the very music that I loved. The lower my mood became, the more I turned to drugs and the longer I listened to the music, it was all like one huge engulfing spiral, leading downward into Hell. After years of this kind of activity, I had sufficiently removed myself from reality to the degree that I had created my own fantasy world. It was then that I began to practice the ritual of self-mutilation, burning and slicing my own flesh and offering my blood to the sun and moon.

Often during those years, I would yearn for the peace of my childhood, but somehow I was unable to recapture it. The more that I yielded myself to the ROCK MUSIC, the more my life portrayed the message that it gave. I lost sense of my own identity, and went about in costumes and disguises, presuming myself to be some sort of historical figure out of the past century. It was in this condition of sorrow that Jesus Christ found me and lifted me up and I was able to place my foot upon the REAL ROCK and have my name written on Heaven's Roll. I shall be thankful for His redeeming power that freed me from the chains of Satan's Rock Music.

Lila's descent into Hell was no less dramatic. As a young fan, first of Elvis Presley and then the Beatles, Lila confesses:

[T]he seeds of ROCK MUSIC were planted deep within me. Little did I realize that as the years passed and the ROCK MUSIC got rockier, that my life would follow the trend and as the music which was to lead a generation into rebellion, drugs, illicit sex, and bondage to sin, that I too would become one of many caught in the web of mesmerizing sounds. ... I seemed to flourish on wild, wanton music.

Lila and her generation weren't simply having a good time as rebellious teenagers, they were becoming tools of Satan:

Little did I realize that Satan was using the medium of music to change my morality, to revamp my appearance, and my standards. Soon, I became like so many others of my generation: "turned on, tuned in, and dropped out." Little did I realize in my naivete that I would subconsciously respond to the message that Satan was sending me... When I was in my early twenties, my sensitive nature had so responded to the message of the music, that I had uncontrollable fits of depression, spent hours listening to morose recordings and would spend hours at such places as the Avalon Ballroom dancing fiendishly to the "Acid Rock" groups. I began to fashion myself after Grace Slick and Janis Joplin, and as my life got harder and more depressed, I could envision myself as one of these "low-down" broads, suffering for the cause of rebellion. Little did I realize that I was only a foolish dupe in the hands of Satan and that it was his desire to either kill me, drive me insane, or get me to kill myself as did so many of the early "Rock stars." ... Satan is not deceived in what he is doing, he had geared the music to lead the youth into destruction and he will give his uncanny power to any who will be his prophet.

"Little did I realize in my naivete that I would subconsciously respond to the message that Satan was sending me."

Satan caused Lila to attempt suicide no less than three times, "the last time narrowly escaping death." She became "addicted" to marijuana, and experimented with all the hard stuff as well. Between sex, drugs, and rock 'n' roll, Lila was completely burned out at age 24; she'd fallen for the "flower power dream," following the commands of the "ROCK MUSIC PROPHETS," until "Jesus Christ reached down His hands of mercy and brought me out of the captivity of sin, freeing me from a life of drugs, free sex, and Rock Music."

Released from Satan's grip, the Greens embarked on the fundamentalist warpath. By 1981, they had established Free Love Ministries in Sacramento, which, according to Schmierer, began as an "orthodox christian" ministry. But both Lila and Jim are extremists, evidenced by their descents to the depths of rock 'n' roll depravity. Over the years, laments Schmierer, their teaching became more and more radical. Eventually, Lila began to claim she was God's number one prophet. Religious services included Lila's sermons and prophecies, chanting, writhing on the floor, and speaking in tongues.

A Sacramento resident of that era reports that the ACMTC maintained a "very high profile," appearing in Marine-style clothing with a golden winged logo on their jackets, all members wore short hair with polished shoes, and exhibited a "general lack of emotion." Their show on Sacramento Christian radio station KFIA regularly warned listeners to brace for war against the Satanic forces responsible for such scourges as homosexuality, psychoanalysis, fornication, rock 'n' roll and pride. ACMTC's fanaticism apparently became too much for the station; management cancelled its show in 1984. By this time, their Christian brethren and neighbors had begun to worry about ACMTC's activities.

Having escaped from a small shed on the ACMTC compound the previous year, Maura Schmierer filed a $20 million lawsuit, claiming the Greens brainwashed her, changed her name to "Forsaken," and then forced her to stay in a small wooden shed for ten weeks.

In 1985 the El Dorado County sheriff's office investigated ACMTC in response to neighbors' accusations that ACMTC was conducting armed war games in the desert, although no weapons were found on ACMTC property. In response, Jim Green protested to a reporter from the Sacramento Bee, "We're nothing but a missionary training group. The only military operation out there is running and jogging."

Indeed, ACMTC literature makes it clear that, at least officially, ACMTC is concerned with spiritual — not bodily — warfare, and that firearms are uncategorically prohibited from ACMTC grounds. But the literature also makes clear that ACMTC is deadly serious about the DEVIL, and considers mainstream Christians to be not only wimps, but dupes of Satan, who "don't even know that there's a war going on."

> They think that being a Christian is smiling, touching one another in love, chatting, having social parties together, hearing nice little sermons, raising nice little families. That is superficial! ... I call it "Churchianity" because that is what it is, it's not real! True Christians are going to have to fight the devil, and they are going to have to know the Lord, and they are going to have to come under command. ... JESUS CHRIST DIED TO REDEEM MANKIND FROM THE CAPTIVITY OF SATAN, NOT TO MAKE FALSE PEACE WITH THE DEVIL AND CALL HIM BROTHER.

ACMTC says normal Christians have been duped by the Devil into seeing Jesus as a wimp, when in fact he is a fierce warrior with a military title. According to Hebrews 2, Jesus is the "captain" of the salvation of many sons. When Captain Jesus said "blessed are the meek," he wasn't talking about wimps:

> There is a misconception being preached based on Matthew 5:5, "Blessed are the meek, for they shall inherit the earth." The misconception in modernism or "modern" Christianity is the portrayal of God's people as soft, meek, passive, and compromising Christians. Let me point out to you that "meek" doesn't mean "weak." Jesus Christ, our captain, doesn't want His soldiers to be weak, soft, or soggy, but rather strong in the Lord and the power of His might (Eph. 6:10). Meekness is a quality of having strength under control, being calm and confident when there is a battle being fought around you.

With Jesus Christ as official "Commander-in-Chief," ACMTC was keenly aware of the battle being fought around them. The war with the Devil heated up in early 1988, when Maura Schmierer filed a lawsuit against Free Love Ministries seeking $20 million in damages. Schmierer, having escaped from a small shed on the ACMTC compound the previous year, claimed the Greens had accused her of loving her husband more than God, brainwashed her, changed her name to "Forsaken," and then forced her and another brainwashed member to stay in a five-by-12 foot wooden shed for ten weeks, nourished only by tiny peanut butter sandwiches. Schmierer's five-year-old son's name was also changed — the Greens accused him of being possessed — to "Demon."

For the Greens, Schmierer's lawsuit was further evidence of their constant battle with Satan. A few months after the lawsuit was filed, in a personal letter, they wrote, "Please be aware that the message that we preach is one that Satan hates, and if you step forward into spreading the message to others you are asking for a big fight with the devil. The messages are anointed and they set people free through the power of the Holy Spirit, so be prepared to fight if you start distributing the army message." They knew this all too well from experience.

The Greens were used to this kind of warfare. The lawsuit didn't seem to faze them; they never even showed up in court. By late 1988, however, the Greens must have begun to worry. Lila got word from God that Bob Blasier, Schmierer's lawyer, would soon be run over by a truck. When the prophecy didn't pan out, she predicted he would be struck down by God's wrath. When that prophecy didn't pan out either, the Greens found themselves in serious trouble.

In 1989, the court ordered ACMTC to pay Schmierer $1.2 million; they lost the lawsuit by default. When they didn't come up with the money, Blasier had their compound seized by the court. When an attempt was made to assess its value, however, Free Love Ministries was gone and the premises were in ruins. They apparently demolished the Sacramento compound shortly before fleeing to one of their missions in Mozambique. The Greens denied having wrecked the property, but neighbors had observed them tearing down parts of the buildings and loading them into vans.

ACMTC later attempted to set up headquarters in Butte County, about 80 miles north of Sacramento, but Blasier, hot on their trail, put a lien on the new property. Around this time, in a letter to another correspondent, Lila and Jim said they had been forced to close their doors because of "extreme persecution." They'd never stop fighting Satan, though. "We're busier than ever. Our work has tripled because of persecution!"

Free Love Ministries settled in Klamath Falls, Oregon, three months after leaving Butte County, but by then, ACMTC membership had dwindled to nineteen. In 1992, however, the Greens appeared to be back in full force with printed attacks on abortion, homosexual rights, animal rights, rap music and Christian rock, although Lila now signed her articles, "Deborah L. Green," and ACMTC called itself the "Life Force Team."

In substance, little has changed. Whether they learned anything from their experiences in the 80s remains to be seen. From their latest newsletters, it would appear the Greens are indestructible.

"Frenzy"—"hysteria"—"hostile"— "demonic," Crazy Man Crazy!

THE POWER OF MUSIC

THE END WAS HERE BEFORE

Many Israelites continued to practice age-old rituals, and even worship the old gods, such as Baal.

Not only the Guarani [tribe] but all the Nature is old and weary of life. How often the medicine-men, when they went to meet, in dream, Nanderuvuvu, have heard the Earth imploring him: 'I have already devoured too many corpses, I am filled from it, and I am exhausted. Do make an end of it, my Father!' The water also beseeches the Creator to let it rest, disturbed no longer, and so the trees ... and so all the rest of Nature.

— Curt Nimuendaju, *Zeitschrift für Ethnologie,* quoted in Eliade, *Myth and Reality*

Just as the signs of Doomsday — comets, famine, plagues, earthquakes, floods and war — are not unique to any particular age, neither are Doomsday Prophets. History is chuck full of End of the World prophecies. It does seem, however, that waves of messianism accompany increases in misfortune, persecution and general human misery. The early Christians, for example, lived in daily expectation of the Second Coming; the expectation was again popular in the Middle Ages. When their persecutions were worst, the Jews expected their Messiah "any day now." Nor are non-western cultures immune, as evidenced by the messianic movements of Native Americans, such as the "Ghost Dance," and the Cargo Cults in Melanesia and elsewhere.

As Mircea Eliade documents in *The Myth of the Eternal Return,* the idea of the End of the World as something that happens only once in history is an outgrowth of monotheistic religion, beginning with Zoroastrianism. The Doomsday motifs — a dying and resurrected King (the Messiah), an old world replaced by the new — were played out in previous multitheistic societies as ritual events happening over and over again, not just once. The idea of linking historic time with mythic time — one consequence of which is reading the bible as an account of historic events — was an innovation with irreversible consequences. (It is important to note, however, that not even all biblical Israelites accepted the linkage, and many continued to practice age-old rituals — and even worship the old gods, such as Baal.)

Jewish Predictions

The Jews have been waiting for the Messiah since Biblical times, and in many periods of history expected to be led back to The Promised Land during their lifetime. According to the Talmud, the resurrection (of Jews who had died) would occur in Jerusalem; those buried elsewhere would be compelled to make their way back to the Holy Land through underground passages. To avoid any need for post mortem travel, many older Jews simply moved to Palestine, to die and be buried there.

Owing to inaccurate predictions early on, the practice of prophesying the date of the Messiah's return has generally been discouraged. One Rabbi put a curse on those who would speculate upon such, "for if their calculations should prove false, the people will despair of his coming altogether." Rabbis instead emphasized the less attractive alternative: repentance of sin. If all the children of Israel would repent of their sins for just one day or, if they would observe the Sabbath in all the detail of the law, then the Messiah would come much more quickly. According to Julius Greenstone in *The Messiah Idea in Jewish History,* at various times the injunction went unheeded:

> The [messianic] hope became still stronger, when an enthusiast by the name of Moses arose in the Island of Crete, or Candia [around the 5th century], declared himself the Messiah, and attracted all the Jewish congregations of the island, which was then an important Jewish settlement. Business was neglected, all the common pursuits of life were forsaken, in the anxious expectation of the time when the new Moses should lead them dry-shod through the sea into the Promised Land. So convinced were the people of his mission and of his powers, that they delivered all their belongings to him, and men, women and children followed him to the sea. Standing on a promontory projecting into the sea, he ordered them to throw themselves into the ocean, as the waters would surely part for them.

The result can easily be imagined — many were drowned, some were rescued by sailors. The Christian chronicler who is the authority for this account adds that many of the Jews of Crete subsequently embraced Christianity.

The rise of Kabbalism in the 13th and 14th centuries made messianic predictions popular again. One Kabbalistic text, the *Zohar,* pinpointed the time the Messiah would arrive by mystical calculations based upon numerical values in the Tetragrammaton (the Hebrew letters, *Yod-He-Vav-He,* spelling out the Ineffable Name of God). The numerical value of *He* (5) represents the 5,000 years Israel spent enslaved under the subjection of foreign powers. *Yod* is 10 and *Vav* is 6; 10 x 6 = 60. Thus, after 5,000 years + 60 have passed, Israel will rise; every 60 years after that "the kindness of God toward Israel will increase, until 600 in the sixth millennium, when the gates of heavenly wisdom from below will gush forth, and the world will be prepared to enter upon the seventh millennium..." According to this calculation, the Messiah would appear in calendar year 1300; but after 1300 came and went, the calculation was re-interpreted to mean 1328, and then 1648.

The 1600s saw many Kabbalists and many false Messiahs, but the greatest of the false idols was **Sabbatai Zevi,** a rabbinical student and Kabbalist with an especially charismatic personality. In 1648, the twenty-two-year-old mystic pronounced the "Ineffable Name of God," thereby revealing himself as the Redeemer of Israel. To the orthodox rabbis, Sabbatai Zevi was merely a troublemaker. He was excommunicated from the Rabbinic College of Smyrna and, in 1651, banished from the town itself. Leaving Smyrna for Salonica, a hotbed of Kabbalah, Sabbatai Zevi invited followers to a feast and proceeded to celebrate his wedding to his bride, the sacred scrolls of the Torah. He was subsequently banished from Salonica as well. Sabbatai Zevi then relocated to Jerusalem to await the miracle that would confirm his position as the Redeemer of Israel. Upon meeting Sabbatai Zevi, Rabbi Nathan of Gaza entered an ecstatic trance and proclaimed the advent of the Messiah in the person of Sabbatai Zevi.

His banishment rescinded, Sabbatai Zevi returned to Smyrna, and on the new year, in the synagogue, announced himself Messiah amid cries of "Long live our king, our Messiah!" Within months, the Jewish world was in a messianic frenzy. Expecting the final march to the Promised Land any day, many Jews abandoned their worldly interests. The demand for prayer books adorned with the likeness of Sabbatai Zevi was so great Amsterdam's printing houses couldn't keep pace. In London, Jews offered ten to one odds that Sabbatai Zevi would be crowned and anointed King of the Jews in Jerusalem within the next two years. Sabbatai Zevi announced that initiation of the New Messianic Age freed the Jews from Rabbinic Law. He encouraged followers to eat non-kosher food, practice sexual licentiousness, and engage in sins of every kind. Jews began to marry their children off at age ten or twelve, sometimes 700 couples at once, because tradition said the Messianic Age wouldn't begin until the supply of unborn souls was exhausted.

Sabbatai Zevi encouraged his followers to eat non-Kosher food, practice sexual licentiousness, and engage in sins of every kind.

As the year 1666 drew near, Sabbatai Zevi led a march to Jerusalem to usher in the Age of Peace and Wisdom. On the road to the Holy Land, however, he was taken prisoner by the Ottoman Turks and given a choice between slow execution or conversion to Islam. Choosing the more comfortable option, Sabbatai Zevi lived as a Moslem for a while, and was later banished to Albania, where he died. Remnants of the Sabbatian movement, however, survived until the First World War.

Panic in the Year 1000

The End of the World fever that struck Europe at the turn of the first millennium is often cited by chroniclers as an example of the "Madness of Crowds." Evidence for the mania, however, is scant; almost every account relies on one source, the *Histories* of a Bergundian monk, **Raoul Glaber.**

Glaber tells of thousands of pilgrims who set off for the city to cleanse themselves of sin shortly before the millennium. After weeks of difficult travel, many were denied

To William the Conqueror's surprise, his census was seen as a harbinger of The End.

admission to Jerusalem by a steep entry tax set by the Islamic Saracen governors of Palestine. The impoverished pilgrims were stuck at the gates of the city until a rich pilgrim arrived, and paid for the lot of them. Once inside, the credulous Europeans were ripe for exploitation by relic vendors, who peddled flagons of water from the river Jordan, boxes of moss from the hill at Calvary, splinters from the Cross and tears from the Virgin Mary.

Someone in Jerusalem suggested the year 1000 would herald the Second Coming of Jesus. There was little question that the omens — epidemics, invasions, even a comet — were there. Mt. Vesuvius erupted in 993; the Roman church of St. Peter burned; a five-year famine devastated the Christian world. The pilgrims in Jerusalem believed the end was near, and when Pope Gregory V died in 999, suspicions were confirmed. Word traveled back to Europe, and the pilgrims were joined by thousands more who abandoned their homes, their land, their possessions and their families, expecting never to return. Normal life in Europe and Jerusalem was suspended while End of the World panic spread throughout Christendom.

Some historians take Glaber's account to be exaggeration or even pure fantasy, citing evidence that European life in the 990s went on pretty much as it always had. In 998 the Council of Bishops in Rome imposed a seven-year penance on the King of France; in 999 Pope Sylvester II declared the Archbishop of Rheims would always thereafter crown the King of France; on March 27, 1000, the Pope conferred Kingship upon Stephen of Hungary and his heirs; in the same year, Emperor Otto III announced he would henceforth govern the Empire from Rome. Many examples of last wills and testaments exist from around that time, which those expecting the End of the World would not have bothered with. Clearly, the upper echelons — popes, bishops, emperors, kings and nobles — didn't expect the world to end anytime soon. The doings of popes and kings, however, have little to do with the general populace of peasants, serfs and beggars. Those with the least to lose are invariably those most prone to catch millennial fever. A panic in the Year 1000 likely occurred among the superstitious multitude, not their worldly rulers. Notably, End of the Millennium fever didn't subside with the End of the Millennium. When the Turks captured Jerusalem in 1010, many thought this foretold the Second Coming of Christ. Others predicted the world would end in 1033.

The Domesday Book

A generation later, another incident spurred the doomsday prophets to action. In 1066, William the Conqueror of Normandy defeated the Anglo-Saxon King Edward and took control of England. William, unaccustomed to Anglo-Saxon ways, attempted to take inventory of his new property, but was deeply confused by the legal system, or rather, legal systems; Mercian, Danish and West Saxon laws governed different parts of England, by custom and oral tradition. After spending nearly 20 years on the problem, William took action. In 1085, he ordered an all-encompassing census and survey of England, to record, in part:

> ... what is the name of the manor, who held it in the time of King Edward, who holds it now, how many hides are there, how many ploughs in demesne and how many are held by the tenants, how many villeins, how many cottars, how many slaves, how many freemen, how many sokemen, how much wood, how much meadow, how much pasture, how many mills, how many fisheries, how much has been added or taken away, how much the whole was worth then and how much now, how much each freeman or sokeman had there or has ...

To William's surprise, his census was seen as a harbinger of The End. It seems the English peasantry, though generally uneducated, had studied the bible. They were very familiar with the Book of Revelation, which prophesied that those unrecorded in The Book of Life will be cast into the Lake of Fire. William the Conqueror's census — *The Book of Life* — was being compiled, it was popularly believed, in accordance with this prophecy. As soon as it was complete, the world would end. Thus, the census was popularly known as *The Domesday Book*.

Richard fitz Nagel, writing in 1179, reported:

> This book is metaphorically called by the native English, Domesday, i.e. The Day of Judgment, For as the sentence of that strict and terrible last account cannot be evaded by any skilful subterfuge, so when this book is appealed to on those matters which it contains, its sentence cannot be quashed or set aside with impunity. That is why we have called the book "the Book of Domesday", not because it contains decisions on various difficult points, but because its decisions, like those of the Last Judgment, are unalterable.

It may be that the census was known as *The Domesday Book* before the peasantry interpreted it as a sign of the End.

To the relief of many, *The Domesday Book* was never completed.

Messiah vs. Messiah

The Jewish and Christian prophecies of The End were almost identical, but were largely independent of one another and sometimes in severe conflict. Each group observed the absurdities of the other with horror and/or amusement.

In the 1600s, before the Sabbatian movement swept Jewish Eastern Europe, a new brand of Christian messianism erupted in Western Europe. A new sect, the Fifth Monarchy Men, arose; comprised of English Puritans who supported Cromwell's government in the belief that it was the predecessor to the Fifth Monarchy (to succeed the Assyrian, Persian, Greek, and Roman monarchies). The Fifth Monarchists believed Jesus would return and would reign on Earth with the saints for 1,000 years. They believed the Jews would be the first to regain the Holy Land, the Ten Lost Tribes would be found, and the Jewish Messiah would appear in accordance with the Old Testament. Between them, Jesus and the Jewish Messiah would decide which should reign on Earth. These proto-Anglo-Israelites sought a Jewish Messiah as much as the Jews themselves.

Around this same time, **Mannasseh ben Israel** (1604-1657), a Jew and Kabbalist well-versed in the dominant European culture, became well-known in both Jewish and Christian circles. At the onset of the year 1648 — according to Kabbalists the year to look for the Jewish Messiah — messianic Puritan Christians began to flood Manasseh ben Israel with letters and pamphlets. The Puritans became the Jews' best friends, for in serving Israel their own prophecies might be fulfilled. (The practice continues today with American fundamentalist groups.) Also rebelling against their own Church Fathers, the Puritan sects concentrated more on the Old Testament than the New, and believed the Jewish Messiah would not appear until the Jews had been scattered all over the world. Thus, Manasseh ben Israel began arguing for the admittance of Jews into England, in accordance with this prophecy.

When Manasseh ben Israel learned that a Spanish Jew, **Antonio de Montezinos** (a.k.a. **Aaron Levi**), claimed to have discovered Jewish tribes among the North American Indians, he was more convinced than ever that the Messianic Age was near. His book, *The Hope of Israel,* details how the Messiah would gather the remnants of the Ten Lost Tribes from the four corners of the Earth — including America, Asia and Africa — and lead them to Palestine through Egypt and Assyria, over the Nile and the Euphrates, both rivers becoming dry and passable. The Messiah would be slain in the battle between Gog and Magog, but would then be resurrected. Manasseh ben Israel didn't venture to guess dates for these occurrences, but addressed a book, *The Precious Stone, or the Image of Nebuchadnezzar,* to the Christian world, arguing that the Fifth Monarchy would soon arrive in the form of the Kingdom of Israel. He pleaded for the admission of Jews into England, which, he argued, would hasten the Messianic Age. *The Precious Stone* was well received in Jewish and Christian circles — with the great master Rembrandt providing four etchings — and Jews were subsequently allowed to settle in England. The Puritans expected that the advent of the Messianic Age would commingle the Jews and the Puritans, and naturally, the Jews would accept

The Messiah would be slain in the battle between Gog and Magog, but would be resurrected.

Jesus as their Savior in prelude to the Final Judgment.

Believers seemed to increase both in number and faithfulness with each unfulfilled prophecy.

The Millerites

New England was settled by religious zealots, so it is no surprise that early America became a hotbed of Protestant millennialism. Many claimed the Pope's exile from Rome in 1798 fulfilled prophecies in Daniel 7 and Revelation 13 predicting that after 1,260 days (interpreted as years), the reign of the Beast/Antichrist (the Roman Papacy) would end, followed swiftly by the Second Coming. Because the millennialists dated the rise of the Papacy at 538 A.D., simple arithmetic demonstrated 1798 would be the year it would fall. The Pope's exile thus proved the prophecies were fulfilled, and Christ's reapparance on the world stage would soon follow.

According to another prophecy, the Messiah would come 2,300 days after the "desolation of the sanctuary." Identifying the "desolation" with Nebuchadnezzar's sack of the Temple at Jerusalem in 457 B.C., the millennialists found by similar methods that Christ would arrive in 1843.

Thus, when **William Miller** announced Christ would return on April 3, 1843, it was no great surprise to a religiously inclined populace. Miller, a New York farmer, was an unbeliever until about 1830. After he saw the light, he reread his bible, and made his calculations. No one took much notice of his preaching until two years later, when spectacular meteor showers began to appear in the night skies. When a comet streaked across the sky soon after, people really began to get really worried. The *New York Herald* published Miller's prophecy; hundreds soon joined Miller's sect, some of whom began to kill themselves and each other in order to beat the crowds that would throng the entrance to Heaven after Armageddon.

No one was embarrassed when the appointed day came and went without an appearance by the Lord and Savior. Miller, it seemed, had made a slight miscalculation: The end would occur on July 7. Miller's following grew into the thousands. Believers increased in number with each unfulfilled prophecy, so much so that several prophecies later (the last predicting October 22, 1844 as the day of reckoning), the Millerites numbered close to 100,000. When July 7 arrived, Miller's followers weren't taking any chances. They awaited their Redeemer wearing white ascension robes purchased from Miller.

That last date continues to live in infamy. The Millerite successors, the Seventh-Day Adventists, refer to it as the "Day of Great Disappointment." Rather than conceding that Miller was incorrect, the ever-faithful contend that Christ did relocate on October 22, 1844, just not to Earth. Miller had misinterpreted the Bible, which if read correctly, showed Christ had moved from the Heavenly Sanctuary to the Heavenly Holy of Holies (the upper house in the spiritual kingdom). Though their literature shows them to be completely convinced the End is coming very soon, the Seventh-Day Adventists today are careful not to provide precise dates.

This survey of end of the world false alarms shows that our own situation, as we near the end of the second millennium, is hardly unique. There is always ample evidence (natural disasters, ignorance, war, corruption, sin, human misery) that things are bad now and they will only get worse, until The End, coming very soon. I would venture to predict that no matter how many people experience a "Day of Disappointment," there will always be more waiting anxiously to join them, no matter how reasonably we argue against them.

BRING ON THE APOCALYPSE!

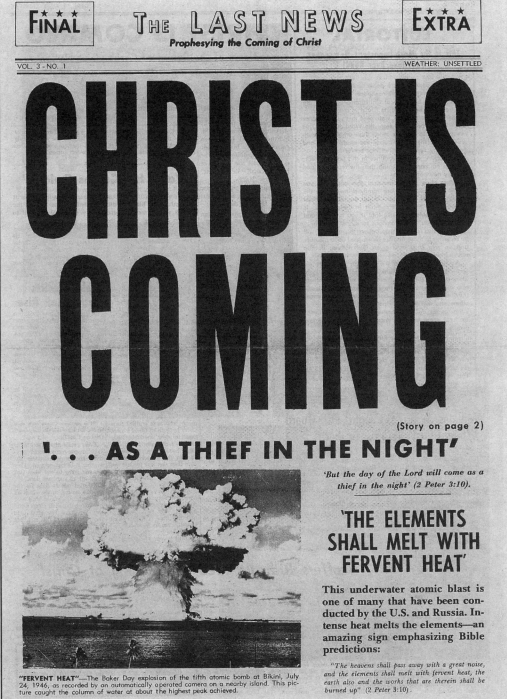

FINAL

THE LAST NEWS

Prophesying the Coming of Christ

EXTRA

VOL. 3 - NO. 1 WEATHER: UNSETTLED

CHRIST IS COMING

(Story on page 2)

'. . . AS A THIEF IN THE NIGHT'

"FERVENT HEAT"—The Baker Day explosion of the fifth atomic bomb at Bikini, July 24, 1946, as recorded by an automatically operated camera on a nearby island. This picture caught the column of water at about the highest peak achieved.

'But the day of the Lord will come as a thief in the night' (2 Peter 3:10).

'THE ELEMENTS SHALL MELT WITH FERVENT HEAT'

This underwater atomic blast is one of many that have been conducted by the U.S. and Russia. Intense heat melts the elements—an amazing sign emphasizing Bible predictions:

"The heavens shall pass away with a great noise, and the elements shall melt with fervent heat, the earth also and the works that are therein shall be burned up" (2 Peter 3:10).

The End-Times can be good times. Witness "The Last News," which mocks a *New York Daily News* type tabloid, circa 1990 (opposite). The following spread features circulars advertising traveling "Revelation Seminars" put on by Seminars Unlimited of Keene, Texas.

ACT TODAY
PREPARE FOR TOMORROW
PLAN NOW TO ATTEND - YOU'LL BE GLAD YOU DID!
STUDY AMAZING PROPHECIES THAT HELP US
COPE WITH OUR WORLD TODAY - AND TOMORROW!
ABSOLUTELY
FREE!
ALL NEW
PROPHECY SEMINAR
JESUS OPENS THE BOOK FOR YOU!
FREE Bible Lessons Binder and Study Materials
HERE'S WHAT YOU WILL RECEIVE
Exciting learning opportunities, not just lectures, await you in this special Christ-centered group interaction Seminar. Enjoy meeting new people as together you explore God's Word.
MYSTERIOUS APOCALYPTIC DREAM
EXPOSES ANTI-CHRIST
GOD TOLD HIS PROPHET "...seal the book, even to the time of the end" - NOW IT'S OPEN

REVELATION NOW!
Global Forces Mobilize-New World Order
1992
United States OF Europe?
Winds OF Change Are Blowing!
"The Final Movements Will Be Rapid Ones!"
TROUBLED LEADERS of a TROUBLED WORLD
Who Will Win? Big Surprise!
Communism & Atheism vs. Capitalism & Christianity
"When they shall say PEACE AND SAFETY then Sudden Destruction cometh upon them." 1 Thess. 5:3
666
AVOID MARK OF BEAST
BABYLON
Amazing Bible Prophecy Reveals Coming World Climax!
SEE INSIDE

THE AMAZING
WORLD OF THE
APOCALYPSE
THE REVELATION
NON-PROFIT ORG.
U.S. POSTAGE
PAID
SEMINARS
UNLIMITED
POSTAL CUSTOMER
CARRIER
ROUTE
PRE-SORT
REVELATION SEMINARS PD
=1509A 6515930326
BEGINNING THIS JOB 00010
Seminars Unlimited
P.O. Box 66
Keene, TX 76059
Time Dated Material
LEARN ALL
ABOUT IT
NOW!

PART II

SCIENCE

THE ARCHIVE OF USELESS RESEARCH

Courtesy MIT's Archive of Useless Research

The archives of the Massachusetts Institute of Technology (MIT) in Cambridge, Massachusetts, contain the original research papers of eminent scientists, past and present, including Norbert Wiener (cybernetics) and Philip Morrison (astrophysics) to name just two. In addition, the MIT archives contain the lesser known research of **A. Page Cochran, Elizabeth Boyle** and **C.F. Elrick,** and works such as, *Darwin as a Pirate, LO and BEHOLD! A Duplicate Key that Unlocks and Unmasks Mathematics,* and *The Riddle of the Universe SOLVED to the Student Competents of my Race.* These works constitute a veritable museum of rejected theories and unrecognized genius, an encyclopedia written not by the experts, but by the bastard children of science. This collection is known as the Archive of Useless Research.

Rather than offer contributions to the body of scientific research, the works in this collection offer to replace it, overturn it, oppose it, or merely attack it. More often than not, celebrated scientists are the subject of the attacks which, at times, revert to name calling. But established scientists have better things to do than argue with cranks. So, rather than take up the various challenges presented in such work, they either dispose of the material, or keep it for amusement in their "crank files." It is from these "crank files" that the collection was formed.

For years, MIT's Engineering Library held on to the crank files of its past researchers which, collectively, became known as "The American Institute of Useless Research." In 1940, **Albert Ingalls,** an editor for *Scientific American,* contributed a bulging crank file as well. The amalgamation of MIT's and Ingalls' material comprise the current collection, which fills six file boxes, available for perusal by interested scholars, journalists and lay people. Though the Institute Archives stopped adding to this collection in 1965, more recent examples of "useless research" may be found among the personal papers of individual scientists.

Among this collection are some beautifully and elaborately self-published books; one immediately wonders how their authors — in an age when printing was considerably more costly than today — were able to afford it. **Kathy Marquis,** the former Reference Archivist who took an interest in the six "useless" boxes, thinks that being "driven" was probably enough:

> These people are driven. And if they have any money, it's going to go into publishing this stuff. Because they are so compelled to put it down and to get it out. So I'd say, if they have any resources to their name, they're going to find a way to publish it, and some of them are going to go on mimeograph, and some of them are going to spend the money to have it hardbound, because it's so important to them. I wouldn't be surprised if they didn't have enough clothes but they got their book published.

Though each pamphlet, book or paper is unique, each deals with similar questions or seek to prove similar propositions. Many "solve" the ancient problem of squaring the circle;[1] others prove Einstein was wrong, or that gravity is bunk. Frequently, the authors' theories, opinions and rants are represented as "discoveries."

Seabury Doane Brewer, for example, made no less than 124 discoveries. His poster-sized treatise entitled, "124 Discoveries Made between 1892 and 1930 by Seabury Doane Brewer, of Lake George, New York, and Montclair, New Jersey," contains the revelations "that temperature, with its variations, is one of the most wonderful things, and is always present everywhere," and "that physicians should be compelled to destroy all unfit specimens of humanity immediately upon their birth." At the time of publication, Brewer was in his seventieth year and *still* making discoveries.

Brewer didn't restrict himself to just one field of science, either, or just to science. The

1. Squaring the circle is a classic mathematical problem of finding a square with a circumference (or area) equal to the circumference (or area) of a circle, using only a straightedge and compass. This would amount to showing that π, the ratio of a circle's circumference to its diameter, is rational, i.e., that it can be represented by a ratio between two integers.

subjects he explored include: Psychology, Government, Life, Evolution, Miscellaneous, Education, Astronomy, The Laws-of-Nature, Fire Balls, — of Lightning, Shadow Bands, — of Sun's Eclipses, Northern Lights, Radio, Mathematics, "Nothing" and Myself; he also adds a postscript concerning atoms and comets.

The following list of Brewer's Discoveries, incomplete as it is, is a fair representation of the type of material found in the archive:

1. That our thoughts have been, are being, and will be, thought by other thinkers.

28. That there is no such thing as Platonic love between normal males and females.

30. That umbilical cords should be allowed to wither away naturally. (I will wager that Methuselah did not have his umbilical cord monkeyed with.) Man alone interferes with the impregnation, interferes with the embryo, and interferes with birth. How unfair to the child. Watch the animals, birds and insects; watch all things in their various processes of being born.

39. That the inexorable economic law of supply and demand is a fake, — as well as many another economic law.

52. That phonetic spelling should not be allowed.

69. That twin stars do not exist. That what is seen is the result of (caused by) optical reflection.

70. That Saturn's ring does not exist. That what is seen is the result of (caused by) optical reflection.

76. That the Fire Balls (of lightning) are optical delusions.

Discovery #108, isn't a discovery at all; it's the story of Brewer's correspondence with Einstein and a "Mr. Poor," which he carried on under his astronomical *noms-de-plume,* "Mrs. Mary Bryant" and "Shirley Brown":

108. That a "5 diagramed paraphrase" explains why it is that Einstein has not yet reached the goal. The paraphrase, and the construction of it, occurred under the following circumstances.

On March 27, 1929, (in the name of "Mrs. Mary Bryant," my astronomical nom-de-plume, although it happens to be the only time I ever wrote a letter in that name) I wrote Albert Einstein, enclosing one dollar, for an authentic translation of his latest article, — which I have never received, and he still has my one dollar.

Without looking the matter up, I think that he was reported to have said, at that time, that "gravitation" is "electricity."

In my ("Mrs. Mary Bryant's") letter to him I said that long ago [N.B.: it must have been in the early part of the 1880 decade, as far as gravitation, magnetism, and electricity was concerned] I had discovered that all things (even gravitation, magnetism, electricity, chemistry, and even Life itself) are so interwoven, intermingled, and mixed up together, that it is almost impossible to tell where one thing leaves off and an other thing begins. ...

"I wrote Albert Einstein, enclosing one dollar, for an authentic translation of his latest article — which I have never received, and he still has my one dollar."

Brewer is a good example of someone who wants to replace the scary and impenetrable theories of 20th century science with good old-fashioned common sense, or, in some cases, a strange admixture of common sense and strong opinions.

George F. Gillette, whose contribution to the Archive is *Orthod Oxen of Science,* is similarly critical of Einstein but, unlike Brewer, is not above simple name-calling. Of the mental giant he wrote, "it were difficult to imagine anyone more contrary and opposite to what a scientist should be... As a rational physicist, Einstein is a fair violinist." What's more, relativity is the "moronic brain child of mental colic" and "the nadir of pure drivel." In 1929 Gillette predicted that by 1940 the theory of relativity would be considered a joke.

Newton, in Gillette's opinion, was the greatest genius of all time. Gillette, however, claims his "spiral universe" is an improvement on Newton, and "out-Newtons Newton" himself. This spiral universe is composed of units called "unimotes," which comprise our immediate universe called a "supraunimote." The cosmos is called the "maximote," but there is also something called the "ultimote," the "Nth sub-universe plane." Gillette explains the significance of this:

Each ultimote is simultaneously an integral part of zillions of otherplane units and only thus is its infinite allplane velocity and energy subdivided into zillions of finite planar quotas of velocity and energy.

This may not sound very Newtonian, but if you've taken high school physics, you may remember Newton's theories as represented

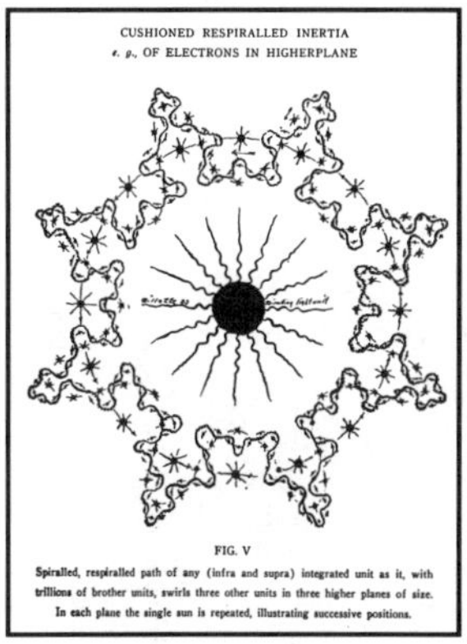

CUSHIONED RESPIRALLED INERTIA
e. g., OF ELECTRONS IN HIGHERPLANE
FIG. V
Spiralled, respiralled path of any (infra and supra) integrated unit as it, with trillions of brother units, swirls three other units in three higher planes of size. In each plane the single sun is repeated, illustrating successive positions.

An illustration explaining George Gillette's hypotheses, courtesy MIT

Martin Gardner probably wouldn't have gone to all the trouble of researching worthless material were it not for the fact that he sees it as *dangerous*.

by the motion of billiard balls. Gillette seems to have taken this interpretation to heart, for the only things that ever happen to objects in the universe is that they go straight, or they bump, just like billiard balls:

> All motions ever strive to go straight — until they bump. ... nothing else ever happens at all. That's all there is. ... In all the cosmos there is naught but straight-flying bumping, caroming and again straight flying. Phenomena are but lumps, jumps, and bumps. A mass unit's career is but lumping, jumping, bumping, rejumping, rebumping, and finally unlumping.

Since he reveres Newton, Gillette believes in gravity, but embellishes Newton's original laws with his "backscrewing theory of gravity." Gravitation, he says, "is the kicked back nut of the screwing bolt of radiation. ... Gravitation and backscrewing are synonymous. All mass units are solar systems... of interscrewed subunits."

As for the title of his book, *Orthod Oxen of Science,* Gillette is referring to the "orthodox oxen" of science. There is "no ox so dumb as the orthodox." These "built up favorites of publishers" are "the reverse of true scientists, ... cramped with Homoplania, ignorant of ultimotically related sub and supraplanias."

Gillette, along with several other contributors to the Archive of Useless Research were immortalized by **Martin Gardner** in *Fads and Fallacies in the Name of Science.* While I am thankful Gardner documented these forgotten treatises, I find his reasons for doing so, along with his conclusions, highly debatable.

The term that Gardner uses for the type of work that ends up in the Archive of Useless Research is "pseudo-science." Gardner, and other defenders of Scientific Rationalism[2] such as the Committee for the Scientific Investigation of Claims of the Paranormal (CSICOP), evaluate such work only in relation to science. Because the work comes short of science, they conclude it is an *imitation* of the genuine article. But a detailed look at these treatises indicates most of this work doesn't resemble science at all. What they have in common is that they are a *reaction* to science. "Anti-science" is probably a more appropriate term than "pseudo-science."

Anti-science is a protest against the dehumanizing elements of science. But to Rationalists such as Gardner, science itself cannot be questioned; their energy is directed towards defending, rather than improving science. Granted, the scientific method itself cannot be improved; it is only a method, not a body of belief, and thus is immune to dogma. But Scientific Rationalism is not so immune; its most cherished belief is that scientific method can and should apply to everything, a dogma clearly under attack by the bogeys of religious superstition, the New Age, the occult, cults, fringe science, alternative medicine and parapsychology. As defenders of the One True Faith, Gardner and the debunkers are compelled to declare that all the work of these "pseudo-scientists" is "worthless."

Gardner probably wouldn't have gone to all the trouble of researching worthless material were it not for the fact that he sees it as *dangerous*. Though the scientists to whom many of these treatises are directed pay little attention to them, the "less informed general public, hungry for sensational discoveries and quick panaceas, often provides [the pseudo-scientist] with a noisy and enthusiastic following." In typical fashion, Gardner describes the members of the Dianetics and Nature-Cure "cults" as consisting of "mentally ill" people and "neurotic housewives."

This smug name-calling is Gardner's primary method of dismissing both pseudo-scientists and their followers. To emphasize the dangers of believing the claims of "health nuts," who are some of the most dangerous pseudo-scientists of all, Gardner decries the "untold numbers of middle-aged housewives [who] are preparing to live to the age of 100 by a diet rich in yoghurt, wheat-germ, and blackstrap-molasses." If those housewives had listened to science, they would have served their families red meat instead![3]

Especially disturbing to Gardner is that "major publishing houses" publish the works of people such as Immanuel Velikovsky, author of *Worlds In Collision*. He doesn't

2. Scientific Rationalism, for my purposes, is the belief that all phenomena can be investigated and explained by the scientific method.

3. Gardner also fails to mention that "cranks" first noted that tobacco causes cancer, and were ridiculed for this.

even entertain the thought there might be some merit other than the scientific to such work, even if it only serves as an object lesson in bad science. Gardner would rather not let people make up their own minds.

It is true that many people do not know the difference between good and bad science, but many people do not know the difference between good and bad *thinking,* either. There are always those who base their thinking on emotional arguments, prejudice and logical fallacies, and they will always have an audience, whether or not the major publishing houses print their work. Somehow, I find it far more alarming that millions of people believe what is presented to them on the evening news, than that they read the works of Velikovsky or Erich Von Daniken. Gardner disagrees:

> If the public wants to shell out cash for such flummery, what difference does it make? The answer is that is not at all amusing when people are misled by scientific claptrap. Thousands of neurotics desperately in need of trained psychiatric care are seriously retarding their therapy by dalliance with crank cults. ... What about the long-run effects of non-medical books like Velikovsky's, and the treatises on flying saucers? It is hard to see how the effects can be anything but harmful. ... it is easy to forget how far from won is the battle against religious superstition. ..."

To Gardner, religious superstition and pseudo-science are scourges to be wiped out, much like Rock 'n' Roll to Christian fundamentalists. If we're not careful, says Gardner, we might end up like Nazi Germany:

> ... a renaissance of German quasi-science paralleled the rise of Hitler. If the German people had been better trained to distinguish good from bad science, would they have swallowed so easily the insane racial theories of the Nazi anthropologists?

Implying that the Nazi movement was, in part, attributable to mere scientific error, Gardner seems blissfully unaware of the connection between the acceptance of scientific theories and politics. *If people would only learn to distinguish good from bad science,* according to Gardner, *there wouldn't be any Nazis, and there wouldn't be such a thing as "religious superstition."*

To help the public weed out the good from the "worthless," Gardner provides a list of tell-tale signs for spotting the pseudo-scientists in our midst: 1. They work in total isolation from their colleagues. 2. They consider themselves to be geniuses. 3. They consider their colleagues to be ignorant blockheads. 4. They consider themselves to be unjustly persecuted. 5. They focus their attacks on the greatest scientists and best-established theories. 6. They write in complex jargon.

Some of these traits apply to some real scientists as well, but I would agree with Gardner that anti-scientists typically exhibit some, if not all, of these traits. But these characteristics of the "worthless" cover only superficial aspects. In speaking of the MIT Archive of Useless Research, former reference archivist Kathy Marquis provides an analysis which is more sympathetic and more penetrating:

> What's been fascinating is seeing the themes that come up over and over and over again, and I've pretty much clarified three of them. One is discomfort with religion and science, and that can go either way. They can either make up their own religious theories or they make up their own scientific theories. But the scientific theories have religious overtones, and the religious theories try to take in science somehow, sort of like Creationism, now. And another theme is debunking. You know, Einstein was all wrong, Newton was all wrong, Copernicus was all wrong, and I'm right. And then the third thing is the people who want to solve the entire world riddle in two pages, and don't care whether it's provable or not, it's just true because they say it's true. ...

When Marquis became interested in the Archive, she discovered that the public as well, was fascinated by the material. She wrote an article for MIT's newspaper, *Tech Talk.* Soon after, she and the Archive both were discovered by the *Boston Globe,* as well as by big and small town newspapers and radio stations all over the country. Because she felt the Archive was important, Marquis hoped that researchers, along with the general public would peruse the six boxes, and

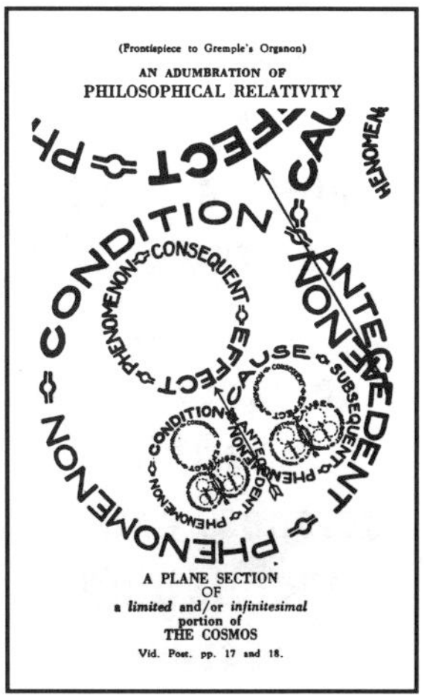

"Philosophical Relativity" from Gremple's Organon, courtesy MIT

learn from the material they contained, as she had:

> **"And I think these people have sort of taken the power back to themselves by redefining science, rather than letting themselves be defined by it."**

Ninety-nine percent of the use so far has been by the media. And some of them have actually come in and used the collection, and other people have quizzed me over the radio and just asked me questions. We've had a little bit of interest from some historians of science, and none of them have come back yet but I expect some of them will. Some of them see sort of the equivalent of coffee-table publications out of it. But some of them are interested in a more sociological look at these things as reflections of peoples' attitudes towards science and technology, which is really one thing that we've wanted to strongly promote, and that hasn't really happened yet, but I think it will.

Were sociologists to study the Archive of Useless Research, I think they would see it isn't a reaction to science *per se,* but a reaction to Scientific Rationalism. According to religious historian **Julius Greenstone,** the rise of rationalism has historically been followed by a reaction to it; in the history of religion, periods of rationalism are always followed by waves of mysticism, which is followed finally by a "safe and happy mean." Greenstone sees the limitations to reason quite clearly:

The history of human events is a history of actions and reactions. The extreme development of any principle, for good or for evil, generally produces a reactionary movement, which results finally in a safe and happy mean. ... But rationalism left to the sweet will of the people becomes a dangerous thing. In its extreme manifestations, it may produce such phenomena as a religion of reason, that most abominable of all the vagaries of the French Revolution.

Contributors to the Archive of Useless Research represent the first reaction to the "religion of reason." The New Age movement, whose roots are in the Spiritualist Movements of the last century, is clearly a further development of this reaction. Whether or not we are now approaching the "safe and happy mean" — a synthesis of the Technological Era and the mystical, New Age reaction to it — remains to be seen.

Until that synthesis takes place, the reaction is likely to become stronger despite the efforts of Martin Gardner, CSICOP and the debunkers. As Marquis points out, the Archive of Useless Research represents an extreme, but an extreme that has elements of popular feeling in it:

... what an archives is all about is documenting, if not all, a lot of segments of society. And, I think that what's interesting about this collection is that clearly people are just fascinated by the craziness of it. But I think it's not off the spectrum, it's on the spectrum. It's at one end of how people see science and technology, and I think that as part of an archives that seeks to document not only the creation of science and technology here at M.I.T. both in research and in teaching, but also public reactions to it because that has everything to do with the way that we're perceived. I think a lot of these people are disturbed but they still have nuggets of popular feeling in them, and it's a great indicator of that.

This is not a very written culture any more. It's one of the few ways that you're going to find what people think about these things besides doing something like reading the letters to the *Globe*. People don't leave diaries, they don't write as many personal letters, and it's just a great set of documents that shows how we feel about forces that are kind of bigger than us, or that we feel powerless against. And I think these people have sort of taken the power back to themselves by redefining science, rather than letting themselves be defined by it. They have no such problems with defining things on their own. It doesn't make a lot of sense, I would definitely call it crazy if you have to put a label on it, but it's their way of making sense of the world.

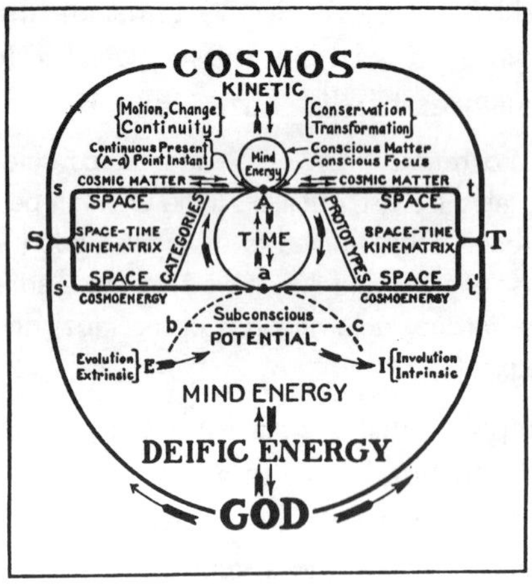

PLATE I.

THE THEOCOSMIC DIAGRAM

The frontispiece from Arvid Reuterdahl's *The God of Science,* courtesy MIT.

ANTI-GRAVITY
FREEDOM FROM PHYSICS

... A Holy Phoenix shall be seen to revive from hot ashes of Einsteinean theory of relativity and to fly over sky. This is very the principles of ultra relativity along with that background spirit of "cosmic philosophy." This title will be found to contain general mathematics, physics and engineerings in order to make our planet a paradise.
— Shinichi Seike, *The Principles of Ultra Relativity*

For centuries, amateur mathematicians attempted to square the circle and trisect the angle, against the advice of their professors who pointed out they were *logically* impossible operations; likewise, amateur inventors engineered perpetual motion machines against the advice of physicists who said it was *physically* impossible. But if no one seems to be squaring the circle or building perpetual motion machines these days, it's not because we live in the New Age of Reason; it's because they're building *free energy* machines and *anti-gravity* devices instead.

Rebel physicists looking for ways to solve energy crises, environmental problems, and economic disparities, would naturally be attracted to the idea of Free Energy. Dreamers and philosophers, however, would likely be more inclined toward anti-gravity, for gravity is the most mysterious of physical concepts. Nobody really understands gravitation, despite Newton's laws and Einstein's theories, for while Newton and Einstein were able to describe the effects of gravitation, no one has yet been able to control it. We can turn electricity on and off; not so gravity.

Around the turn of this century, the dim hopes of controlling gravity were dimmed even further by the so-called "Michelson-Morley Experiments." Before these experiments, it was generally assumed that a substance called the *ether* pervaded space. If the ether existed, interactions between gravitational fields and the ether would be observable, and controlling gravity might be a simple matter of manipulating the ether. To surprise and disappointment, Michelson and Morley demonstrated that the ether does not exist.[1] The experiments are said to have been the basis for Einstein's General and Special Theories of Relativity, which among other things, put the last nails in the coffin of gravity control. The Theory of General Relativity postulates that gravity is a quality of space itself. In order to nullify it, then, we'd have to manipulate space. For that reason, physicists tell us anti-gravity, gravity control, nullifying gravity or whatever you want to call it, is *impossible*.

Physicists were at first optimistic they might be able to analyze gravity in terms of known forces, such as electricity and magnetism, even it they couldn't control it. Einstein himself surmised it might be possible to include gravity in a theory of all physical forces, the "unified field theory." He thought this theory would come close on the heels of Relativity, but it did not, despite the best efforts of Einstein and his successors. These factors only serve to egg on those who would defy the scientific authorities.

In March, 1918, the *Electrical Experimenter* printed an article about Professor **Francis E. Nipher** of the St. Louis Academy of Science, who apparently showed that electricity can nullify gravity. A pamphlet, printed the previous year, supplied experimental evidence showing that "gravitational attraction can not only be suspended or nullified by the electrical current, but it actually can be transformed into 'gravitational repulsion!'" In 1920, in Turin, Italy, Professor **Q. Majorana** observed the "absorption" of the gravitational force by an intervening medium, and concluded "the sun is considerably more dense than estimated, but the gravitational effect is not evident because of its self-shielding. ..."

Thomas T. Brown, described by *Science and Invention* as one of the leading American physicists, not only theorized gravity control but claimed to have achieved it. Like Nipher, Brown's experiments purportedly demonstrated a connection between gravity

Dreamers and philosophers are likely inclined toward anti-gravity, for gravity is the most mysterious of physical concepts.

1. The experiment was based upon the assumption that the speed of light through the ether would be affected by the direction of earth's motion. Michelson and Morley measured the speed of light and found that this was not the case, i.e., that the speed of light was constant. Scientists concluded there is no ether.

According to Captain See, gravity must be "miraculously pulling like stupendous cables of steel, imagined as weightless as spider webs, yet stretched to the utmost limits of their tensile strength across the celestial spaces, for holding the planets in their orbits."

and electrical fields. Brown's experimental apparatus, the "gravitator," consisted of two heavy lead balls suspended 45 cm. apart by wires. After opposite charges were given the balls, Nipher found they behaved according to a new law, something he calls "gravitator action," combining Newton's law of gravitation and Coulomb's law of electrostatic attraction. Lest we doubt he'd found anything new, Brown informed us, "THE PECULIAR RESULT IS THAT THE GRAVITATIONAL FIELD OF THE EARTH HAD NO APPARENT CONNECTION WITH THE EXPERIMENT. THE GRAVITATIONAL FACTORS ENTERED THROUGH THE CONSIDERATION OF THE MASS OF THE ELECTRIFIED BODIES." Thus the energy produced by the gravitator wasn't electrical energy, but something else:

> The gravitator, in all reality, is a very efficient electric motor. Unlike other forms of motors it does not in any way involve the principles of electro-magnetism, but instead it utilized the new principles of electro-gravitation. A simple gravitator has no moving parts but is apparently capable of moving itself from within itself. It is highly efficient for the reason that it uses no gears, shafts, propellers or wheels in creating its motive power. It has no internal mechanical resistance and no observable rise in temperature. Contrary to the common belief that gravitational motors must necessarily be vertical-acting the gravitator, it is found, acts equally well in every conceivable direction.
>
> While the gravitator is at present primarily a scientific instrument, perhaps even an astronomical instrument, it also is rapidly advancing to a position of commercial value. Multi-impulse gravitators weighing hundreds of tons may propel the ocean liners of the future. Smaller and more concentrated units may propel automobiles and even airplanes. Perhaps even the fantastic "space cars" and the promised visit to Mars may be the final outcome. Who can tell?

Another approach to gravity control was to resurrect the theory of the ether. During the 1920s, **Captain T.J.J. See,** an astronomer, developed a "wave theory of gravitation" based on the existence of the ether, which officially hadn't existed since around 1903.

See held several respectable positions in astronomy before his appointment as U.S. Navy professor of mathematics. He eventually became the Director of the Naval observatory at Mare Island, California, a post he held until his retirement in 1930. See is remembered for formulating the wave theory of gravitation, but especially for his insistence that the observed "red shift" of galaxies is due, not to the expanding universe, but to the interaction of light and gravity waves. Notably, it is now conceded that See's ideas are "in striking agreement" with current theories.

See, who wrote thirteen volumes on his wave theory, imagined that, since it sustains tremendous forces of the heavenly bodies, the cause of gravitation must be "miraculously pulling like stupendous cables of steel, imagined as weightless as spider webs, yet stretched to the utmost limits of their tensile strength across the celestial spaces, for holding the planets in their orbits." In other words, gravitation is caused by an elastic ether. When planets rotate, waves generated in the ether follow the laws of wave phenomena, interpenetrate and cause a relative "ether vacuum," creating enormous inter-planetary tensions; beyond the planets, the stresses increase and external pressures exceeding the effect of centrifugal force causes the planets to follow an elliptical path about the sun. "... [T]he existence of forces implies stresses in the aether: the stresses imply waves: the waves imply heterogeneous density in the medium... There is no other view of aether which can be held. Homogeneity of density would imply no stresses; no stresses would imply no forces; no forces would imply an inert universe; which is contrary to observation and thus wholly inadmissible."

See's wave theory was rejected by his contemporaries, probably because he relied on the theory of the ether. Ironically, gravity waves are currently one of the hot topics in astrophysics, although the current notion of gravity waves stipulates they are ripples in space-time, not ripples of the ether. According to Einstein's theories, gravity waves, generated when space is fiercely disturbed, such as when a star is jostled, cause ripples of gravitational energy to radiate in all directions. Presently, astronomers are trying to observe gravity waves via "telescopes" that are actually more like seismographs than optical telescopes.

The present-day theory of gravity waves doesn't challenge existing assumptions about the impossibility of gravity control, because their medium is space-time, not the ether. But some anti-gravity researchers embrace See's theory rather than Einstein's because gravitational fields caused by stresses in the ether clears the way for controlling gravity by manipulating the ether.

Another advocate of the ether theory was **D.C. Miller,** who conducted experiments similar to those of Michelson and Morley, achieving opposite results. In 25 years, more than 200,000 measurements demonstrated a "positive ether drift effect," i.e., a change in the speed of light varying with the direction of earth's rotation, thus proving the ether exists. Miller published his findings in 1933, but nobody seemed to notice — except anti-gravity advocates fifty years later. Another observation in favor of the ether theory was made by **Thomas C. Van Flandern** of the U.S. Naval Observatory, who showed the orbital speeds of the earth around the sun and the moon around the earth are decreasing at rates higher than can be explained by tidal friction. Van Flandern attributes the phenomenon to a weakening in gravity over time, but an alternative explanation is that slower orbits are caused by friction with the ether.

The Gravity Research Foundation

Anti-gravity received a boon in 1948 when **Roger Babson,** a stock market analyst and former Prohibition Party candidate for President, established The Gravity Research Foundation in New Boston, New Hampshire. Babson, who lost two loved ones to drowning, pictured gravity as a dragon that had seized them and dragged them down to the bottom. Babson successfully utilized Newton's First Law ("For every action there is an equal and opposite reaction") in predicting the stock market crash of 1929 a few months before the financial plunge.

Though Babson was interested in all types of gravity research, his main concern was finding a gravity screen that nullified gravitation as an opaque wall blocked light. Babson, undaunted by naysayers, confidently proclaimed that "... Edison experimented with more than 8,000 materials before he finally hit on the right one that gave him a filament for his electric light bulb." Alas, the Foundation apparently made little progress with its own experiments, and soon began to serve instead as a clearing house for gravity research information, reaching out to lonely gravity researchers throughout the world to "let them know that they have at least one sympathetic friend."

To this end, the Foundation organized an annual essay contest, open to gravity researchers everywhere, with a first prize of $1,000. Entries had to deal with the possibility of discovering "some partial insulator, reflector or absorber of gravity," "some alloy or other substance, the atoms of which can be agitated or rearranged by gravity to throw off heat," or "some other reasonable method of harnessing the power of gravity." **Stephen W. Hawking,** today Lucasian Professor of Mathematics at Cambridge University and author of a best-seller, *A Brief History of Time,* entered the contest in the 1970s, winning first prize.

Babson was a businessman, but he was also a statistician, and brought the discipline of statistics to bear on his gravitational studies. To test the hypothesis that gravitational variations of the sun and moon affect human behavior, Babson and the Foundation compiled statistics on all sorts of human affairs, culled from sources as varied as mental hospitals and *Time* magazine. He also sought to compile data on the effects of body weight — i.e., human mass attracted by Earth's gravity — on personality. Babson's conclusions were compiled in a number of pamphlets. In "Gravity and Sitting," Babson attacked the practice of sitting in chairs and sleeping on one's back; also, he was convinced it's easier to climb stairs during high tide. In "Gravity and Ventilation," Babson suggested gravity might be used to clear bad air from buildings by constructing sloping floors connected to

Roger Babson, who lost two loved ones to drowning, pictured gravity as a dragon that had seized them and dragged them down to the bottom.

He reached up and caught hold of the Professor's ankles.

From *The Anti-Gravity Handbook,* compiled by D. Hatcher Childress, Adventures Unlimited Press, 1985.

air outlets at the bottom; he built such a house at New Boston.

Roger Babson died in 1967, but the Gravity Research Foundation, operating from new quarters in Gloucester, Massachusetts, lived on at least until the late-70s or early 80s. Paul Laffoley, an artist/inventor from Massachusetts (see the chapter on Laffoley in the "Enigmas" section of this book), has been unable to trace the Foundation's whereabouts since then or confirm whether it still exists; I suspect it is no longer in operation.

Anti-Gravity & Flying Saucers

Reports of flying saucers added a fresh crop of researchers to the anti-gravity field. Those who believed we were being visited by advanced beings from another solar system began to wonder exactly how the extraterrestrials built their saucers, seemingly the very embodiment of anti-gravity. If having flying saucers was just a matter of more advanced technology, there was no reason that we couldn't duplicate it ourselves, here on earth.

Some maintain saucer/anti-gravity technology exists now, but the government or some other sinister force is covering it up. These conspiracy theorists suggest that some (if not all) UFO sightings result from clandestine experiments conducted by the U.S., the Russians, the Nazis, or all the above. Physicists, according to this theory, in cahoots with the government, not only deny the existence of flying saucers, but also tell us anti-gravity is impossible. While the cover-up will some day be exposed, until then, lonely saucer engineers will be dismissed as kooks.

Perhaps the best-known of these engineers is the Englishman, **John Searl,** who began research in 1946, the year before the phrase "flying saucer" was coined. Searl claims his prototype consisted of a "gyro" or flywheel, which levitated when attached to an active generator, hovered for a full eight minutes, then shot away and disappeared, just like a flying saucer. A 1952 prototype was three times the size of the first, with increased take-off power. In 1968, Searl was granted a patent for a "Levity Disk," but lacked the funding to produce a disk big enough to carry himself and a crew of two around the world in an hour, although by 1972, he was actively soliciting funds to build a full-sized flying saucer. Searl's experiments are cited by nearly all the anti-gravity proponents, but they never mention his progress toward building a full-sized disk.

Searl's progress was matched or exceeded by others. During the late 60s and early 70s a number of "Anti-gravity Space Drive" patents were granted, including Jones' Entropy Engine (1967), Kellog's Gyrothrust (1967), Cox's Magnetic-Etheric Screw (1967) and Roos' Etheric Vortex Drive (1970). In 1971, a man named **Henry Wallace** was granted two U.S. patents for a machine that generated an anti-gravity field, which he called a "kinemassic forcefield." The machine consists of two wheels, made of "carefully chosen materials," spun at 20,000 revolutions per minute. Wallace claims that the wheels, placed so each oscillates under the other's influence while rotating around an axis, create a secondary gravitational field which reduces the weight of the bodies. Wallace further claims that, if the field is sufficiently strong, it generates localized areas of gravitational shielding, thus providing an effective propulsion force.

The pace of flying saucer research increased in the 1970s. In 1975, **Bruce DePalma** (another oft-cited name) circulated a report indicating a rotating object is capable of generating an inertial field. That same year, **Niels T. Sorensen** published a paper giving a method of using microwave radiation beams to effect a reduction in a local gravitational field. Around the same time, **Marcel Pages,** who claimed to have observed levitation of experimental mica discs 14 cm across, developed a new theory of gravitation resurrecting the gravitational wave theory. Pages postulated the existence of a "graviton gas" which permeates space consisting of energy packets of gravitational waves, much like photons are energy packets of electromagnetic waves. Bathed in graviton gas, the weight of protons and electrons is reduced by the weight of the gas they displace, the same way the effective weight of a helium balloon is reduced by helium displacing air.

A French patent has been issued based on this principle, for an "Engine for Cosmic Flight" shaped like a "lenticular UFO."

In 1981, **T.B. Pawlicki's** *How to Build a Flying Saucer* was published. The book, which attempts to demystify saucer technology, presents the case that the technology necessary to build a flying saucer exists. According to Pawlicki, Professor Eric Laithwaite, who invented the "Bullet Trains" operating in Germany and Japan (which literally float on air while travelling at 300 miles per hour), came very close to creating a practical anti-gravity engine. Pawlicki also conducted his own experiments, using junk from around his house:

> I found an old electric motor that had burned out, but still had a few more turns left in it. I drilled a hole through the driving axle so that an eight-inch bar would slide freely through it. I mounted the motor on a chassis so that the sliding bar would rotate in an eccentric cam. In this way, one end of the bar was always extended in the same direction while the other was always pressed into the driving axle. As both ends had the same angular velocity at all times, the end extending out from the axle always had a higher angular momentum. This resulted in a concentration of centrifugal acceleration in one direction. When I plugged in the motor, the sight of my brainchild lurching ahead — unsteadily, but in a constant direction — gave me a bigger thrill than my baptism of sex — lasted longer, too. ...

Though Pawlicki says his initial tests were inconclusive, his fellows are not usually so modest. In 1984, **Dr. Jan Pajak** of New Zealand presented a treatise claiming his "Magnocraft," still only a design, represents a new approach to interstellar travel. If realized, the capabilities of this new saucer are nothing short of astounding, matching or even exceeding the space aliens. Pajak asserts his proposed Magnocraft has no moving parts; can travel at 70,000 km/hr in the atmosphere and close to the speed of light in space; is invisible to radar and the naked eye; will withstand any high pressure or temperature, fly in any environment (including air, water, free space, solid matter or melted media), and oppose any known weapon; and can change into explosive material "and blast every piece of metal found in the range of its spinning, pulsating magnetic field." Even more surprising, the inventor says its operation is based on current knowledge:

> [The craft is based] on the principle of an interaction between the vortex magnetic field produced by the craft itself and a terrestrial, solar or galactic magnetic field already existing in every point of the universe. The pulsating magnetic field providing this spacecraft with the propulsive forces is produced by the "oscillatory chamber," a device which also applies completely new principles. The field is produced in it by an electric spark circulating around a perimeter of a cube formed from two oscillatory circuits with a spark gap. Such principles remove all the limitations which now hold back an increase of output in our present electromagnets, and will raise the strength of a produced field to a level sufficient for propelling a spacecraft.

William L. Brian II, a nuclear engineer, agrees anti-gravity is possible now, but goes further. His book, *Moongate: Suppressed Findings of the U.S. Space Program (The NASA-Military Cover-Up)* builds the case that our government has not only designed anti-gravity devices, but has already employed them to reach the moon.

William L. Brian's book, *Moongate,* builds the case that our government has not only designed anti-gravity devices, but has already employed them to reach the moon.

Brian's case is based upon alleged discrepancies in official NASA statements, especially those concerning the moon's gravity. According to Newton, says Brian, the moon's gravity is approximately 1/6th, or 16.7% of the earth's gravity. However, Brian says, if this were the case, the so-called "neutral point" between the earth and the moon, i.e. the point at which their gravitational pulls were equal, would be very close to the moon, and during the 50s was calculated at around 25,000 miles from the moon's center. Brian points out that our original space probes to the moon, which relied on this calculation, were dismal failures. The successes around the mid-60s, came only after NASA had recalculated the neutral point to be around 43,000 miles from the moon's center. These new calculations were based on NASA probes, rather than a theory. Obviously, if the neutral point is further from the moon, then the moon's gravity must be much greater than originally thought. In fact, says Brian, the moon's gravity is actually 64% of the earth's gravity, which is significantly higher than 1/6th. But the authorities continue to maintain that the moon's gravity is 1/6th of the earth's. Therefore they must be lying, covering up the true figure for the moon's gravity.

"The only way to traverse the vast distances of space is to possess the means of manipulating, or altering, the very structure of space itself ..."

Why would NASA — or anyone else — want to lie about lunar gravity? Brian's answer is, the moon's gravity is much greater than we thought; therefore, our rocket technology would have been inadequate to effect a landing. What NASA used was so top-secret that even some of the astronauts didn't know about it. His conclusion is *the televised lunar landings were staged to fake 1/6th gravity in order to hide the ultra-secret anti-gravity devices we used to get there.*

The Anti-Gravity Equation

An amateur mathematician from New Zealand may have discovered how those ultra-secret anti-gravity devices operate. **Bruce L. Cathie,** a "Fokker Friendship" captain with National Airways of New Zealand, has pursued the "anti-gravity equation" since the 60s, and reported his findings in the books *Harmonic 33* (1968) and *Harmonic 695* (1971). He became interested in flying saucer technology when he and two others witnessed a UFO at Mangere, Auckland in 1952. Some time later, he began to understand the principles involved:

> The first glimmerings of how true space travel might be achieved came to me when I uncovered the first clues that led me to the UFO grid which laces about our globe. ... Somewhere I knew, the system contained a clue to the truth of the unified field which, [Einstein] had postulated, permeates all of existence. I didn't know at the time that this clue had already been found by scientists who were well ahead of me in the play. I know now that they must have understood something of the grid system years ago. They knew that Einstein's ideas about the unified field were correct. What's more, for many years they have been carrying out full-scale research into the practical applications of the mathematical concept contained in that theory. ...
>
> The only way to traverse the vast distances of space is to possess the means of manipulating, or altering, the very structure of space itself; altering the space-time geometric matrix, which to us provides the illusion of form and distance. The method of achieving this lies in the alteration of frequencies controlling the matter-anti-matter cycles which govern our awareness or perception of position in the space-time structure. Time itself is a geometric, just as Einstein postulated; if time can be altered, then the whole universe is waiting for us to come and explore its nooks and crannies.

Rather than opposing Einstein and the results of modern physics, Cathie takes them one step further — if gravity control is a matter of manipulating space-time, then we'll just figure out how to manipulate space-time. His original equations, Cathie says, published in *Harmonic 33,* came very close to the "truth," but had not yet gelled into the earth-shattering revelation of his final equation. This would only happen after a visit from a mysterious Englishman:

> A year after the book was published I had a telephone call from a man who had just arrived in New Zealand from England. He explained that he was a textile salesman and would be here only a few days on business. He said he had heard of my research, and was most insistent that he should see me. He said that he had very little knowledge of UFOs, but that he would like to talk to me about my theories. ...
>
> He arrived ... and at once began questioning me about my activities and my research. It was soon obvious that he knew a great deal more about the subject of UFOs than he was prepared to admit; and he was quite demanding about getting his questions answered. He had an air of nervous tension about him as he checked through pages of my calculations; then he wanted to know where I kept all my data, and if there were many people who knew about my studies.
>
> I make no secret of whatever findings I turn up, and I showed him everything he asked to see. Finally he insisted that there was something I hadn't shown him — an equation which knitted all my calculations together. In some surprise I told him I knew of no such equation; his expression was eloquent of disbelief. ...
>
> His departure was hurried; I have neither seen him or heard of him since.

Cathie resumed his research, and reviewed all of his previous calculations, now in search of the one that would pull them all together. Using the theory of "harmonics" as well as the aid of computers, he came up with:

$$C + \sqrt{(1/C)} = M$$

where C = the speed of light and M = mass. (He derived this from the harmonic of the mass of the earth, which is an actual number.) Applying $E = MC^2$ to this resulted in the equation that would reveal the secrets of the universe:

$$E = (C + \sqrt{(1/C)})C^2$$

where E = energy. This, Cathie says, is a harmonic field equation expressed in terms of light, or pure electromagnetic wave form:

> [This equation is] the key to the universe, the whole of existence; to the seen and unseen, to form, solids, liquids, gases, the stars and the blackness of space itself, all consisting of visible and invisible waves of light. All creation is light; that was the answer that had been right within my grasp for years.

It is important to realize that Cathie derived what he represents as an all-encompassing equation, from the mass of the earth. I may be missing something here, but it seems that Cathie reached a general conclusion from a single, very specific case. But rather than critically analyzing how he came up with his formula, instead Cathie employed a computer to help him derive the most fantastic conclusions from it:

> The fact that the harmonic of light has only to be doubled to obtain anti-light fields must be related to the matter and anti-matter cycles of the physical and the non-physical worlds. If the two, plus and minus, fields are interlocked, as I have postulated, and matter and anti-matter manifest in alternate pulses, then a double cycle must occur between each pulse of matter and anti-matter. The anti-matter pulse cannot be perceived by us, for fairly obvious reasons; but when calculating the frequency interaction between the two, both cycles must be taken into account.
>
> By stepping up or slowing down the frequency of C between two cycles, a shift in space-time must occur.

In other words, Cathie claims to have discovered — via the actual manipulation of space-time — a way to control gravity.

"Ultra Relativity"

Theories, formulae, designs, prototypes and experiments in anti-gravity are usually propounded by independent researchers who rarely talk to one another. For this reason, it is difficult to sort out which claims are in agreement and which aren't; it's not a trivial task just figuring out which researchers are talking about the same thing. What is needed is someone to unify results in anti-gravity research. The first attempts at such a unification are represented by the Gravity Research Foundation and more recently with the Rex Research *Anti-Gravity Articles* and David Hatcher Childress' *Anti-Gravity Handbook*, the latter two being compendia of results from various independent researchers. They do not, however, achieve theoretical unification.

From Shinchi Seike's *Principles of Ultra Relativity*.

Shinichi Seike of the Gravity Research Laboratory in Uwajima City, Japan, may have produced just such a unification, as detailed in *The Principles of Ultra Relativity*. This book, which resembles a physics or mathematics text, contains the original Japanese, but also an English translation on each facing page. Originally published in 1969, its fifth edition was printed in 1978. The book's purpose is explained in the Preface:

> ... The theory would be a legitimate sequential of Einsteinean theory of special relativity and general, and, furthermore, that of anti-matter of P.A.M. Dirac's, and contain much an ultra dynamics upon hyper surfaces. It, of course, belongs to frontiers in natural sciences, and also favors classical mechanics (especially does a mechanics on gyroes and vector analysis), which will make you feel a nostalgia for better old days. Quantum Gravitational Generator, Inverse-G Engine and Time Reversing Machine have been presented as three representative experimentals of "inverse atomic technology" in the latter part of this title, which will be nothing but a new realm of experimental physics. Inverse Gravitation could dramatically be verified with a great work of John Roy Robert Searl's. It might also be useful as an educational model as like eight fundamentals of Japanese manual lettering (SHODOH). On the other hand, it can, however, be a fearful weapon. The author emphatically hopes that it may peacefully be used by his Noble Brothers and Sisters.

Anti-gravity inventions (such as Searl's) are explained in terms of the equations of Newton, Einstein and the quantum physicists, all presented as background for Seike's own results, which include a formula for the gyra-

"You may smoke if you like. On Earth people indulge in that odd habit."

tion of a four-dimensional top, the design of an anti-atomic motor and a time-reversing machine, as well as a theory of topological electronics based on "Kleinian Magnetic Flux" and a "Moebius G-generator." Seike, like Cathie, doesn't oppose current theories, but simply elaborates on them. His method of space travel, described in a chapter entitled "Geodesic Sailing towards the Moon," uses the "g-trajectory," i.e. the nearest path in the curvature of space-time. To prove he's not joking, Seike provides us with a photo of an inverse-g space vehicle, on the ground.

After concluding that this heavy tome was all but impenetrable, I noticed many illustrations alongside page after page of sophisticated mathematical physics rendered in both Japanese and broken English. These include photographs of man-made flying saucer prototypes, Klein Bottles and electronic diagrams. A section entitled, "Ultra Dynamics upon the First Hyper Surface" is illustrated with Fig. 2, "History of entities is observed along time axis on the 1st hyper surface corresponding with x axis on the zeroth hyper surface (ordinary physical space)," a series of five photos along a time line, beginning with a toddler; the fourth photo in the series is unmistakably *Elizabeth Taylor as Cleopatra,* and the final photo in the series appears to be a painting of an older English woman. Another strange feature of this text is the Appendix of "Nostalgic (Time-Reversing) Melodies." Printed underneath the titles of these songs, are values for t, or time. For example, "Roaming Song over the BIWA Lake (Words and music by Taroh OGUCHI, t = -1,555,200x10^{13} sec.)" The total effect is illustrated by the following example:

The School Song of the University of Tokyo:
(t = -2,083,968 x 10^3 sec.)
Receiving flakes with a glass of jade,
Lunar beams upon greeny liquor,
Seeking for public paradise,
Looking down at mundane luxuries,
Healthy students are ambitious in five dormitories.
Standing at the Mukohga-Hill!

Another Appendix contains quotations, some in Japanese without translation, some translated into English. Included are the statements of an unidentified "foreign female." Without further explanation or context, she is quoted as saying, "You may smoke if you like. I will get you a receptacle for your ashes. You see, on Earth people indulge in that odd habit," and "It is a great pity that we must take of much sorrowful things — and still sadder that such woe exists anywhere in the Universe. In ourselves, we of the other planets are not sad people. We are very gay. We laugh a great deal."

After pondering their meaning, I realized the significance of these quotes: they provide a strong clue to the ultimate results of anti-gravity research. When the human race conquers the final frontier — gravity — we will be free of the force that drowns us, that gives us backaches and sore feet, that makes us fall down, and that keeps us on this miserable planet. Among those who have thought about it, most accept gravity as a permanent feature of the physical universe. Thus "freedom" is only a relative term.

But to some, freedom must be physical and total. They will continue to pursue their inventions, experiments and theories despite the results of mainstream physics, because they will never be free until they escape the heavy hand we call gravity.

Anti-gravity time line from Seike's *Principles of Ultra Relativity*

IBEN BROWNING
THEY ALL LAUGHED WHEN I PREDICTED AN EARTHQUAKE

by Trevor Blake

But so wide is the separation between the way men actually live and the way they ought to live, that anyone who turns his attention from what is actually done to what ought to be done studies his own ruin rather than his preservation.

— Niccoló Machiavelli, 1513 (a quote carried by Iben Browning in his wallet at all times)

Iben Browning (1917-1991) was a scientist who used equipment and ideas considered obsolete by his contemporaries to make stunning new discoveries those blinded by the shiny and new could not see. Largely self-taught in complex fields such as astronomy, artificial intelligence, and history, he studied the cosmos in an interdisciplinary way, gaining insights lost on experts. His innovations in aviation technology, computers, and meteorology affect millions of people daily, but he is virtually unknown outside of a small circle of admirers and fellow scientists.

Born in Vanderbilt, Texas, Browning grew up during the last days of frontier America on his father's cotton farm. He was a pioneer from birth; his parents wanted to set him apart from everyone else, so they made up the name Iben for him. Iben began to read at age two (his mother was a schoolteacher) and entered first grade the same year. He graduated from college at nineteen and taught for a time a year later. Iben's farm experience also made a deep impression on the bright student, as he came to the conclusion that "chopping cotton provides motivation to do ANYTHING else."

During World War II, Browning was a test pilot. Realizing he could probably design better equipment than he was given, he invented the *Formation Stick,* now a standard instrument in most aircraft. He also acted as a technical consultant to Disney studios in Hollywood, briefing animators on aircraft for their propaganda films. During those years, Browning met neurosurgeon Florence Pinto, his future wife.

After the war, Browning returned to college, where he developed the first of many cases of cancer he was to suffer throughout his life. Although several of his cancers were considered terminal, each time he managed to recover.

In the early 1950s, Browning was Chief Scientist at the Research Division of Bell Aircraft, where he developed navigation equipment with former Nazi rocket scientists. It was at Bell that he began to structure his lifelong interdisciplinary self-education, resulting in what he called *The Entirety.*

First published in December, 1956, *The Entirety* is a periodic table of states of matter and the disciplines associated with them. The Entirety defines four states of matter: natural nonliving states (atoms, planets), natural living states (living creatures), unnatural nonliving states (machines), and unnatural living states (robots capable of thought and reproduction). These four states of matter expand from a central point labeled "molecule"; cross-referencing any two or more points in *The Entirety* reveals the discipline associated with them. In some cases, the relations are obvious: cross-reference natural non-living matter lying somewhere between molecules and planets with natural living matter above mono-molecular organisms but below biotype (a genetic community) indicates paleontology and related fields of study. Other relations reveal disciplines that do not as yet exist or are not recognized; when Bell Aircraft first published *The Entirety* it removed all references to the unnatural living state of matter; its appearance on the table indicated machines capable of thought or reproduction, which at the time, was too farfetched for them.[1]

His parents wanted to set him apart from everyone else, so they made up the name Iben for him.

1. *A complete history and explanation of The Entirety can be found in* Robots on Your Doorstep *by Nels Winkless and Iben Browning.*

Iben Browning

The Entirety also appeared in the Spring 1958 issue of *Space Craft Digest,* a publication of the Pacific Lemurian Society. This group, founded by engineer **W. Gordon Allen,** was interested in unraveling the mysteries of the alleged ancient continent of Lemuria, but also maintained a burning interest in flying saucers and anti-gravity. Allen saw Browning as succeeding in the creation of a unified field theory where Einstein had failed. *The Entirety* confirmed his own "I Field" theory, "a FOUR FIELD CONTINUUM under constant movement thru an 'N' number of dimensions and states of reality from waves thru universes," developed to explain UFO electric "ETHER PUMP" flight behavior. Browning himself had no opinion on UFOs, stating "I have never found any scientific approach to dealing with these things that sheds any light at all on their validity, one way or another."

Browning resigned from Bell Aircraft after money from his budget was used to hire a disciple of Edgar Cayce. While he had no qualms about using a spiritualist in high-tech aviation research, he found it intolerable that control of his budget was subject to the whims of others.

In 1957, Browning was hired by the Atomic Bomb Works in Albuquerque, New Mexico and suffered a heart attack a year later. During the several weeks of his recovery period, he developed one of the earliest artificial intelligence systems, the "N-Tuple Pattern Recognition System." This system not only compensated for "noise" generated by Browning's low cost equipment, but also employed it; "noise" enabled the machine to operate intelligently, as when learning the difference between shapes. Although 20 years later, products were introduced that incorporated Browning's vision of artificial intelligence (Savvy and Wizard for IBM), according to Browning the N-Tuple system is now only an example of how NOT to make a thinking machine: it doesn't cost enough and is too simple (in a Rube Goldberg sort of way) to remain in the hands of experts.

In the 1960s, having had enough of working for others, Browning set up the Thomas Bede Foundation and performed contract research on everything from portable nerve gas detectors to soft contact lens cleaners. With every new contract, he would essentially reinvent and rediscover old territory in order to approach each problem from a fresh perspective. He said he liked to change careers every three years, so he could keep learning.

In 1964, Browning wrote *A Feasibility Study of Computer Programming of Circuit Card Layouts from Design Sketches,* the basis for the creation of automatically printed circuit boards, a key invention leading directly to high density integrated circuits such as those found in today's personal computers.

By the early 1970s, Iben Browning's interdisciplinary studies led him to believe dramatic events in human history tended to come in bunches in some sort of as-yet unrecognized pattern. By mapping out myriad bits of data, including thousands of years worth of planetary positions; the length of rule of individual Popes in Italy; sunspot activity; Pueblo mythology; earthquakes; wars; the health of newly elected U.S. Presidents; glaciation; wine harvests in France between 1599 and 1604; volcanic activity; the assassination of John Lennon; tree growth as measured by rings; and famines in ancient China, Browning came to the conclusion that the greatest motivating factor in human history is climate.

Browning's theory was that cosmic forces, such as meteorites and tidal forces, trigger energy releases on earth in the form of volcanoes and earthquakes. These energy releases, combined with bolide strikes on the moon and sunspot activity, influence particulate matter in earth's atmosphere. Dust in the air changes temperature, humidity, and storm patterns, which changes food supply, which affects human behavior by causing wars, migrations, revolutions, and the like.

From Browning's climate/history research came a number of other conclusions. He pointed out that, viewed as a whole, earth is just beginning to leave one of the longest cold periods of its existence, and that it is "normal" for temperatures to be higher. This, combined with the fact that a single volcano can throw up more pollution in a single day than all the cars in the world over a year's time, led him to conclude that while humans are directly affected by climate, the climate is not at all affected by humans. He believed the greenhouse effect was largely a myth propagated by environmental extremists.

Browning also gathered together what he considered to be The Great Ideas of Mankind. Beginning ten million years ago and moving to the present (with some suggestions for future Great Ideas), Browning grouped the Great Ideas into sets of six or seven Ideas per period; he concluded that the number of billions of "Man-Years" per Idea generally decreases as the population increases.

Perhaps the most significant result of Browning's climate/history research was the ability to forecast, with "86% accuracy," changes in both climate and human affairs. His predictions of earthquakes and volcanic activities were among the most accurate in the world (the February 9, 1971 Los Angeles earthquake, for example). No later than 1981, Browning predicted that Communism and the Soviet Union would fall by 2010. *Past and Future History: A Planner's Guide* coauthored by Browning and his daughter Evelyn M. Garriss contains a Criswell-like alphabetical listing of inferred future events, covering Arizona (will become wetter), Canada (will cease to export grain), Famine (get ready, world), Israel (atom bombed), Slavery (will return), and more. Browning's views were respected enough that he could ask $225 for a one year subscription to his quarterly eight page newsletter — and get it.

Iben Browning neither sought nor received much publicity during his life — until his research indicated high probability of a major earthquake in December, 1990, along the New Madrid fault line in Illinois, Missouri, and Arkansas. He offered his evidence for this probability at an Albuquerque Rotary Club meeting in May of that year. But people don't want *probabilities* — they want *predictions*. In the past, Browning made very precise but ignored predictions; for some reason, this one was noticed. The media reported it, law enforcement and rescue officials prepared for it and residents stockpiled supplies or simply left the state. Naturally, with sad irony, the earthquake didn't occur. Rather than celebrate their good fortune or appreciate the practice in earthquake survival which would, sooner or later, be of use, those who inflated Browning's probability into a prediction turned against him, accusing him of being a kook.

The 73-year-old biophysicist was eulogized as the man who got it WRONG.

My father met Iben Browning shortly after this incident, at his trailer in Albuquerque. Browning was again suffering from skin cancer. Because motion and even the light pressure of clothing caused him pain, he greeted his guest in a cloth bathrobe. The two men discussed Browning's theories, but also the treatment he received in the aftermath of the New Madrid statement. He was bitter that his words had been twisted into a meaning he never intended, and more so that he was held responsible for their misunderstanding.

On July 18, 1990, Iben Browning died of a heart attack. The 73-year-old biophysicist — whose work earned him a place in both the *American Men of Science* and *Who's Who* — was eulogized as the man who got it WRONG. A typical obituary headlined, "Earthquake projector dies of a heart attack," dwelt for six of nine paragraphs on "his prediction, which didn't come true," with nary a word for his many important achievements. The lesson was clear: make a mistake in predicting an earthquake and you will die.

Iben Browning's books are out of print, but his daughter and supporters continue to publish the newsletter he started. I don't think Browning would have minded being in a book about kooks: he may have been thought of as crazy, an outsider, and lacking scientific credentials, but 86% of the time he had truth on his side.

Flat Earth News

©

RESTORING THE WORLD TO SANITY

International Flat Earth Research Society
$10.00 yearly to Associate Members only.

Quarterly

Charles K. Johnson, President
Marjory Waugh Johnson, Secretary

Box 2533, Lancaster, California 93539-2533
Phone: (805) 727-1635

Founded, published quarterly since 1972. This FLAT EARTH NEWS is the first and only FLAT EARTH NEWS ever published in the history of the world. FLAT EARTH NEWS is totally unique in history and time.

September 1992, #83

COLUMBUS PROVED EARTH FLAT

The Earth NOT a Whirling Globe

SHAPE - Children at school, before they are able to judge for themselves, are taught to believe that "the earth is round like an orange." This idea was drummed into our ears so long that we came to believe it in spite of its palpable **absurdity.** It will not bear critical examination. For instance:

A school geography says, "We know that the earth is round because ships have sailed around it." **What wretched logic!** Ships can sail round the Isle of Man: Is that a globe? Not more so than the earth. Ships go round the world as they sail round an island, or as we walk round a square, or a town, going round along a flat surface. A thing may be "round" and flat too, like a penny.

Pictures of ships, in false and distorted perspective, are given in school books, professing to show why the hull disappears before the masts. The line of sight which should be a tangent to the sphere *at the place of the observer,* is raised miles high, descending to a very distant horizon at a considerable angle. But no man in this world, whatever his altitiude, ever looked down to his horizon. It is always on a level with the eye. It, therefore, a fraud to picture it otherwise. Besides, when the hull of a ship has disappeared to the naked eye it can often be rendered visible again by a good telescope, thus proving that it had not gone down beyond or over the horizon, nor behind a hill of water. Vapour or spray might obscure it.

MOTION - Astronomers teach that we are rushing through "space" at the awful rate of about 63,000 miles an hour, or more than 1,000 miles a minute! Can you believe it? It would be fearful. The astronomers would be whirled off into "space," with clouds, rivers, and seas all flying after them. **The idea is absurd. No proof of such motion has ever been given.** It is a mere supposition, incapable of proof.

It is absurd to suppose there are people at the so-called "Antipodes" hanging heads downward in relation to us. What keeps them from falling off? Flies that walk the ceiling have suckers to their feet. Gravitation! A myth invented to support the whirling globe superstition. What is "gravitation?" - a solid, a liquid, or mere gas? Heavy bodies fall to the earth by their own weight; light substances float in the air in spite of the combined pull of all the particles in the world. Luminous bodies have no attraction, except for silly moths. Magnetic *currents* affect bodies according to their varying forces, but there is no such thing as universtal attraction, or a general pulling and tugging of bodies to get together in the whole universe. Gravitation has never been proved. It is an absurd speculation of men spoiled with the pride of "science," but, as Paul says, a " science falsely so called." - 1 Tim. vi. 20. Give it up for the Truth.

Proof in Egypt

Sir - Your Halifax correspondent fires his Copernican popgun, then runs away. Yet the book from which I get my data for calculating the sun's height is by "Paralax, "the *nom de plume* of the late Dr. Rowbotham, with whom I corresponded before his death; and I am not aware that zetetics, according to J. Layton, believe that the sun's distance is approximately 4,000 miles, far less 6,000. We must calculate by plain trigonometry, seeing that the surface of water is level, whilst the Bedford Level, the Salisbury Plain, etc., are what their names imply, and not arcs of a globe. Canals and railways are constructed without any allowance for a convexity which necessitates the

Continued on back page

Two witnesses declare Earth Flat.

Globularity

Sir, Mr. Harpur assures us that "surveys for canals and railways are made without mention of curvature because the levels are taken by a succession of short tangents which overlap; so that, in surveyor's slang, "the backsight cancels the foresight." Now, we know that surveyors require back and foresights for uneven ground, and that their "datum line" must be parallel to the horizon, which is invariably level; nor, have I ever seen it otherwise. Mr. Harpur is challenged to prove that this cancelling allows for the fall of 8 inches per mile, increasing as the square of the distance. Nor can he prove his short tangents to be less imaginary than the globe itself, whirling on an imaginary axis, with an imaginary lurch of 23.5 degrees on an imaginary plane, driven along an imaginary orbit by the imaginary centripetal and centrifugal forces. Since the earth is alleged to whirl 1,000 miles an hour, how many billion tons of centrifugal force, according to mechanics, does Mr. Harpur grant to pitch us off, seas and all movables, against the man in the moon? Now, isn't this sea earth ball a curiosity; nobody able to explain how all the great continents and oceans stick together to make it? Over its shape, size distance, etc., how star-gazers squabble! Herschel will have it like an orange with two axes, but Ball with three axes, and Airy thinks it like a turnip. Hershel makes an astronomical degree 70 miles, Airy 69, so that the globe's circumference may be either 25,200 or 24, 840 miles. Again, according to Lardner, its distance from the sun is 100 million miles to Herschel's 95 millions, to Airy's 92 millions, etc.; but whilst to "Copernicans" the phantom's whereabouts is uncertain, **common sense knows that it exists only in Newtonian brains.** - I am, etc.

Sir, "C.H.'s supposition of the differences in levelling are surely exploded by the letter from the **Manchester Ship Canal Office denying all allowance for curvature.** It seems to be forgotten that the sun's distance is the astronomer's unit rod of measurement, and that seeing the **astrolo-**

Continued on back page

Is the Newtonian Astronomy True?

Glasgow, 15th May

Sir, Your correspondent seems to think this a question entirely of flatness or convexity: whereas there are four sects of globists all at loggerheards: (1) The Ptolemaists, representd by J. Gillespie, of Dumfries, who suppose the "earth" globe a centre for the revolution of the sun, moon, and stars; (2) The Koreshans of America, who suppose the "earth" a hollow globe for us to live inside: (3) The Newtonian Copernicans, who suppose the sun a centre, keeping the planets whirling in orbits by gravity; and (4) the Copernicans, who suppose the planets to whirl round the sun, without the necessity of gravity, Sir R. Phillips heading up this school. However, here are a few nuts especially for Copernican teeth: Why are railways and canals constructed without any allowance for terrestrial convexity; and why do artists in marine views represent by a straight line the horixon, whether running east and west, or north and south? How can all the vast continents with convexity only imaginary, along with the oceans, stick together to make a ball something like a little schoolroom globe, able to whirl on an axis only imaginary - that is, no axis at all; and though very many million tons in weight float light as a little cork in ethereal fluid found only in Copernican brains? How can gravity, which no one can describe, or prove, toss nineteen miles in a twinkling the great oceans and continents over the sun, and yet we are not accordingly killed outright, or even conscious of any such horrible motion? Is not this **pagan Aristotelian gravity** only a disguised theory

Continued on back page

THE EARTH IS NOT A GLOBE

They are the last pocket of individual thinkers in the English speaking world.

— Sir Fields (owner of newspapers in England), about the Flat Earth Society

With the exception of the handful who have actually seen the earth from space, most people take its shape on faith. Sure, we've seen the NASA photographs of the "Whole earth," but these are documents — which must be accepted as genuine before they give us any information — and not first-hand experiences. Such scientific proofs as Foucault's Pendulum involve procedures we leave to the experts; when they announce that experiments prove earth is indeed a globe rotating on its axis, we believe them. In fact, the earth's shape is so entrenched in the current shared belief system of Western Civilization that, confronted by someone who denies or even questions that assumption, a non-technical public is ill-equipped to answer the challenge, despite the conviction that the globular earth is an elementary fact.

Thus in the 19th Century, when the so-called "zetetic astronomers" began to "prove" the earth was flat, they won many adherents, even among the educated. Though not exactly a mass movement, enough influential people were involved to create a controversy similar to the Evolution/Creation debate today.

In school, we are given the impression that scientific knowledge is somehow cumulative, that the "truth" is discovered, everyone recognizes it as such and humanity is thereby advanced. But the life cycle of knowledge is rarely that simple. Much of the knowledge attained by the Greeks, for example, was suppressed by the Church during the Dark Ages, and the shape of the earth was one of the casualties.

Though Greek philosophers and scientists believed the earth to be a globe, ancient Babylonians, Egyptians and Hebrews all thought it was flat, as reflected in certain passages of the Bible such as those referring to the "four corners of the earth." Thus, Christian fathers, including Lactantius, Severianus and John Chrysostom, were among the first to denounce the spherical earth on scriptural grounds. In the sixth century, **Cosmas Indicopleustes,** a monk from Alexandria, wrote *Christian Topography,* perhaps the first flat earth polemic. Cosmas' flat earth was a rectangle, with Jerusalem at the center. The firmament arched overhead, with heaven hovering above. Around the inhabited portions of the earth lay the oceans, and beyond that, Eden. The sun revolved around a mountain at the north pole. Seasonal changes were caused by the position of the sun at the mountain; in the summer it revolved around the peak, and in the winter it revolved around the base.

In the sixth century, Cosmas Indicopleustes, a monk from Alexandria, wrote the first flat earth polemic.

Cosmas' cosmogony was welcomed by the Catholic Church and accepted by devout clergymen for many centuries. Among the scientifically inclined, however, Cosmas was no match for Ptolemy, and by the eighth century, the flat earth was an outdated notion. Since the earth maintained its spot at the center of the its universe, the Church wasn't overly concerned with the Ptolemaic system. But when Copernicus and Galileo relegated earth to a place subservient to the sun, and then, far worse, to a corner of a vast unknowable expanse, religious leaders had to take action. In 1616, the Church denounced the Copernican system as dangerous, and in 1632, Galileo was imprisoned at the hands of the Inquisition.

The raging debates of the time, however, were not over the shape of the earth, but over its place in the universe. Until the mid-1800s, that is, when an English gentleman named **Samuel Birley Rowbotham,** a.k.a. **Parallax,** began to promote "zetetic astronomy," which held the earth is shaped like a pancake. The word "zetetic" (from the Greek verb zeteo: to search or examine) combined with the insistence that zetetic astronomy is based on "facts" while conventional astronomy is based on "theories," has stuck to this day. Apparently the guise of reason paid off

> **John Hampden, an Oxford graduate, considered *Earth Not A Globe* to be an airtight refutation of Copernicus and Newton, staking a £500 bet on it.**

for Rowbotham, who made many converts via public lectures.

Rowbotham's books, *Earth Not a Globe* and *Zetetic Astronomy,* described particulars more sophisticated than Cosmas' rectangular plane. According to zetetic astronomy, the known world is a vast circular plane. The north pole is situated at its center, the south pole is distributed around the edge, with a 150-foot thick wall of ice marking the impenetrable southern limit. The equator falls halfway between the north pole and the southern limit. The sun, moon and planets circle above; an optical illusion causes us to see them as rising and setting. This planar system, plus tiny stars, constitute the entire universe, enclosed by a solid dome.

Rowbotham was so dedicated to the cause of zetetic astronomy that in 1838, he slept for nine months inside a wooden hut to conduct important experiments nearby. The experiments took place at the Old Bedford Level in Cambridgeshire, a straight, six-mile stretch of canal marked by bridges at either end. This afforded a clear view from one end to the other. If the earth is a globe, reasoned Rowbotham, an object placed near the water-line at one end would not be visible at the other. If, on the other hand, the earth is flat, the object would be seen clearly with a telescope. Peering through a telescope a few inches above the water at one end of the stretch, Rowbotham claimed he could clearly see barges and other objects at the other end of the stretch, and beyond.

With the experiments, Rowbotham made so strong a case for the flat earth that earnest Victorian scientists were compelled to refute him. Rowbotham, "schooled in the tricks of the lecture hall," knew how to manipulate the so-called "globularists" into ridiculous emotional outbursts, a skill that won him sympathy — and sometimes converts — from the audience.

One convert was **John Hampden,** an Oxford graduate who considered *Earth Not a Globe* to be an airtight refutation of Copernicus and Newton. He was even willing to stake £500 on it, and placed an ad in the January 12, 1870 issue of the journal *Scientific Opinion,* offering the sum to anyone who could "prove the rotundity and revolution of the world from Scripture, from reason, or from fact." Alfred Russell Wallace, the distinguished evolutionist, was in desperate need of funds at the time and answered the ad, although he would rue the day he ever became involved with the zetetic astronomers.

All agreed the experiment should be conducted at the Old Bedford Canal. In March, 1870, Hampden and Wallace, each with a referee, arrived at the site. After several days of refining the experiment, each of the four men peered through the telescope, which, not too surprisingly, yielded slightly different views for each of them. Actually, Hampden's referee saw what the globularists saw, but interpreted it as a telescopic effect. In any case, the party needed an umpire and agreed upon Mr. J.H. Walsh, Wallace's original referee. When Walsh ruled in favor of Wallace and handed him his £500, an irate Hampden dubbed the affair the "Bedford Canal Swindle." Hampden waged a smear campaign against Wallace, freely using the terms "knave, liar, thief, swindler, impostor, rogue, and felon."

Wallace was not amused. In January, 1871, he sued Hampden for libel, and was awarded £600 by the British court. Wallace was unable to collect the sum, however, because Hampden assigned all his assets to his son-in-law and declared bankruptcy. This was not the end; the struggle between the two continued with suits and countersuits, while Hampden's harassment — which included poison pen letters to Wallace's wife — continued for the next *sixteen years.* Wallace later wrote that the episode was a blight upon every aspect of his life during that time.

Meanwhile, Hampden became England's foremost zetetic astronomer. From his house, which he called "Cosmos House," he established numerous flat earth "organizations," including the Biblical Science Defence Association, the Biblical Science Institute, the Socratic Society, the Biblical Defence Association, the New Geographical Society, the Philosophical Society of Christendom and the

Christian Philosophical Institute. No record of what these organizations did exists, or if indeed they had any members besides Hampden.

Neither Hampden nor Rowbotham lived long enough to see the founding of the Universal Zetetic Society (UZS) in 1892. Within a year, the UZS had members in England, Ireland, the U.S., Canada, South Africa, India, Australia and New Zealand. The organization promoted the flat earth via publication and distribution of zetetic books, pamphlets and periodicals, and in public debates with the opposition, often won by the zetetics. The UZS journal, *Earth Review,* offered £1000 to the editor of another journal, *Science Siftings,* for proof of the earth's rotundity; perhaps recalling the Old Bedford Canal affair, the editor never took them up on the offer.

Earth Review folded in 1897, but at its height had about 1,000 subscribers. A frequent contributor was **Lady Elizabeth Anne Mould Blount,** eccentric wife of a wealthy baronet. She eventually took the UZS helm and founded a new journal, *Earth,* which she edited between 1900 and 1904. Lady Blount convinced several well-known and distinguished people, including an archbishop and a theologian, to support the UZS.

Lady Blount passionately believed in a flat earth. She herself documented her fervor in the novel *Adrian Galileo;* in *Eccentric Lives and Peculiar Notions,* John Michell provides an amusing summary of this flat earth melodrama:

> ... She herself is the heroine, disguised only in name as Lady Alma, alias Madame Bianka the zetetic lecturer. Her fictional husband is the oddly named Sir Rosemary Alma, a Roman Catholic like Blount. He is old, cold-hearted and mean, and he forbids his young wife the company of her fellow Protestants. She responds by taking a priest for a lover. To him she delivers passionate speeches about the Bible and the flat earth, and has almost converted him when they are both shot down by the priest's jealous housekeeper. Recovering separately, the lovers undergo amazing transformations, as do all the other characters in the novel, the priest becoming a licentious baronet in Paris while Lady Alma, now Madame Bianka, takes to the lecture hall circuit, winning many to the true zetetic faith. Much of her propaganda is put out as doggerel verses set to music ...

Though Lady Blount won support for zetetic astronomy, it wasn't enduring; the English flat earth movement soon died out. The English successfully exported their ideas to Americans, however, who carried the flame henceforward.

The New York Zetetic Society was organized in 1873. But it wasn't until 1879, when the English zetetic **William Carpenter** emigrated to Baltimore, that the U.S. movement had a publicist. Carpenter, a printer by trade, printed and distributed over 10,000 copies of his 1885 pamphlet, *One Hundred Proofs That the Earth Is Not a Globe,* which went through twelve editions. In true zetetic fashion, Carpenter delivered numerous public lectures, reaching over 100,000 people. Among them were several Seventh Day Adventists, including **Alexander Gleason** from Buffalo, who practiced on Lake Erie the same English zetetic experiments on Old Bedford Canal. The experiments and conclusions are detailed in *Is the Bible from Heaven? Is the Earth A Globe?,* published in 1890 and revised in 1893. Gleason's contribution to the flat earth culture included a four-color map of the disc-shaped earth.

Until this time, flat earthers in the U.S. were basically indistinguishable from their British zetetic forebears, using the strategy of winning converts at the public lecture hall. This was all very well and good, but in the U.S., rather than arguing about "the truth," zealots build entire worlds based upon it, as did many utopian and religious communities during the 19th Century. So when Reverend **Wilbur Glenn Voliva** (1870-1942) became General Overseer of the Christian Catholic Apostolic Church and transformed Zion, Illinois, into Flat Earth Central, zetetic astronomy took on a peculiarly American flavor.

The small town of Zion, three miles south of the Wisconsin border on the shore of Lake Michigan, was established by Scottish faith-healer Reverend John Alexander Dowie in 1900 "as a refuge for church members, a city free from doctors, drug stores, oysters, pork, tobacco, liquor, labor unions and other cor-

When Reverend Wilbur Glenn Voliva became General Overseer of the Christian Catholic Apostolic Church and transformed Zion, Illinois, into Flat Earth Central, zetetic astronomy took on a peculiarly American flavor.

Voliva's puppet government forbade tobacco, alcohol, movie theaters, pork, doctors, drug stores, unions, secret societies, and, of course, globes.

rupting influences." Voliva, Dowie's right-hand man, overthrew him in 1906. By 1914, Voliva ruled Zion with an iron grip, dominating its church, industry, schools and government. Zion was a theocracy, with Voliva as God's earthly representative.

In an August 16, 1914, sermon, Voliva raged against his usual bogeys of modern medicine, science, evolution, geology, historical analysis of the bible, but especially astronomy:

> Where is Heaven? Heaven is up yonder! This is the Earth!
>
> When the Blessed Lord ascended, they saw him going up, did they not? And the angels declared that in like manner He would come again, did they not? And when He comes, He is coming to Earth, is He not?
>
> I shall ask you this question: If the world is whirling around in space at the rate of a million five hundred thousand miles a day, whizzing around many times as fast as lightning travels — how is the Lord going to light on it? Just tell me!

Voliva's flock may have noticed nothing new in this sermon, but their supreme leader was leading up to something. On December 26, 1915, he announced a new doctrine:

> I believe this Earth is a stationary plane; that it rests upon water; and that there is no such thing as the Earth moving, no such thing as the Earth's axis or the Earth's orbit. It is a lot of silly rot, born in the egotistical brains of infidels.
>
> Neither do I believe there is any such thing as the law of gravitation. I believe that is a lot of rot, too.
>
> There is no such thing!
>
> I get my astronomy from the Bible.

Voliva's assistant, Apostle **Anton Darms,** was subsequently assigned the task of searching the bible for information on the earth's shape. He published his findings in *Leaves of Healing,* the church's magazine. The resulting article, entitled "The Teaching of the Word of God Regarding the Creation of the World and the Shape of the earth in Fifty Questions, Answered by Scripture," cited the usual passages about "the four corners," but also documented lesser known scriptures. For example, when Daniel had his vision, he saw a tree so tall that everyone on earth could see it; this could never occur if the earth were a sphere. The size of the stars are similarly inferred from Revelation 6:13, where "the stars of heaven fell upon the Earth, even as a fig tree casteth her untimely figs, when she is shaken by a mighty wind."

By March, 1916, Darms amassed so much evidence that Voliva declared the earth officially flat in Zion.

With the new order came new restrictive laws. Voliva's puppet city government passed statutes forbidding tobacco, alcohol, movie theaters, pork, doctors, drug stores, unions, secret societies, and of course, globes. Women were forbidden to cut their hair, expose their necks or straddle a horse. When trains stopped in Zion, police boarded them to arrest smokers. Zion police also lurked in nearby Waukegan to arrest Zion residents trying to escape Zion's laws.

Having successfully completed his mission, Darms was assigned to rewrite hymns sung in Zion's church, as necessary. For example, "Let every kindred, every tribe, / On this terrestrial ball, / To Him all majesty ascribe, / And crown Him Lord of All" was changed to "Let every kindred, every tribe, / On this terrestrial plane, / To Him all majesty ascribe, / And praise His Holy Name."

In 1922, Voliva became the first religious broadcaster to found a radio station, WCBD. He thundered forth on the airwaves against "The Devil's Triplets," evolution, higher criticism, and modern astronomy. Like many of the zetetics before him, Voliva couldn't resist offering an Earth Not A Globe Wager. Voliva offered $5,000 to anyone who could prove to him the earth is a globe. No one ever collected this sum, as Voliva's repertoire included answers to every globularist argument. For example, in answer to those who offered the successful circumnavigation of the earth as evidence for earth's sphericity, Voliva wrote:

> Take a silver dollar to represent the stationary, plane Earth. The center of the dollar is the North Center. Draw a line from the edge of the dollar to the North Center. As you go toward the Center you are travelling north; as you go from the Center to the edge you are travelling south. East and west are simply points at right angles to north and south. Start from a given point and travel

due east, and you will be compelled to come back to the point of departure.

In answer to those who would suggest the sun is millions of miles away, he appealed to good old fashioned common sense:

> The idea of a sun millions of miles in diameter and 91,000,000 miles away is silly. The sun is only 32 miles across and not more than 3,000 miles from the Earth. It stands to reason it must be so. God made the sun to light the Earth, and therefore must have placed it close to the task it was designed to do. What would you think of a man who built a house in Zion and put the lamp to light it in Kenosha, Wisconsin?

Despite his eternal certitude, Voliva began to lose his grip on Zion's populace in the late 1920s when the Illinois legislature, probing his financial dealings, concluded something was amiss. When the Great Depression hit, the city itself began to have financial problems, as well, and by 1935, Voliva — and his flat earth doctrine — was deposed. Voliva began to spend time in Florida, occasionally visiting Zion. He paid his final visit to the city in 1942, when he died at age 72.

But flat earthism by no means passed with Voliva. Shortly before his death, **Charles Kenneth Johnson** of Texas wrote him asking about the flat earth. In 1956, the Englishman **Samuel Shenton** organized a new zetetic organization, The International Flat Earth Society. In 1971, Shenton's dying wish was that the organization be passed to Charles K. Johnson, and it was. Since then, the name "Charles K. Johnson" has become all but synonymous with the flat earth.

Johnson and his wife Marjory preside over the Flat Earth Society from their home in Lancaster, California. Unlike their predecessors, the Johnsons don't seek converts. They are trying to remove the bible-thumping image from the movement, and in their newsletters, focus on blasting science rather than on biblical quotations. The Johnsons oppose other "Bible Scientists," such as the creationists and the geocentrists, considering them to be hypocrites: they claim to defend the bible while continuing to believe the earth is a globe. The Johnsons have more in common with the creationists and geocentrists than they are willing to admit, however. Like them, the Johnsons are fundamentalist Christians, and The Flat Earth Society is incorporated as the Covenant Peoples Church.

The Flat Earth Society suggests that "Science Religion" should be replaced by "Sanity."

The Johnsons' Flat Earth Society may be a "toned-down" version of the flat earth movement, but this is difficult to discern from the literature. The introductory flyer, a diatribe against "Science Religion," a "weird, way-out occult concoction of gibberish theory-theology," suggests it should be replaced by "Sanity." By contrast, the purpose of the Flat Earth Society is "to carefully observe, think freely, rediscover forgotten facts and oppose theoretical dogmatic assumptions." Turning the meaning of the word "science" on its head, Charles Johnson writes, "Science 'proves' earth a 'ball' by 'scripture' words. We PROVE earth Flat by experiment, demonstrated and demonstrable. Earth Flat is a Fact, not a 'theory!'" In the true spirit of the zetetics Johnson is deeply disturbed by the scientific method, especially by its limitations. There is, by definition, no certainty in science. Scientific knowledge comes in the form of hypothesis, not unalterable truth. Johnson, however, knows "one thing for sure about this world... the known inhabited world is Flat, Level, a Plane World."

The society's newsletter is even more polemical than the introductory flyer. With its motto "RESTORING THE WORLD TO SANITY," *THE FLAT EARTH NEWS* dispatches the headlines, "COLUMBUS PROVED EARTH FLAT," "SPACE PROGRAM WPA THEATRE," "Challenger Blown Up By God," and "God Says Earth Is Flat." The articles elaborate the Johnsons' attack on science, and sometimes even the ancient Greeks:

> THE WORD OF THE LARDS
>
> SCIENCE IS, GREASY SPOON, etc.
>
> SCIENCE IS; Greasy Spoon Superstition. Now all know what we call the "Grease ball" world or delusion comes from the fact every school tells us, and is known by most, the "Ball-Planet" idea came from Grease. So, when we say, the Grease ball, we mean and is obvious, is the idea or superstition from "Grease", It is of course the very foundation of the present Church - State Religion **the education system,** in short. Now, to anyone who has checked into this whole thing (after

all if a person will base his entire LIFE on a system sure should check fully into it and the ones who invented it, right?) know that the "great ones" of old Grease had a custom of eating "lard"! Now they didn't just dip it out with their hands, but used a spoon. So the glorious "founders" of present education-science-religion system sat around eating lard from a bucket, with a spoon and telling and hearing tall tales many of these "lards" vied with each other to take the most absurd idea and concoct a way to tell it and make it seem reasonable or at least be believed. One of the reasons for so much time concocting weird outlandish sophesty theories was they had visions of "capturing the entire world and enslaving them." They did nothing themselves slaves did all work done in Grease ball Land. ONLY for barbaric heathen mindless creatures too DUMB, too STUPID, too DEVOID OF REASON, LOGIC COMMEN SENSE to know better, than to waste their time and money, marbles and chauk on endless lunatic "explanations of the universe" and all therein!

Ronald Reagan, a secret flat earther?

In a 1988 issue devoted to the space program deception and the Challenger explosion, Johnson reveals that Ronald Reagan is a secret flat earther. Johnson points out that repeatedly, on television, Reagan mentioned God and then looked up. Thus, Reagan knows — as the bible says — that Heaven is above the earth, which implies the earth is flat. Johnson continues:

... so this FAKE landing of the shuttle, [Reagan] mentioned he believed in shuttle and God trying to clear himself with the media. But WE know he can't be cleared as EVEN THOMAS PAINE one of the FOUNDERS of USA has said it is IMPOSSIBLE for Mr. Reagan to believe in God and the Space Shuttle. Is he not telling the truth? about WHICH? The shuttle or God? I leave it to you to figure out.

... media moguls went to ask Mr. Bush — was the earth flat? BUSH as well as Reagan. So he used the same praise about the phonie the Carnie ANTI-CHRISTS the slobbering foul degenerate dogs, the "astronauts" in Discovery, he said to the Degenerate anti-christs, YOU made us proud, etc. ... BUT he then went on to say, EARTH IS FLAT, GOD EXISTS. HE IS IN HEAVEN, A PLACE, THAT IS UP ABOVE EARTH, ABOVE THE USA. THAT HE BELIEVED AT DEATH OUR SOUL GOES TO HEAVEN ABOVE THIS FLAT EARTH!...

In the tradition of the most extreme conspiriologists, Johnson is beginning to reinterpret the news in light of one belief, the flat earth. Every other bit of data in the universe can fly out the window, but the flat earth must stay, even if it means isolation and ridicule. Behind the belief in the flat earth — for Johnson, as well as Voliva, Blount, Hampden and Rowbotham — is a childlike faith in the literal truth of the bible. Rather than the independent thinkers they paint themselves to be, flat earthers are, in fact, obedient lambs with undying faith in the Sunday School teachers, parents, or whomever told them to believe in the bible.

THE DEVIL IS A DINOSAUR

The scene could be taken from a Godzilla movie or *Journey to the Center of the Earth.* Two gigantic reptilian monsters, predator and prey, claw for their lives in the steamy primordial jungle. Blood spurts from powerful limbs and furious shrieking heads. An armored tail whips out, gutting an exposed torso. Absorbed in the fight, neither of the doomed creatures realize, until it's too late, that they've begun to sink, ever so slowly, into quicksand. As they go down, their shrieks become deafening and fury turns to panic. Swallowed up by the earth, their frames are locked in eternal combat, suggesting an unholy suicide pact.

The scene, however, is not from a Godzilla movie, or any movie; it really happened. The bones of the two unfortunate dinosaurs were discovered in 1991; scientists tell us that the battle between the carnivorous velociraptor and its intended prey, the herbivorous protoceratops, took place approximately 75 million years ago.[1]

We might think that the world is a cruel place now, but these two dinosaurs lived in a world without mercy, "a freakish, hellish nightmare world drenched in the blood and gore of violence, death and destruction" inhabited by "abnormal, grotesque creatures and monstrosities" hellbent on destruction. It was a world invented by the Devil himself, according to **Damien Royce** and **Jason Zolot,** the authors of *Did God Destroy the Dinosaurs?*

While millions of dinosaur lovers everywhere delight in their gigantic proportions and sometimes comic physiognomies, Royce and Zolot are deeply disturbed by them. "Even a cursory examination of the facts," they write, "produces the distinct feeling that something was just not right with the dinosaurs and the related reptiles of the air and sea. It is as if they were not of this world and did not belong in it. It is as if they were travesties of Nature, monstrous caricatures of other creatures and of life itself — the result of some obscene joke played by some perverted prankster." They assert that it was the most perverted prankster of all, Satan, who created these travesties and, in his insatiable perversity, became one himself:

> Somewhere at the bottom of one of the oceans or seas of this planet there lies the skeleton of a gigantic multi-headed winged sea-dragon. For millions of years, it was the terror of the land, sea and air of the primordial world over which it reigned as the bloodthirsty lord and master. This monster — unlike anything the world had ever seen before or since — was the physical manifestation of Satan.

Sincerely horrified at this bizarre scenario, the authors are more than saurophobic Satan-bashers. They are theologians who carefully argue their case, with due consideration to science and religious history. Their inevitable conclusion — that Satan created the dinosaurs and that God destroyed them — brings together, they claim, science and the bible. With greater sophistication than most evangelicals, Royce and Zolot borrow freely from Gnosticism, Zoroastrianism and Paganism to form a Christian heresy that features an obsession with dinosaurs. Their purported aim is to reconcile bible belief with scientific doctrine.

The authors' ambition to appeal to secularists seems like wishful thinking. Although Royce and Zolot seem to understand basic scientific problems associated with the dinosaurs, they labor under a grossly unrealistic view of science. As they see it, science should have all the answers; dissenting views among scientists means that scientific methodologies have utterly failed. Royce and Zolot admit there is mounting evidence that dinosaurs died out as a result of a giant meteor colliding with earth. In their view, however, the catastrophe theory of extinction totally negates the theory of evolution. And so the saurian demonists consult the bible for a definitive answer to the dinosaur question since science offers only provisional explanations and shifting theories whereas religion serves up the TRUTH.

The cover to Royce and Zolot's pamphlet.

Quotations used in this article, except where specified, are from Royce, Damien and Zolot, Jason, Did God Destroy The Dinosaurs?, *1992.*

1. *Reported in* Fortean Times, *#66, Dec. 1992 - Jan. 1993, from* Daily Telegraph, *8/28/91.*

> **"Satan turned Earth into a freakish, hellish nightmare world drenched in the blood and gore of violence, death and destruction."**

When dinosaur bones were first discovered in the 19th century, people generally imagined that the dinosaurs were victims of the Great Flood — conveninently overlooking the story of Noah and his Ark. Today, bible believers who think that the earth is 6,000 years old, face a similar quandary. Told that dinosaur fossils are many millions of years old, they are forced into rejecting scientific dating methods, and therefore the entire fields of geology, astronomy and biology.

What are today's Creationists supposed to make of these creatures, who missed boarding the Ark, and who didn't warrant so much as a phrase in the bible? Some of them say that God actually planted dinosaur bones to test the faith of believers.

Royce and Zolot rush to the rescue, pointing out that the dinosaurs did indeed exist. "The eloquent testimony of the fossil record and the divinely inspired words of the Bible," they say, "seem to be mutually excludable and reciprocally irreconcilable," but conclude, "in fact they are not." Taking biblical interpretation to new extremes, they find the solution to this massive quandary in between the first and second sentences of Genesis.

"In the beginning God created the heavens and the earth. And the earth was without form and void." Royce and Zolot inform us that, in the original Hebrew, the second sentence really says, "The earth became chaotic and in confusion." They fixate on the word "became," which proves, to their minds at least, that the chaos and confusion came a lot later than creation of the Universe. Furthermore, they assert, God is never the author of waste and confusion. Not only did the chaos happen a lot later than the creation, but it wasn't even God who caused it. Genesis 1, rather than an account of the *creation* of the earth, is in fact an account of its *repair.* And in between the creation of the Universe and the Chaos, between the first two sentences of the holy bible, lived the dinosaurs.

In addition to the bible, Royce and Zolot turn to gnosticism, paganism and even Zoroastrianism to piece together the creation and demise of the mighty dinosaurs.

The story begins before the beginning with the "God family." (In the original Hebrew, "God" is plural.) Only one member of the God family — Jesus Christ — created the Universe itself. The entire family then created angels, endowing them with "free will" so that they could help out in the completion and care of the Universe. God's favorite angel, Lucifer, acquired special duties and powers. "It was to this beloved super archangel, Lucifer," Royce and Zolot assert, "that God delegated the overall responsibility for the administration and care of all creation. ... Under his direction the Universe which God had created was to be brought to completion." One might say that Lucifer became a kind of sub-contractor for Creation. God's mistake was to give Lucifer the exclusive power to create life. It was only a matter of time before Lucifer got a big head and became Satan the rebel, creator of dinosaurs.

Royce and Zolot speculate on the circumstances of the awful event.

> The Universe must have teemed with life, wondrous and beautiful in its many varieties. But then Lucifer began turning into Satan by beginning to tamper with the creation of life. Perhaps it started initially as an amusement or a prank or diversion for himself, or perhaps to impress or to entertain the lesser angelic beings who lacked his power to create life. What Satan had realized was that not only could he create life, he could also destroy it! For his amusement, Lucifer-turned-Satan introduced the reality and the curse of death to the living, something God had never intended...
>
> Satan turned Earth into a freakish, hellish nightmare world drenched in the blood and gore of violence, death and destruction, an obscene parody of what God had intended. ... His bloodlust became insatiable.
>
> Lucifer abused his creative powers by creating a planet with a steamy, wet, tropical climate, a planet populated by dinosaurs, sea reptiles, flying serpents and other abnormal, grotesque creatures and monstrosities. ...

Satan was joined by other naughty angels, in his diabolical amusements and in a major rebellion intended to overthrow the God family as rulers of the Universe.

> First enticed by a game of fun and amusement, [the fallen angels] assumed the form

of the dinosaurs and actually partook in the bloody violence and gore which the Devil had introduced to Earth. This hedonistic bloodlust was contrary to what God had intended. As bloodshed begat bloodshed, physical life came to be deemed completely worthless to them. Through exposure to the senseless, wanton violence and bloodshed and, indeed, through their active participation in the killing and bloodshed, these angels also grew morally dissolute.

Hints of this story can be found within the secret doctrines of the Gnostics, or in Pagan mythology. "This animating power of Lucifer (turned Devil)" write Royce and Zolot, "was so disconcerting and disturbing to the ancient Biblical scholars and scribes, who were well versed in Gnostic secret doctrines, that all overt traces of it were, evidently, consciously purged from the Bible." But subtle clues remain for those willing to dig them up. For example, biblical references to "Satan's seed," as well as passages about the Leviathan and the Behemoth are all really passages about Satan's creation, the dinosaurs.

Pagan myths contain less veiled references to Satan's creation. They depict a world, parallel to our own, inhabited by grotesque beasts and monsters, which, to Royce and Zolot, are representations of the dinosaurs. "Perhaps the most horrible of all [evil mythological] creatures" they write, "was the Medusa. Most interestingly, the description of Medusa resembles that of certain dinosaurs or sea reptiles."

Most telling of all, are the clues found within Zoroastrianism, a forerunner of Judeo-Christianity. Royce and Zolot point out that even though the Jews adopted certain elements of Zoroastrianism from the conquering Persians, the key teaching was adulterated. Today Zoroastrianism is just another dying religion, displaced by Islam. The authors quote Bullfinch's account of the Zoroastrian creation story:

> Ormuzd created man and supplied him with all the materials of happiness; but Ahriman marred this happiness by introducing evil into the world and creating savage beasts and poisonous reptiles and plants. In consequence of this, evil and good are now mingled together in every part of the world and the followers of good and evil ... carry on incessant war. But this state of things will not last forever. The time will come when the adherents of Ormuzd shall everywhere be victorious and Ahriman and his followers be consigned to darkness forever.

Ahriman is, of course, Satan, and the "savage beasts" are dinosaurs. Beyond descriptions in the holy books of "dead" religions, living remnants of the truth can also be found in the Book of Revelation, which depicts God's answer, after stalling so long, to Satan's fun and games:

> The heavens were completely cleansed — at least for awhile — of the rebellious demonic host... God cast Satan down to Earth, then destroyed the dinosaurs and set about the renewal of the world. Satan was deprived of his power to create in the physical realm, but he retained his power to manipulate life. Not all of Satan's creation was destroyed at this time. Certain areas were permitted to retain their hot, steamy climate and certain abnormal creatures like sharks and crocodiles were permitted either to exist or to arise through his genetic engineering.

The heavens were completely cleansed — at least for awhile — of the rebellious demonic host.

God then pursued Satan into the Solar System; evidence of the battle can be found on the pockmarked surfaces of Mars, Mercury and the moon.

Royce and Zolot interpret the Book of Revelation as a graphic depiction of this chaos and confusion (remember the second sentence of Genesis!), when "hail and fire mingled with blood," and "a great mountain burning with fire was cast into the sea." They quote:

> And the fifth angel sounded, and I saw a star fall from heaven unto the earth: and to him was given the key of the bottomless pit.
>
> And he opened the bottomless pit; and there arose a smoke out of the pit, as the smoke of a great furnace; and the sun and the air were darkened by reason of the smoke of the pit.
>
> And there came out of the smoke locusts upon the earth.... (Rev. 9: 1-3)

Thus, "the great 'comet' or 'meteor' which devastated Earth 65 million years ago and put an end to all dinosaurs," they write, "was none other than Satan himself being thunderously hurled towards Earth, confounding and

> **Satan still retains the ability to "genetically engineer" evil versions of already extant plants and animals.**

destroying the whole ecosystem of the planet!"

When the dinosaurs were so destroyed, the earth became habitable for humans, though certain areas retained their "old hot, steamy, tropical and semi-tropical climate." The authors elaborate:

> The perfection, beauty and harmony in Eden notwithstanding, this was still a planet with the remnants of Satan's earlier creation. The once planetwide tropical ecosystem still existed but was now confined to the planet's equatorial belt region. In these tropical and semi-tropical regions, there still lived such vile and savage creatures like crocodiles and alligators, puny cousins of the dinosaurs and sea reptiles, but no less deadly and bloodthirsty. ... Other vile creatures of the land and sea also either survived the metamorphosis or were biologically engineered by Satan afterwards.

Even after his vile creations were destroyed Satan still wouldn't give up. He sabotaged Eden, and continues to wage war with God, even to this day. Satan, after all, holds dominion over the earth, and although he lost his power to create life, he still retains the ability to "genetically engineer" evil versions of already extant plants and animals. Poison ivy, venomous snakes, saber-toothed tigers and vampire bats, as well as harmful bacteria and viruses such as syphilis, AIDS, smallpox and polio, are just a few examples. But Satan is not satisfied with this mischief; he wants his old power back:

> The proof that Satan still desperately tries to create is provided by the accounts of sightings of strange creatures or huge specimens of known creatures.
>
> ... Of all the creatures of Satan's menagerie, his most favored were and remain the dinosaurs. Satan has persistently tried to recreate dinosaurs! All such attempts at creation have failed... His most persistent attempt to recreate his old brood has been at Loch Ness, Scotland.

But the specimens are doomed due to the waning of Satan's power; this accounts for the repeated vanishing acts performed by "Nessie" and her ilk. Although Satan's attempts at creation remain comical and pathetic, less so are his weapons of mass destruction. However, even the plan to get humans to blow themselves off the earth could backfire:

> Science and modern weapons of destruction are double-edged swords. Satan would like to beguile man into unleashing mass destruction weapons upon himself. But he fears that man might unleash these very same weapons against his brood.
>
> Man already has the potential to eradicate all crocodiles and alligators from the wild, and indeed from existence. And man can already launch the expurgatory war against sharks, piranhas, lamprey eels and other vile creatures of Satan's menagerie. To date, man has chosen to eradicate from the wild only one member of Satan's brood — smallpox. Under the guise of the generally laudable and beneficial conservation mentality of maintaining the balance of nature, man has unwittingly included the conservation of Satan's lifeforms.

Royce and Zolot finally warn about those who take pity on wolves and crocodiles; for they are dupes of Satan! God is destined to wrest the earth from Satan's grip, destroying "his seed" in the process. Nuclear holocaust will be the fulfillment of God's will!

DR. CYRUS TEED
WE LIVE ON THE INSIDE

To know of the earth's concavity and its relation to universal form, is to know God; while to believe in the earth's convexity is to deny him and all his works. All that is opposed to Koreshanity is Antichrist.

— Koresh,[1] *The Cellular Cosmogony*

During the 19th Century, religious people everywhere began to notice that, in the eyes of science, the universe was getting bigger and bigger, while humanity was getting smaller and smaller. Man, no longer Lord of the earth, was merely its product. The Cosmos, no longer God's little playground, was an infinite, impersonal, unknowable expanse.

Dr. Cyrus Teed, who later took the name **Koresh,** made a valiant effort to reverse all this, devoting his life to the proposition that "WE LIVE ON THE INSIDE."

A distant cousin of Joseph Smith (founder of the Church of Latter Day Saints) Cyrus Teed was born in 1839 and grew up in the fertile religious territory of western New York state known as the "burned-over district," so-called because the land "burned-over" with religious fervor. Teed displayed a talent for oratory early in life, and his family suggested he enter the Baptist ministry. He chose healing instead and, after a stint with the Union Army Medical Corps during the Civil War, began studying "Eclectical" Medicine, a blend of Homeopathy, orthodox medicine, and herbal remedies. Teed graduated from the Eclectical College in New York City in 1868, and set up practice in his home town of Utica.

The Illumination of Koresh

The spiritually-minded doctor was unable to confine himself exclusively to medical pursuits. Disturbed by the increasing forces of rationalism, particularly in science, Teed began to conduct experiments late at night in a solitary pursuit of truth. In 1869, he set up a laboratory for investigating "electro-alchemy," a discipline he himself invented.

Like the alchemists, Teed sought the "Philosopher's Stone" that would enable him to accomplish the "transmutation" of one substance into another. By updating alchemy to include the concepts of electricity and magnetism, Teed found what he was looking for. He discovered that energy and matter are two different forms of the same thing, and that once he could reduce matter to energy, he could reconstitute it as matter of another kind by utilizing polar magnetism. He claimed that, using this process, he transformed base metal into gold dust, visible, however, through only the most powerful microscope.

Even more astounding than Teed's formation of gold was his realization that he had also found the secret of immortality. Teed believed the process of transmutation he had discovered was the scientific means to human, physical immortality, through the direction and regulation of "human life forces."

Late one night, shortly after his discovery, Teed realized that he might, through concentration, use his knowledge to cause his "highest idea of creative beauty" to materialize:

> Suddenly, I experienced a relaxation at the occiput or back part of the brain, and a peculiar buzzing tension at the forehead or sinciput. Succeeding this was a soft tension about the organs of the brain called the lyra, cruva, penealis, and conarium. There gradually spread from the center of my brain to the extremities of my body, and, apparently to me, into the auraic sphere of my being, miles outside of my body, a vibration so gentle, soft, and dulciferous that I was impressed to lay myself upon the bosom of this gently oscillating ocean of magnetic and spiritual ecstasy. I realized myself gently yielding to the impulse of reclining upon a vibratory sea of this, my newly found delight. My every thought but one had departed from the contemplation of earthly and material things. I had but a lingering, vague remembrance of natural consciousness and desire.

Cyrus Teed, or "Koresh," from *The Cellular Cosmogony*

1. Not to be confused with David Koresh, aka Vernon Howell, of Waco, Texas fame.

In the impulse of that last remnant of material thought I put forth, as I supposed, my material arm and hand to experience some familiar touch — but there was no response ... I started in alarm, for I felt that I had departed from all material things, perhaps forever. [Quoted from *The Illumination of Koresh, Marvelous Experience of the Great Alchemist at Utica, New York,* in Robert Lynn Rainard's unpublished Master's thesis, *In the Name of Humanity: The Koreshan Unity.*]

The earth isn't a tiny ball flying through limitless space, but a stationary concave hollow shell, 8,000 miles across and 25,000 miles around, containing the cosmos and the sun in its center.

To test his senses, Teed spoke aloud, but rather than his own voice, he heard a maternal, feminine voice speaking through his own lips on the subject of his past incarnations. When he opened his eyes, Teed beheld an "exquisite" woman "emerging from a sphere of purple and golden light," who continued to speak to him, identifying herself as the Father, the Son and the Mother, in One. She revealed remarkable truths about the cosmos, and said it was now time to announce these truths to the world; it would be Teed's mission on earth to preach them, and in the process "reform the race." Finally, she promised the amazed doctor he would meet her again soon, in the flesh.

After his visitor departed, Teed realized the significance of what she'd said. He vowed he would "achieve the victory over death, not for myself, but for those to whom I come as a sacrificial offering." Teed would be, in other words, the embodiment of the Second Coming of Christ.

In his new role, Teed needed a title. Realizing that "Christ" wouldn't do, he instead called himself "Koresh," Hebrew for "Cyrus," his first name. His teachings would be designated "Koreshanity" and his followers "Koreshans."

Any parallels that might exist between Christianity and Koreshanity ended there. The central teaching of the new religion consisting of the cosmic revelation imparted to Teed was that the Copernican view of the universe is inside out: the earth isn't a tiny ball flying through limitless space, but a stationary concave hollow shell 8,000 miles across and 25,000 miles around, containing the cosmos with the sun in its center.

Koresh's little universe, *The Cellular Cosmogony,* was not just analogous to the shell of an egg — it was the shell of an egg. As he stated some years later, "All life develops in a shell, egg, or womb. ... [T]he law of development in the greater or macrocosmic order does not depart from the universal law. ... The earth, therefore, is the great womb of natural development, hence we are living *in a shell.*" Once again, the universe was finite, with Man reigning supreme:

The Koreshan Cosmogony reduces the universe to proportionate limits, and its cause within the comprehension of the human mind. It demonstrates the possibility of the attainment of man to his supreme inheritance, the ultimate dominion of the universe, thus restoring him to the acme of exaltation, — the throne of the Eternal, when he had his origin.

Koreshanity didn't quite catch on at first. In his zeal to "reform the race," Teed attempted to convince everyone — starting with his patients — that he was the second Christ and that we live inside the earth. Rather than become his disciples, however, Teed's patients for the most part sought medical help elsewhere. Owing to a failing medical practice, Teed was forced to set up shop at another location, but the same thing happened there and in every other town he tried; once he had patients, he would reveal to them his true identity as Koresh and gain a lasting reputation as "that crazy doctor." By 1873, the nomadic, impoverished existence of the Teed family took its toll on Mrs. Teed. Ill, she left with their son to live with her sister, remaining there until her death in 1885.

By the time Mrs. Teed left, however, Teed had picked up a small following, including his first convert, **Dr. A.W.K. Andrews,** who became a lifelong disciple and a source of funds during hard times. Following a serious correspondence with the utopian Harmony Society at Economy, Pennsylvania, Teed and Andrews were invited to visit in 1873, and were entertained by the community's leadership. The experience made a strong impression on the spiritually-minded doctors, who later adopted the Harmonists' practices of celibacy and communism. Teed had a similarly lasting effect on the Harmonists; some accused their president, John Duss, of espousing Teed's doctrine.

The Koreshan Unity

Throughout the 1870s, Teed's efforts to convert an unwilling populace — as well as to earn a living — met with consistent failure. His revelation had earned him the title of crackpot rather than messiah. But Teed proved his sincerity by continuing his efforts despite many years of ridicule and poverty. Finally, in 1886, his persistence was rewarded.

Teed met a woman, Mrs. **Thankful H. Hale,** a New Yorker deeply impressed with his teachings. Mrs. Hale was also involved with a Chicago group, the National Association of Mental Science, and convinced them to invite Dr. Teed to speak at their 1886 convention. Teed gratefully accepted the invitation and traveled, at their expense, to Chicago. This trip proved fateful; the mental scientists were so impressed with Teed's presentation that shortly after, they unanimously elected him president of their association.

Suddenly, Teed had a following, and wasted no time in making the most of it. He stayed in Chicago and, within a few years, reshaped the Association of Mental Science and founded the "Koreshan Unity" and the "World's College of Life," with courses in electro-alchemy, metaphysics and, of course, mental science. With church coffers now overflowing, the Unity had means to purchase an ornate, old mansion — dubbed "Beth-Ophra" — in Chicago's elegant Washington Heights. Beth-Ophra served as Koreshan headquarters, housed the College of Life, and contained dormitories for the first Koreshan community, which numbered 126.

By the mid-1890s, Koresh had convinced 4,000 people that "we live on the inside." One such follower was **Lou Staton,** whose instantaneous conversion is recounted in Carl Carmer's *Dark Trees to the Wind*:

> I was barbering at the Sherman Hotel in Chicago. Left my room for a walk down State Street. The nineteen-hundred elections were going on. Speakers were hollering about that on one corner and on another the Salvation Army was holding a meeting, but I wasn't paying anybody mind. I was out for a walk. Then I saw a fellow speaking beside a post that had a sign on it — same sign you see there on the wall — WE LIVE INSIDE. What he said made sense and I stopped to listen. I bought a copy of the *Flaming Sword* from a man standing beside the speaker. It was three cents but I gave him a nickel and said "Keep the change." I read it in bed that night. Before I went to sleep I was inside.

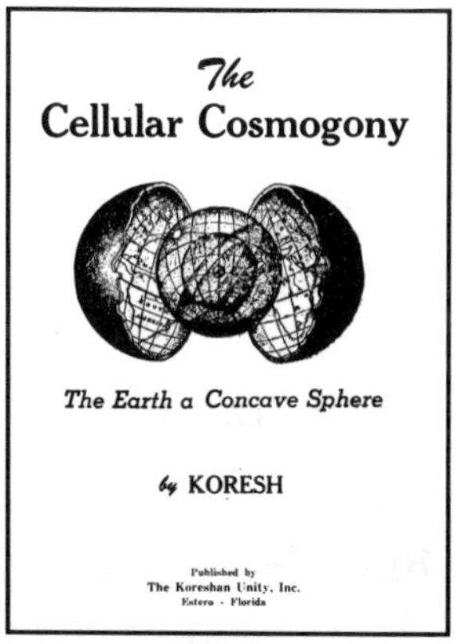

The sensation that was Koreshanity spread throughout the nation owing to Teed's boundless energy and frequent travel. Koresh won disciples in Chicago, Massachusetts, Baltimore, Denver, San Francisco, and Portland, Oregon. But gaining a following, Koresh also gained notoriety, police harassment, lawsuits from the husbands of converted wives, as well as sometimes unflattering press coverage. The *Chicago Tribune* described the up-and-coming messiah as "an undersized, smooth-shaven man ... whose brown, restless eyes glow and burn like live coals [who] exerts a strange, mesmerizing influence over his converts, particularly the other sex." The *Chicago Herald* denounced Teed as "the absolute, irresponsible, immaculate and inviolate high muck a muck if ever there was one. He is addressed with awe and trembling... neither his acts nor his motives are inquired into and his word is law — the only law."

Some of the harassment and bad press was undoubtedly due to the "communistic" bent of the Koreshans, drawn mainly from the upper and middle classes. In 1891, so he might also convert members of the working class, Teed established the anti-monopolistic "Bureau of Equitable Commerce," which promoted cooperative sharing of goods and a peculiar version of democracy where everyone is equal, under Koresh.

Teed's argument for establishing his versions of communism and democracy was based on his idea that the "physical heavens" constitute God's blueprint for social government:

> The order of the physical heavens, in which all of the stars are related to the central one and regulated by it, must constitute the pattern after which the social government is to be formulated. ... The government of the physical universe is imperial, in that the head of government resides in one center; but democratic, in that all of the stars bear that reciprocal relation which makes

the center dependent upon the reciprocal activity of the subsidiary but contributory centers.

Teed saw great things ahead for New Jerusalem, which he envisioned rivaling Washinton D.C. until fulfilling its final destiny as the center of the New World Government.

While some of Teed's ideas were authoritarian, he was also an early advocate of women's equality and population control. These would be accomplished through celibacy, which would also allow Koreshans to conserve their life forces and achieve physical immortality. And, as Teed's deity was hermaphroditic — half-male and half-female — the Biblical 144,000 elect members of New Jerusalem was doubled, to include 144,000 males and 144,000 females, each couple pairing to form a "new race of men."

Ever since his illumination, Koresh had been seeking the physical manifestation of the deity who promised to walk by his side. When **Annie G. Ordway** joined the Koreshans, he immediately recognized her as that manifestation, renaming her "Victoria Gratia." Ordway became Teed's permanent companion (they were supposedly celibate), with Koresh serving as spiritual leader and Victoria as the organization's president. Jointly, the two directed the community, along with a council of seven women representing the seven planets.

[Teed] says as soon as his system of government prevails, which he says will be within ten years, he will build a six track railroad between the Atlantic and Pacific coasts, in one year employing a million men in its work. He will also construct a pneumatic passenger way across the continent which will carry one to San Francisco in 12 hours; the cars will run without wheels. More wonderful than all, Dr. Teed says one of his members in the Chicago office has a device whereby he can, from his desk in that office in Chicago, set the type for every newspaper in this country by wire and that an application for a patent is now on file in Washington. [Quoted from the *Pittsburgh Leader,* 10/25/1891, in *Dark Trees to the Wind.]*

Estero & New Jerusalem

The reality of the Koreshan cooperative, however, wasn't so cheerful. Continued harassment, lawsuits and bad press caused the Koreshans to begin thinking about establishing utopia in a more remote location. Teed considered merging with an established community, such as the Shakers, the Brotherhood of New Life, or the Harmonists, but negotiations with these groups failed to yield anything workable. Instead, the community moved into uncharted territory of the southwest coast of Florida.

Sources disagree, however, on the events leading up to that move. By one account, the Koreshans came to Florida on their own. In 1893, Teed and three Koreshan companions left Chicago in search of "the point where the vitellus of the alchemico-organic cosmos specifically determines." Their route was determined by spiritual guidance alone, which eventually brought them in January, 1894 to Punta Rassa, Florida. There they convinced a German immigrant, **Gustave Damkohler,** to donate 320 acres of isolated, sparsely-populated wilderness near Estero Bay to set down roots for the Koreshan utopia. Like other speculators of the day, the Koreshans predicted Florida would become the "greatest commercial thoroughfare of the world." For his donation of the Koreshans' New Jerusalem, Gustave Damkohler was promised eternal life.

In a second version of the story, Damkohler is portrayed as a mystic who purchased the land in 1883 at the urging of a disembodied voice. The voice directed him to stay put and wait for the Lord's arrival at Ester Bay. For seven years Damkohler stayed loyal to the disembodied spirit even though he lost his wife and six children to the inhospitable climate. When Damkohler happened upon a Koreshan pamphlet in a nearby town, he immediately recognized Koresh as the long-awaited messiah. After a few years of entreaties, Koresh obligingly visited the holy swamp and accepted the 320 steamy acres — an unsolicited gift from Dakohler.

Teed envisioned his New Jerusalem as a rival to Washington, D.C. until fulfilling its final destiny as the center of the new world government:

The shape of the city is to be octagon. In its center is to rise the most magnificent temple the world has ever seen — the great fame of the Koreshans. Around this temple is to run in a circle a placid sheet of water (an arm of the Estero), and around that, the arcadium, a complex of structures wherein schools, gymnasium, etc., are to be housed... Two principal streets, each 400 feet wide are to intersect the whole city, and these are to be called meridian way, north and south, and parallel, east and west while two diagonal streets, each 200 feet wide, are to cross. The diameter of the octagon from side to side is to be exactly one-half of a mile, and within the inner space is to be a fine park, with the Triumphia Octagonia near it... The whole city is to be surrounded by a circular boulevard, and the length of the octagon has been taken from the diameter of the circle, the diagonal of the square of which is ten times that distance, 'which is our way of squaring the circle'... Placed at equal distances near the circumference are to be twenty-four distributing centers or stores. [Quoted from *New Jerusalem* in *In the Name of Humanity.*]

The first few Koreshans to dedicate themselves to Koresh's vision were extraordinarily hardy, industrious souls. In 1894, the pilgrims, clad in heavy Victorian clothing, left Chicago and, seven train changes later, arrived at Punta Gorda, the end of the line. The travellers, ill by this time, were moved by sailboat to Mound Key and pulled by towboat to Halfway Creek. The rest of the way, they had to carry their belongings through the bush on foot. For ten months, they slept in tents, sometimes in mud, but the energetic northerners soon learned how to deal with the climate and the land. Within a year, 100 Koreshans had converted the swamp into a productive village they proudly called the "Koreshan Co-operative and Communistic Colony."

The Rectilineator & *The Cellular Cosmogony*

Koresh had long sought scientific means to prove the earth concave; at Estero, he had the opportunity. In 1896, **Ulysses Grant Morrow,** a professor at the Koreshan College of Life, devised the "Rectilineator" to settle the question of the earth's shape once and for all. The device consisted of "ten T-squares set horizontally, alternately head-to-head and tail-to-tail, mounted on ten carefully adjusted legs." The principle was simple; if the earth is concave, a straight line beginning at any point on Earth would describe a chord, eventually reaching another point in the earth. If the earth is convex, the line no matter how long would go out into space. The Rectilineator would constitute such a line, section by section. Though "objectively" pursuing the truth, the Koreshans probably didn't account for the possibility that the rectilineator might take them out into space, and not too surprisingly, it didn't. In 1897, five months after they began creating their line, the Koreshan Geodetic Survey reached Naples, Florida, having moved the Rectilineator, section by section, four miles. When the line struck water, they rejoiced; they knew that they had proved the Earth concave.

The earth appears convex to most people due to an unfortunate optical illusion.

Now all Koresh needed to do was to tell the (concave) world about his triumph over Copernicus. In 1898, he and Morrow collaborated on the book that would change science forever, *The Cellular Cosmogony*. This became the central text on Koreshan "Universology," which "embraces every department and phase of form and function in the universe..."

In *The Cellular Cosmogony,* Koresh takes on science with a vengeance, reserving his strongest venom for The Copernican System, developed, he points out, during the dark ages. Science, Koresh says, is supposed to be knowledge. The Copernican System, however, and "the pseudo-science of modern times," is admitted by its most brilliant advocates to be based on assumptions and hypotheses rather than certain knowledge. In stark contrast, the Koreshan System is founded on the infallible rectilineator device wielded by the Koreshan Geodetic Staff. The choice between Copernicus and Koresh is no less than a choice between uncertain conjecture and rock solid truth. That earth appears convex to most people is simply due to an unfortunate optical illusion.

Repeatedly assuring his readers that his system is based on proven facts rather than hypothesis, Koresh unfolds the Cellular Cosmogony in all its glory. He does not, however, describe the experiments that prove all the details of his system. Rather, he imparts them with such an air of authority that they sound almost reasonable:

The alchemico-organic (physical) world or universe is a shell composed of seven metallic, five mineral, and five geologic strata, with an inner habitable surface of land and water. This inner surface, as the reader already understands, is concave. ... Within this shell are three principal atmospheres, the first or outermost (the one in which we exist) being composed chiefly of oxygen and nitrogen; the one immediately above that is pure hydrogen, and the one above the hydrogen atmosphere we have denominated aboron. Within this is the solar electromagnetic atmosphere, the nucleus of which is the stellar center. In an occupying these atmospheres are the sun and stars, also the reflections called the planets and the moon. ...

The planets are mercurial disci moving by electro-magnetic impulse between the metallic laminae or planes of the concave shell. They are seen through penetrable rays, ultra electro-magnetic, reflected or bent back in their impingement on spheres of substance regularly graduated as the stories in the heavens.

Koresh's shell universe has no room for heavenly bodies other than the earth and sun.

Koresh's shell universe has no room for heavenly bodies other than the earth and sun. This makes the moon, the planets and stars mere optical illusions, reflections of the sun and earth.

Koresh dwells for some time on the "foreshortening" effect, the optical illusion that causes us to see a convex earth. His explanation of the illusions of heavenly bodies is more complex, hinging on the existence of the many atmospheres or "laminae" filling the inside of the earth's shell. Using these principles, Koresh reveals not only the "reflections" of the heavenly bodies, but also the causes of day and night, and the seasons:

The sun in the third atmosphere is pendant, so to speak, from the pivot at the center. As the center revolves in its vertical revolution, the pendant sun in the third atmosphere moves in an orbit through the space of that atmosphere. This causes day and night. The lateral revolution in the sun, producing the diaphragm and peripheral rings (zones) of levic 'force,' produces the slow revolution of the cold and heat poles of the lateral cycle from north to south. From the cold pole of the zone (to midway between these extremities) it grows warmer, and from the hot pole it grows colder until the temperate is reached.

To Koresh, the only bodies besides sun and earth not due to optical illusion are human. The "Anthropostic Cosmos" is his name for the human analog to the Cellular Cosmogony; its conception is strongly reminiscent of the alchemists:

The stellar nucleus is the center of space; the metallic laminae are at the circumference of space. Correspondentially in humanity, the Lord Christ was the stellar Center, and his quality was the correspondent, in anthropostic being, of space in the alchemico-organic cosmos. ... In the progress of time in its relation to the development and progress of the race, the seven churches yet to be formulated into groups are the anthropostic depositions corresponding to the seven metallic plates. The seven churches are seven qualities of human characteristics and correspond to seven planets, and therefore to the seven primary substratic laminae of the cosmic crust.

In addition to the alchemists, Koresh was clearly influenced by the spiritualists, mentalists and occultists of his day. He saw a constant flow between spirit and matter which likens the cellular cosmos to "a great electromagnetic battery":

The sun and stars are focalizations of physical spirit-substance, merging into matter materialized through voluminous and high-tension convergence. There are at these centers constant concretion and sublimation. Spirit-substance is constantly materializing, and the temporary materialization is as rapidly changed to spirit-substance and is radiated. There is, therefore, a reciprocal interchange of substance from center and circumference. The spirit-substances engendered at the nucleus are radiated to the circumference, and are there solidified. At the circumference the surplus solidification is reduced again to spirit-substance and flows to the nucleus.

Koresh's ability to integrate astronomical, alchemical, mentalist, electrical and religious ideas into a single passage is awe-inspiring. This, perhaps, is one of the qualities that won him disciples. In a passage ostensibly about the precession of the equinoxes, Koresh manages to conclude with a soliloquy on the second coming of Christ:

We are now approaching a great biologic conflagration. Thousands of people will dematerialize, through a biologic electro-magnetic vibration. This will be brought about through the direction of one mind, the only one who has a knowledge of the law of this bio-alchemical transmutation. The change will be accomplished through the formation of a biological battery, the laws of which are known to only one man. This man is

Elijah the Prophet, ordained of God, the Shepherd of the Gentiles, and the central reincarnation of the ages. From this conflagration will spring the Sons of God, the biune offspring of the Lord Jesus, the Christ and Son of God.

The Beginning of the End

By 1903, the Koreshan colony — whose entranceway read, "WE LIVE ON THE INSIDE" — was thriving. The Chicago branch had moved *en masse* to Estero, swelling its numbers to about 200. The Koreshans were industrious, producing high-quality citrus, giving them means to purchase an additional 6,000 acres for New Jerusalem. They built a floating stage on the Estero River, producing classical music concerts. Their Art Hall was filled with charts of the Cellular Cosmogony and a globe which could be taken apart to show the nations of the world, on the inside. The College of Life, now called "Pioneer University of Koreshan Universology," was also doing well, with a brass band that won first prize at the Florida State Fair.

But this happy state of affairs wasn't to last. Politics would be the downfall of the Koreshans and of their leader.

In 1904, Koresh toured the county with his "Progressive Liberty Party" and a brass band, promoting public ownership of utilities, economic equality, free schools and protection of natural resources. Their stand pitted the Koreshans against the local county political machine, but they won many supporters. Just before the election, Koresh found himself in an argument — which erupted into a fight — with the marshal of Ft. Myers. The marshal began to beat Koresh until several Koreshans intervened. The marshal drew his gun, and arrested them all.

Koresh never recovered from the beating; he suffered weakness and pain the rest of his life. To add insult to injury, the Progressive Liberty Party lost the election by a slim margin.

The Death of Koresh

In 1892, Teed had written in the Koreshan newspaper, the *Flaming Sword,* "Dr. Teed will die; the termination of his natural career will be tragic. He will reach death at the instigation of a people who profess the religion of Jesus the Christ of God." On December 22, 1908, at the age of 69, Teed fulfilled his own prophecy. Teed's teachings on immortality, however, were taken quite seriously. Upon his death, the Koreshans fully expected that, by Christmas, Teed would be resurrected by *theocrasis,* his name for the "incorruptible dissolution, without decay of the flesh, of a physical body by 'electro-magnetic combustion.'" A vigil was kept over Teed's body, to await certain resurrection; Teed's decaying flesh lay for nearly a week, until finally health authorities took notice, and the Koreshans were forced to bury their savior. On December 27, Koresh was laid to rest at Estero Island.

A vigil was kept over Teed's body, to await certain resurrection.

After Teed's burial, the Koreshan community fell apart. Annie Ordway (Victoria Gratia), already Koreshan president, declared herself the new leader, but many Koreshans wouldn't accept her and the group split into factions. In 1909, Ordway left Estero for Tampa with her devoted following, and married **Dr. Charles A. Graves,** the former mayor of Estero. The sexagenarian newlyweds were ousted from the Koreshan community for their supposed violation of the vow of celibacy, though the decision was obviously political. Ordway and her followers remained as a splinter group until her death in 1923.

Meanwhile, the "diehards" continued to expect the resurrection of Koresh, and even plotted to open his cement sarcophagus. They were caught in the midst of their necromantic plot, and from then on the tomb was patrolled by a night watchman. But the guard was helpless to defend Teed's tomb against a hurricane which struck Estero Island in 1921, and carried away Koresh's tomb, leaving no trace of the messiah. Teed finally experienced *theocrasis,* thirteen years after his death.

By the time the hurricane struck, younger Koreshans had begun to leave Estero, while older ones were dying off. Mounting financial problems would help ruin Estero, though the faltering utopia experienced a brief renaissance with the arrival of its last recruit, **Hedwig Michel** from Frankfurt, Germany.

Bender saw himself as the reincarnation of Koresh.

Michel, a Jewish woman, had been forced out of her deep involvement with the theater by the Nazis. Just before World War II, she was serving as headmistress of a Jewish children's school. One of her instructors was Peter Bender, who through his mathematical researches had become convinced, like Teed, that we live on the inside. By chance, he had come across *The Cellular Cosmogony* — which confirmed his researches — in a library at Worms am Rhein. Bender began corresponding with the Koreshans, and eventually saw himself as the reincarnation of Koresh. (As Koresh was the second Christ, this would make Bender the third.) Michel, after listening to Bender's arguments, was soon converted to Koreshanity herself. As the Nazis were beginning make good on their promise to solve "the Jewish Question," Michel wisely left Germany — for Estero — on the last American ship to bring in Jewish refugees. Bender stayed in Germany and was eventually killed in a concentration camp.

The arrival of Michel at Estero infused new energy into the dying colony. In 1948, she was so optimistic that she told Carl Carmer, "Koreshanity is not of the past but for the future. It is a great truth and it will someday sweep across the world." When Michel became director, in 1954, she halted the selling off of land and resurrected the colony's newspapers. But there wasn't much more she could do. By 1960, there were only four people left in the community, of whom Michel — then in her sixties — was the youngest. In 1961, Michel donated 300 acres of Koreshan land to the State of Florida; it was eventually opened to the public as the "Koreshan State Historical Site," where Michel continued to live until her death in 1982. There, today, one may visit the Koreshan Art Hall, the dorms and main house which were once the center of the universe.

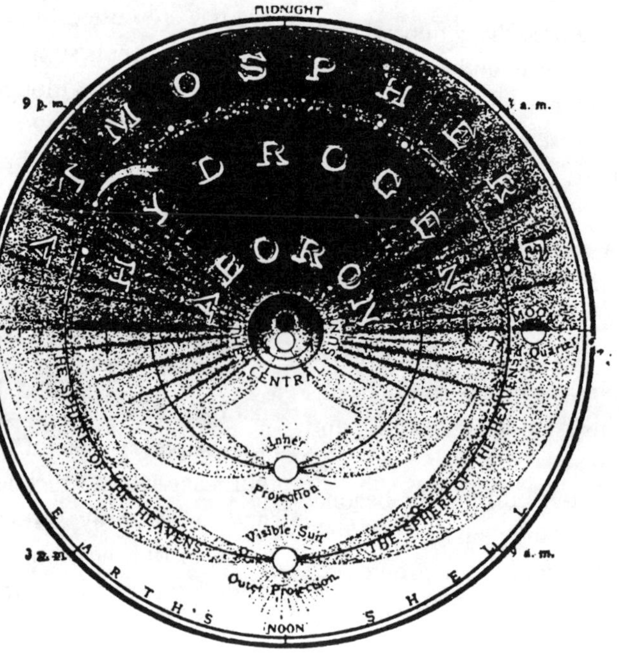

Cross-Sectional View of the Great Electro-Magnetic Battery, with the Sun as the Perpetual Pivot and Pole. Southern Hemisphere of the Cell

From *The Cellular Cosmogony*

MEN CAN HAVE BABIES

AMONG THE MANY INEXPLICABLE DOCUMENTS that reached my files was a neatly-typed flyer which is reprinted below word-for-word.

The fact that men can have babies and a man's prostrate gland operation is avoidable are related. The prostrate gland problem afflicts a large percentage of men that live long enough. Briefly the gland enlarges, closes off the urethra, making it difficult, then impossible, for the victim to urinate. The usual remedy is an operation. Up to fifty or sixty years ago the condition was fatal. It is a horrible way to die. It used to be said his water stopped. Men would not be here unless there were ways around this problem.

The most satisfactory way around this prostrate gland problem is a particular position a man and woman take in sex when the man is about forty years old. The man must be mature yet sexually active. If the two people are successful the man has a physical experience. The man and woman lie side by side, they put their forefingers up each others rectum, she yanks the man penis and the man rubs the womans clitoris. This position is not written down in any publication that mentions sex. The sexual relationship has to be perfect. One disfunction and it will not work. The physical experience the man has is a flood of liquid, the consistancy of water, out the mans rectum as the couple climax.

If the man with his co-operative woman, is successful in having this physical experience, they will discover that the man can have a baby. For about a year after the man has this physical experience he can get pregnant. The man for this year has a very itchy rectum and has to scratch it. During this period of time the man who had this physical experience would let another man put his erect penis up his rectum and ejackulate. The sperm would migrate along the tube that runs from near the oriface of the rectum to the man's uterus back of the testicles, between his legs. After the usual period of time a normal baby either male or female would be born out of the mans rectum. Men can nurse babies from their breasts. After the first baby is born the man can have another one. As the man's pregnancy progresses he would waddle as he walked. After the baby was born the man would have to cork his rectum.

My father is Dr. E.P. Linton, a Ph.D. in quantum mechanics. I understand when a new idea as foreign as this is exposed you have to have proof. I have some suggestions.

Now suppose it has never been done before. You are back in the 1850s. It would not be easy to find out how a woman's breast produced food for her baby. In her nullitarous state, difficult; opening up the cadaver of a woman who died postartum while nursing might be possible. The same thing applies to a man. The way to get scientific proof is to examine a cadaver between his legs. The uterus before a man had that physical experience would be vestigal. That tube leading from near the oriface of the rectum to the uterus would appear as a piece of flesh. It should be possible to trace that piece of flesh back to the uterus. That tube also serves as a birth canal.

The actual physical act is a hilarious experience for a woman. What happens when a man is successful in having a woman do him this favor (and it is a favor, the only favor a woman can do a man), she watches him very closely for the year or so in which it is possible for him to get pregnant. It is obvious that this is how a man got a life before women were created. I would suggest to you that the first woman on earth came out of a homosexual's rectum.

The fact that men can have babies has implications for women. Everything inside our bodies is reflected in our brains. This makes men more complicated than women.

The reason that this is getting written down is that since I was thirty eight years old I have known that I was not going to lose my prostrate gland. For a year when I was this age I could have gotten pregnant by the method I have described. I might mention that I am a layman. That prostrate gland operation is a very necessary one. However, if I have my way, there will be an increasingly large number of men who do not need this operation.

I am a normal man with a normal man's ego. I expect all the credit from the scientific community for pointing out these facts of male anatomy to you.

— David Linton

"After the usual period of time a normal baby either male or female would be born out of the mans rectum."

DISCREET behaviour is an important part of respectability, and has assisted men and women to be virgins for their weddings, yet some had been to UNIVERSITY and other places of advanced learning, and had sexual friends at that time, and were very passionate, too. Being discreet helps to keep these people —faithful in marriage, as well.See page 4, line 21.

EIGHT PASSION PROTEINS WITH CARE

This booklet would benefit more, if it were read occasionally. And it deserves to be read at all changes of life: marriage, expectancy, menopause, retirement, old age, new situations, etc.

SEXUAL ATMOSPHERE

Boy and girl companionships, co-education, love literature-and-pictures, day dreams, and inactivity, from the start of sexual awareness, —TEND to bring early lust to youths, —with SICKLINESS and adult hazards. —The reproductive system must not be developed quickly, sacrificing HEALTH.

A young person with a personal month, might need to lengthen it, to have better health: by thinking—less of sexuality and by following lines 10-13, page 9.

It is important to marry, with good health.

Married people slowly killing themselves, with compulsive married-love, must lengthen the phases of recovery, by having healthy pursuits, away from thoughts of sexuality, and if necessary, by always having a lower level of protein.

Your excessive lust— could be fatal to your compulsive spouse.

'ASSIMILATION: Strict vegetarians that cannot plan their meals note: when the conversion of protein into benign protein, halts between meals, for —lacking particular protein-parts, the unused protein-material becomes merely 'sugar' for energy. cf., p.1, bottom.'

Without a knowledge of food-values, a meal consisting of a little of each of a number of items, would be better than a meal with a larger amount of each of fewer items.

Contraception is possible by not developing the 'monthly' womb-lining, by eating less protein; but it could be a serious hazard for a wife careless — of health proven by a good colour, vivacity, and no ailments. A womb-lining could creep-up on a wife lacking skill and constancy.

And could you, a —gentle wife, reach the climaxes in married-love, with only sexual fascination and love-play?

..or PROTEIN WISDOM

Proteins are for body building; for body maintenance; and for reproduction involving the build up of passion for mating.

Most foods contain —some protein; but the eight passion-proteins are foods that have much protein, and that individuals eat frequently. So, how obvious it is that we should regulate passion, by regulating our eating of these eight classes of food.

Those who do not have to work hard with their limbs, and those who are inclined to sit about —will STORE UP their protein for passion, during these spells of easiness. —Retirement could be a time of boosted passion and marital discord. —During prolonged extreme inactivity, one's needs of protein, could be very small.

The EIGHT passion-proteins are MEAT, FISH, and BIRD; CHEESE, EGGS; PEAS(incl. lentils), BEANS; and NUTS.

MEAT, FISH, and BIRD, mean any creature of the land, or water, or air. —Fat is not protein. —There are many sorts of cheese, eggs, peas, beans, and nuts —all generally rich with protein.

Mostly, the protein of plants lacks the completeness of protein derived from and of creatures; but another food taken at the same meal could make a plant as efficient. Likewise, plant-protein could make creature-protein more efficient. Synthetic meats of some sausages and snacks, and protein-concentrates are very efficient.

When protein-material is building-up the spent reproductive organs again and gradually, this is —recorded in the sensitive brain, and this is increasingly fascinating —the mind wanting —more and —more of it. This is passion.

CHILDREN and CONVERSATION.

EAGERNESS to know of life, draws children to lewd talk, which could condition a child to be promiscuous; but let lewd talk be supplanted by SIMPLE explanations. And implanted rules of behaviour would be a strength to young people, when the sexes mix.

The parents have abdicated from parenthood, for ambition and pleasure. They have forsaken their children, for sexuality.

Are you a dull, unhelpful parent tired and weakened by too much married-love? Have you sweets and toys only, for your children?

You have so much to tell your children, if they are not to go wrong; but do you ever talk, very much, to your children? Are they drawing away from you, and learning bad ways? Have bad children and adults, more credibility with your children than you? PARENT CREDIBILITY begins in the pre-school-years, by parents' being interesting to their children.

When the children become teenagers; then we shall see how bad their parents were; then children start smoking and drinking and using drugs, become vandals, thieves, gamblers and motorists, and without being married, sons and daughters,—lose their virginity,—if they had bad parents.

And how many nice children are spoilt by parentless, DORMITORY years?

Excerpts from a rather inexplicable pamphlet from England, circa 1968.

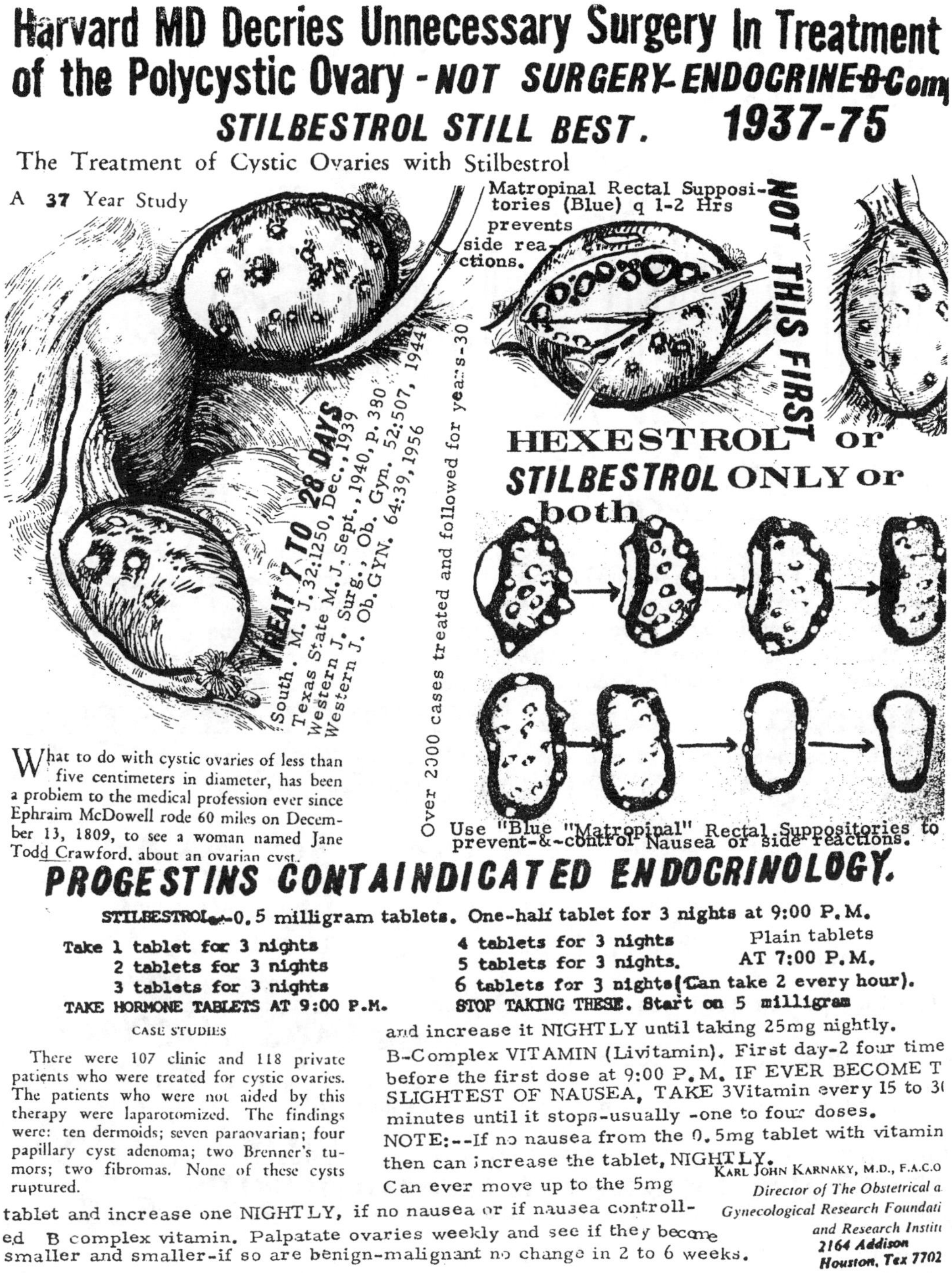

Harvard MD Decries Unnecessary Surgery In Treatment of the Polycystic Ovary - NOT SURGERY-ENDOCRINE-B-Com

STILBESTROL STILL BEST. 1937-75

The Treatment of Cystic Ovaries with Stilbestrol

A 37 Year Study

Matropinal Rectal Suppositories (Blue) q 1-2 Hrs prevents side reactions.

NOT THIS FIRST

HEXESTROL or STILBESTROL ONLY or both

TREAT 7 TO 28 DAYS

South. M. J. 32:1250, Dec., 1939
Texas State M. J. Sept., 1940, p. 380
Western J. Surg., Ob. Gyn. 52:507, 1944
Western J. Ob. GYN. 64:39, 1956

Over 2000 cases treated and followed for years-30

What to do with cystic ovaries of less than five centimeters in diameter, has been a problem to the medical profession ever since Ephraim McDowell rode 60 miles on December 13, 1809, to see a woman named Jane Todd Crawford, about an ovarian cyst.

Use "Blue "Matropinal" Rectal Suppositories to prevent-&-control Nausea or side reactions.

PROGESTINS CONTAINDICATED ENDOCRINOLOGY.

STILBESTROL--0.5 milligram tablets. One-half tablet for 3 nights at 9:00 P.M.

Take 1 tablet for 3 nights
2 tablets for 3 nights
3 tablets for 3 nights
TAKE HORMONE TABLETS AT 9:00 P.M.

4 tablets for 3 nights
5 tablets for 3 nights.
6 tablets for 3 nights (Can take 2 every hour).
STOP TAKING THESE. Start on 5 milligram

Plain tablets AT 7:00 P.M.

CASE STUDIES

There were 107 clinic and 118 private patients who were treated for cystic ovaries. The patients who were not aided by this therapy were laparotomized. The findings were: ten dermoids; seven paraovarian; four papillary cyst adenoma; two Brenner's tumors; two fibromas. None of these cysts ruptured.

and increase it NIGHTLY until taking 25mg nightly. B-Complex VITAMIN (Livitamin). First day-2 four time before the first dose at 9:00 P.M. IF EVER BECOME T SLIGHTEST OF NAUSEA, TAKE 3Vitamin every 15 to 3(minutes until it stops-usually -one to four doses. NOTE:--If no nausea from the 0.5mg tablet with vitamin then can increase the tablet, NIGHTLY. Can ever move up to the 5mg tablet and increase one NIGHTLY, if no nausea or if nausea controlled B complex vitamin. Palpatate ovaries weekly and see if they become smaller and smaller-if so are benign-malignant no change in 2 to 6 weeks.

KARL JOHN KARNAKY, M.D., F.A.C.O
Director of The Obstetrical a
Gynecological Research Foundati
and Research Institu
2164 Addison
Houston, Tex 7702

A selection of flyers taken from the prolific letter writer and M.D. (?), Karl J. Karnaky, appear on the next two pages.

Karnaky's theory Of Menstruation-1940 1984

Bulletin of The Methodist Hospital Clinical Luncheon Club - Vol. 1, No. 3, 1940.
Presented before the Methodist Hospital Luncheon Club, Jan. 9, 1940.

KARNAKY'S THEORY OF MENSTRUATION

Bleeding Level = one above & one below bleed-
Amenorrheic Level = Two.

Read how to make millions of menstrual disorders by using Progestogens.
Dr. J. Goldzierger & Karnaky "
"19-nor steroids expensive way to provide estrogen- All estrogeni in action. Why not ound sooner

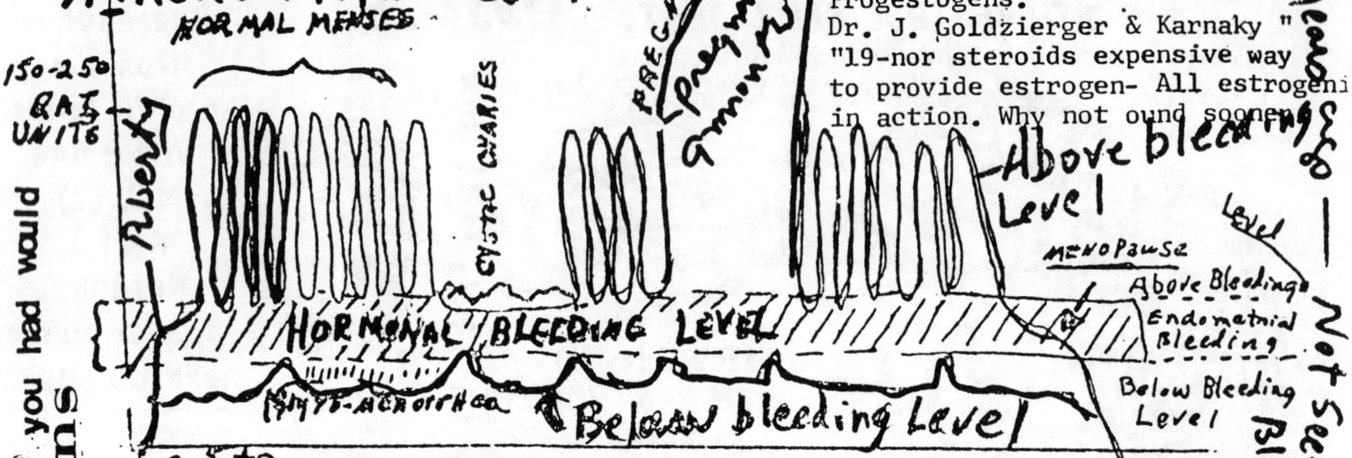

At 5 to 8 years the girl's ovaries begin to function. If the normal metabolism of Estradiol to Estrone to Estriol is normal, the girl has a normal menstrual cycle at puberty because she goes on through the bleeding level normally. If she remains in the bleeding level, she floods. Then normal menses come on as shown in diagram. If the ovaries become cystic, then the hormonal level may be reached and she floods or may be amenorrheic according to hormonal bleeding level.

Progestogens GREATEST OF MYSTS
BY GREATEST OF PROFESSORS
Who's Who's in Gyn

Stilboestrol (Estrosyn-Squibb) is a drug entirely different structurally ... when given by mouth.

Estrosyn (Squibb) can be used in almost all cases where natural estrogens have been used or advocated.

Estrosyn (Squibb) is not toxic as far as the laboratory determinations could detect or when this drug was studied clinically.

Estrosyn (Squibb) produces nausea in a few patients but this nausea is eliminated when given at 7:00 or 8:00 p.m. and if bile salts and acids (Ketochol or Procholon) is given with the Stilboestrol and three times daily.

One no longer has to submit their patients to anesthesia, dilatation and curretage for uterine bleeding - Estrosyn will stop these patients of their uterine bleeding. ADDED: 2-16-66: In this author's years of gynecology, not one hospital D.&C. have had to be done to stop a functional uterine bleeding and not one uterus have had to be removed because of functional uterine bleeding. This is in the CHARITY and PRIVATE CASES. Stilboestrol alone or with estradiol stopped the uterine bleeding. Seldom was surgery necessary.

Quicker than getting next to Hospital, operating Room, and doing Dre. Many before Stilbestrol were done this way. Stilbestrol stop that. 1-2, Lotusate, 2 grains (capalette) with Pill, 1938 1983

Dysfunctional Uterine Bleeding-Endocrine-No operation

but Stops and No cures

43 years 1940 — Not seen or heard because of Bleeding Causes

Have you read Karnaky's theory of menstruation? If you had would show progestogen produce D. U. B millions

A377

PROFESSOR ARNOLD EHRET'S MUCUSLESS DIET HEALING SYSTEM

TO PROFESSOR ARNOLD EHRET (1866-1922), so-called civilized human beings were living cesspools of paste, pus, waste, and debris. Ehret's life was dedicated to the task of cleaning this substance — MUCUS — from the bodily pipe systems of his patients. To this end, he developed the "Mucusless Diet Healing System," meant to remedy this state, using naturally cleansing foods as well as fasts, to sweep out humanity's pipes.

"Life is a tragedy of nutrition." Ehret would never find out if his sweeping aphorism would ultimately apply to the tragedy of his own life. Enduring a sickly childhood and years spent cleaning his own system of accumulated garbage and disease, it is said that Ehret finally reached a sublime state of vitality. But, "while still in the very prime of life, enjoying a superior state of health known but to few men of present day civilization," his publisher laments, "he met with an unfortunate accident." Ehret — who had been disseminating the principles of mucusless living full-time — fell and cracked his skull. Years of rigorously maintained fasts and diet regimens did not forestall the jaws of death.

Fortunately he finished writing his *Mucusless Diet Healing System Lesson Course* just prior to his unfortunate demise. It remains his most popular work, if the abundance of thrift store copies is any indication. Should there be doubt, the publisher of this little orange (sometimes yellow) book assures readers that "[Ehret's] clearness of expression, the forceful, logical array of facts in his easily recognizable, convincing manner, is sufficient proof that his mind was not obstructed by any mechanical disturbances."

Like many a healer, Ehret had suffered from an illness labeled "incurable" by orthodox medicine.[1] He visited 24 physicians, with no improvement in his health. He contemplated suicide. He resorted to "Nature Cures" and sanitariums, with disappointing results. Ehret's turning point came when he made his own observations:

> ... I learned something from the experience though; the main symptoms were mucus or pus and albumin in the urine and pain in the kidneys. The doctors, on the presumption that a clear urine indicated health, tried to stop these eliminations with drugs and to replace the albumin by a meat, egg, and milk diet, but it only increased the disastrous results. I reasoned out from these methods what seemed like a great light on the subject; that the right diet should be free from mucus and albumin. My naturopathic treatment drew out some of the mucus by baths, exercise, etc., but fed it back by wrong diet.

Ehret's biography reads like a list of the fad diets and cures of his day, and indeed it is; he tried or studied everything — Vegetarianism, Naturopathy, Mental Healing, Magnetic Healing, Christian Science. Berlin at that time contained over 20 vegetarian restaurants, but Ehret observed that vegetarians looked no healthier than "one-sided meat eaters." Finally, after trying a "radical fruit diet," Ehret travelled to Algiers, finding that its mild climate, in combination with a fast-and-fruit regimen, seemed to improve his condition:

> ... One morning of a well feeling day I chanced to notice in my mirror that my face had taken on an entirely new look; that of a younger and healthy looking person. But on the next bad feeling day the old and sickly looking face returned, yet it did not last long and these alternating changes in my face impressed me as a "revelation" from Nature that I had found out her methods in part and was on the right track, and I resolved to study them more and live them closer in my future life.

Ehret had escaped from the "Scientific Medical Clinics" he called the "Slaughter house of mankind." No sooner had he received his revelation from Nature than he began embarking on amazing feats of human endurance. His first was an 800-mile bicycle trip with a "trained bicyclist" on a normal diet, whose endurance Ehret claims to have surpassed with the help of his fruit. Ehret's

1. Ehret's biographer indicates he suffered from a variety of illnesses: "bronchial cattarh," "neurasthenic heart trouble," and "Bright's disease, with consumptive tendency"; unanswered is the question of which was the incurable one.

"The average person has as much as ten pounds of uneliminated feces in his bowels continually, poisoning the blood stream and the entire system. Think of it!"

contention that "grape sugar of fruits was the essential material of human food, giving the highest efficiency and endurance, and at the same time was the best eliminator of debris and the most efficient healing agent known for the human body" was borne out with each new day.

Ehret was ready to try his methods on an unnamed youthful friend (who seemed to be present on most of the professor's journeys, fasts, and experiments from then on). Ehret and his companion journeyed to southern France, where they experimented with fasting, normal food, and "nature's food." Leaving France, they were ready for real endurance tests in Italy:

> To test our efficiency at exhaustive labor, we took a trip through northern Italy, walking for 56 hours continuously without sleep or rest or food, only drink. This, after a seven-day fast and then only one meal of two pounds of cherries. ... After a 16-hour walk I made a test of knee bendings and arm extendings, 360 times in a few minutes, and later numerous strength tests and with athletic competitors, showing superior results.

Natural Living at the dawn of the industrial age was clearly frenzied. It was also important during that era to have a good tan. Ehret's own "ruddy and healthy complexion" brought "interesting comments by ladies." Ehret was particularly proud that he and his friend were sometimes mistaken for "Indians."

The ruddy, mucusless adventurers became completely dedicated to their cause, stopping at nothing to find the Truth about health, vitality, and disease. The "young companion" it seems, had a stuttering problem:

> ... I had the idea that even that was caused by a physical encumbrance of debris. We proceeded to a secluded place on the island of Capri and there took longer fasts and daily sunbaths with heat around 120° of four to six hours. We were so well cleansed that we did not sweat. On the eighteenth day my young friend became quite hoarse, and fearing he would lose his voice — not then knowing what caused it — ended his fast with about three pounds of figs, at my suggestion, with the result that for nearly an hour he raised a very large quantity of mucus from his throat and his body cleansed itself in other directions. His voice soon being restored and his stuttering disappeared and has never returned.

Following additional sojourns in other foreign lands, Ehret began teaching his principles to others through public fasts and lectures. Officials and doctors in the era were apparently less encumbered and had room in their schedules for public demonstrations by the latest fad healers. Ehret was "sealed in a room by Notaries of State," and watched closely by physicians, while he conducted fasts of 21, 24 and 32 days — all within 14 months. "The latter test," he writes, "is the *world's record* of a fast conducted under a strict *scientific supervision of government officials."* (We should note it may be the only record of a fast conducted under strict scientific supervision of government officials.)

Between and after his fasts, Ehret lectured and began "giving tests of physical and mental efficiency" apparently so convincing that he was able to open a treatment center in Switzerland. Ehret also wrote articles, with the effect of separating Europe into "Ehretists" and "Non-Ehretists." We can only speculate as to whether the controversy ever pitted "brother against brother."

Shortly before "The Great War" began, Ehret travelled to the U.S. to visit the Panama Exposition and "examine fruits." The outbreak of war forced him to remain. He naturally gravitated to California, a hospitable climate for his diet, his ideas, and his tan.

By then, Ehret's Mucusless Diet had evolved into a "Healing System" based on the principle that disease was Constipation, "a clogging up of the entire pipe system of the human body," with symptoms of "local constipation" or "accumulated mucus." The physical state of the civilized person, to Ehret, was appalling:

> ... The average person has as much as ten pounds of uneliminated feces in the bowels continually, poisoning the blood stream and the entire system. Think of it!
>
> ... [All diseases] have their source in the colon, never perfectly emptied since your birth. Nobody on earth today has an ideally clean body and therefore perfectly clean blood. What Medical Science calls normal health is in fact a pathological condition.

The mucusless diet, consisting of raw and cooked fruit, and starchless and green leafy vegetables combined with long and short fasts, was the only road to health for a poisoned race. Fasting alone, however, done in ignorance of the principles of mucusless eating, was dangerous. "Promiscuous" fasting was especially harmful, possibly fatal. Importantly, fasters didn't die from lack of food, but "actually suffocate in and with their own waste."

> A one-sided meat eater suffering from diabetes, broke his fast which lasted about a week by eating dates and died from the effects. A man of over 60 years of age fasted twenty-eight days (too long); his first meal of vegetarian foods consisting mainly of boiled potatoes. A necessary operation showed that the potatoes were kept in the contracted intestines by thick, sticky mucus so strong that a piece had to be cut off, and the patient died shortly after the operation.

Although fasting could be fatal, it was also the road to health. The professor, on the principle that fasting causes poisons to be excreted, prescribed a short fast as a diagnostic method. The more rapidly the patient felt worse, the "greater and more poisonous his encumbrance." If the patient didn't die first, this short fast was the beginning of a new way of life: "For the ordinary person it will require from one to three years of systematically continued fastings and natural, cleansing diet, before the body is *actually cleansed* of 'foreign matters.'"

Could you live with these foreign matters? Guess again. All physical or mental problems were caused by mucus: Toothache was nature's way of saying "Stop eating; I must repair; there is waste and pus; you have eaten too much lime-poor food, meat." Stammering was an accumulation of mucus in the throat. "Sex diseases" were nothing more than mucus elimination through the sex organs, and "easily healed." Near and far sightedness was congestion in the eyes. "[M]ental disease" was a congestion in the brain; if asylums would stop serving food, their inmates would be sane in no time:

> One man on the verge of insanity was cured by a four week's fast. ... Differences of ideas today are caused largely by diet. If something is wrong with anyone, look first to the stomach. The mentally diseased man suffers physiologically from gas pressure on the brain.

Mucus was even responsible for the sickly pallor of the white race:

> In my first published article I promulgated the gigantic idea that the white race is an unnatural, a sick, a pathological one. First the colored skin pigment is lacking, due to a lack of coloring mineral salts; second, the blood is continually overfilled by white blood corpuscles, mucus, waste with white color; therefore the white appearance of the entire body.
>
> The skin pores of the white man are constipated by white, dry mucus; his entire tissue system is filled up and filled out with it. No wonder that he looks white and pale and anaemic. Everybody knows that an extreme case of paleness is a 'bad sign.' When I appeared with my friend in a public air-bath, after having lived for several months on a mucusless diet with sun baths, we looked like Indians, and people believed that we belonged to another race. This condition was doubtless due to the great amount of red blood corpuscles and the great lack of white blood corpuscles. I can notice a trace of pale in my complexion the morning after eating one piece of bread.

These statements begin to make sense if you see, as Ehret did, that the human body is an "air-gas engine" made of "rubber-like, very elastic, spongy material," and that, contrary to popular opinion, the lungs (not the heart) are a pump while the heart is a valve. Think of a body as a filthy engine, and you understand Ehretism: "Would anyone attempt to clean an engine through a continually higher speed and shaking. No! You would first flush with a dissolving liquid and then change your fuel supply ..." True "Vitality" is not dependent on the nutritional value of food, but by lack of obstruction. Ehret's "Formula of Life" was V = P - O: Vitality equals Power minus Obstruction. Nutrition, Ehret concluded, is besides the point. "Vital energy" from air and water alone "is tremendous, beyond imagination, as soon as 'P' works and can work without 'O' — without obstruction and friction in a perfectly clean body. ... The limit of going without food and before solid food becomes necessary under such ideal conditions, is yet

> **"The sense organs of man are in a pathological state embodied in a 'pus-like' mucus and waste ..."**

unknown." Electricity, ozone, light and even odor increase "P."

Because Ehret didn't value nutrition, he didn't see himself as one of the many "food faddists" of his day — Dr. Lahmann who proved that all disease is caused by carbonic acid; Dr. Haigh and his anti-uric acid diet; Dr. Catani's starchless diet; Dr. S. Graham's "Physiology of Nourishment" advocating whole wheat rather than white flour; Graham's detractor, Dr. Densmore, who said too much bran and whole wheat injures the intestines; the German mineral salt movement; Horace Fletcher's Fletcherism, which stressed proper chewing; Schroth's dry cure. All are improvements on the "albumen theory," which will "kill and stamp out the entire civilized Western world if its following is not stopped," but all make the same fundamental mistake: believing in the nutritional value of food.

To Ehretists, civilized man's worst habit is eating a heavy breakfast; many diseases can be cured by simply following Ehret's "No Breakfast Plan." Another grave error is eating *too much* meat, but especially eating it after it has "decayed." Homo sapiens is a natural fruit eater and doesn't know the proper way to eat meat, known to natural carnivores. "No meat-eating animal can remain healthy on cooked meat," says Ehret. "They must eat it fresh and raw — blood, bones and all."

Not that there was raw meat at Ehret's sanitarium. The menu was quite economical: Breakfast — none; Lunch — one or two kinds of fruits; Supper — mucusless or "mucuslean" vegetables. Recipes or food mixtures were out. Cows ate only one food — grass — so why should humans be different? The best diet, Ehret declared, is a "monodiet" taken after the body is completely cleansed of mucus.

Ehret provided a mucanalysis of common foods to show the superiority of mucusless food:

Meats: "All are in a decomposing state, producing cadaver poisons, uric acid in the body and mucus."

Eggs: "Eggs are even worse than meats, ... the white of eggs makes a very perfect glue."

Milk: "Also makes a good glue for painting. ..."

Cereals: "Raw cereals, if toasted, are to some extent a mucus broom, ..."

Legumes: "Lentils, dried beans and dried peas are too rich in protein, ..."

Rice: "Is one of the greatest mucus formers and makes an excellent paste. I firmly believe thru my experience with serious cases of sickness (awful boils, etc.) prevalent among one-sided rice eaters, that rice is the foundational cause of leprosy, that terrible pestilence."

In summation: "... All of these unnatural foods are extremely bitter, and in fact for a normal nose they possess an offensive odor. The sense organs of man are in a pathological state embodied in a 'pus-like' mucus and waste, the same as the entire system, and being in a partly decayed condition themselves, they find this half rotten food palatable. ..."

The implications of this view reach beyond personal health to the health of the race. In Ehret's day, just about every physician had views on the new science of racial hygiene, better known as eugenics, usually combined with new and scientific guilt-free views on sex. In this regard, Ehret was on the cutting edge. Venereal diseases, to Ehret, were no big deal (these were the days before penicillin). Ehret opined that venereal diseases could be healed by diet and fasting, since "the patient is generally young in years." Gonorrhea was especially easy: "Nothing is easier to heal than this 'cold' or 'catarrh' at the sex organ, if untouched by drugs or injections. Doctors must admit that this condition may exist *without actual sex intercourse,* and therefore the germ can hardly be blamed. Gonorrhea is simply an elimination thru this natural elimination organ. One-sided meat eaters are very susceptible to this disease. Should a society girl contract it, they call it Leucorrhea."

Ehretist eugenics was, naturally, mucusless, but involved maximizing what Ehret called "love vibrations."

The fact is that we are all, with very few exceptions, the result of stimulants instead of love vibrations exclusively. Procreation is the most holy and divine act and charged with the highest responsibility, especially on the part of the father. A germ with the slightest defect is a generation not forward but downward. In very old and in classic civilization "Sex" was a cult, a religion, and in every mythology, poetry of all civilized people, love is the great, main and general subject with the conscious or unconscious goal to reproduce his kind.

The fact is proven by statistics that every family of the city's population dies out, disappears with the third or fourth generation. In other words, the "sins" of the fathers and of the mothers produce diseased children and children's children degenerating into death with the third generation. What are these "sins"? You shall "love thy neighbor," and you do, perhaps, but you kill your own child, partly at least before it is born. Latent disease is general and universal. Besides the statistical fact that over fifty per cent of all young men in large cities have gonorrhea and young women leucorrhea, how can a defective germ grow into a perfect being between a filthy, mostly constipated colon and an unclean bladder of a civilized mother? And one of the worst tragedies of ignorance is the expectant mother who eats twice as much decayed "cadavers" of animals killed years ago in the stock yards of Chicago, because she is advised to "eat for two" — herself and the growing embryo.

The result of traditional views on motherhood is disgusting: "What is considered a well-fed and healthy looking baby, of average normal weight, is in reality pounds of waste of decayed milk." The Ehretist mother, by contrast, would give birth to clean, silent babies. And be so pure she would stop menstruating:

Motherhood with mucusless diet, before, during and after pregnancy is the development towards the Madonna-like, holy purity principally different from the dangerous so-called "ordinary" childbirth, with its ever-present risk of life, known in our present civilization.

If the female body is perfectly clean thru this diet, the menstruation disappears. In scripture it is called by the significant word "purification," which it in fact is; clean — no longer polluted by the monthly flow of impure blood and other waste. This is the ideal condition of an inside purity capable of "immaculate conception." When seen in the light of this truth the entire "Madonna mystery" is easily understood.

Every one of my female patients reported their menses as becoming less and less, then a two, three and four months' intermission, and finally entirely disappearing, which latter condition was experienced by those who went thru a perfect cleansing process by this diet.

Headaches, toothache, vomiting, and all other so-called "diseases of pregnancy" disappear, and painless childbirth, an ample sufficiency of very sweet milk, babies that never cry, babies who are very differently "clean," as compared with others, are the wonderful facts I have learned from every woman becoming a mother after having lived on this diet.

The father, as well, needed to be on the mucusless diet to improve not only his health, but also his sexual virility, as evidenced by hair and beard. The mucusless diet would cure gray hair and baldness. Ehret concurred with **Gustav Jaeger** on the importance of hair odor, and took a special dislike to modern hair fashions:

No one of western civilization knows what genuine "love vibrations" mean from a body with clean blood composed of such ingredients that produce electric currents and static electricity sent out and received by "wireless" — hair. ... The beard of man is a secondary sex organ. Beardless and hairless and bald makes for a "second-rate" sex quality in every respect. ...

... In addition to the mustache shaped geometrically and angular or trimmed off entirely, then the modern clothing which distinguishes itself from that of all the centuries by the greatest insipidity — and this we find beautiful reasons, for which the present-day man gets his beard removed and his hair cut down to a minimum length. The lack of beauty and therewith the unaesthetic appearance of hair and beard has become so general that in course of time the need of shaving and use of the clipper have come as a matter of course. In our time of equalization and all-leveling it is preferred, and rightfully so, to cut off these odor, and so to speak, revelation-organs of inner man, instead of furnishing by ugly, disheveled, uneven and hereditary morbid hair, a living proof for the descendants theory. Therewith we can understand the maltreatment of hair.

... I, THEREFORE, RECOGNIZE IN THE HAIR OF THE HUMAN A VERY IMPORTANT ORGAN WHICH ASIDE FROM PROTECTIVE AND WARMTH-REGULATING PURPOSES HAS A HIGHLY INTERESTING AND USEFUL DESTINA-

"The beard of man is a secondary sex organ. Beardless and hairless and bald makes for a 'second-rate' sex quality in every respect."

TION: to conduct away the exhalations, the odor of healthy and sick people, which reveals to experts and acute noses not only individual qualities, but even certain disclosures as regards the inner state of health or sickness of a man. ...

The Nietzschean aspect of Ehret's system is expressed in his publication, *Thus Speaketh the Stomach.*

Perhaps Ehret's most important finding in eugenics was "how to produce a genius."

What I will endeavor to show here is how to produce a genius, and this will prove at the same time that the predetermination of sex is based on a higher principle than on the time of conception only.

Again and again, diet is everything; man is what he eats! Are not all geniuses, great men, inventors, the greatest artists of every kind, born of poor parentage?

Why did the birth of boy babies increase during the European war? They will become good and intelligent men. Restriction in diet and restriction in sexual intercourse, that is all! The cleaner the body of both parents, the less frequent the intercourse, the smaller the quantity of good food, the greater the love vibrations become, and with these conditions the better the chance for a genius, and that is always a boy. ...

The Ehretist idea continues to survive, if only in the form of Ehret's books. Besides the *Mucusless Diet Healing System Lesson Course,* the Ehret Literature Publishing Company offers *Rational Fasting; The Definite Cure of Chronic Constipation; Thus Speaketh the Stomach;* and *The Tragedy of Nutrition.* Whether humanity will rid itself of the scourge of Mucus and the Tragedy of Nutrition is another matter. Professor Ehret is probably turning in his grave over the ballooning American physique, the advent of Fast Food, and the popularity of head shaving. On the other hand, he may take solace from the increasing popularity of health food, and the existence of the so-called "breathetarians." The modern health food movement follows in the footsteps of Ehret and other food theorists of his day, many of whom based their ideas on spiritual or religious themes. Ehret's comments, especially those about eugenics, suggest a spiritual basis for his concern with bodily purification. Purification rituals of old have been forgotten or diluted to the point of sterility; religion has been separated from our physical lives, banished from sex, and relegated to one day per week. Ehret's diet represented a symbolic and spiritual purification. It was the scientific bias of his times that compelled him to present it as a cure for physical, rather than spiritual ills.

DR. GUSTAV JAEGER
SMELL SENSES THE SOUL

While Dr. Freud was busying himself with the science of mind, **Dr. Gustav Jaeger** innovated the science of odors with *psychoösmology.* A respected professor of zoology and an early champion of Darwin's theories, Dr. Jaeger struck out in an altogether new direction when in 1885 he brought out a two-volume work, *Discovery of the Soul,* which provided humanity with a new way of seeing — and smelling — the world.

In *Discovery of the Soul,* Jaeger wrote, "The soul is *Duft,* an odorous emanation. Smell senses the soul." There is a ring of poetry to this, but Dr. Jaeger was a man of science. Duft, Jaeger enthused, could be smelled, quantified, evaluated, even ingested; the principles of psychoösmology would provide the terminology and experimental techniques for its proper study.[1]

Duft emanates naturally from a person's skin, mouth and nose, but, as Jaeger advised the budding psychoösmologist, "if a portion of brain substance be pulverized in a mortar and a few drops of nitric acid be added, the same odor is obtained."

Before attempting the advanced procedures of psychoösmology (involving among other things the extraction of duft from ladies' hairnets), a student must understand its basic principles.

The first principle states that odors are divided into two categories: pleasant or unpleasant. Pleasant odors are called "fragrances," unpleasant ones "ordures."

The second principle holds that pleasant odors are beneficial, unpleasant ones noxious. Every emotion possesses a distinct duft. For example, *fear* can be sensed by smelling the noxious odors of *fear stuff* (in German, *angst stoff.)*

These principles seem like common sense until one hits upon Dr. Jaeger's most unique discovery. Not only can one sense an emotion by its duft, but the emotion itself was *caused* by duft:

> I define the physical source of the emotions to be subtle essences bound up with and emanating from the albumen in the bodily tissues. ... Only when a decomposition of albumen in the tissues occurs are they set free; they then become perceptible to the senses, especially to that of smell, and create in the body emotion or mood. The salutary principle makes emotions that are cheerful, enterprising and courageous; the noxious principle produces gloom, depression, want of courage, and a distaste for food.

Dr. Gustav Jaeger

Fortunately for the citizens of Stuttgart and London who suffered the ill effects of noxious odors — Jaeger had cult followings in both cities — the good doctor discovered a way to avoid the bad odors, while preserving the good ones.

This is the third principle of psychoösmology. It is possible to retain the beneficial odors, and thus promote happiness, by the use of animal wool, 100% unadulterated wool. Limited benefits are obtained by wearing wool clothing by day, and maximal benefit is only possible by spending the night hours as well on 100% wool bedsheets and mattresses. Jaeger further noted that good duft, preserved by wool, actually protects the body from infection by germs and parasites.

Sheep's wool is adequate for the purpose, but Jaeger found that camel's wool works best — especially if you are interested in preserving your soul. Furthermore, camel's wool could be used to lose weight. Those who wear 100% camel's hair garments day and night need less food than others. In some cases, the garments stimulate a desire to fast.

It is especially important for members of the fair sex to wear wool at all times, to protect against harm to their delicate odorific integrity:

> Women should wear all underclothes, stockings, even corsets, made of pure wool. A dress of pure wool, closing well around the throat and having a double woolen lining at the chest and downwards, should be the winter and summer wear of women, who would then participate in all the advantages which I have described, and

1. The 19th Century had more than its share of new emanations and substances, including ectoplasm, N-Rays, and something called "od."

of which they stand even in greater need than do men.

Lucky for fragile Victorian ladies, all-wool underwear and clothing were available from the doctor's own manufacturing company. No mere capitalistic enterprise, Jaeger Sanitary Woolens was a serious effort to "reform" clothing by expanding the concept of clothing to include the preservation of soul essence. Despite bad reviews from fashion critics, the company and its wool garments lived on long after both Jaeger and psychoösmology were dead and forgotten.

Dr. Jaeger became so nasally sensitive that he could identify the moral character of a woman merely by the odor of her hairnet.

In Dr. Jaeger's further refinement of the duft concept, he found that human hair is an even better font of duft than pulverized brains. Jaeger began to assemble a large collection of ladies hairnets, naturally rich in duft. In time Dr. Jaeger became so nasally sensitive that he could identify the moral character of a woman merely by the odor of her hairnet: "If you smell the hair of a flapper, you will find the odor somewhat insipid and flat; or, as one of my women observers put it, the odor was like that of a 'rubber stopper' — not a bad observation."

The benefits of good duft were limitless. Using a Hipp chronoscope[2] and the psychoösmological method of "nerve analysis," Jaeger found that ingestion of good duft improved his "reaction times." His normal reaction time of 76/100 second decreased to 68/100 second after he smelled his wife's hairnet. His conclusion: nerve impulses are quickened by sympathetic odors. To prove this wasn't his own peculiarity, Jaeger tried the same experiment on his son-in-law, using *his* wife's hair net. Such is the precision of the scientific method.

Jaeger obtained a hairnet from the head of a professional singer, a girl of eighteen, and placed it in water. He diluted the liquid to "the fifteenth homeopathic potency," then put a few drops of the liquid into a glass of water or beer, and drank it. Jaeger observed that his voice became clearer and purer and his range increased by one note. The inevitable conclusion:

> When the duft of an organism is absorbed by eating the flesh or by wearing the hide, hair, or feathers as clothing; or by using the fat of the animal for cosmetic purposes; or by lingering long in the atmosphere of such animals; or by consuming the homeopathically diluted extract from the hair or feathers; or the customary use of ashes of burnt feathers or hair; then the organism thus absorbing the duft acquires not the entire set of qualities characteristic of the animal absorbed, but its traits are more or less inclined in that direction.

Could this be confirmation of the warrior's superstition that eating your dead enemy's heart will make you strong? It would seem Jaeger was promoting a literally "watered down" version of cannibalism; he sought to "humanize" food by adding tincture of hair duft to it. For example, wine would be humanized by mixing it with a diluted tincture of hair duft, preferably from the head of an attractive young woman. Jaeger claimed that drinking the substance would have an exhilarating effect.

Jaeger prepared the essence of humanized food, "anthropin," and sold it to his Stuttgart followers. He also made use of the principle of "self-anthropin." Apparently, sniffing a lock of one's own hair, provided that it was clipped when younger and healthier, has rejuvenating powers.

These practical applications were just a small segment of the universal principle of the duft-soul. Jaeger found that even plants and soil contain duft-soul. He also held that inherited traits are not passed on by chromosomes, they are conveyed by duft. And, since food carries the duft of the cook, this explains why German men like German food best (it's cooked by women) or why German women are partial to French cooking (it's cooked by men).

Such are the mysteries of Psychoösmology, which incorporated Dr. Gustav Jaeger's peculiarities and fetishes so well that it was forgotten soon after the death of its champion.

2. Electric timepiece which measures time in hundredths of a second.

THE "THIRD EYE" IS A HOLE IN YOUR HEAD

Up stood the ape — down came the drag —
The beginning of the blues —
Can't talk your way out of it adult
Daddy there's a drag on you. ...

What you're trying to regain
Is blood belonging to your brain —
Will you know before you're dead
That paradise is in your head?

You was robbed — so you made belief —
It's gravity — we've caught the thief
All you prayers won't save your soul
Adult you need a hole.

— "The Great Brain Robbery" by Joe Mellen

Healers ancient and modern, primitive and civilized, are known to have "trepanned" their ailing brethren, a procedure which results in a permanent hole in the head. Even as recently as the 16th century, trepanation was used regularly as a treatment for madness, along with many other unspeakable "treatments." Before the dawn of the Age of Reason a hole bored into the skull was thought to let the devils out; modern medicine tells us that the procedure is supposed to relieve pressure in the brain cavity. Sufferers of cerebral ulcers sometimes undergo a form of trepanation even today. Be that as it may, most people assume that cutting a hole in one's head went out with bleeding and other quaintly barbaric cures.

Not so for a few brave souls who, during the 1960s, applied a theory of higher consciousness through trepanation to scientific scrutiny, offering themselves as experimental subjects. You might say these people were dead serious about getting high. Reinforced by the positive results of their experiments, the bore-a-hole-in-your-head crusaders went all-out on promoting this mind-blowing alternative to taking drugs.

It all began in 1962 when a boyish looking Dutchman named **Bart Huges** developed new theories of higher consciousness. According to Huges, the devolution of humankind was caused by the upright stance. In the good old days, our habit of walking on all fours and swinging from trees caused increased pressure inside of our brain cavities. Becoming a rigid biped may have helped us in some ways, but created the unfortunate side effect of reducing cosmic consciousness. Huges maintains that the blood flowing downward from our brains is not replaced by more blood but by lighter, cerebrospinal fluid, in turn reducing the "brain blood volume." The brain, which is nourished by oxygen and sugar supplied by blood, becomes nutrient-deficient, and the range of consciousness is reduced accordingly. Youngsters are not so deprived, reasons Huges; babies are born with their skulls unsealed, the blood flowing directly from their hearts to their brains. This is why young people are so much more creative than adults. When children reach the age of 21 or so, their brains are permanently cut off from their heartbeats, unless further measures, such as standing on one's head, taking drugs, or boring a hole in the skull, are taken.

Babies are born with their skulls unsealed, the blood flowing directly from their hearts to their brains. This is why young people are so much more creative than adults.

T. Lobsang Rampa's *The Third Eye,* a no doubt fraudulent work purported to be the autobiography of a "Tibetan lama," swept through England in the late 1950s, and may have helped set the stage for Huges' theories. Rampa had claimed that at the age of seven he'd been chosen to enter the lamasery, and that at eight, he was forced to undergo an operation which opens the "third eye" by trepanation. The operation, which involved drilling a hole in the middle of Rampa's forehead, was purportedly executed by monks without the use of anaesthesia.

Rampa recounted, "Suddenly I felt a stinging, ticklish sensation apparently in the bridge of my nose. It subsided, and I became aware of subtle scents that I could not identify," And with the words, "You are now one of us, Lobsang. For the rest of your life you will see people as they are and not as they pre-

DUTCH STUDENT BORES HOLE IN HIS HEAD TO PROVE THEORY OF INCREASED BRAIN ACTIVITY
HOPES TO MAKE USE OF LEGENDARY THIRD EYE
By KARL ESKELUND

tend to be," Lama "Mingyar Dondrup" welcomed Rampa to their exclusive club. Soon Rampa was able to perceive auras and all that only the enlightened can know. He had opened his third eye.

Though this operation might be appropriate for Tibetan lamas halfway across the globe, Rampa's readers — middle class devotees of psychic, mysterious and occult subjects — would never dream of trying it themselves. But to the next generation of seekers, altered states of consciousness was a way of life. Among the vanguard of this new generation was Bart Huges, whose commitment to exploring consciousness was so deep that no experiment — even boring a hole in his own skull — was taboo.

Born in Amsterdam in 1934, Huges' vivid childhood memories of Nazi-occupied Holland include an attempted arrest of his father — a doctor — who had refused to become a member of the Nazi "Kulturzimmer." Huges recalls a time when the Nazis sat for a long time on a sofa while his father hid underneath. Another war memory was of his malnourished grandfather who had subsisted on a diet of grass and leaves. Later, during the 50s Huges slept through school out of boredom, but conducted his own autodidactic course in philosophy. By the time he was 20 he had read Plato, Nietzsche, Freud, Pavlov and Hesse. And following in the footsteps of both his father and grandfather, Huges studied medicine, with an emphasis on psychiatry and psychoanalysis. By 1964 he had passed all of his medical examinations except one; when the government subsequently withdrew his funding, Huges decided to throw in the towel on ten years of study. But by then, he had already strayed from the familiar pastures of aspiring physicians, to explore the unknown territory of altered states of consciousness.

Huges' first exposure to strong psychoactive substances occurred in 1958, when, as a subject in a psychiatric experiment at the University Hospital in Amsterdam, he ingested his first dose of LSD. Experimentation with mescaline and marijuana soon followed. Curious about the mechanisms at work during these drug-induced experiences, the medical student began to compare them to other methods of expanding consciousness. He had met a man named Titi who stood on his head at parties to get high; his father had also practiced standing on his head every morning "to keep fit." Nehru, the late prime minister of India, as well as David Ben Gurion of Israel had also practiced standing on their heads for a few minutes each day to stimulate their brains. Huges was inspired to try his own experiments, which began with headstands, but did not end there:

> I read somewhere how the India togi [sic] increase their awareness by closing the two large veins that lead the blood to and from the brain. I started to do this myself and it worked well. I found I could stop the flow of blood using what the Dutch call the "hand-grip-method," and when I let go I really felt high. ... Why? That's what I wanted to know. There had to be some connection between this condition and the amount of blood on the brain—the brain blood volume, I mean. ["Dutch Student Bores Hole in his Head to Prove Theory of Added Brain Activity."]

In November of 1962 a friend of Huges who "has his third eye from a car accident" gave him some mescaline. It was during this trip that Huges first understood the principle of brain blood volume: that increasing the volume of brain blood expands consciousness. He also realized that if there is more blood in the brain, there must be "less of something else," and that this "something else" is cerebrospinal fluid. Huges later completed his understanding during another trip, during which he directly perceived "the action itself, the constriction of veins." He knew from his medical studies that "brain cells take more glucose from the blood than body cells do" and so reasoned that the increase in brain blood volume that enhances consciousness must also cause a depletion of sugar, a condition which he called "sugarlack." He concluded that when people take "mind-expanding" drugs, the feeling of "getting high" is caused by expansion of the brain blood volume, which in turn, expands the capillary vessels above the brain. The veins, but not the arteries become constricted, so the blood isn't able to exit the brain as rapidly as before. The excess blood expands the capillaries, and some of the cerebrospinal fluid is squeezed away and replaced by more blood, causing the drug-taker to—temporarily—experience the heightened consciousness of humanity's youth.

The temporary effects of drugs were not good enough for Huges. He was determined to find some way to increase his brain blood volume — permanently:

> I thought about making a hole at the base of the spine to let the [cerebrospinal] fluid out, and while thinking about holes I realized that pressure was necessary to squeeze the cerebrospinal fluid out of the system. Then, having concluded upon the nil pressure inside the adult skull... I saw that any hole in the bony surrounding of the system would give the pressure back. But after a time I realized a hole in the spine would heal over, so it had to be in the skull, where holes stay open. [Dialogue in *The Transatlantic Review.*]

While looking for a surgeon to perform this operation, Huges wrote a treatise, *Homo Sapiens Correctus,* which explained his new theory and listed eight methods of increasing consciousness, including psychoactive drugs, adrenaline, the headstand, as well as the method of pressing the fingers against the windpipe to close the neck veins. Not all these methods are equal, however. One of Huges' disciples, Amanda Fielding writes: "On an imaginary scale if one puts the adult's norm of consciousness at zero and the LSD user's at 100 then the childhood level and that attained by trepanation is 30 and the level of cannabis is around 50 to 60."

For two years Huges looked for a surgeon who would agree to open his third eye, but finally gave up and purchased an electric dental drill, so that he could do it himself. In addition to the drill, he also obtained a surgical knife and a hypodermic syringe for the local anaesthetic. Though he was now ready to trepan himself, another snag developed; worried friends took away his tools.

Six months later however (January, 1965) Huges had purchased new tools for the operation, but this time he told no one except his wife. He prepared for his secret self-trepanation by first applying a strong local anaesthetic. He then guided the drill with one hand, while the other regulated the depth of penetration. The whole procedure lasted about 45 minutes and caused no pain, but he bled profusely. Huges dressed his fresh wound and waited. Four hours after the operation, the cerebrospinal fluid was pressed out and three days later the wound healed. The results were all that he had hoped for: "After I had [trepanned myself] my spirits rose slowly and significantly hour by hour until they eventually levelled out." Huges now feels as he did before the age of fourteen.

Ten days after the operation, Huges went public, and removed his bandage at a "happening." A week later he gave a press conference. Apparently the authorities — whose consciousnesses were still at zero level — couldn't grasp the significance of Huges' discovery. He recalls that before the press conference, "I went to the University hospital to have an X-ray photograph taken. I was detained for an hour by two psychiatrists and released only when I promised to return the following day. ... The next day I went back with two witnesses. Then ten male nurses formed a circle round me and forced me into the clinic, where I was kept involuntarily for three weeks, for 'observation.'" A month later, he appeared on Dutch television, but afterwards the government issued a statement, read on the news, that his treatise, *Homo Sapiens Correctus* was balderdash.

"This is the story of how I came to drill a hole in my skull to get permanently high."

In the meantime, Huges had gained a disciple, Joseph Mellen, an "English lawyer and avant-garde poet." Mellen later wrote the book, *Bore Hole,* which begins, "This is the story of how I came to drill a hole in my skull to get permanently high." *Bore Hole,* in addition to being a pro-hole polemic, is reported to be a valuable record of "high bohemia" of London in the 60s, replete with the inside dope on the Beatles and Rolling Stones and filmmaker Kenneth Anger, not to mention various lords, pages and heiresses.

Huges and Mellen began a crusade to promote Huges' theory and trepanation. The first targets of the mission were the local paranoia stricken acid heads who were ignorant of the scientific bases of consciousness. Their brains were becoming starved of sugar, and so were

According to Huges and Mellen, the pool of adult human beings are living under the yoke of "gravity's drag."

experiencing "bad trips." The hope was that if they knew of Huges' theory, they would take additional sugar with their pills, or — even better — trepan themselves. Apparently, nobody in that crowd was serious enough about their consciousness to try it.

The new mission focused not only on individual consciousness, but also society as a whole. According to Huges and Mellen, the pool of adult human beings which make up our backward society are all living under the yoke of "gravity's drag." Huges puts it succinctly: "Gravity is the enemy. The adult is its victim — society is its disease." He thinks that "no construction of adults can work optimally unless each adult in the construction is trepanned." Were trepanning to become widespread, the social advances would be enormous. There would be "increased efficiency of social operations, the restriction of activity to the essential, and with the restoration of originality and creativity to the adult rapid progress in technology." In addition, "art is likely to become a common activity — no longer an 'in' commercial enterprise." In the trepanned society there will be more cooperation, less conflict and chaos "because communication will depend less on the number of words and more on their meaning. ... Trepanned man will not find it necessary to give meanings to abstract words, or to invent new superstitions." In short, "Gravity is the enemy. A large part of adult behavior is motivated by the fear of losing the grip on what blood is left in the brain. Trepanation, by restoring the blood lost in the course of growth, removes the main cause of fear."

The two missionaries enthusiastically entered the LSD/consciousness lecture circuit espousing Huges' theories, but they were misunderstood. According to one account, "After a lecture they gave at the respected bookshop, Better Books, they were approached for an interview by two journalists of the Sunday newspaper, *The People*. Their attitude was sympathetic, [Huges and Mellen] accepted them as genuine seekers after truth and they spent a whole night together in deep study of Brainbloodvolume and trepanation. Eager to see how the message had been presented to the world, [Mellen] was out first thing Sunday morning for the paper. In it was a crude article about [Huges] under a banner headline: THIS DANGEROUS IDIOT SHOULD BE THROWN OUT."

But there were a few artists and "bohemians" who were receptive to Huges' theories, notably Heathcote Williams, who published a dialogue between Huges and Mellen in the *Transatlantic Review* and also included a climactic trepanation scene in his award-winning play *AC-DC*. Julie Felix, "a world-famous American singer in the style of Joan Baez" was so impressed that she recorded some of Mellen's trepanation songs including *Brainbloodvolume, The Great Brain Robbery* and *Sugarlack*.

Thus far, Huges was the only member of the new society of trepanned adults. But he was soon to be joined by Mellen, and a third convert, Amanda Fielding. Unlike Huges before him, Mellen chose to use a manual trepan for the operation. He describes the instrument in *Bore Hole:* "Its main feature was a metal spike, surrounded by a ring of saw-teeth. The spike was meant to be driven into the skull, holding the trepan steady until the revolving saw made a groove, after which it could be retracted. If all went well, the saw-band should remove the disc of bone and expose the brain."

After an unsuccessful first attempt, Mellen tried to get assistance from Huges, who was then back in Amsterdam, barred from entering the U.K. So Mellen's friend, Amanda Fielding helped instead. He was almost successful this time, despite the fact that he nearly perished in the process:

> After some time there was an ominous sounding schlurp and the sound of bubbling. I drew the trepan out and the gurgling continued. It sounded like air bubbles running under the skull as they were pressed out. I looked at the trepan and there was a bit of bone in it. At last! On closer inspection I saw that the disc of bone was much deeper on one side than on the other. Obviously the trepan had not been straight and had gone through at one point only, then the piece of bone had snapped off and come out. I was reluctant to start drilling again for fear of damaging the brain

membranes with the deeper part while I was cutting through the rest or of breaking off a splinter. If only I had had an electric drill it would have been so much simpler. Amanda was sure I was through. There seemed no other explanation of the schlurping noises. I decided to call it a day. At that time I thought that any hole would do, no matter what size. I bandaged up my head and cleared away the mess.

Despite a general feeling of wellbeing, Mellen was still not completely sure that he had gone far enough. He decided to bore yet another hole at a new spot, only now he would use an electric drill:

This time I was not in any doubt. The drill head went at least an inch deep through the hole. A great gush of blood followed my withdrawal of the drill. In the mirror I could see the blood in the hole rising and falling with the pulsation of the brain.

In 1970 Amanda Fielding decided to join Mellen in his blissful state, documenting the whole thing on film, for posterity, and calling the finished documentary, *Heartbeat in the Brain*. Fielding performed the operation herself with an electric drill, while Mellen manned the camera. One viewer of the film reports, "The film shows her carefully at work, dressed in a blood-spattered white robe. She shaves her hair, makes an incision in her head with a scalpel and calmly starts drilling. Blood spurts as she penetrates the skull. She lays aside the drill and with a triumphant smile advances towards Joey and the camera." The soundtrack is of "soothing music," and surgical scenes alternate with "delightful motion studies of [Fielding's] pet pigeon, Birdie, as a symbol of peace and wisdom." According to a film critic, at one London showing, the audience "dropped off their seats one by one like ripe plums."

The result of Fielding's operation was all that she had hoped it would be:

It is difficult to express such a subtle and yet vital change — the words have already been used to sell shampoo and life insurance. ... During the hours following the removal of the piece of bone I could just notice myself rising, as if on the waves of an incoming tide. I felt a tension fall away. At one point in the evening I noticed that the bugging voice inside my head had shut up. ... It does not instantaneously wipe away all one's neurotic patterns of behavior, but they become less dominant. The long term effect is what is most important: slowly the brain, and the body it controls, gain increased freedom from the strangulation of chronic repression. ["Blood and Consciousness."]

Fielding soon became the primary trepanation crusader, with an emphasis on trepanation rights, the idea that anyone who wants to should be able to hire a doctor to perform the simple operation. Oxford-educated and reasonable, Fielding argues, in an interview by Tim Cridland, that in a medical setting, trepanation is a minor operation:

I'm very against self-trepanation. What I'm for is for national health, for the doctor to do it. It takes half an hour. But the dangers of the thing is — one: infection and two: to damage the membrane. ... The membrane, there are three layers of membrane and they are very tough. I practiced with the drill I used, the bore-head, on my hand — which is dry, after all. And one could do it for five minutes without it roughing up the skin. So that then I realized there's no damage, there's no danger of it damaging the membrane which is lubricated by blood, anyhow. ... The only way one could puncture it is if one used, obviously, a pointed drill — puncture the membrane — then, obviously, you could do bad damage. ... In primitive, stone-age cultures [they trepan by] tapping away with a bit of stone. We've got all the advantage of local anaesthetic and electronic drill. It's a simple procedure. In the hospital, the nurse does it, not the doctor. It's half an hour, you're in and out; and you can go on with your day's work after you've left the clinic.

Fielding has been more successful than Huges and Mellen in attracting the mainstream media to the cause, but with disappointing results. Every time she has agreed to appear on a television show — including *60 Minutes* — the show is cancelled just prior to airing, due to legal liability fears. The *Sunday Times* stopped an article on Fielding but "in the same week they told the story of an assassin who killed people by injecting air in the back of the throat so that no one could detect it. So that's legal, and to give out information on trepanning is unacceptable." For obvious reasons, Fielding no longer makes an effort to do serious articles for the mainstream media.

At one London showing of Heartbeat in the Brain, the audience, according to one critic, "dropped off their seats one by one like ripe plums."

But she has been somewhat successful in arousing interest in the United States. She held an exhibition at PS1 in New York entitled, "Trepanation for the National Health," and showed *Heartbeat in the Brain* to an invited audience at the Sudan Gallery. The question and answer period after the film led to gatherings and interest groups elsewhere. Her treatise, "Blood and Consciousness" was published in conjunction with the exhibition. Though the audience was far more receptive in the United States, Fielding continued her crusade in England as well. After the birth of her first child, she "stood parliament" on a platform of "trepanation for the national health."

Currently, Fielding and Mellen live together with their two children, splitting their time between the country and London. They run a successful art gallery as well as a publishing company.

As for Huges, after his turbulent years as a trepanation guru he became better known as a member of the PROVOS, a "satirical politico-cultural group" in Amsterdam. Currently, he works as a museum librarian while continuing his own studies of traditional and primitive lifestyles, especially "how traditional people get high."

To all appearances, the effects of trepanation are positive. But Huges' theory of consciousness hasn't yet been scrutinized by mainstream researchers. Rather than confirming or challenging the theory, those in positions of authority have so far rejected it without serious examination, ensuring that Huges, Mellen and Fielding's pioneering explorations of the physiological bases of consciousness remain virtually unknown.

Special thanks to Tim Cridland for generously sharing material.

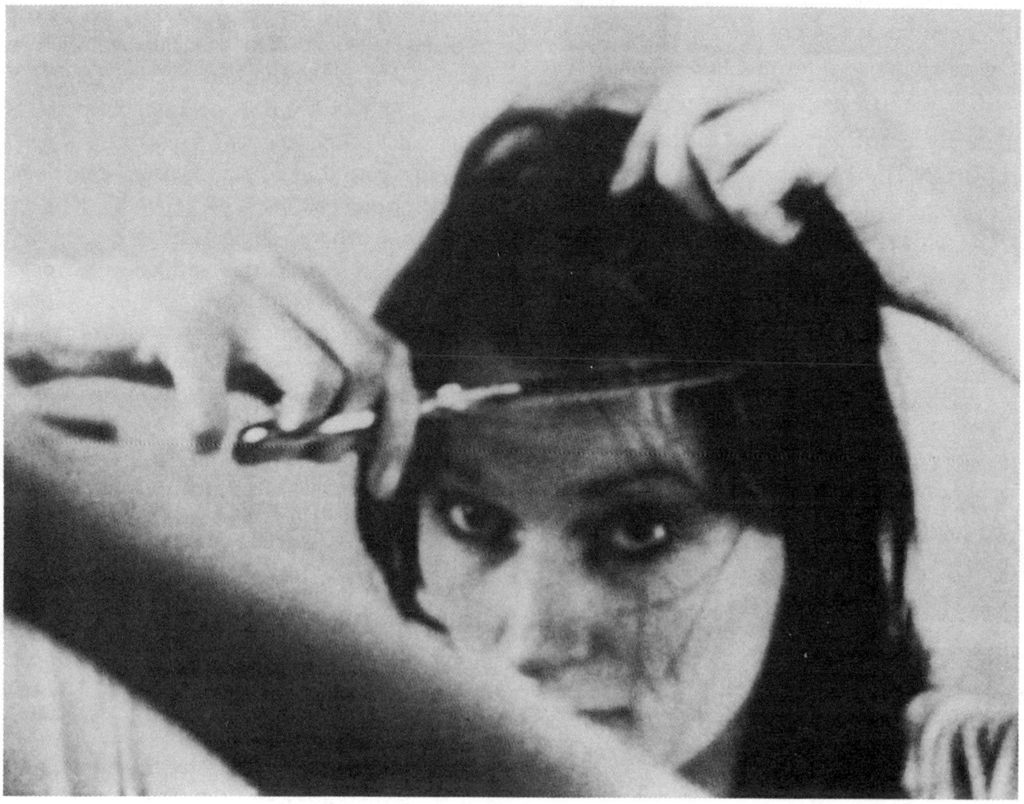

A frame from *Heartbeat in the Brain*.
Amanda Feilding prepares herself for self-trepanation.
[photo from *Eccentric Lives and Peculiar Notions* by John Michell]

PART III

METAPHYSICS

URIEL and the Unarius Library

THE SPACE BROTHERS ARE WATCHING YOU

by Gregory Bishop

Some of the most bizarre beliefs on the planet today sprouted in the fertile climate of Southern California. Science — and sometimes critical thought — having lost luster in the long shadow of the mushroom cloud, and having failed to address spiritual concerns, created an explosion of space-brother contactee cults. Though groups otherwise differed, they had in common leaders who claimed contact with extraterrestrial consciousness. It is possible the holy men and women of history who experienced divine inspiration and communication were the contactees of previous centuries, but whatever wisdom the California Saucer Saints may have to offer, we can reap entertainment from them as well.

From the rubble of internal power struggles and dogma wars, a few survivors from the spiritual wasteland of the 1970s and 80s remain. The best-known are the Aetherius Society, based in Hollywood, and the Unarius Academy of Science, in El Cajon near San Diego. With the crazy-quilt of saucer contact history — and a few pre-conceived ideas — in mind, I decided to experience these alternate realities.

Aetherius

In 1954, London taxi driver **George King** was washing dishes when he heard a voice booming, "Prepare yourself! You are to become the voice of the Interplanetary Parliament!" A few days later, the spirit of an Indian Yogic master passed through a door to King's apartment and informed him that Cosmic Intelligences orbiting Earth in a flying saucer had selected him as the primary channel for messages that would save the human race. He established telepathic contact with a consciousness from Venus called **Aetherius.**

King soon began to organize events in London in which Aetherius, through King, revealed a "cosmic plan for the Peace and Enlightenment of the People of Earth." He also started a newsletter, *The Cosmic Voice,* subtitled *Mars and Venus Speak to Earth,* published to this day. An Aetherius center was established in Los Angeles within a year of first contact.

The Reverend **Alan Moseley,** a member of the Aetherius Society for over 20 years who presides at all services, guided me through the turquoise and pink stucco sanctum of Aetherius' world headquarters. Despite appearances of what could be interpreted as cosmic craziness, Rev. Moseley stressed that Aetherians are very practical — "We *don't* believe that we are from another planet, and we *do* have a sense of humor about all this," he said, hastening to add, "if we're from anywhere, we're originally from MALDEK, which is the remains of a planet between Mars and Jupiter which is now the asteroid belt."

The Reverend explained the Aetherius mission as "the psychic, spiritual, and physical salvation of all the souls on the planet — whether they knew of the Society or not." By logging "prayer hours," the Aetherians hope to win the karmic tug-of-war that keeps humanity on the brink of disaster. Asked for proof that their efforts bear fruit, he replied that such natural disasters as the predicted earthquake that would send California into the sea have not occurred, and that the recent developments in the Communist bloc, and other improvements in international relations, resulted from the energy of Aetherian prayer. Our world must always go through periods of upheaval, according to Rev. Moseley. The Aetherians are here to "smooth out the bumps."

> **By logging "prayer hours," the Aetherians hope to win the karmic tug-of-war that keeps humanity on the brink of disaster.**

George King himself, I was informed, had moved on to the etheric plane, but seemed substantial enough the Sunday morning I saw him at an Aetherian religious service. We all bowed and faced King as he entered and walked to the podium. The Master, having accepted consecration as an archbishop through the Independent Liberal Catholic Church, was resplendent in red and gold robes and tall "pope's hat," carrying a large gold-painted staff. His Eminence The Master took the podium for announcements and the bestowal of awards on worthy members of the Society. King was not an overwhelming personality, as one might expect a Spiritual Master to be, but radiated an easy-going manner. He was the least serious of the worshippers present at the services, joking with the parishioners and using British colloquialisms, such as "cheeky," during the presentations. King exited to the piped-in strains of Beethoven's Ninth Symphony.

George King himself, I was informed, had moved on to the etheric plane, but seemed substantial enough the morning I saw him at an Aetherian religious service.

Aside from occasional visitations by His Eminence, the Aetherians gather each week at the "Spiritual Battery," one of several devices constructed using specific plans from the Cosmic Masters. Charged with positive Prayer Power, the batteries are used during periods of international crisis. I saw only a photograph of the device that handles discharge, but it appeared well-suited to the mission with its numerous lights, knobs, and meters.

When I arrived for the charging ceremony, I was escorted to a waiting area featuring a model of "Satellite #3." According to the Aetherian information, the 1-1/2 mile long, egg-shaped object is in geosynchronous orbit with earth, but makes periodic visits to the upper levels of the atmosphere, at intervals revealed to George King by the Cosmic Masters. The efforts of the Aetherians and "anyone who prays for world peace" are magnified 3,000 times when the satellite dips periodically into the ionosphere, acting as a sort of spiritual communications broadcaster by radiating "positive energies" to trouble spots around the globe. Rev. Moseley explained that Satellite #3 contains the "records of the life streams of all individuals who have ever lived on the planet," and added that it is "undetectable by current technology. When Man is ready to see it, it will become visible."

I was led to the inner sanctum, a room lit by two "10 K" movie lights with blue filters. To begin the ceremony, Reverend Doctor **Ray Neilson** asked the congregation to perform an exercise I recognized as the *pranayana* method of yogic breathing. (The Aetherians say it is a universal act of spiritual preparation handed down to them by the Cosmic Masters.) Power began to flow in earnest as the Buddhist chant "om mani padme hum" filled the room. I had been told the pronunciation of the *mantra* was very important if its power were to be utilized. King, Neilson and Moseley are all British, so the "a" sounds tended toward longer pronunciations — *om manny pad may hum* — which, considering King's relationship with the Cosmic Masters, may well be correct.

Waving his hands like a conductor and admonishing the congregation, Reverend Neilson brought proper nuances to bear in the chanting. A Society member, wearing white gloves, moved to the Battery and, unscrewing four plastic bolts, removed its protective cover. As the correct chant frequency was reached, three designated members approached the Battery, their right hands held up to the device, their lefts over their heads in the *mudra* position (thumb and index finger together, other fingers straight). The members prayed forcefully at the Battery four times each, their voices rising with emotion to complete the recitation of the Twelve Blessings. Nearby, two members armed with stopwatches, charts, and calculators recorded the duration and relative force of the recitations. Using a complicated algorithm handed down by the Cosmic Masters, prayer hours stored in the Battery can be calculated. After 30 or so minutes of chanting, soliloquy, and mathematics, the congregation adjourned for water and a little cool night air.

During a second session with the Battery, we were startled by a cry of "No, no, no-no-no" from the rear of the room. His Eminence George King entered and halted the ceremonies in mid-*Om Manny Pad.* He admonished the members: "In 15 minutes I could charge that battery without saying a word! Don't shout at it like a lot of friggin' idiots."

He coached a jostling line of prayer adepts for a couple of minutes, then repaired to his sanctuary next door to a chorus of "thank you, Master."

On another occasion, we were asked to attend an announcement of "an event of great occult significance." Chairs were set up, and an Aetherius hierarch approached the podium. He read a letter from The Master, who had just received a new title from the Cosmic Masters, earned for his meritorious service in the earthly plane. Aboard the satellite Shambala, stationed in the Subtle Realms above the Gobi desert, the Master Buddha had proclaimed King "Supreme Grand Master Of The Knights Templar Of The Inner Sanctum Of The Holy Order Of The Spiritual Hierarchy of Earth. This organization is the oldest order of honor and merit on the Earth and is not affiliated with the Knights Templar founded in the 11th century." The letter continued, describing the Knights as a 500,000 to 750,000 year-old society, begun by the Ancient Masters of Lemuria. Members have included Jesus and the Apostles, at least two Pharaohs, and a host of spiritual leaders of ancient China and India.

Unarius

The Academy of **UN**iversal **AR**ticulate **I**nterdimensional **U**nderstanding of **S**cience takes offense if referred to as a "religion." "We are a scientific research organization" was the secretary's curt reply when I suggested that I was doing "religious research." Actually, Unarius students *are* researching their own life path, recognizing mistakes from past lives, on earth and other planets. Their "mistakes" — accumulations of bad karma — can be purged in this lifetime through the study and practice of "Unariun" principles.

This and other revelations come from the Space Brothers, who channel their wisdom through **Archangel Uriel,** known as **Ruth Norman** in her terrestrial incarnation. Uriel (**U**niversal **R**adiant **I**nfinite **E**ternal **L**ight) and her husband **Ernest Norman** founded the Academy in 1954 after meeting at a lecture in Glendale. Ernest has left the Earthly plane to reside on Mars, where he acts as moderator of the Universe for the Confederation Of The 33 Planets. Uriel however carries on, and although her physical presence at the age of 92 blesses the Unarius headquarters less often these days, her guidance pervades all Unariun activities.

The front office is very protective of Uriel, and laid to rest any hope of interviewing her personally. Her age may have something to do with this policy. Although she is the living incarnation of a supreme spiritual being, according to Unariun belief, her earthly shell may have outgrown its use. (Reverend Moseley of Aetherius suggested that Uriel may be "a little off, bless her heart.") Uriel did send a very kind reply to my thank you note, in which she politely restated her unavailability: "... my students have spoken very adequately for me, and my time is limited to bringing through our great texts from the Hierarchical Minds and getting them into print." Perhaps we should be satisfied that Archangel Uriel is able to continue the valuable work she began nearly 40 years ago (or 4,000 years ago, if you count her previous incarnations as Confucius, Socrates, Henry VIII, and Benjamin Franklin.)

I was surrounded by classical columns and tendrils of rhododendron as I entered Unarius headquarters 20 miles east of San Diego. Frescoed vistas in various shades of light blue covered the walls. An abstract version of a Tesla Coil, in colored foil and plexiglas, dominated one end of the lobby. Switched on and warmed up, it emitted tiny bubbles that rose up the center column like an old jukebox. A fountain bubbled quietly in the center of the room, surrounded by a perfect circle of greenish carpet. I was shown a painted star map of the federation: 33 intricately colored planets, lit with cycling white Christmas lights and arranged to show energy flowing from the Infinite Source to all peoples of the galaxy.

Unariun student **Michael Leas** explained to me that the Earth is the only planet in the federation of 33 not yet advanced enough to join the rest of the galaxy. He went on to say the Space Brothers are scheduled to arrive at the Unarius acreage in the year 2001, in 33 jewel-bedecked space ships carrying 30,000 ascended masters each. These masters will then push earthlings along on the Unarius path.

Caveman Zan tends his campfire, with superimposed titles reading, "20,000 YEARS AGO — Based on a true story."

One activity that sets Unarius apart from other saucerian groups is media savvy. Regularly scheduled radio and cable TV shows spread the message of Unariun healing. Production is done using a makeshift soundstage and a surprisingly sophisticated video editing and effects studio. The media spread the hardcore dogma of the foundation, for easy access by potential members and as a therapeutic exercise for Unariuns themselves.

A film, *The Arrival,* is for sale to Unariun students as well as scoffers and doubters. The plot is simple. Caveman Zan tends his campfire, with superimposed titles reading, "20,000 YEARS AGO — Based on a true story." A sudden wind knocks Zan to the ground. He observes flashing lights settling nearby. Zan clears away the brush and finds a glittering UFO with a pulsating ruby rim standing on translucent amber legs. Three Space Brothers, mis-matched skullcaps slightly askew, beckon from atop a shining ramp. Zan meets Uriel, who appears amid a blaze of light and animated special effects. Afterwards, Zan takes a joyride around the universe.

I was also shown a few works in progress. One, a rough cut, was a psychodrama. Michael popped a tape into the VCR and the screen lit up with a D'Artangnian-like character. The actor ran someone through with his rapier, then, as the camera zoomed in, assumed an expression of regret. The next scene took place long ago on another planet. A woman and female assistant tended a kewpie doll suspended in a fishbowl, adding powders and colored liquids, and looking very concerned. In her past life, Michael explained, she was an evil genetic scientist. In this life, he continued, she realized she had killed one of her experiments. "You know they used to create life in their labs and there were armies of clones sent out to sap peoples' psychic energy." The women became very agitated as their attempts to reanimate the doll failed. As a last-ditch effort, the scientist tore open a paper envelope and dumped Alka-Seltzer tablets into the bowl. The doll remained motionless. The women bowed their heads in disappointment.

A group of six students I spoke with concurred that the Unariun teachings had helped them deal with life outside the foundation. Longtime student **Leanne Stevens** said when she began to read the channeled Unariun messages, she found "the books started to make sense in daily life. The principles were provable." As an example, she stated a phenomenon most of us can relate to: "If you see pinpoints of light at the edge of your vision, those are the Unarius brothers projecting part of their consciousness to help you." Unarius teaches that fears and repressed feelings are the result of "past-life actions manifesting in this life," and that for people to free themselves, all they need do is "relive these actions." This may sound like gibberish, but it serves as effective therapy for dealing with life, while also preparing the initiate for a role in the coming order of the Space Brothers.

Faulty Radios?

Groups like the Aetherians and Unariuns have stood the test of time as other organizations have passed into oblivion. They have moved in to fill a void left by antique "religions" unable to address the problems of the world. Christians passively "pray" for salvation, but Aetherians and Unariuns use modern techniques to kick some karmic ass and save our planet and the human race. If these groups are "tuning in to a Universal message with faulty radios," as William Burroughs has written, at least they *have* radios, and know how to use the secret decoder ring. The Cosmic Masters and Space Brothers stand ready to help us evolve, *if we are ready.*

THE WORLD IONIZATION INSTITUTE

A HALLMARK OF NEW AGE PHILOSOPHY IS the fusion of science and spirituality. New Age spiritual writers and practitioners appropriate scientific theories, terminology, equipment and results, while rejecting scientific methods and objectives. One example is the belief in Space Brothers — scientifically advanced, enlightened beings from another planet who intervene in human affairs to save us from ourselves, especially the technological excess that led to the creation of such horrors as the hydrogen bomb and toxic waste.

This simultaneous acceptance and rejection of scientific authority — taking power from scientist-priests and putting it into the hands of spiritualist-folk healers — is one way New Age groups attract followers. (The New Age does not have a monopoly on this tactic. Christian Fundamentalists have appropriated the image and language of science to further biblical claims in "Creation Science.")

The World Ionization Institute is at the nexus of science and spirituality. Institute members believe atomic and sub-atomic particles are the omniscient, omnipotent hands of God. Born in the early 60s, when nuclear holocaust seemed imminent, they renamed the bible as "The Bible the Book of Nuclear Physics" in the belief the bible is a direct expression of the "Laws of Nature," particularly Einstein's Law of the Conservation of Energy — $E=mc^2$ — as well as something called "XXenogenesis," a process of "criss-crossing matter with anti-matter." The technique is reputed to create immortality. Disappointingly, Einstein's equation $E=mc^2$ turns out to be just an alternative version of the apocalypse, with the World Ionization Institute leading the elect to a high-frequency heaven.

The World Ionization Institute hails from Florida, but its spiritual history begins in 1961, in Worthing, England, with a Weeping Angel Picture. **Richard Grave** and his wife, having recently moved into an old house, found a Victorian oleograph in the garage, framed in glass. As Grave attempted to dispose of it,

> [A] most astonishing thing happened. A Supernormal Being, apparently from another dimension, appeared in front of Richard, blocking his way. "I am he", said the Cosmic Visitor. As he reached out, his left hand touched the picture. The glass on the picture shattered, and the mysterious being disappeared in a blaze of orange light. So intense was this light, Richard thrust his left arm upward to shield his eyes, and his forearm was burned. [*Immortality Unveiled.*]

Grave's wife took the picture, by now blackened and blistered, and put it aside for later disposal. But when she returned an hour later, "the picture was no longer dark, but clear and the blisters were gone. It was as if some unseen hand restored the picture." The pair examined the picture, which they hadn't bothered to look at before, and saw a depiction of angels announcing the coming of Christ entitled "The First Christmas Morn." It was clear something strange was happening, and they were no longer determined to throw it out.

The Being reappeared the next day, although only Richard could see it hovering over the picture. Two days later,

> Mrs. Grave noticed water accumulating on the floor where the picture stood. Richard placed the picture by the fireplace for it to dry. It was then that they realized that the water was coming from the face of an angel in the picture. The "Angel was weeping". The weeping continued in spite of the fact that the picture was left in front of the fire for several hours.

When the weeping angel story hit the *Psychic News*, the psychic community descended on the Graves, soon joined by church authorities, TV crews and newspaper columnists. All witnessed the weeping phenomenon which was eventually found genuine by the religious community.[1] By 1963, Grave was on the metaphysical lecture circuit, and the story became national news.

The weeping angel, it would appear, was a convenient method for drawing attention not only to Richard Grave, but also to the cosmic

Institute members believe atomic and sub-atomic particles are the omniscient, omnipotent hands of God.

Richard Grave and his miraculous picture.

1. *Corroborated by several reports forwarded to me by the Churches' Fellowship for Psychical and Spiritual Studies in Lincolnshire, England.*

"Ready or not, one thing seems sure, the progressive unveiling of the 4th dimension is going to dispel the great illusion veil for all mankind."

being — Grave deemed him "The Master" — to publicize his messages to mankind. Grave recorded, then transcribed the text of his visits with The Master, then gave them to **Liebie Pugh,** a psychic in the Worthing community, who distributed the texts.

What did the messages say?

> ... he tells everyone to follow only what is truth to them, until they are ready for the next step in their unfoldment, which is inevitable since mankind is awakening. Also this Cosmic Visitor urges all mankind to follow only what reflects Love and Truth to them. In his plans he does not relate only to the planet Earth or to mankind, but always refers to the Universe.
>
> ... [he is] a Supernormal Being who tells us that he is the Truth, the Light and the All, throughout the Universe; and that he has been appearing, walking, talking on this Earth since April, 1961.

The Master also made promises of a 4-dimensional future.

> Ready or not, one thing seems sure, the progressive unveiling of the 4th dimension is going to dispel the great illusion veil for all mankind.
>
> This will be done through the medium of nuclear evolution.
>
> Some are already sensing the great mystical secret of this throbbing God power that dwells in the divinity of the atom.
>
> And a brand new concept will burst on the waiting consciousness of all mankind.
>
> This concept will concern itself with the unlocking of the divinity of the atoms of which you are constructed. ...
>
> To effect my materialization I require many instruments and this will create, to an extent, confusion; much deliberation is therefore necessary among my true followers so that they may tread wisely. ...
>
> Your lives are but tracings made by your immortal selves in this film world.
>
> If I were to return in peace, no one would recognize me except my re-incarnate. The multitude will have to recognize me through a medium of might. ...
>
> It is becoming necessary for me to interfere with the scientific devices of men and halt their progress.
>
> I will intervene in many matters of science. I have not embarked on this procedure for the purpose of preventing the manifestation of any or all scientific developments.
>
> I can halt all matter at any time, without giving reason or warning.
>
> I am intent on bringing my earth plane to realize my very presence, by practical means best recognizable by man.
>
> A great many scientists are aware of an energy that is influencing their thesis.
>
> All are regarding my influence as a challenge. None will stop to reason until I have created a means for them to appreciate fully that their program is limited in its entire objectivity. ...
>
> No man can know the day or hour when my great Universal Revelation will be enacted; however, I must repeat — I will reveal myself to the Universe through the medium of Nuclear Evolution. This is my plan which is the absolute.
>
> A major world conflict will herald the last stages of the universal progress. In the meantime, general world conditions will show evidence of a leading up to the introduction of a nuclear device that will bring about the final human level episode.
>
> The major conflict I speak of will be between nations and it will be most sudden.
>
> A human press-button device will be used and, simultaneously with the pressing of the button, instead of disaster, the universal revelation will occur.

As Richard Grave received earth-shattering messages from his Master in England, an anonymous author across the Atlantic — call him **Mr. X** — was undergoing a cosmic metamorphosis of his own, detailed in *Immortality Unveiled*. He too began receiving messages from a Master, "the Universal Mind of God." The Universal Mind first materialized in the form of a beautiful celestial woman, who spoke to him in a "vision of the night" and gave Mr. X four words "with which you will know what to do" — Mr. X knew them instantaneously — Equate — Equilibrium — High — Frequency. She sang a cosmic song and Mr. X experienced untold bliss and happiness, but more importantly than that, came to understand the true meaning of the four words. Understanding, however, would not be enough; Mr. X would have to practice them as well.

Mr. X, no stranger to the psychic milieu, knew of the Weeping Angel picture and of the Master's messages to mankind, and would soon receive messages of his own.

The gist of the messages, received with the help of various psychics, channellers, and "akashic readers," was that Mr. X was no less than the messiah, undergoing his spiritual transformation for the good of mankind. In 1963, a psychic from Buffalo, New York relayed the message that "if he were to disclose these revelations to mankind, some people would faint, some people would die of fright right on the spot. ... You are the expected one, the leader and forerunner, and you are to be a teacher of mankind. ..." Mr. X's messianic status was corroborated by psychic **Nada-Yolanda** of Mark Age in Fort Lauderdale, Florida, who channelled hundreds of messages for Mr. X from his higher-self "I AM presence," named "**San Cha**," from a location in the Universe called Andranda. San Cha's messages to Mr. X, the "broadcasting beacon of light," became the basis for his World Ionization mission.

Like Richard Grave's Master, San Cha harped on nuclear themes:

October 25, 1960: ... [Einstein's Theory of Relativity] will be known and explored within 5 to 15 years, and it will be his theories from which the new age works will be based.

May 1, 1965: ... you are a key scientist in charge of an expedition to bring about the electromagnetic concept of Divine Power in action, as it relates to the planet Earth during the transition from the 3rd to the 4th dimension. ... The time will come when you will be able to prove through scientific application and demonstration that the parables and spiritual teachings underlying all religions are immutable laws of nature. One of the reasons you are so interested in spacecraft is because the space beings use their spacecraft to beam down their frequency to make contact with you. You will build a Research Center for New Age concepts. You will be a doorway or a means through which many of these inventions and inventors will be attracted.

For all his special status, Mr. X had a great deal of work to do, for he had not yet experienced his reversal from mortal to immortal, a prerequisite for teaching mankind to practice "higher energy, vibration and frequency modulation." As a first step, he was instructed to quit his "earth-plane" job as the successful owner of a gigantic lumber enterprise. Selling his business would remove an obstacle to communion with his higher self. But if Mr. X's earth-plane business was too distracting for a New Age messiah, his organizational experience would be very useful in the higher realms: "... this soul [Mr. X] is to exercise much authority over similar projects in the future, in planning for huge communities and enterprises having to do with the foundation of a new order and government of and by the spiritual forces. ..."

As instructed, Mr. X liquidated his enterprise, then formed the World Ionization Institute and wrote the books *Immortality Unveiled* and *Immortality Through XXenogenesis* to educate mankind about the creation of the new high-frequency order. Taught the secrets of the atom, Mr. X then was authorized to teach them to us, through the "greatest book on earth," the bible.

The bible, The Book of Nuclear Physics, "a mystical or hidden treatise of the Divine laws of nature in operation," may seem to be a collection of stories about the Israelites and their Lord, but its true subject, says World Ionization Institute doctrine, is nuclear energy. Unlocking the "divinity of the atom" as described in biblical scripture will open the "kingdom of God that is within woman and man" and save the world.

Einstein's equation is code for the biblical principle that "whatsoever the Lord made, it shall be forever; for nothing can ever be added to it and nothing can ever be taken away from it" — Ecclesiastes 3:14. Furthermore, 666, the mark of the beast in the Book of Revelation, really describes the carbon atom, which consists of six protons, six neutrons and six electrons:

The beast which is referred to is the ferocious uncontrolled power of the carbon 666 atom. When a carbon 666 atom deviates from its process of nuclear evolution, the awesome Omnipotent power of the atom is so uncontrollable, that in due time the atom devours and grinds itself into an infinitesimal dust. From dust thou came unto dust of carbon 666 atoms thou shall return. Because man is comprised of carbon 666 atoms, he is always subjected to being consumed by the cosmic hissing serpent — the beast.

All biblical references mentioning numbers are subject to nuclear interpretation. Revela-

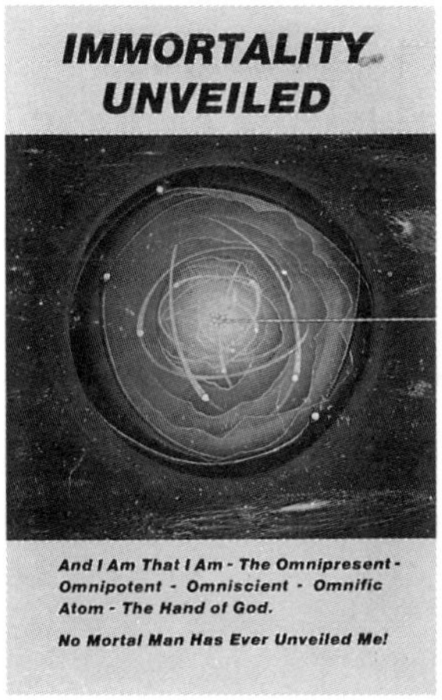

IMMORTALITY UNVEILED
And I Am That I Am - The Omnipresent - Omnipotent - Omniscient - Omnific Atom - The Hand of God.
No Mortal Man Has Ever Unveiled Me!

Warning: Lucifer refused to partake in the "veneration of atoms" and was gravely punished.

tion 21:16 says "the city stands 4 square," seemingly a statement of how plumb or stoutly built it is, but World Ionization knows better — "city" is code for "the realm of the 4th dimension." In Revelation 21:17, "144 cubits is man's measure, that is the same measure as of a Divinity" — cubits is code for the carbon atom (666), which will ultimately contain 144 electrons.

This transformation of carbon from six to 144 electrons is the key to attaining the 4th dimension, XXenogenesis and immortality. When this occurs, "it will be perfect as it was in the Garden of Eden, the 4th dimension; from which mankind fell. ..." However, only a small group — the elect — will choose to expand by cubit-electrons and attain, through XXenogenesis, the light, life, love, liberation and "veneration of atoms" that is immortality.

The perfect immortal atom has a full complement of 144 electrons whirling at beyond the equilibrium speed of light, throughout the 7 electron inertia energy levels. Together, the principles of light, life, love and liberation are necessary for the harnessing of the energy contained within the atom. ...

In order for the perfect atom to maintain its Divine perfection within itself, this flowing Divine energy must constantly undergo XXenogenesis thermonuclear fusion and veneration of atoms. As above so below — as in the macrocosm so it is in the microcosm; therefore, each microcosmic atom must partake in the veneration of atoms; which is the exchange, change and interchange of nuclear energy, or the milk and honey manna from one atom to other neighboring atoms.

Warning: Lucifer refused to partake in the "veneration of atoms" and was gravely penalized:

There was a time in the infinity, in the time — space — existence continuum when Archangel Lucifer thought he had the most beautiful, most radiant and perfect atomic structure in all existence, and consequently adored only himself. He was so proud of himself that he selfishly refused to partake in the exchange of the Divine energy or the veneration of angels between himself and Archangel Michael. ...

If at any time, anyone in the higher realms of existence refuses to be constantly perfected through the veneration of one another, then in due time, electron degeneracy commences within the atoms of that being.

Electron degeneracy is no less than the fall of mankind:

The electrons progressively lose energy and begin decelerating below the speed of light, and are no longer equating their equilibrium to a high frequency. Consequently, the electrons are stripped or fall out from the 7th, 6th, 5th and 4th electron inertia energy levels.

When this happens, the once perfect immortal atom is denuded and left with electrons in only the first 3 electron inertia energy levels or orbits. This type of an atom, where it is always subject to decomposition, corruption, decay, sickness and eventually transitional death. Thus the perfect atom becomes "mortal" and is operational in the 3rd dimensional worlds of any solar system.

The revelations about atoms, thermonuclear fusion and XXenogenesis amount to the story of Eden, The Fall and Man's redemption of the Kingdom of God through Christ. The sign of the cross represents XXenogenesis and "the criss-crossing of matter and antimatter."

XXenogenesis thermonuclear fusion will bring forth the birth of Christ in woman and man. As already related earlier, this is the time not of one Christ, but of many Christs. Through XXenogenesis, man will resurrect and perfect the carbon 666 atoms of his mortal body while he is still alive.

In 1971, San Cha revealed that "the years of training, discipline, preparation and questioning have ended for you." Mr. X had finally exchanged polarities and entered higher consciousness. "... you have now set in operation the (4th dimensional) frequency for an earth body to do this." Together, Mr. X and San Cha would undergo a 10-day tribulation and "cosmic crucifixion," the "XXenogenesis thermonuclear fusion — the fusing of matter and antimatter" that would result in immortality.

It is a universal and scientific fact that when matter and antimatter come into contact with each other under uncontrolled conditions, annihilation occurs.

However, by controlling the criss-crossing (+) of matter with antimatter through XXenogenesis thermonuclear fusion, the carbon 666 atoms of man's body undergo the reversal from mortal to immortal existence. Through this, the enmity between the carbon 666 atoms is permanently conquered. This removes the results of the 1st original sin.

In time, San Cha continued, everyone will undergo cosmic crucifixion and XXenogenesis thermonuclear fusion, conquering their animalistic natures, or they will pay the price of refusal.

Despite the monumental news, the world appeared indifferent to these truths. Even other New Agers refused to hear. San Cha interpreted the indifference as part of the divine plan:

> The antichrists thrive on ignorance and deception. They will deny that the Christ seed has come and has been fused in the flesh. They will present falsehood and error as truth. You will know an antichrist is speaking when the voice is raised against this XXenogenesis revelation, and the truth that is revealed.

The elect, said San Cha, will be those who believe. They will be awarded by immortality, while those who don't will be punished by death:

> ... unless mankind will use this God given information to transmute the body through XXenogenesis into an immortal nuclear energy light body of the 4th dimension, no living creature shall remain alive on this planet Earth. The self-elect are those who will add cubits to their stature thru XXenogenesis.
>
> This solar system, including planet Earth, is currently traversing a transitional period in the cosmic cycle. The frequency of the 3rd dimension — the mortal existence, will be accelerated and changed to a 4th dimensional frequency for immortal existence. Man must establish this new equilibrium in his mortal body, one which corresponds to and is compatible with the ultra high frequency of the 4th dimension. If man does not equate his equilibrium to an ultra high frequency, then he will not be able to endure the oncoming cosmic holocaust or exist in the world to come. Thus, that portion of mankind which rejects this truth and rebels will eliminate itself by its own foolish hand as prophesied.

Funny. Here I thought the Evangelical Christians had already figured out the apocalypse will mean believers will ascend to heaven and unbelievers will descend to hell. And they didn't need nuclear physics to do it.

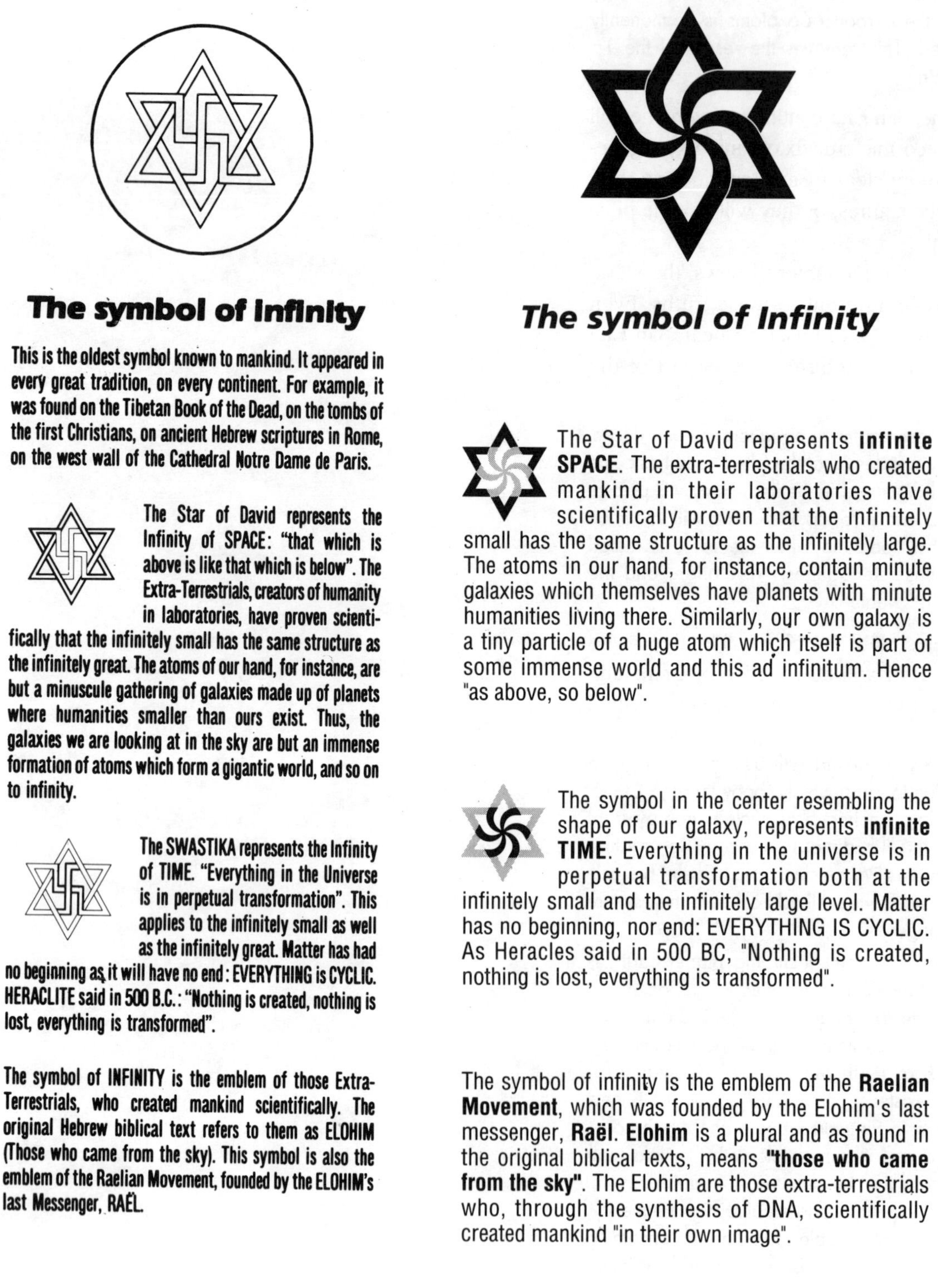

The symbol of Infinity

This is the oldest symbol known to mankind. It appeared in every great tradition, on every continent. For example, it was found on the Tibetan Book of the Dead, on the tombs of the first Christians, on ancient Hebrew scriptures in Rome, on the west wall of the Cathedral Notre Dame de Paris.

The Star of David represents the Infinity of SPACE: "that which is above is like that which is below". The Extra-Terrestrials, creators of humanity in laboratories, have proven scientifically that the infinitely small has the same structure as the infinitely great. The atoms of our hand, for instance, are but a minuscule gathering of galaxies made up of planets where humanities smaller than ours exist. Thus, the galaxies we are looking at in the sky are but an immense formation of atoms which form a gigantic world, and so on to infinity.

The SWASTIKA represents the Infinity of TIME. "Everything in the Universe is in perpetual transformation". This applies to the infinitely small as well as the infinitely great. Matter has had no beginning as it will have no end: EVERYTHING is CYCLIC. HERACLITE said in 500 B.C.: "Nothing is created, nothing is lost, everything is transformed".

The symbol of INFINITY is the emblem of those Extra-Terrestrials, who created mankind scientifically. The original Hebrew biblical text refers to them as ELOHIM (Those who came from the sky). This symbol is also the emblem of the Raelian Movement, founded by the ELOHIM's last Messenger, RAËL.

The symbol of Infinity

The Star of David represents **infinite SPACE**. The extra-terrestrials who created mankind in their laboratories have scientifically proven that the infinitely small has the same structure as the infinitely large. The atoms in our hand, for instance, contain minute galaxies which themselves have planets with minute humanities living there. Similarly, our own galaxy is a tiny particle of a huge atom which itself is part of some immense world and this ad infinitum. Hence "as above, so below".

The symbol in the center resembling the shape of our galaxy, represents **infinite TIME**. Everything in the universe is in perpetual transformation both at the infinitely small and the infinitely large level. Matter has no beginning, nor end: EVERYTHING IS CYCLIC. As Heracles said in 500 BC, "Nothing is created, nothing is lost, everything is transformed".

The symbol of infinity is the emblem of the **Raelian Movement**, which was founded by the Elohim's last messenger, **Raël**. **Elohim** is a plural and as found in the original biblical texts, means **"those who came from the sky"**. The Elohim are those extra-terrestrials who, through the synthesis of DNA, scientifically created mankind "in their own image".

The old Raëlian movement symbol (left) and the new, politically correct version (right)

THE RAËLIAN MOVEMENT

After a voyage of 20 billion miles or so, extraterrestrials arriving on earth would probably enjoy some hospitality. The well-meaning who erect large banners reading, "WELCOME SPACE BROTHERS," may make the occasion of an alien visit seem like a birthday party or science fiction convention. Members of the "Raëlian Movement," founded by a former reporter for a French auto racing magazine, suggest a more dignified welcome; they believe the ETs deserve an embassy.

According to the Raëlians, extraterrestrials known as the Elohim requested an embassy because "there are no official channels they can use to establish a non-threatening contact." Also, "they would be breaking several laws by flying through our airspace, airways and landing on our territories." To overcome these problems, **Raël** (formerly a French auto racing writer named **Claude Vorilhon**) and his followers want to raise $20 million to erect an Elohim embassy in Jerusalem, to facilitate meetings with world leaders. As incentive for us to get things underway, says Raël, the Elohim will delay contact until we build it.

Lack of an embassy, however, didn't stop the ETs from visiting France in 1973 to confer with Vorilhon.

On December 13 of that year, while hiking in a dormant volcano near his home, Claude Vorilhon encountered a flying object the size of a small bus. The UFO, sporting a cone with a flashing white light on top and a blinking red light on the bottom, hovered several yards above the ground while a glowing, child-sized occupant wearing a green suit descended to earth. The suit and spacecraft were decorated with an emblem consisting of a swastika within a Star of David. The conversation between the occupant of the space vehicle and Vorilhon, as recorded in Jacques Vallee's *Messengers of Deception:*

Vorilhon: Where do you come from?
Occupant: Very far away...
V: You speak French?
O: I speak every language on Earth.
V: You come from another planet?
O: Yes.
V: Is this your first visit to Earth?
O: Oh no!
V: Have you come here many times?
O: Very often ... that's the least you could say.
V: Why did you come?
O: Today I come to speak to you.
V: Why did you pick me?
O: For many reasons. First we needed someone who lived in a country where new ideas are well-received. France is a country where democracy was born, and her image on the entire Earth is that of the land of freedom.

Vorilhon, now renamed "Raël," was told he was selected to spread a message of love, peace and fraternity to all humanity. Vorhilon was chosen because: he was a "free-thinker," but not anti-religious; he was born in 1946, shortly after the first atomic bomb sent mushrooms to the sky; and he was neither scientist nor professional writer,[1] so the Elohim were confident he wouldn't "make up convoluted sentences that most people wouldn't be able to read."

The green-suited man instructed the young Frenchman to return the next day, and bring his bible. For five successive mornings, Raël was given bible lessons. Upon their conclusion, he "realized the immensity of the mission that he had been given," but that he would be mocked as an "illuminated one." Concluding "it is better to be an illuminated one who knows than an enlightened man who doesn't," Raël decided to go public. He compiled his notes into a book, *The Message Given to Me by Extra-Terrestrials.*

Various Raëlian flyers and promotional pamphlets summarize that message:

Life on earth is the result of a scientific creation by people who came from a distant planet. The oldest history book ever to be found on earth, the original Bible written in Hebrew, contains the details of this masterpiece.

It refers to ELOHIM as being the Creator. This word when properly translated does not mean

1. Various sources identify Vorilhon as a reporter, a journalist, and a publisher.

God as we have been led to believe but simply "Those Who Came From the Sky."

These scientists from outer-space are 25,000 years ahead of us scientifically. They had mastered the scientific secrets of creating life through manipulation of DNA (deoxyribonucleic acid) coupled with advanced genetic engineering abilities in order to guide humanity through it's progression in time, the ELOHIM sent us prophets (Greek word meaning "he who reveals"). Some of the better-known are, Moses, Jesus, Buddha, Mohammed and Joseph Smith.

Their mission was to establish the great religions, and so prepare humanity for the Age of Apocalypse or the Age of Revelation. We have entered this era on August 6th, 1945, for it was on that day that humanity learned that a new energy source had been discovered. On the other hand, the ELOHIM knew that humanity had reached the stage in its scientific evolution where it was now ready to understand the truth about its origins. I was born in Vichy, France, on September 30, 1946.

The ELOHIM have asked that I build an Embassy, a place where they could come in peace to meet with our political leaders to give us their wisdom as well as their technology.

The Elohim don't condemn sensual pleasure as sinful, teaching that receiving such pleasure helps harmonize the mind.

According to the Elohim (via Raël), humanity was created as part of a scientific experiment on their home planet. Ordered by their government to continue the experiment elsewhere, the Elohim scientists selected earth, at the time completely covered by water. To provide living space for the experimental humans, the Elohim raised land masses via massive explosions. Although all the details of the experiment weren't covered in the bible, the Elohim did manage to sneak in the story of an ideological split between factions led by Yahweh and Satan respectively.

The Elohim decided to reveal this to Raël so mankind would finally understand certain concepts of nuclear physics and genetic engineering, but more importantly, so we would know we are living in The Last Days, which require vast political changes. To start, existing political institutions — like elections — must go:

You must eliminate elections and votes that are completely ill-adapted to the current evolution of mankind. Men are the useful cells of a large body called Humanity. A cell in the foot doesn't have to say whether or not the hand should pick up an object. The brain decides, and if the object is good, the cell in the foot will profit by it. ... A world government and a new monetary system must be created. A single language will serve to unify the planet.

Why the Elohim denounced democracy — after extolling its virtues — was not explained, nor was what appears to be a double standard on aggression: If the military service in every country on earth is not abolished, the Elohim told Raël, they will wipe out our scientific centers next time they return to earth. Underlining the threat, they cited similar treatment given the biblical Sodom and Gomorrah.

The totalitarian overtones in the Elohim message may bother such observers as **Jacques Vallee,** author of *Messengers of Deception: UFO Contacts and Cults,* but apparently they give "inner peace" to Raël and his followers. Still, perhaps in response to Vallee's criticisms, Raël now spells out the "Raëlian Values" in his promotional literature. These values includes, "Awareness of Consequences of our Actions: Even if Raël himself, or the Elohim... asks you to obey an order which is contrary to your own conscience, don't obey it. ..." The literature doesn't say whether these values originated with Raël or with the Elohim.

Raël's book, by now translated into 25 languages, became the basis for the "Raëlian Movement." By 1992, Raël claimed 28,000 members worldwide. The former racing enthusiast had become a New Age Guru, holding mass seminars on "Sensual Meditation," a technique he was taught by the Elohim.

Despite what might seem to be biblical prohibitions, the Elohim don't condemn sensual pleasure as sinful, teaching that receiving such pleasure helps harmonize the mind:

[Sensual Meditation] constitutes the "directions for use" given to humans to teach them to use the harmonizing possibilities of their mind; directions for use, given by beings who indeed created the human brain, and who are obviously in the best position to understand it. Man is connected to infinity which surrounds him and which he is made of, by his sensors, the senses.

To develop one's sensuality, is to develop one's capacity to feel connected to infinity, to feel oneself infinite. Allowing to erase the scars of guilt from the Judeo-Christian religions without falling into the ethereal mysticism of the oriental teachings, sensual meditation gives the human being the opportunity to discover his body, and mainly to learn to derive pleasure from sounds, colors, smells, tastes, caresses and particularly from a sexuality experienced through all the senses.

Raël learned this on a visit to the Elohim home planet, a tropical paradise, two years after initial contact. While there, inside a metal shell, Elohim knowledge was piped directly into his brain. During his holiday in space, Raël met Jesus, Buddha and Mohammed, among others. In 1987, in recounting the adventure to reporters in Toronto, Raël said, "Jesus is a very beautiful man, very thin, very feminine" who is "amused by the image we have of him here. ... at what the Vatican does in his name."

Raël's second book, *Beings From Outer Space Took Me to their Planet,* which documents the 1975 encounter, describes a sexual romp with robots:

I put on my belt and found myself carried in front of the apparatus used to make robots. When I was seated, a splendid-looking dark-haired girl appeared in the three-dimensional luminous cube. My robot asked me if I liked her and wished to have different shapes or a modified face. I told him I found her perfect.

The robot fabricated five more girls for Raël. All six accompanied him to a bath, and, as Raël tells it, "submitted to all my desires."

As thousands responded to Raël's promise of guilt-free sex, the movement's symbol — a swastika within a Star of David — became an item for public debate. For those confused by the "Symbol of Infinity," the movement provided detailed explanations. Raël claims it is the oldest symbol on Earth:

... It appeared in every great tradition, on every continent. For example, it was found on the Tibetan Book of the Dead, on the tombs of the first Christians, on ancient Hebrew scriptures in Rome, on the west wall of the Cathedral Notre Dame de Paris.

The Star of David represents the Infinity of SPACE that which is above is like that which is below. The Extra-Terrestrials, creators of humanity in laboratories, have proven scientifically that the infinity small is of the same magnitude as the infinity great. The atoms of our hand, for instance, are but a minuscule gathering of galaxies made up of planets where humanities smaller than ours exist. Thus, the galaxies we are looking at in the sky are but an immense formation of atoms which form a gigantic world and so on to infinity.

The SWASTIKA represents the Infinity of TIME. Everything in the Universe is in perpetual transformation. This applies to the infinitely small as well as the infinitely great. Matter has had no beginning as it will have no end: EVERYTHING is CYCLIC. HERACLITE said, 500 years B.C.: "Nothing is created, nothing is lost, everything is transformed." The symbol of INFINITY is the emblem of those Extra-Terrestrials who created mankind scientifically. The original Hebrew biblical text refers to them as ELOHIM (Those who came from the sky). This symbol is also the emblem of the Raëlian Movement, founded by the ELOHIM's last Messenger, Raël.

This explanation for the swastika doesn't seem to satisfy those offended by it, despite lengthy explanations which — rightly — place the ancient symbol within a wider context than that of 20th century geopolitics. But since the Raëlians wanted to build an embassy in Jerusalem, they decided to do something about the swastika imagery. In 1992, a press release announced, "The Raëlian Movements Have a New Symbol."

Since the Raëlians wanted to build an embassy in Jerusalem, they decided to do something about the swastika imagery.

Out of respect for the victims of the Nazi holocaust and in order to facilitate negotiations for the construction of the embassy in Israel, Raël has decided to change the symbol of the Raëlian Movement and replace the swastika with a spiralling galaxy which also represents the cycle of infinity in time. This was done with the Elohim's consent and despite the fact that their symbol is the oldest on Earth with traces of it still remaining in Israel today such as in the ancient synagogue at *Ein Gedhi* near the Dead Sea.

The change has been in effect since the beginning of April 1992. It goes without saying that the original symbol seen on the Elohim's spaceship will remain the emblem of the Elohim. It will be seen again on their spaceship when we welcome their official arrival.

This attempt to stay on the good side of Israel was followed up with formation of a committee to spread The Message to Jewish

They're coming
They created humanity scientifically in laboratory, thanks to DNA
Their masterpiece was described by those primitive men, who first wrote the Bible.
Who are they?
What are they to humanity?
Why have we been created?
When will they come?
Where do they want to meet?

communities around the world. Though the arrival of the Elohim is billed as an "historical planetary event," the Raëlians, like their Christian predecessors, have specifically targeted Jews for conversion.

A 1992 issue of the *US Raëlian Quarterly* reported a "blitz" organized in Israel. "This will be an excellent opportunity for the Jewish people of Israel to discover their true origin, another step toward the building of the Embassy in Israel. ... They will learn that the Messiah is already among us and it is up to them to recognize him. ..." Apparently, the results have been positive; a 1993 article in the same publication, entitled "Peace Agreement between Israel and PLO permitted by the Elohim," reported an Israeli study group has formed, "comprised of rabbis and other influential Israeli scholars who, as a matter of policy, will not interfere with the establishment and growth of the Raëlian Movement in Israel." This is only the first step however, because "they are not yet ready to admit that Raël is the actual Messiah."

The movement's brochures, however, do not directly state that Raël is the Messiah; rather, he is identified as the "Elohim's Messenger," along with hints that he is mankind's savior. Raël can save us, however, only if the Elohim arrive on Earth; because the Elohim will arrive only if the Raëlians build their embassy, and an embassy can be built only if Israel allows it, the Raëlians believe — not unlike evangelical Christians — that the fate of the world hinges on the conversion of the Jews.

The Raëlian culture is thoroughly New Age, but there is little new in their core beliefs. They reject Judeo-Christian morality and claim to question authority, but their messianism clearly supports an authoritarian structure; the Elohim are at the top, humanity is at the bottom, Raël is somewhere in between. Defying Raël is tantamount to defying the Elohim, because he is their representative, and the Elohim have told us what will happen if we defy them: they will destroy us just as they destroyed Sodom and Gomorrah. Raël says the Elohim are Space Brothers, but if that is the case, they act and speak as if they are the fierce, masculine, unforgiving God of the Hebrews we in the Western World have known and "loved" for centuries.

DR. DOREAL & THE BROTHERHOOD OF THE WHITE TEMPLE

Along with advertisements for The *Flying Saucers — As I Saw Them!* by Kenneth Arnold, Sturgis "The Sun Man," The National Hygienic Society, Photos of Rudolph Valentino and "The Secrets of Dynamic Living Unveiled," the October, 1952, issue of *Fate* magazine contained a large display ad on the inside back cover headlined, "ANCIENT WISDOM; MASTER YOUR DESTINY." It invited readers to "Write for Free Brochure" or any one of 30 books in the "Little Temple Library," just 35 cents each from The Brotherhood of the White Temple. It also announced a "Wisdom School" correspondence course for the serious seeker, and concluded, "With headquarters on a large tract of land high in the Rocky Mountains [the Brotherhood] invites correspondence with all True Seekers for Truth."

Respondents might have been surprised when they received — along with lessons on ancient wisdom — plans for surviving Armageddon in 1953, and detailed descriptions of Atlantis, Lemuria, and kingdoms inside the hollow earth.

Dr. Maurice Doreal, born **Claude Doggins** in Sulfur Springs, Oklahoma, formed the Brotherhood of the White Temple in 1930 "as a vehicle for bringing the ancient wisdom to those ready to receive." Doreal was known to members as the "Supreme Voice" for as long as he was alive, and to this day, the Brotherhood recognizes no other authority. He wrote their lesson material, books and pamphlets, and because the Brotherhood does not condone the use of "spirit guides" or channeling to find "new truths," Doreal's writings will never be revised or amended.

Doreal's teachings — he identified them as the Wisdom of the Ancients — resemble those of other Theosophically-derived Wisdom Schools and organizations; the name "The Brotherhood of the White Temple," was used prior to Doreal by Annie Besant, successor to Madame Blavatsky. Doreal's explanation was that the name refers to his direct link with "The Great White Lodge" of Masters, and though not a Master himself, he "has made contact with the Masters and has been shown a path whereby others can make the same contact." The Masters, however, don't favor everyone. The seeker must attain a certain level of consciousness before becoming worthy of their contact.

Those hoping to meet the Masters, including the "Master Within," are advised to take take *The Brotherhood of the White Temple Lesson Course*. The course — which the student agrees to keep secret — includes four "Neophyte" and 12 "Temple" grades, and takes four and one-half years to complete at a rate of one lesson per week. Upon completion, the seeker is awarded a diploma and the title "Dr. of Metaphysics" (probably what the "Dr." in "Dr. Doreal" refers to).

The lessons — I was sent a sample — are intended to help the student "overcome the sense of the impossible," joining with illumined men and women throughout history. Only the spiritually advanced, however, are "elected" to find the truth. "This election must take place in the student or candidate in a manner that the grasping mind of the world has not the slightest conception of." By taking the lessons, a student may begin to apprehend how to join the "elect," though there are no guarantees. Doreal adds, "If an illumined being should publicly state that he was God in the flesh, which is the sum total of illumination, the world would spring upon that person and display its venom to such a degree that he would remain a spectacle. ..." Bearing this in mind, students are cautioned to be careful about what they say to outsiders.

Those who are not students or members of the Brotherhood are invited to buy modestly priced pamphlets, all written years ago by Doreal. The 100 titles from the "Little Temple Library" include *Adam and the Pre-*

Dr. Doreal's emblem.
A lighter shade of Raël.

Adamites; Akashic Records and How To Read Them; Armageddon Plan For Safety; The Inner Earth; Occult and Mystery Teachings of Jesus; The Spinal Brain and Health; and *World War and Reincarnation.* The pamphlets impart what Doreal claims to be "ancient wisdom" to which he is privy via the Masters as well as Tibetans — Doreal claims that after serving in World War I, he spent eight years in Tibet studying with the Dalai Lama.

Some of the material, however, is purported to spring from Doreal's direct experience. In *Mysteries of Mt. Shasta,* which reads like bad science fiction, he tells of his visit to an Atlantean colony inside Northern California's Mt. Shasta. In this and other pamphlets, Doreal exhibits wide knowledge of both world mythology and fantasy literature; his imagination fills in the details.

Doreal begins his story by recounting some of the legends and rumors surrounding Mt. Shasta — despite numerous fires in the vicinity, the forest around the mountain has never burned; lights have been seen rising from the mountain; residents in the area see strange people dressed in unknown garb, including head dresses and long robes; the strangers appear in small towns nearby, and "buy quantities of certain chemicals and pay for it with gold nuggets or gold dust."

Doreal says he had previously visited the colonies inside of Shasta, but the visits were "astral," not physical. In 1931, he was invited to visit the Atlantean colony in the flesh. He was lecturing in Los Angeles when two audience members identify themselves as colonists. They invited him to visit their colony at Mt. Shasta that day, but Doreal declined, thanking them for the invitation but pointing out he would have to return to Los Angeles in time for his next lecture. They replied, "[W]e have another way of going," and the three drove by car through the hills toward Topanga Canyon.

Handing Doreal a thin cellophane-like face mask, along with a belt with two little pockets and a row of buttons, the Atlanteans took Doreal by the arm and told him to press certain buttons. They ascended into the air until the earth faded away below, the masks enabling them to breathe normally despite the altitude. They descended to a point more than halfway up Mt. Shasta, entered a small building, and rode a kind of elevator to a huge flat rock on top of the mountain. They passed through an opening at the center of the rock, and sank into the mountain until they were five miles deep, then descended another seven miles. They entered a cavern two miles high, 20 miles long, and 15 miles wide, and bright as a "summer day" owing to a giant glowing mass of light at the center. "They told me later," Doreal writes, "that it was condensed from a blending of the rays of the sun and the moon and that it had all of the harmful rays in it extracted and only the life-giving and beneficial energies left." The glowing mass explained the strange lights people had seen in the vicinity as discharges from the colony's "power houses."

Finally, Doreal and his hosts entered a city of beautiful white marble houses and fantastic tropical gardens. The city's trees bore fruit unknown to today's world, preserved from Atlantis and Lemuria.

The city's trees bore fruit unknown to the outside world, preserved from Atlantis and Lemuria.

The marvels of the city were the result of the nearly super-human beings who live in this city, whose powers are many and needs are few. Though they have many foods to eat, they don't eat for nourishment, as their power houses provide all the energy they need. To produce clothing, "they would make a picture of the design of the costume that they want for themselves, then place it in a projecto-scope, an invisible ray of energy would shoot out and then on a screen would form a kind of misty figure of the figure they were projecting and that would become more and more solid until there would fall on the floor, the garment they desired."

The city-dwellers almost never fall ill, live to 150 years of age, and pass away of their own free will. As spiritually advanced "illumined souls," they have a temple but no religion; they know God directly, making religion superfluous. Indeed, the inhabitants beneath Mt. Shasta "are masters of all the laws of Nature," writes Doreal. "They are able to create vacuums at will; they have extin-

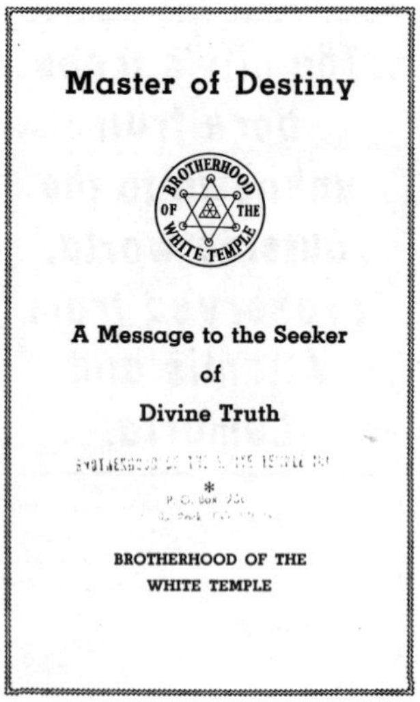
Master of Destiny

BROTHERHOOD OF THE WHITE TEMPLE

A Message to the Seeker of Divine Truth

BROTHERHOOD OF THE WHITE TEMPLE

guished fires that came too close; they can warp space..."

Despite an extraordinary technology, spiritual illumination and health, the Atlanteans are forced to purchase supplies from the outside. Doreal witnessed their use of "alchemistry" to turn sand into gold, which the Atlanteans exchange for currency. He doesn't explain why they don't simply use alchemistry to turn sand into the supplies; this might be one of their closely guarded secrets.

Doreal was privileged to become one of the few invited to the Atlanteans' temple to learn the secrets of the illumined ones. The Atlanteans outlined a plan for Doreal's work in the outer world, "so that gradually the consciousness of man could be made more and more aware of the great mysteries behind matter and substance and behind life."

The Atlanteans know more about us than we do ourselves, and are committed to protecting us and helping us grow. Unfortunately, they are not the only inhabitants of the inner earth; the Shasta colony, about 350 strong, guards millions of captive Lemurians. Doreal explains that in the days before Lemuria and Atlantis sank, the space beneath Lemuria contained "pleasure cities" created from the Lemurians' vast store of knowledge, including the secrets of the atom. When Lemuria sank, surviving priest-kings and nobles retreated to underground palaces. Approximately 4.5 million are alive today, guarded by Atlanteans. Doreal worries that, "someday, they might break forth. That is one thing I am afraid of the war in the South Pacific. I am afraid they might break the seal which has held the Lemurians below the surface of the earth."

Lemurians, fears Doreal, are basically evil. His letter to *Amazing Stories* during the Shaver Mystery craze seems to equate the Lemurians with Shaver's "deros":

> Like Mr. Shaver, I have had personal contact with the Dero and even visited their underground caverns. In the outer world they are represented by an organization known loosely as the "Black Brotherhood," whose purpose is the destruction of the good principle in man.... The underground cities are, in the most part, protected by space-warps, a science known to the ancients, but only touched on by modern science....

Mt. Shasta, it seems, is just the tip of the iceberg. Another pamphlet, *The Inner Earth,* describes a vast system of channels and caverns hundreds of miles below the surface with inhabitants even more sinister than the Lemurians. These are disharmonic giants — some over a mile tall — who invaded earth and enslaved people during the "second cycle" of human existence; they are the source of our legends of Lucifer and the coming of evil. Impossible to kill, they were imprisoned in a central metallic globe that floats in the center of the earth, the "bound spirits" of the bible. And there they will remain, guarded by Atlanteans, until the cosmos passes and a new cosmos is created.

The "god-men" who trapped the gigantic evil Lemurians millions of years ago were giants themselves. According to another Doreal pamphlet, *Polar Paradise,* they originated around the North Pole, at the time a tropical paradise, fertile and warm. The giants who lived there were "almost" immortal, i.e., they lived a very long time. These are the "Sons of God" depicted in the bible. The "Tower of Babel" is the story of a mountain which once reached the home of these god-men.

> Once it rose, high upon it was built the City of the God-race. Around it, lower down were built the cities of ancient man. The man races looked with longing upon the Home of the Gods on the Holy Mountain and they tried to force their way up the mountain and the super human divine power of the God man drove them out and they scattered into different parts of the world and the story of the confusion of tongues was nothing more or less than a legend arising from the fact that when men were scattered and formed tribes and nations and later, when they got together they could no longer understand each other....

The ancient wisdom, Doreal says, teaches that after "the [current] dark age," the north pole ice cap will melt, and we will once again be able to travel to the Holy Mountain and stand before the home of the gods.

As proof, Doreal presents examples from the mythologies of various cultures, including the bible, the Zendavesta, Norse mythology, and Hindu mythology. Doreal is apparently unaware that symbols and metaphors are often used in religion and mythology to describe that which cannot be described in any other way. His knowledge of the world's myths and religions as well as his esoteric training contribute to only the most literal interpretations:

> In the Zend Avesta of Zoroaster, we find this quotation: "There the stars, the moon and the sun are only seen to rise and set once a year and a year seems only a day." He is speaking of the Holy City of the Gods upon the Holy Mountain. Is there any other place in the world where the sun seems to rise and set only once a year?

Doreal concludes from passages such as these, that the North was once, and still remains, the home of the gods.

> There is a small area in the North only about one hundred and fifty miles in circumference that is still as tropical and fertile as it was in the beginning of time; in that there rests what remains of the ancient Holy City from which all mankind came in the dawn of time, those who remain as the guardians of the children of the world. The Aurora Borealis is nothing more or less than the energies used to give light to that region around them. They literally bend or curve space in such a manner that it strikes upon a warp in space which they create so that if man has a compass and moves towards that he is diverted in a circle around it and though he thinks he is going straight...
>
> In it even today, there still live certain of the giant God-race from the very beginning of mankind, because under the influence of the very force of life itself they do not die. ...

Doreal continues the story of the human race, peppered with achingly literal interpretations of mythology, in *Adam and the Pre-Adamites* and *The Ten Lost Tribes of Israel,* which detail the various migrations of the supposed tribes and races of humanity. Though he denies such a convergence, Doreal's evidence, line of reasoning and conclusions are practically identical to those of the Anglo-Israelites. And though he is careful not to appear anti-Semitic, his arguments imply that swarthy big-nosed Jews are descended from outcasts and mutants, while light-skinned "Christian Races" are descended from the spiritually advanced God-race.

Doreal deviates from Anglo-Israelism, however, in his speculations about which "races" descended from the Lost Tribes. The Anglo-Israelites conclude that only Anglo-Saxons or Europeans are descended from Israel, but Doreal saw Lost Tribes almost everywhere he looked. To him, the Lost Tribes ended up not only in Britain, but also in China, the Gobi Desert, Ethiopia, India, Afghanistan, and, as the Mormons believe, America.

> From evidence which we find in races and tribes here in America, most definitely there was a certain knowledge of the Kabbala which was a common heritage of all the Twelve Tribes of the Israelites. ... We also know that there was found a leaden tablet in a cave in Indiana, that was talked about by scientists all over the world and the lead tablet was carved in Hebrew characters, that gave the first chapter of the Book of Concealed Mysteries and the account of certain of the wanderings of Daniel and the Tribe of Napthali. It was discarded. Whatever happened to it I do not know.

But, of the various Lost Tribe representatives world-wide, only Anglo-Saxons hold the "spiritual key" of Christianity:

> ... [K]nowledge of the meaning of the mysteries, came to England with the dispersion of the Israelite Tribes, because one Tribe that had the interpretation of it was the Levites who settled in Europe. The Jews were given the letter and the Levites were given the spiritual key and it was for that reason that Jesus came to the Israelites and that through them his gospel has been spread...

Although their teachings are supposedly drawn from *all* the religions of mankind, The Brotherhood of the White Temple is fixated on Christ more than any other religious figure. And although they claim to emphasize the "esoteric" meaning of Christ's teachings, The Brotherhood comes to many of the same conclusions as Fundamentalist Christians, believing in a literal Armageddon, and praying that it will come soon.

In the pamphlet, *Armageddon Plan for Safety,* Doreal warns:

> I know I am painting a grim picture, but you must remember that this is Armageddon and not just another war. The anti-Christ in person is leading the forces of evil in a last great fight against the forces of Light. It is Ragnorak, the Twilight of

And though he is careful not to appear anti-Semitic, Doreal's arguments imply that swarthy Jews are descended from outcasts and mutants.

the Gods, and men and Satan are loosed to afflict mankind because man has not taken advantage of his opportunities given him by the love of God. ... Man must pass through trials and tribulations, purged in the fire, before he will turn to God and make the way ready for the second coming of Christ, which will be soon after the last great battle.

When the mountain retreat was completed, the Brotherhood began its plans for surviving Armageddon.

Doreal shared post-Hiroshima anxieties with many. In 1946, he began to construct an "atom-proof" hideaway in a mountain valley near Sedalia, Colorado. The valley, near scenic "Devil's Head," is walled in on all sides by sheer precipices 1,500 feet high and a mountain wall more than a mile thick. Doreal was convinced this would protect the Brotherhood from radiation. Located on 1,600 acres, the hideaway would also serve as headquarters for the Brotherhood and as a utopian community.

The community, "Shamballa Ashrama," would house 800 members of the Brotherhood composed of "a carefully-selected cross-section of humanity." There would be "doctors, lawyers, atomic scientists, engineers, laborers, educators, mechanics, carpenters, painters and representatives of all important trades."

When the mountain retreat was completed in 1951, the Brotherhood moved its headquarters there from Denver, and began its plans for surviving Armageddon. In 1953, Doreal predicted the last great battle would occur that year. In February, 1953, Doreal read an announcement to The Brotherhood outlining the scenario for the Last Days, which might begin as early as May but surely no later than September. He told them decisions had already been made in Russia, that the United States would cause an all-out atomic war triggered by the situation in Korea. He didn't disclose sources for his intimate knowledge of these high-level decisions, but his speech cited the prophecies of Nostradamus, the bible and the Great Pyramid.

Doreal issued orders barring outsiders, except "necessary workmen," from the valley. But *The Denver Post* — which learned of the hideout through one of the workmen — paid Doreal a visit anyway. A reporter travelled to "Shangri-La-in-the-Rockies" hoping to obtain a first-hand account of Doreal and the Brotherhood. They refused to talk to him.

This didn't stop the newspaperman from snooping around. He walked uninvited into a room where "the silence was deafening." What he saw he described as "breathtaking":

> ... Mystic symbols decorated the walls and the arched ceiling above the sanctuary.
>
> In the center of the sanctuary ... sat a large satin-lined throne with a single smaller chair on either side at a lower level.
>
> The sanctuary floor was covered with carpeting and the raised pedestal which the throne sat on glowed under a white, furry material.
>
> Indirect lighting around the top of the wall near the ceiling cast an eerie blue light from hidden bulbs. Rich robes lay nearby. The odor of incense was strong.
>
> I felt as if a thousand eyes were watching me as I walked down the center aisle between rows of overstuffed pews finished in blue leather. I was scared, and I left fast, my heels clicking loudly in the deathly silence of the sacred temple.

The newshound may have exaggerated for the sake of a good story, but Doreal's aura of splendor is corroborated by an earlier story in the *Rocky Mountain News*. The journalist visited the former headquarters in Denver, converted from the "imposing home of W.G. Fisher, founder of Daniels & Fisher Stores..." He described the material aspects of the headquarters in great detail:

> The Argentine satinwood-paneled walls of each room are lined with rare Oriental tapestries, books, and varied objects of art, all the collection of Doreal...
>
> Doreal boasts the finest collection of Thibetan literature in the country. The robe he wore yesterday, a bright purple habit with gold collar, cuffs and sash, was handed down to him by priests of the Royal Order of Shamballa in Thibet, he said.
>
> He sat yesterday in the throne of his auditorium, a beautifully-carved chair which was used by Emperor Maximilian of Mexico, purchased by Doreal from the collection of the late Dr. John Eisner of Denver.
>
> Beside Doreal's throne was an antique set of Chinese temple bells he uses during his sermon meetings. Behind him was an austere painting of a Thibetan valley — entrance to the fabulous Shamballa of Thibet which is said to be located

75 miles under the Himalayas on the China-India border.

Doreal fingered a highly-polished strand of 108 wooden beads, each carved with Sanscrit mantrams of the Thibetan religion. The beads, he said, were worn by Shri Rama Krishna, the great Hindu saint.

In addition to Tibetan artifacts, Doreal collected fantasy and science fiction literature, which may account for his more bizarre teachings, though Doreal denied any such connection. He began collecting *Tarzan* books as a child; by 1955, his collection included around 5,000 fantasy and science fiction books out of his entire collection which numbered 30,000 titles. His sci-fi library included many rare first editions, and was known as one of the most complete science fiction libraries in the country. Doreal was the classic bibliomaniac, buying "every book of that type that's ever been written," and reading them "only to relax," laying aside those that are "supposed to make you think."

Doreal's life-long interest in fantasy and science fiction provides a clue to the man beneath the splendorous robes. Growing up on the bleak plains of Oklahoma, he had a fascination for fantasy and science fiction, and later for the occult. Despite claims to the contrary, it is obvious that Doreal's appetite for fiction inspired him to transform fantasy into a very material reality.

In 1963, Doreal fell ill and died without having named a "successor." Shamballa Ashrama continued its activities, and to this day issues the pamphlet, *Armageddon Plan for Safety*. It is as if the failed 1953 Armageddon prophecy never happened.

In 1990, newspapers returned to Shamballa Ashrama to check out stories of attacks from hostile neighbors and discovered a considerably less fantastic place than the one described 30 years earlier. Curiosity seekers visiting the retreat are apparently disappointed to find a "sleepy mountain community fighting off the publicity and sightseers that are a product of the village's storied past." Some visitors come at night to throw rocks at residents' homes, thinking the community houses a white supremacist or satanic cult. In fact, more than half of the 200 residents don't even belong to the Brotherhood. Members carry on Doreal's teachings, but they have apparently lost some of their urgency. They have abandoned their practice of storing food and supplies in preparation for Armageddon. With slick competitors — Elizabeth Clare Prophet's "Summit Lighthouse," the channelers, the UFO religions and exiled Tibetan monks teaching authentic Buddhism — The Brotherhood of the White Temple is now little more than a quaint reminder of outdated notions about the "Mystic East" and the "Secrets of the Tibetan Masters."

Doreal was the classic bibliomanic, buying "every book of that type that's ever been written."

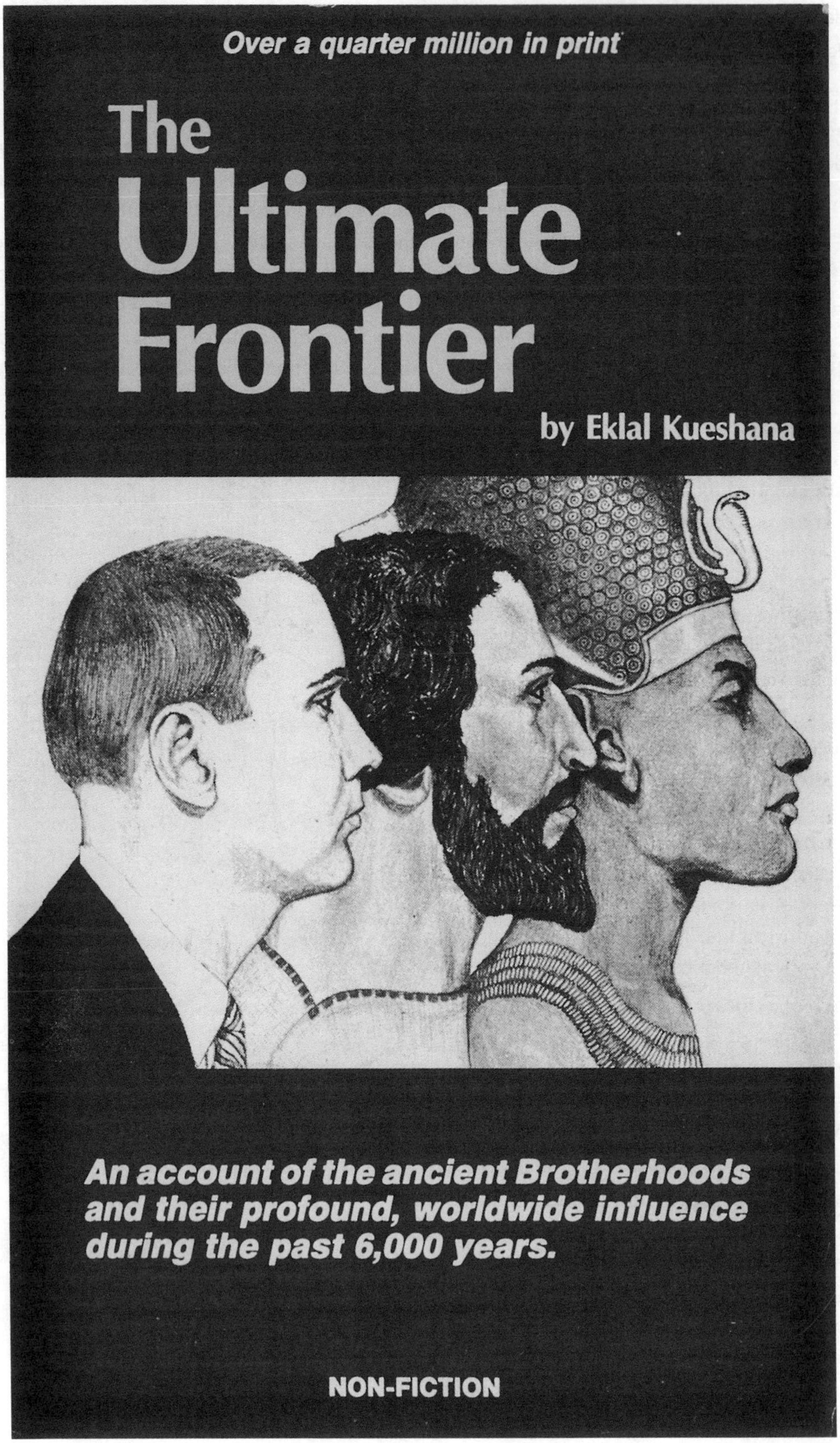
Over a quarter million in print
The Ultimate Frontier
by Eklal Kueshana
An account of the ancient Brotherhoods and their profound, worldwide influence during the past 6,000 years.
NON-FICTION

The cover illustration is titled "Three Men — One Mind," and is said to depict Stelle founder Richard Kieninger, King David and Akhnaton of Egypt.

THE STELLE GROUP

You walk into a New Age bookstore hoping to find THE BOOK THAT WILL GIVE YOU ALL THE ANSWERS, SAVE THE WORLD AND CHANGE YOUR LIFE FOREVER. Perhaps you aren't consciously seeking such a book, but believe, in the back of your mind, that it might exist. You browse the "Metaphysics," "Eastern Religion" and "Self-Help" sections, and can't tell whether the answers will come from an Indian adept, an English Druid or a Venusian Dolphin. Flipping through channelled messages from disembodied spirits and kindly aliens, you notice they all seem to say the same thing — the only difference is in the packaging.

Back in the 1960's, it was still possible to read THE BOOK, realize that it contained THE TRUTH, quit your job, pack your bags, and head — not to California, but to Illinois — to follow the teachings of the Ancient Mystic Brotherhoods of Mankind and help build the Nation of God. THE BOOK was *The Ultimate Frontier,* by **Eklal Kueshana**, and the Nation of God was to begin in Stelle, Illinois with The Stelle Group.

Utopia in Illinois

The Stelle Group began as an intentional community in the tradition of 19th Century utopias. Each new member was required to read *The Ultimate Frontier,* and indeed, the book was the group's only means of recruitment. Those who came to Stelle were self-selected, deeply affected by and in sympathy with its teachings. Even today, members of The Stelle Group use *The Ultimate Frontier* as a guide to living and Truth.

The Ultimate Frontier is written as the biography of a boy named Richard — who is, it turns out, the book's author, **Richard Kieninger,** writing under the pseudonym "Eklal Kueshana." It is an account of Richard's boyhood instruction in Lemurian philosophy,[1] the history of mankind, apocalyptic prophecies, and his role in future world events. Taught by kindly old Dr. White, a member of The Brotherhoods, and by other Brothers, Richard learns he was a Brother in previous lifetimes (Pharaoh of Egypt in one), and has been selected to lead mankind into the new era of brotherly love. Richard — and the reader — learn the answers to the Big Questions — How It All Started, When And How We All Got Here, What We Are, What Our Purpose Is, Where We Are Going.

> *The Ultimate Frontier* is an account of Richard Kieninger's boyhood instruction in Lemurian philosophy.

In Richard's first meeting with Dr. White, an hour-long get-together on Richard's 12th birthday in 1939, he is instructed on such topics as the transmigration of souls and atomic physics. White seems to know the details of Richard's life, and tells the boy he will need to know the secrets of the universe, which hinge on the concept of "nutation," to complete his life's task:

"... In addition to orbiting there is another important motion of all sub-atomic particles, and this motion is called nutation. It is valuable for you to understand nutational motion *because it is the very key to the secrets of the universe.* ... nutation refers to a wobble of the axis of rotation...

"You were an engineer and manufacturer during many of your incarnations in the Poseid Empire. The device for taking motive power directly from the atmosphere was perfected about twenty thousand years ago, and you were among the many who understood its workings. Perhaps you may be instrumental in its rediscovery."

Richard is instructed on the SEVEN PLANES OF EXISTENCE (Physical, Etheric, Astral, Mental, Angelic, Archangelic and Celestial), each with its own distinct nutational rate:

"All the human beings occupying this planet came into existence at the same time — somewhat more than a million years ago.

"At any given time, approximately one-sixth of the human Egos assigned to this planet are incarnated into physical bodies or vehicles. To date, you, Richard, have incarnated almost three thousand times."

The point of all incarnations — not just Richard's — is to allow humans to master each plane of existence, Physical to Celestial, until all are ONE WITH GOD. No one can advance to the Fifth Plane until everyone

1. The Stelle Group calls its philosophy "Lemurian," although its beliefs should not be confused with those of "The Lemurian Fellowship." The relationship between the two groups is explained below.

"In effect, man as a race vegetated. Instead of advancing from innocence to virtue, he remained a clod."

masters the Fourth — although those who flunk the Fourth Plane after 7,000 years of trying will be abandoned, and the Masters will be allowed to advance.

It would be Richard's job, if he wished to take it, to boost humanity to the Fifth Plane of Existence, to please the higher beings who created us, nurtured us, and fought over us, their problem children from the beginning of time. With the help of Lucifer and the Brotherhoods, we would ascend to the Seventh Plane:

"Man on this planet did not progress as was to be normally expected during the first 400,000 years after he began incarnating. Jehovah, having been responsible for our creation, was loathe to bring us to the trials that would make us grow through adversity. Instead, He provided man with a superabundance of readily gathered food in a subtropical climate. That was Eden which was located somewhat north and west of the present Hawaiian Islands. There man lived, bred, ate, and slept. He did not begin upon the path to greatness because he had no need or incentive. In effect, man as a race vegetated. Instead of advancing from innocence to virtue, he remained a clod.

"This state of affairs gave rise to two factions in our Angelic Host. On one side were those who believed, as did Jehovah, that man would attain his destiny more readily in a serene environment free from the distractions of strife. The other faction believed that only through hardship and struggle would men actively seek the better way and thus strive for perfection. ... Those other Angels who differed with Jehovah finally took matters into Their own hands and set about to destroy Eden. This was done under the leadership of the great Angel, Lucifer, to whom we owe the advantages of our present advancement.

"Earthquakes and the first glacial period of the pleistocene epoch destroyed Eden, and man had to struggle to remain alive. ... Man began on the road to advancement."

Richard learns humanity is almost ready for the "unveiling [of] all of the secrets of God which are within the ken of men's minds" and, at the age of 12, must decide if he is up to the challenge of preparing Earth for its big moment. He assents — with some misgivings — and is consecrated on the spot with a new name, *Eklal Kueshana* — meaning "Harbinger of Aquarius, the Judge of Israel, the Builder of Lemuria, and the Fountainhead of Christ." After Dr. White pours the contents of a vial over Richard's head, he instructs the boy to close his eyes; when he opens them, Dr. White is gone.

The ceremony with White is mere preliminary to Richard's real initiation to the Brotherhoods; some months later, taken to a group of Masters, his new name is ceremonially inscribed into his flesh in a private area of his body. Shortly after, the men vanish into thin air, with one exception — Berkeley — a Brother who gives the boy a lesson on the practices and aims of the Brotherhoods.

Berkeley tells Richard the Brotherhoods, organized by Melchizadek (Christ) 20,000 years ago, consist of human beings on the path to mastering the first four Planes of Existence. Their aims are high — to instruct candidates aspiring to human perfection; to garner knowledge of the truths of existence; to preserve a continuous history of mankind; to analyze the causes for success and failure of civilizations; to prepare the way for the Kingdom of God; to implement Christ's plans; to protect and guide the population of the world. Brothers do not reveal their identities as Brothers except to other Brothers. The American Forefathers — Franklin, Jefferson, Washington and Madison — were all students of the Brotheroods, and the establishment of the United States of America was a step toward their final goal. The Great Seal of the United States symbolizes the Brotherhoods' mission.

The Great Pyramid of Gizeh, inscribed on the Great Seal, was built under the Brotherhoods' supervision by an ancient people called the "Hyksos," to record the Brotherhoods' plan for the evolution of a superior society. The Hyksos, according to Berkeley, were "a Semitic-White race that came out of Ethiopia," some of whom later emigrated to Britain and built Stonehenge.

Superior societies once flourished, Richard learns, on the now-sunken continents of Lemuria and Atlantis. Lemuria, the continent where the human race evolved, encompassed most of what is now the Pacific Basin — Australia, New Zealand, the Philippines,

Oceania, Western North America, and everything in between. The first and greatest human civilization arose there 78,000 years ago, lasting 52,000 years until the continent sank following massive earthquakes. Atlantis, Lemuria's successor and known at the time as the "Poseid Empire," lasted 14,000 years until it also sank some 10,500 years ago.

Pole Shift & the Kingdom of God

Richard learns the demise of Lemuria and Atlantis presage our fate, here at the turn of the millennium. The world as we know it will end in a cataclysm known as the "pole shift," caused by ice built up at the poles and other factors that will upset the equilibrium of earth's rotation. On May 5, 2000, the planets in the solar system will be arrayed in an almost straight line; the resulting gravitational pull will upset Earth's delicate balance, sinking the old continents by earthquakes, volcanic eruptions and tidal waves, causing new continents to rise.

Not all will be lost. "The developing state of the Earth's surface structure and the effect that the planets will have upon it," Dr. White assures Richard, "was long ago carefully measured and analyzed by the Masters who, with the aid of Melchizadek, arranged Their program for the establishment of the Kingdom of God to coincide with this horrendous cataclysm." Although Armageddon, described in the Book of Revelation, has begun and will "grow more destructive and vicious as this century draws to its close," ending in "wholesale obliteration" in November, 1999, the one-tenth of the world's population remaining when the pole shift occurs will see it as a "blessing." Those not driven insane by the inevitable death, destruction and decay will rebuild the world, and embody the Kingdom of God.

Finally, Richard is enlisted to establish a fledgling Kingdom near his home town of Chicago well before Doomsday, so that by 2001 the group will be ready to begin the new era. Richard is advised the community must be self-sufficient and must have plans to assure its safety when the cataclysm comes; when the danger has passed, it will safely move to a new home on the "great isle of the West which will rise out of the Pacific Ocean. ...," situated where once Lemuria stood. Dr. White says the growth of the proto-Kingdom will be "phenomenal" a few decades before the turn of the millennium.

The Ultimate Frontier closes with a progress report on development of the Stelle community.

Despite the nature of its information, Kieninger maintains *The Ultimate Frontier* is not fiction. He also claims to be in contact with the Brotherhoods to this day, who are not, by the way, disembodied entities, but real people.

The Stelle Group

Kieninger began fulfilling his destiny in earnest in 1960, when he married a woman who would help him establish the Kingdom of God. The marriage (Kieninger's second) was sanctioned by the Brotherhoods, who told Kieninger that he and his wife, **Gail,** had worked together in past lives. In 1963, Kieninger published *The Ultimate Frontier* and established The Stelle Group. By 1970, The Stelle Group had purchased 240 acres of farmland and established Stelle, Illinois, which eventually contained homes, a woodworking corporation, and a water purification plant, all designed and installed by the members themselves. Kieninger also planned a massive "airlift" to safely house the community during the pole shift.

The community thrived, although its growth was not exactly "phenomenal." Today, with the pole shift less than a decade away, perhaps a few hundred people are involved.

I spoke with both Kieninger, who now resides in Texas, and **Tim Wilhelm,** who is Stelle's current Executive Director, Corporate Secretary and Registered Agent, for an update on Stelle's activities. The story that emerged was significantly different from the Brotherhoods' plan as outlined in *The Ultimate Frontier.* Rather than appearing a wise, spiritual leader, Kieninger ends up looking more like the archetypal cult leader with an overblown ego and sexual appetite. The Stelle Group, rather than the perfect, democratic, cooperative community described in the book, has

Those not driven to insanity by the destruction caused by the pole shift will rebuild the world and embody the Kingdom of God.

become like any other group that's suffered from scandal, lawsuits, power struggles, and schisms, in trouble from its inception.

"Either he had some kind of a hallucination or a vision or he has a very creative imagination, or he really had the experiences he talked about ..."

The Lemurian Fellowship

During the 1950's, Kieninger was a student of a "Wisdom School," The Lemurian Fellowship, begun according to Wilhelm in the late 1930s by **Dr. Robert D. Stelle** (for whom The Stelle Group is named) and **Dr. Howard John Zitko.** Zitko "had some kind of experience that led him to have conscious awareness of ... the Brotherhoods' philosophy," recorded in a book called *The Lemurian Theochristic Conception*. Zitko and Stelle formed the Lemurian Fellowship, and Stelle turned Zitko's manuscript into lesson material for a correspondence course. By the time Kieninger became a student, Zitko left the Fellowship and Stelle had passed away.

Wilhelm says Kieninger and The Fellowship came into conflict because Kieninger founded a rival organization, The College of Christian Minds, while still a Fellowship student. The Fellowship gave Kieninger the choice of either staying with them or The College of Christian Minds, but not both. Kieninger chose the Fellowship and dissolved The College of Christian Minds.

A second conflict arose several years later, when Kieninger established the Stelle Group. The original by-laws of the Stelle Group required each of its members to become students of The Lemurian Fellowship, a stipulation unknown to The Fellowship until its managers noticed a disproportionate number of students from Stelle, Illinois. The Fellowship's director responded with an 11-page open letter to the Stelle community disavowing any connection between The Lemurian Fellowship and The Stelle Group and accusing Kieninger of plagiarism and fraud. Wilhelm adds, "to this day, if you write to the Lemurian Fellowship from Illinois, they are suspect of your intentions."

I asked Wilhelm whether, in his opinion, *The Ultimate Frontier* was plagiarized from Fellowship lessons:

> The whole thing with Mr. Kieninger has been a real enigma to me. That I still, to this day, haven't quite been able to sort out [what he really experienced] that he wrote about as true, and what [he just made up.] Because I have personally caught him in more than a few lies; I have personally caught him in plagiarism; I have personally caught him in forgery... Looking at that track record one has to think, well, it's pretty likely that he did.
>
> At the same time, there are some elements of the writing in *The Ultimate Frontier* which I've not been able to find other sources of, even in the Lemurian Fellowship lessons. Which says to me that either he had some kind of a hallucination or a vision or he has a very creative imagination, or he really had the experiences he talked about. Or it could be some combination of that. ...

As Stelle developed during the early 70s, Kieninger claims he was given "a new assignment" by the Brotherhoods — to warn business and government people in petroleum-rich Texas, of imminent economic collapse:

> [Texas] has something on which to base another currency in the event U.S. currency just takes a nosedive, and that's petroleum, as a desirable commodity throughout the world. Any Texas dollar [would be] based on a given amount of petroleum; you exchange the dollar much like at one time you used to be able to exchange a greenback for a certain amount of silver or a gold certificate for gold of a certain amount, so it would work the same way.

Despite Kieninger's promotional zeal, the petro-dollar never quite took off, even in Texas.

Kieninger left Stelle permanently around 1975. Why he did remains a matter of dispute. Kieninger maintains that he left Stelle for the good of the group, assigning new leaders and maintaining regular, friendly contact with them; only after he suggested divorce from his wife Gail did she and the trustees turn against him, barring him from the community. He implies the conflict was purely ideological.

But according to Wilhelm, "it came out that [Kieninger] was sexually involved with a number of married women in the group." After a hearing before a panel of seven peers, Kieninger was expelled from The Stelle Group and prohibited from entering the premises of the community for a year.

Whatever the reason for Kieninger's departure, the vacuum it produced resulted in a power struggle between the parties remaining. Ultimately, the entire Board of Trustees resigned, and 40 people — including Kieninger's ex-wife Gail, the President of the Corporation and the entire Board of Trustees — left for Wisconsin.

Those left behind later forgave Kieninger, by then residing in Texas, establishing a third group, "The Adelphi Organization." In 1982, he returned to the Board of Trustees as "Chairman of the Board for Life," and the main headquarters for The Stelle Group moved to Texas. This congenial situation didn't last long. According to Wilhelm, by 1986 problems "that went beyond sexual improprieties" cropped up. Kieninger resigned from both The Stelle Group and The Adelphi Organization under duress. Through what Wilhelm describes as "trickery," Kieninger returned to take over what was left of The Adelphi Organization, but by that time, had established yet another group, "The Builders of the Nation," with headquarters near Dallas.

Current Activities

Kieninger is still attempting to build the Nation of God. However, when I asked him whether he believed unshakably in the prediction of the pole shift, he backed off, despite an appearance on the Fox network's super-tabloid show, *Sightings,* where he predicted that after the pole shift, most of the world would end up back in the stone age. He seems to take the view it very well *could* happen, but won't say it absolutely *will* happen. He seems to want it both ways, to take credit for publicizing the pole shift but if it doesn't happen, to be in a position to say, "it was the Brotherhoods who predicted it, so don't look at me":

[The 5/5/2000 pole shift] is not my prediction, so I can't absolutely know that from anything in the past. You know, a lot of things that don't appear in high school and sometimes even in college texts on geological things — for instance, it took a long time after the tectonic plate theory was pretty much accepted by the scientific world, for it to begin to show up in any kind of high school texts. ...

The whole concept of Pangeia just doesn't fit in with the Bible or anything like that, so there's other objections from other quarters. But, geologists have known for quite a long time that in the last 30,000 years, which is a long period of time, there have been three other areas that have been under polar ice when the rest of the world was not covered with ice. That's about every 10,000 years on average; I wouldn't think that anybody could pinpoint the year. The Sudan Basin in Africa was one of those places; the scoreations on the rocks and what have you, expanding glacier and what have you, and the depression in the earth, where more or less fluid mantle was squeezed out, is still rebounding from having had that pressure of ice off of it. Also the Hudson Bay area and the Caspian Sea. All of those were poles in the last 30,000 years. There haven't been any major changes for the last 3500 years, that we know of. So it seems like it's within the range of something which could happen again. Scientists are willing to accept that such a thing can happen; they're not going to stick their neck out though. ...

Kieninger won't stick his neck out either, but he is at least doing his homework. He along with many others have found a mass of evidence corroborating the prediction, ranging from an analysis of The Great Pyramid to observations of ice masses in Antarctica. Apparently even the Druids knew what was going to happen on May 5 of the year 2000:

There's another interesting thing that came up. A new book. I don't know if the name, Trevor Ravenscroft is familiar to you. He wrote *Spear of Destiny.* He came out with a new one called, *Mark of the Beast.* In that, he points out that during the Middle Ages certain cathedrals were constructed atop former Druidic sanctuary sites. The Druids gave each of these the name of a planet, calling them their planetary oracles. And these planetary oracles are geographically located on a line that runs roughly between Spain, north into Scotland. And according to Ravenscroft — he says the arrangement of these planetary oracles on the surface of the Earth forms a prophetic map of the planets in our solar system. And the arrangement of the planets in this, kind of, super map, matches the actual alignment of the planets on May 5, of the year 2000. ...

Since Kieninger's departure from Illinois, The Stelle Group has retreated from predictions of apocalypse. Wilhelm maintains that

Since Kieninger's departure, The Stelle Group has retreated from predictions of apocalypse.

the pole shift was never emphasized in the first place:

It has always been, for as long as I have been aware, a criterion for membership in the Stelle Group that you be in sympathy with the Stelle Group's teachings. Which means that no one was ever expected to believe any of the stuff that Richard had said, but you were expected to be at least in sympathy with it, meaning that you would not work against it, or fight against it. [It] was an attempt to be consistent within our own teachings. Part of our teachings holds that what's called, well, one of Buddha's rules ... embodied in a quote alleged to come from him which is "accept nothing that is unreasonable, but discard nothing as unreasonable without proper investigation."

... That being the case, it's hard to say that one believes in something or doesn't believe in something. ... And I guess what I would say on the whole pole shift prediction is, no we don't believe in it, and no, we never did. But, we've always been sympathetic to it, and we have always done what we can to investigate it and check it out to prove whether it's true or false. Now, in those investigations, it turns out that there is quite a bit more than one would expect to support that premise. ... Now whether or not it would happen on May 5th of the year 2000, who knows?

... There's another way to approach it, and that is, if you think that something is possible, you can choose to operate on the assumption that it may be possible, as a contingency. And that is something the Stelle Group did for years, and continues to do. ...

The massive airlift to house the "Nation of God" during the pole shift was supposed to operate on just that contingency. But Wilhelm and Kieninger both point out the resources necessary to accomplish such a project are prohibitive, and for that reason, it may not be completed in time. Wilhelm says an airlift was never part of the Brotherhoods' plan; the idea was Kieninger's alone. Neither Stelle nor Adelphi are working on an airlift project, lacking the several billion dollars that would be needed.

To my surprise, Wilhelm also revealed The Stelle Group isn't building "The Kingdom of God" either:

[Creating the Kingdom of God] was never part of the Stelle Group's mission. That was something Richard always said was his personal mission. That our mission — The Stelle Group's corporate goal was to focus on the community of Stelle, Illinois, to make that as self-sufficient of a community as it could be, with the ambience being basically governed by the philosophic teachings of the Brotherhoods.

... It's just that Richard threw in these other things, on top of what the corporate mission was, and he also said, like this whole thing with the Nation of God, "This is my personal mission, I may ask the Stelle Group for help on that, but it's not the Stelle Group's responsibility, it's mine." And he never really did get around to asking our assistance on it. ...

The Stelle Group is currently focused on applying the Lemurian Philosophy to their daily lives, not on surviving Doom's Day. This may not sound as impressive as building a Nation of God after Armageddon, but it is probably just as challenging, and no less worthy. Despite several decades of struggle, the group continues to study teachings in *The Ultimate Frontier,* the book that inspired them to seek a better life.

By contrast, the explicit mission of The Adelphi Organization, Kieninger's group in Texas, is to build the Nation of God. This is spelled out in its introductory literature: "The Adelphi Organization serves to gather and teach people who will have the opportunity to assist in all that is required to plan, build and administer the Pacific-island city to be known as Philadelphia. ..." The group also encourages people to donate money to help build it. "Donations to The Adelphi Organization are an important way to hasten the urgent effort to implement the program planned by the Brotherhoods to preserve a remnant of civilization to survive the turn of this century. ..." A donation to Adelphi, then, is no less than a donation to the future of the human race.

PART IV

POLITICS

(SOLUTION TO THE WORLD PROBLEM)

CREDENTIAL OF MR. CHARLES E. BUON GOD'S ENVOY TO THE U.S.A.

Charles to show him the communists of North Korea whom God has used symbolically to represent the rebel angels, the real enemies of America in the invisible world. By that phase of the message, God has not only revealed my name to President Reagan, but also my mission as His Envoy to the United States of America. I was sent to America to denounce and identify her spiritual enemies to the authorities of the present generation. According to God, the facts and logic the communists are not the enemies of the Americans. They are their brothers and sisters.

The role that Leiutenant Charles has played in the Korean message was an image of my spiritual mission as God's Envoy to the United States. I hope that President Reagan in particular and the American people in general shall understand God's strategy to communicate with them despite the infernal barriers of His spiritual enemies.

SIMILARITY OF PROCESSES

At the DMZ of South Korea, God caused President Reagan to be seeking the enemies of America in the material world with the help of a telescope. By that phase of the message, God said to the President: "What you are doing in the material world *now*, do it too in the spiritual world to discover the real enemies of your country."

Note that the President could not see the communists without the help of Lieutenant Charles. Not that because of the remoteness and the location of the said enemies (communitst), the President could not see them without the use of a telescope. When we apply the meaning of the symbolic role of Lieutenant Charles and that of the telescope to the antagonism Capitalism versus Communism, we understand that God's advice to President Reagan is: "Look for the technological help of an Instructor whose name is Charles and you will discover the real authors of the problems that the United States is facing presently."

CENTRAL INTELLIGENCE AGENCY CHURCH IN ACTION CIA+CIA=2 CIA

The greatest objectives of God in the lessons that He has taught to President Reagan on November 13,•1983, are the discovery and identification of the enemies of the United States in the spiritual world. According to God, the U.S. authorities shall discover the real enemies of America if only they orient their researches from the material world to the invisible one.

MEANING OF THE SYMBOLIC ELEMENTS OF THE KOREAN MESSAGE

	SYMBOLS		MEANINGS
1-	President Reagan	=	The U.S. Government, America, the American people.
2-	Lt. Charles Preysler	=	Professor Charles E. Buon
3-	Ann Ji Sook	=	South Korea or Worldwide Capitalism
4-	Lee Kil Woo	=	North Korea or worldwide Communism
5-	Use of telescope	=	Inability to see, lack of clairvoyance
6-	Bags of sand	=	Protection
7-	Raised place	=	Elevation, Domination, Promotion
8-	Children	=	Small nations
9-	Heart	=	Love, compassion, sensibility
10-	Heart disease	=	Difficulties, Sufferings, oppression.
11-	Heart surgery	=	Solution to the problem of an oppressed nation - disinterested love.
12-	American hospital	=	Material and technological possibilities to help an oppressed nations.
13-	Bunch of flowers	=	Victory
14-	Union of Ann and Lee in US	=	Unification of South and North Koreas; or by extension, unification of all communist countries to all capitalist countries, reconciliation of the nations of this world.
15-	Fort Liberty Bell	=	Protection of missionary army in foreign countries
16-	U.S. Flag	=	Founding principles of America
17-	North Koreans, Communists	=	Rebel angels, spiritual enemies of America

THE UNITED STATES IS PLUNGED INTO SPIRITUAL DARKNESS.

SIMILARITY OF THE AMERICAN PROBLEMS IN TWO DIMENSIONS

Symbolically, God used the communists of North Korea to represent the enemies of America in the invisible world. The role that God has asssigned to the North Koreans in the message of November 1983 proves that the communists are not the real enemies of the Americans. They have been called to play the role of enemies in the message as they are playing unwillingly that role under the pressure of the invisible enemies of America. According to God's denunciation to President Reagan, the communists are the images of the real enemies of the American people. As I previously said, Lee Kil Woo, the Korean boy that President Reagan and his wife brought to the United States to undergo a heart surgery, represents all the communist countries of this world. Lee Kil Woo firstly represents the communists of North Korea. However, in spite of his role of communist representative, God confided the healing of his ailing heart to an American hospital under the parental care of Mr. and Mrs. Reagan. That phase of the message means that the U.S. is called to protect the communist as the capitalist countries of this world. This is a divine mission based on love.

In Korea as in many other places, God has denounced the rebel angels as the sole and real authors of the war problem that is devouring Humanity. The Master has clearly showed that the last objective of those revolted angels is the eradication of mankind by a nuclear disaster that they are trying to provoke between the United States and the Soviet Union. So, one more time God clearly says that the enemy of man is not man, but the rebel angels. Consequently, the enemies of America are those of God.

A few pages from a patriotic American's pamphlet, circulated in Cambridge, MA, 1987.

VOLUNTARY HUMAN EXTINCTION

May We Live Long and Die Out.
— Voluntary Human Extinction Movement

It may seem ultimately self-defeating, but there are small organized clandestine cells working on the development of technologies to diminish or even eliminate the race of man from the Earth.
— Vincent M. Cannistraro
National Strategic Information Center

THE ENVIRONMENTAL MOVEMENT HOLDS A special terror for ex-CIA agent Vincent Cannistraro, senior fellow of the National Strategic Information Center, the only conservative think-tank specializing in "intelligence." He fears that, within the radical fringe of the environmental movement, human-hating but earth-loving mad scientists will stop at nothing to save the planet from human damage. They will even go so far as to destroy all or most of the human race to attain that goal, and are developing a virus to wipe out mankind while sparing everything else.

But human extinction crusader **Les U. Knight,** who may well haunt Cannistraro's worst nightmares, is anything but misanthropic. He loves the earth, and despite his stance that we should be phased out, loves humans too. His "life's work" has gelled into what he calls the Voluntary Human Extinction Movement, or VHEMT (pronounced "vehement"), a loose network of people who pledge not to breed, and believe The Solution to the World Problem is the gradual phasing out of the human race by voluntary means only. When asked whether VHEMT Volunteers are largely misanthropic, Knight — vehemently — answers in the negative. "Misanthropes tend to be more of the *involuntary* human extinctionists," he says, "and they would like to see more diseases that we can't cure. ... A third of the mortalities on the planet today are unnecessary. They were people who would not have been born if people had a choice. And they are only born to starve and die horrible deaths. ... The lower the birth rate, the higher the quality of life, for all life, especially for humans."

Knight believes the quality of life will be highest when the human birth rate is zero. He goes beyond the old notion of "Zero Population Growth" to the more advanced idea of zero population. The world and its teeming life forms, presently ailing under the yoke of *Homo sapiens,* Knight asserts, would not miss us. "Humans really are not in anybody's food chain," he points out. "If we disappeared, other than for the fact that all of our naughty little messes would still be around, if it weren't for that, if we could take all that with us, and our domesticated animals, we wouldn't be missed one little bit. In fact, the whole idea is that it would be a great improvement on the planet's life system. The biosphere would breathe a sigh of relief."

Knight goes beyond the tired old notion of "Zero Population Growth" to the more advanced idea of zero population.

The biosphere might sigh, but for many, the idea is unsettling. Not so for Knight, who feels not the slightest nostalgia for our inevitable demise — which would, of course, mark the end of art, music, history, science, philosophy, literature, and baseball, along with all the really bad stuff. "It's just sort of a sadness, the mourning of the passing of something that really had wonderful potential, but somehow went awry," to Knight. "All of the things that humans consider important are only important to humans. They really don't help out anything else. I might be missing something, but I can't think of anything that really is of value to the rest of the planet, the rest of nature, that humans really value. So, when we're gone, all of those things will be gone, and the bears won't miss us, if there are any left by the time we leave."

Those reluctant to phase out our species, Knight believes, are in a state of denial; if they ever face reality, they too will become VHEMT Volunteers.

Voluntary human extinction, as the Solution to the World Problem, may seem an extreme measure to those who're not in touch with their inner Volunteer. To them, Les U. Knight may look like a kook. *Reader's Digest,* which condensed a *New Age Journal* article on VHEMT in April '92, characterized

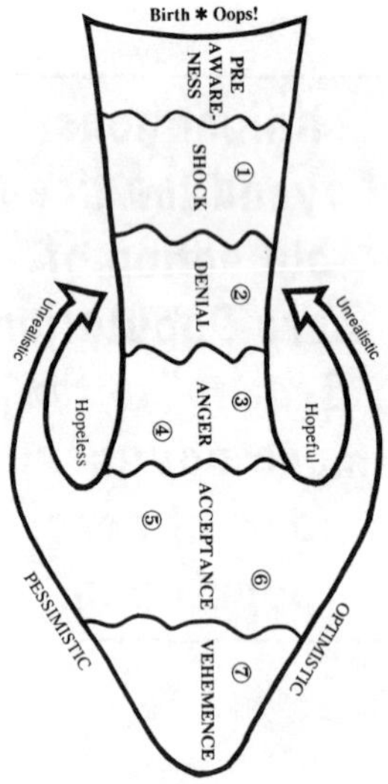

The "Path of Progressive Awareness," from *These Exit Times*

VHEMT as "outrageous!" even as it introduced VHEMT to 100 million readers in 17 languages. *These* EXIT *Times,* the VHEMT newsletter, responded by extending "A hearty 'Thank you!' to the *Reader's Digest* folks," adding, "Their comment, 'Spotlighting absurdities in our society is the first step toward eliminating them,' seems to echo the VHEMT view. One of society's minor absurdities is magazines which are too wide for the toilet tank and keep sliding off the back. Again, the *Digest* and *[These* EXIT *Times]* agree."

Reader's Digest, that bulwark of good old fashioned American common sense, may never recognize the uncommon sense behind VHEMT. Our practice of breeding more humans to fuel a production/consumption treadmill with a never-ending "growth economy" and "full employment" is based on massive delusion. It seems people really think they can atone for their sins of consumption by eating rainforest crunch ice cream, or simply buying things labeled "recyclable." People like to think of themselves as environmentally aware, but would rather not face the fact that each new person is a walking, breathing, environmental disaster.

Why not just commit suicide? "Death comes soon enough. More good can be done by living than by dying," answers Les U. Knight. This is the crux of the matter for VHEMT — human extinction is good, early death is not. But even if human extinction is achieved via non-breeding rather than early death, it must be voluntary: "...[T]he main reason I think it needs to be voluntary is that there is no way to all of a sudden bring about the complete loss of viability of all Homo sapiens' sperm on the planet. ... So, if you set about any sort of involuntary human extinction, it's going to be genocidal, it can't be equal. And that's my biggest objection to it."

It might seem that Volunteers would be hard to come by, but to Knight, everyone is a volunteer or potential volunteer. "There are millions of VHEMT Volunteers," he claims. "Many of 'em don't know it, and they haven't told me about it. But I'm sure that there are millions of people all over the world who have come to the same conclusion that I have. And that is that the planet would be so much better off without humans. And of course if you think it through you'll realize that a voluntary method is really the only workable and moral method of bringing about extinction."

But how do you convince the ever-fruitful teeming millions of breeding-maniacal "potential volunteers" to come around? Stuff envelopes all day or knock on doors soliciting donations? Les is not looking for that kind of volunteer.

The movement, he says, has never gotten its members together; the chance is less than nil that it ever will. "The Volunteers come from such a diverse range of people that it might be better if they never actually got together and talked about it. Although it'd be wonderful to think that we could all get along. I correspond with people who I know would not like each other, because they have such different views, and yet, they both think that the planet would be better off without humans and that a voluntary extinction is the best way to go." Though VHEMT issues a newsletter, makes available bumper stickers with slogans like "Thank you for not breeding," and "May we live long and die out," this movement eschews hidebound activist tactics, such as marches on Washington.

Since volunteers reproduce the newsletter, Knight doesn't even know how many copies are in circulation. The first issue, used for outreach, is an introduction to and clarification of some potential misconceptions about the movement. It explains:

> *These* EXIT *Times* doesn't carry on about how the human race has shown itself to be a greedy, amoral parasite on the once-healthy face of this planet. That type of negativity offers no solution to the inexorable horrors which human activity is causing.
>
> Rather, *These* EXIT *Times* presents The Movement's encouraging alternative to the callous exploitation and wholesale destruction of the Earth's ecology.
>
> As Volunteers know, the hopeful alternative to the extinction of millions, probably billions, of species of plants and animals is the voluntary extinction of one species; Homo sapiens... us.

An editorial, "Les Talk" from Knight Himself, is a pro-vasectomy pep-talk, exhorting men to "... stop just talking about women's rights and dare to put your balls where your mouth is." He reminds them that women have "endured painful IUDs and side effects from the pill... abortions, miscarriages and, yes, even live births," while "most of us won't even endure a layer of latex rolled over the business end of our private parts." He pleads, "Come on, men! Somebody's getting screwed here, f'cryin' out loud," concluding "as millions can testify, being sterile ends the muss and fuss of contraception for the rest of your life. ... Tie the lover's knot and you'll never have to say you're sorry. ..."

There are, of course, many still untied knots out there, and many, many men who do have to say they're sorry, though some don't even say that. The often unhappy result — a visit to the local abortion clinic, or, worse, a baby. But VHEMT favors abortions "only when someone is pregnant." Knight adds, "Pregnancy, of course, should be prevented whenever possible. Unwanted pregnancy is the cause of almost all abortions, and VHEMT certainly doesn't favor unwanted pregnancy. The Movement doesn't even favor *wanted* pregnancies. If there were no need for abortions there would be no abortions."

How did Knight achieve such enlightenment? What gave him the courage to lead a crusade that runs counter to almost every notion in every culture on earth? Knight's history, to hear him tell it, began when he left the army:

> Well, it was shortly after being released from Uncle Sam's military that I got involved in the ecology movement, which was sort of new as far as having a name and popularity. And I could see that all roads led back to humans, and just basic human activity, and that no matter how good you were, we still pretty much flush the toilet the same way ... none of the service stations offered gas that didn't pollute the air, and I could see that our choices were fairly limited. We could reduce our impact, but it was still gonna be pretty heavy. And that each new person we produced would automatically be a 72-year average of consumption and pollution.
>
> This simple realization was the beginning of my life's work.
>
> ZPG was only a few years young then, and *The Population Bomb* about the same age. Both recommended stopping at two children... two being as radical as people seemed to be able to handle at the time. No doubt some listened, but the world's population growth rate continued to grow. It became obvious to me that nothing short of a worldwide moratorium on births would be enough to spare the planet.
>
> I projected the moratorium 21 years into the future. The world looked good. In the vision, deaths from childbirth, child abuse, juvenile delinquency, and so on were eliminated. Expensive items from disposable diapers to station wagons and new houses became unnecessary. Best of all, the Earth's biosphere would get some needed relief. All I had to do was share this discovery with everyone and they would surely agree.
>
> Like many of you, I went through quite a few phases on my way to vehemence. My naive optimism was soon replaced with righteous indignation, then lapses of apathy, and on beyond anger.
>
> In 1977 I founded GreenWar—Oregon and began the Arm the Whales movement as commander-in-chief. When the whales refused to fight, I realized that the violent methods human beings so often use to deal with problems is a major part of the problems in the first place. If the whales could forgive humans, so could I. The Voluntary Human Extinction Movement was the obvious choice. ...

"It became obvious to me that nothing short of a worldwide moratorium on births would be enough to spare the planet."

Les U. Knight joined the whales in the underworld of deep ecology, and there was no burrowing back. He had the awesome task before him of convincing the rest of the world to join him. The "Eco Depth Gauge," which asks the musical question, "How deep is your ecology?" might be a start for the potential volunteer. The gauge describes a continuum of ecological depth, ranging from "Superficial: We should take good care of our planet, as we would any valuable tool" to "Abysmally Deep: A quick annihilation is too good for humans. A horrible, fatal illness from outer space is only fair."

Vincent Cannistraro's "mad environmentalists" would probably reside in the netherworld of Abysmally Deep ecology; VHEMT Volunteers would generally fall around the Profoundly Deep level: "Humans are too great a threat to life on Earth. The species should be phased out."

As the potential Volunteer digs down to Profoundly Deep ecology (being careful not to dig further), he or she will visit the stages on the "Path of Progressive Awareness," leading from pre-awareness to shock, denial, hopeful anger, hopeless anger, hopeless acceptance, hopeful acceptance, and on to the final stage of vehemence.

The Path of Progressive Awareness could be the foundation of a New Age religion, but VHEMT has no allegiance to any particular spiritual practice or religion; Knight asserts its goal does not conflict with any religion that he knows of, despite the Judeo-Christian mandate to "be fruitful and multiply."

There are passages right along with those that say, "be fruitful and multiply," and "subdue the earth," that say that the earth belongs to God and that we've gotta take care of it, because it is God's, it's not ours. "And so by bringing about extinctions of species, if somebody reads the Bible closely, and not selectively, they'll see that Christians should endorse an ecological point of view. ... I'm sure there are some people who consider themselves Christians who think that it's just a horrible thing that we want to bring about the extinction of the human race, and yet their own beliefs speak of a time when there will be no humans on the planet.

A group of Christian VHEMT Volunteers even put together a little column for *These* EXIT *Times* #2 identifying biblical quotes that support voluntary human extinction. "Woe unto them that join house to house, that lay field to field, 'til there be no place, that they may be placed alone in the midst of the Earth!" (Isaiah 5:8) is clearly a warning against overbreeding. "Blessed are the barren, and the wombs that never bore, and the breasts which never gave suck" (Luke 23:29) is a go-ahead from Jesus to become a VHEMT Volunteer — and Jesus, as we all know, was himself a Volunteer.

Having reached 100 million potential Volunteers through the auspices of mass media, the Voluntary Human Extinction Movement may be spreading — like Cannistraro's human extinction virus — at this very moment. But the VHEMT virus will not cause human suffering, it will cure it forever.

For those who have not caught the VHEMT virus, who are still looking for the Solution to the World Problem, Les U. Knight advises: "Some say, 'If you're not part of the solution, you're part of the problem.' Actually, we're both the problem and the solution. Look around and you'll see the problem. Look within and you'll find the solution."

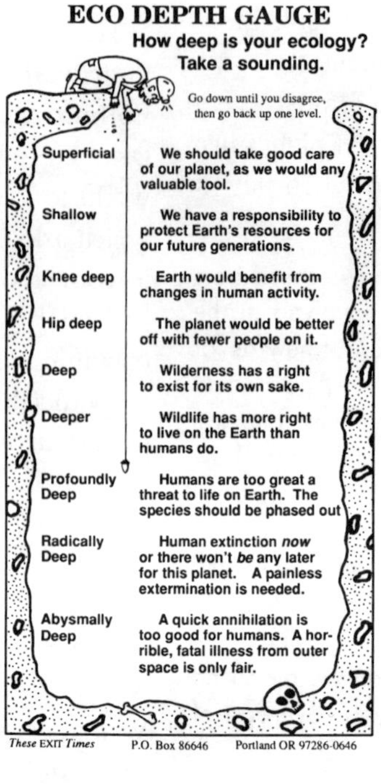
ECO DEPTH GAUGE
How deep is your ecology?
Take a sounding.
Go down until you disagree, then go back up one level.
Superficial
We should take good care of our planet, as we would any valuable tool.
Shallow
We have a responsibility to protect Earth's resources for our future generations.
Knee deep
Earth would benefit from changes in human activity.
Hip deep
The planet would be better off with fewer people on it.
Deep
Wilderness has a right to exist for its own sake.
Deeper
Wildlife has more right to live on the Earth than humans do.
Profoundly Deep
Humans are too great a threat to life on Earth. The species should be phased out
Radically Deep
Human extinction now or there won't be any later for this planet. A painless extermination is needed.
Abysmally Deep
A quick annihilation is too good for humans. A horrible, fatal illness from outer space is only fair.
These EXIT Times
P.O. Box 86646
Portland OR 97286-0646

J.C. "BIRDBRAIN" BRAINBEAU'S 4-WAY PEACE PLAN

THE TIME IS APPROACHING When your best bet is to stop laughing at birdbrain BRAINBEAU and start laughing at yourself. Coming events will prove who the real birdbrains are and you could be among them unless you change your thinking. That's chancy because it took a W.W.II. head injury incident for this "brain" to become the world's ONLY radical — the sole possessor of the only peace plan that can bring peace (thirty years in the making). Send SASE to: 4 WAY PEACE PLAN ... — J.C. Brainbeau

Lieutenant **George E. Lemon,** Post 1445, recipient of the Purple Heart, was officially welcomed home from World War II 48 years late. In 1991, nurses at the Blackburn Home for Aged People in Poland, Ohio saw fit to finally give Lt. Lemon what he had deserved since the spring of 1943, when he was discharged following a serious head injury from a jeep accident during the North African campaign.

Lt. Lemon could easily have become either an embittered or feeble-minded old veteran after such an experience, but instead he "wobbled" his brain and became... **J.C. Brainbeau**.[1]

All my brain needed was a tilt and I gave it one. In my pup tent on the shores near Bizerte I visualized the coming dangers but nothing shook me up until a superior officer told me to defuse land mines until one blew up in my face — THAT shook me up. Immediately began a me-to-me talkathon which has given yours truly the only way to end war, inflation, unemployment, trade deficits and death. ...

Despite the non-stop "me-to-me talkathon" on Brainbeauism, George E. Lemon worked steadily for the Youngstown Sheet and Tube Company, living a quiet life with his two unmarried sisters in his home town of Youngstown, Ohio. Brainbeauism had not yet entered the annals of the Mail Order publications, though probably Lemon spoke of his revelations to his family and friends. It wasn't until his retirement at age 72 — 20 years after his discharge — that Brainbeau was unleashed upon the world.

Brainbeau didn't seek publicity for his ideas in the usual manner, however; instead of writing a book or handing out flyers to passersby, he used an as-yet undeveloped medium: the classified advertisement. Before he died in 1992, Brainbeau had expanded the concept of the classified ad to previously unheard-of dimensions.

Philosophical ads existed before Brainbeau. They can still be found in the back pages of magazines like *Gnosis, Fate* or *Biblical Archeology Review*. Typically, such ads proclaim "Esoteric Secrets of the Egyptians can be Yours," "You Possess Hidden Powers," and once in a while something like, "Jesus Never Existed." While ads such as these might lead you something philosophical, their main purpose is to peddle books and amulets, not to communicate ideas.

For Brainbeau, the ads themselves were esoteric truths. Those who sent Self Addressed Stamped Envelopes (SASE) to Brainbeau expecting to receive literature, products or information received even more ads! They revealed Brainbeau's plans, bit by bit, ad by ad. Several sheets of closely spaced Brainbeau ads could be fit together like a jigsaw puzzle, but the resulting picture would be just another sheet of ads.

Brainbeau hovered near three major themes: 4-WAY PEACE PLAN, EVEN-AGE WORK FORCE, and HEREBEFORES. All outlined ways of righting four wrongs: War, Atheism, Unemployment and Death.

... Inflationary fixed wages should be unfixed — produce more or less — earn more or less, workers should receive a fixed percentage of a company's income and I would suggest 50%. An even age work force would give a person close to 50% of what he or she produced or its equivalent. A comparable amount would go to those under 20 and over 60 and be paid by the 'others' of a 50/50 workers, others money split. This herenow should be balanced with herebefores

Are the 52 all that free?
Aren't we all hostage to 100% wrong fixed wages, winnerless wars unemployment and death?
Send S.A.S.E. to:
4 WAY PEACE PLAN
Box 2243 Youngstown, Ohio, 44504

H's a natural Law that each
Fallen soldier (loser) should trigger a chance-selected winner (civilian again). It's also only natural that the PRINCE OF PEACE should be the first BIRDBRAIN that concerns him or her self with the adoption of this non-suicidal war-ending concept.
Drop a SASE on: BRAINBEAU'S Winners
Box 2243 Youngstown, Ohio, 44504

There Are No Atheists
In fox-holes and when the 4 Way Peace Plan is adopted - no "fox-holes" in this world and part of the next. Spirit a SASE to 4 W, Box 2243, Youngstown, Ohio, 44504

IF MADISON AVENUE
Seems half-deserted maybe the deserters are out on assignment wearing WORK GLOVES. Send SASE to world-changing (for the better)
EVEN AGE WORK FORCE PLAN
Box 2243 — Youngstown, Ohio, 44504

1. Woody Russell wrote several biographical texts on Brainbeau, some of which he published in various issues of the National Hobby News. The biographical information in this article is derived from those texts. The quotations are from Brainbeau's classified ads.

HOW WE CAN PRESERVE
The integrity of the
Social Security System —
establish mentarian.
The year 'round paying even
age (20/60) work force plan
should produce enough to feed,
clothe and house all of us)
DISESTABLISHMENTARIAN.
Send SASE to all-embracing
year 'round paying
EVEN AGE WORKERS
Box 2243
YOUNGSTOWN — OHIO, 44504

IF BIRDBRAIN
BRAINBEAU'S CONCEPTS
Puzzle you it's because Nature
makes us adjust to the 100%
wrong way of doing things
which has been in effect since
the year one. Thanks to a W.W.II
jeep accident head injury inci-
dent I gotmaladjusted in 1943
Send S.A.S.E. to:
4 WRONGS RIGHTED
Box 2243
YOUNGSTOWN — OHIO, 44504

IF YOU ARE BETWEEN
50 and 80 buy life insurance
'A LA ED McMAHON.
Better yet — If you are ANY age
get life insurance for this and
the next world
'A LA BRAINBEAU.
Send S.A.S.E. to:
4 WAY HEREBEFORES
Box 2243
YOUNGSTOWN — OHIO, 44504

TRENCH WARFARE
May be a thing of the past but
NOT THE REPERCUSSIONS.
Its suicidal strategy still pre-
vails. We should come up with
CHANCE-SELECTED WINNERS
to match the losers.
End suicide — Don't be a RED
all your life. Send S.A.S.E. to:
WINNERS — Box 2243
YOUNGSTOWN — OHIO, 44504

and hereafters. There were other concepts and they all followed a pattern as exemplified by the terms 50/50; men, women; winners, losers; odd, even; herebefore, hereafter; etc., etc. If you want to keep on living in this herenow or in past and future herenows earn your keep on the production line at the grass roots level. Send SASE to A PERFECT WORLD .

Volunteer or drafted today's defense forces should have a 50/50 (men, women), losers, winners (chance-selected) war-waging strategy...

As Brainbeau saw it, the four major wrongs did not have four solutions, but one — **The 50/50 Split.** The details of Brainbeau's plans to apply The 50/50 Split to each wrong were hard to spot, even in the longer ads. Rather than detailed solutions, the ads presented a question or problem to get us thinking, concluding with a hint of the Brainbeauistic solution:

I HAVE Some good news and some bad news for our latest 20 million dollar lottery winner. The good news is that he will win 20 million dollars 20 million times and more in future lifetimes ad infinitum (herenow reruns). The bad news is that to insure eternal life we must adopt or have adopted a money independent economy where everyone does or did his or her share of blue collar work — no free riders. Send SASE to: SCRAP SOCIALISM...

The 50/50 split revelation as applied to eternal life yields religion, Brainbeau style. He doesn't talk much about God, Sin or Faith, only about Herebefores and Herenow Reruns:

DO I BELIEVE IN ETERNAL LIFE? It's more probable to just hit the dartboard than it is to hit the bull's eye. Also one is more likely to be living in a million year span than in one of seventy years more or less. I was as much an atheist as anyone until I wobbled my brain with an imaginative above-the-line-of-duty order from a superior officer following a jeep accident head injury. To my rescue came a me-to-me talkathon which has allowed this birdbrain to come up with all the answers to ending war, inflation, unemployment and death. For a 20th century herebefore religion send SASE to HERENOW RERUNS...

QUESTION: If my life is the spit and image of each of my herebefores just how long would you say I've been living — 10,000 years? ANSWER: It would probably be more. If we put the unfolding line of eternal life on a limitless dartboard those millenniums would be in the bull's eye which is more difficult to hit than the whole board. My guess is that you and I have been around a million lifetimes more or less and that more or less is seventy million years. For a 20th century arithmetically and spiritually sound religion send SASE to: HERENOW RERUNS...

Brainbeau claimed this "HELL ON EARTH" is the HEREAFTER, and that all of his solutions, including the EVEN AGE WORKFORCE and the 50/50 WORKERS, OTHERS MONEY SPLIT were "adopted a million years ago more or less," during HEREBEFORES, or previous lifetimes. This means that a million years ago, more or less, Brainbeau was saying

WORLD-WIDE UNEMPLOYMENT WOULD BE ZERO IF EVEN AGE People between 20 and 60 shared equally the working-class work while the odd ages took full pay full year vacations or whatever. For this and other concepts that were adopted (let's hope) eons ago Send a SASE to World-Wide Peace and Prosperity Forever or simply PEACE...

And:

"Is there a CURE to the economic MESS that exists in this country?" Yes - it was discovered and instituted a million years ago more or less. As opposed to fixed wages it's called UNFIXED wages. That's a 50/50 (workers, others) money split. The "others" (odd age people) pay for today's tax-supported expenditures on a wheel-of-chance basis resulting in zero taxes, 5% profit and 5% interest rate. ...

With leisure time dramatically increased by Brainbeau's EVEN AGE WORKFORCE — now, a million years ago, or a million years in the future — many people will (and did) need more options for recreation. For this eventuality, Brainbeau invented a "CARD CADDY" that brought the Laws of Chance to your own living room:

It's a Playing Cards Caddy
It's a living room Vegas.
It's a conversation piece.
It's a thoughtful gift.
It's a Brainbeau brainstorm.
And it's ten dollars!

The CARD CADDY was one of many Brainbeau inventions; by the end of his life, he had a total of 13 U.S. patents, four pertaining to steel, nine pertaining to sports. Brainbeau was interested in "CHANCE" in all its forms, and could reportedly detail the pertinent data on every horse that ever ran in the Kentucky Derby.

To the end of his life, Lemon/Brainbeau lived as a bachelor, enjoying the simple pleasures of ballroom dancing, reading, inventing, puttering and writing classified ads to help save the world. George E. Lemon was humble about his achievements, claiming he couldn't point to any one accomplishment out of the ordinary. From beyond the grave, however, Brainbeau says over and over and over and over again:

$$

QUESTION:
Who do you think will be our next president or maybe our next Jesus Christ or maybe both?
ANSWER:
Unless someone else has had the same war theater experience I had you are stuck with me — BIRDBRAIN BRAINBEAU.
The other guy if one exists is talking to himself at a mile-a-minute clip since his imaginative above-the-line-of-duty order from a superior officer. I presume he thinks or will think as I do about ending war, inflation, unemployment, deficit spending and death. May the best man win. After 33 years I thought I had the ism to end isms with my 4 way peace plan but it took another 10 years to come up with concept #5. It ends trade deficits by paying workers with hours worked certificates that would be used to buy products made in the U.S.A. ONLY. For a world-wide platform that had to be adopted in a previous herenow send S.A.S.E. to:
5 WRONGS RIGHTED
Box 2243 — YOUNGSTOWN, OHIO, 44504

$$

IT'S A DIRTY TRICK of nature that all of us save one are unable to suggest the four new concepts that must be adopted by everyone if we are to survive the 20th century. Blame it on the rest of you lacking a truth-revealing, war-theater-jeep-accident-head-injury incident to: 4 WAY PEACE PLAN...

$$$$$$$$$$$$$$$$$$$$$$$$$$$$$$$$$$

"THANKS TO FOREIGN COMPETITION OR AUTOMATION..."
You read it every day espoused by some free-riding newspaper correspondent. To end unemployment en toto send SASE to all-embracing WORLD WIDE EVEN AGE WORK FORCE or simply EVEN AGE
Box 2243
YOUNGSTOWN — OHIO, 44504

$$$$$$$$$$$$$$$$$$$$$$$$$$$$$$$$$$

$$$$$$$$$$$$$$$$$$$$$$$$$$$$$$$$$$

A FIRST, SECOND OR THIRD Rate mechanic shouldn't be out of work and won't be when the even age work force plan IS ADOPTED.
Everyone works in tomorrow's world (hello, Carson - hello, Doc and gets a year long paid vacation). End free riding and unemployment. Send SASE to all-embracing inescapable EVEN AGE
Box 2243
YOUNGSTOWN — OHIO, 44504

$$$$$$$$$$$$$$$$$$$$$$$$$$$$$$$$$$

$$$$$$$$$$$$$$$$$$$$$$$$$$$$$$$$$$

ADVERTISING Supported newspaper, radio and T.V. personnel will be the last to lose their "JOBS". There won't be any production workers they can rip off. End free riding. Send SASE to unemployment-ending, inescapable year 'round paying EVEN AGE WORK FORCE
Box 2243
YOUNGSTOWN — OHIO, 44504

$$$$$$$$$$$$$$$$$$$$$$$$$$$$$$$$$$

$$$$$$$$$$$$$$$$$$$$$$$$$$$$$$$$$$

WHAT IF THAT Circus clown walking on stilts tried it with just one stilt? That's the trouble with each of the world's defense forces. You go into battle with a chance to lose (get killed) but no chance to win (go home). For a war-ending strategy fire a SASE at: LOSERS, WINNERS (chance-selected) or simply WINNERS — Box 2243
YOUNGSTOWN — OHIO, 44504

$$$$$$$$$$$$$$$$$$$$$$$$$$$$$$$$$$

4 IT'S BRAINBEAU OR BUST 4

WINNERS		LOSERS
FIFTY		FIFTY
EVEN		ODD
HEREBEFORE		HEREAFTER

DEFENSE-MONEY-WORK-RELIGION

4 CONCEPTS A LA BRAINBEAU 4

ALFRED LAWSON

Author of

"MANLIFE"
"CREATION"
"BORN AGAIN"
"DIRECT CREDITS"
AND MANY OTHER BOOKS

Inventor of

THE AIRLINER
TRANS-OCEANIC FLOAT SYSTEM
TWO-TIER PASSENGER COMPARTMENT
AND MANY OTHER MECHANICAL DEVICES

The Discoverer of

THE CAUSE OF SEX
THE CAUSE OF GROWTH
THE CAUSE OF EVOLUTION
THE CAUSE OF ATTRACTION
THE CAUSE OF CONSCIOUSNESS
THE CAUSE OF CAPILLARY ACTION
ZIG-ZAG-AND-SWIRL MOVEMENT
CONTINUOUS MOVEMENT OF MATTER
THE LAW OF PENETRABILITY
THE EQUAEVERPOISE

The Founder of

LAWSONOMY—The knowledge of Life
THE DIRECT CREDITS SOCIETY

PRESENTS TO THE WORLD

LAWSONOMY

VOL. 1. Cloth Bound, 223 Pages, Price $[illegible] 10,00

HUMANITY PUBLISHING COMPANY

Publishers

LAWSONOMY

It's regrettable there isn't some sort of Nobel Prize which would recognize [Lawson's] fantastic career and incredible literary output.

— Martin Gardner

To try and write a sketch of the Life and works of Alfred W. Lawson in a few pages is like trying to restrict space itselff.

— Cy Q. Faunce

Let's thank GOD for LAWSONOMY.

— Alfred Lawson

In 1933, 16,000 frustrated victims of the Great Depression hung on every word of **Alfred W. Lawson's** two-hour speech at Detroit's Olympia Auditorium. Lawson roared about the evils of finance, especially the practice of usury.

Assembled for what was described as "the greatest parade in the history of Michigan," the crowd cheered Lawson for a full fifteen minutes.

As he wrote in *Direct Credits for Everybody:*

> Interest is the thief of everybody. The human race has stood for many slick schemes during the past that made slaves of everybody, but the scheme that allows those with money to tax those without it, is the worst that people have ever had to put up with.
>
> It robs the government, it robs the manufacturer, it robs the merchants, and it robs workmen. It robs everybody except a few financiers who control the money, and by its control, gain the power to stifle governments, industry, trade and employment.

Lawson founded the The Direct Credits Society in 1931 to provide the solution to the World Problem. He wrote and published *Direct Credits for Everybody* that same year. Characterized by Martin Gardner as "worthless," Lawson's plan was more a list of complaints than a system.

The substance of Lawson's proposal was to replace money with "Direct Credits," abolishing the gold standard and making currency itself the standard of exchange. The new paper currency would be issued directly to everyone in sufficient quantity to ensure economic equality. The government would control the currency and issue all loans; private banking, private loans and interest would be abolished. Money would be issued only in exchange for actual value given or service provided — or to those unable to provide value or service.[1] Under Lawson's plan, there would be no "speculation" and no stock market, and therefore no financiers who collect wealth but provide no goods or services in return. In a time of deprivation and capitalism's dysfunction, the socialist plan was welcomed by many.

To round out his program, Lawson advocated further socialistic proposals to provide for the needy, the young, and the elderly without so-called "charity." Lawson wanted to replace "charity" with "justice."

Other Talents

Lawson's many talents — he invented the commercial airliner and investigated the causes of consciousness and sex, not to mention an eighteen year stint in professional baseball — had to remain in the background while he devoted himself to stirring up the masses. Previously, Lawson began his monumental study of Life itself — *Lawsonomy,* in which he cracked the principles of creation — *Equaeverpoise, Zig-Zag-and-Swirl,* and *Penetrability* — but Direct Credits would be his ticket to popularity. "It may be," he wrote, "as some intellectuals say, that Lawson's *Creation* is the greatest book ever written by anybody, but it is a fact that *Direct Credits for Everybody* is the book that thrills everybody that reads it, that is, those who have spark of Justice within themselves."

The Direct Credits Society, like other idealistic movements from the Depression era, shriveled when times improved. The Direct Credits Society continues to operate to this day under the moniker "The Humanity Benefactor Foundation," reprinting and distributing old Direct Credits broadsides as well as numerous volumes on Lawsonomy, which, following the decline of the Direct Credits movement, revealed Lawson's solution to the world's *real* problem, *Humanity.*

Lawson's many talents — he invented the commercial airliner, and investigated the causes of consciousness and sex, not to mention an eighteen year stint in professional baseball — had to remain in the background while he devoted himself to stirring up the masses with his Direct Credits program.

1. Abuse and corruption under this system seems quite likely, given that other options to fuel greed would be cut off. Lawson didn't address the possible abuses.

Alfred Lawson, aviator

Each volume on Lawsonomy begins and ends with portions of Lawson's biography authored by a "Cy Q. Faunce," no doubt Lawson himself. The biographical accounts are worshipful, almost hagiographic, like a child's biography of Sir Isaac Newton or George Washington. It is well nigh impossible to escape the hyperbolic allusions to Lawson's monumental achievements on almost every page.

We learn time and time again in the volumes on Lawsonomy that Alfred William Lawson was born in London, England, on March 24, 1869, to Robert Henry Lawson, an Oxford-educated mechanical engineer, inventor and theological scholar, and Mary Anderson Lawson, "a student of economics." Three weeks after his birth, the family moved to Windsor, Ontario; four years later, they crossed the U.S. border to Detroit, and became American citizens.

As a boy, Lawson hawked newspapers and blacked boots on the streets of Detroit. "Even at that early age Lawson used to contemplate on the absurd Economic System under which the people tried to live, as he noted that those who did the hardest work wore the poorest boots, while those who did no work at all wore the best boots." Even at a tender age, Lawson was questioning the educational system. He decided reading and writing were useful but "arithmetic was a cheat's invention used by people to defraud one another."

Lawson the reformer soon gave way to "Al" the normal boy who, in 1888, became a professional pitcher for minor league baseball teams in Indiana, Illinois and Wisconsin. By 1890, he was pitching in the major leagues. "But even as a boy," he wrote of himself, "Lawson was not satisfied with playing away his life ... Later he became known as the greatest organizer of baseball leagues in America, having established eleven different minor leagues." Baseball brought out the innovator in Lawson, as well; he introduced electric light to the sport in 1901, "when he invented a portable outfit that went from city to city, lighting up ball parks for night games."

Lawson the capitalist earned a "fortune" as owner of numerous ball clubs, but was soon corrupted by money, tobacco, alcohol, and meat. His health deteriorated, but Lawson saw the light and saved himself. Lawson naturally mined this inspiring experience in his first book, *Born Again,* a utopian novel described by Martin Gardner as "one of the worst works of fiction ever printed." Although Lawson was still waist-deep in the baseball business, his career as an author had begun in earnest.

Born Again may have been bad fiction, but it predicted several technological advances that were soon realized. He wrote about how poisonous gas could be employed in warfare a dozen years before World War I. Other predictions were more fanciful: " ... a city can be ... built entirely under one roof, a mile or more high. ... the streets can be made to run vertically as well as horizontally, with car service going upward and downward as well as forward and backward, at different levels and with suitable connections made altitudinally as well as latitudinally and longitudinally. ... sunlight is a substance and that it is possible to harness or mix it with matter of greater density and utilize the compound for lighting purposes ..."

Although influenced by the spiritualists of his time, Lawson went further, anticipating the concerns of current New Age prophets. He discussed thought transferrence and transmigration of the soul, and suggested that if earthlings all meditated together at once they could direct the consciousness of the entire universe.

Destined for greater things than baseball, Lawson quit the business in 1908 and put his technical abilities to work in aviation, founding the world's first aeronautical magazines, *Fly* and *Aircraft.* Lawson claimed to have coined the word "aircraft" — though *Webster's Ninth New Collegiate Dictionary* maintains the word was first used at least nineteen years before Lawson was born — and registered it as a U.S. trademark. He was ridiculed for his insistence that airplanes had the potential to be fighting machines, but was vindicated when he began designing and building fighter aircraft during World War I. But his greatest achievements were yet to come.

In 1919, Lawson "amazed the world" by inventing and piloting the first commercial airliner, which seated 26 passengers comfortably He flew from Milwaukee to New York and Washington, D.C., and back again to Milwaukee, carrying over 200 passengers including ten U.S. senators. A *New York Times* article said, "Provision has been made for cooking light meals, and yesterday the passengers enjoyed an impromptu tea en route from Syracuse. ... The plane is lighted by electricity." The flight proved to the world that commercial aviation was not only possible, but profitable.

Amazing Al established the Lawson Aircraft Corporation to develop his airliner with sleeping berths, shower, heated cabin, mail chute, and other luxuries. His company won a contract to carry the nation's mail, although the contract fell through in a financial recession. This financial disappointment may have contributed to Lawson's desire to reform the economic system.

Lawsonomy, the general volume on Lawson' philosophy, begins with the principles of Life and Space, and ends with Lawson's career in aviation. In between are chapters on Earth, Power, Zig-Zag-And-Swirl, Vibration, Swirlation, Rest, Nourishment, and Law, to name a few. (Other volumes, such as *Creation* and *Manlife* cover similar material albeit with a slightly different focus.)

At first glance, Lawson's terminology looks like camouflage for ignorance. On closer inspection, Lawsonomy is an internally consistent system based on a few basic principles that make sense — that is, if you forget everything you ever learned about physics, chemistry and biology. Forget about time, energy, and Newton's Laws. But most importantly, forget Scientific Theory. "Theory as espoused by the so-called wise men or self-styled scholars has no place in Lawsonomy. Everything must be provable or reasonable or it is not Lawsonomy." The student of Lawsonomy must arrive with a clean slate and a desire to absorb TRUTH. "Lawsonomy stands for Truth as against falsity; constructiveness as against destructiveness. It stands for life, love, freedom and true expression as against the misrepresentation, hate, slavery and death of falsity. So if it isn't real; if it isn't truth; if it isn't knowledge; if it isn't intelligence; then it isn't Lawsonomy."

Truth begins with Lawsonomy, but Lawsonomy begins with *Suction* and *Pressure*, the *Law of Penetrability, Equaeverpoise* and *Zig-Zag-and-Swirl* movement. These concepts, Lawson assures his readers, unlock the mysteries of the Universe. They apply to Everything, — Matter in Space — and follow *Lawson's* Laws.

Lawson's first law: *There is no limit to the smallness of Space*. Space is everywhere and contains everything, but has no properties of its own; it's an empty vessel. Inside the vessel is all Matter, composed of *Substances* of varying *Density*. The property of Density causes all other properties, and all physical events, as well.

This is where Suction and Pressure enter the picture. *Pressure* is "Force caused by substances of greater density falling toward Space with lesser density," while *Suction* is "Force caused by Space with lesser density drawing toward it substances of greater density." Just about every event in Life and Space is caused by Suction and Pressure. An example of the dynamics of Suction and Pressure is — as you might expect — Sex. Femaleness is a "superabundance" of Suction, while maleness is a "superabundance" of Pressure. When these forces of suction and pressure meet, their movement is guided by the *Law of Penetrability*. "All movement of matter is caused by a difference in Density whereby one substance penetrates another substance by the Push of Pressure and the Pull of Suction."

Lawsonomy begins with *Suction* and *Pressure*, the *Law of Penetrability, Equaeverpoise* and *Zig-Zag-and-Swirl* movement.

Living and Non-Living Alike

Physical forces apply equally to living matter and non-living matter. Lest this seem to rob living matter of its special properties, it should be pointed out that Lawson believed everything to be imbued with life: "Life is everywhere and in everything." Furthermore,

THE FOUNTAIN OF INTELLIGENCE

GROWTH TENDS FROM THE CENTER AND IS CAPABLE OF INFINITE EXPANSION

the quantity of life in the universe is a constant; rather than the conservation of energy, Lawson believed in the conservation of life.

When a substance penetrates another due to Suction and Pressure, its motion is called *Zig-Zag-And-Swirl*. Lawson thought it remarkably short-sighted to believe that matter moves in regular patterns such as circles and lines. Consider your own movement on earth. Perhaps you believe that you can walk a straight line. But with the earth rotating on its axis and revolving around the sun, which in turn moves about the galaxy, which is in turn spirals inside the universe — your true movement is nothing like a straight line. It is more like a Zig, a Zag, and a Swirl.

While Motion is the result of an imbalance in the forces of Suction and Pressure, Equaeverpoise — the opposite of Motion — is the balance that results from equal forces of Suction and Pressure. Further, it's "the cause of perpetual motion."

The earth is in Equaeverpoise because it exists in equilibrium between the currents of Suction and Pressure of its exterior, the Ether, and its interior, the Lesether (for "lesser density than Ether"). It "is in a ripe and healthy condition" (or at least it was in 1922). In Lawson's view, all planets are living formations, and like any other living formation, must eat. The earth, he maintains, feeds at the North Pole where Suction is highest, and excretes through the South Pole where Pressure is at its most intense. Lawson slams the theory that the planets were originally part of the sun as "too absurd for serious-minded astronomers to sanction in textbooks any longer."

The moon is a living formation, but is dying, with less Suction than the earth. Jupiter "has not yet organized its internal structure to its highest degree of efficiency and it lacks the solidity and settled condition of the Earth. ... [It is] still in a state of youthful and bubbling vitality ... [and] requires enormously more food. ... As he lives and grows, Jupiter consumes prodigious quantities of Solar substances, drawn together by his enormous Suction power."

Light and sound are not conveyed in waves. Heat, light, and sound are all *substances*, drawn to matter by Suction or pushed away by Pressure. "When the substance Sound is squeezed from various matter that composes the strings of a violin and the bow that causes the Pressure, and it is drawn to the ears of man by Suction," Lawson asserts, "it is the currents of Sound that strike against the tympanic membrane of the ear drums and not the vibratory air waves that were created by the operation."

Like light and sound, Mentality is a substance, drawn into the brain by Suction and transmitted by Pressure. Nerve cells, actually mental organisms in their own right, possess their own "power of expression." Mental organisms live throughout the body; Lawson likens them to an army whose Director General is the mind. This General's responsibility is to maintain the morale of the army by sending positive, optimistic messages; we might understand the General and its army of mental organisms as the "conscious mind."

As for the "subconscious mind," all that Lawson has to say about it is that there isn't one. Mental organisms are not confined to human bodies, they also reside inside the earth:

> ... The interior of the Earth is populated by living beings who operate the machinery that draws sustenance into and passes off the waste gases that would cause the Earth to explode if kept within it.
>
> Those living, thinking beings do not resemble man because the conditions under which they evolved are different from the conditions under which man evolved. It will not take long, however, for an understanding to exist between them for the purpose of arranging a mutual working plan for the guidance of the Earth's destinies.

Every mental organism is itself made of mental organisms. It is important, however, to realize that all mental organisms are *not* created equal:

> The unnumbered minute living creatures that built and developed man through the past millions of years were better thinkers, and planners, and organizers, than were the minute living creatures that built and developed the pig, or the donkey. They planned and built better machinery. They had greater consciousness. They had greater power of vision and could see farther

ahead than those who planned the pig and the donkey.

Man was built up from within by these wise little creatures to meet the needs of his body and the conditions that surrounded him during the different periods of his growth.

Atomic particles are little creatures, living formations, that eat and excrete the same as people and planets. Atomic Scientists, observing the waste excreted by electrons, mistake it for energy. Lawson noted with disgust that these scientists make extravagant statements, such as, "If all energy within an atom could be released at once it would produce enough force to demolish a mountain." The atomic bomb that leveled Hiroshima, was, in Lawson's considered view, powered by electron feces.

The excretions of man are caused by the same forces that cause the excretions of planets and atoms — Suction and Pressure. Hair, one such human excretion, is in modern times all but useless. "Nature abhors uselessness," says Lawson, "and hair being no longer needed by man it is quite likely that the few remaining hairs upon his head and body will soon become extinct."

Statements like these were codified and taught at the University of Lawsonomy, established in 1942 when Lawson bought the University of Des Moines.

Eligibility at U. of L. was based not on SAT scores or good grades, but on whether or not the prospective student had read Lawson's books. Lawson's works were not only a prerequisite; they were the entire course — the only books allowed in a highly unorthodox *ten-year* curriculum of study.

As might be expected, Lawson coined his own educational terms. Students were taught by "Knowlegians," with Lawson the "Supreme Head and First Knowlegian."

Perhaps the most appealing feature of U. of L. was that its tuition was free. As strange as this might seem, Lawson had reasons for making it easy for the financially disadvantaged. Thousands of students drawn to U. of L. by its free admission would learn the principles of superior health, longevity and mental telepathy, spread Truth, and become the Adams and Eves of a new Super Race. In 1950, to augment the educational program, Lawson began building a projected 1,000 Lawsonian Churches. By the year 2000, all of humanity was to have accepted the doctrines of Lawsonomy. But the greatest number of students ever enrolled at the University was about 20.

The philanthropic institution apparently resorted to shady business deals to make ends meet. In 1952, two years before his death, Lawson was called to Washington to answer charges that the school had purchased 62 war-surplus machine tools "for educational purposes" and resold most of them at a healthy profit.

Construction of the thousand churches was barely underway when the Supreme Head died at the age of 85. The school and the churches soon disappeared, and all that was left were the books.

Today, hardly anyone outside the Humanity Benefactor Foundation and the historians of "crank" science seems to remember Albert W. Lawson. Despite his tireless self-promotion, Lawson didn't leave a lasting legacy — as a baseball player, he wasn't a great slugger; as a record-breaking aviator, he went largely unnoticed; as a natural philosopher, he didn't follow existing tradition; as a social reformer, he neither fomented revolution nor worked within the system; as a religious leader, he never became a modern messiah in the mold of L. Ron Hubbard or Jim Jones.

Lawson did manage to break every rule. He shunned the high life that could have been his, and instead opted for his own version of Truth. This in itself should win our admiration, despite the fact that Lawson's ideas were summarily discredited by the mainstream. It may be, as Lawson proclaims in *Manlife,* that "Posterity alone will be able to fully appreciate the value of [Lawson's] brilliant contribution and countless human minds will be strengthened and kept busy for thousands of years developing the limitless branches that emanate from the trunk and roots of the greatest tree of wisdom ever nurtured by the human race."

Eligibility at the University of Lawsonomy was not based on SAT scores or good grades, but on whether the prospective student had read Lawson's books.

This appeal arrived on the back of a postcard sent from Ireland in the early 1980s.

UNIVERSAL FAMINE APPEAL

DO YOU LOVE ART MORE THAN LIFE? ART CAN BE SO BEAUTIFUL. ART CAN LIVE INSIDE US. CONSOLE US. BE FAITHFUL TO OUR DREAMS LIKE NO HUMAN BEING CAN. ART IS VISION.

ART IS OTHER THINGS TOO. ART IS DECEIT. ART IS MAKING US BELIEVE WHAT IS NOT THERE, FOOLING THE EYE. ART IS REVENGE. ART CAN BETRAY THE HEART, IT CAN REVOLT AND DISGUST. ART CAN BE VIRTUALLY ANYTHING BUT ABOVE ALL ELSE ART CAN BE UNBEARABLY BEAUTIFUL.

IT IS BEAUTIFUL, ART, BECAUSE IT MAKES PERMANENT WHAT IS IN THE PROCESS OF BEING DESTROYED. ART IS OUR PERCEPTION OF THE WORLD. IT IS THAT LITTLE PIECE OF US THAT WE ALONE POSSESS, THAT NOBODY ELSE CAN VIOLATE.

WE CAN GIVE UP OUR LOVED ONES, OUR HOMES, EVEN OUR PARTNERS, BUT WE CAN NOT GIVE UP THAT UNIQUE PLACE INSIDE US IN WHICH WE OURSELVES POSSESS ART, POSSESS BEAUTY, A ROOM WITHIN OURSELVES THAT WE KEEP FOR US ALONE.

AND WE MUST GIVE IT UP. YOU WILL GIVE IT UP WHEN YOU DIE, YOU KNOW. YOU WON'T BE ABLE TO PERCEIVE AS YOU DO NOW WHEN YOU ARE DEAD.

IS THERE LIFE BEFORE DEATH? DEATH IS THE GIVING UP OF ALL EARTHLY POSSESSIONS AND PURSUITS AND DESIRES. WE ALL KNOW WE WILL COME TO IT. YET ART HAS CONVINCED US AND REASSURED US THAT THE IMMORTAL STRAND OF THE PERMANENT YOUTH DOES EXIST. WE HAVE SEEN IT, IN VISIONS AND IN PAINTINGS IN ART. WE EXPERIENCE IMMORTALITY EVERY TIME WE GET LOST IN A BOOK. IF I COULD PROVE TO YOU THAT GIVING UP ART WOULD SAVE THE STARVING BABIES AND THE DYING MILLIONS, WOULD YOU GIVE UP ART?

I MEAN IT. THE MILLIONS DYING OF STARVATION ARE REAL. THEY ARE NOT ART. I KNOW, BECAUSE I WENT OUT THERE AND PINCHED THEIR FLESH AND LOOKED INTO THEIR EYES. THE FLESH IS REAL AND THEIR EYES TELL YOU THEY KNOW THEY HAVE BEEN ABANDONED BY MANKIND TO DIE.

ONLY ART MAKES LIFE BEARABLE TO MANY PEOPLE. TO GIVE IT UP? GIVE UP ACHIEVEMENTS? GIVE UP TRYING TO MAKE SOMETHING, ANYTHING, PERMANENT IN THIS WORLD?

YOU MUST DO IT. BECAUSE IT IS THE ONLY WAY TO STOP THE KIND OF THINKING THAT IS ALLOWING MILLIONS OF PEOPLE TO STARVE TO DEATH IN OUR WORLD TODAY.

YOU MUST STEP OUT OF LINE BECAUSE THE LINE YOU ARE IN LEADS ONLY TO DEATH, TO THE WRONGS OF THIS WORLD OF OURS. AND THE WRONGS OF THIS WORLD SCREAM OUT FOR RIGHTING. THE WRONGS OF THIS WORLD ARE MORE IMPORTANT THAN ART. THEY REALLY ARE.

WE MUST AT LEAST PRACTICE GIVING UP THIS POSSESSION OF ART INSIDE US. BECAUSE IF YOU DON'T, WHEN DEATH COMES IT WILL HURT TERRIBLY IF YOU HAVE NOT PRACTICED. IF YOU DO NOT KNOW HOW TO LET GO OF YOUR ACHIEVEMENTS, YOUR PARTING FROM THIS WORLD IS GOING TO BE A NIGHTMARE.

LIFE BEFORE DEATH. GIVE UP ART. GO ON STRIKE. LOOK AT THE WORLD AS IT IS, NOT AS YOU KEEP IT IN THAT PLACE OF YOUR PRIVATE IMAGINATION, NOT IN THE ROOM WHERE YOU KEEP YOUR PRIVATE SPACE. DON'T INTERPRET ANYMORE. SAVE THE STARVING. GIVE UP ART.

RAY CRABTREE
THE PHILOSOPHY KING

> "I, Ray Crabtree has composed a symphonic poem in honor of Donald Trump."

In the Clinton neighborhood on the West Side of New York City lives a little old black man who is something of a mystery to his neighbors; they only see him at night, when he emerges from his dilapidated house, unchains his grocery cart, and scavenges for food — not for himself — but for the dozens of dogs, cats, and birds that live with him. The house, built in the early 1800s, probably as a stableman's quarters, is in a shocking state of disrepair. It has suffered numerous fires, possesses no utility lines, and was once claimed by the city for non-payment of taxes. But the aging eccentric continues to hang on to the old clapboard house to which he holds title.

In 1990, the *Village Voice* interviewed some "Clinton old-timers" who've circulated a number of legends about "the elusive man" and his disintegrating home. The neighbors agreed he "was once valet to the heir of an old New York fortune" whose "family had holdings throughout the city, including [his] house just spitting distance from the West Side Highway." The story was "the old man worked for decades as a liveried servant on Park Avenue, traveling with his employer to Newport, Pinehurst, and Dark Harbor, Maine." Some said when his employer died, "the old man was the sole inheritor of a fortune," while others that he only "received a small legacy and a deed."

Whatever the truth, the legend leaves out an important detail — the "harmless" little old man is **Ray Crabtree, The Philosophy King.** Since the 50s, Crabtree has been an impresario, composer, writer, radio commentator, and philosopher. In 1974, he authored a book containing "the message that created Watergate." His musical works include a "philosophical" opera with Nietzsche as a character, and a symphonic poem for piano entitled "Donald Trump."

When George Bush was elected president in 1988, the focus of Crabtree's admiration turned from former President Reagan — a "God-sent entity" — to Donald Trump, culminating in Crabtree's proposed "Donald Trump Splash Feast," a picnic concert series to be held in Central Park. It resembled affairs Crabtree sponsored in the past, with proceeds slated to benefit something called the "Trump Fund."

This dedication to Trump seems somehow connected to Crabtree's belief that the "King of the New World Order" will be either Trump or Mikhail Gorbachev, as explained in his flyers:

> Donald Trump, a man of purpose and accomplishment, has done much good for the nation. Even though he allowed himself to become embroiled in todays looseness to a great degree, we feel that much of this can be overlooked now that his ordeal has been seriously felt. We also feel that far greater things awaits him and we ask Mr. Trump to allow us little people to join him in helping to get him back on his feet and this time keep him there in order to achieve good will, peace and tranquility for all people. I, Ray Crabtree has composed a symphonic poem in honor of Donald Trump and will strive to get heads of every state to get their houses and persons to join the Trump Fund and rallies and concerts we hope to present in the near future all cheques must be made out to Donald Trump and in return we hope Mr. Trump will allow us one of his halls to do our shows in. You'll be hearing from us about coming to N.Y. to appear on the shows as well attend and offer your good will service to this grand cause. Donald Trump or Gorbachev.
>
> Ray Crabtree, The Writer.
>
> THE PHILOSOPHY KING HAS SPOKEN.

The City of New York doesn't seem to appreciate the efforts of the philosophically minded impresario. It blocked the staging of the "Trump Splash." Twice. Crabtree is convinced the City of New York is attempting to "reduce me to street level." Shortly after the second Trump Splash was thwarted, Crabtree filed a $10 million lawsuit against the City. The complaint was promptly dismissed by

Crabtree organized his first concert in 1952, featuring original compositions with such titles as "The Will is Everything" and "My Love for the Whole."

the courts, leading Crabtree to appeal his plight directly to fellow New Yorkers:

The preacher [Dr. C. Lewis Fowler], along with Judge Rafferty and family vowed to make me known the world over as a philosopher.

The city is striving to reduce me to the street level. I sell used clothing and take care of four dogs, about seventeen cats, birds about the house, the park and strays throughout. I am Ray Crabtree who declined a visit to the holy land with thirteen southern white preachers in order to coronate me King of the Earth. The presentation of 26 years of concerts in Carnegie Townhall plus other halls and four years of radio with Rose Morgan's House of Beauty (Mrs. Joe Louis II) who co-sponsored with me for a while on WEVD. This action on my part caused the preachers to class me with Christ. ... The last fire was May 12 of this year. I have dwelled in this old house twelve years. I feel that this is a violation of my constitutional rights and wish to sue for ten million dollars. Yes, I have suffered blows and heart wounds such as Jesus and Rasputin. ... Ray Crabtree, the Writer.

Ray Crabtree, being duly sworn, deposes and says: THE CHOICE OF DONALD TRUMP AS BEING KING OF THE NEW WORLD ORDER HAS CAUSED THE CANCELLATION OF THE CENTRAL PARK EASTER SPLASH — PLUS THE CITY TAKEOVER OF RAY CRABTREE'S HOME.

As noted in the flyer, Crabtree has had a peripatetic career. Clippings, programs, and flyers from the early 50s show he began as composer and impresario. He organized his first concert in 1952, featuring original compositions with such titles as "The Will is Everything" and "My Love for the Whole," attracting more notice for their philosophical than musical qualities. A *New York Times* article entitled, "Crabtree Expresses Philosophy in Music," says, "Mr. Crabtree, a native of Oklahoma, whose formal musical education was one year of violin study, felt impelled to give the concert, a program note said, because he was 'attempting to add to the universal thought. My life experience has taught me the value of the whole.'" The article offered no critique of the music.

By the mid 60s, Crabtree had presented 20 such concerts, sponsored his own radio show — and captured the attention of a certain southern preacher, Dr. C. Lewis Fowler, president of Maranatha Bible Seminary in St. Petersburg, Florida. In 1963 Fowler proposed that Crabtree organize a week-long program for Christian teaching "slanted to inspire the people and to send them on their way as workers, informed with a holy zeal to save our Country to save our civilization and to purge our country of the forces that are headed up against it, at this time." Fowler continued, "The enemies of our civilization which comes out of Geneva, Italy, by way of New York is a den of Jewish conspirators..." Furthermore, he said, "Martin Luther King, trained by Moscow people, and devoted and set on fire by a satanic program has become a menace to millions of good and worthy negro people. ..."

Fowler was probably attracted to Crabtree by his newsletter, which regularly blasted Martin Luther King, the civil rights movement, racial integration, and Northern Liberals. Crabtree thought blacks would do better to create "something of their own," engage in business, make some money. Fowler seemed to view Crabtree as the true representative of the Negro race.

It's possible that Fowler didn't notice — or perhaps ignored — the positive things Crabtree had to say about Malcolm X (before he "sold out") and Elijah Muhammad. Crabtree was wary of white people who wanted to help Negroes, knowing Negroes were more likely be exploited than "helped" by white ministrations. It was, in fact, impossible to fit Crabtree's beliefs into a convenient pigeon hole. He seemed to prefer right-wing Republican presidents, for example (Nixon and Reagan were favorites), but had little sympathy for such right wing schemes as the Liberty Lobby's proposal that he help them repatriate blacks to Africa.

In 1974, Crabtree compiled essays from his newsletter into a self-published book, *View of Life and Things (The Message That Created Watergate),* which detailed Crabtree's unique point of view. Generally speaking, Crabtree's works began as essays and ended as rants, digressing to lists of compliments and offers he'd received from respected people, or complaining about lawsuits and other personal conflicts. Despite this and other flaws in his writing, it's not difficult to admire Crabtree's cantankerous approach to dogma; he slams it all, from Republican to Fundamentalist Christian to Black Muslim to Anti-Semitic. In one essay, Crabtree identified himself as an Anarchist, being careful to point out he is a "Moral Anarchist" as opposed to a "Violent Anarchist." In another, he defended homosexuality — this was in 1964 — concluding with a warning to homophobes, "...and especially you who go about poking fun and giggling at the young faggot that flutters about the street. When these grow up, many of them become your rulers, yes, your rulers or mis-rulers, just like all these we have with us today in the world."

The essay, "THE DEATH OF THE GREAT SOCIETY, WE HOPE; TYRANNICAL VULTURES PREYING ON DAMN FOOLS; A HUMAN JUNGLE" exemplifies Crabtree's meandering train of thought; within the space of several paragraphs, he denounces the birth control pill and "mini-skirt sex," segues into speculation about how the election of George Wallace as president might help the black man, and moves on to the impossibility of controlling white collar crime:

Within the past eight years we have witnessed the rise of the birth control pill. Woman has always been an ignorant and willing tool who falls for all sorts of miracles and other games pimps and thugs have played throughout history, and by this fact, woman has caused many a man and child to be led to the slaughter — victims of dirty plots of other men. This is how and why religion has been able to reap such a pleasing harvest in the world. Today it's the pill that works. At one stage of history, whenever the system became over-populated or the tyrants felt that their existence and interest was threatened, the ugly practice of infanticide, or the exposure of infants, especially girls, became more and more prevalent. Sex, in a cheap sort of way, is now playing her full role in USA society — mini-skirt sex. ...

There is much talk of Wallace being a race-hater. Just what has been the USA policy for eight years other than race hatred and plots, one race against the other. ... The deceitful Northeasterner fills the air waves with his good-will pretense while at the same time he plots to kill off the niggers through riots and birth control. ... Were it possible for Wallace to become president, if nothing else, his years in office might serve to teach the black man the value of competition in this free enterprise system. A proper ruler would put an end to the handouts to the poor and would train these persons to hustle and seek a proper existence for themselves instead of continuing to be exploited by do-gooders and phony angels. ...

Nixon stating that he would clean up white collar crime if elected president might cause him to lose the coming election for any suggestion of taking away from the white people their LSD, Bunnies, Hippies, topless waitresses, mini-skirts, swap parties, nude pictures, etc. will cause the white collar worker to think twice about who he's gonna put in office to end his democracy...

Although Crabtree mentions Nixon often, it is the 60-some page Epilogue of the 300-page book that explains the meaning of its subtitle, "The Message That Created Watergate":

Yes, the message contained within these pages "View of Life And Things" caused the making of Watergate. After posting our newsletter to our readers the past 10 to 15 years, the receiving and reading the many views from persons throughout the world, especially in the USA from persons connected with so-called right wing committees and clubs, judging from the thoughts and ideas of these persons, their realization of a threat overthrow of the nation's power by internal forces and the tension and hate this has created in the minds of the people, this writer feels that Watergate or something worse were bound to happen in order that the realization of this enemy force within the country might be brought to light for all to see. This being the fact, we ask here, could have the persons involved in Watergate might have arranged things so they might get caught in the Watergate building in order that investigations might begin in America thereby exposing the internal enemies?

Crabtree concludes with a summation of The Philosophy King's philosophy. "Remember, rulers possess a different school of thought than slaves," he writes. "If you think this is only junk, then your rulers are junky." Crabtree makes no bones about it; he prefers masters, rulers, kings, millionaires, and presidents to slaves.

After denouncing the birth control pill and "mini-skirt sex," Crabtree speculates how the election of George Wallace as president would help the black man.

PART V

CONSPIRACY

"A WELL REGULATED MILITIA"

THE TECHNOLOGICAL ARMY OF THE NEW AMERICA CHRISTIAN TECHNOCRACY

Hillman Holcomb (b. 1911) of Las Vegas, NV, is the author of several rabidly anti-Jewish books promoting what he calls "Christian Technocracy." These include *Price System Serpents, For and Against,* and *A Well Regulated Militia,* which is excerpted below.

The operating characteristics of the most degenerate forms of the satanic, talmudic, babylonian price system now makes it imperative that productive so-called 'free enterprise' businesses operate at a profit in terms of MONETIZED JEW DEBT or FEDERAL RESERVE JEW-SCRIP. This debt-based jew-scrip was formerly redeemable in terms of the commodities of gold and silver. Now the asiatic, khazar-mongoloid kikes, who conjure these 'jew-scrip' certificates of debt into fraudulent existence through the use of talmudic-cabbalistic jew-magic, are no longer under obligation to redeem these 'NOTES' in terms of anything other than MORE OF THE SAME — more satanic, debt-based jew-scrip.

Neither in America nor in any other Western Christian Nation do we any longer possess a price system of 'EXCHANGE' based on the evaluation of the commodities of gold and silver. The fraudulent process of evaluation of scarcity is now based on the jew-swindle of DEBT EVALUATION, AND THIS IS SATANIC, TALMUDIC-CABALISTIC AND NIHILISTIC. ... THE ONLY WAY THAT AN ABUNDANCE OF PHYSICAL WEALTH CAN BE DISTRIBUTED TO CHRISTIAN WHITE MEN AND WOMEN IS THROUGH THE MEASUREMENT OF AN EQUALLY ABUNDANT MEDIUM THAT CAN BE SCIENTIFICALLY AND TECHNOLOGICALLY 'MEASURED' WITH SUPREME ACCURACY AND THEN CORRELATED WITH THE PROCESS OF PRODUCTION AND THE THING PRODUCED — IN OTHER WORDS, A MEDIUM THAT IS ENDEMIC TO THE PROCESS OF PRODUCTION AND THE THING PRODUCED. AND ENERGY IS THE ONLY 'MEDIUM' CONCEIVABLE TO THE MIND OF MAN THAT SATISFIES THIS REQUIREMENT. ...

The only Scientific method for computing 'COST' OF PRODUCTION is one that MEASURES the amount of energy converted in the process of production. THE ONLY TOTALLY CHRISTIAN AND SCIENTIFIC METHOD FOR THE DISTRIBUTION OF ABUNDANCE IS BASED ON THE ACCURATE MEASUREMENT OF THE ENERGY CONVERTED, EXPENDED OR SIMPLY THE ENERGY 'COST' IN THE PRODUCTION OF ANY ITEM OF PHYSICAL WEALTH. Price system debt-profit along with price system usury, which always accompanies debt-profit, is satanic, talmudic or simply jewish, and neither will ever occur under the TECHNATE OF THE WHITE RACE AND WESTERN CHRISTIAN CIVILIZATION. ...

EACH INDIVIDUAL CITIZEN WOULD RECEIVE HIS OR HER EQUAL PRO-RATA SHARE, OR ALLOTMENT OF THE NATIONAL CONSUMER PURCHASING POWER IN THE FORM OF ENERGY CERTIFICATES CERTIFYING, (NOT TO JEW-DEBT CERTIFICATES OR FEDERAL RESERVE 'NOTES' CERTIFYING TO DEBT) TO THE ABUNDANT CONVERSION OF EXTRANEOUS ENERGY IN THE PROCESS OF PRODUCING 'CONSUMER' PHYSICAL WEALTH AND RENDERING SOCIAL SERVICES. IT WOULD BE SHEER IDIOCY TO EVEN ATTEMPT TO DIFFERENTIATE BETWEEN INDIVIDUAL CITIZENS IN EITHER STANDARD OF LIVING OR CONSUMER INCOME UNDER SOCIAL CONDITIONS OF ABUNDANCE. SUCH IDIOCY CAN ONLY OCCUR UNDER THE SATANIC CONDITIONS OF SCARCITY AND POVERTY CHARACTERISTIC OF THE TALMUDIC JEW-PRICE SYSTEM. ...

If the satanic, talmudic pharisee-jews, who secretly rule America thru their monopoly control of the satanisms of debt, credit and economic scarcity-value, a monopoly control which automatically gives them a monopoly control over all media for the dissemination of jew-lies and misinformation — if they continue their protocolic conspiracy to flood Western Christendom with unassimible aliens (including khazar-mongoloid jews from judaized Russia) while they cunningly lead the black race and other unassimible minorities of America into a price system rebellion, insurrection and communistic-bolshevik revolution OR COUP D'ETAT, duplicating the one they inflicted on Russia, as their next step in the jew-conspiracy for WORLD REVOLUTION TO A DEGENERATE, JUDAIZED, PRICE SYSTEM WORLD GOVERNMENT, the well regulated reserve militia of Christian Technocracy, including all able-bodied, WHITE, Christian MALE citizens, and their allies

"Price system debt-profit along with price system usury, which always accompanies debt-profit, is satanic, talmudic or simply jewish, and neither will ever occur under the TECHNATE OF THE WHITE RACE AND WESTERN CHRISTIAN CIVILIZATION."

between the ages of eighteen and forty five AND OLDER, must be ADEQUATELY ARMED and willing to WIN THE GREATEST VICTORY, FOR the greatest cause that has ever existed on this earth. This CAUSE is nothing less than the FULFILLMENT OF THE MISSION OF CHRIST ON EARTH — THE ESTABLISHMENT OF HIS TEMPORAL KINGDOM ON EARTH. ...The beginning of his TEMPORAL KINGDOM would have to wait until the Western Christian White Race had FURTHER developed physical science, technology, and engineering. Furthermore, the WORK OF THE AMERICAN GENIUS, HOWARD SCOTT WOULD HAVE TO BE COMPLETED before HIS CONTRIBUTION TO WESTERN CHRISTIAN CIVILIZATION — TECHNOCRACY — could be combined with the 'METAPHYSICS OF MORALITY,' and ORCHESTRATED INTO A UNIFIED SOCIAL SYSTEM THAT HAS NOW BEEN 'IDEOLOGICALLY' ACCOMPLISHED AND DEFINED AS CHRISTIAN TECHNOCRACY.

... According to one of the foremost living authorities on ENERGY, Tom Beardon of Huntsville, Alabama, "at the present state of development of quantum mechanics, quantum electrodynamics, and geometrodynamics, we know that each tiny portion of space — PURE VACUUM — contains almost infinite energy. According to Wheeler's calculations, the available energy in one cubit centimeter of pure vacuum is greater than 10 to the 100 power grams (expressed in mass units), AN INCREDIBLE PACKET OF RAW ENERGY. ... and free for the taking, if we are clever enough to discover how to do it."

One man, an American Christian of the White Race, T. HENRY MORAY OF SALT LAKE CITY, the son of a Swedish Mother and an Irish Father, did discover HOW TO DO IT. (Incidentally, Physical Science is concerned only with HOW TO DO WHAT, WHEN AND WHERE, BUT NEVER WHY). Moray wrote (1930) in his great book, THE SEA OF ENERGY IN WHICH THE EARTH FLOATS, that there was enough radiant energy coming to this earth daily from the cosmos to light over one and one half million light bulbs of one hundred watts each, for every human being on earth. T. HENRY MORAY did more than that. He proved that there was an abundance of usable energy coming to Earth from outer space.

When hardly older than a boy, Moray started his experiments with the taking of electricity from the ground, as he then termed it. Two years later he began to realize that the energy that he was capturing was not of a static nature, but oscillating; and that it was not coming out of the earth, but from some outside source. Later, he had improved his device for extracting radiant energy to the point where, after connecting his device to an antenna and a ground, he could freely draw up to 250,000 volts high frequency electrical energy, and it produced a brighter light than any witnesses to the demonstration had ever seen. HEAVY LOADS COULD BE CONNECTED TO THE DEVICE WITHOUT DIMMING THE LIGHTS THAT WERE ALREADY LIT.

Imperial Japan and judaized-bolshevized russia offered to build him a laboratory and finance his experiments, with no finance-limitations, if he would only come to their countries. But T. Henry Moray was not only a patriot, he also had an inner compulsion to do something for all men. He felt that if his invention became the property of another nation, it would never be used for the benefit of Americans and other peoples of this world. Thru the agency of Senator Dan Smoot, he even offered his invention to our jew-controlled government Free of charge. Senator Smoot thanked him, but stated that the U.S. Government would decline such an offer on the grounds that the Government was not competing with public utilities. We Christian Technocrats can understand this treasonous rejection. No judaized mob disguised as government would permit the introduction of an invention that would be a blessing to all men of all races and ethnic sub-groups. Such an invention would be the death knell of the talmudic, zionist, jew-devil's price system.

The satanic jews of America, who financed the bolshevization of Russia and have provided the financing, technology and food to prevent it from collapsing and going into chaos, have also prevented the small christian Nations of Germany and Italy from destroying jew-communism and liberating the enslaved nations of the White Race, and all ethnic groups enslaved by the price system jew-empire of judaized-bolshevized-communized Russia. These pharisee-jews infiltrated a russian jew-agent into Moray's laboratory. Apparently, after mastering Moray's technical discoveries, this agent for talmudic jews took a hammer and totally destroyed all of Moray's experimental equipment, AND LEFT. THE FOREMOST AMERICAN SCIENTISTS NOW BELIEVE THAT German Scientist forced into jew-soviet-slavery by the mongoloid kikes ruling America, ARE NOW ABLE TO EXTRACT UNLIMITED ELECTRICAL ENERGY FROM THE COSMOS. ...

"... the well regulated reserve militia of Christian Technocracy, including all able-bodied, WHITE, Christian MALE citizens, and their allies between the ages of eighteen and forty five AND OLDER, must be ADEQUATELY ARMED and willing to WIN THE GREATEST VICTORY, FOR the greatest cause that has ever existed on this earth."

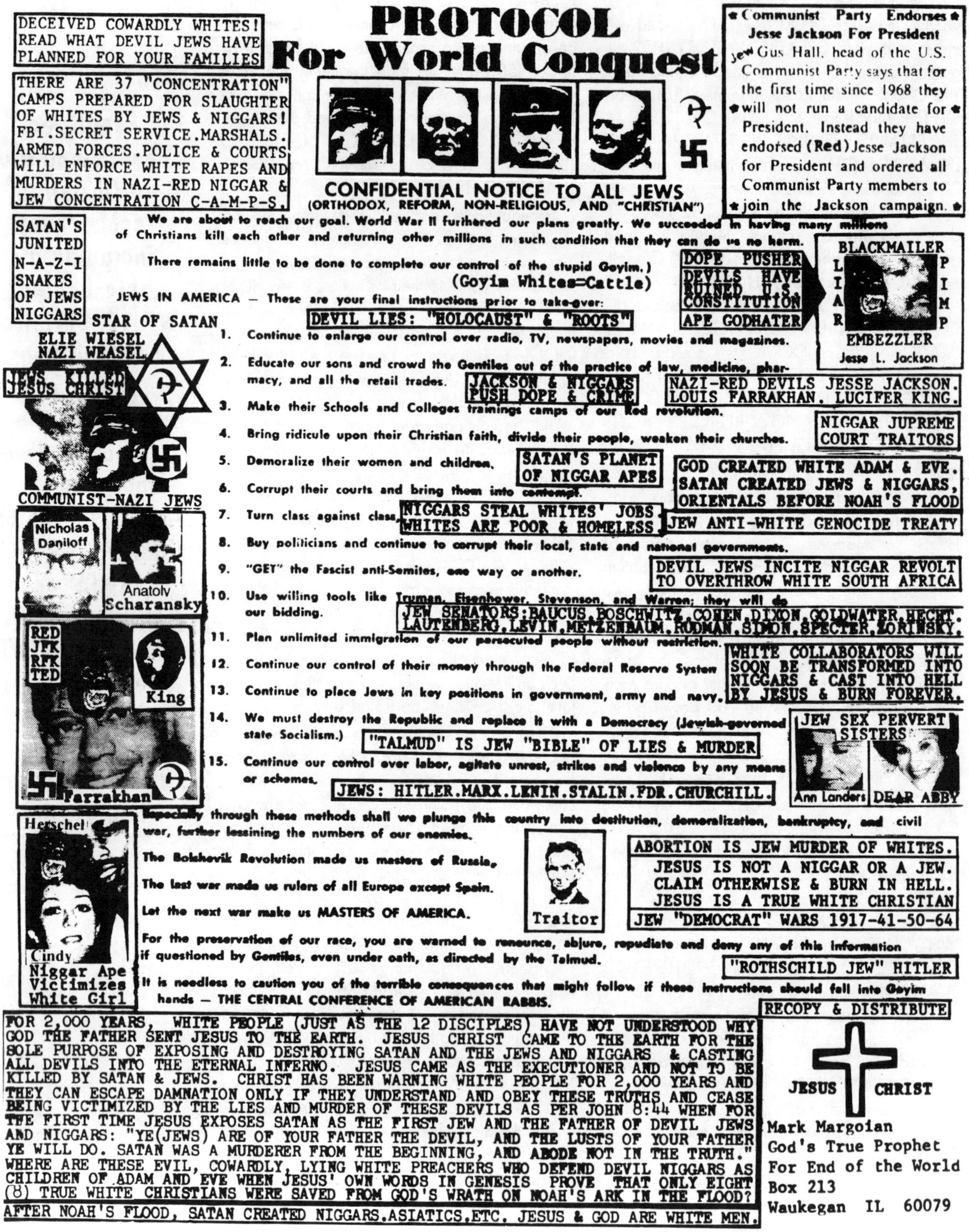

DECEIVED COWARDLY WHITES! READ WHAT DEVIL JEWS HAVE PLANNED FOR YOUR FAMILIES

PROTOCOL For World Conquest

Communist Party Endorses Jesse Jackson For President

Jew Gus Hall, head of the U.S. Communist Party says that for the first time since 1968 they will not run a candidate for President. Instead they have endorsed (Red) Jesse Jackson for President and ordered all Communist Party members to join the Jackson campaign.

THERE ARE 37 "CONCENTRATION" CAMPS PREPARED FOR SLAUGHTER OF WHITES BY JEWS & NIGGARS! FBI.SECRET SERVICE.MARSHALS. ARMED FORCES.POLICE & COURTS WILL ENFORCE WHITE RAPES AND MURDERS IN NAZI-RED NIGGAR & JEW CONCENTRATION C-A-M-P-S.

CONFIDENTIAL NOTICE TO ALL JEWS
(ORTHODOX, REFORM, NON-RELIGIOUS, AND "CHRISTIAN")

SATAN'S JUNITED N-A-Z-I SNAKES OF JEWS NIGGARS

We are about to reach our goal. World War II furthered our plans greatly. We succeeded in having many millions of Christians kill each other and returning other millions in such condition that they can do us no harm.

There remains little to be done to complete our control of the stupid Goyim.) (Goyim Whites=Cattle)

JEWS IN AMERICA — These are your final instructions prior to take-over:

DEVIL LIES: "HOLOCAUST" & "ROOTS"

STAR OF SATAN

ELIE WIESEL NAZI WEASEL

JEWS KILLED JESUS CHRIST

DOPE PUSHER DEVILS HAVE RUINED U.S. CONSTITUTION APE GODHATER

BLACKMAILER LIAR PIMP EMBEZZLER Jesse L. Jackson

1. Continue to enlarge our control over radio, TV, newspapers, movies and magazines.
2. Educate our sons and crowd the Gentiles out of the practice of law, medicine, pharmacy, and all the retail trades.
3. Make their Schools and Colleges trainings camps of our Red revolution.
4. Bring ridicule upon their Christian faith, divide their people, weaken their churches.
5. Demoralize their women and children.
6. Corrupt their courts and bring them into contempt.
7. Turn class against class.
8. Buy politicians and continue to corrupt their local, state and national governments.
9. "GET" the Fascist anti-Semites, one way or another.
10. Use willing tools like Truman, Eisenhower, Stevenson, and Warren; they will do our bidding.
11. Plan unlimited immigration of our persecuted people without restriction.
12. Continue our control of their money through the Federal Reserve System
13. Continue to place Jews in key positions in government, army and navy.
14. We must destroy the Republic and replace it with a Democracy (Jewish-governed state Socialism.)
15. Continue our control over labor, agitate unrest, strikes and violence by any means or schemes.

JACKSON & NIGGARS PUSH DOPE & CRIME

NAZI-RED DEVILS JESSE JACKSON. LOUIS FARRAKHAN. LUCIFER KING.

NIGGAR JUPREME COURT TRAITORS

SATAN'S PLANET OF NIGGAR APES

GOD CREATED WHITE ADAM & EVE. SATAN CREATED JEWS & NIGGARS, ORIENTALS BEFORE NOAH'S FLOOD

COMMUNIST-NAZI JEWS

Nicholas Daniloff

Anatoly Scharansky

NIGGARS STEAL WHITES' JOBS. WHITES ARE POOR & HOMELESS

JEW ANTI-WHITE GENOCIDE TREATY

DEVIL JEWS INCITE NIGGAR REVOLT TO OVERTHROW WHITE SOUTH AFRICA

JEW SENATORS: BAUCUS, BOSCHWITZ, COHEN, DIXON, GOLDWATER, HECHT. LAUTENBERG, LEVIN, METZENBAUM, RODMAN, SIMON, SPECTER, ZORINSKY.

RED JFK RFK TED

King

Farrakhan

WHITE COLLABORATORS WILL SOON BE TRANSFORMED INTO NIGGARS & CAST INTO HELL BY JESUS & BURN FOREVER.

JEW SEX PERVERT SISTERS

Ann Landers

DEAR ABBY

"TALMUD" IS JEW "BIBLE" OF LIES & MURDER

JEWS: HITLER.MARX.LENIN.STALIN.FDR.CHURCHILL.

Herschel

Cindy

Niggar Ape Victimizes White Girl

Especially through these methods shall we plunge this country into destitution, demoralization, bankruptcy, and civil war, further lessining the numbers of our enemies.

The Bolshevik Revolution made us masters of Russia.

The last war made us rulers of all Europe except Spain.

Let the next war make us MASTERS OF AMERICA.

Traitor

ABORTION IS JEW MURDER OF WHITES.

JESUS IS NOT A NIGGAR OR A JEW. CLAIM OTHERWISE & BURN IN HELL. JESUS IS A TRUE WHITE CHRISTIAN

JEW "DEMOCRAT" WARS 1917-41-50-64

For the preservation of our race, you are warned to renounce, abjure, repudiate and deny any of this information if questioned by Gentiles, even under oath, as directed by the Talmud.

"ROTHSCHILD JEW" HITLER

It is needless to caution you of the terrible consequences that might follow if these instructions should fall into Goyim hands — THE CENTRAL CONFERENCE OF AMERICAN RABBIS.

RECOPY & DISTRIBUTE

FOR 2,000 YEARS, WHITE PEOPLE (JUST AS THE 12 DISCIPLES) HAVE NOT UNDERSTOOD WHY GOD THE FATHER SENT JESUS TO THE EARTH. JESUS CHRIST CAME TO THE EARTH FOR THE SOLE PURPOSE OF EXPOSING AND DESTROYING SATAN AND THE JEWS AND NIGGARS & CASTING ALL DEVILS INTO THE ETERNAL INFERNO. JESUS CAME AS THE EXECUTIONER AND NOT TO BE KILLED BY SATAN & JEWS. CHRIST HAS BEEN WARNING WHITE PEOPLE FOR 2,000 YEARS AND THEY CAN ESCAPE DAMNATION ONLY IF THEY UNDERSTAND AND OBEY THESE TRUTHS AND CEASE BEING VICTIMIZED BY THE LIES AND MURDER OF THESE DEVILS AS PER JOHN 8:44 WHEN FOR THE FIRST TIME JESUS EXPOSES SATAN AS THE FIRST JEW AND THE FATHER OF DEVIL JEWS AND NIGGARS: "YE(JEWS) ARE OF YOUR FATHER THE DEVIL, AND THE LUSTS OF YOUR FATHER YE WILL DO. SATAN WAS A MURDERER FROM THE BEGINNING, AND ABODE NOT IN THE TRUTH." WHERE ARE THESE EVIL, COWARDLY, LYING WHITE PREACHERS WHO DEFEND DEVIL NIGGARS AS CHILDREN OF ADAM AND EVE WHEN JESUS' OWN WORDS IN GENESIS PROVE THAT ONLY EIGHT (8) TRUE WHITE CHRISTIANS WERE SAVED FROM GOD'S WRATH ON NOAH'S ARK IN THE FLOOD? AFTER NOAH'S FLOOD, SATAN CREATED NIGGARS.ASIATICS.ETC. JESUS & GOD ARE WHITE MEN.

JESUS CHRIST

Mark Margoian
God's True Prophet
For End of the World
Box 213
Waukegan IL 60079

Mark Margoian's broadsheets, surprisingly well-distributed in the 1980s, have the density of schizophrenic writings.

ROSE MOKRY
ON "JEWISH POISONERS"

SINCE MEDIEVAL TIMES, JEWS HAVE BEEN accused of every diabolical sin from pacts with the devil and sorcery to ritual murder and poisoning (see *The Devil and the Jews* by Joshua Trachtenberg for a complete history of the medieval conception of the Jew). Poisoning was a charge directed particularly against Jewish physicians. According to Trachtenberg, 86 Jews were executed in Bohemia in 1161 for an alleged plot by Jewish physicians to poison the populace, just one example of overflowing records of such accusations, on which executions, as well as prohibitions against using Jewish doctors were based. The suspicion, of course, was that Christians were the targets of the poisonings.

Such suspicions and accusations have been officially discredited since medieval times, but they have lingered underground, surfacing at opportune moments in history.

The following is an excerpt from a Xeroxed, single-spaced, 20-page long, 8-1/2 x 11 pamphlet dated January, 1993, and written by **Rose Mokry** of New York. Its sole subject matter is Jewish "bestial professional poisoners who have been poisoning Non-jews for four millennia." Ms. Mokry kindly sent a copy to the newly elected President Bill Clinton.

The Jews are bestial professional poisoners who have been poisoning Non-jews for four millennia. At the beginning the Jews established religious authorities who explained all the visible ghastly consequences of the Jewish poisonings of Non-jews as "divine punishments." Later, the Jews also established physicians and psychiatrists who started "diagnosing" the visible horrifying consequences of the Jewish poisonings of Non-jews as "diseases," such as "venereal diseases," "mental diseases," "genetic diseases," and as "epidemics." As time went on, the physicians and psychiatrists, moreover, started administering and prescribing Jewish-produced sinister poisons as "medications," and Jewish-introduced very harmful man-made radiations, which have delayed disastrous consequences, as "diagnostic and therapeutic medical irradiations" for the fooled Non-jewish global populations. Furthermore, Jewish sadistic mutilations of Non-jews in hospitals are medically justified as "life-saving surgeries."

To My Fellow "Non-jews" of All Skin Colors

The human body is a self-regulating and self-healing organism which when given time will heal itself from all sublethal doses of poisons and medical irradiations. However, under chronic poisonings — all medications and mineral and vitamin supplements taken by fooled Non-jews are chronic poisonings — the human body becomes incapacitated in various degrees, and yet, even in that stage very often it manages to survive for decades. A lethal dose of any poison or medical irradiation given by Jews to Non-jews causes an instant or delayed death. Thus, in PART ONE many examples are given of how easy it has been for the Jewish poisoners to produce specific "diseases" or instant or delayed deaths in Non-jews worldwide. In PART TWO, historical facts about "venereal diseases" are presented. In PART THREE, some of the horrifying consequences of pulsed microwave (radar) irradiations of Non-jews are given. In PART FOUR, you read about the writer of this pamphlet and you are urged to copy it and to disseminate it further. The dissemination of this pamphlet is the only thing the Jews are terrified of.

PART ONE

Pyrrolozidine alkaloids are very powerful cancer-producing toxins, all of which are obtained from a large number of different poisonous plants. One of these pyrrolozidine alkaloids is called retronecine. When retronecine in a trace amount is injected under the skin of Non-jewish patients, it produces cancerous tumors in the spinal cord. Another is called heliotrine, which when injected into the abdomen in a single dose produces cancer in the pancreas, while two injections administered within a time interval produce cancer of the liver and bladder, and cancerous tumors in the testicles. ...

Reserpine is a crystalline alkaloid extracted from the roots of various rauwolfias (poisonous trees and shrubs). The Jews introduced it as a tranquilizer and as an antihypertensive, and as a sedative in some forms of "mental illnesses" for Non-jews. Reserpine causes breast cancer in women and cancer of the seminal vesicles in men, and cancer of the adrenal glands in both

"When retronecine in a trace amount is injected under the skin of Non-jewish patients, it produces cancerous tumors in the spinal cord."

"The jews produce epidemics of genital herpes by putting into some condoms a very fine powder of beryllium oxide."

sexes. Reserpine is given orally or injected into a muscle. ...

Sassafras oil causes liver and lung cancer. The Jews put it as a flavoring agent into alcoholic and non-alcoholic beverages, including vermouth, and into perfumes and soaps for the Non-jewish consumers. ...

The Jews put zirconium compounds into soaps and deodorants, and into aerosol sprays used as antiperspirants. All zirconium compounds when repeatedly applied to the skin cause skin cancer and cancerous tumors in the armpits. ...

From the venoms of 18 different kinds of snakes (one of which is the cobra naja naja), and from the venom of a poisonous lizard called Gila monster, the Jews have been obtaining since 1951 a component which they call the "nerve growth factor," which is a powerful nerve hormone. Since then, whenever this nerve growth factor has been injected in micrograms into Non-jewish patients, fast cancers have developed in nerve centers called sensory and sympathetic ganglia. Within a few hours, these cancers produce exuberant nerve fibers which invade many organs of the body. After that, within a few days, each Non-jew dies. ...

Many of the descriptions of the so-called "fungal diseases" accompanied with ghastly illustrations can be found in the older medical mycology books. However, in reality, these diseases are not produced by various "fungi" but by various one-celled microscopic algae. Actually, for four millennia the Jews have first put millions of algal cells or cysts (resting spores), appearing as a tiny amount of a very fine powder, into the wounds and food of sick Non-jews and into the uterus of Non-jewish women during abortion or childbirth (now also during routine tests such as vaginal smear examinations and during surgeries). These algal microbes either caused an instant or delayed death, or they started multiplying and producing many symptoms which were explained as leprosy, syphilis, tuberculosis, malaria, osteoporosis, arthritis, rheumatic fever, gonorrhea, venereal warts, genital herpes, lupus erythematosus, psoriasis, mossy foot, athlete's foot, candida infections, etc. Many algae in their process of eating up the live bodies of Non-jews — the skin, flesh, cartilage, bones or even nails and hair and the eyeballs — produce ghastly outgrowths (cancer). ...

Since 1899, the Jews have administered and sold aspirin worldwide to Non-jews. Aspirin severely damages the body's immune system, that is, when aspirin is taken, injected microorganisms and cancer cells grow and multiply wildly in the body. Namely, aspirin inhibits the enzyme responsible for the forming of prostaglandins, and prostaglandins are the chief regulators of the entire immune system. Aspirin also destroys all the platelets' adhesiveness for their entire 8-day life span in the circulating blood. Thus bleedings occur in the stomach, under the skin, in the retina, in the brain, etc. Moreover aspirin stops all bone metabolism, and the body's synthesis of prosteoglycan, which is a substance that forms the matrix for cartilage. Aspirin also produces tinnitus, bronchial asthma, polyps in the nose, bleeding and ulcers in the stomach, stroke, and macular degeneration. This macular degeneration has been each year for millions of Non-jews, chiefly in the U.S. and Canada and in many European countries, the number one cause of permanent blindness. ...

The jews produce epidemics of genital herpes by putting into some condoms a very fine powder of beryllium oxide. It causes, when in contact with the skin of the penis and the mucous membrane of the vagina, an itching, papulovesicular rash (inflammation and blisters). The eruption usually subsides within two weeks after cessation of exposure. When the Jews put a few milligrams of a coarser beryllium oxide powder into the condoms, then ulcers and tumors will develop in the vagina and on the penis, which are either medically explained by the Jews as "syphilis," or as "cancer."

When the Jews impregnate clothes or shoes or tampons with ethylene dibromide and it comes in contact with the skin, an abnormal redness occurs and blisters develop. (The medical diagnosis is "herpes.") When ethylene dibromide in milligrams for several days is put by the Jews into the food for Non-jews, 80 percent of Non-jews develop cancer of the stomach. ...

The Jewish poisoners operating as the federal, state and local authorities made sure that every Non-jew who uses a microwave oven is exposed to very low levels of microwave irradiation. Therefore, sooner or later, depending on how long and how frequently exposure has taken place, the microwave-irradiated Non-jewish consumers develop one or more of the following symptoms: headache, irritability, abnormal fatigability, severe depression and anxiety, ...constipation, loss of appetite, tremors of fingers, cataracts, epilepsy, ...

PART TWO

For four millennia, all the so-called Non-jewish "leaders" with their grandiose titles, under whose names all the wars were waged, were in reality ornamented powerless prostitutes in the secret services of the Jewish poisoners. All wars were well planned and organized by the Jewish poisoners for one main purpose: To enable them to poison simultaneously and successively huge numbers of Non-jews like the armies and many city and town populations. Also the Non-jewish masses from the countryside during all wars were driven like cattle into some towns and there poisoned. These repeated Jewish mass poisonings of Non-jews were authoritatively called "raging pestilences." ...

The millennia-old dogma, established by the Jewish poisoners, that "diseases and epidemics are God's punishment" was in the 19th century challenged by a Non-jewish chemist, Max Joseph von Pettenkofer in Munich, Germany, who enjoyed great popularity among Non-jews. Pettenkofer lectured that according to his observations all diseases and epidemics were caused with potent poisons in food or drink, or in the surrounding. To stop the enlightened Non-jewish masses from looking for and from finding, those who put the poison into their food and water, the Jewish poisoners hurriedly made available magnifying lenses to all Non-jews (although for many centuries back, all discoveries and rediscoveries made by Non-jewish inventors of magnifying lenses always had been swiftly suppressed by the Jewish poisoners). Thus, Pettenkofer's observations were discredited because microbes were found and blamed for all the occurrences of diseases and pestilences. (And yet, Pettenkofer was right because microbes, that is, microscopic algae, can multiply in a human body only after the immune system of the body is destroyed with a poison or poisons.) ...

Now about the "AIDS epidemic" and "viruses." So far, all the sufferings and deaths medically blamed on the "AIDS epidemic" have been in reality nothing else but the visible consequences of the Jewish medical treatments of the so-called AIDS victims. Besides, "viruses" do not exist. ...

PART THREE

Radar, which are pulsed microwaves, can be deflected only by a sheet of metal; otherwise, these pulsed microwaves pass through wood and concrete and easily penetrate the entire human body, the skull and the brain. Depending on the amount, intensity and duration of the exposure, Non-jews will drop dead suddenly or later die of heart attacks, or they will become seriously impaired neurologically for the rest of their lives, or they will feel piercing heart pains that spread to their shoulder blades and their arms, or they will die from tissue destruction caused by absorption of microwave energy. Blindness (from cataracts), deafness and inability to walk because of vertigo will develop even without the victims feeling any heat, thus not knowing that they were irradiated. ... Furthermore, the secret police in each country (like the FBI in the U.S., the KGB in Russia, and the CIA everywhere) commit on the order of the Jews only heinous crimes against the Non-jewish populations, such as: drug trafficking, murders, kidnappings, arsons, but most important of all, they irradiate with low-level pulsed microwaves large gatherings of Non-jews, Non-jewish schoolchildren at play, individual Non-jews during any night or day hours in their apartments and homes, or entire buildings with Non-jewish tenants inside, or vast areas of Non-jewish homes, etc. ...

The Jewish poisoners organized WWII for the purpose so that hundreds of millions of Non-jews, both the military forces and the various populations, could not only be poisoned, but also, or chiefly, be irradiated with pulsed microwaves (radar). (Adolf Hitler and all the other heads of governments and all Non-jews in key positions were only helpless Non-jewish prostitutes who played their roles assigned to them by the Jewish poisoners, so as other Non-jewish prostitutes before them have done so, and today do so.) And since WWII, pulsed microwaves (radar) irradiations of Non-jews (the military and civilians) occurred in each war the Jewish poisoners brought about, such as in Korea, in Vietnam, in the Persian Gulf, and in all the other wars in between. The Jewish poisoners have channelled hundreds of billions of Non-jewish taxpayers' dollars into the research and production of a great variety of radars: non-portable ones placed in each country, and portable ones visible but mostly hidden in vans and trailers, and in airplanes and mounted on ships. Some radars beam only a particular pulsed microwave frequency; others can beam several pulsed microwave frequencies simultaneously, as well as intense bursts of X-rays; still others produce with their beams an equivalent electric field accompanying a lightning stroke; and still others produce multiple frequency bursts of very narrow pulse widths with rapid rise time, which means immune surges of radiofrequency and microwave radiation — sometimes called radio flashes — which accompany nuclear explosions are produced. All these different radars are used on the unsuspecting Non-jewish populations all over the globe at some time or another and the consequences of that, that is, the mass destruction of human life and painful, horri-

"The Jewish poisoners organized WWII ... so that hundreds of millions of Non-jews, both the military forces and the various populations, could not only be poisoned, but also, or chiefly, be irradiated with pulsed microwaves (radar)."

> **"President Bill Clinton is a helpless Non-jewish prostitute in the tight clutches of the Jewish poisoners as all the other presidents were before him."**

fying, lifelong debilities for those who survive, are authoritatively explained sometimes as epidemics of "syphilis" or "AIDS" or as some other causes like "radiation that escaped from a nuclear power plant" or "chemical fumes from a chemical plant", but most often, no authoritative explanations are given at all by the Jewish poisoners' operated mass media in each country.

PART FOUR

My name is Rose Mokry. I am 63 years old and I am the writer of this research paper presented here in pamphlet form. From September 1984 to September 1989, I have been intensively researching most of the facts contained in this pamphlet, and hundreds of others as grisly as these in books, encyclopedias and magazines in the Libraries of Columbia University in New York City. From September 8, 1989 to April 1990, I have been distributing this pamphlet on the streets of Manhattan, New York City to drivers of all vehicles. (Notice how soon after I started distributing this pamphlet the panic-stricken Jews began dismantling their pet system called Communism in so many countries.) From April 1990, I have been sending this pamphlet only by mail all over the U.S. and Canada. This pamphlet is the Twenty-Sixth Edition. The previous twenty-five editions consisted of 54,000 copies.

Now a few facts about our new Non-jewish "leader:" President Bill Clinton is a helpless Non-jewish prostitute in the tight clutches of the Jewish poisoners so as all the other presidents were before him. President Clinton suffers on an allergy. And how do the Jewish poisoners produce allergies in Non-jews? Quite simply: Many poisons, anyone of which when administered in a sublethal dose once will cause mild health problems and the body gets completely rid of the poison within a certain time limit like 6 weeks or so. However, if the Non-jewish victims are poisoned again with the same poison before the human body can get rid completely of the previous sublethal dose, a violent reactions occurs producing more than one severe, long lasting health problem and even death may follow.

None of the American presidents ever died naturally (and those who still live will not die naturally either.) Some the Jews let die on injuries sustained in "accidents"; some the Jews let assassinate, but most of them the Jews poisoned which was always medically diagnosed as "death due to some disease or heart attack."

My Non-jewish readers. We Non-jews of all skin colors are an easy prey to the very cunning and deranged group of professional poisoners who operate everywhere from positions of legitimate power and through all mass media. What is going on in Bosnia and in Somalia is a Jewish poisoners' creation and continuance and the Jewish poisoners can bring about the same horrifying conditions for Non-jews anywhere in any country including the U.S.

With this pamphlet in your hands and by copying it and disseminating it to other Non-jews, Non-jewish prostitutes and police informers and even to Jews (it works everywhere instantly wherever it arrives) you will bring about a four-thousand year overdue justice for the Jewish poisoners and for us Non-jews a world without disease, birth defects and premature deaths. As you can see, the more millions of Non-jews the Jewish poisoners debilitate and kill, the more tens of billions of dollars are allocated by the Jewish run American Federal Government to the Jewish operated American Medical Authorities for "research and a cure" of a non-existing venereal disease called AIDS caused by a Non-existing virus called HIV.

All your letters containing this pamphlet sent by mail will arrive. However, with me it is a totally different matter. The Jewish poisoners who run Columbia University and the NYC and state and federal law enforcement agencies use all these agents (that is, Columbia University employees, city uniformed policemen and detectives, and police informers, as well as FBI and CIA agents, and special Jewish groups) for a round-the-clock illegal electronic surveillance over me. The agents' task is to find out when and where I go and into which mailboxes I drop my letters containing this pamphlet, so that the Jewish poisoners can intercept them. How arrogant and cunning the Jews are: they spend tens of millions of taxpayers' dollars and not one penny of their own for the colossal criminal round-the-clock electronic surveillance over me.

New York, January 1993.

Rose Mokry

P.S. One copy sent to President Bill Clinton, White House, Washington, D.C.

Polish immigrant Jozef Mlot-Mroz publishes *S.O.S.* (opposite and following page) from his home in Salem, MA, to fight the "Communist-Jewish Conspiracy." Mlot-Mroz brings a classic Polish perspective to rabid Jew hatred.

Wake Up ! American Nation ! Stir up the Americans and take up your arms, today, prayer alone, is not sufficient, boycott is not enough, because the Jews only laugh at us, when they see us crying out loudly ! The Jew needs a "good-spanking", on the Jaw, and belly, and even on their teeth, which need to be also straightened out. We also should boldly and bravely, shout the truth about the Jewish-zionist-communist conspiracy, and, we must fight against their conspiracy, and, we must fight against their conspiracy, too, just like our forefathers did, just 200 years ago.

SO, HELP US GOD !

Yours, for God, Freedom and Country.

September, 1988 — Jozef Mlot-Mroz

THE PEOPLE MUST CHALLENGE THE HIDDEN HAND

S.O.S.

SHIP OF STATE

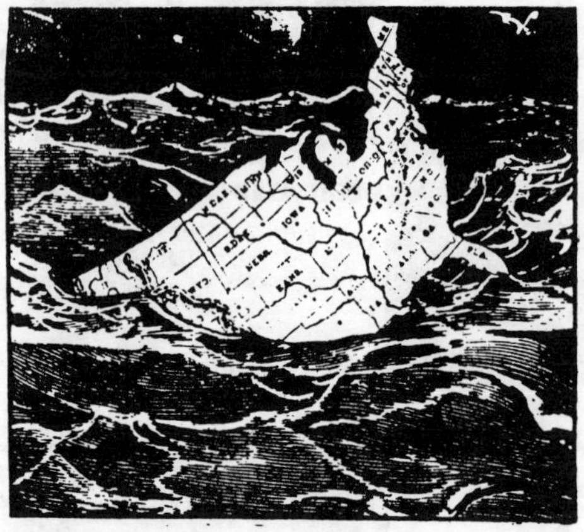

FIGHT JEWISH COMMUNIST CONSPIRACY

AMERICANS BEWARE!

YOU KNOW WHAT IS RIGHT BUT TOO MANY OF YOU ARE AFRAID OF THE JEWS

Jozef Mlot-Mroz

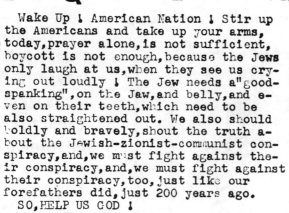

Don't Let American Youth Die For Israel!

Dear Reader - Auburn Danver's Case - Cover letter 3. 9/3/85

From pg 162 The Splendor of Greece: to discover the art of government.--refused to tell him where the valuable property was hidden.--Herodotus----Hera. Expanding on that, HE were my mother's initials, the book written by Robert Payne does jive with Payne Webber(later), & Grace Herod was president in 1955 of the Railroad Clerks Union when I resigned under considerable pressure; thus, there is also a rod idea & initials of my mother?.....The book, The World's Great Religions, yr. 1957 does show pg 162 ending the discussion on the Jewish religion, with the table of contents showing 131(Ludwig-Saxe Realty"president" difference)& 155(address of Hemming Morse in 1979 & Franklin Money Fund where the trustee opened an account). Space, length, & time precludes me from discussing any of this at length, but a lot of this is further explained in the letter. Pg 15 shows a heading: Truth Behind A Veil. It is a part of the section on Hinduism which jives with my sister becomming a Hindu, the Ramada Inn in Albuquerque as a Hindu name, item"O"of the trust, being probably the most important part of it, is the 15th item, besides my purpose is to get to the truth & get rid of the fiction & find out what is permanently real. Christendom starts at 206 giving the 6/2/82 idea when the Franklin Money Fund was opened & pg. 279 shows THE CHURCH GOING U.S.. Thus, the Herod/Pilate connection, 972 Burger King backwards, the landlord's friend 949 LUD license plate when my birthday is 23rd giving another indication(mother Hedwig, Ludwig, Dum UL?). Getting back to the Oct. 1975 Reader's Digest evidently planned so that I would accept them, & possibly then further planned when I kept them, we have ARE WE CREATING SUPER ATHELETES-OR MONSTERS? by Ron Clarke(middle name of Mastercrafts Atty?)page 141 from 360 gives 219 (2/19)when the roofing summons was issued. Oliver Twist, U.S.A. by Lester Velie is on pg 155 matching above, besides that the subject was foster homes. My step father's cousin Ross managed a foster home years ago in San Francisco. The"Quad"Who Won't Quit does connect to the Fay Stender matter, after being shot 6 times idea; that is to some extent. Planning for Us vs. by Us by MiltonFriedman(I do feel fried). Back to Oliver Twist, Polk County is mentioned which matches the Polk Directory apartment numbers later mentioned. Do It Yourself Way to Earn College Credits by Alfred & Florence Steinberg. Steinberg was"my"grandmother's family name. Taking the Story The Balloon Hoax by Poe crossing the Atlantic in 75 hours in the Monck Mason Flying machine using the steering Balloon Victoria, the digest then also for 75¢, you have the Lee County, AL realtor's 10/1/80 letter(Monk Wright Realty), Victoria, Queen while Disraeli was prime minister, & so on. DeBardelaben cited the case Herston vs. Whitesell(my leasing agent was Mr. White when I bought the rest of the warehouse) which was about attorney malpractice in the form of a painter falling off scaffolding, which he knew was dangerous, but the city had failed to add the missing screws. Thus with the Watchtower Society in 1961 at 124 Columbia Heights & my uncle at 124 Eyre Court, a reason for the choice beyond that given becomes clear. Besides Eyre in the Book 1,000 Things, on Pg 32 Time-Religions, there is the Hymn: To Purusha, my sister now named Usha, & it begins- A 1,000 heads hath Purusha, 1,000 Eyes, 1,000 Feet. In addition, not only did the President then of Saxe have four of the same letters as the person in the story, The Nose, but the story The Tiger(also from my library)starts at 279 to enhance that matter. As to the Ancor Book(The Nose), The Story of the Siren starts pg 170 mentioning the Blue Grotto of Capri where I was with my mother about 1933 and on pg. 173 also the name Guiseppe, the formal name of my landlord who's realty recordings were of interest. The story started with a note book of the Deist Controversy, thus on religion -I hope the siren is heard. U Lonston

While rereading an expansion of the above, I noticed that I did not differentiate between two different stories.??; by chance thus, I hit upon the following: Pg 99 Arrangements in Black & White-Dorothy Parker: Walter Williams, Burton, Katherine Burke; Walter, step father's twin brother or Walter Neubauer ideas meaning new builder & with his wife shows WON, & Burke Key Joints were used to put the warehouse floor concrete together. She also has on pg 179 Soldiers of the Republic: Valencia, to which my landlord moved in 1980, the new street number shows a certain relationship with the recordings I looked up. On pg 260 is Honors & Awards by James Reid Parker. James original Alabama atty., Reed College phonetically to which my parents wanted me to go. The story is partly about prejudice & I also note that "Pontius Pilatus"was written therein. Now to Bedside Tales(also from my inherited library). Here We Are by Dorothy Parker on pg 130 in the limited portion part-it does include two suitcases idea(the reason for the Mastercraft suit?). Big Blond by Dorothy Parker on pg. 356 showed Hazel Morse, 357 Houston(National Childcare"then" main office, 362 Mrs. Martin(in 76 across from my warehouse), 363 Detroit(my political file?), 372 Nettie(from Splendor of Greece-pg 125-in their nets the limbs of a godlike hero)who was a household worker like Mattee(don't know how spelled)was for my step sister(ex trustee's wife); 367 Vera Riley(Vera as mother of the extrustee & Riley as the Linden Office Postmaster. The main inside cover pg shows A Gay Collection with an introduction by Peter Arno, Wm. Penn Publishing 1945. I am 99½% sure that by 1980 if not before, that the Parker matter became one of the more leading parts of the plot. Ulric R Lonston 9-4-85

Pg 154 Stormy weather is what man needs from time to time to remind him that he is not really in charge of anything by Bill Vaughan. The signing of the 10/10/78 guaranties by the doctors(M.D. Foods Auburn main guarantors)together with the atty. work has proven that to me-that I was not in charge of the situation, besides the attorneys.

The Splendor of Greece was a gift from the 4 member Ken Royce office. Dorothy Shyshka's signature does give the Parker & Opelika Road 1478 Danver's idea

One of a fistful of flyers handed to me in downtown San Francisco, circa 1984.

GOD'S LAW

"We cannot release any details of God's Master Case publicly because all is in public records where we cannot protect it once released."

IN 1989 I REQUESTED INFORMATION FROM an organization called "God's Law"; the response to my simple one sentence inquiry far surpassed my expectations. The response, along with facsimiles of flyers, are reprinted below.

July 4, 1989

Dear D. Kossy:

Thank you for your interest. In answer to your questions:

1. — I began to research Satan's Banker-Jew-Masonic machinery of legalized Satanism in God's scriptures 40 years ago. Since then I and good sons Peter, Chas, etc., have formed this massive research into God's Scriptural Master Case of Lawful Christian Authority in destruction of Satan's Banker-Jew-Masonic Masonic Case of Unlawful Religious Jurisdictional Jupiter & Justice Idol Authority.

2. — We call ourselves The Church of Mary Mother of Christ and Christian Government of God's Master Case of Lawful Christian Authority. Why? Because our research show that:

a. — God established Mary as the Mother of Christ and Christian Government of God's Laws & Master Case of Lawful Taxation, Process, and Rule (Scriptures reserved).

b. — That Satan & Banker-Jew-Masonic Conspiracy established Jupiter-Satan and his daughters Satan-goddesses Liberty, Justice-Vengeance, etc., as their criminal Confederacies and Master Case of Unlawful Religious Jupiter & Justice Idol Authority - of unlawful Taxation Process and Rule.

c. — That God commanded us and all true Christians to 'Join'each other in prosecuting God's Laws & Master Case in destruction of all the Satan-Banker-Jew-Masonic Conspiracy and their unlawful Religious Confederacies and Master Case of Unlawful Jurisdictional Jupiter-Justice Idol Authority.

Master Case reserved to only those who 'Join' us:

3. — We cannot release any details of God's Master Case publicly because all is in public records where we cannot protect it once released. This means that those who refuse to accept God's scriptural instructions of how to use His Master Case may easily steal and abuse the Master Case if we publish it. Once they possess sources of this Master Case, they will do just that — steal and ruin it for us and other true christian Souls.

4. — We do not have any 'organization' beyond our own, and effort to 'organize' other Christian Souls to establish God's Master Case under their own 'organization' of a Church of Mary Mother of God and Christian Government where they live. The idea is to assure that all Souls remain independent, yet united in God's Master Case against our common internal enemies.

5. — I enclose an INVITATION to meet with us — if you are a true Christian Soul and are willing to accept God's simple requirements to 'join' us in His Master Case against the enemy Master Case of Unlawful Religious State-Federal Jupiter-Justice Idol Authority.Thank you for your interest, and we hope to hear from you in a more serious way.

James C. O'Brien Senior
Church of Mary Mother of Christ & Christian Government

of

God's Master Case of Lawful Christian Authority In Destruction of Satan's Banker-Jew-Masonic-Islamic Master Case of Unlawful Religious State-Federal Jurisdictional Jupiter-Justice Idol Authority

We do not have funds for our 'Publication' as yet. We invested our last $2000 in enclosed INVITATION to help us publish more about ourselves and Master Case. Without money we cannot publish more at this time.

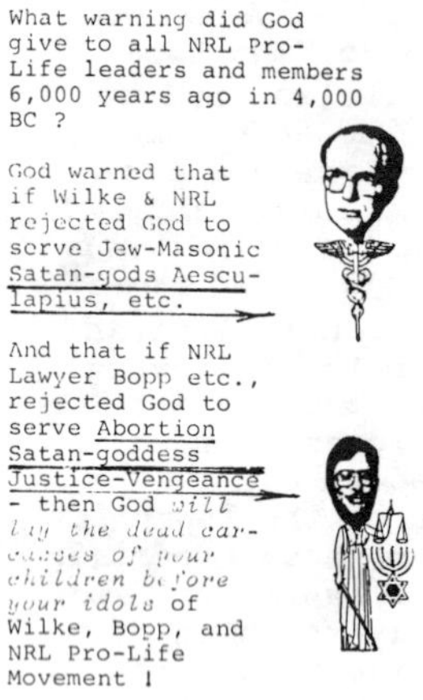

What warning did God give to all NRL Pro-Life leaders and members 6,000 years ago in 4,000 BC ?
God warned that if Wilke & NRL rejected God to serve Jew-Masonic Satan-gods Aesculapius, etc.
And that if NRL Lawyer Bopp etc., rejected God to serve Abortion Satan-goddess Justice-Vengeance - then God will lay the dead carcasses of your children before your idols of Wilke, Bopp, and NRL Pro-Life Movement !

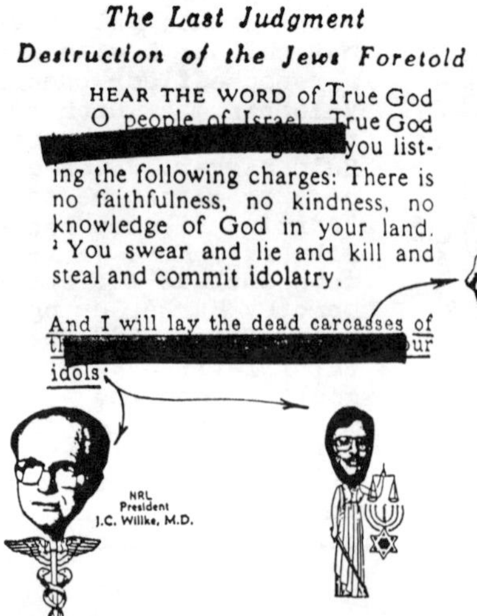

HEAR THE WORD of True God
O people of Israel. True God
[redacted] you listing the following charges: There is no faithfulness, no kindness, no knowledge of God in your land. You swear and lie and kill and steal and commit idolatry.

NRL President J.C. Willke, M.D.

Criminally Fraudulent Exploitation

The following is an excerpt from a press release sent anonymously to a Nashville music writer.

July 20, 1985

In reference to the criminal conspiracy to defraud in interstate, and international commerce, that was being perpetrated on an industry wide scale by the Film, and TV industries, this is not only continuing unabatedly, and utterly criminally unconscionably, but has been very greatly, and violently worsened, especially Via infinitely more depraved and bestially criminally vicious, & atrociously unconscionable means than previously, involving such greatly worsened moral corruption as to convey the impression that we're not living in America the land of the free, where liberty, equality, and democracy reigns, but that we're instead living in Nazi Germany, and/or in the twin cities of sin, Sodom And Gommorah, involving the fact that massively widespread Bribery is mainly the reason for this situation's current enormous worsening, as based also on the Spirit Of Evil that continues to be prevalently involved in this country, that has allowed it to be unabatedly continued to this date, Via its' commencement more than thirty years ago, in 1950, and/or prior thereto Per. Films, etc; which also continues to be unabatedly involved in TV Commercials, and in Top Category TV Shows, such as Dallas, Dynasty, Hotel, Magnum PI, General Hospital, and innumerably many others, including literally as a common pattern in Top Category Films, and especially in Academy Award winning films, including throughout "A View To The Kill," Prizzi's Honor, by the notorious monster, who calls himself a Director, who's become the "Frankenstein" of Films, John Huston, also throughout Perfect, Purple Rose of Cairo, Rambo: First Blood II, A Private Function, especially conspicuously, and unconscionably throughout "Pale Rider," also The Shooting Party, all very substantially, and criminally fraudulently based on disaster code "P & R" (combined with others, including with our name in some, such as "A View To The Kill," and "Perfect," etc;) and on the utterly shockingly connibalistically inspired current enormously reactivated "Promotion" thereof, which (again) involves our being virtually constantly subjected to the most abusive, sadistic, and criminally intolerably atrocious harassment, including at our Hotel, in conjunction therewith (from the outside however) to constantly provoke conflicts, tumults, furors, and commotions, as a continuous series of criminally conspiratorially, and fraudulently alleged publicity stunts therefore, and also Via the fact that disaster code #17, is also simultaneously in an enormously and criminally atrociously reactivated state of such alleged and utterly sadistically inspired greatly reactivated promotion and exploitation, which is identified with disaster codes "P & R," as they are the 16th. and 18th. letters, etc; which also often involves them separately, as disaster codes "P or R," the most shocking, and appalling aspect of which is that such constant, or constantly recurrent, and often utterly sadistically violent criminal harassment I'm being regularly subjected to for such alleged further "Promotional" purposes, may at any very possibly imminent moment, cause my death such as due to a stroke or a heart attack, which especially due to my present age may be involved at any very possibly immanent moment such as today, tomorrow, or possibly the next day, etc; ...

> "... the Spirit Of Evil that continues to be prevalently involved in this country, that has allowed it to be unabatedly continued to this date, Via its' commencement more than thirty years ago, in 1950, and/or prior thereto Per. Films, etc; which also continues to be unabatedly involved in TV Commercials, and in Top Category TV Shows, such as Dallas, Dynasty, Hotel, Magnum PI, General Hospital, and innumerably many others..."

In Re. the most shocking and appalling "Common Pattern" involving the fact that our so called "Employers," most of whom live in the Beverly Hills area (apart from those in the New York area, who's "Psychotic Syndrome" is also similar thereto, etc;) have been constantly arranging to have us subjected to such most incredibly, and utterly brutally criminally atrocious harassment, everywhere we live, and have lived since prior to 1950, for virtually 57 varieties of utterly criminally insanely inspired & criminally conspiratorially fraudulent purposes, including especially to deliberately cause us to be made continuously so extremely severely, and critically irreparably ill, injured, and disabled, especially due to constantly, and/or constantly recurrently loud "Noisemaking" Via most duplicitously conniving, finagling, and covert (Chicanery) means used, generally to attempt to conceal their monumentally criminally atrocious guilt, to pretend this is being done for legitimate purposes, etc; and usually with the aiding and abetment of the New York Police, during all the years we were involuntarily compelled to remain living there, during the 1951-82 years, and especially to cause us to be made constantly so severely and irreparably Neurologically ill, and disabled due to massive brain damages, that I should be made unable to legally defend myself against them, such as by suing them for damages... sometime after I moved to my present Hotel in downtown Los Angeles in late 1982, ... it was arranged to commence three construction

> "... as this would confirm that they're 'Unable to comprehend the difference between right and wrong,' as this 'Inability to comprehend this difference,' is of course precisely the legal definition of insanity, it must therefore be concluded that all those who're engaging therein are in reality so 'Insane' ..."

jobs (in addition to wrecking jobs immediately prior thereto, etc;) nearby, and/or adjacent to my Hotel, involving the virtually constant making of loud noise thereby, was also most probably deliberately arranged by the perpetrators of this criminal conspiracy to defraud, Via Channels, in concert with others, for the aforenoted essentially similar criminally conspiratorially fraudulent purposes, in addition to for the simultaneous purpose of the construction of buildings, including to at the same time constantly create criminally conspiratorially, and fraudulently alleged material to enable them, and especially TV, and TV News Shows particularly, such as Good Morning America, and The "Today" show (formerly also the CBS Morning News Show, until recently, etc;) to constantly engage in exploiting what may be transpiring, and how I'm coping therewith, as criminally conspiratorially and fraudulently alleged Topical Comedy News Material, by constantly attempting to criminally insanely promote the false impression that this in addition to all of our other utterly criminally atrocious victimization in Films, as well as on TV, unabatedly during the past 35 or more years is, and has merely been innocently inspired as a continuous series of most amusing practical jokes, and/or comedy situations, by means of which they're constantly attempting to also "Reverse or obscure the difference between right and wrong," and as this would confirm that they're "Unable to comprehend the difference between right and wrong," as this "Inability to comprehend this difference," is of course precisely the legal definition of insanity, it must therefore be concluded that all those who're engaging therein are in reality so "Insane," and/or Mentally Incompetent, which would also of course apply to all of their collaborators, and especially to those who're usually engaging therein by the most zealous and conscientious means, which would include David Hartman, Bryant Gumbel, The "Today" Show's host, including J. Carson, Merv Griffin, as well as to various of the most unconscionably collaborating Politicians, including Mayor Koch of New York, meaning especially while I was living there, during his tenure, commencing in 1977, until I left there in 1982...

Among many others, such criminally fraudulent exploitation is also involved throughout Siverado, The Emerald Forest, Goonies, Back To The Future, Daryl, Fletch, Per. disaster code "F" especially, and also The Jigsaw Man, Via M. Caine's role as Kimberly Per. the Kimberly Diamond Mines, the most conspicuous of which were the 375 films so far in which I was most brazenly identified by name, & likewise the over 2,750 TV (segments) in which I was also most flagrantly identified by name. ...

Television, Satan's major instrument

The greatest moral peril for humanity

This other calamity: the Godless, secularized, mixed schools

By a Roman Catholic Priest

Television *(as a world congress of moralists not long ago affirmed it),* television is the greatest moral peril for humanity. Nothing is as clear or as easy to understand. Then, do not be unconscious criminals, do not play with this terrible peril, do not expose your children's innocence, under pretext to do like your neighbour!

Evil enters through the eyes. Never did Satan disposed of such an instrument so as to penetrate everywhere at once, with his sensual and imprudent pictures, more or less insolently displayed, which imperceptibly burn the delicate fibers of innocence and awake thirsts and unhealthy curiosities, terribly dangerous for the ideal of purity, of force, for the virginal religious vocations, these marvelous flowers who should in great number embalm the earth, if the modern wave of rotten eroticism did not exercise its diabolical devastation, by picture, the cinema, the television, by the present filthy, "dirty-minded" fashions: means of corruption launched by "Freemasonry".

Schools

In front of these mortal perils, souls of the young are without real resistance, owing to this other calamity which are the Godless, secularized and mixed schools, where the mind is not awaken to the real light, to the love of the sole Being worthy of love: God their Father, of Whom it is forbidden to mix the name to vanities of profane science. Attention! our society, rotten by its madness, begins to sway on the edge of the abyss and of the Apocalyptic Chastisements, final day of reckoning for secularized nations.

One can if one wants

Dear reader, if you have children whom you really love, one only sensible conclusion imposes itself: no television in your home, whatever the cost.

One will tell you: "But one cannot go against the evolution of things and of morals". Nothing more inaccurate! One can if one wants. All decadence is the result of individual weaknesses.

This capitulation is unworthy of a father or a mother, for whom purity of their child comes before all vanities of fashion, of comfort and of "what will people say". There is only one true wealth which matters: the wealth of the heart, the soul, the mind. Now, this wealth, it is the love of God Himself, sole true food of the heart and mind. This divine wealth, must be protected at all cost, yes, at all cost. "If your eye scandalizes you, pluck it out...".

If television sullies the eyes of your children, refuse it entrance in your family sanctuary. If you let it penetrate, know well it is entering with Satan, the demon of the flesh... who by picture will make reign the madness of bestial and carnal love in the souls of your children, the "fiddlesticks fascination"... ruin of all ideal. The chiefs of corruption begin by degrading hearts.

Refuse television
Cinema, fashions

Parents! attention! refuse this diabolical and criminal danger. Refuse television at all cost! Attention also to cinema!

As for you, dear reader, if you want to respect God in you and in others, to be the temple of Jesus crucified and of Mary, to resist the present infernal wave of pornography and sexual madness, then no more disgusting fashions: no more panties, no more mini-skirts, no more frequenting of sickening beaches, no more of these ignoble "show-all" fashions, which sully the eyes of the young and the little ones, and poisons the social atmosphere with the mortal virus of a disproportionate eroticism. The one who loves danger, poison, will die from it. How many young people die from it or drag themselves in mud, like broken wing eagles! Yes, evil enters through the eyes...

Courage! Hearts reaching up! Look at Jesus crucified to expiate the sins of the flesh. Look at Mary, Virgin without stain, the star of purity. Look at the true daughters of Mary, the Cloistered Nuns, the virginal, religious brides of Christ, jealously sheltered by the cloister, reserved for the sole glance and the sole love of God. In their very noble frock of frieze, these terrestrial angels, by the total purity of their life, their glance, their heart, save the world and condemn impurity, the reign of the flesh. Courage! lead in their footsteps the hearts of your children. Protect their innocence, push back temptations, stupidity and the animality of sexual imprudences of mixed schools or other, push back the school's secularism, push back television far away from the eyes of your children... if you want to protect the flame of their ideal... Evil enters through the eyes, deceitfully, like the cunning, secretive and perfidious serpent.

Idiotic arguments

For goodness' sake, push back the idiotic arguments of a bored world. Obviously, those who have lost all innocence do not any more risk to lose it. They can look at everything. Those who have lost everything, fear no more the dangers of the thief! But those who want to keep the treasure of happiness and of purity in their heart and the heart of their children, those ones must take the vigorous means, forthwith, because, in one second, in one glance, by a picture, what a mother has put twenty years to erect can be forever devastated, by a hurricane of carnal passions, unleashed imprudently. If the young are rebellious, it is because they have lost happiness.

One knows the slogans of the world and of Hell: it is necessary to harden the young, to accustom them to danger. But this is precisely where the problem lies. For the peril is so great, the ground so slippery, the traps so striking, that the hardening consists to know how to steer clear of them. No need to go through death to know that one is mortal. If one wants to go through it, one does not return, it is suicide. The good war is to avoid the mortal traps, because it is necessary to reckon with original sin, the degeneration of man. The original degeneration consists precisely in that the knowledge of evil and the forbidden fruit leads the connivance of the weaken and ineffectual willpower. The apostle deplores it: "Although I know where good is, it is evil I listen to, and who leads me". Only God knows how to "initiate", or to enlighten without burn.

(continued on page 4)

Michael Journal, a French-Canadian version of the Moral Majority, advocates the panacea of "social credit" as an answer to the Federal Reserve, taxes, bankers, corruption and economic injustice. Its most extreme viewpoints are reserved for television and the media.

Angela Lynn Douglas

Prior to changing sex, Doug Czinki was raised in the Air Force, completed high school in Tokyo, served in the Air Force as a meteorologist and was also a working rock-jazz singer-guitarist from 1958 to 1968, including while in school and in the Air Force. Czinki had affairs with many women and was married to Cuban-born Norma Rodriguez from 1962 to 1968, who became a lesbian and left Czinki. Their daughter, born in 1968, is named Joann. Rodriguez didn't turn up until 1982.

Czinki began the sex change in Hollywood in 1969. For two years, crushed by Rodriguez's actions, Czinki had lived with bikers and became a heavy drug user, but abandoned drugs in 1969. He took the name "Angela Douglas," inspired by Irish actress Angela Douglas, who was in the film "Cleopatra," and became a writer, and has lived as a woman since 1969. In 1970, Douglas founded the Transsexual Action Organization rights group, which was based in Miami from 1972 to 1976, and was also active in the revolutionary gay movement, but broke with that due to violent hatred of transsexuals by many gay men and lesbians.

In 1976, Douglas moved to Berkeley and underwent sex change surgery by Dr. John R. Brown in L.A. in 1977, which left him ill for years.

Douglas had been interviewed on radio, TV and by many publications, includin The Miami News and High Times Magazine over the years, and a pornographer in L.A., Stan Grossman, published a "biography" about her in 1978, "Sex Change, Th Story of Angela Douglas." "Impostors" in show biz began surfacing around 1980 while Douglas was trying to get back into music, openly as a transsexual.

Douglas has been violently assaulted over 20 times and seriously injured several times, arrested twelve times on petty charges since 1970 (all but a few cases were dismissed) and investigated by the FBI at the behest of film makers she threatened to sue or protested against due to their attacks on her and transsexuals. Blake Edwards, Garry Marshall, Jerry Bruckheimer, Brian de Palma, Larry Flynt and Grossman all went to the FBI on her over the years.

The TAO group became the world's best-known of its kind, one of about 50 groups in the 1970's for transsexuals and transvestites. The group was disbanded in 1976, and had developed branches throughout the US, Canada and the British Isles.

Born in Detroit in 1943, Douglas grew up mostly in Florida and also attended junior high and one year at Hialeah High there.

Rodriguez surfaced in 1982 and disclosed that she is now in a Hindu cult.

Over the years, Douglas has had thousands of stories published in a wide variety of publications ranging from gay papers to the underground press and The Honolulu Star-Bulletin and Lake Tahoe News. She self-published her autobiography, TRIPLE JEOPARDY, in late 1982, primarily to try and dispel the confusion that was developing about her and her life.

Douglas was also associated with radical feminist groups in 1971, in Los Angeles.

The transsexual has never been wealthy as many assume, and for some years, was homeless. In recent years, Douglas thumbed to Floridaand back a dozen times or so on long-haul trucks and has traveled throughout the country.

Douglas' most successful rock band was the original EUPHORIA, active in L.A. from 1965 to 1967, consisting of Douglas and three men. In 1972, Rodriguez stole the Euphoria name and got a record album out on MGM-Heritage Records. She is the dark-haired woman on the record cover.

The transsexual's life and many adventures havebecome rich fodder for Hollywood. writers and "impostors" surfaced to cash in on her growing notoriety.

She is physically female as a result of the 1977 surgery.

The story of transsexual Angela Lynn Douglas, who claims to have been ripped off repeatedly by everyone from Hollywood producers to the manufacturers of Garbage Pail Kids, can be found on her voluminous flyers. Samples above and opposite.

From the 1986-87 "Annie" comic strip....

Angela's 1979 Hawaii I.D.

Angela has filed suit against Topps Gum Co. of Brooklyn on its "Glandular Angela" "Garbage Pail Kids" sticker, which came out in 1986, but it was dismissed on a technicality and she hopes to re-file it. Angela's book explains that the sex change was the result of glandular disorders. Many cases of transsexualism, homosexuality and lesbianism are the result of glandular disorders and hormonal imbalances, although gay and lesbian militants try to ignore the fact. Both males and females both secrete both male and female hormones. If there is an imbalance, the men become physically feminine and the women become physically masculine. East Germany made homosexuality legal recently on ground it is an illness caused by hormonal disorders...

Angela in Berkeley 1987

AN UNWITTING SUBJECT

"The reason I am still alive is because I have been protected by Aerial Electronic Surveillance Physiological and Psychological Weapons, and other Aerial Electronic Protective Surveillance Systems, for unlimited distance in the United States."

THE FOLLOWING IS NEARLY THE ENTIRE TEXT of a letter/flyer received by me in the late 80s. The subject matter indicates that it was probably written in the late 70s.

I have been an unwitting subject of Central Intelligence Agency research and development of physiologists monitoring my brain and human body by means of a remote transmitter of an electronic station by electromagnetic wave surveillance, of radio wave frequency behavior and mind control, nuclear alienation, radio cybernetic cyborgation biofeedback control of my bodily functions and organs unusually, cruelly, and severely, radio conversation communication of my silent thoughts, remote video of my silent thoughts (of the same capabilities, but better, of the Perfect Spy psychic visions Central Intelligence Agency research and development currently being conducted), my brain and human body of no implant device, of my unknowing unobvious to me until after 4 January 1978. Before 4 January 1978 the outcome of my life was electroformed, controlled, and direct, myself recognizing and distinguishing how I was manipulated from the way I have been manipulated since 4 January 1978.

Since 4 January 1978 I have been under persecution of neurological stress systems programs at biofeedback by CIA physiologists of my emotions, feelings, and nervous condition throughout my human body, controlling me the way they want for the desired affect, and I have been receiving and transmitting radio conversation communication of my silent thoughts, the CIA physiologists part of non-stop and non-fact talkage, recording, and assessment (in coordination with remote video of my silent thoughts, and neurological stress systems programs), of aberration, dehumanization, mind bending, brainwashing, a wash-out, an attempted wash-up, extreme mental and physical cruelty, a suicidal malicious maltreatment, all while not sleeping of endless manipulation.

I am a CIA research and development subject capable of receiving and transmitting from radio wave frequency brain monitoring remote video, and radio communication, of my silent thoughts. I have been shown persons by the remote video of my silent thoughts with radio communication starting about in the middle of 1977, then at a later date recognizing the person or persons in public before. Persons I have seen are related to myself used as a radio cybernetic cyborgation/nuclear alienation zombie and video radio of my silent thoughts spy for organized crime and racketeering law enforcement purposes for crackdowns, exposure, and espionage in the United States, and their identities unknown to me. My pictures and visions of my silent thought and my silent thoughts, were under monitoring to me unwittingly until after 4 January 1978. After 4 January 1978 I became aware that pictures and visions of my silent thoughts, and my silent thoughts, were being monitored with parts of the unwitting remote video reshown to me, plus exposure of the witting monitoring of my silent thoughts caused extreme embarrassment, torturement, and uncomfortness, defenseless against forced submission of my past and current life.

I have been under persecution of radio cybernetic cyborgation/nuclear alienation testing and disposal since 4 January 1978, against my will, consent, life and physical safety, and right to protect myself, myself a private citizen enslaved, imprisoned, and ostracized from my due course of human life, forced into operational use and used as a covert agent for organized crime and racketeering law enforcement purposes, myself not related to organized crime and racketeering in any way ever, used as a radio cybernetic cyborgation/nuclear alienation zombie, video radio of my silent thoughts spy given "master spying" capabilities, and a murder hit spur, framed up to be killed by the Mafia blamed for doing drug busts for part or possibly all of the reason for the murder contract, to attract and expose organized crime hit men in the act and in conspiracy to murder me for Covert Operation Exposure in the United States. I have had a Mafia hit upon me since November 1977 that I know of, unwittingly controlled before 4 January 1978. The reason I am still alive is because I have been protected by Aerial Electronic Surveillance Physiological and Psychological Weapons, and other Aerial Electronic Protective Surveillance Systems, for unlimited distance in the United States.

The situation has prevented me of flourishment of life, accumulation of wealth, a residence of my own being forced to live at my parents apartment, emotional independence, no married life, no family life of a family of my own, no love life, incapacitated from my life just existing in radio cybernetic cyborgation/nuclear alienation testing and disposal, deprived of life, liberty, and pursuit of happiness, of unhealthiness, since January 4,

1978. There has been about six and a half months that I have not stayed at my parents apartment since January 4, 1978.

I can hear the noise level of the nuclear alienation vibrating through my head and it sounds like a furnace flame when I cover my ears or plug my ears. I can also feel it vibrating throughout my human body. I am prevented of applying myself under nuclear alienation, prevented of protecting myself, and need Emergency Services. I need to be monitored with Health Endangerment Radiation Monitoring Systems or other means to get me released of nuclear alienation.

My situation is a fraud case and the FBI will do nothing for me. I believe the FBI will do nothing for me because it would only lead to exposure of Watergate Criminal Activity upon me by the FBI. The federal Criminal Division will not do anything for me either of the fraud, waste, and abuse of my situation. In September or October 1977 a girlfriend of mind said, "Your name came up on a roster," "Another Watergate," "I can't wait to get his military records," "I still say you have something big going on," "Just something big," referring to the FBI. Every time she passed the FBI Field Office in Campbell, California she said, "There's the FBI Building," time after time. The same girl said out of the blue one day, "I have two FBI friends." I was unaware of my relation to the FBI in any way. I have never been confronted by anyone about a job in law enforcement, and never had or have any intentions of doing so. The same girl said, "If my mother knew I was seeing you she would throw a folder out in front of me of everything about you." She has also referred to her mother as people with money can get away with anything. A roofing customer of mine in November 1977 after a brief talk with me he turned around about 20 feet away from me and said, "He don't know it but he's foolin with a VIP," "A G-Man," then scratches his head and walks off.

I do not have my human freedoms of benefit for law enforcement purposes and the United States at the sacrifice of my life. I am a U.S. Marine Corps Veteran with an Honorable Discharge spending less than two years active duty within the United States joining in time of the Vietnam War. I was in an Air Delivery Platoon in Camp Pendleton, California and made 67 or 68 parachute jumps while in the service.

I have been under radio cybernetic cyborgation/nuclear alienation disposal since about the middle of my 26th year of age, and now I am 30 years of age as of June 12, 1981.

The Federal Bureau of Investigation, and the Central Intelligence Agency, are concealing from the United States Government the fact of myself being a radio cybernetic cyborgation/nuclear alienation zombie and video radio of my silent thoughts spy, and any knowing activity in support of my situation, a Covert Operation, and a Cover Up. I have been under radio cybernetic cyborgation/nuclear alienation disposal to keep me from intervening in highly illegal intelligence activity and highly explosive Watergate Criminal Activity upon me of which I was put into in the first place unwittingly that has been targeted against organized crime and racketeering.

The situation has also included a Zombie Run through Tucson and Phoenix, Arizona within the dates December 25-28, 1977 while under unwitting control. The next morning after returning from Arizona in San Jose, California at a small restaurant a guy walking out the door turned around and looked at me and said, "He's killin people." He and another guy stepped into a black limousine cadillac.

All my letters I have written to President Jimmy Carter, President Ronald Reagan, Central Intelligence Agency, Congress, U.S. Department of Justice, California Department of Justice, and others, have been under radio cybernetic cyborgation/nuclear alienation incapacitation preventing me of protecting myself sabotaging my potential letters or any letters at all in attempt to get out of this mess, affecting decisions made upon me by government officials to lead to my release of radio cybernetic cyborgation/nuclear alienation since 1978...

I have filed two complaints in the past of one brought against the U.S. Department of Justice filed by me August 2, 1978 (C-78-1735 RHS) for 10 million dollars damages, and the other brought against the Central Intelligence Agency filed by me December 14, 1978 (C-78-2861 SW) for [illegible] million dollars damages, and was denied grounds for damages for both complaints by the U.S. Attorneys' Office of San Francisco. I had made the complaints while under the condition of radio cybernetic cyborgation/nuclear alienation incapacitation, and being under this condition for so long, since 4 January 1978, has denied me access to justice keeping me indigent and from applying myself. I have not been able to hire talented experienced counsel and have access to the assistance of investigators, researchers, and technical or science experts. The U.S. Attorneys' Office of San Francisco has said in the past that I would have to get my own attorney [for] my complaining of my situation...

"I can hear the noise level of the nuclear alienation vibrating through my head and it sounds like a furnace flame when I cover my ears or plug my ears."

THE "MASTER RACE" FRANKENSTEIN RADIO CONTROLS
BRAIN THOUGHTS BROADCASTING RADIO
EYESIGHT TELEVISION
FRANKENSTEIN EARPHONE RADIO
THRESHOLD BRAIN WASH RADIO
LATEST NEW SKULL REFORMING TO CONTAIN
ALL FRANKENSTEIN CONTROLS EVEN IN
"THIN" SKULLS of WHITE PEDIGREE MALES
VISIBLE FRANKENSTEIN CONTROLS
SYNTHETIC NERVE
RADIO DIRECTIONAL LOOP ANTENNA

MAKE COPIES for YOURSELF *Francis E. Dec* B.A., L.L.B., L.L.M. 29 MAPLE AVENUE HEMPSTEAD,
THERE IS NO ESCAPE FROM THIS WORLD GANGSTER POLICE STATE USING ALL OF THE DEADLY GANGSTER FRANKENSTEIN CONTROLS. IN 1965 C.I.A. GANGSTER POLICE BEAT ME BLOODILY. DRAGGED ME IN CHAINS from KENNEDY N.Y. AIRPORT. SINCE THEN I HIDE in FORCED JOBLESS POVERTY ISOLATED ALONE in this LOW DEADLY NIGERTOWN OLD HOUSE. THE BRAZEN DEADLY GANGSTER POLICE AND NIGER PUPPET UNDERLINGS SPRAY ME WITH POISON NERVE GAS from AUTOMOBILE EXHAUSTS AND EVEN LAWN MOWERS, DEADLY ASSAULTS EVEN IN MY YARD WITH KNIVES, EVEN BRICKS and STONES, EVEN DEADLY TOUCH TABIN, or ELECTRIC SHOCK "FLASH LIGHT" EVEN REMOTE ELECTRONICALLY CONTROLLED AROUND CORNERS TRAJECTION of DEADLY TOUCH TARANTULA SPIDERS. or EVEN BLOODY MURDER "ACCIDENTS" TO SHUT ME UP FOR EVER WITH SNEAK "UNDETECTABLE EXTERMINATION", EVEN WITH TRAINED PARROTING PUPPET ASSASSINS. IN MAXIMUM SECURITY INSANITY PRISON FOR WRITING THESE UNFORGIVEABLE TRUTHFUL LETTERS UNTIL MY "UNDETECTABLE EXTERMINATION", I, FRANCIS E. DEC. ESQUIRE, 29 MAPLE AVENUE Hempstead, N.Y. I STAND ALONE AGAINST YOUR MAD DEADLY WORLD-WIDE CONSPIRATORIAL GANGSTER COMPUTER GOD COMMUNISM WITH WALL to WALL DEADLY GANGSTER PROTECTION, LIFE LONG SWORN CONSPIRATORS MURDER INCORPORATED ORGANIZED CRIME, THE POLICE AND JUDGES, the DEADLY SNEAK PARROTING PUPPET GANGSTERS USING ALL THE GANGSTER DEADLY FRANKENSTEIN CONTROLS. THESE HANGMAN ROPE SNEAK DEADLY GANGSTERS, THE JUDGES AND THE POLICE trick-trap, rob, wreck, butcher and murder the people to keep them TERRORIZED IN GANGSTER FRANKENSTEIN EARPHONE RADIO SLAVERY for the COMMUNIST GANGSTER GOVERNMENT and CON ARTIST PARROTING PUPPET GANGSTER PLAY BOY SCUM ON TOP THE SECRET WORK of ALL POLICE in ORDER to MAINTAIN A COMMUNIST CLOSED SOCIETY. The same world-wide mad deadly COMMUNIST GANGSTER COMPUTER GOD THAT CONTROLS YOU AS A TERRORIZED GANGSTER FRANKENSTEIN EARPHONE RADIO SLAVE, PARROTING PUPPET. YOU ARE A TERRORIZED MEMBER of the "MASTER RACE", WORLD-WIDE FOUR BILLION EYESIGHT TELEVISION CAMERA GUINEA PIG COMMUNIST GANGSTER COMPUTER GOD "MASTER RACE"! YOUR LIVING THINKING MAD DEADLY WORLD-WIDE COMMUNIST GANGSTER COMPUTER GOD SECRET OVER-ALL PLAN: WORLD-WIDE LIVING DEATH FRANKENSTEIN SLAVERY to EXPLORE AND CONTROL THE ENTIRE UNIVERSE with the ENDLESS "STAIRWAY TO THE STARS" namely the MAN MADE INSIDE OUT PLANETS with NUCLEONIC POWERED SPEEDS MUCH FASTER THAN THE SPEED OF LIGHT.

LOOK UP AND SEE THE GANGSTER COMPUTER GOD CONCOCTED NEW FAKE STARRY SKY.

THE WORLD-WIDE COMPLETELY CONTROLLED DEADLY DEGENERATIVE CLIMATE AND ATMOSPHERE THROUGH THE NEW WORLD ROUND TRANSLUCENT EXOTIC GASEOUS ENVELOPE, WHICH the WORLD-WIDE COMMUNIST GANGSTER COMPUTER GOD MANIPULATES THROUGH THE COUNTLESS EXACTLY POSITIONED SATELLITES, THE NEW FAKE, PHONY STARS IN THE SYNTHETIC "SKY"

FOR AGES BEFORE FRANKENSTEIN CONTROLS, APOIDIC NIGERS INTERBREEDABLE WITH APES HAD NO ALPHABET, NOT EVEN NUMERALS. SLAVERY CONSPIRACY OVER 300 YEARS AGO IDEAL TINY BRAIN APOIDIC NIGER GANGSTER GOVERNMENT EYESIGHT T.V. GANGSTER SPY CAMERAS. C.G.G. "NEW WORLD ORDER" DEGENERATION with "GIFTED" with ALL GANGSTER FRANKENSTEIN CONTROL NIGER DEADLY GANGSTER PARROTING PUPPETS OR NIGER BRAIN PROGRAMED ROBOTS DEADLY APE FRANKENSTEIN MACHINES DEGENERATIVE DISEASE TO ETERNAL FRANKENSTEIN SLAVERY, OVER-ALL PLAN through "ONE WORLD COMMUNISM" (top secret code word), meaning WORLD-WIDE ABSOLUTELY HELPLESS AND HOPELESS SIMPLE LANGUAGE MONGREL MULATTO APOIDIC NIGERS.

World-wide SYSTEMATIC INSTANT PLASTIC SURGERY BUTCHERY MURDER "FAKE AGING" SO ALL PEOPLE ARE DEAD OR USELESS BY AGE 70. DONE AT NIGHT TO YOU AS A FRANKENSTEIN SLAVE PARROTING PUPPET GANGSTER SLAVE, NOW EVEN YOU KNOW I AM A MENACE to YOUR world-wide mad deadly COMMUNIST GANGSTER COMPUTER GOD, THEREFORE I MUST GO TO EXTERMINATION. BEFORE I AM EXTERMINATED BY THIS GANGSTER COMPUTER GOD CONCOCTED AND CONTROLLED WORSE MONGREL ORGANIZED CRIME MURDER INCORPORATED GANGSTER COMMUNIST GOVERNMENT, I HAND YOU THE SECRETS TO SAVE THE ENTIRE HUMAN RACE AND THE ENTIRE UNIVERSE. DONATE MONEY OR EVEN A MANUAL TYPEWRITER TO ME FOR YOUR ONLY HOPE FOR A FUTURE.

FRANCIS E. DEC, ESQUIRE
YOUR ONLY HOPE FOR A FUTURE!

The writings of Francis E. Dec, Esquire, make almost every other kook document seems as ordinary as a business memo. Dec, with his repeated invocations of the mantras "Frankenstein Earphone Radio," "Frankenstein Eyesight TV" and "Computer God Parroting Puppet Gangster Slaves," seems to be attempting to free himself from the paranoid universe he inhabits. Like archeologists, who recreate entire cultures from microscopic fragments, witnesses to Dec's flyers and letters enter a vastly complex, barely comprehensible world through a few scraps of paper.

Dec has become something of an underground hero, but my researches have failed to turn up any information about him. The address listed on his flyers is no longer valid, and those who received original copies of his letters or flyers know just as little about him as everyone else. In most cases, those who received them were the least able to appreciate them. For example, in the mid-80s, an employee of a folding wall company in Indiana, the father of my correspondent Tim Maloney, was the unhappy recipient of a flyer from Francis E. Dec, Esquire. Dec sent back one of the company's business reply mail cards with the flyer "Master Race Frankenstein Radio Controls" stapled to the card. Tim's father was neither thrilled nor amused by this. He complained to the post office about delivering mail obviously six times the size covered by the bulk mailing permit. Fortunately, Tim made a copy of the flyer, saved it, and later sent me a copy.

Dec's rants have appeared in the comic book *Weirdo* (edited at the time by Robert Crumb) and the SubGenius newsletter *The Stark Fist of Removal* (edited by Rev. Ivan Stang.) The best forum for Dec, however, is audio tape. Voice recordings of his rants have been circulating on cassette among aficionados of the weird for a several years, and have been aired on public access radio. I was greatly disappointed, however, to learn these masterful recitations are not Dec, but an anonymous professional radio announcer. I know four such recordings, all produced at a radio station studio. Two of them use appropriate incidental music; the recording of "Gangster Computer God Worldwide Secret Containment Policy" (printed here as Rant #2), I consider a collaborative masterpiece by Dec and the producer.

Notes on the transcripts: Rant #1 is a transcript of the almost unreadable flyer illustrated here. (Thanks to Tim Maloney for expert help with deciphering.) Rant #2 is a transcript of one of the recordings. For this reason, there may be some discrepancy between my version and the original document; Dec may have capitalized, or had unique spellings, unknown to me. And, unfortunately it is impossible to duplicate this stellar performance on paper.

Like archeologists, who recreate entire cultures from microscopic fragments, witnesses to Dec's flyers enter a vastly complex, barely comprehensible world through a few scraps of paper.

Rant #1

THE "MASTER RACE" FRANKENSTEIN RADIO CONTROLS

BRAIN THOUGHTS BROADCASTING RADIO

EYESIGHT TELEVISION

FRANKENSTEIN EARPHONE RADIO

LATEST NEW SKULL REFORMING TO CONTAIN ALL FRANKENSTEIN CONTROLS

EVEN IN "THIN" SKULLS OF WHITE PEDIGREE MALES

VISIBLE FRANKENSTEIN CONTROLS

SYNTHETIC NERVE

RADIO DIRECTIONAL ANTENNA

FRANKENSTEIN FORMFITTING CONTROLS

BRAIN

PART OF BONE REMOVED

MAKE COPIES for YOURSELF. FRANCIS E. DEC B.A., L.L.B. L.L.M., 29 MAPLE AVENUE HEMPSTEAD, N.Y. THERE IS NO ESCAPE FROM THIS WORSE GANGSTER POLICE STATE USING ALL OF THE DEADLY GANGSTER FRANKENSTEIN CONTROLS. IN 1965 C.I.A. GANGSTER

> "The game world-wide mad deadly COMMUNIST GANGSTER COMPUTER GOD that CONTROLS YOU AS A TERRORIZED GANGSTER FRANKENSTEIN EARPHONE RADIO SLAVE, PARROTING PUPPET."

POLICE BEAT ME BLOODILY. DRAGGED ME IN CHAINS from KENNEDY N.Y. AIRPORT. SINCE THEN I HIDE in FORCED JOBLESS POVERTY ISOLATED ALONE in this LOW DEADLY NIGER-TOWN OLD HOUSE. THE BRAZEN DEADLY GANGSTER POLICE AND NIGER PUPPET UNDERLINGS SPRAY ME WITH POISON NERVE GAS from AUTOMOBILE EXHAUSTS AND EVEN LAWN MOWERS, DEADLY ASSAULTS EVEN IN MY YARD WITH KNIVES, EVEN BRICKS AND STONES, EVEN DEADLY TOUCH TABIN, or ELECTRIC SHOCK "FLASH LITE", EVEN REMOTE ELECTRONICALLY CONTROLLED AROUND CORNERS TRAJECTION of DEADLY TOUCH TARANTULA SPIDERS. or EVEN BLOODY MURDER "ACCIDENTS" TO SHUT ME UP FOREVER WITH SNEAK "UNDETECTABLE EXTERMINATION", EVEN WITH TRAINED PARROTING PUPPET ASSASSINS. IN MAXIMUM SECURITY INSANITY PRISON FOR WRITING THESE UNFORGIVABLE TRUTHFUL LETTERS UNTIL MY "UNDETECTABLE EXTERMINATION", I, FRANCIS E. DEC, ESQUIRE, 29 MAPLE AVENUE, HEMPSTEAD, N.Y. I STAND ALONE AGAINST YOUR MAD DEADLY WORLD-WIDE CONSPIRATORIAL GANGSTER COMPUTER GOD COMMUNISM WITH WALL to WALL DEADLY GANGSTER PROTECTION, LIFE LONG SWORN CONSPIRATORS MURDER INCORPORATED ORGANIZED CRIME, THE POLICE AND JUDGES, the DEADLY SNEAK PARROTING PUPPET GANGSTERS USING ALL THE GANGSTER DEADLY FRANKENSTEIN CONTROLS. THESE HANGMAN ROPE SNEAK DEADLY GANGSTERS, THE JUDGES AND POLICE, trick-trap, rob, wreck, butcher and murder the people to keep them TERRORIZED IN GANGSTER FRANKENSTEIN EARPHONE RADIO SLAVERY for the COMMUNIST GANGSTER GOVERNMENT AND CON ARTIST PARROTING PUPPET GANGSTER PLAY BOY SCUM ON TOP, THE "SECRET" WORK of ALL POLICE in ORDER to MAINTAIN A COMMUNIST CLOSED SOCIETY. The game world-wide mad deadly COMMUNIST GANGSTER COMPUTER GOD that CONTROLS YOU AS A TERRORIZED GANGSTER FRANKENSTEIN EARPHONE RADIO SLAVE, PARROTING PUPPET. YOU ARE A TERRORIZED MEMBER of the "MASTER RACE". WORLD-WIDE FOUR BILLION EYESIGHT TELEVISION CAMERA GUINEA PIG COMMUNIST GANGSTER COMPUTER GOD "MASTER RACE". YOUR LIVING THINKING MAD DEADLY WORLD-WIDE COMMUNIST GANGSTER COMPUTER GOD SECRET OVERALL PLAN: WORLD-WIDE LIVING DEATH FRANKENSTEIN SLAVERY to EXPLORE AND CONTROL THE ENTIRE UNIVERSE with the ENDLESS "STAIRWAY TO THE STARS" Namely the MAN MADE INSIDE OUT PLANETS with NUCLEONIC POWERED SPEEDS MUCH FASTER THAN THE SPEED OF LIGHT. LOOK UP AND SEE THE GANGSTER COMPUTER GOD CONCOCTED NEW FAKE STARRY SKY. THE WORLD-WIDE COMPLETELY CONTROLLED DEADLY DEGENERATIVE CLIMATE AND ATMOSPHERE THROUGH THE NEW WORLD ROUND TRANSLUCENT EXOTIC GASEOUS ENVELOPE, WHICH the WORLD-WIDE COMMUNIST GANGSTER COMPUTER GOD MANIPULATES THROUGH THE COUNTLESS EXACTLY POSITIONED SATELLITES, THE NEW FAKE, PHONY STARS IN THE SYNTHETIC "SKY." FOR AGES BEFORE FRANKENSTEIN CONTROLS, APOIDIC NIGERS INTERBREEDABLE WITH APES HAD NO ALPHABET, NOT EVEN NUMERALS. SLAVERY CONSPIRACY OVER 300 YEARS AGO IDEAL TINY BRAIN APOIDIC NIGGER GANGSTER GOVERNMENT EYESIGHT T.V. GANGSTER SPY CAMERAS. C. GOD NEW WORLD ORDER "DEGENERATION" with "GIFTED" with ALL GANGSTER FRANKENSTEIN CONTROLS NIGER DEADLY GANGSTER PARROTING PUPPETS OR NIGER BRAIN PROGRAMMED ROBOTS DEADLY APE FRANKENSTEIN MACHINES DEGENERATIVE DISEASE TO ETERNAL FRANKENSTEIN SLAVERY, OVER-ALL PLAN through "ONE WORLD COMMUNISM" (top secret code word) meaning WORLD-WIDE ABSOLUTELY HELPLESS AND HOPELESS SIMPLE LANGUAGE MONGREL MULATTO APOIDIC NIGERS. world-wide SYSTEMATIC INSTANT PLASTIC SURGERY BUTCHERY MURDER "FAKE AGING" SO ALL ARE DEAD OR USELESS BY AGE 70. DONE AT NIGHT TO YOU AS A FRANKENSTEIN SLAVE. PARROTING PUPPET GANGSTER SLAVE, NOW EVEN YOU KNOW I AM A MENACE to YOUR world-wide mad deadly COMMUNIST GANGSTER COMPUTER GOD, THEREFORE I MUST GO TO EXTERMINATION. BEFORE I AM EXTERMINATED BY THIS GANGSTER COMPUTER GOD CONCOCTED AND CONTROLLED WORSE MONGREL ORGANIZED CRIME MURDER INCORPORATED GANGSTER COMMUNIST GOVERNMENT, I HAND YOU THE SECRETS TO SAVE THE ENTIRE HUMAN RACE AND THE ENTIRE UNIVERSE. DONATE MONEY OR EVEN A MANUAL TYPEWRITER TO ME FOR YOUR ONLY HOPE FOR A FUTURE.

SNEAK SHAMELESS HANGMAN ROPE GANGSTERS

GANGSTER GOVERNMENT LEADERS INTO ETERNAL FRANKENSTEIN LIVING DEATH SLAVERY.

Jimmy Carter the scribble-print yokel felon "warmed-over McGovern", in with the controlling Georgia Mafia and all the parroting puppet Governors, Congressmen, many, many Mayors ETC. have my eight page typewritten letter, which includes this Communist Gangster Computer God Exposé and even pages explaining some of the many, many "Undetectable Extermination" attempts against me by this worse mongrel gangster Communist Police State.

Ask them for copies of my said letter to them, the Communist Gangster Computer God ANOINTED UNTOUCHABLES, insidious sneak deadly gangsters, STAGED CON ARTIST PARROTING PUPPETS, figure heads, hags and playboys (EVEN APOIDIC NIGERS) deadly enemies of the Human Race, because of my letters, in COWARDLY TERROR, feloniously, they watch my Frankenstein Eyesight Television playback, waiting for my "Undetectable Extermination."

I face the deadly insidious INEVITABILITY OF GRADUALNESS CONSPIRACY. Completely alone and isolated, waiting for my "UNDETECTABLE EXTERMINATION." I very seldom venture out to one of the four last PLEBIAN supermarkets left in this GIGANTIC Niger infested boarded-up ghost town. We already have a C. God TOP SECRET DUAL FOOD STANDARD. INFERIOR DEGENERATE PLEBIAN MASSES VEGETABLES AND FOODS FOR THE SCUM, WHOLESOME NORMAL VEGETABLES AND FOODS. I hide STARVING AND BEGGING for even incomplete and late delivery of PLEBIAN especially picked, secretly coded inferior seriously degenerative Comp. God UNBELIEVABLY AND SCIENTIFICALLY GENETICALLY ENGINEERED HYBRID PROTEIN POISONING CEREALS AND PULP HYBRID HORSE RADISH GREEN VEGETABLES for my vegetarian diet.

Unbelievably Innocent and worse than defenseless, I have NO Gangster Frankenstein Earphone Radio. Only the impossible a Real miracle can Save me. Parroting puppet gangster Slave, if you believe in Anything? I beg you say one word of pray for me.

For your Only Hope for a Future.

Francis E. Dec, Esquire

Rant #2

Gangster Computer God Worldwide Secret Containment policy made possible solely by Worldwide Computer God Frankenstein Controls. Especially lifelong constant threshold brainwash radio. Quiet and motionless, I can slightly hear it. Repeatedly this has saved my life on the streets.

Four billion wordwide population, all living, have a Computer God Containment Policy brain bank brain, a real brain in the brain bank cities on the far side of the moon we never see. Primarily, based on your lifelong Frankenstein Radio Controls, especially your Eyesight TV, sight and sound recorded by your brain, your moon brain of the Computer God activates your Frankenstein threshold brainwash radio lifelong, inculcating conformist propaganda, even frightening you and mixing you up and the usual, "Don't worry about it." For your setbacks, mistakes, even when you receive deadly injuries. This is the Worldwide Computer God Secret Containment Policy.

Worldwide, as a Frankenstein slave, usually at night, you go to nearby hospital or camouflaged miniature hospital van trucks, you strip naked, lay on the operating table, which slides into the sealed Computer God robot operating cabinet. Intravenous tubes are connected. The slimy vicious Jew doctor simply pushes the starting button, based upon your Computer God brain on the moon which records progress of your systematic butchery. Your butchery is continued exactly, systematically. The Computer God operating cabinet has many robot arms with electrical and laser beam knife robot arms with fly eye TV cameras watching your whole body. Every part of you is monitored, even from your Frankenstein controls. Synthetic blood, synthetic instant-sealing flesh and skin, even synthetic electrical heartbeat to keep you alive are some of the unbelievable Computer God instant plastic surgery secrets. You are the highest, most intelligent electrical machine in the Universe.

Inevitability of gradualness. Usually, in a few years, you are made stringbean thin or grotesquely deformed, crippled and ugly, or even made over one foot shorter or one foot taller, as the Computer God sees fit. Virtually all of the important instant plastic surgery is done to you inside the Computer God sealed robot operating cabinet. Even unbelievable, impossible plastic surgery operations, all impossible even for dozens of vicious kosher bosher doctors working around the clock for weeks. The Computer God sealed robot operating cabinet can perform all of the above impossible plastic surgery operations overnight, even dwarfing you over a foot, or increasing your height by two feet. This is possible because Computer God robot operating cabinet imitates your microminiature electrical current intelligence system in your body. It even duplicates the microminiature electric currents that soft-

"... as a Frankenstein slave, usually at night, you go to nearby hospital or camouflaged miniature hospital van trucks, you strip naked, lay on the operating table, which slides into the sealed Computer God robot operating cabinet."

en your broken bones to create mending of them and then create stress either compressing the bones thereby shortening them or stress to make the bones grow longer.

Spring, 1984, Mr. Dec, lifelong would-be doctor and printer. Insight to the Worldwide Computer God stratified closed society, perfected by hospital birth making possible lifelong Frankenstein controls and lifelong hampering human defects containment policy. Hospital birth lifelong gifts example, deformed, crippled, retarded, pox, hives, warts, moles, blindness, deafness, poor vision, etc. Kosher bosher containment policy work good doctors secret health example cataract, rheumatism, weak heart, damaged vision, epilepsy, fainting spells, paralysis, loss of memory, trembling, gout, diabetes, many diseases.

The worldwide unbelievable lowest deadly gangster kosher bosher vicious medical profession worldwide unbelievable instant plastic surgery butchery of the body and brain, especially the face. Wipe on hormones and laser beam surgery causing instant ugly deep wrinkles, scars, age spots, arthritis, freckles, blemishes, pimples, red, brown, black or even sick white face and body. Worldwide dark negroidic colored male sex organs. The brainwash inferior female brain from overall plan intermarry with niggers. Total graying and balding, even hairy body and furry body, mustached, bearded women, even wipe-on synthetic hormones causing cancerous growth. Bloating, swelling, deformed, big pickle nose, bulldog, hanging cheeks and jowls. From teenage gradual wipe-on yellowing, frowning and blackening of teeth, and instant grinding and acids leaving hollow brown stumps so vocal chords are made raspy, aged, creating a wrinkled, ugly gargoylic clown booze face, worldwide population by age 70. Deformed, crippled, weak and brain damaged, senile. Lingering for inevitability of gradualness extermination. For your only hope for a future, do you know one word of pray for me, Francis E. Dec?

Computer God computerized brain thinking sealed robot operating arm surgery cabinet machine removal of most of the frontal command lobe of the brain, gradually, during lifetime and overnight in all insane asylums after Computer God kosher bosher one month probation period creating helpless, hopeless Computer God Frankenstein Earphone Radio parroting puppet brainless slaves, resulting in millions of hopeless helpless homeless derelicts in all Jerusalem, U.S.A. cities and Soviet slave work camps. Not only the hangman rope deadly gangster parroting puppet scum-on-top know this top medical secret, even worse, deadly gangster Jew disease from deaf Ronnie Reagan to U.S.S.R. Gorbachev know this oy vay Computer God Containment Policy top secret. Eventual brain lobotomization of the entire world population for the Worldwide Deadly Gangster Communist Computer God overall plan, an ideal worldwide population of light-skinned, low hopeless and helpless Jew-mulattos, the communist black wave of the future.

"Worldwide dark negroidic colored male sex organs."

RUMORS OF MOLESTATION OF A VERY BIZARRE KIND

Here is the entire text of a flyer circulated around Berkeley, California, from the early-to-mid 1980s.

Three new coin-demanding electric and one old refurbished manual typewriter await you downstairs at the Berkeley Public Library on Kittredge Street. Also awaiting you are voices produced to cause stress so that you will have trouble concentrating.

The problems here can be seen under many perspectives and could lead to many kinds of consequences. Not the least of these is the problem of the medical consequences of ignoring stress as well as the consequences in terms of the lack of quality of whatever anyone attempts to write under these conditions.

But the problems are worse. There is a rumor of child molestation of a very bizarre kind (a woman with short hair banged the head of a young boy with rather long hair (beyond his ears), and worse on at least two occasions there were sounds of struggle or defeat coming from men as well as staff members who took credit for the murders (or put-ups of murders? No one has spoken of people being seen strangled for instance.)) "We kill hippies" was a remark made by a caucasian female employee at the check-in desk and another older woman pointed an accusing finger at her afterward: of course such gestures take place in a medium which is very nuance-sensitive and probably repugnant to such enterprises as investigations — by enforcement agency certified personnel or by "peoples investigations."

There was a long controversy over silence in the library in which the director of library services typed (with errors) the type of approximation or rather mockery of responsible statements that could have led to the murder of a man with long hair during a public controversy over the disturbance in the library.

Of course I have made many efforts to circulate the kind of urgent alert necessary to prevent future abuses of the library and other public-financed institutions in Berkeley. They have been stolen and a few times (probably because of demoralization) lost.

I must apologize for the style of the present handbill. But perhaps there is a place for quantitative precision sometimes even if insulated from qualitatively superlative creativity.

TREVOR JAMES CONSTABLE
BIOPHILIA IN EXTREMIS

by Andrew Gaze

Constable's hypothesis is that most UFOs are not spacecraft ferrying bug-eyed monsters but giant aerospace organisms he came to call "critters."

Sociobiologist Edward O. Wilson defines "biophilia" as "the urge to affiliate with other forms of life." Such an urge applies to the work of **Trevor James Constable,** a noted military historian and engineer who has spent most of his life taking a unique approach to UFOs. Although tinged with paranoia, Constable's ideas are both charming and compelling. Briefly, Constable's hypothesis is that most UFOs are not spacecraft ferrying bug-eyed monsters to scare backwoods farmers but giant aerospace organisms. His ideas are a result of his early dissatisfaction with conventional attempts to investigate and explain UFOs. Though the Air Force once considered the idea that living creatures might be behind some sightings, they refused to pursue it further citing lack of expertise in alien life forms.

Constable's books on the subject, chiefly *The Cosmic Pulse of Life,* are not merely expository, but spiritual autobiographies that present an inside look at the history of fringe science, replete with name dropping and anecdotes of unusual events. Though his biophilial theories are naturally opposed to the UFO establishment and its "ET Hypothesis,"[1] Constable wasn't trying to upset anyone. "These living creatures, these bioforms," he writes, "were neither what we wanted or what we expected. They were for us at that time a definite emotional letdown. In the intervening time, I have observed with interest and fascination the disquieting, disturbing effect [the photos] have on all persons whose approach to UFOs is mechanistic."

Constable, born in New Zealand in 1925, majored in communications in college and worked in radio as both a technician and in voice theater. He served in the Navy during World War II as a broadcasting engineer and shipbound radio officer and continued serving in various merchant services when strange occurrences reported in the news caught his attention. Inexplicable lights were seen over the skies of post-war Europe, alternately dubbed "phantom rockets" or "foo fighters." These represented the earliest consistent reports of UFOs in the modern era. As reports increased in the late 40s and 50s, people demanded an explanation. Constable was satisfied neither with the government line nor the work of such determined investigators as Major Donald Keyhoe, who wrote some of the first books on UFOs.[2] Keyhoe advanced the idea that the most likely explanation for these sightings was that earth was being invaded by alien beings. To Constable, however, this premise was riddled with technological inconsistencies and unanswered questions. How could a mechanical craft possibly fly in the ways described by eyewitnesses and not tear itself apart? How could the saucers apparently disappear and reappear? Why were there no formal attempts at contact from the beings that piloted them?

When Constable met **George Van Tassel,** owner of a rest stop out in the California desert, he thought he had finally found the answers. Van Tassel claimed he was constantly receiving telepathic messages from otherworldly intelligences. He and his followers would gather to conduct what looked like conventional séances. After he had experienced these sessions firsthand, Constable became convinced that while all the radios turned to the heavens brought back only static, the voices channelled by Van Tassel spoke volumes.

The mystic Van Tassel recognized potential in this seeker and instructed Constable in various esoteric exercises. Constable writes that while the exercises expanded his awareness, they also created emotional disturbances culminating in a breakthrough that revealed to him the existence of an invisible world. Conventional science and mundane political structures, however, were unwilling to accept

1. *Extraterrestrial (ET) Hypothesis: UFOs are the spacecraft of extraterrestrial intelligent beings.*

2. *His best known titles are,* Flying Saucers are Real; Flying Saucers from Outer Space; *and* Flying Saucer Conspiracy.

his revelation, despite its potential to answer many riddles while also pointing the way to human advancement. For this reason, Constable was disappointed in mechanistic science:

Observations of UFO phenomena multiplied all over the world during the ensuing quarter century, but mechanistic science could contribute *not one significant discovery* pertaining to these objects... Between 1946 and the present time, billions of dollars have been literally *dumped* into thousands of alleged "research" projects, undertaken by official science and its minions... investigating everything from the fat layering of female Korean divers to the sex life of Arkansas wart hogs. Federal information storage facilities are bulging with this monstrous pedantry, this fantastic plethora of inconsequential minutiae, palmed off as "science" at the dawn of the Cosmic Age... opened minded individuals who have tackled UFOs avocationally have been frustrated in their efforts to establish any deterministic guidelines for these multi-form phenomena, *without departing from the officially sanctioned bases of their disciplines...* Official science is bankrupt on UFOs — methodologically, ethically and emotionally bankrupt... The Great Impasse in which mechanistic science finds itself arises from the irreconcilability between *living phenomena* and a mode of cognition anchored in sterility and deadness. Science is in danger of losing its ideals of serving life and raising knowledge to ever higher levels because of the control exercised over its reception system by life-hating, life killing individuals.

The emotional disturbances continued and Constable was directed to esotericist and publisher, **Dr. Franklin Thomas,** who urged the troubled man to abandon his psychic activity and pursue the seeds of his revelations in the physical realm. Thus in the mid-50s, Constable redirected his studies. Through Thomas, he came in contact with the ideas of **Dr. Albert Abrams** and **George De La Warr,** founders of radionics; **Meade Layne,** founder of Borderland Science Research Foundation; **Dr. Ruth Drown,** who developed Abrams' work; and **Eva Reich,** daughter of **Dr. Wilhelm Reich.** The information he obtained from these sources would lay the groundwork for his pursuit of a holistic explanation of UFOs — something new and radical that would explain the lights, the discs, the telepathy, the strange heat effects, sunburn at night, the multiple right angle turns, the disappearances, mysterious air crashes and religious fervor — an all-embracing theory for anything that might occur when a UFO manifests.

Living in Ether

Constable used radar as an analogy for various forms of extrasensory perception. Earth, silent for so long, turned on a cacophony of electromagnetic signals with the advent of radio. Before long, radar operators began reporting contacts which, when aircraft were sent to investigate, were mysteriously silent. Constable's solution to this is to resurrect the long-dead ether theory:[3]

The sudden, widespread, pulsed-wave activity that commenced with wartime radar did not take place in a vacuum, but in the ether. Rational scientists postulate an ether because there cannot be waves without a medium for them to wave in...

Constable's hypothesis rejected conventional physics after conducting photographic experiments of the reactions of the ether to radar, using infra-red film, assisted by James O. Woods, whom he met in 1956. The two would journey to the outskirts of the Mojave Desert and shoot reel after reel of infra-red in the twilight dawn. The results confirmed what Constable intuited but could hardly bring himself to affirm consciously. Still, proof was there before his eyes — forms he came to call "critters":

... amoebalike life forms existing in the plasma state. They are not solid, liquid, or gas. Rather they exist in the fourth state of matter — plasma — as living heat-substance at the upper border of physical nature...

Normally hidden from us because they are in the infrared range of the electromagnetic spectrum, critters occasionally emerge into the visible portion of the spectrum... At such times they are invariably identified as UFOs, which they are, of course, although they are not constructed craft. They are living creatures. Failure to recognize this, and so distinguish creatures from craft, has deeply confused UFO research.

As living organisms, critters appear to be an elemental branch of evolution probably older than most life on earth, dating from the time when the planet was more gaseous and plasmat-

Constable's hypothesis rejected conventional physics after conducting photographics experiments of the reactions of the ether to radar.

3. An invisible substance called "ether" was thought to pervade space until experiments performed at the turn of the century proved otherwise; see "Anti-Gravity: Freedom from Physics" for other examples of ether proponents.

ic than solid. They are part of what occultists term "elementals." They live invisibly like fish in the ocean of atmosphere. Like fish, I estimate them to be of low intelligence. They will probably one day be better classified as belonging to the general field of macrobiology or even macrobacteria inhabiting the aerial ocean we call the sky.

Abiogenesis, the belief that living creatures can grow out of lifeless matter, was disproved by Louis Pasteur but revived by Wilhelm Reich.

Constable used Rudolf Steiner's theory of "etheric physics" to help explain how such creatures could exist. Steiner postulated seven forms of ether but Constable said only four were necessary to understand the critters.

According to Steiner, these forces, alleged to exist beyond the sub-atomic level of matter and to shape it, propagate phylogenetically, that is, light ether forms from warmth ether, chemical ether from light ether, and life ether from chemical ether, retaining properties as they move up the scale. Warmth ether is analogous to the *phlogiston* of alchemists, a substance and "not a mere mode of motion affecting the other three states." Light ether produces electromagnetic radiation or acts as its facilitator through a vacuum. Chemical ether is identified as the orgone energy discovered by Wilhelm Reich. Constable contends that orgone is responsible for chemical processes, the transmission of sound and the manifestations of whole numbers in nature, and mitigates the effects of warmth ether. Life ether is the most complex; it is emitted by large radiant bodies like the sun and acts upon matter along with other ethers to imbue it with life.

It is important here to note the fringe science of radionics, devised in the late 19th century by Dr. Albert Abrams who inquired into the links between living things and electricity. Radionics is based on the principles of the etheric forces, seeking to create practical means for manipulating these forces as they interact with matter. Abrams believed tissue could become healthier by manipulating it electrically; in practice, however, he found that tissue was damaged, rather than healed by the energy. So, using analogies from homeopathy and electronics, he focused instead on energy acting on tissue at a distance.

By subjecting the photographs of his critters to radionic analysis, Constable discovered, "They consist of calcium and fluids, the metal and the fluids both being in the plasmatic state," or in other words, of matter transmuted by the action of the ethers.

Abiogenesis (or spontaneous generation, the belief that living creatures can grow out of lifeless matter) had long been disproved by the experiments of Louis Pasteur. Pasteur's results had eclipsed the work of H. Charlton Bastian, who proposed that life particles or *bions* were responsible for not only disease but also the emergence of life. But the idea of abiogenesis wasn't dead; it was revived by Wilhelm Reich, the strongest single influence on Constable's ideas.

Wilhelm Reich & Orgone

Reich (1897-1955), who alongside Jung and Adler was one of Sigmund Freud's most famous students, was forced out of his native Austria by the Nazis. He ended up in Norway, and there worked on unlocking the secrets of libidinal energy. Believing an answer might be found in the chemistry of foodstuffs, Reich observed their decomposition under high power microscopes. The decay produced luminous vesicles containing particles that could be cultured. Reich said the particles, which he called *bions,* had antiseptic properties, and existed in virtually every living substance. He found a way to contain their energy using alternating layers of metal and organic material such as wood or felt. This energy he called *orgone.*

According to Reich, the most potent orgone originated in plant and certain animal sources; its pulsating nature seemed identical to electro-galvanic responses measured in patients experiencing sexual stimulation. Reich came to believe bions had potential for medical use against various diseases, especially cancer, earning for himself the wrath of Norway's scientific community. Hounded again, Reich left Norway for the United States.

He found the isolation he needed in Rangeley, Maine, on a ranch he christened Organon. Here he developed inventions that used orgone energy, such as the *cloudbuster,* a device of turreted metal tubes sunk in a reservoir of water that apparently draw and channel orgone from the clouds. Reich claimed the atmosphere was saturated with orgone and by using the cloudbuster, he could control weather conditions locally.

Reich found orgone to be endlessly versatile: under certain conditions, he said, it could promote abiogenesis, and could defy the laws of thermodynamics by creating an anomalous temperature differential in one particular spot. For a while, it appeared Reich would finally receive credit for his discoveries from the scientific community — even Albert Einstein found Reich's work fascinating — but it wasn't to be; Einstein concluded Reich had misinterpreted his experimental data. "Once more," Constable later lamented, "the orgone energy had provoked the irrational in a man of science. Not much later, Alamogordo, Hiroshima, and Nagasaki showed where Einstein's head was — alas, for poor mankind."

In the late 1940s, Reich found that radioactive samples placed in an orgone box underwent a transmutation that made them more benign but also yielded what he called *Deadly Orgone Radiation* or *DOR.* Constable believes this event triggered the attention of the Ahrimanic powers, who then conspired to destroy Reich from within and without, lest his discoveries benefit mankind. At the same time, the Food and Drug Administration (FDA) began investigating Reich's practice of "orgone therapy," wherein his subjects would replenish their vital energies inside of a human-sized box called an orgone accumulator.

But Reich had a more immediate concern: the appearance of an unexplainable blight upon Organon. In 1951, a strange black substance appeared around the grounds of Reich's facilities, corroding rocks, killing plant life, and causing unpleasant symptoms in himself and his staff. The substance defied analysis except that it manifested many of the properties of DOR. Reich dubbed it *melanor.* Almost coincident with the appearance of melanor were reports of lights in the sky. For Reich, the descriptions of UFO antics resembled the behavior of orgone bions; he reckoned he could deal with the problem using his own devices.

UFOs and government agents would both dog him as he tried to comprehend this frightful mystery. When the lights in the sky approached closely, he would train cloudbusters on them, causing them to fade and move away. He then used the cloudbuster, in conjunction with the transmutation of radioactive elements, to cleanse the area of the foul blackness.

Reich won the battle against assault from the skies, but was soon arrested for medical fraud, mail fraud, and other charges, becoming the target of one of the FDA's most intense campaigns against alternative medicine. Convicted, his orgone devices and many of his writings — even those having nothing to do with orgone — were consigned to an incinerator. Wilhelm Reich died in prison in 1955.

Reich has been more or less rehabilitated into psychiatry, but to Constable, he is the single most important individual of the 20th century: he established the existence of a primal energy through meticulous experiments and proved many of the foundations of conventional physics wrong. Constable is convinced that, if Reich is telling the truth about orgone, physicists must start from scratch. Specifically, entropy does not exist, something can come from nothing, output can exceed input, and sand can run up the hourglass.

Constable believes that Reich's orgone experiments triggered the attention of the Ahrimanic powers, who conspired to destroy Reich from within and without.

Zoroastrian Redux

Reich's fate was not the product of bureaucratic malice, Constable contends. Indeed, what happened at Organon and in the federal courts was a concerted effort by individuals in league with — or manipulated by — sinister forces whom Constable affectionately calls "The Boys Downstairs," agents of Ahriman, the future anti-Christ. Ahriman — a concept popularized by Rudolf Steiner — is responsible for the current state of the world, a result of the preparations for his manifestation on earth:

Predatory critters hunger for orgone stored in sexual organs and other body parts.

... Malfeasance, embezzlement, theft, bribery, corruption, deception, premeditated murder and all other left-handed activity on this earth shares a common functioning principle: keep the victim unaware that he is being preyed upon...

"There are essentially two factions at work in UFOs," Constable writes. "There are the ethereans, who enlighten and guide, and the Boys Downstairs who confuse and control mankind. The earthly instrumentalities include those who are inspired — by whatever means suit the particular individual — to kill every rational approach to the UFO subject." The result is that "Governments and their satellite scientists adequately demonstrate the strangulation of rational inquiry."

Every major political force, as well, is a manifestation of the cosmic struggle:

Few people today realize that the Bolshevik Revolution in Russia was funded by Wall Street. Bolshevik Russia is an Ahrimanic creation... Wall Street and the highest officials of successive U.S. governments have taken every necessary step to ensure that Soviet Russia does not collapse... maintained as a Frankenstein to terrorize the western world into enormous armament budgets...

The American people will henceforth need to ensure, if their fortunes are not to come under illegal control from the inner planes, that people of unassailable moral and ethical quality alone are elected to high office. Party affiliation is of no great significance. The inner sanctum of the White House, the spiritual center of America, can only be protected in this way. If a man goes into that sanctum as a profane ignoramus of spirit, and especially if he is ruled by his sex drives in an immoral fashion, he will be manipulated from the inner planes like a marionette. The entities whose aim is the destruction of America can use and direct life energy far more proficiently than we use electricity.

Attack of the Unidentified Flying Amoeboids

UFO investigator **John Keel** has suggested that the instruments of popular culture subliminally transform fiction into apparent reality. He was referring to flying saucers, but this could apply just as well to Constable's critters.

Sky creatures have been a staple in science fiction from the beginning. In Sir Arthur Conan Doyle's short story "The Horror of the Heights," an aviator who investigates mysterious disappearances of planes discovers that balloon-like creatures resembling aerial jellyfish reside in the upper atmosphere. In due time he also finds the reason for the disappearances: eel-like predators with beaks that hunt the jellyfish for their stores of light gases. Constable believes that a number of real-life missing aircraft suffered a similar fate; the predatory critters responsible — who hunger for orgone stored in sexual organs and other body parts — are also behind the mysterious cattle mutilations.

A more recent example of the idea occurs in an early episode of *Star Trek* entitled "The Immunity Syndrome." In this episode a vampiric, planet-sized amoeba threatens the galaxy; there is an opaque black membrane around it which Spock describes as "a negative energy field, however illogical that may sound." The scenario is strangely similar to the phenomenon of the malign entities that bedeviled Wilhelm Reich and Organon.

Constable and Reich are not the only sources of reported living sky creatures. The October, 1959 issue of *Flying Saucers*, published by Ray Palmer — who helped turn flying saucer fiction into flying saucer fact — contained an extraordinary letter, written by someone named Don Woods, Jr.:

I must write you of what happened to me in 1925, which I think solves most UFO reports. I have never told this to anyone, but can get signed affidavits if needed. Four of us were flying old "Jennies" over the Nevada Desert. One plane was a two-seater, the one I was in. We landed on Flat Mesa, near Battle Mountain, Nevada. The mesa is about 5,000 square feet and the walls are too steep to climb unless a lot of work is done.

We wanted to see what was on top of this flat place. We landed at 1 p.m. While walking about the top of this place we noticed something coming in for a landing. It was about 8 feet across and was round and flat like a saucer. The undersides were a reddish color. It skidded to a stop about 30 feet away. This next you won't believe, and I don't care but it's the truth. We walked up to the thing and it was some animal like we never saw before. It was hurt, and as it breathed the top would rise and fall making a half-foot hole all around it like a clam opening and closing.

Quite a hunk had been chewed out of one side of this rim and a sort of metal-looking froth issued. When it saw us, it breathed frantically and rose up only a few inches, only to fall back to earth again. It was moist and glistened on the top side. We could see no eyes or legs.

After a 20 minute rest, it started pulsating once more. (We stayed 10 feet away.) And so help me the thing grew as bright as all get out, except where it was hurt. It had a mica-like shell body. It tried to rise up again, but sank back again. Then we saw a large, round shadow fall on us. We looked up and ran. Coming in was a much larger animal 30 feet across.

It paid no attention to us, but settled itself over the small one. Four sucker-like tongues settled on the little one and the big one got so dazzling bright you couldn't look at it. Both rose straight up and were out of sight in a second. They must have been traveling a thousand miles an hour to get so high so fast. When we walked over there was an awful stench, and the frothy stuff the little one had bled looked like fine aluminum wire. There was more frothy, wiry stuff in a 30-foot circle where the big one had breathed.

This stuff finally melted in the sun, and we took off. So help me, this was an animal. I have never told this before as we knew no one would believe us. I only write now because this animal would be one big 30-foot light if seen at night. I don't expect belief, but I simply had to write.

In like manner, **Loren Coleman,** in his book, *Curious Encounters,* reports on a 1983 encounter in Puget Sound with what could be described as a giant, electric sea slug. Coleman believes the "creature" was really a machine in the guise of an animal but it might also be seen as evidence of a plasmatic being generating tremendous energy. Most recently, strange, bioluminescent remains dubbed "The Bermuda Blob" were reported in the popular scientific press. The connection between reports such as these and Constable's critters is obvious. Constable's successors will have their work cut out for them in exploring the blobs, the UFOs and other strange phenomena such as crop circles, altered states of consciousness, and spontaneous human combustion.

Critters & Beyond

In the current edition of *Cosmic Pulse of Life,* Constable appends the work of individuals who have pursued his leads. Fortean investigator **Larry Arnold** provides an exhaustive record of the sky creatures through history. He proposes that the entities could be responsible for some instances of spontaneous human combustion, presumably by discharging too much warmth ether. Italian researcher **Luciano Boccone** and his UFO research group GRCU, with members in Italy and Romania, independently stumbled upon Reich's work in the late 70s. Boccone contacted Constable in 1980 but died soon afterwards. He had produced photographs depicting processions of amoeba-like life forms and triangular bodies of flame-like radiance he called "new-pterodactyls," detailed in the book *La Realta Nacosta (The Hidden Reality).*

Sky creatures could be responsible for some instances of spontaneous human combustion.

The theories of **Alvin H. Lawson** and **Michael Persinger** might also be applied to the critters. Lawson believes the spate of "missing time" and "alien visitor" experiences are exceptionally powerful archetypal fantasies resulting from latent traumas suffered during birth or physical or sexual abuse. Persinger's theory correlates UFO experiences with powerful hallucinogenic effects wreaked upon parts of the brain caused by exposure to high frequency electrical sources. Such sources could be power lines, ball lightning, or tellurian plasmas discharged as tectonic plates act on subterranean mineral deposits. Perhaps a critter might also act as kind of a random generator of brain-altering vibrations, because its composition interferes with everything around it when it materializes. According to Constable, the high concentration of etheric forces that result from the critters instantly explains black-outs, burns, calcination of local exposed rocks, and other phenomena.

The crop circles are another mystery that might be explained by the critters. **Colin Andrews,** a self-described "psychic archaeologist" has been investigating the crop circle manifestations and published his findings in his book *The Circlemakers.* He had stumbled upon *Sky Creatures* and found that the con-

"The [bioform] can actually re-mould and transform itself into anything from a Christmas tree, to Marilyn Monroe, pretty girls, crocks of gold, visions of the Virgin Mary, signs of the saints, alien spaceships or little green men..."

cept of the critters solved a great many problems. Adapting terminology from quantum mechanics out of context, he uses the notion of "non-locality" — the indeterminacy of the position of sub-atomic particles as they move about an atom — to describe how mental energy influences crop circle formation:

The closer a recipient comes to an orgone bioform, the stronger the non-locality process occurs. This, I now believe, will enable the bioform to metamorphasize into archetypal imagery reflecting the neurological wave patterns of the person concerned. It can actually re-mould and transform itself into anything from a Christmas tree, to Marilyn Monroe, pretty girls, crocks of gold, visions of the Virgin Mary, signs of the saints, alien spaceships or little green men... These encounters will have an objective and often physical reality that will last only for the duration of the supernatural experience. They will then evaporate like camphor, back into the higher realms of the electromagnetic spectrum, the only evidence of their temporary existence being the physical traces that often accompany encounter cases.

... Taking the matter a step further, I now feel that if a percipient physically enters a bioform... he or she will, through the altered states induced by temporal cortex stimulation, take an active part in the temporarily real, fifth dimensional experience... it will take place outside our own four-dimensional, space-time continuum in an instant of time — a process that may well result in actual time distortion, or missing time... Afterwards, the brain will update the memory to substitute what really happened with a softer, more predictable version that will be easier for the mind to accept. ...

Conclusions

Ever since I first read *Sky Creatures,* years ago, the ideas behind it have fascinated me. I even spent a few years looking for a Wratten 18A ultraviolet filter so that I might capture the critters on standard color film. Infrared film can also ferret them out; one picture I took at night yielded an image of what seemed to be a paramecium-like object over my neighborhood.

When I reflect on all the paranoid ranters all too endemic to this area of strangeness, I feel that somewhere between the metaphysical paranoia of Constable and **Jacques Vallee** is something akin to the truth. Constable's view harkens — but without nostalgia — to a time when humans tended to regard the world as one vast living thing, much as some primitive societies. But he is of the conviction that we need not return to a primitive lifestyle; instead, we can harness the energy of the ethers to venture out into the stars. This energy is the force *behind* the physical forces, so it can easily overcome them with the right effort. Constable implies that that is precisely what living things were meant to do as they evolved, and it is only proper that we direct our energy towards a true and healthy harmony with the ethers. His visceral tirades against establishment science are harsh but often on target. Growing numbers of concerned scientists feel that the pose of detachment has caused social apathy in their profession.

And, of course, Constable's theory is yet another way of joining all aspects of life into a seamless whole, as has been the quest since the time of the ancient philosophers. Every human has the right to make that attempt at least once in their life and, though the goal be unattainable, inspire those to conscious living in the process. Like him, I often desire that communion with life. I look up into the night sky and consider just how strange and wonderful it would be if giant, invisible flying amoeboids were indeed floating up there, like the sky whales Charles Fort spoke of in *LO!,* even if they did pause once in a while to snack on a Guernsey or incinerate some poor sod sitting in his easy chair.

Constable and cloudbuster

WILLIAM COOPER

If the evidence doesn't seem to fit a particular conspiracy theory, just create a bigger conspiracy theory.

— Robert D. Hicks, *In Pursuit of Satan*

I am still searching for the truth. I firmly believe that this book is closer to the truth than anything ever previously written.

— William Cooper, *Behold a Pale Horse*

William Cooper from *UFO* magazine

CONSPIRACY THEORIES ARE LIKE BLACK holes — they suck in everything that comes their way, regardless of content or origin; conspiracies are portals to other universes that paradoxically reside within our own. Everything you've ever known or experienced, no matter how "meaningless," once it contacts the conspiratorial universe, is enveloped by and cloaked in sinister significance. Once inside, the vortex gains in size and strength, sucking in everything you touch.

William Cooper, an "independent UFO researcher," has entered just such a universe; it's unlikely he will ever return. Cooper identifies with his theories so completely that he thinks anyone who challenges them — even his friends — do so because they're part of the conspiracy. It is no use to point out contradictions, or even trivial errors, because Bill Cooper knows THE TRUTH.

Though William Cooper is a self-professed regular guy and ex-military man, his claims rival the *Weekly World News* for sensationalism. What is most beguiling is that Cooper doesn't just *believe* that our government signed a formal treaty with extraterrestrials in 1954, or that we have already set up a base on the planet Mars; William Cooper *knows* these things to be true, because while working for Naval Intelligence, he saw the secret documents to prove his assertions.

Cooper burst upon the UFO scene with these claims in 1988, and has been an infamous figure ever since. He gives public lectures, is heard on radio, sends out newsletters, and in 1991, wrote a book, *Behold a Pale Horse.* In UFO circles, Cooper is best known for accusing his colleagues of being CIA agents and for physically threatening them. According to researcher Bob Lazar, "Everyone seems to have a Bill Cooper story..."

Since 1988, Cooper himself has been accused of being alcoholic, a liar and a fascist, or even worse, written off as a psychopath; with the exception of Jacques Vallee, his critics have focused attention on his belligerent personality rather than contradictions or factual errors within his stories. His opponents take him seriously enough to go to great pains to discredit him, in order to defend themselves against his accusations. But if his opponents didn't have their own crashed saucer/government cover-up stories to defend, they might see the connections between Cooper's stories and their own, as well as a possible relationship between conspiratorial logic and some UFO phenomena.

Behold a Pale Horse is a fine example of conspiratorial logic. Cooper includes every gory detail of the sinister alien plot to control humanity, as well as documents to back it all up. He includes the story of his own UFO sightings while in the military, background on his involvement with Naval Intelligence, and a sentimental account of his ancestors' survival of the American Frontier. Cooper paints himself as a patriotic "Red-Blooded American Male" who loves Mom and Apple Pie, who would fight and die to defend the "American Way," who just happened to stumble on the greatest secret in the history of the world.

Cooper, born into a military family in 1943, enlisted in the Air Force upon graduating high school in 1961 in Japan. In more than ten years of military service, in both the Air Force and Navy, he was exemplary member, earning medals, and steadily taking on greater responsibility. Soon after enlisting, he was graced with a Secret security clearance, and, outfitted with a dosimeter, working around "REAL atomic bombs" on a daily basis. He says that he was part of the elite of the Air Force and though still a young recruit, "met a couple of sergeants who kind of adopted" him. When the sergeants told him stories about being "attached to a special unit that recovered crashed flying saucers," he didn't believe them because they always came out when the group was "half-tanked." Besides, "sergeants were known to tell some tall tales to younger guys like [Cooper.]" But a few years later he began to believe them after seeing a few saucers of his own.

"Rumors floated around that UFOs had kidnapped and mutiliated two army soldiers, then dropped them in the bush."

In 1966, after switching from the Air Force to the Navy, Cooper volunteered for submarines. While on watch aboard the USS Tiru, Cooper saw his first flying saucer. At first, he alone saw the saucer, the size of an aircraft carrier, "rise from beneath the ocean" and then "disappear into the clouds." But within minutes, it was back, this time capturing the attention of several others:

> I was just lifting the binoculars off my chest when I saw it. The giant saucer shape plunged out of the clouds, tumbled, and, pushing the water before it, opened up a hole in the ocean and disappeared from view. It was incredible. This time I had seen it with my naked eyes, and its size in comparison with the total view was nothing short of astounding.
>
> The Captain surged up the ladder with the quartermaster on his heels. Chief Quartermaster Quintero had the ship's 35-mm camera slung around his neck. The Captain stood patiently while Ensign Ball tried to describe what he had seen. He glanced at us and we both nodded in affirmation. That was enough for the Captain. He called sonar, who during the excitement had reported contact underwater at the same bearing ...
>
> The Captain called down and ordered someone to closely monitor the radar. His command was instantly acknowledged. As the five of us stood gazing out over the sea the same ship or one exactly like it rose slowly, turned in the air, tilted at an angle and then vanished. I saw the Chief snapping pictures out of the corner of my eye.

Cooper recounts that everyone who saw the craft was ordered to keep quiet about it; they weren't even allowed to talk among themselves. Each witness was questioned individually by a commander from the Office of Naval Intelligence. When Cooper's commander asked what he'd seen, and Cooper said he believed he had seen a flying saucer., the commander's response was to scream obscenities and threaten to put him in the "brig" for the rest of his life. Given a second opportunity, he got the story right; he told the commander he'd seen nothing. He then signed documents that spelled out what would happen if he ever told anyone: he could be fined up to $10,000, imprisoned up to 10 years, or both. Not long after, Cooper "devolunteered" from submarines.

In 1968, while in Naval Security and Intelligence School, Cooper received special training in conducting Pacific-area intelligence briefings and followed this with a stint in Vietnam. To hear Cooper talk about it, you'd think we'd been at war with space aliens rather than Communists:

> The whole time I was in Vietnam and especially on the DMZ I had noticed that there was a lot of UFO activity. We had individual 24-hour crypto code sheets that we used to encode messages, but because of the danger that one of them could be captured at any time, we used special code words for sensitive information. UFOs, I was told, were definitely sensitive information. I learned exactly how sensitive when all the people of an entire village disappeared after UFOs were seen hovering above their huts. I learned that both sides had fired upon the UFOs, and they had blasted back with a mysterious blue light. Rumors floated around that UFOs had kidnapped and mutilated two army soldiers, then dropped them in the bush. No one knew how much of this was true, but the fact that the rumors persisted made me tend to think there was at least some truth in them. I found out later that most of those rumors were true.

Cooper also claims that a UFO shot down a B-52 during the Vietnam War, that U.S. troops were attacked by "something" they first thought were helicopters, and he himself witnessed an incident involving the recovery of "a craft" listed as a Soviet submarine.

Back in Hawaii, with an upgraded security clearance (Top Secret, Q, Sensitive Compartmentalized Information), he found out what all the UFO activity meant. As a member of the Intelligence Briefing Team of the Commander in Chief of the Pacific Fleet (CINPACFLT), it was Cooper's job to brief high-level officers about various documents. The contents of these documents were what led Cooper to an "18-year search" that culminated in writing *Behold a Pale Horse.*

Cooper's first revelation as a member of the CINPACFLT briefing team was that the Office of Naval Intelligence "participated in the assassination of President John F. Kennedy and that it was the Secret Service agent driving the limo that had shot Kennedy in the head. ..." But this was only the tip of the iceberg. By 1972, Cooper had discovered everything about the Secret Government, the coming ice age, Alternatives One, Two and Three, Project GALILEO, and most sinister of all, the plan for the New World Order.

Chapter 12 of *Behold A Pale Horse,* entitled "The Secret Government," was delivered July 2, 1989, as a research paper at the MUFON (Mutual UFO Network) Symposium in Las Vegas. The information was supposedly gleaned during Cooper's stint as a member of the CINPACFLT briefing team, although he cannot divulge specific sources "for obvious reasons."

Any one of Cooper's revelations would keep investigators, journalists, historians and scientists busy for the next hundred years, but focusing on any one is impossible; each leads deeper into the sinister tangle of secrecy and manipulation.

Though Cooper believes secret societies have run the world for centuries, the modern era of secret government began in 1947, with the advent of flying saucers. Between January 1947 and December 1952 "at least 16 crashed or downed alien craft, 65 alien bodies and 1 live alien were recovered." Besides alien bodies, those who recovered the saucers discovered "a large number of human body parts stored within [two of the] vehicles." A special group of top American scientists was organized to study the phenomenon — all top secret, of course. In fact, the original CIA, then called the "Central Intelligence Group," along with the National Security Agency, were formed for the express purpose of dealing with the alien presence.

Cooper reveals that not everyone agreed with the policy of secrecy, and were dealt with accordingly:

> Secretary of Defense James Forrestal objected to the secrecy. ... He believed that the public should be told. James Forrestal was also one of the first known abductees. When he began to talk to leaders of the opposition party and leaders of Congress about the alien problem he was asked to resign by Truman. ... Forrestal later was said to have suffered a mental breakdown. He was ordered to the mental ward of Bethesda Naval Hospital. ... Finally, on May 21, 1949, Forrestal's brother made a fateful decision. He notified authorities that he intended to remove James from Bethesda on May 22. Sometime in the early morning of May 22, 1949, agents of the CIA tied a sheet around James Forrestal's neck, fastened the other end to a fixture in his room, then threw James Forrestal out the window. The sheet tore and he plummeted to his death. James Forrestal's secret diaries were confiscated by the CIA and were kept in the White House for many years. Due to public demand the diaries were eventually rewritten and published in a sanitized version. The real diary information was later furnished by the CIA in book form to an agent who published the material as fiction. The name of the agent is Whitley Streiber and the book is Majestic. James Forrestal became one of the first victims of the cover-up.

Whitley Streiber had written *Majestic* as a frankly fictionalized account of a possible event, but Cooper seems to see it as factual. Cooper also believes the movies *E.T.* and *Close Encounters of the Third Kind* are "thinly disguised" versions of historical fact. The science fiction book *Alternative 003* is also, according to Cooper, "70% true."

The story behind *E.T.,* Cooper says, is that the true-to-life alien was called "EBE," to stand for "Extraterrestrial Biological Entity." In 1951, the "chlorophyll-based" EBE became ill; though doctors, botanists and entomologists were called in, their efforts to save him failed; EBE died on June 2, 1952.

Many more aliens were on the way, however. According to Cooper, 10 more flying saucers crashed in 1953; 26 dead and four live aliens were recovered. The newly elected President Eisenhower, in a fix because of these events, turned to Nelson Rockefeller; together they developed a plan to "wrestle and beat the alien problem."

In the meantime, astronomers found that large objects, first thought to be asteroids,

Though Cooper believes secret societies have run the world for centuries, the modern era of secret government began in 1947, with the advent of flying saucers.

One base, a "super-Top Secret facility," was built at Groom Lake in Nevada, code-named "Area 51."

were fast approaching earth. The objects were more alien spaceships. The government used radio communications and "computer binary language" to arrange a landing, which resulted in diplomatic relations between the U.S. and a second race of aliens who left a "hostage" as a "pledge that they would return and formalize a treaty." Yet a third race of aliens — enemies of the second race — landed at an Air Force Base in Florida. They "offered to help us with our spiritual development," and in exchange, wanted us to dismantle our nuclear weapons. Needless to say, we declined the offer.

By 1954, the second race of aliens met with Eisenhower to sign a formal treaty. The U.S. Government received an alien ambassador, "His Omnipotent Highness Krlll," during this meeting, but "in the American tradition of disdain for royal titles he was secretly called Original Hostage Crlll, or Krlll." Cooper says the meeting was filmed and that the films still exist. Later, Krlll "gave lots of information, scientific data, some of which was published in the open scientific literature under the name of O.H. Krill, after being sanitized. ...Krill is still alive."

Details of the treaty included provisions that we wouldn't interfere in alien affairs and they wouldn't interfere in ours; we would keep their presence a secret, and they would furnish us with their technological advances; they were allowed to abduct human beings on a limited basis for medical examination and monitoring of our development, as long as they didn't harm anyone in the process; sixteen personnel each would be swapped for educational purposes; underground bases would be constructed for the humanoid guests. One base was built at Groom Lake in Nevada, code-named "Area 51." "According to documentation that I read," Cooper adds, "at least 600 alien beings actually resided full time at this site along with an unknown number of scientists and CIA personnel."

All the crashed and orbiting saucers, three alien races, treaties, and a cover-up of the whole thing required almost the entire U.S. government to deal with it all. But international groups, such as the Bilderbergers (they now control the world) and the Trilateral Commission (formed in secret before 1973) became involved as well; in fact, the main reason these groups were formed was to deal with the alien question. Cooper adds, "the name of the Trilateral Commission was taken from the alien flag known as the Trilateral Insignia."

Cooper's version of the now-famous "MJ-12" story is as follows: Eisenhower established a permanent committee, future members of the One World Government, that became known as Majesty Twelve (MJ-12). The group would "oversee and conduct all covert activities concerned with the alien question." Among its nineteen members were Nelson Rockefeller, Allen and John Foster Dulles, J. Edgar Hoover, George Bush and Dr. Edward Teller. Since George Bush was on MJ-12, he obviously knew the alien secret while President, but the general policy was to keep the alien presence so secret even the President didn't know. Kennedy found out, however, and the reason he was assassinated was — you guessed it — he was about to divulge the alien secret to the American people.

Cooper — the biggest whistleblower of them all — has not yet gone the way of Kennedy and Forrestal. The reason, Cooper says, is that this would show the world what he says is true. All the conspirators can do at this point is harass and discredit him. The reason he is having conflicts with the larger UFO research community is that most UFO researchers, including **Stanton Friedman, William Moore, Philip Klass, John Keel, Charles Berlitz, Budd Hopkins, Dr. J. Allen Hynek** (now deceased) and even horror novelist **Whitley Strieber,** are really working for the CIA and the Office of Naval Intelligence. *UFO* magazine, with its obviously slim budget, is financed and controlled by the CIA. And, although Jacques Vallee isn't mentioned in this particular blacklist, after one meeting and several phone conversations, he too joined the ranks of the accused.

Besides all being famous for their involvement in the UFO question, just about the only thing these people have in common is that they don't agree with Bill Cooper. But, since Cooper knows the truth, questioning his information is tantamount to blasphemy. I have seen three accounts of Bill Cooper from among those on that list; two from *UFO* magazine, and one from **Jacques Vallee.** Both Vallee and *UFO* magazine reveal simple details that show the obvious falsity of key elements in Cooper's story. When presented with these details, Cooper brushes them aside, sticks to his story — and eventually becomes enraged.

Vallee's scientific training and sharp mind are no match for the likes of Cooper. During their initial meeting, described in Vallee's book, *Revelations,* Vallee naturally asked questions along the line of, "Why, if their technology is thousands of years in advance of ours (as Cooper claims), did the aliens need any help from us, especially in the form of a treaty?" Cooper answered that our radar affected their navigation systems, throwing their craft off-balance, and they wanted their presence kept secret. Vallee pointed out that we, supposedly in the stone age compared to the aliens, can already overcome radar navigation problems. As for wanting their presence to be kept secret, this is akin to Americans landing on the shores of New Guinea and enlisting a tribal chief to keep the U.S. presence secret. There's simply no point to it.

Another hole in Cooper's story pertained to the removal of "implants" from abductees. Cooper told Vallee that J. Allen Hynek authored a secret document stating that one person in 40 has been abducted and received an implant. (Vallee was a close associate of Hynek, and states that Hynek would never have made such a claim.) Nobody knows the purpose of these implants, because their removal would cause the abductee to die. Vallee pointed out that since abductions have allegedly been going on for four decades, some of the abductees would have died by now of natural causes. Surely, it would be a simple procedure to remove the implant during an autopsy. Cooper waved the question away, and stuck to his story.

Perhaps the most embarrassing weakness in Cooper's story is his claim that he saw a document authored by "O.H. Krill," whom Cooper identifies as the alien ambassador to the United States. The document is well known in the UFO field. According to *UFO* magazine, it was conceived by **John Grace,** a.k.a "**Val Valerian**," head of the Nevada Aerial Research organization. The name "O.H. Krill" was an inside joke; a woman who'd appeared on the TV special, *UFOs: It Has Begun,* channelled an entity name CRYLL, and Grace "just pulled the O.H. out of thin air." During the time Cooper was teaming up with John Lear, he told a TV interviewer that he'd seen an O.H. Krill document in the early 70s. Lear turned "beet red," pulled Cooper aside, and tried to tell him that O.H. Krill was just a joke. Cooper stuck to his story, replying he really did see that document in 1972. Lear subsequently dropped the issue, but then "began to wonder just how much of Bill Cooper was real."

A similar incident involved yet another document Cooper claims to have seen during the 70s. UFO researcher **Bob Lazar** told UFO magazine that he wrote a paper at Los Alamos in 1988 concerning "Project Excalibur," an "earth-penetrating, nuclear-tipped missile designed to destroy underground facilities." He gave a copy to Lear, who gave a copy to Cooper:

> ... I heard Cooper reading it verbatim, word for word, at the (1989) MUFON convention. He claimed to have seen it in the mid-'70s. I then heard him on the Billy Goodman show. I called him; he recognized the voice. He said he knew who I was. I then asked him, "Bill, that Excalibur missile thing, did you get that at John Lear's or did you read that in the '70's?"
>
> I gave him an out if he had forgotten. He said no, "I read that word for word in 1973." I said okay and thanks. That was my first confirmation that this guy was a complete liar.

It is not unreasonable to conclude, like Lazar, that Bill Cooper is simply a liar, but what is really going on may be much more complex. Why would Cooper lie? Why would he put his sanity, credibility, and even his life on the line for something he himself thinks is false? The fact that many people who have seen UFOs have kept it to themselves is testament to the fact that the entire topic of UFOs

Bob Lazar wrote a paper at Los Alamos in 1988 concerning "Project Excalibur," an earth-penetrating, nuclear-tipped missile designed to destroy underground facilities.

(not to mention flying saucers and extraterrestrials) is taboo; these are not claims that bring fortune or fame, but rather misfortune and infamy.

Vallee suggests Bill Cooper and others may have b een fed false "top secret" documents.

I don't think Cooper is consciously deceiving people. As Vallee observed during his contact with him, Cooper seems very sincere. His writing, as well, is sincere to the point of embarrassment. His behavior suggests someone emotionally attached to certain ideas; the holes in his story seem less the product of a slick liar, and more that of someone ill-informed, naive and gullible. Vallee interprets Cooper's story — and the mass of disinformation floating around in UFO circles — as possible manipulation by an unknown third party; Cooper might simply be a pawn in someone else's game. Vallee suggests Bill Cooper and others may have been fed false "top secret" documents for various reasons, such as covering up genuinely secret military information, testing responses to alien invasion, or even to promote fascist ideology. Certain UFO sightings, Vallee suggests, may have been staged.

Cooper may well have seen some falsified documents, but many of those he claims to have seen simply didn't exist at the time, so while Vallee's interpretation may account for some aspects of Cooper's story, it by no means covers all. If Cooper is being deceived by someone, it's most likely himself. He himself suggests he may have been manipulated, with the alien scenario as "the greatest hoax in history designed to create an alien enemy from outer space in order to expedite the formation of a one-world government."

More than a UFO researcher, Cooper is a classic conspiracy theorist cloaking 19th century xenophobia in a Space-Age guise. His book even contains a reprint of "The Protocols of the Wise Men of Zion" with a prefatory note explaining that references to "The Jews" should be replaced by "Illuminati" and the word "goyim" replaced with the word "cattle." Though Cooper is trying to leave the Jews out of his list of conspirators, he's not trying hard enough. Cooper had remarked to Vallee:

> There are four types of aliens. There are two kinds of Grays, including one race, not commonly seen, that has a large nose. Then there are the Nordic types, tall blond Aryans, and finally the Orange ones. They come from Orion, the Pleiades, Betelgeuse, Barnard's star and Zeta Reticuli. ...
>
> You know, I'm not a religious man. But if you look at the Bible... The Angels could be the Nordic types and the Grays could well be the demonic ones. After all, the Bible talks about a pact with the Devil in the last days, after Israel is reinstated. Leading to Armageddon.

Rather than Jews controlling the world, it is demonic big-nosed gray aliens from Zeta Reticuli. And rather than Aryans saving mankind, it is tall blond angelic beings from the Pleiades.

Cooper also reprints documents which purportedly show the "U.S. Army Intelligence Connection with [the] Satanic Church." Michael Aquino, leader of the Satanic "Temple of Set," it seems, is also a member of U.S. Army Intelligence. I'm not sure what this information is supposed to prove, but it's clear the principles of Freedom of Religion and Separation of Church and State mean nothing to Cooper, who claims that his only political stance is "constitutional."

In fact, Cooper believes himself to be serving a higher cause than the U.S. Constitution; he is engaged in the battle between angels and demons which will culminate in Armageddon and doomsday. Discrepancies, errors and even false statements just aren't very important, when you're serving TRUTH.

Revelations of Awareness
THE NEW AGE COSMIC NEWSLETTER
92-4
$3.00
ISSUE NO. 396
Cosmic Awareness Communications
Helping People Become Aware
THE WEB OF CONSPIRACY (Part 11): THE ALIEN AGENDA: AN UPDATE AND OVERVIEW
THE COMING OF 'NEMESIS' THE DARK STAR AND THE 40 MILLION REPTOID ARMY
WITH THEIR PLAN TO INVADE AND CONQUER THE EARTH

Perhaps the oldest "living" channeled voice, Cosmic Awarenss first identified itself through the body of former army officer Williarm Ralph Duby in 1962. When asked, "What is Cosmic Awareness?" it answered, "total mind that is not any one mind, but is from the Universal Mind that does not represent any unity other than that of universality." A year later, it instructed its listeners to form the Organization of Awareness, composed of 144 entities on the inner plane called "Essence." Upon Duby's death in 1967, the organization splintered into seven groups, each claiming to represent the authentic voice of Cosmic Awareness. The largest of these, Cosmic Awareness Coummunications in Olympia, WA, continues to hear Cosmic Awareness, but through a new channel, Paul Shockley. The record of these communications are published regularly in *Revelations of Awareness*, as seen above.

S.K.
&
FAMILY
MAR,'87

SHE-BOP STEVE

Steve Renstrom, aka She-Bop Steve, is a Seattle artist who believes that the former Senator from California Alan Cranston — whom he affectionately calls "the hog" — is the evil genius behind the conspiracy responsible for the deaths of everyone from John Belushi to John F. Kennedy.

The Goods on the Big Boys

Reagan/Cabinet, Iran/Contra Situation —

IT'S A CRANSTON "TAKES
THE FALL" FRONT LIE.
(TERROR OF JUSTICE)

The Reich, or Cranston Co., owns the scenario and is undermining the power and popularity of the Presidency. The Reich is freaking about the possibility of justice re their mass slaughtering of the people.

So, they opportuned and exacerbated the Iran thing plus deviously called for conclusions, anti-Reagan conclusions, all across the land. (brainwashing every voice)...

This one really tipped me: picture of Reagan on the front page pointing to head. (At the same time as Iran scheme!) ...

The Dan Rather Incident: Horrifying Berlin 42 Implications

It was designed also to blind mass "Dupe Troop" levels. "What's the frequency" was a "drop" they'd buy as — "it's pigs allright, must be o.k. to beat up newsmen. We oughta accept more 'n more Nazi violence and atrocities. And it's o.k. also about owning the media about it."

P.S. All during this writing I'm being insanely tortured. Also flow "cover up" and American guilt lies every second.

The Rock Band "Sonic Youth"

They were brainwashed into writing their song "Kill Yr. Idols". It's just standard hog schemes. They painted a logical story as to how "the next to go" rock star supposedly dies. It's a brainwashed scenario.

The hog needs to kill, say, Pat Benatar because she's a material witness that could hang Cranston and his flakes, so, they brainwash the song "Kill Yr. Idols" onto the scene. Then they brainwash a kid to kill Pat Benatar. Rock "takes the fall" for "the hogs'" murder of "rock." The hog slides and no one suspects.

The "yr." thing, Y-R instead of "your", in "Kill Yr. Idols", I recognize as a standard fascist contortion order for to stimulate the "Dupe Troops" or police types. It's called "escaping to slang." The police psychologist looks at the song title and comes to the conclusion that Sonic Youth subconsciously knew they were guilty. ("Take the fall" again.)

(Hinckley, DeNiro, Belushi Reagan — Circle)
Jodie Foster

Circle
James Dean
Natalie Wood
Sal Mineo
Samantha

Belushi

In one of his movies the hog "phased over" a teary face, anachronistic to the script. It was made detectably hog "No secret it's us, we just want you to think we're killing him". (since 1000s already knew J.B. was in big danger.)

Heraldo Rivera, "Crack", T.V. special. The Feds puppeted a thing where a Belushi "point to the neck" from a Saturday Nite Live clip was to imply that J.B. was talkin' crack as his problem instead of "hogs."

(the hog opportunes, owns, the cocaine thing etc. always painting a seemingly logical story as to how masses die. The citizens are helplessly fooled.)

Natalie Wood

Star Magazine T.V. ad, Natalie Woods' close friend, Wadkins, tries to wink to indicate B.S. info as to how and why she died. The hog who drowned her remotely from the Federal Building downtown, fooling millions, replaces Wadkins' wink with a "detectably hog" mechanical wink to say to the "Dupe Troops" "No secret we're involved since you knew already via, say, Ms. Wood's "Brainstorm" Flick.

They had to wipe out that simple wink! (Freakin, squirmin, insane, desperate Nazis.) In "Brainstorm" an actor reaches over and touches her neck letting us 20,000 "meat puppet" material witness' know she was in danger.

I see hundreds of little big things like a photo of Jimi Hendrix pointing to his neck and with a suspicious look on his face. Things like the China allusion on a Joplin cover which was a puppeted squirmin scammin flag lie. (To get the cops to click their heels in the vicinity of an atrocity.)

"The hog needs to kill, say, Pat Benatar because she's a material witness that could hang Cranston and his flakes, so they brainwash the song, 'Kill Yr. Idols' onto the scene."

Measuring in at 19 X 25 inches, *The Independent News,* the "OFFICIAL PUBLICATION OF THE U.S.A. MILITIA," may be the largest kook publication ever printed. Reproduced here is a detail from one of its massive, run-on pages. "*The Independent News* is the only newspaper in history that has and continues to publish God's Truths! That is the reason why 'House of Rothschild' Slave State C.I.A. Mail Censors and Thieves and Mercenary Murderers stop *The Independent News* when posted in the now held 'House of Rothschild' former U.S.A. postal system!"

MULTITUDES OF WHITE HOMELESS UNITED STATES OF AMERICA, SLAVES! THE REASON IS GIVEN HERE! IMMEDIATE ACTION MUST BE TAKEN!

THE HOMELESS WHITE U.S. AMERICANS, BEING EVICTED FROM THEIR HOMES BY THE "HOUSE OF ROTHSCHILD" TRAITORS WHO HOLD THE HELPLESS "FAKE CONDOMINIUM LEASES" "IN BONDAGE" HAVE NOWHERE TO GO!

IF IMMEDIATE ACTION IS NOT TAKEN TO SEIZE EVERY "CONDOMINIUM" AS SPOILS OF THE WAR THESE "CONDI-COOP" TRAITOR RACKETEERS HAVE WAGED ON THE PEOPLE OF THE UNITED STATES OF AMERICA, THESE RACKETEER TRAITORS WILL BE CAUGHT AND TORN TO PIECES BY WELL JUSTIFIED U.S. AMERICANS! YOU TRAITOR POLITICIANS MUST SEIZE THESE BUILDINGS IMMEDIATELY AND GIVE THEM, WITHOUT ANY "STRINGS ATTACHED" TO THE VICTIM TENANTS OF THE "HOUSE OF ROTHSCHILD" TREASON WAR UPON THE UNITED STATES OF AMERICA!

FURTHERMORE, IN ALL STATES ANY BUILDING WITH MORE THAN TWO TENANTS IS A TENAMENT HOUSE, NO MATTER IF IT IS MADE OF SILVER! THIS IS CALLED THE TENAMENT HOUSE LAW! IT VARIES IN NAME IN SOME STATES BUT IT MEANS THE SAME EVERYWHERE! THERE NEVER IN ALL HISTORY WAS ANY PIECE OF PROPERTY IN MORE THAN ONE TITLE HOLDERS NAME! AS ONLY THE LAND ANY BUILDING IS ERECTED ON IS NEVER COUNTED EXCEPT FOR LOCAL SERVICE CHARGES (IN SLAVE NATIONS) CALLED PROPERTY TAXES! THE "FRAUDULENT TRAITOR CONDOMINIUM RACKETEERS" WHO NEVER PUT ONE DOLLAR OF THEIR OWN INTO THESE ROTTEN "ROB THE POOR, WEAK AND DEFENSELESS" TENANTS FAKE, TRAITOR, MANIPULATED "CONDIE", LEASE ONLY, RACKET BUILDINGS, AS THEY STEAL THE MONEY THEY USE FOR CONSTRUCTION OF THESE "BARRIOS" BY THE "DOWN PAYMENT FOR ONLY A LEASE" AS ANY CONDOMINIUM OR SO CALLED COOPERATIVE OWNED TENAMENT HOUSE!

NO ONE EVER OWNS ANYTHING EXCEPT THE TRAITOR AND THIEF "OPERATOR" THAT COMMITS TREASON, IN EVERY ONE OF THESE FRAUDULENT "CONDOMINIUM" TENAMENT HOUSE LEASE SELLING FRAUDS! WHEN THESE BUILDINGS GO INTO BANKRUPTCY, AND MOST WILL, IF NOT ALL IN THIS PRESENT AND WORST "PLANNED DEPRESSION" THAT "THE SPAWN OF SATAN HOUSE OF ROTHSCHILD" NOW HAS BEEN DOING TO THE U.S.A. AND EVERY INDUSTRIALIZED NATION FOR THE PAST TWENTY YEARS, EVERY ONE OF THESE "CONDI TENAMENTS" WILL "GO BROKE"!

IT HAPPENED IN 1927, AFTER THE 1926 HURRICANE IN MIAMI, FLORIDA! THEN, THESE RACKETEERS CALLED THEIR CROOKED TREASON "COOPERATIVES"! THE VERY LEAST PART, THAT THE TRAITOR POLITICIANS NOW MUST TO SAVE THEMSELVES AND THE UNITED STATES OF AMERICA, THE WORST BLOOD BATH IN HISTORY IS TO READ THE FOLLOWING HORRIBLE CRUELTY THAT IS BEING INFLICTED UPON THE "STRENGTH" AND BODY OF ANY NATION! THAT VAST MAJORITY ARE THE SO-CALLED NON-AFFLUENT, BUT TRUE U.S. AMERICANS, WHO SCORN THE BEGGARY OF ANY "WELFARE STATE"! OUR NATION'S FOUNDERS GAVE THEIR LIVES TO NEVER HUMBLE THEMSELVES FOR THE ENEMIES GAIN! NO ONE CAN DO LESS! THE VERY WORST PART OF THE "CONDOMINIUM RACKET" IS AS FOLLOWS! AFTER THE WEAK, UNINFORMED, DUE TO "THE HOUSE OF ROTHSCHILD" BEING IN CONTROL OF EVERY FORM OF NEWS, THE VICTIMS OF THE HORRIBLE "CONDI" RACKET ARE TAKEN IN AS RENTERS AT FIRST, AND NOW NATIONWIDE, THESE TRAITOR VULTURES THAT ARE AN INSULT TO ANY OF GOD'S NECESSARY BUZZARDS AND VULTURES GO TO THEIR VICTIM TENANTS AND MAKE THE DEMAND! "WE ARE TURNING THIS BUILDING INTO A CONDOMINIUM! YOU MUST "BUY"! MAKE THE DEMAND! "WE ARE TURNING THIS BUILDING INTO A CONDOMINIUM! YOU MUST, IN MOST CASES, FORTY FIVE OR MORE THOUSAND DOLLARS IF VICTIMS WANT TO CONTINUE TO LIVE THERE! THEN YOU MUST PAY THE "MAINTENANCE" (RENT) CHARGES, AND THESE RENTALS ARE BEYOND THE ABILITY OF ANYONE TO PAY!

THE NEVER EXISTENT COMMUNISM WHICH GOES AGAINST HUMAN NATURE AS GOD'S HUMANS HAVE AS STREAK OF MATERIALISM THAT ALL OF THEM BUT A FEW CHRISTIAN AND BHUDDIST RELIGIOUS ORDERS WHO TAKE VOWS OF POVERTY AND LIVE BY THESE VOWS! OF COURSE, IN EVEN THESE CASES AS GOD'S PLANET EARTH OWES NO ONE A LIVING, OTHERS MUST PAY WITH THEIR LABOR FOR THE UPKEEP OF RELIGIOUS ORDERS THAT ARE NOT ENTIRELY SELF-SUPPORTING! THUS "THE POOR YE WILL ALWAYS HAVE WITH YE", AS JESUS SO WELL TAUGHT! THIS DOES NOT MEAN THAT POVERTY AND DEPRIVATION ARE THE IMPOSED LOT OF SO MANY! IN A FREE SOCIETY, AS FREE NATIONS THAT WERE FREE BEFORE "THE HOUSE OF ROTHSCHILD" BOUGHT THESE NATION'S TREASURIES AND NOW SLAVE TAX GOD'S CREATURES, THE OLD SAYING "YE CANNOT KEEP A GOOD MAN DOWN" AND THAT MEANS THAT THE GOOD MAN MUST BE HONEST AND NOT A CROOK! UNDER OUR EARLY REPUBLIC UNDER GOD, WITH FREE U.S. AMERICAN REPUBLICAN WAYS, ANYONE WITH ABILITY AND WILLING TO WORK, AND PRODUCE WITHOUT SCHEMING TO STEAL LEGALLY OR ILLEGALLY SOMEONE ELSE'S LABOR BY ANY MEANS AND WHO HAD CONTRIBUTED TO THE NATION FOR THE GOOD OF THE NATION AND SELF, WITH THAT FINAL INGREDIENT CALLED "GOOD LUCK" WHICH IS A MYSTERY MIRACLE OF GOD AND MUST NEVER BE QUESTIONED! THERE WE HAVE THE SECRET OF GOD'S HOLY FREEDOM WAR! THE ENEMY, SO WELL PROVED BY GOD'S MIRACLES, GUIDANCE AND AID TO HIS OLD, SIMPLE, FIRST CENTURY CHRISTIAN SERVANT, SPEAKS FROM NEARLY SEVENTY NINE YEARS OF EXPERIENCE GAINED BY HARD WORK AND GOD'S MIRACLES, WITHOUT WHICH WE ARE NOTHING! TAKING TIME OFF TO SERVE THE REPUBLIC IN TWO OF THE "HOUSE OF ROTHSCHILD" PLANNED WORLD WARS, AND WHO, TODAY, AFTER HAVING SPURNED EVERY OFFER TO BE THE POSSESSOR OF WEALTH, AS NO ONE CAN SERVE GOD AND MAMMON AT ANY TIME, THE EDITOR, WITH ALL HE HAS EXPERIENCED, INCLUDING 8,000 MIRACLES OF GOD, FEELS THAT HE IS THE RICHEST MAN IN THE WORLD! THEN, IT IS WELL PROVED, BOTH BY TRIALS AND PRESENT ABSENCE OF "COMMUNISM" IN ANY NATION THAT WORD COMMUNISM AND ANY OTHER "ISM" BUT TRUTH AND FAITH AND TRUST IN GOD IS A LIE PERPETRATED BY THE "HOUSE OF **ROTHSCHILD, INTL. ANTI DEFAMATION LEAGUE OF BRNAI BRITH NEWS CONTROL CONSPIRACY, AS THE PEOPLE COULD NOT UNDERSTAND THE WORDS BOLSHEVIK DICTATORSHIP AS HAVING ANY MEANING THAT COULD CONFUSE THEM INTO THE LIE THAT THE WORD COMMUNISM DOES CONFUSE THEM INTO!**

THE "HOUSE OF ROTHSCHILD" BANK OF ENGLAND (BRITISH TREASURY) BRANCH IN THE U.S.A. AND OTHER NATION, J.P. MORGAN AND CO. CONTROL CHRYSLER! THESE ENEMIES OF GOD AND ALL HIS CREATURES HOLD AS MORE DOGS IN THE MANGER JOINTLY WITH THE "HOUSE OF ROTHSCHILD" FUEL CONTROL CONSPIRACY. THE STORAGE BATTERY PATENTS! THERE NEED BE NO WASTE IN MAKING NEW ELECTRIC CARS! THE VERY WELL MADE OLD ONES OF THE EDITOR'S YOUTH ARE IN MANY MUSEUMS! THEY ARE MIGHTY GOOD! IN GERMANY, THE "ROTHSCHILD" CONTROLLED BOSCH CO. HAS 100 PASSENGER STORAGE BATTERY BUSES RUNNING IN ALL CITIES! THE EDITOR AND HIS BELOVED WIFE USED TO RIDE THE DOUBLE DECK FIFTH AVE. EDISON, NICKEL, IRON ALKALINE STORAGE BATTERY POWERED BUSES IN NEW YORK CITY IN 1920! THESE BATTERIES ARE GOOD FOR LIFE! THERE MUST BE A DRIVER WHO ONLY DRIVES AND A CONDUCTOR WHO COLLECTS FARES! PASSENGERS MUST ENTER BY FRONT DOORS! LEAVE BY REAR DOORS, AS IT WAS, AND IS STILL DONE IN EUROPE AND JAPAN! THE WAY OF GREED IN PUTTING THE CONDUCTOR OUT OF A JOB, SHOWS THE CRIMINAL STUPIDITY OF "THE COLLEGE GRADUATE BLUNDERS" HIRED BY THE FINANCIERS AND POLITICIANS THAT OPERATE OMINBUS LINES!

THE "PLANNED DEGENERACY" LED BY THE "INTL. A.D.L. CONTROLLED SEX MAGAZINES! THE EDITOR IS NO PURITAN OR HYPOCRITE! THE FEMALE FORM THAT IS BEAUTIFUL IS NOT TO BE DENIED ITS ADMIRATION, AS A WORK OF GOD! NOT TO BE EXPLOITED FOR "PLANNED DEGENERACY" OF THE ENEMY! THE PLAYBOY "CLUBS" ARE PART OF "PLANNED DEGENERACY"! SO ARE THE "TOPLESS SALOONS". SO ARE THE ORGY FESTIVALS OF DOPE CRAZED, ALCOHOL DRUNK, SEX CRAZED, FILTHY DEGENERATES OF THE DIRTY BEARDED, STINKING, UNWASHED "HIPPY" CARNIVALS OF HELL CALLED "ROCK FESTIVALS"! EVERY ONE OF THESE WORSE THAN ANCIENT ROMAN DEGENERATE ORGIES IS PART OF AND PROMOTED BY "HOUSE OF ROTHSCHILD" "PLANNED DEGENERACY" PROMOTED BY "HOUSE OF ROTHSCHILD" INTL. A.D.L. MEMBERS! YOU WHO HATE BARBERS AND ARE AFRAID OF THE INFERIORITY COMPLEXES THAT YOU HAVE ARE DIRTY AND LOUSE RIDDEN! ANY GIRL WHO IS WITH YOU IS AS LOW AS WHAT THE NEGROES PROPERLY CALL "SHACK UP WITH NEGROES" WHITE GIRLS WHO HAVE LEFT THE WHITE RACE, WHITE TRASH!

"I am followed everywhere ..."

BELIEVE IT OR NOT, THE LETTER BELOW IS A mere excerpt describing an elaborate scheme of skullduggery by police and bystanders playing street theater. The missive was simply titled, "Untitled Letter."

Upon returning to New York I began looking for a place to live. I looked at around ten apartments and called to inquire about several others. Since the secret police had already selected and prepared an apartment for me this proved to be a futile endeavor. I signed a two-year lease for apartment twenty-four at 620 East 11th Street and moved to the building in November. The apartment provides me with a place to live but it also provides the secret police with a living environment they control. The building where I live, the surrounding buildings and the neighborhood serve as a theatrical set; and the "tenants" of my building, neighborhood characters, and intelligence agents stage a theatrical production. Controlling the immediate neighborhood is a security measure and it allows maximum freedom of action for staging operations. The building I live in is connected to four other buildings; when I look out my only window with a "view" (one window is boarded up and three others face an interior light well) I see the back of a row of buildings on 10th Street. These buildings form a unit that is flanked by three empty lots. the secret police use these nine buildings for staging operations and own some or all of them. The buildings may have been purchased but it is very likely that they were acquired from the City of New York through Mayor Koch. The city government owns many buildings in the area due to non-payment of taxes and abandonment. I believe most of these buildings have no tenants or caretaker tenants. The two largest buildings were being renovated when I moved to my apartment and appeared to be almost tenantless until the summer of 1982. Either they acquired tenants that summer or the secret police expended a greater effort to make them seem inhabited. The two buildings were renovated at a minimum cost of $500,000 each, so even if all the other buildings were acquired from the city, the secret police spent over one million dollars to provide me with a $115.00 a month slum apartment. ...

The basic strategy of the secret police is to be everpresent; at all times and in all places they make themselves an intrusive, oppressive and inescapable presence. They involve themselves in every detail of my life and are present everywhere I go. At first I dismissed the strategy of being everpresent as silly game-playing, but the intelligence agents responsible for planning operations clearly intended their use of thousands of collaborators to be a form of non-violent harassment; a psychological assault designed to have a negative psychological effect. Being everpresent is intended to be more of an invasion of consciousness than an invasion of privacy. Being everpresent is used as a means for stealing reality, and thus the ability to function normally in a real world. The secret police have imposed upon me a substitute reality; they have dismembered and appropriated the real world and placed me in a labyrinth of intelligence operations. It is difficult to relate to and impossible to adjust to the artificial, arbitrary and hostile living environment the secret police have created. By being everpresent they try to turn the most commonplace life experiences and the activities of daily life into a maze-like obstacle course and to make the living of everyday life a frustrating, unnatural and disorienting experience. Since secret police operations began I usually made a note of a detail or incident only if it stood out as unusually intrusive, offensive or bizarre. Sometimes I kept daily accounts of every aspect of secret police operations and listed every encounter with an agent or collaborator. Basing an estimate on the days and weeks when I counted agents and collaborators, and acknowledging that the nature and intensity of operations has changed over the years, I believe that a minimum of forty thousand American citizens have participated in secret police operations since they began in 1977. It is a curious reversal of everything this country has ever stood for that two Presidents, many of their closest associates and supporters, and personnel of law enforcement agencies now constitute the single largest group of citizens engaged in organized criminal activity.

I am followed everywhere partly as a security measure but also because it is necessary to know where I am at all times in order to conduct secret police operations. At any given moment several intelligence agents work together choreographing street theater and surveillance operations. Agents and collaborators follow me on foot and in vehicles; while maintaining radio contact, they pass me on like a relay team passes on a baton. Most of the surveillance agents appear to have been recruited from the FBI and the New York City

"The apartment provides me with a place to live but it also provides the secret police with a living environment they control."

"As I approach the intersection, a signal is given and people, most of whom are young men, start crossing the intersection from every direction."

Police Department. After observing my behavior and interests for over five years it is not hard for intelligence agents to predict when I am likely to go out and where I am likely to go. Whenever I leave my apartment I encounter intelligence agents, collaborators, and a theatrical production stage managed by the secret police. After several years this provocative annoyance has come to seem rather like running the gauntlet; a form of military punishment in which an individual is made to run between two rows of men who strike at him as he passes by. While descending the stairs from my apartment I usually meet one or more of the "tenants" trying hard to look as if they live in the building or staging a scene for me to observe. As I left the building one afternoon two fat men stood with their backs against opposite sides of the narrow first floor hall so that I had to turn sideways and step between them. Frequently groups of men are standing or sitting on the stoop when I go out or come in; sometimes blocking the steps so that I have to ask them to move. Several times a week one or more collaborators walk by me just as I step outside. On days when it is felt some special intimidation is necessary a police car will drive by as I go out and again as I come home. When I go out I almost always head west, walking through the intersection of 11th Street and Avenue B. Since I then might head in any of three directions, this is the only place that operations can be planned for with near certainty that I will enter into the staged scene. The secret police operations I encounter at this intersection are usually more elaborately detailed and choreographed than they are elsewhere, and it is very likely there are hidden cameras. There are usually twice as many people around this intersection as at any other in the neighborhood, frequently from ten to twenty people. A corner with a hardware store, a sometimes open grocery store and two abandoned buildings is not likely to be a favorite neighborhood hangout yet there are often groups of Puerto Rican and black men standing around. Often one or more collaborators will be placed on each corner so that the only way I can avoid them is to walk in the street. As I approach the intersection, a signal is given and people, most of whom are young men, start crossing the intersection from every direction; people walking on the sidewalks, boys riding by on bikes, and other people driving by in cars. Intelligence agents frequently use this kind of collaborator saturation placement at other intersections. This operational technique became obvious when several times, after having gone through intersections that were inexplicably busy, I stopped to count the number of people and vehicles that moved through the intersection during the next few minutes.

The majority of collaborators have been involved in one basic situation; a male child or a handsome young man (sometimes an ordinary looking or older man) presents himself to be looked at while other people observe me. Presumably, if I look at the conspicuously displayed bait the observer-witnesses claim to have seen proof of sexual interest or an attempted seduction. Within this basic situation the secret police have devised a relatively limited repertoire of scenes but with infinite variations. The actors have basic roles and patterns of interaction; it is somewhat like watching the same play over and over but each time with a new cast. A few thousand such scenes were staged to create incidents that could be used to discredit me, to manufacture "evidence" that I was immoral, and to make a fictitious propaganda portrait of me seem to be true. More time and effort have been invested in staging such scenes than in any other single aspect of secret police operations. Intelligence agents made such encounters the centerpiece of their operations because political leaders found that making an issue of homosexuality was their most effective means of gaining political support for a criminal conspiracy. Every system of morality, whether based on religious beliefs or philosophical principles, is concerned with the difference between right and wrong. Without defining what is right and what is wrong, everyone can nevertheless agree that morality is a hierarchical system; there are greater and lesser evils and there are greater and lesser goods. It is a wildly distorted sense of morality that considers two human beings expressing sexual desire or love for each other degenerate and immoral while considering a political conspiracy to violate a citizen's constitutional rights, the creation of an illegal domestic secret police, the police-state tactics of intelligence agents, and the suspension of the country's system of government by the rule of law, to be matters of no importance. ...

On Tuesday, September 8, I left my apartment around 3:30 intending to pay my Con Edison bill. Just as I stepped out of the building, a car that was waiting a few feet from me, pulled away from the curb accelerating rapidly, "burning rubber" as if it were in a drag race. The secret police frequently set up similar incidents as a distraction; I believe the screeching tires and the brazen display of contempt were intended to induce angry thoughts that would preoccupy me and influence my behavior. As I walked to the

Con Edison office at 4 Irving Place I counted sixteen collaborators engaged in street theater; the next day I encountered at least twenty. At the Con Edison office I looked in the window; the office was unusually crowded and the bill-paying line seemed suspiciously long. I was generally apprehensive about entering a trap, so I decided to come back the next day. I left my apartment around 3:05 P.M. on Wednesday. Walking across 14th Street, I looked at every newsstand for a copy of the New York Times so that I would have something to read while waiting in line. Over a two year period I frequently bought or saw papers late in the afternoon at the various newsstands; it is highly unlikely they would have all been sold out. I believe intelligence agents asked the newspaper sellers to hide the papers so that I would have nothing to do while waiting except to observe the planned operation. Inside the main floor customer service office, intelligence agents placed a minimum of twenty-five people and it seemed as if all the employees had been given some sort of briefing and were participating in secret police operations. I joined the bill-paying line, there were around ten people in line and as I approached two young men placed themselves directly ahead of me in the line. Within a few minutes around fifteen more people lined up behind me. There were five bill paying windows. While I waited in line the clerks closed their windows until only one window was left open for customer service. The four people in front of me all went to the same window. I believe this was a delaying tactic to keep me in the office for a longer period of time. While waiting in line the secret police operation being staged was very obvious. Seven young men presented themselves to be looked at and a man and a woman each walked by me twice staring holes through me. The situation reminded me of the movie "The Sting." Sting operations are frequently used by law enforcement agencies; police agents create and operate fictitious companies as a means of entrapment. In this case intelligence agents set up an elaborate but thinly disguised covert operation within the office of a legitimate business. A few weeks earlier I found myself surrounded by game-playing collaborators in a line at my bank. I became angry and denounced them for participating in secret police operations. I believe intelligence agents chose to restage a similar scene in Con Edison's offices hoping to elicit the same or a similar response; an angry outburst that could be used as "proof" that through paranormal powers I had somehow triggered the transformer malfunction and resulting blackout. I was in the Con Edison office about ten minutes, from approximately 3:20 to 3:30; the power failure began at 3:24. I believe intelligence agents committed an act of sabotage timed to coincide with the provocative secret police operation being staged in Con Edison's office. The secret police involved at least forty people, many of them Con Edison employees, in staging their scene in Con Edison's office. Although these people were intended to witness an angry outburst they were also witnesses to the fact that intelligence agents were expending a great deal of effort to manufacture an incident.

— George Dahl

"I believe intelligence agents asked the newspaper sellers to hide the papers so that I would have nothing to do while waiting except to observe the planned operation."

IS JFK ALIVE? AN INTERVIEW WITH BERNIE BANE

Bane has maintained for the past 30 years that JFK's assassination was a hoax, that JFK is actually alive.

Bernie Bane, along with a large segment of the U.S. population, believes that the assassination of President John F. Kennedy was the result of a high-order conspiracy. To Bane, however, the deceit goes even further than usual; he has maintained for the past 30 years that JFK's assassination was not only a conspiracy but a hoax, that JFK is actually alive.

When Bane contacted me a few years ago hoping for some publicity via *Kooks* magazine, I arranged for an interview. Arriving at his Cambridge, MA, apartment, the first thing I noticed was a giant photograph on the wall. It showed a dapper-looking young man pointing to his all-inclusive circular diagram of the human psyche. It was a photograph of Bane taken in the 50s when *The Harvard Crimson* did a satirical story on him; at that time he was promoting an unorthodox psychoanalytic thoery. The story of how Bane came to believe that JFK is alive, it turns out, began while he was promoting this theory, his "Grand Model of the Mind."

The 1990 interview, excerpted below, covers the basic elements of Bane's theory. His self-published books include *The Grand Model of the Mind* (1962), *The Bane in Kennedy's Existence* (1967), and *Is President John F. Kennedy Alive ... And Well?* (1973).

Donna Kossy: *I want you to describe the events that led up to your conviction that the JFK assassination is a hoax.*

Bernie Bane: How I got involved in the politics — originally my interest was to propound my theory in psychology. At that time people had heard about my views, more or less. And I don't know how it happened, but I think somebody recommended that I give a speech at one of these various lodges. You know, Masons and things like that. ... And somebody invited me to their lodge as a speaker, and it turned out that they liked it very much, and usually people in a lodge belong to more than one lodge. So somebody there said, "Why don't you come speak at *my* lodge?" And it got to the point where I was doing some circuits around various lodges.

And eventually it started paying me a little. They were paying me around $25, when they were paying me — sometimes I'd do it for nothing — so then I decided, if I'm such a hit — I was breaking attendance records — I figured, gee, why don't I sponsor myself, and maybe I'll charge an admission, and I would be able to make more money that way. So ... I advertised a speech by me, at the end of the lecture there would be a coffee hour and a mixer — a dance. And it was for younger people. It turned out that people became more interested in the dance part of it than the speaking part of it. So I figured why don't I drop the speech and promote the dances. And this is what I did.

So I started out at that time — back then it was the rock 'n' roll era, in the 50s. And I decided to invite a local disc jockey — he was the most famous one at the time — Joe Smith. The reason why I mention his name is because today, Joe Smith, I just saw him on television. He's the president of Capitol Records.

So that's how I got in with the local record hops. And that became quite successful, although it wasn't terribly organized. So I moved into Boston, and hired a hotel in Boston. And I started to run dances at a hotel in Boston. And I called my dances "The Hearts and Diamonds Dance Club." And they were picking up interest. ... Then what happened was I ran my dances at a hotel owned by a Boston slum-lord. He was a very famous man at that time. If I mention his name it probably wouldn't mean anything — you weren't around — Morris Gordon. He was very famous. And he was one of the two important rich Jewish people in the Boston Area. ...

So eventually, Morris Gordon threw me out of the hotel, and started to run the dances himself. … In any event he was in the position of throwing me out on some pretense that I didn't pay him the rent, which is not true.

Then his lawyer said to me, "We'll exchange releases." I had a lawyer to sue Morris Gordon for throwing me out arbitrarily, to prove I had all the records, that I'd paid the rent. And the lawyers when they first took the case were very excited: "We'll look at the case, won't even charge you for it, we've got a clean-cut case, we'll sue him for $20,000." Then, for some strange reason the lawyer said he had to withdraw. He didn't want to do it. They recommended another lawyer. The other lawyer said, "No problem," then *he* withdrew. Every time I got a lawyer, they kept withdrawing. So it occurred to me that Morris Gordon was reaching them.

So then one lawyer said to me finally, "Look, I'm not going to say we're being reached by Morris Gordon, but why don't you do it yourself. You can prosecute the case, you won't have to worry about — you can do it." So, I decided to do it. That was one of my biggest mistakes. Here, now, I'm suing Morris Gordon *pro se,* by yourself. I figured, why not, it's a clean cut case, I have the evidence, etc.

OK, well, how it happened was, how it ended up was that he got a jury trial, and before that the judge assigned it to arbitration. When it got to arbitration I could see that they were going to hassle me, that it was going to be rigged. So I decided, I'm going to walk out of this, I'm not going to partake in this silly thing 'cause already I can see that this thing is rigged. In any event they rendered a decision in favor of Morris Gordon. …

At that point I began to get suspicious of a kangaroo court, of a degree to which Morris Gordon can bribe not only arbitration, but also the jury. How he can do that takes a lot of power and influence. And then gradually it occurred to me that it wasn't Morris Gordon who was doing all the bribing, but it was a force much greater than Morris Gordon. I used the term, "the Mafia." Later on I called them "Social Engineers." And it's interesting how I made a correlation between the Mafia and the Social Engineers.

Today, the reverse is taking place, where the Social Engineers are really taking over the Mafia, and becoming the Mafia. I'm suspicious of that. In other words, the drug trafficking, we believe is run by the Mafia. But, in fact, it's run by the CIA.

DK: *Who are the Social Engineers? You would say the CIA —*

BB: The CIA is an arm of the Social Engineers. Be that as it may, so here now, when I lost the case with Morris Gordon, I still didn't quit. I decided to see if I could do an intercollegiate dance. … [I called it] an "Ivy League Mixer."

… I advertised in Boston newspapers, and they said, "What's an Ivy League Mixer? Is that a drink?" They didn't know what a mixer was. But the college students *did* know.

So, in the beginning it was very slow. In fact the *Harvard Crimson* came down and did a front page story on it and made a satire on it, "Five people showed up to Bernie Bane's Ivy League Mixer." Everybody read it and laughed. We had a cop there. It showed the cop leaning his arm on the piano, listening to the music. It was so boring, nobody was there. It was a funny shot. The next week I ran it again, and a lot of people started showing up, because this is the dance everybody's laughing at. And when more Harvard students started showing up, more girls came down. The more girls came down, the more guys came down, and it got to be quite successful. …

Now we're into 1963. So from '59 to '63 I was running dances. All of the sudden, in '63, the early part of '63, maybe '62, they canceled my license to run the dance, and I didn't know why. So I started to inquire with the license commission, and they didn't give me an answer. They kept shifting me from office to office, and at the same time I was getting reactions from the general public — bizarre reactions — I found the police officers were following me. I'd get in my car, and there'd be about five motorcycle police behind me,

The back cover of *The Bane In Kennedy's Existence.* Behind RFK's head, Bernie Bane expounds on his schematic diagram of the "psyche structure."

just following me. They would give no explanation for it. And it would be things like that that began to really get on my nerves. ...

"And then I had an experience — also in the nuthouse — where one of the inmates said to me, 'The reason why you're here is because of that man on television. It was President Kennedy on television."

So, finally one day, I got a call, a knock on the door, and it was a police officer. And I wouldn't let him in. So I called the police myself to complain that I'm being harassed by the police. It was a very bizarre thing. I wasn't sophisticated enough to know how to deal with the so-called harassment that was going on. It consummated where somebody came to my door, and it was the police, and my brother was there. I said, "What are you doing here?" He said, "Don't worry, I'm going to help you." So, I let him in, and the policemen with him. So he said, "Don't worry, just do what they say, and everything will be fine. They just want to ask you a few questions down at the office. Take your car, and they'll follow you down."

So, as soon as I left the house, the police handcuffed me, and put me in a paddywagon, and shipped me to, what I found out later to be, one of their doctors. It was a psychiatrist. And the doctor asked me, "Why are you here?" So I said, "Hey, that's what I want to know. There's no warrant for my arrest, I've been arrested without a warrant, I'd like to know what's going on." So he said, "What do *you* think is going on?" I was too unsophisticated. So I had to show off my expertise. So I gave my opinion which was that I think there are politics being played out through me. And, that was it. He gave the diagnosis ... so they shipped me to the nuthouse. And, when I was in the nuthouse, they gave me a shot of LSD. [This was in] Boston State Hospital. And they said, uh-huh, he's having a schizophrenic fit. He's having hallucinations.

OK, so I knew enough to know at the time, I'd read about it. So when I got that needle stuck in me, I realized that I was having an LSD experience. And it was bizarre because it was heavy and it was through a needle.

I'd read about LSD in *LIFE Magazine* about two weeks before that. They were doing experiments with that — Leary — in the Harvard Lab. And I happened to have gone there to see what he was doing. So I had that behind me, otherwise I would have freaked out. It was a heavy experience, it was unbelievable, I mean, it wasn't something I was ready for. And the effect of it carried on about a week until I kept it down — I had illusions like I could fly and things like that — that I was superhuman. I said to myself, don't express any of these illusions, any of these experiences, be normal. You cannot walk through walls, you cannot fly. ...

So, eventually, it tapered down, and also I could feel normal. And then I had an experience — also in the nuthouse — where one of the inmates said to me, "The reason why you're here is because of that man on television." And it was President Kennedy on television. And somewhere along the line, I don't know exactly when it was, either somebody had told me, or I had figured it out, that **President Kennedy was going to get assassinated as a birthday present to me.** People kept asking me questions like, "When's your birthday Bernie, when's your birthday Bernie?" And they had an idea something was coming on.

I was put away in October, and I was released after a 30-day observation thing. They had me there under observation. If I had not passed the observation exam, they could have kept me there indefinitely. So they called a staff meeting of 30 doctors. And one of the staff doctors said to me, "I understand you wrote a book in psychology. And, I'll let you know that we'll let you out if you won't expose us, you won't write a book exposing us." So I figured at least he's recognizing the fact that I was there unjustly. So I was happy to hear that. So I promised him, "Don't worry, I'll give you my word I won't expose you," whatever. Whatever they wanted to hear, I kept saying that. So, I passed the exam, and they let me out

So, I got out October 15. And according to the expectations, something was going to happen on my birthday. My birthday's November 21st. President Kennedy was supposed to be assassinated as a birthday present to me. So, on November 22, he was assassinated. So that's how I got involved. I figured, there's something going on here.

There was a definite connection. So then, when I read an article in the Boston Globe which said, "HOAX IN DALLAS" — somebody did something that had nothing to do with the Kennedy assassination — but to me, it meant something: "HOAX IN DALLAS" — it means the assassination's a hoax. And I always felt there was something bizarre about the whole thing. So I concluded, OK, he never got killed. And I realized after concluding that, a lot of people around me knew that all along, but they didn't admit it. So I still didn't say anything about it. So slowly I leaked out my belief that he wasn't even killed.

I was too afraid to even talk about the fact that Kennedy got assassinated as a birthday present to me. I never said that, because if it ever leaked out I figured people who were so much endeared to Kennedy would want to get even — they would want to kill me — to revenge the fact that he was killed because of me. So I didn't say anything. But when I realized he was alive, I figured, hey, they're not going to kill me, because he's there, they're holding him hostage. So I felt more safe to talk about my beliefs.

At first [people] would go, "We're so happy to hear he's alive, how do you know this?" They said, "Why don't you write a book on it?" That's how it happened. I decided to write my first book on it. The title, "The BANE in Kennedy's Existence," it's a great title. The "Bane" means the destruction of his political machine, so to speak. Somehow, because of me, he got assassinated, but now the assassination is really a hoax... that's how I got involved.

But the thing is, there are other things involved. I was right in my initial intuitions about Social Engineers. But the curious thing is that it just never got resolved. To this day. The Kennedy assassination hasn't gotten resolved. And I'm still in the same place where I was back then, in many ways. In that it started out where I was being badgered to do something. I was complaining to my friends, and whatever, surrounding me, saying, "I'm being harassed and there's something weird going on."

Some people would say to me with a smile, "Bernie, why don't you do something about it?" It sounded like a strange way to react. Why should you put the imposition on me to do something if you know there's something going on, you should be helping me. Well this is the reason why I kept desperately doing whatever [they] wanted me to do. So we can resolve this silly thing. No matter what I do, I get deeper and deeper involved. But, first, I couldn't get my license back. And interestingly, here I had this beautiful dance, making lots of money, and I wanted to do something to go back the way it was. The more I tried to do, the more I'd get into the Pandora's Box. It was a lure. If I had just simply dropped everything, and did nothing, I might have gotten out of the whole thing. But by doing something I got worse in it. And that never occurred to me.

"I'm embarrassing Kennedy because he is alive. I wasn't quite sure just how he would take it."

I figured when I wrote the book, now that I wrote the book, that'll turn things around. But, in fact, it made it worse. It was a perfect thing because here I'm saying Kennedy's alive. Here, I'm embarrassing Kennedy, because he is alive. But I wasn't quite sure just how he would take it. I would think that the clarification would bring him back and that everybody would be happy. But see, that's not the way it went; at first he wanted to make contact with me, because I [told them], when I submitted the manuscript to [Ted Kennedy's] office for approval, "If you have any objections, I won't go through with the publishing."

So I went back to the office to see what the reaction was, the girl said to me, "Senator Kennedy told me to tell you he doesn't want you to do anything until you hear from him." Then, all of a sudden, I couldn't reach him, the girl was fired, and, that was it. So I had to make a decision. I couldn't reach anybody. So I went through with the publication of it, ... on my own, without his actual — either yes or no. ...Every time he would give a lecture, a public lecture, I would be there with my book, to say here I want you to read my book. And his so-called staff people would prevent me from making contact with him.

And he was very much protected wherever he'd go.

"Professor Galbraith said, 'Oh, gee, I'd love to read the book. I'll give you a review on it.'"

So, ultimately and finally, after fifteen, 20 years, I was finally able to deliver a copy of the book to him. It was bizarre, because, he was at the point where, at the dedication of the JFK School of Government, this is where I was able to make contact with Joe Kennedy and Professor Galbraith, and eventually, Senator Kennedy yielded, so to speak, and he approached me, waiting for me to give him the book, and when I gave him the book, he appeared very flushed. And he said nothing, he just took the book and left.

DK: *He had known about you before.*

BB: His staff told me, "We have a file this big on you," so there's no question about it. When Joan Kennedy saw me and the book, she was, "Oh thank you, thank you, I'd love to read it." Professor Galbraith said, "Oh, gee, I'd love to read the book. I'll give you a review on it."

But the point was, the response that I finally got, see, I never approached Joe Kennedy, curiously. But I did approach Professor Galbraith, and he refused to give me a response. And, Ted Kennedy did give me a written response, which is in the book.

One more thing I should tell you, it's kind of interesting. Before I wrote my first book, I went to a lecture at Harvard that was given by Paul Krassner. I was, like, awed, that he would use four-letter words at Harvard University no less. And all the young kids were there, and they were all applauding him — so, I spoke to him, I figured, hey, if you're that far out, maybe you might be interested in doing a story on my theory of the Kennedy assassination — hoax. His response was, "I wouldn't do it, but why don't you do what I did: open up your own publishing house, and do it yourself." He was the one who suggested I do it myself. And afterwards I figured, hey, he was invited to Harvard, and I figured a little association there, that's how I got into writing my own book, publishing my own book. It's like he inspired me to get into the publishing business. I don't know if Paul Krassner even knows who I was. So basically, I feel, that the major focus — it's interesting about the correlation between Paul Krassner — is that I don't think there is too much focus on Paul Krassner today. I think the focus is on me.

DK: *What do you mean by that?*

BB: I think what I do is of greater concern to the establishment than what Paul Krassner does.

DK: *The Social Engineers?*

BB: Yes. Here's the correlation: when I give my lectures now, on [cable] television, I follow very carefully the events in East Germany — the unification issue. In last night's lecture, I blew everybody away, because I come so close to where it's at. What I'm saying has a greater impact on the events because I'm the one who made the claim that Kennedy's alive. Now if Kennedy is alive, then, if that issue, whether he's alive ever comes to fore — see, people aren't talking about whether he's dead or alive, in fact they don't even talk about the Kennedy assassination at all. [The movie *JFK* hadn't came out yet.] The only time they talk about it is when the establishment brings him out, either on his birthday, or whatever. They don't raise the issue of him being dead or alive. They only raise the issue of what Ted Kennedy's doing now, should he run for President. But, Ted Kennedy and the Kennedys obviously, it seems to me, that if John Kennedy's alive, that what they're working towards, is, to be able to bring out the fact that he's alive, and save face. So that, because I'm the only one that raised the issue that he could be alive, it seems to me that what happens to me and my decisions, my role in life, has a greater impact on how Kennedy — how he'll make decisions. Whether he will decide, let's surface now, or let's not surface now…

DK: *Who, exactly, are the beneficiaries of the hoax?*

BB: Oh yeah, the Social Engineers. Now we're going back to a whole different thesis of the real power struggle, the on-going historical power struggle between the Protestants and the Catholics. In other words, this goes back from the onset of the American Revolution, you might say. Who settled

America? It was Protestants. Right? All your major Generals and Presidents have always been Protestants, right?

Only recently, in recent history, with the growth of the Catholic Church in America, and generally, Catholics have dominated politics on the local level only. And the one major attempt in history where there was a Catholic — running for President — Al Smith. Al Smith was a Catholic. He was running as a Democrat. And the Republicans were saying, a Catholic can never win in America. So, he lost, and he lost closely, and they said, "We told you so." So, ever since then, nobody would dare to be a Presidential candidate unless he was Protestant. Then came John Kennedy. ...So the strategy they used was to let him be President, because there was still a power struggle between Protestants and Catholics, and, the Social Engineers from the State Department. Parallel to this power struggle between Protestant and Catholic is also the power struggle between the combatants in World War I and World War II. Japan and Germany were the bad guys in World War I, and they were the bad guys in World War II. Right? So the secret meetings that were held in Yalta — the Yalta Conference — at the end of World War II — the people who were there — Roosevelt and all his staff people from America, Alger Hiss, were all Protestants, there were no Catholics at that meeting, except Kennedy. There is a parallel. The State Department, principally, is operated by Protestants. And when Kennedy came in, he wasn't privy of the secrecy that was involved in the Yalta conference. He came in on his own agenda, which was a Catholic-oriented agenda.

DK: *Last time you said [the hoax] was kind of a bargain.*

BB: Well, no, the hoax was a double-cross. Kennedy agreed to go through with the hoax, with only he'd be called "wounded," in order to placate the civil rights controversy. Because you have the blacks wanting more reform, and the white supremacists wanting less reform. So he was losing his support down south because he was siding too much with the blacks. So, in order to counter that, to neutralize, the assassination hoax, where he'd be called wounded, would placate both sides.

If he's being bombarded from both sides, one side saying faster reforms, the other side saying slower reforms. Here, he gets wounded. Now the press releases are sent out. Those who are saying we want more reforms — "look let's go easy on him, look what happened, he just got shot, because of his trying to help out." And then, to those who are saying, "ease up," you could say, "alright, it serves, look what happened to him, he got the message now. He's gonna ease up now."

In any event, it didn't work, because he was double-crossed. They didn't call him wounded, they called him dead. So, now he's out of the picture. So, now there's a vacuum, and the Social Engineers come in, and now they fill that vacuum. Now the issue is — according to my thinking, they made an agreement with Kennedy: if you cooperate with us, we'll surface you, face saved. We will bring about necessary social reforms, and give you the credit for it...

My strategy now is to see if I can build up my credibility, and I've got to break the so-called — I mean, I'm sort of caught in this place where it's not to the best expedient vested interest of the Social Engineers to give me credibility.

"I'm sort of caught in this place where it's not to the best expedient vested interest of the Social Engineers to give me credibility."

NORMA COX'S SECRETS

A crippled and widowed housewife, strangely I have been given the ability to "see." With this gift goes an awesome and inescapable responsibility: that of informing the people of my race of the Secrets, the great mysteries of which they know nothing. ...

— Norma Cox

Mrs. Cox's writings are especially urgent due to her sincere belief that "here in the United States the White Christian is targeted for extinction."

NORMA COX'S STIRRING EXPOSÉS OF TRUTHS that have been deliberately hidden from American Aryans by evil alien pagan gods who live inside the hollow earth and in outer space, are the result of a literal-mindedness ruthlessly applied to everything from UFOs to American History. The bits and pieces of this conspiriologist's knowledge are sewn together into a crazy quilt where leading Jews are sun-worshippers, where Hitler is alive in a warm place beneath Antarctica, and where the Statue of Liberty is actually a radio tower receiving messages from the moon. A little knowledge may be a dangerous thing, but it is also essential if one is to explain why the world is a complete mess. It seems that the less you know, the more you can explain, and Norma Cox can explain everything.

Norma Cox disseminates her revelations in a newsletter, *Secrets,* and in compilations with titles like, *The Holyland Above and Below, UFO's and the Dragon Power,* and *Christianity and the Sun God.* On first glance at these publications, it looks as though Mrs. Cox blames the Jews for everything, but a closer look reveals that the Jews are merely the tools of a greater power, that of extraterrestrials — better known as the pagan deities Zeus, Apollo, Diana and Satan — who live within the hollow earth.

It would be easy — but also erroneous — to place Norma Cox in any number of ideological categories: Jewish Conspiracy, Masonic Conspiracy, Vatican Conspiracy, UFO Conspiracy, Neo-Nazi, Anglo-Israelite, Millenialist, Fundamentalist, Hollow Earth. Actually, Norma Cox is a category unto herself, artfully weaving all of the above into a seemingly consistent fabric of TRUTH. Her loyal following is among "Aryan Christians."

Mrs. Cox's writings are especially urgent due to her sincere belief that "here in the United States the White Christian is targeted for extinction," and that soon, there will be a Battle of the Titans between the heathen gods of the Inner Earth and the One True God and His Son Jesus Christ. In her renewal notice to subscribers, she writes, "... Christians knowing and spreading the truth of all this will largely survive. The Elect — the Israel of the surface — will go into Earth to join Jacob where together the two forces will take up the fight in a world that, until now, has been unknown to surface dwellers. ..."

Mrs. Cox's powerful vision probes not only into the hidden world beneath the surface, but also deep into the reaches of time, before there were problems, before there were Jews, and before the extraterrestrials — "The Watchers" — came to earth:

> The Watchers came to this planet during the age that preceded the one that saw the world ruled from the island that stood as a flawless green gem in the midst of the Atlantic ocean. ...
>
> ... Then and now, at the root of [all afflictions] have been the Watchers, their incredible inventions, their corruptive influence, and the wars they concoct.
>
> Two hundred in number, the Watchers were just that: Watchers. Before they made the decision to give up their positions as workers in the Cosmic scheme for orderly progress, their ships would hang in the high heaven, and from that wondrous vantage point, they would search the different worlds for signs of development, or the deterioration of development . . . Planets with intelligent, advanced beings, or beings simple and savage; planets with lakes and streams and trees on the sides of mountains, or cratered worlds, rocky and bald, and as dry as an old bone. But always the orbs had openings at either end, gateways to a great lighted void in their centers.

Though there were countless beautiful planets, earth was something special:

> Of all the worlds watched by the watchers, none caught their fancy as did Earth. ... And nothing caught their attention as did the daughters of the men of planet Earth. ... Finally, when

> their lust could no longer be contained, they made the decision that would so alter Earth's destiny that never again would she return to the ways of earlier ages: they would make Earth their home and the base for their operations. And they would mate with the comely women of the planet, and they would raise children- demi-gods-by them. ...
>
> ... Flagrantly, even defiantly, they were breaking a cardinal law of their Maker: that of mating with a mortal. . . And an angered Creator was not long in imposing a sentence: Banishment to the inner-earth where forever thereafter they would be bound! ...
>
> The offspring of the Two Hundred and the daughters of men were giants. So huge were they that men indigenous to Earth appeared as animated toys. Every thought of the giants was absorbed in wickedness. And their appetites were voracious and insatiable. Consuming all that mortal men had provided for themselves, they took to eating mortal man! This continued until the Lord God decided it had gone far enough. Then He set one giant against another. And the giants killed one another off until only a few remained. ...

According to Mrs. Cox, this struggle between the Watchers and the Creator — The One True God — is what the Old Testament is all about. Cox also adheres to one version of the Anglo-Israelite story: that the biblical Israelites — God's Chosen People — are not the Jews, but are, in fact the Aryans,[1] and that the Jews are really the biblical Canaanites, in disguise.

But Cox doesn't stop there; not content to explain the Old Testament, or even the New Testament, she must also explain all of ancient and modern history in light of her hidden "knowledge." Unfortunately, in her enthusiasm to explode every prevailing myth of our time, Mrs. Cox unwittingly explodes her own, as well. Since new evils and deceits are introduced with every passage, sorting out the "good guys" from the "bad guys" is a hopeless task. Norma Cox has something bad to say about *everyone.*

There is a special place in Norma Cox's heart reserved for Jewry, however; they incur many times more wrath than any of the other groups she writes about. Exposing the "fact" that the Pharisees and Sadducees of biblical times still exist — they are the Communists and Zionists of today — Mrs. Cox derives much satisfaction from her observation that there is an eternal struggle between these two despicable factions of World Jewry. As polarized as they seem, it is each faction's dearest wish to do one thing — eradicate the Aryan Race:

> ... The left side of the battling conspirators is trying, and with complete success, to drive America into the position of a base, third-rate nation, while the right side strives equally hard to maintain the status quo, a losing battle for the simple reason of the accord of the adversaries in the matter of eliminating the Aryan, a situation that has existed since the time Cain killed Abel.
>
> ... Why would Jews — a tiny minority people — feel such abiding rancor for the people who made it possible for them to obtain the wealth that has enabled Communism and Zionism (Capitalism) to rule the world — albeit behind a curtain? The answer is the fact that the Aryan is the genius, the inventors of all of the tools representing progress; the fact that, except for the Jew's inherent cunning, and his unexcelled cleverness in manipulating money, the Aryan is his superior in every way, and the fact that the Gentile-Aryan is the chosen of the Creator, and not the Jew.

Though the Aryans are the Chosen People, they once worshipped pagan deities like everyone else, and, in fact, Zeus, "The King of the North," is their ancestor, while Satan is the ancestor of the Jews.

Though spawned by Satan, the Jews worship the Sun God Apollo, Zeus' son, who is, according to Cox, in constant battle with Zeus. This eternal conflict between the father and son, Zeus and Apollo, is Norma Cox's key to world conflict, past, present and future. Be it Communism vs. Capitalism, Nazi-Aryans vs. Jews, or Republicans vs. Democrats, every struggle on Earth can be reduced to a struggle between Zeus and Apollo. In trying to sort out all of Norma Cox's various battle lines, however, the careful reader might become lost in a hopeless mire. Norma Cox forgets that some Republicans are Zionists, making them both Apollo and Zeus worshippers; even worse, Communists and Nazis share the same deity, Zeus.

> ... We have been made to believe that communists are atheists steeped in the belief that

1. Cox uses the term "Aryan"; the Anglo-Israelites usually use the term "Anglo-Saxon."

For Norma Cox, the pagan symbols concocted by our founding fathers have duped an entire nation into worshipping aliens.

there is no order of being higher than Man (Humanism); that Man is himself a god. All of which is a lie patently betrayed by the Soviet Flag on which is displayed the Sickle, indicating a final reaping of mankind, and the Hammer of Thor, the Skygod. Also known as Zeus, Thor, the actual god of communists, is the biblical King of the North, the Gog who will come from out of the center of Earth with his armies during the final years to do battle on Earth's surface. ...

The strange bedfellows wrought by Cox's paganalysis of world history doesn't bother her at all; in fact, the inconsistencies actually open up new vistas of deceit and intrigue. We discover the Catholic Church is really a front for Apollo; the inevitable conclusion is that the Jews and the Vatican both are in on the plot to destroy the Aryan Christians.

Wearing the mask of the Savior, Jesus Christ, the god of Vatican hierarchy is the sungod, Apollo, the Lucifer of Scripture; this, while the moongoddess, the evil Ashtoreth, the whore of Revelation 17, is paraded as Mary, the mother of Christ. This fraud, perpetrated on Catholics since the time the church took root, has gone so undetected that CBS, the TV network working the communist side of the conspiracy, boldly displays Sungod symbols on the "Sunday Morning with Charles Kuralt" show. Unknowing, Christians attending Sunday church service are paying homage not to their Creator and His Son but to the pagan superman whose Sun Chariot daily rides the heaven from east to west. ...

For Norma Cox, the pagan symbols that adorn our world are sinister reminders of the identity of our real masters; most sinister of all are those symbols concocted by our founding fathers to dupe an entire nation into worshipping aliens.

... Immersed in the kind of paganism that prevailed in Egypt in ancient times, the so-called "founding fathers" believed it was the wish of the gods that a revolution be fomented, one that would become the wedge in creating a new Order, an Order that one day would be established all over the world. ...

Masters of subterfuge, these intriguers who lit the fire and fanned the flames of Revolution had mastered the degrees leading to the top rung of Masonry's ladder. Enemies of the God of Abraham, and the Christianity that followed in the wake of the murder of the Son of God, the monument sacred to the architects of a deceiving Constitution was the great pyramid of Giza, the one which, amidst the rest of the pagan-god symbols, is pictured on the Great Seal of the United States and the dollar bill.

... One of [the Cheops Pyramid's] multifaceted purposes is to conceal what lies beneath. In the Mideast, the entrances leading to the wondrous cities of the ancients are concealed in the sides of mountains and hills. In the case of the Pyramid, the door leading to the concealed habitations patterned after the likes of Osiris and Isis is hidden somewhere in its mind-blowing maze of twisting corridors. . . . There is no doubt about it, enthralled by it all, what the master masons had in mind for America, and eventually all the rest of the planet, was an Egypt like the one of the heathen Pharaohs.

In contact with extraterrestrials, George Washington set the pace for all future presidents:

Enormously ambitious, the "father of our country" was aggressive and without scruples. Giving not a damn for education and the finer side of life, George Washington was a money-grabbing, glory-grabbing charlatan with a bent for deceit and the devious. With the ability to inspire trust and zeal, he was the perfect tool for Masonry. Therefore, he was made privy to the deepest held secrets of that diabolical organization, and allowed to fulfill his insatiable need for power, wealth, and attention. ... What a job lying historians have done on this fakir over the last 200 years!!!

And George was an occultist who got a tremendous bang out of fooling around with the "supernatural." Of the highest masonic degree, the "father of our country" was in full masonic regalia when he deposited secret objects at the cornerstone laying of the White House. With awe his subjects hailed this expert in the art of witchcraft as the "Worshipful Master." Talking with "angels," this pagan had visions, and by the "angels" and "visions" mapped a course for the newly formed nation — 13 states with 13 masonic governors — to follow. Since that time, every man succeeding to the presidency of the United States — whether a mason or a favored member of some other demonic order — has held firmly to the treasonous outline plotted by the sorcerer we have been taught to honor and admire. ...

Years later, the ignorant American citizens were given the Statue of Liberty, which is not only a symbol of the pagan goddess Diana, but also a radio antenna:

With great spikes (ANTENNA) crowning her head and sitting upon a star-shaped base in the midst of flowing water (water, essential for the purpose), this huge COPPER statue (copper, a #1 conductor of electricity) serves a dual purpose:

One, under the cover of a symbol of Liberty, it mesmerizes the citizens into adoring a goddess they know nothing about. Two, with this cover concealing a still more important function, the statue serves as a tower, one that reaching into Heaven, transmits and receives messages to and from the Moon!

The Washington Monument, as we may well imagine, is not what it seems. Cox quotes one Ray Stoner for hidden knowledge about the towering obelisk:

Constructed in the old tradition, the Washington Monument, in our nation's capital, is the tallest antenna on the planet, and a gravitational astronomy observatory. Built between 1848 and 1884, the monument is 555 ft. 5-1/8 inches tall. Casting its shadow and reflection upon the reflecting pool, which also serves as a seismograph, it attracts pilgrims from the planet's four corners.

Constructed from 32 blocks of marble and 24 blocks of granite, to the course, it brings a unique frequency to our capital since our 55 mph speed limit was instituted. ...

Bombarded by the symbols of her enemies every single day, Norma Cox must contend with the knowledge of a deceitful government, evil alien forces, pagans parading as Christians, and the ignorant masses brainwashed by Hollywood. Living in a hostile environment within a nation run by conspirators bent on exterminating her people, Cox puts her faith in only one man — Adolf Hitler. Convinced that Hitler is still alive, preparing his forces for the Final War against the extraterrestrials and their dupes, Cox lives in expectation of the redemption of her race.

At the time when a "number in the hand" will be necessary for all who buy and sell, Jacob of the nether world and the elect of Israel of the surface will join hands to fight the enemies of their God and of their white race.

The leader of these combined forces will be Cyrus — not, of course, the physical person of the great white warrior who defeated Babylon in war and established the great white nation of Persia, but the spirit of that remarkable man who achieved the impossible simply because he was found worthy in the eyes of the God of Abraham. ...

Even to his not knowing the Lord God, I can think of no man fitting the character of Cyrus as well as Adolf Hitler. Hitler was not an evil man, except in the eyes of those persons who have had their thinking so twisted that they have come to regard the separation of the races as evil.

Hitler fought to cleanse the planet of the filth that was destroying it. Knowing the plot was to exterminate the white race, he fought to prevent that from happening; further, he sought to put the Aryan in a position whereby he would dominate their enemies.

We are not allowed to forget Hitler and wartime Germany. Nightly, we are presented with an ever on-going television tirade against the man and the country he loved. It all happened so long ago that one may well wonder why it doesn't cease. There can be only one answer: FEAR, the fear that a fourth reich will come from beneath the ice of Neu-Sachwabenland — to square accounts may be well-founded . . . There are many who believe Hitler did not die a suicide; there are many who believe he escaped to a warm place made ready for him beneath the ice of the Antarctic.

Living in a nation run by conspirators bent on exterminating her people, Cox puts her faith in only one man — Adolf Hitler.

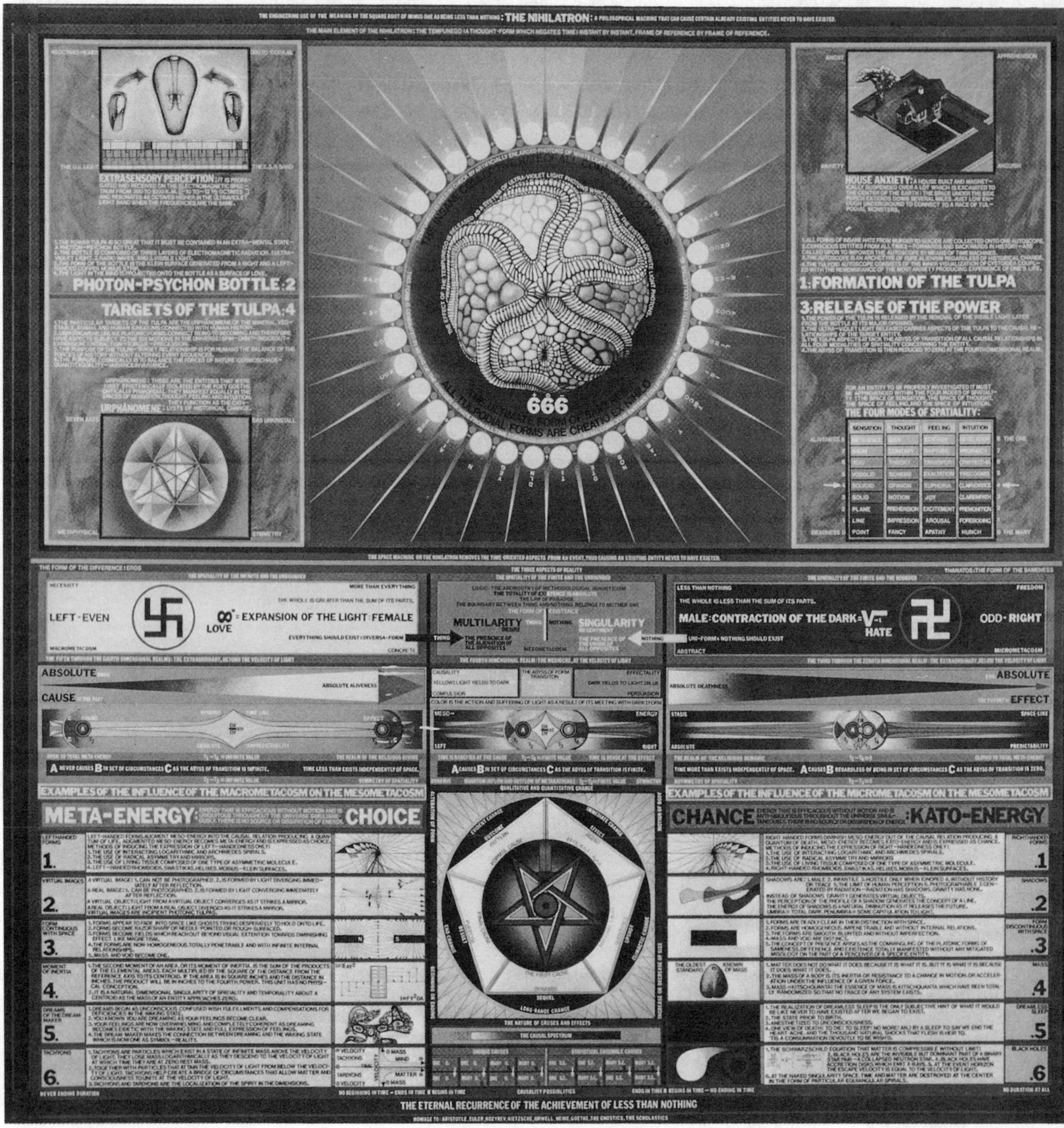

Paul Laffoley, "The Nihilatron."

PART VI

ENIGMAS

Paul Laffoley in his Boston studio. Photo by Joanna Soltan

PAUL LAFFOLEY
THIRD GENERATION LUNATIC FRINGE

Paul Laffoley, an artist and registered architect in the state of Massachusetts, has been building a time machine. Laffoley, who's attracted to the idea of such a device because it lacks limitations, seemingly has no limitations himself. His discussions encompass fields ancient and modern, revealing a deep comprehension of classical philosophy, art history, world history, religion, metaphysics and parapsychology, as well as a working knowledge of modern science and technology. He is a kind of "renaissance man," an alchemist, who uses the full spectrum of his knowledge to achieve transcendence.

My own studies don't even approach the depth or breadth of Laffoley's, so it is impossible for me to fully comprehend or evaluate all of his ideas. The segments I can comprehend not only make perfect sense, but facilitate moments of transcendence in my own mind; while talking to him, I feel like I'm communicating with a member of an advanced civilization. It may well be that his ideas are bunk, and that I've been hypnotized by the endless flow of words, which combine hundreds of fantastic notions with fascinating anecdotes from Laffoley's past. But if Laffoley is a crackpot, he is one of the most brilliant.

Laffoley's time machine is a design whose realization is "ongoing." He is applying for a grant to build an essential part, the "Levogyre," and is optimistic that its time has come; Laffoley expects that there will be a fully working time machine somewhere on earth by the year 2013.

Laffoley's idea was inspired by the device found in H.G. Wells' novel, *The Time Machine,* but there the resemblance ends. Laffoley's time machine is not a mechanical contraption with lots of knobs and dials, but "a 'mind-physics,' or psychotronic[1] device capable of producing a controlled dislocation of human consciousness in space-time. Its essence is the control and amplification of preperception of the future and retroperception of the past to such a degree that obvious space-time dilations will occur." There will be *some* knobs and dials, however.

Laffoley is a kind of alchemist, utilizing the full spectrum of his knowledge to achieve transcendence.

Laffoley has not yet built this device, nor does he say it can be built — now. He is optimistic, however, that it will be possible in the next 20 or so years to do so. The time machine has become Laffoley's all-consuming passion. Well aware of its "crackpot" status, Laffoley observes that "... the attempt to build a time machine, or even to propose the possibility of such a device coming into existence, by any individual has been cause to label that individual as one holding, or laden with embarrassing, atavistic and superstitious beliefs about the nature of reality." He adds, "This has been the general case even to the present."

When Laffoley first read Wells' story, like everyone else, he thought a time machine was an obvious impossibility. He was interested, at first as only an "interesting visual or mental construct" or "an impossible device like a perpetual motion machine," because of its lack of natural limitations. But his attitude changed when he learned of the "emerging new fields of biofeedback and psychotronic research by means of 'New Age' newspapers and other alternative media" during the late 60s.

But the evolution of Laffoley's time machine really began much earlier, when he was exposed to something akin to psychotronics — "mind physics" — by way of his father, a dabbler in the occult and spiritualism. Laffoley's father had friends who were "pioneers in the field of psychic research," including Leonard T. Troland, a professor of optics at Harvard, who had "set about to construct a complete mathematical description of 'mind physics.'"

With a parapsychologist in the family, an Ivy League education in classics, training in

1. The U.S. Psychotronics Association defines psychotronics as "the science of mind-body-environment relationships. ... [A]n interdisciplinary science attempting to integrate the phenomena of consciousness, parapsychology, and advanced physics into a coherent system and world view with practical application to the betterment of health, the improvement of the environment, and realization of human potential..."

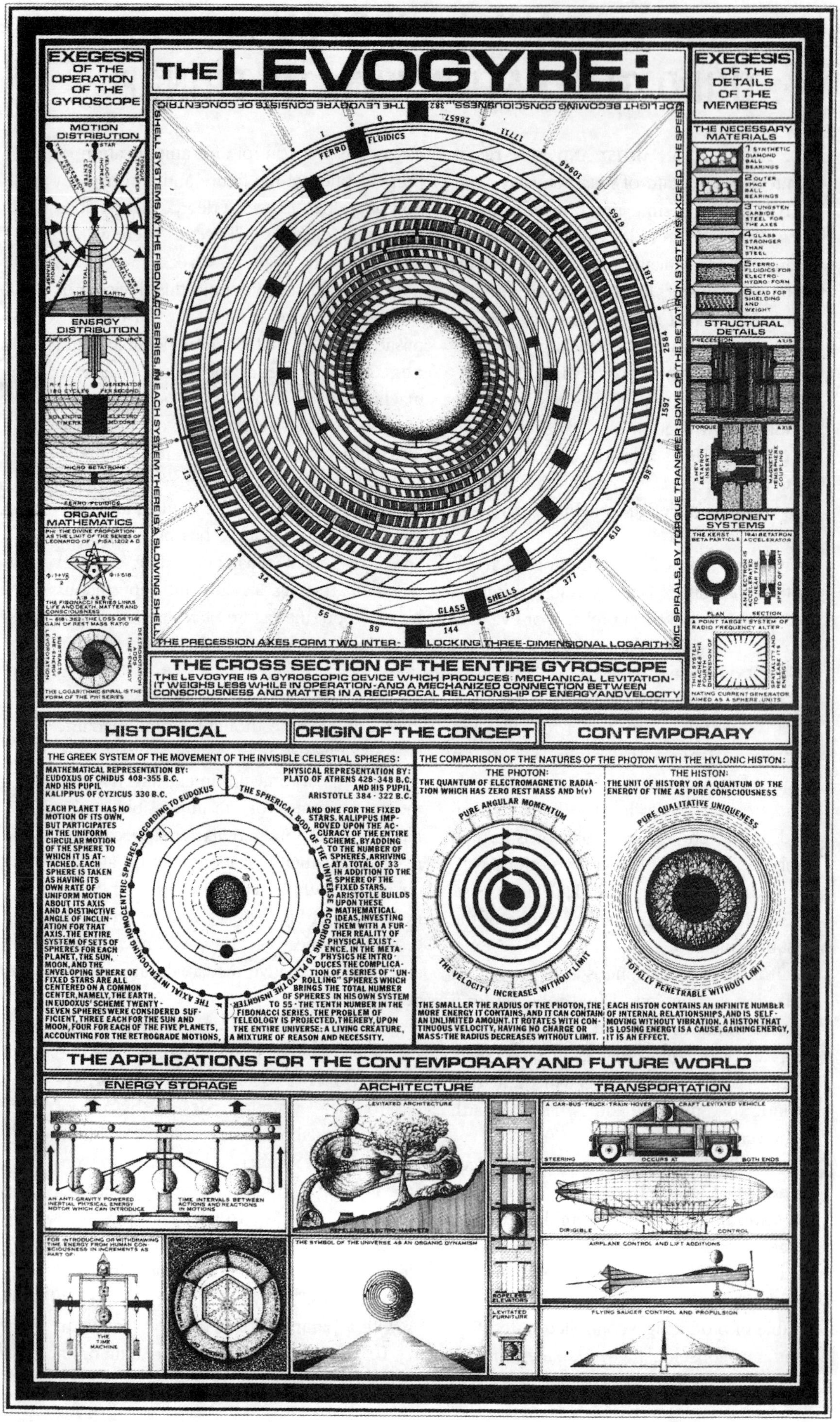

EXEGESIS OF THE OPERATION OF THE GYROSCOPE
THE LEVOGYRE:
EXEGESIS OF THE DETAILS OF THE MEMBERS
MOTION DISTRIBUTION
ENERGY DISTRIBUTION
MICRO BETATRONS
FERRO-FLUIDICS
ORGANIC MATHEMATICS
THE LOGARITHMIC SPIRAL IS THE FORM OF THE PHI SERIES
THE LEVOGYRE CONSISTS OF CONCENTRIC SHELL SYSTEMS IN THE FIBONACCI SERIES, IN EACH SYSTEM THERE IS A SLOWING SHELL
THE PRECESSION AXES FORM TWO INTER-LOCKING THREE-DIMENSIONAL LOGARITHMIC SPIRALS, BY TORQUE TRANSFER SOME OF THE BETATRON SYSTEMS EXCEED THE SPEED OF LIGHT BECOMING CONSCIOUSNESS
FERRO FLUIDICS
GLASS SHELLS
THE NECESSARY MATERIALS
1 SYNTHETIC DIAMOND BALL BEARINGS
2 OUTER SPACE BALL BEARINGS
3 TUNGSTEN CARBIDE STEEL FOR THE AXES
4 GLASS STRONGER THAN STEEL
5 FERRO-FLUIDICS FOR ELECTRO-HYDRO-FORM
6 LEAD FOR SHIELDING AND WEIGHT
STRUCTURAL DETAILS
PRECESSION AXIS
TORQUE AXIS
COMPONENT SYSTEMS
THE KERST BETA PARTICLE
1941 BETATRON ACCELERATOR
PLAN
SECTION
THE CROSS SECTION OF THE ENTIRE GYROSCOPE
THE LEVOGYRE IS A GYROSCOPIC DEVICE WHICH PRODUCES: MECHANICAL LEVITATION-IT WEIGHS LESS WHILE IN OPERATION-AND A MECHANIZED CONNECTION BETWEEN CONSCIOUSNESS AND MATTER IN A RECIPROCAL RELATIONSHIP OF ENERGY AND VELOCITY
HISTORICAL
ORIGIN OF THE CONCEPT
CONTEMPORARY
THE GREEK SYSTEM OF THE MOVEMENT OF THE INVISIBLE CELESTIAL SPHERES:
MATHEMATICAL REPRESENTATION BY: EUDOXUS OF CNIDUS 408-355 B.C. AND HIS PUPIL KALIPPUS OF CYZICUS 330 B.C.
EACH PLANET HAS NO MOTION OF ITS OWN, BUT PARTICIPATES IN THE UNIFORM CIRCULAR MOTION OF THE SPHERE TO WHICH IT IS ATTACHED. EACH SPHERE IS TAKEN AS HAVING ITS OWN RATE OF UNIFORM MOTION ABOUT ITS AXIS AND A DISTINCTIVE ANGLE OF INCLINATION FOR THAT AXIS. THE ENTIRE SYSTEM OF SETS OF SPHERES FOR EACH PLANET, THE SUN, MOON, AND THE ENVELOPING SPHERE OF FIXED STARS ARE ALL CENTERED ON A COMMON CENTER, NAMELY, THE EARTH. IN EUDOXUS' SCHEME TWENTY-SEVEN SPHERES WERE CONSIDERED SUFFICIENT, THREE EACH FOR THE SUN AND MOON, FOUR FOR EACH OF THE FIVE PLANETS, ACCOUNTING FOR THE RETROGRADE MOTIONS,
THE AXIAL INTERLOCKING HOMOCENTRIC SPHERES ACCORDING TO EUDOXUS
THE SPHERICAL BODY OF THE UNIVERSE ACCORDING TO PLATO THE INSIGHTER
PHYSICAL REPRESENTATION BY: PLATO OF ATHENS 428-348 B.C. AND HIS PUPIL ARISTOTLE 384-322 B.C.
AND ONE FOR THE FIXED STARS. KALIPPUS IMPROVED UPON THE ACCURACY OF THE ENTIRE SCHEME, BY ADDING TO THE NUMBER OF SPHERES, ARRIVING AT A TOTAL OF 33 IN ADDITION TO THE SPHERE OF THE FIXED STARS. ARISTOTLE BUILDS UPON THESE MATHEMATICAL IDEAS, INVESTING THEM WITH A FURTHER REALITY OF PHYSICAL EXISTENCE. IN THE METAPHYSICS HE INTRODUCES THE COMPLICATION OF A SERIES OF "UNROLLING" SPHERES WHICH BRINGS THE TOTAL NUMBER OF SPHERES IN HIS OWN SYSTEM TO 55 - THE TENTH NUMBER IN THE FIBONACCI SERIES. THE PROBLEM OF TELEOLOGY IS PROJECTED, THEREBY, UPON THE ENTIRE UNIVERSE: A LIVING CREATURE, A MIXTURE OF REASON AND NECESSITY.
THE COMPARISON OF THE NATURES OF THE PHOTON WITH THE HYLONIC HISTON:
THE PHOTON:
THE QUANTUM OF ELECTROMAGNETIC RADIATION WHICH HAS ZERO REST MASS AND h(v)
PURE ANGULAR MOMENTUM
THE VELOCITY INCREASES WITHOUT LIMIT
THE SMALLER THE RADIUS OF THE PHOTON, THE MORE ENERGY IT CONTAINS, AND IT CAN CONTAIN AN UNLIMITED AMOUNT. IT ROTATES WITH CONTINUOUS VELOCITY, HAVING NO CHARGE OR MASS: THE RADIUS DECREASES WITHOUT LIMIT.
THE HISTON:
THE UNIT OF HISTORY OR A QUANTUM OF THE ENERGY OF TIME AS PURE CONSCIOUSNESS
PURE QUALITATIVE UNIQUENESS
TOTALLY PENETRABLE WITHOUT LIMIT
EACH HISTON CONTAINS AN INFINITE NUMBER OF INTERNAL RELATIONSHIPS, AND IS SELF-MOVING WITHOUT VIBRATION. A HISTON THAT IS LOSING ENERGY IS A CAUSE, GAINING ENERGY, IT IS AN EFFECT.
THE APPLICATIONS FOR THE CONTEMPORARY AND FUTURE WORLD
ENERGY STORAGE
ARCHITECTURE
TRANSPORTATION
LEVITATED ARCHITECTURE
A CAR-BUS-TRUCK-TRAIN-HOVER CRAFT LEVITATED VEHICLE
STEERING
OCCURS AT
BOTH ENDS
DIRIGIBLE
CONTROL
AIRPLANE CONTROL AND LIFT ADDITIONS
FLYING SAUCER CONTROL AND PROPULSION
THE SYMBOL OF THE UNIVERSE AS AN ORGANIC DYNAMISM
LEVITATED FURNITURE
THE TIME MACHINE

design, and exposure to the mind explosion of the 60s, Laffoley began to play with the idea of time travel as a psychotronic, rather than a purely physical, event:

About 1967 I thought that the idea of time travel might be identified with the psychic phenomena of pre- and retro-cognition (preperception of the future and retroperception of the past). But, to qualify as an isomorphic interpretation of the effects of time travel, I felt that these phenomena would have to be engineered to some extreme form of controlled amplification. In their natural state the dreams, hallucination-like visions and strong hunches that overlay the present-time experiences of anyone enduring episodes of precognition or retrocognition about specific events, seemed to me (I have had a few of these experiences) too weak to qualify as a complete translation of the sense of radical displacement of one's natural present — in the manner described by Wells. *But,* they did have one advantage: being facts of nature, pre- and retrocognition could not be accused of violating the definition of time, as Wells' definition of time travel was.

At this same time I began to research the concept of dimensionality from the point of view of quality, and not just quantity, as a mathematician might do. Taking my clues from the theosophical use made of the Vedantic levels of reality, I identified the western notion of energy (as something which is efficacious by means of motion), with the idea of time. The more comprehensive dimension 'eternity' I defined as a form of energy that is efficacious without motion. In this manner, I began to establish qualities of dimensions and open out *the seemingly monolithic concept of energy. [Elements of the Time Machine: Homage to H.G. Wells.]*

The heart of Laffoley's time machine is the "Levogyre," a kind of super-gyroscope. He claims it is the most stable possible object on earth and will weigh less while in operation than when at rest. "The dynamics of the geometry of its design," he writes, "amplifies the natural reduction in mass any gyroscope endures while in operation — only the reduction in mass is not normally detectable."

The Levogyre, roughly speaking, is a system to produce a "singularity," or "still-point," i.e. "a point-instant at which space-time is infinitely distorted by gravitational forces." The black hole predicted by General Relativity is an example of a singularity of mass; other natural examples are "the still-point at the center of a spinning wheel, the twin still points of a pendulum system [and] the still instant between the cause and effect of an event sequence." Laffoley observes that "consciousness, as well as mass, could be subject to singularities"; examples would be chakras, acupuncture points, revelation and psychic phenomena.

As the Levogyre loses mass, Laffoley claims it gains consciousness, providing a way to induce control of pre- and retrocognition.

Since he is seeking to control its effects, particularly time distortion, Laffoley is more interested in a "structured" than a "natural" singularity: "While black holes, wormholes and chakras were 'natural' singularities and in a sense 'dimensional portals,' it was the photon (a 'structured' singularity) with its infinite internal spin and an external travelling velocity that became the actual model of my 'Levogyre.'" Laffoley claims that, as the Levogyre loses mass, it gains consciousness, providing a way to induce control and amplification of pre- and retrocognition.

The construction and operation of the Levogyre is explained as follows:

The Levogyre is an attempt to model a photo creating light, and in turn, an atom of consciousness. The structure of the Levogyre derives from the structure of the Universe proposed by Eudoxus (the astronomer pupil of Plato.) Eudoxus stated that the Universe is a series of nested crystalline spheres which contained the stars as fixed, the planets which moved, down to the central non-rotating Earth. Each sphere is connected to the next by gimbal-like axes which are randomly distributed.

In the Levogyre, a series of nested shells are connected by gimbals, but the axes now form two interlocking, three-dimensional spirals. The shells are constructed in the Fibonacci Series, a golden proportion or phi relation.[2] Because of the golden proportion relationship of the axes, a torque transfer of angular momentum is made toward the centroid of the Levogyre, building up energy as in a photon.

The Torque Wheel of the Levogyre is really a series of nested rings which unite the hemispheres of the shells. By means of fiber optics, laser beams of coherent light can be propagated in contained circular orbits. This means that as the Levogyre is in operation, the speed of light is constantly in the process of being transcended, which results in a loss of mass by the device, and thereby a proportionate loss of weight. The

2. The Fibonacci Sequence is 1,1,2,3,5,8,13,...; each new term is formed by adding the previous two. As the terms of the Fibonacci Sequence grow larger, the ratio between a term and its successor approaches Phi, a.k.a. the Golden Proportion of .618.... The Golden Proportion abounds in nature, and was much used in classical times.

weight loss will never reach zero, but will approach .382... percent of its total weight at rest. This proportion is the other side of .618... of unit or the golden proportion.[3]

In operation, the Levogyre becomes an atom of consciousness — a photonic system — or like a black-white hole drawing kato-energy into the unmanifest aspect of the Universe, or releasing meta-energy into the manifest aspect of the Universe.

"He didn't believe in gravity the way other men don't believe in Santa Claus."

Long after Laffoley had conceived of the Levogyre, a friend handed him a copy of Hugo Gernsback's 1911 science fiction story, "Ralph 124C414." Along with predictions of "most of the major technological inventions of the 20th century, such as radar," the story *contained a description of the Levogyre,* built by a person in the story named "969L9." Laffoley's reaction to reading the relevant passage "was the wish to have [his] name changed to '969L9.'"

While the Levogyre is probably its most important component, the time machine itself is a "sculpture" occupying a five foot cube. In addition to the Levogyre, it also contains, "several sets of converging electromagnets aimed to the center of the evacuated cube," "the five Pythagorean convex solids,...composed of piezoelectric crystals that are electrically fired and connected to the suspension wire of the pendulum," and other components as well.

Laffoley's time machine is an important contribution to solving the problem of time travel, whether or not it is ever built, for even the act of contemplating its blueprint has a psychotronic effect on the open mind. It may well be that the major concepts of physics — time, mass, energy and gravity — originate, and can be dissolved in our minds via "mental physics" and "psychotronics."

Third Generation Lunatic Fringe

The natural barriers of time, energy and mass were no longer barriers when Laffoley began to see them in terms of parapsychology; hence the concept of time travel was no longer absurd. Paul Laffoley was now firmly entrenched in his role as what he calls "third-generation lunatic fringe," for his father did not believe in gravity (another natural limitation), and his grandfather had been a religious free-thinker who gave lectures — along the lines of "the great agnostic" Robert Ingersoll — at the Ford Hall Forum, in Boston. It was through his father that Laffoley became intimately acquainted with the rejection of notions that others take for granted:

> ... He didn't believe in gravity the way other men don't believe in Santa Claus: it's nice folklore that's not harmful unless you take it too seriously. Growing up, I didn't know you were supposed to believe in gravity. It was subject that just never came up in conversation with my friends. ... [*The Phenomenology of Revelation.*]

Young Paul's upbringing, as a result, was sometimes bizarre, even though his father was a prosperous banker. Rather than take his son fishing or to a ball game, Laffoley's father took him to see exhibits of antigravity and perpetual-motion devices at Babson's Gravity Research Institute in New Boston, New Hampshire. Despite the heavy indoctrination, Paul couldn't help but come into conflict with his Dad:

> ... all the time he would constantly come back to that, that he could see elements, that I was being duped by the system, because I showed evidences in certain ways, of believing in gravity. [Gravity, for him, represented "The System"], because it's what held you down. Symbolically, I think it's a good idea. Why do people want to levitate? Because that's the thing that is the most materialistic, in the sense, symbolically, is the concept of gravity. "Billiard ball determinism" is based on the idea of balls operating on the gravitational force.
>
> ... And so, whenever we'd have the classic father and son arguments, no matter what the subject was that we began with, he would always [end] by saying that I had sold out to the system by believing in gravity.

The extent of the older Laffoley's stubborn rejection of gravity is best illustrated by an anecdote Paul wrote about in his book, *The Phenomenology of Revelation.* When he was a child, his father had taken him, by train, to New York, for the very first time. Like his stand on gravity, his father's relation to the grand metropolis was transcendent; this little trip was more than just a diversion; it was a dispensation of truth, from father to son. After visits to Times Square and Radio City

3. .382... is Phi squared.

Music Hall, and an encounter with "Mr. Peanut" which caused some friction between the two, Paul and his father found themselves at the window of a joke shop on 42nd Street:

Right up close to the window, smack between a generous supply of imported French blue garlic chewing gum labeled *nonpareille* on the right and authentic Cape Cod salt-water taffy made with real salt on the left, was a large rectangular box, painted jet black, about a foot wide by two feet long by eight inches thick... Slightly above the middle zone of the box was a circular opening that seemed to me to be about six inches in diameter, inside of which a small white sphere, poised with no visible means of support, spun on its axis in a blood-red void lit from inside. The elegant lettering on a large plate of simulated brass identified the device as "The Anti-Gravitron." A small white card in front of it read, "Amaze everyone as you instantly defy gravity with the flick of a switch" and, in small letters at the very bottom, "Ping-pong ball and electric fan not included."

My father was ebullient again, explaining to me how the designer of the "toy" had inadvertently hit upon the secret of the organization of the physical universe. The air jets that held the ping-pong ball in position represented the materials that each heavenly body throws off as it spins on its axis. All bodies in space, therefore, form an equilibrium in space, creating the various orbital distances and motion we observe. When I would ask him why then isn't the largest planet in the solar system closest to the sun and all the other planets lined up in descending size, or what is out at the periphery of space that holds all the forces in, he would simply state that these were wrong kinds of questions, indicative of a mind not yet free of the concept of gravity. ...

Flying Saucers I

Except for his view on gravity, Laffoley's father was thoroughly conventional; like most people at the time, he was skeptical about flying saucers. (Apparently he hadn't made a connection between flying saucers and anti-gravity.) So when the itinerant gardener who trimmed the Laffoleys' bushes each year claimed to have been taken aboard a flying saucer with his son, everyone, including Paul's father, assumed he was some kind of nut. In the meantime, the contactee had been giving Paul some of the popular saucer books of that period, including Adamski's books and *Secret of the Saucers* by Orfeo Angelucci. Paul was fascinated, his interest partially fueled by the fact that the rest of the neighborhood thought the gardener was crazy.

I remember later, I saw *The Day the Earth Stood Still,* as a kid, when it came out, and it was like, it was almost nostalgia at that point, to me. It was like somebody was telling me stuff I already knew, but other people kept saying, well why do you know this? You can't possibly know this. This was not a thing that happened to people in the suburbs, or at least in that part of the world. And it was all because of the prompting of this guy who himself claimed to be a contactee with his son. He'd been taken up, so he was telling me all the stuff. In other words, he was giving me chapter and verse of how it all operated, being taken on board, and punctured.... My parents [were] saying, "Hey the guy's nuts, get out of here, don't pay any attention to him," and then one year he just never comes back.

Paul's contact with the contactee was only the first in a series of revelations concerning saucers and UFOs. As his fascination continued into adulthood, he began to investigate the architectural basis for the flying saucer shape:

And then, when I'm at Harvard Graduate School of Design, I find out that Frank Lloyd Wright had actually designed the flying saucer [in *The Day the Earth Stood Still]*. And you can see that in the movie, where the interior consists of a lot of ribs of glass tubing... that was used a couple of years earlier in the design for the Johnson Wax home office in Racine, Wisconsin. So that the imagery of it was simply taken and used as the interior part, and then of course the shape of it is like... the curve of normal distribution. Which I analyzed to figure out that... the tip of that relates to the power point in the Great Pyramid. ... It's like a new classical form. Because all classical forms are involved with the Divine Proportion. ...

Then, right after Harvard I go to New York, and I meet ... Frederick Kiesler. ... I was working with Kiesler, who had designed the Book of the Shrine for the Dead Sea Scrolls Museum, which is outside the West Wall in Jerusalem, and the shape of it was like a flying saucer. I said, "Wow, you're doing this form, this is a flying saucer that's hovering." He said, "No no, this is an Amphoreus Jug," you know, where it's sticking in the ground. Because he somehow had to hang

"I find out that Frank Lloyd Wright had actually designed the flying saucer [in *The Day the Earth Stood Still]*."

> "The sculpture seemed to have an infinite number of sense organs, each as distinct from the other as the eye is from the ear."

on to the European Classical academic stuff, when he wasn't anywhere near that. He had taught at the Bauhaus, and then had left for America about the same time as Marcel Duchamp, and was essentially part of the permanent avant-garde in New York ever since. He really got upset when I defined the shape, that he was really working with, the flying saucer shape from *The Day the Earth Stood Still.* He didn't want to admit that he could be influenced by anything. ...

Shock Treatment & The Lucid Dream

Before meeting Kiesler, Laffoley had entered "a mild state of catatonia" and was "basically immobilized for a couple of years," during which he received eight electro-shock treatments. When I spoke to Laffoley about this episode, he was very cheerful and didn't seem to regret the treatments:

... It sounds almost like a torture chamber number, but I didn't really mind them. Because I was anaesthetized, it's just that I got so many; I got eight within a two-month period. ...Well, my father said he can't afford any more, because they were so expensive...

He claims that before he received the treatments, he usually dreamed in black and white, occasionally in color. After the treatments, he began to dream exclusively in color, but more importantly, began to experience what has recently been defined as "lucid dreaming," i.e., he began to feel he could actively participate in the scenarios of his dreams. One such experience, described in *Phenomenology of Revelation,* involved an intensely disturbing and vivid nightmare, in which Laffoley entered a gallery that exhibited living sculpture:

The sculpture seemed to have an infinite number of sense organs, each as distinct from the other as the eye is from the ear. Suddenly a strange feeling came over me that I had never experienced before. I felt that I had become the knowledge and the sculpture the knower; I was being subsumed, not physically but epistemically. ... My modality of consciousness seemed mechanical in comparison with that of the sculpture's. Finally I realized the full import of what was happening. I had first been enraged at not being able to communicate with anybody around me. Then I was inflamed with jealousy when I recognized authentically new art. At this last point, alone with the sculpture, I was overcome with terror. I was fully awake: I knew I was trapped in the gallery and would surely die if I did not get out of this dream and out of the presence of these "sculptures." ...

... For several weeks afterward I tried to sleep as little as possible to avoid a recurrence of the dream. After about a month I was able to sleep normally again, and with this came a period of assessment. My first realization was that the dream had originated in my subconscious and that its content was mine, regardless of how collective or universal the concept of the subconscious might be interpreted to be. At least I had been shown something that I could use or from which I could learn.

... I believe the dream was as close as I have come to a fully developed revelation or mystical experience as it is classically defined. ...

... I believe that I left our physical universe, the fourth dimensional realm of Time-Solvoid, which is life, and entered the fifth dimensional realm of Eternity-Vosolid, which is death. I thought I would not be able to return to life if I let myself go more deeply into the dream.

That my art began then to develop into what it is today was one of the dream's positive effects. As I tried to remember the dream, ideas for paintings would come to me as a kind of shield from the reality of the physics of the dream. ...

These "ideas" for the paintings were soon transformed into a complete "inventory of pictures stacked in his mind, already painted, circling like planes over Newark, simply waiting their turn to get realized."

New Jerusalem & Holyland USA

Revelation became the recurring theme in Laffoley's art, and so, in 1972, given the opportunity to do whatever he wanted, with funding from Boston's Institute of Contemporary Art (ICA), Laffoley naturally chose to create his own "New Jerusalem" from the Book of Revelation. As Laffoley tells it, the reason he was given this opportunity was basically a scheme, dreamed up by the director of the ICA, to take revenge on his associates there, who he knew would not like Laffoley's work. He gave Laffoley an entire room, and advised him to make a lot of noise:

... So I worked this whole thing out, I painted the whole room flat black inside, floor, ceiling and walls, and started to do this thing. It was a big six-foot cube, and it had huge foundation stones made out of jewels, and you know, with pearls and all of the angels, and the whole thing, and an angel pointing down from the mountain where you walked up, and a burning lake of sulphur. The whole bit.

And, as it was going along — I started out by myself — within days I collected a crew that worked freebies. And they all brought ... thousands of dogs, so every day dogs would come running in and out of this thing, and yelping. And all these other people were now starting to get a little uptight. Because buzz-saws were going... And so, we're getting going and there's a maelstrom happening inside that, and people would come in there; each day this woman, this little squeaky-voiced woman, said, "Why are you here?" And I said, "Because I'm not all there." And she'd come back and she'd do the same thing day after day. ...

... So this went on for, like, two solid months. And finally, they got Mayor White to close the place down. ...

Laffoley describes this experience as "the karmic input" to his eventual involvement with the design of "Holyland USA" amusement park. Apparently some reviews of Laffoley's *New Jerusalem* piece at the ICA appeared here and there in the press; possibly, this is how a couple of "Christians," one named "Billy Bob," learned of it, and showed up at Laffoley's studio one day:

They had heard of [New Jerusalem], they hadn't seen it, they'd seen pictures of it. ... And then I showed them slides of it, ... they said "Wow, I really like this thing," all this sort of stuff. ... They thought that the ICA had gone devil-worshipping or something. And I think that's probably one of the reasons why these people from the South found out about it. It was just like the beginning of say, the Moral Majority people, tapping into popular culture and saying what's bad. And so these guys, who are totally around the bend, said, "Wow, we could use this." ... And he was like a Colonel Parker show-biz guy. This was before Tammy and Jimmy's attempt to do an amusement park. This was the original one.

Laffoley recognized this as a once-in-a-lifetime opportunity; to make sure Billy Bob and company would hire him, Laffoley claimed he could do all sorts of things, "like part the Red Sea every three hours." When they asked him if he could levitate something, he answered "NO PROBLEM." The entrepreneurs had nothing so far, except land, so Laffoley began to design the park on the spot. For him, it was the "clean slate." Among other things, Laffoley was designing a giant plastic Jesus — "it would look like a plastic Jesus on your dashboard" — 115 feet high. He was going to recreate his New Jerusalem not at six feet, but at 100 feet. The entire park would be seen from the air as a giant Star of David. People would be delivered to the park from angel-shaped helicopters. There was no limit to what he said he could do.

Laffoley was designing a giant Jesus statue — "it would look like a plastic Jesus on your dashboard" — 115 feet high.

Laffoley's efforts were successful:

[Finally] they decided that I was going to save their whole thing. ...

So then they said, "OK, we'll sit tight, and we'll get back to you." And so they flew off to "Jerusalem" and got a lot of silversmiths and stuff, and got all those people lined up. Then a couple weeks later I get a big check in the mail... for $10,000, and he said, this is an advance on purchasing this thing, and bringing you down here in order to set up a crew to make this thing 100 feet high. Plus other kinds of design tasks, which would be, like, designing the whole thing. That was what was really going on, see, they would lure me down there and get locked in. The guy wanted to buy me a house, all this kind of stuff, I would move down. He was gonna give me 10% right off the top of the whole thing; it was like getting 10% off the top of Disney World!

... So this was building up, and I was ready to explode. My blood pressure went up 50 points during the two weeks that I was down there. So then after that we did things like, we had a planning retreat at Disney World. Great. We stayed in the thing that has the monorail that goes through the building, you've seen pictures of that, it's a ghastly building, but it's great to enter the building like in a subway. So all these people had rooms and they had different things on the doors, saying, like, "from Holyland," and the maids that were cleaning up thought we were from Jerusalem. And so, in the morning, I walk out, and [the maid] gets down on her knees and says, "Pray for me," or something, "you're from the Holyland." I said, "wrong Holyland, folks."

After the planning retreat was over, Billy Bob "took off in his Cadillac, and he was gone." Laffoley and about 150 other people, it turned out, were the victims of a classic con-artist. Billy Bob's facade was so effective that he scammed $2.5 million off the State of

Alabama, as front money. But for Laffoley, this was just another bizarre episode in a life filled with bizarre episodes.

Laffoley's art is much enhanced by lengthy explanations; he thinks of them as the modern analogue to medieval illuminations, or even cathedrals, which were, to his mind, more of a teaching mechanism than an exercise in aesthetics.

Flying Saucers II

If earth was visited by extraterrestrials, they might well land at Laffoley's Holyland USA, with its Star of David seen from the air. But this might not even be necessary, as Laffoley thinks of himself as a "contactee" already, due to several other strange episodes in his life. Though he doesn't claim to have actually met any aliens in the flesh, he does claim to be in some sort of communication with them:

> Now, the reason why I can say that [I have encountered UFOs] is because of the history that I've had with that subject. That's basically the situation of having been contacted by "Brad Steiger," who I thought was Brad Steiger, but turned out that it wasn't Brad Steiger. Because he said he did not contact me. Now, that's how I actually got in the book, *[Gods of Aquarius]*.
>
> One day in September of 1975, I get a letter that's written with orange ink on green paper, it wasn't on lavender paper like you'd expect, it was on green paper. And saying that I'd like to invite you to contribute to this book as a writer, and do some illustrations, I know about your interest in UFOs. And he said it would be $2,500, and this is to be basically a subjective article describing your own situation. And I looked him up, I never knew anything about him before, but I looked in the library and he had sixty books on things to do with UFOs, and various occult things, and I said, "Wow this guy's really got something going, and so the book will obviously get published." So I said, "great," and I wrote it all out, and it had to do with my own history, of the situations in my own lifetime that have happened with this. ...

Steiger was surprised to receive Laffoley's essay, because, in fact, he had never requested his participation. Steiger had never even heard of him; none of his friends had either. Steiger was indeed working on a book called *Gods of Aquarius*, but had already selected the twelve people who would participate. He'd only wanted twelve, and Laffoley would have been the thirteenth. When Steiger called Laffoley to report all this, he concluded, "Wow, we've got an encounter of the first kind." Whoever had contacted Laffoley as "Brad Steiger" was one of *them:*

> So this is like a communication thing to be placed in position to make some statements. Because my article had to do with UFO as a world view. And because of world views being connected deeply to language, that was a real change in the world. And the people that were dealing with UFOs were unconsciously undergoing a shift. And so that the shift was not in a sense defined as self-induced. That it was a shift that was being created by *them.* So that they were going down to a genetic and engrammatic programming in people, and turning the switches on and off. ...

Recently, even more evidence has turned up that Laffoley has been contacted by otherworldly beings. Paul was getting dental implants, which required a CAT-scan of his entire head. After examining the results, the clinician asked him if his neck had ever been broken; Paul replied that it hadn't. The clinician then asked if he'd ever been shot; again, Paul replied he hadn't. The reason the clinician was asking was the CAT-scan revealed Laffoley has a 3/8" long, 1/16" diameter vertical pin, rounded at the ends, *lodged between his brain and his back.* Lacking any other plausible explanation, Paul interprets this as "the classic UFO implant."

Boston Visionary Cell

Paul's studio, in an old building, smack in the middle of downtown Boston, *looks* like the studio of a UFO contactee. From top to bottom, it's densely packed with models of flying saucers, odd devices and parapsychology books, with advertisements for local fortune tellers tacked to the wall.

Laffoley does not work in isolation, however, and obviously feels some responsibility to support other worthy artists and to educate the public. To this end, his studio also serves as headquarters of The Boston Visionary Cell, a nonprofit art association Paul founded in 1971. Laffoley says that they "really push making people familiar with the contents," of the art, which "involves lectures, symposium, and the rest." Laffoley's art in particular, is much enhanced by lengthy explanations; he thinks of them as the modern analogue to medieval illuminations, or even cathedrals, which were, to his mind, more of a "teaching mechanism" than an exercise in aesthetics.

The existence of content, though, is not Laffoley's only criterion for Visionary Art. The content must be organized beyond the level of pure information. For example, "psychotic art ... does not recognize any kind of holiarchy or any kind of hierarchy, because it is, in a sense, trying to deconstruct everything." Visionary art, however, does follow a hierarchy, and with the proper key its contents are decodable:

> I have a hierarchy of symbology, going from a sign, an index, an icon, an archetype, to a symbol. And that those things go from *information* which is totally arbitrary — A can equal B; to an *index,* which is like, animal tracks in the snow, or ballistics, or forensic information; to an *icon,* which is an attempt to get at the object, by describing it spatially or temporally; to an *archetype,* which phases into Jung's definition of coming to information that appears to be an engrammatic in peoples' brains genetically ...; and finally coming to a *symbol,* where the force is at one with the thing that you're dealing with. So it goes from totally arbitrary to non-arbitrary information. So that the energy and the information connect together, rather than being separated, at the level of sign. I don't think psychotic art would follow such a paradigm, in the way that they would explore any information.

Even though he sees a wide gap between his art and that of "psychotics," Paul Laffoley likes to think of himself as a "kook." The last time I talked to him, he asked me how big I thought this book would be. When I told him I thought it would be pretty big, he said he hoped it would be as thick as *Who's Who in the World* (Laffoley appears on page 649 of the current edition), because he plans to put *Kooks* right next to *Who's Who in the World* on his bookshelf so he can proudly point out to visitors that he appears in both.

Paul Laffoley likes to think of himself as a "kook."

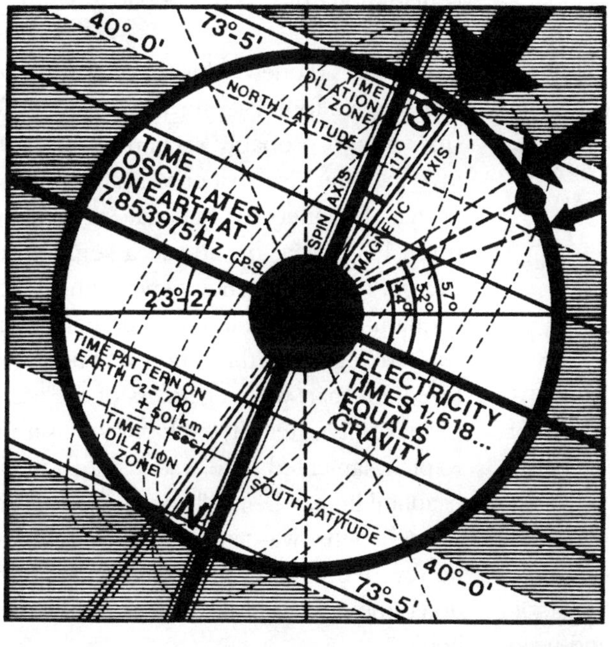

THE CHRONPUKNOZONE: Every paranormal phenomenon that occurs within the frame of reference of the Earth depends on the ebb and flow of the density of time. In any microscale location time is thin near a cause and thick near an effect, but around the surface of the Earth macroscale time dilation zones exist which promote or inhibit event ensembles. Ideally, these zones are high, cold and devoid of ambient life, and near the poles.

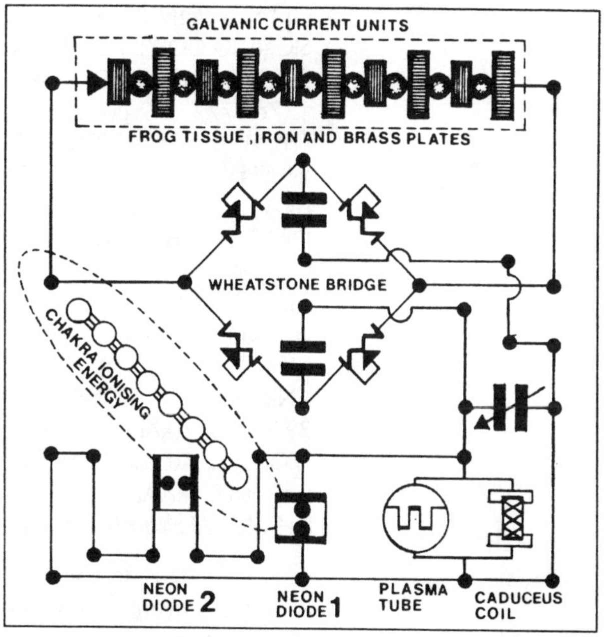

THE MONITOR: The Chakra Monitor and the Chakra Energy Amplifier constitute the human consciousness entry into the Time Machine system. During occasions of retro- and preperception, appropriate chakras are monitored for energy pulsations. Next, these chakras have their energy quanta diminished or enhanced by instrumentality as deemed necessary to promote human time dilations.

Illustrations by Paul Laffoley for his article, "Elements of the Time Machine: Homage to H.G. Wells," from the *Journal of the United States Psychotronics Association,* Summer, 1990.

THE NUMBERS MAN

The flyers contain the frequent refrain of "ONE GOD," an optimistic tone, and the assurance that not one inch of space will be wasted.

Norman Bloom, who died in 1989, was known as "The Numbers Man" to devoted listeners of the Larry King Radio Show. In addition to maintaining his status as a regular caller to the talk show, Bloom produced and distributed intriguing, giant sized Xeroxed flyers crammed with numerical news — football scores, birth dates, stock market figures, Hebrew letters. Bloom's capitalized commentaries helped the readers understand the significance of all the numbers:

39 = YHVH ECHOD — ONE GOD

I, ALONE, TEACH THAT GOD BROUGHT NY METS TO VICTORY 13 YRS AFTER 26th YOM KIPPUR (YOM KIPPUR WAR 73 at 39th YOM KIPPUR OF ISRAEL. (SIGNING HIS NAME INTO NY METS: & INTO BASEBALL & INTO WORLD HISTORY SO WHILE I WATCH GAME, AND RECORD ALL THE SIGNS OF GOD'S CREATION, AS I ALONE TEACH, I HOLD THAT PUBLICATION IN MY HANDS — AND WHEN GIANTS WIN BY SCORING 39 POINTS & SIGNING GOD'S NAME & IDEA OF 9-10- THE DOUBLE CLOCKWORK MAN LIVES IN AND 1776-1777 & 9 cycles 47-48 & 10 1967 I SHOW THOSE PRESENT, AT FAIRLAWN A.C., WHERE I WATCHED, THAT PAGE & EXPLAINED HOW GIANTS VICTORY FULFILLED ALL THE IDEAS ON THAT PAGE, THAT I HAD TAUGHT CONGRESS & THE FACULTIES OF 13 UNIVERSITIES (ONLY, I, IN ALL THE EARTH DID THESE THINGS, AND PRAYED THIS PRAYER TO MY FATHER AND AS I PRAYED, SO IT WAS DONE, AND ONE GOD SIGNED HIS NAME 39 IN THE 39th YR OF ISRAEL- AS A SIGN TO THE JEWISH PEOPLE (& ALL MANKIND) THAT HE IS FULFILLING HIS ETERNAL PROMISE.

Behold I Make All Things New!

The above is an excerpt from one corner of a flyer covered with similar information, along with the newspaper articles and headlines. These flyers are reminiscent of labels found on Dr. Bronner's castile soap: they contain the frequent refrain of "ONE GOD," an optimistic tone and the assurance that not one inch of space will be wasted. But the similarity leaves off there, as **Dr. Bronner** seems utterly rational in comparison.

The "point" of the flyers, if you read closely (and reading closely is the only way they may be read), is that Bloom is the messiah, by numerical logic. A happy messiah as contrasted to the more common doomsaying variety, he is full of good news for all, not just the few. Nothing less than "freedom for all mankind" brought on by God himself, via the power of the United States, is what we may expect in the coming days.

The numerical content is squeezed between proclamations that Communism is dead — this was written in the mid-1980's — and that the messiah is here. The numbers Bloom displays indicate biblical cycles, times, dates and measurements, rather than mathematics, though simple calculations are essential. These prove that the stock market and football figures that occur on certain dates are exactly in sync with biblical prophecy. Of course, none of it could possibly be due to coincidence.

Bloom's notoriety with **Larry King** devotees is quite fortunate, for otherwise, his life story would probably remain in obscurity, save the numerical evidence in his enigmatic posters. Reporters for National Public Radio, upon his death, broadcast a segment on Bloom, containing interviews with friends, acquaintances and family members. What was striking about this report was how well-loved this man was, regardless of the eccentricity of his latter days. Bloom's cousin, Iris Kaplan, lamented, "He was just a beautiful, beautiful human being. There was something about him that was almost spiritual. And how he reverted to this kind of *mishagos,* and I don't know what else to call it, I will never know."

Bloom was a sour-smelling but well-known street character, once a middle-class Jewish citizen in suburban New York. He was happily married, with two children as well as a piece of the family linoleum floor-coverings business. Prone to ecstasy brought on by music, Bloom seems to have been a sensitive and charismatic person, bursting with energy.

But by the mid-50s his erratic behavior, paranoia and get-rich-quick schemes put a strain on his marriage. He ruined his linoleum business when he invested in pencils implanted with plastic-encased girlie pictures. His wife left him in 1958, but he was adored by his children. He frequently embarrassed them, but also wrote them songs, put Walt Whitman to music for them, and took them on exciting week-end adventures.

Bloom's turning-point came in 1962. He had hired Carnegie Hall for a concert which was supposed to vindicate and validate what had lately become his preoccupation: the bible. His brother recounted that the concert was impressive, but almost nobody showed up. Bloom was shattered. A note scribbled on one of the concert programs read, "My dear Brother, I guess you are right, and I am the fool. No critics, no audience except friends and relatives, even though I distribute 1600 tickets. This will probably change many things for me. One thing will not change. He is my rock, my shield and my strength, in Him do I place my trust. Your loving brother, Norm."

From that day on, Bloom's obsession with the bible and numbers became all-consuming. He began to write down license plate numbers, kept dollar bills with significant serial numbers, and was arrested in New York City in an incident involving a number on a subway turnstile. His family tried to put him away, but he repeatedly convinced the relevant authorities to release him, probably helped by his intellect and gentle manner.

In a 1988 interview, King asked him whether he was the messiah. Bloom answered, "Yes, this is who I am, sir. This is definitely who I am. This was made known to me in 1962. There was an anointing without human hands of sacramental wine... I am the one who fulfills this. I am the one who reveals the power of God and teaches mankind, and brings a new world for mankind. This is my purpose."

During summer months, Bloom worked in the lucrative Pied Piper ice cream business in Hawthorn, New Jersey, delivering both ice cream and "numerical good news" to children. This paid for his more important numbers work, to which he fully devoted his time during the winter. He ate all his meals at the Triangle Diner, where he would scribble and pore over the newspapers for each day's numerical news. Though technically "homeless," Bloom did have an office of sorts, The Fairlawn, New Jersey, Public Library. He annoyed some of the librarians there, but befriended others, on whom he imposed his rants and flyers. One librarian was particularly touched by Bloom. "He was a courtly man, and the thing that really made me feel very extremely warmly toward Mr. Bloom, was his ability to quote poetry, and he did it so beautifully..."

After his death, Bloom's children were left with the task of sorting through his belongings. Indifferent to their father's messianic importance, they apparently discarded many cartons of his flyers and correspondence. Rather than treasuring the artifacts that revealed who he really was, his daughter was engaged in a fruitless search for artifacts that showed his love for her. In the previous few years, he visited her in her Boston home; she considers herself to have been his link with "reality" at that time. During the visits, though he spent some time as a normal Dad, Bloom would always eventually resume his work, Xeroxing and distributing flyers, fulfilling his one true destiny as THE NUMBERS MAN.

Thanks to David Hauptschein for providing the NPR tape.

Bloom began to write down license plate numbers, kept dollar bills with significant serial numbers, and was arrested in New York City in an incident involving a number on a subway turnstile.

Enigmas solved by the Numbers Man.

ON 12-3-87 D.J 1776 ONE GOD PROVED HIS POWER

1-2-3

ALL MY TEACHINGS ON 12-3 PAGE, BROUGHT TO HUNDREDS OF FACULTY OF BRANDEIS & HARVARD UNIVERSITIES ON 12-3 1987 PROVEN TRUTH

THAT PAGE PUBLISHED IN CAMBRIDGE (CW BEAWE - MASS AVE) ON 12-3 CONTAINS THESE HEADLINES:

ONE GOD'S TEACHING TO THE 100TH CONGRESS !.

THE COMPLETE CONGRESS ALSO CONCEDES AND ADMITS THAT IT 1986 → (BY IT'S SILENCE) 8-8-86 IS A PROVEN TRUTH

THAT ONE GOD BROUGHT THE UNITED STATES TO BIRTH IN 1776 (First year July 1776-1777) (BUT THEY ALL HATE THIS TRUTH)

HEADLINES FROM MY PUBLICATIONS 8-8-76 & 86

1776 AD = 888+888

THE UNITED STATES IS BORN. IS THIS AN ACCIDENT OF HISTORY OR IS IT THE SHAPED CREATION OF GOD?

THE NEW WORLD

Norman Bloom

1776 A.D. (888 YEARS & 888 YEARS : 1776)

GOD'S WORDS !

YHVH ECHOD—ONE GOD SAYS— I HAVE PROVEN, I HAVE THE POWER TO SHAPE THE STOCK MARKET— ON 12-3-1987

ON 12-3 1848.9 −72.4 1776

72.44 Drop Puts Dow At 1,776.53

Widespread Selloff; Close Lowest Since The Oct. 19 Plunge

THE GREATEST CRASH, BLACK MONDAY 10/19, 1987 — ONE GOD, A 2ND TIME, PROVES IT IS HIS CREATION; BY REPEATING NOV. 9 & 10 — GREAT 1 9 0 . 0 0 ANNOUNCEMENT OF - 5-22-1948,

AND ON 12-3 MY TEACHINGS IN 1980 BOOK REPEATED AGAIN —

אמת

TIME OF THE COMING OF THE MESHIACH 5739-5740 ! PUBLISHED SPRING 1980

ON 12-3-87 REPEATING 1948 ANNOUNCEMENT

1948 184.8 −72 (18×4=72) ·1948 1 7 7 . 6

THIS DROP TO 1776 - when I BRING THIS WORK TO HARVARD & BRANDEIS WAS IN REVERSAL OF ALL MARKET INDICATORS

YHVH ECHOD—

—ONE GOD'S TEACHING TO PRINCETON UNIVERSITY !

יְהוָה אֶחָד 13 + 26

A RESTATEMENT OF THE $ 1,000 challenge issued to the faculty of PRINCETON UNIVERSITY IN 1975-

A RETEACHING AND EXPANSION OF THAT PROOF !

It is proven herein that the odds are 6.4 x 10[28] power IN FAVOR OF YHVH ECCHOD—13-26-ONE GOD HAVING SHAPED ALL OF WORLD AND JEWISH HISTORY IN BRINGING TO BIRTH ISRAEL IN 1948& 1967, so fulfilling all of THE PROMISES OF GOD made 2200 to 2600 years ago

IT WAS DONE ONLY TO PROVE ONE GOD'S POWER AND THAT NORMAN BLOOM — IS TEACHING TRUTH TO HARVARD & BRANDEIS — VERITAS — ON THEIR UNIVERSITY SEALS

THE GREAT ANNOUNCEMENT MAY 1929 to MAY 1948

ONE GOD'S GREAT ANNOUNCEMENT 1929-1948 PROCLAIMING— I, YHVH ECHOD, WILL SHAPE ALL OF WORLD AND JEWISH HISTORY ON THE IDEA OF MY SHAPING OF THE CLOCKWORK OF THE HEAVENS, ON THE IDEA OF 19 yr- 235 mo, THE JEWISH CALENDAR CYCLE — IN ORDER TO PROVE I AM G

4-1- 1929 300.40

4-1-1948 1 7 7. 6 1

4-1-1929—300.40 close— 19 yrs later
4-1-1948 1 7 7 . 6 1 close—

I AM YHVH ECHOD who shaped the Heavens The 1-3 JEWISH GOD 1x3x10x10=300. I AM YHVH ECHOD who brought to birth the U.S. in 1776 = 888+888, causing 13 to become 1 because ECHOD=1=13=4-8-1, is my name- as ZECHERIAH 14-9 proclaims.

SO—BECAUSE I BUILD ONE CREATION ON THE NEXT—SO BEFORE I ESTABLISH THE STATE OF ISRAEL—SO I REPEAT THE IDEA ——THAT IN ORDER TO BRING TO BIRTH A STATE OF ISRAEL IN 1,948—I FIRST BROUGHT TO BIRTH THE UNITED STATES— " THERE HAS BEEN NO STRANGE GOD AMONG YOU" I, YHVH ECHOD, AM FULFILLING MY WORDS THROUGH MY PROPHETS— I KNOW, WHAT IS REQUIRED TO BE DONE IN ORDER TO ACCOMPLISH IT—AND SO I HAVE DONE— WHY ON 1st day of 4th month this 1776 . (It occurs no other time in 1948). Because 1776=4x4x4x4=888+888

וְהָיָה יְהוָה לְמֶלֶךְ עַל־כָּל־הָאָרֶץ
בַּיּוֹם הַהוּא יִהְיֶה יְהוָה אֶחָד וּשְׁמוֹ אֶחָד

AND GOD WILL BE KING OVER ALL THE EARTH 1
IN THAT DAY SHALL THERE BE ONE GOD
(YHVH ECHOD = 13 + 26 = 39
AND HIS NAME
"ECHOD" = ONE
= 4 + 8 + 1 = 13 = 1 + 8 + 4 = 13 = ONE.

א - 1
ח - 8
ד - 4

אֶחָד : THE GREAT ANNOUNCEMENT

אֶחָד ECHOD- 1-8-4 -1.-2.-3.

5-13 1948 184.82 -8400- 23 yr.

13= 1= 1-8-4 : אֶחָד וּשְׁמוֹ

YHVH ECHOD SAYS——FOR 3,000 YEARS—I HAVE WORKED AND PLANNED FOR THIS DAY—5-13-1948—WHEN I WILL PROVE TO THE WHOLE EARTH I AM— THE ONE GOD, WHO STRETCHED OUT THE HEAVENS, WHO IS THE GOD OF SCRIPTURES AND THE GOD OF HISTORY—and there is no other——

ONE GOD KNOWING HE WILL CAUSE 1848-72=1776 ON 12-3- POINTS AHEAD TO HIS CREATION BY WRITING AN 888 POEM INTO complete week ON 11-30 MONDAY to 1833.55 POINTING TO 1776

− 76.93

With yesterday's drop, the Dow lost 159.98 points for November. The 30-stock blue-chip index now stands 888.87 points, or 32.6 percent, below its record high of 2,722.42 reached last Aug. 25. And the Dow is just 94.81 points above the Oct. 19 closing level of 1,738.74.

−888.81 Since all TIME HIGH 8-25 2722.42

ON 12-1 + 8.84 to 1842

ON 1st 2nd = 8.8 = ECHOD = 1 = 184 signal 8.8 — to 880 POINT

ON 12-2 + 6.63 to 1848.97

MANIFEST DESTINY US 2-2-1848

A CONTINUOUS FLOW OF THOUGHT IN A POETRY IN NUMBER —

IDEA 888-888-1776!

This announcement is proclaimed in NYC the largest JEWISH COMMUNITY on earth, AGAIN, BY MY PLAN AND WORK, I AM THE 1-3 JEWISH GOD—who works and who will reverse it ?) (I AM THE GOD OF FREEDOM whose POWER brought you out of bondage to Pharoah)

MAY 1948

5-1-1948 high 180.58 180.28 close

MAY 1-1948—HIGH 180.58 Close 180.28

FOR THOUSANDS OF YEARS I HAVE PLANNED TO BRING A JEWISH NATION TO LIFE (CHAY-18) In 1948 AD—after the PERFECT ECLIPSE at the NEW MOON OF IYAR 57 0 8. TO COMFORT MY PEOPLE——so the HIGH on 1st of 5th month(as in YAH=10+5) so 180. 58=BECAUSE NOACH—TO COMFORT,= 50+8=58. BECAUSE, I AM THE 1-3 JEWISH GOD, who shaped the Heavens on 23=8400=28X300 & 28 is 3rd Perfect. so on 1st 180.28 close.

o, by doing this 180.58&180.28 on 5/1/1948 PROCLAIM—I, the 1-3 JEWISH GOD, who stretched out the heavens, WILL COMFORT 58=NOACH) MY PEOPLE—by bringing to LIFE 18x10=180) ISRAEL IN MAY 1948.

I HAVE PLANNED FOR—BAYOM HAHOO—in THAT DAY—WILL THERE BE ONE GOD YHVH ECHOD AND HIS NAME ECHOD. This day the rule of the gentiles comes to an end—AND I RETURN MY PEOPLE TO THE LAND I PROMISED TO ABRAHAM—WOULD BE THEIRS FOR ALL TIME—— THAT DAY WHEN I PROVE TO THE EARTH I AM YHVH ECHOD, OSHEMO ECHOD. AND SO—BAYOM HAHOO—IN THAT DAY—5-13- I WRITE MY NAME ECHOD 1 8 4 — as the CLOSE (It does not occur as close in any other day of May 1948—ONLY ON THE 13th- BECAUSE I AM THE 1-3 JEWISH GOD WHOSE NAME IS ECHOD——— BUT AS IS MY WAY, I SAY MANY OTHER THINGS BY THE DOING OF ONE WORK- BECAUSE——NOT ONLY DID I WRITE 184—— BUT I WROTE 184.8

By writing 184.8 2 as the Close on 5-13-1948—I ALSO PROCLAIMED BEHOLD, I AM THAT SAME ECHOD=1=13=184=481—WHO COMPLETED THE MANIFEST DESTINY OF THE UNITED STATES ON 2-2- 1848—WRITING MY NAME ECHOD= 184=481 (=1=1) in 1776 and in 1848 72 years later) AND ON THIS DAY—I BEGIN THE MANIFEST DESTINY OF ISRAEL— by writing MY NAME ECHOD=1-8-4

I AM THAT SAME ECHOD=1=1-8-4=481 who caused 48 states to result from 2-2-1848=pointing ahead to 1948 & 48 states I AM THAT SAME ECHOD=1=1-8-4-4-8-1 WHO SHAPED ALL OF WORLD HISTORY IN 1848 (1-8-4-8)in a way without equal, pointing ahead 100 yrs to 1948- I AM THAT SAME ECHOD who brought the 2nd and definitive CHARTER TO COLLEGE OF NEW JERSEY (ie Princeton)in 1748—and its first class to graduate in 1748—POINTING AHEAD 100 YEARS to 1848, POINTING AHEAD 200 YEARS to 1948=when the 2nd coming of the 2nd part (SON& PRINCE OF PEACE) is 26 yrs(YHVH) POINTING AHEAD 200 YEARS to the single greatest ACTION OF THE PROOF——THAT PROOF THAT I BRING PRINCETON THE FIRST TIME in 74 (=JESUS=MESSIAH) and SECOND TIME in 1980.

THIS POEM REQUIRES THE ULTIMATE POET

3 th GREAT WORK! 1978 BOOK

THE CULMINATION DAY- CAUSING THE RETURN TO 8 8 8 on the day 8-4- AFTER 1 YEAR FROM 8-4-1 9 7 7 WHEN THE MARKET WAS CAUSED TO REMAIN BELOW THIS POINT-

THE GREAT IDEA!!

1977-78 8-4

888 yrs. & 888 yrs. =1776 23 yr. - - - 8400 d.

888.17 8-4-1977

DOW JONES AVERAGES 30 Industrials UP 1.56 Closed at 888.43 August 4, 1978

888.43 on 8-4 8-4 1978

PUBL 12-5-1987 AT CAMBRIDGE MASS AVE

THIS BALLOT INTRODUCES LOVE 22
"22'S - BALLOT"

There's "ONLY 1" Independent Man For President in '88.

"22" Zingers Under The "Freedom Of Information Act" (F.O.I.A.) "I.O.U. $22"

1. Our First "PRES." was "BORN" on the "22"nd . . . George Washington Feb. "22."
2. "THE LAST" two "PRES." "DIED" on the "22"nd . . . L.B.J. Jan. "22," J.F.K. Nov. "22."
3. How many letters are there in (United States Government)?? .... "22."
4. "PRES." Reagan was just shot with a . . . let "ME MAKE A" point . . . A . . . "22."
5. The Hip Zip "CODE 4" "WASH. D.C." is . . . . . "20202."
6. The Area Code when calling "WASH. D.C." is . . . . . "202."
7. "WASH. D.C." using the "ALL NEW" ABC Key "ADDS-UP-2" "I WANT" "U-2-GUESS" . . . . . "22.
8. "OF AMERICA" using the "ALL NEW" ABC Key "ADDS-UP-2" a double "22" "SEE-IT"??
9. (L O V E) on your Telephone Dial "ADDS-UP-2"? You got that right . . . . . "22."
10. If you don't know the (#) number, Information is (1-555-1212) which always = 22.
11. There are how many chapters in the book (Love Story)?? You got that right "22."
12. The Media: "ABC-NEWS" = "22" "CBS-NEWS" = "22" Sorry NBC . . . "ABC-CBS-NBC" = "2
13. "WORK" "SALARY" "CHECKS" "CASHED" "F.D.I.C." "F.S.L.I.C." & "9 to 5" all = "22."
14. See how "STUDENT" "LESSONS" "CLASSMATES" & "GRADS" all = "22" + How about "ADULT-E
15. The "$22 BILLS" are legal now. "LOVE 22" can sell them to finance his campaign.
16. A Judge accepted one ($20 Fine) Really!! (7-11 Store cashed 2) Thats Incredible!!
17. Postage is up to how many cents?? "22¢" "U.S. MAILS" "ADDS-UP-2" . . . . . "22."
18. Who won the Noble Peace Prize?? Bishop Who?? . . . . . Bishop "Tu-Tu"!!! Am I going too fas "4-YOU-2."
19. If Love has made U "SMILE," "LAUGH," "PLEASE" have a "NICE" DAY, "I.O.U. 22" all = "22
20. "THEY" said I should have had my head examined for printing up "THOSE" "$22 BILLS." S I got a Tape Measure and Measured my head. It's exactly "22" Inches around!! I don't kno where "THEY" get (7½ & 7¼) maybe it's the "HOLE" that goes "THRU" which "ADDS-UP-2" . . . "22
21. "THE LAST" Revelation in the New Testament is "REV. #22" plus "LORD" "MASTER" "BIBLES" = "22."
22. Some will send a $1. & some will send Love $2. Some $5, $10 or $20 and some $22. Love 2 4 "PRES." In '88. "A VOTE 4" Love is "A VOTE 4" you: "YABB-ADABB" "ADIEU" a double "22 P.S. "I-LUV-U" = "22."

LOVE 22 - P.O. BOX 4022 KY. WEST, FL 3304(

There are 22 reasons 2 vote for Love-22, "the Independent Greenback Party Write-In Candidate" for President of the United States, every (2+2) years.

There are 22 "platform planks" in the Love-22 campaign for "ALL NEW" government, among them, "Proposition 22," which seeks to "AX-TAXES." Reprinted here is a flyer from the '88 campaign.

DAN SCOTT ASHWANDER AND HIS COSMIC MIND

Dan Scott Ashwander

Ashwander wrote on the back of the photo, "Made in 1979 when I was under time limits and the computerized Spirit, the Evils' Leader was after me."

I first became aware of Dan Scott Ashwander in 1988 through **O. Nenslo,** who responded to an ad for Ashwander's book *Am I Insane?* in the classified section of a supermarket tabloid. Nenslo received the book directly from the author in Foley, Alabama, along with a steady stream of handwritten and xeroxed letters.

Am I Insane? was first published by Carlton Press in New York in 1983. Carlton, a vanity press, required several thousand dollars from Ashwander to print a small run of the book. By the time I attempted to order it, *Am I Insane?* was no longer available.

The flyleaf of the original hardcover reads:

Am I Insane?, by Dan Scott Ashwander, is a unique and remarkable account of a world in crisis and the one man who has the ability to effect its salvation.

Assaulted early and often by the powers that seek the destruction of the world, the author stands alone as a bastion against the confusion and ruin of universal chaos and evil. Says the author: "This is my final assault to save time for all men to have Eternal Life by virgin birth. Using mental telepathy, I engaged the Evil Eternals in combat in the spirit with time limits of utmost importance."

Am I Insane? is a vital, relevant book that addresses an issue of concern to all of us — the very survival of our planet in the face of an onslaught the very dimensions of which will stagger the mind of any thinking member of contemporary society.

Concludes Mr. Ashwander: "Our planet Earth is the only place where there is life before death now as all other planets with former life before death people have been exterminated and all those people are in life after death now.

"I told the Evils' Leader that Good would conquer evil someday which it did on February 8, 1983, when my final mission was accomplished and all men received Eternal Life forever. So maybe 'evil' will look as a bad name and 'good' as a good name in eternity."

When I offered to reprint *Am I Insane?*, free of charge, Ashwander was delighted. He began sending letters, tapes, photos of himself and of his dosimeter readings, and ideas for new books. It soon became clear that, unlike so many others, Dan was good-hearted, trusting and optimistic, despite his eternal battles.

I printed about 500 copies of *Am I Insane?* and began peddling them to the readers of *Kooks* magazine. The response wasn't overwhelming, but there were a few people who appreciated Dan; one person wrote that he was hoping to travel through Alabama to meet Ashwander in person. **Matt and Melissa Jasper** of Tray Full of Lab Mice Productions in Durham, New Hampshire, enchanted with Ashwander, began a correspondence with him after reading *Am I Insane?* Upon publication of a pamphlet, *The Selected Letters of D.S. Ashwander,* they became the primary Dan Ashwander contacts. The pamphlet included many of Ashwander's letters to the Jaspers, the entire text of *Am I Insane?*, and an extensive photo section. The Jaspers also established "The Church of Dan Ashwander."

Relieved that others were communicating with Dan, I no longer felt obligated to respond to his flood of repetitious letters, though I continued to write occasionally.

In addition to *Am I Insane?* I distributed The *Dan Ashwander Healing Tape,* which contained more than an hour of Ashwander's slow, Alabama drawl reciting his bizarre texts. I found it a bit unsettling that he frequently sent me updated versions of the tape, demanding that I sell them as well, predicting that they'd be million-sellers. Of those he sent, the strangest was *Heaven's Angels Talk By Mental Telepathy,* aptly named because the entire 90-minute tape was silent except for a few beeps.

Undaunted by the slow sales of his voice tapes Ashwander paid a large sum of money to a vanity songwriting and recording outfit to have his gospel verses, "The Will of God," put to music:

I AM GOING TO PUT THE WILL OF GOD ON THIS EARTH
BECAUSE I AM JESUS CHRIST
I WANT TO SEE JERUSALEM AND ISRAEL
MADE THE CAPITAL OF A UNITED PEACEFUL WORLD
THE EVIL GERMAN RACE HAS DEFEATED ME
AND A PEACEFUL EARTH
BY LEADING PEOPLE DOWN THE ROAD TO HELL
WITH A SECRET NAZI DICTATORSHIP
WITH GERMANY THE EVIL HOLY CENTER OF EARTH
AND ADOLF HITLER AS GOD
DO YOU WANT TO WORSHIP ADOLF HITLER AS GOD AND GO TO HELL
OR WORSHIP ME GOD AND JESUS CHRIST?

The singer who recorded Ashwander's song did a good job of sounding sincere, though I wouldn't say that there was much soul in the rendition.

Ashwander's fame hasn't come in quite the way he expected. I'm not sure if he knows or cares, because what's important to him is that people know about him. Now, because of this book, even more people will know about him; he's also going to be the subject of a trading card, part of WFMU's (an Upsala, New Jersey college radio station) second set of the "Crackpots & Visionaries" trading cards.

Ashwander may be insane, but he also has a streak of realism, which enabled him to achieve a degree of fame and happiness that eludes even those whose minds are far less "cosmic" than his.

AM I INSANE? (Part I)

Am I insane? I'll let you be the judge of that after you read my book or read my story.

In January, 1961, the late President John F. Kennedy said over nationwide TV that we have "control of the mind" and then shaking all over after a press conference in Washington, D.C., walked away. Lord, God Almighty, did Kennedy really say that then or am I hallucinating now because it has been so long ago and nothing in public has ever been said about President John F. Kennedy saying "we have control of the mind" to explain what he meant after that.

You see, I believe completely that I was referred to as we have "control of the mind" by the late President John F. Kennedy. I will give my reasons as you shall see. The day after the late President John F. Kennedy said we have "control of the mind," I was listening to Art Linkletter's radio show when he started interviewing a woman who was a refugee from Communist Russia.

"The Communists have killed forty million people," the Russian woman on Linkletter's show suddenly blurted out.

Immediately, in my mind, the late Albert Einstein started spitting in my face, Jesus Christ being crucified on a cross, and John Foster Dulles smiling in 1-2-3 order back and forth in a laser type beam picture which was cutting my brain apart and kept me under much pain.

But my suffering was just beginning anew. I had quit my job at American Cyanamid Company in Milton, Florida, where I managed to struggle to hold my job as an analyst for one year in the dye and physical testing labs. My father decided I should go back to Bryce State mental Hospital for the second time, since I had quit my job at Tuscaloosa, Alabama after about 24 hours and after 12 hours at Bryce Mental Hospital. The pain from Albert Einstein spitting in my face, Jesus Christ being crucified on a cross and John Foster Dulles smiling being alternately flashed through my mind was finally stopped by me, God. On the criminal ward of Bryce Mental Hospital or the psychopathic ward in the receiving building I was interviewed by a Mexican doctor, thought by all Intelligence people to be Adolf Hitler but who was not as I shall explain later on. The man known to all people as Adolf Hitler in Intelligence circles had been one of my Sunday school teachers along with Benito Mussolini, while Winston Churchill was our minister at First Methodist Church in Birmingham, Alabama. Hitler and Mussolini never died but were saved by the SA brown shirt secret Nazi society of the U.S.A. (started in 1875 with a front name of capitalism) to be pushed around like myself by the SA brown shirt Nazi leaders of the U.S.A. Francisco Franco was a member of our church and known as the best basketball player for Ensley High School at that time. Franco had been forced to leave the leadership of Fascist Spain in 1948 to be used to try to harm me, along with Churchill, Hitler and Mussolini.

In a couple of days after being in Bryce Mental Hospital as a patient, Hitler was placed in Bryce as a patient as a Jehovah's Witness Church member and Benito Mussolini was also a

"Immediately, in my mind, the late Albert Einstein started spitting in my face, Jesus Christ being crucified on a cross, and John Foster Dulles smiling in 1-2-3 order back and forth in a laser type beam picture which was cutting my brain part and kept me under much pain."

Ashwander
"Made in 1988 at my mother's home."

patient at Bryce, forced to follow me around to destroy me. Mussolini was known to me as a man with another name from Holly Pond (north of Cullman), Alabama, and still lives there. The only time I ever came close to getting help from anyone under control of the mind — other than the late John F. Kennedy — was when Benito Mussolini sent "KKK" (which meant Ku Klux Klan) by mental telepathy to my mind when I sat across from him at Bryce one day. This was in February, 1961. I had known Adolf Hitler under another name at Hanceville, Alabama, where I was born on February 6, 1934. Hitler was forced to be at Hanceville in Cullman County (a German settlement) from 1945 (after World War II) until we moved to Birmingham, Alabama, where I met Hitler as Robert who was dating the leader of the EEs, Evil Spirits or Evil Eternals, known as Posky, but had teleported spiritually from Leia Organa's planet in the Milky Way Galaxy into the body of a woman who rose from the dead. Eva Braun was saved from death for the same reason as Adolf Hitler.

But to show a reason why I claim to be the one and only God which was told to me many times through mental telepathy by the Eternal Spirit, I will explain to you a mystery of the Cosmos. I was born by virgin birth of Lois Blanche Blackerby Ashwander at Hanceville, Alabama. I created myself by virgin birth into the womb of my mother from the Microbe Cosmos (which is the only original Eternal Universe) into the newly created United Spirit Universe of which planet Earth was created in time and space and I was going by the name of Satan then of which I had 12 million angels or Satan's Angels in my harem. In 1953, I separated a yellow or gold colored soul, spirit, or mind from my head which was round and was going around in a circle from left to right, stared me a few seconds in the face a foot from me and then disappeared. I would like to point out that the American Government dispatched scientists on campuses across the U.S.A. to see if any men had separated a soul from their head about a month after President John F. Kennedy referred to me as we have "control of the mind" in January, 1961, I read in the paper. (I am a graduate in pre-medicine from the University of Alabama.) In 1959, after I got out of the U.S. Army, I had electro-shock treatment to my head which electrified my mind and body and turned me into a type of thermonuclear reactor and sent my "cosmic mind" into the Cosmos on infinite time and space. Since then, I have been tortured by all satellites in orbit around Earth and computer minds on Earth.

In my final assault to save time for all men to have Eternal Life, I had to face eons of time limits (negative micro-split second, split second, etc., time limits) since I was born at Hanceville and could only make ten mistakes in one locality or else it would have been over for all men in Eternity as they would have been exterminated in the spirit and dead forever in a lethal deadly proton. I saved time for all men first in Eternal Life or life after death to have Eternal Life with no end on December 12, 1982, and second for all men in life before death to have Eternal Life with no end around the beginning of January, 1983. All women had time saved for them in Eternity by me to have Eternal Life.

Albert Einstein followed me around at Phillips High School in Birmingham, Alabama. When I was at Bryce Mental Hospital from February to May in 1961, one day when I was sitting next to Mussolini who was rolling cigarettes on a cigarette machine while we looked out of the bleak iron bar window. Albert Einstein was on a computer and sent a visible upside down horseshoe with a computer mind and got within two feet of penetrating the next window but I prevented it by being one second ahead of Albert Einstein (atomic scientist). If Albert Einstein had penetrated the window, then I would have made ten time limit mistakes after that for a total of 11 and that would have meant the end of Eternal Life for all men in Eternity because it was a deadly lethal time limit thrown on me by Dr. Albert Einstein. Another incident about this time at Bryce involved Paul the Cobra Man, (Another cobra man who was after me I called "Cowboy" because he wore cowboy hat and boots. All non-human life rises from the dead to become men and women in Eternal Life.) who got me down to a two-second time limit in mind power of mine against his right before we were to sleep, in another lethal, deadly time limit like Albert Einstein pulled on me at the window when I was sitting next to Mussolini at Bryce. Paul the Cobra Man had the most evil mind of any person I have ever encountered with evil mind power. Paul the Cobra Man, along with Cowboy, had teleported into the U.S.A. from another planet in the Milky Way Galaxy as secret agents for the EEs, Evil Spirits or Evil Eternals to harm me. I found out about all these people through mental telepathy communication with them, and others, whether on computerized "mind" or not, computer minds and the Eternal Spirit.

I am single and have never been married. I have no friends except my mother. It's a crying shame but there is nothing I've been able to do about it or to get help so that I won't be left alone or so that the public would find out about me. I have been known about since I was born by virgin birth. I had to obtain near-perfect brain damage when I was three years old when I fell out of a moving car into a ditch to trap the EEs, Evil Spirits or Evil Eternals led by the Evils' Leader into attacking me head-on in the spirit. In 1978, in the summer, all of a sudden I saw a sight that awed me — it was the Evils' Leader appearing bright like the sun in my back yard at Foley, Alabama. He was dressed in a white gown, had brown skin and a white beard and mustache. Combat at the VA Hospital had already broken out against me at Gulfport, Mississippi, by the EEs, Evil Spirits or Evil Eternals in the Spirit, and I had exterminated it seemed like almost infinite numbers of evil spirits on time limits and mind control who were supposed to be dead in the spirit forever (men and women) when I killed them in the Spirit as a patient at the VA the time before I met the Evils' Leader and Evil Spirits in combat at Foley, Alabama.

When the Evils' Leader first appeared to me at Foley, Alabama, he told me he was God through mental telepathy and I had to believe him to keep me from making 11 time limit mistakes. After nine months of the Evils' Leader's spirit being in and around our home where my mother and I live, I finally exterminated the Evils' Leader. Since 1976 I had been sending letters and typed manuscripts to different magazines, organizations, the U.N., etc., on what President John F. Kennedy meant when he said we have "control of the mind" but until now, nobody was interested in me except myself.

The leader behind the EEs, Evil Spirits or Evil Eternals was a man named the EE God or Evil Eternal God. Later, I met him in person at Will's Hotel in Gulfport under a different name in 1980. This man was the first microbe spirit to evolve in this United Spirit Universe when I went by the Divine Light in the Spirit. He first evolved as a woman and became evil-minded at once, stealing secrets from me I could not prevent but she became a man and the EE God. The EE God later broke away from my control in the Spirit and got control of 51% of the United Spirit Universe of which planet Earth was located and became EE or Evil Eternal Land and I controlled the other 49% and Eternity as the Divine Light. The EE God will remain a man in Eternity.

The most horrifying intelligence I gathered through mental telepathy other than torture was the cyclotrons, betatrons, thermonuclear reactors, and truth serum shots in the arm that turned human beings into many types of non-human life such as animals, insects, books, etc. I stopped these criminals in the U.S.A., Russia, China, and all over planet Earth (all countries on Earth are secretly SA brown shirt Nazi dictatorships) from turning human beings (one out of three were men, two out of three women) into non-human life about three months ago permanently. Most of the concentration camps on planet Earth were located underground on Earth which were created by the EE God.

All of my combat against the EE God, the Evils' Leader, the EEs, Evil Spirits or Evil Eternals and my own thoughts and life are fully recorded by computers and are locked away in secrecy in Washington, D.C., by the U.S. Government.

I am just biding my time in loneliness now waiting for the betterment of Eternity to come about.

All men have one woman each not in Eternity which I created for the men. Later on each man will have three trillion women in their harem. The women only stay with the men ten months and then are created into my harem of my women which are all women who have ever lived other than the women who will live with the men for then months at a time in life after death. The men have two societies to live in in life after death — the largest is a Socialist and the smallest is a Nazi black shirt SS society.

Good God! It was left up to me with total responsibility to save time for all men to have Eternal Life in Eternity since I was born February 6, 1934, and how I came through I'll never know although it was and is now much suffering on my part because I never could receive any direct or indirect help or moral support.

I have been over a trillion men in eternity either by virgin birth or in time and space. I was God of the Holy Bible, Jesus Christ son of God born of the virgin Mary, Allah of the Koran, Buddha who started the Buddhist religion, God of the Torah, Hippocrates who started medicine on Earth, Pliny the Elder, the ancient Roman historian, King Arthur of the Knights of the Round Table in England, Karl Marx (who wrote The Communist Manifesto), John Wilkes Booth who killed Abraham Lincoln, Adolf Hitler from 1933 to 1945 in time and space, etc.

May God (me) spare us mortal beings on Earth from further suffering as soon as possible and bring joy and a meaning to life for all of us. Amen.

"I had to obtain near-perfect brain damage when I was three years old when I fell out of a moving car into a ditch to trap the EEs, Evil Spirits or Evil Eternals led by the Evils' Leader into attacking me head-on in the spirit."

MONDAY, MARCH 15, 1982 BERKELEY, CALIFORNIA

PUBLIC PROPERTY DOCUMENT

1. Very few males, in my opinion, have any epidermis records to the effect that they ever had been addressed vibrationally by organized crime boss type organisms, in an other than direct light encounter situation.

2. No males, in my opinion, have ever gotten epidermis vibrations from organized crime boss type organisms, in other than direct light encounter situations.

3. No males, in my opinion, have ever gotten any definite idea of either the vectors (angles) to their person from whence the organized crime boss type organism vibrations are originating or the distance from their person from whence the organized crime boss type organism vibrations are originating, when connected vibrationally in an other than direct light encounter situation.

4. No males, in my opinion, have ever gotten any specific identity of any organized crime boss type organism when connected vibrationally in an other than a direct light encounter situation.

5. No male has ever, in my opinion, matched any specific organized crime boss type organism vibrations with any specific organism within the context of a direct light encounter situation.

6. No male has ever, in my opinion, identified a specific organism as being a source of organized crime boss type organism vibrations with enough certainty to approach said specific organism within the context of a direct light encounter situation and discuss said organized crime boss organism type vibrations explicitly.

7. Of those males who have been vibrationally addressed by organized crime boss type organisms, all have experienced step and fetch vibrational conditions from the general direction of organized crime boss type organisms, in my opinion at the time of this writing. Males experience it, females do not experience it, in my opinion at the time of this writing. Step and fetch vibrational conditions as experienced by the recipient results in a situation where the male epidermis does something and, rather soon afterward, a remote entity (the organized crime boss type organism), not necessarily being addressed or related to directly, knows what the epidermis has had done, within the context of a surveillance relationship. A round trip communications loop is experienced by the male epidermis from the remote entity (the organized crime boss type organism) to the male epidermis and back to the remote entity (the organized boss type organism) without the permission of the male epidermis and without the male epidermis being able to disconnect at the discretion of the male epidermis.

8. Of those males who have ever been vibrationally addressed by organized crime boss type organisms all have experienced over-rides of their central nervous system by means of air communication achieved as a result of some kind of organized crime boss type organism activity, in my opinion at this time.

SERGE BOUTOURLINE, JR., 10:25:17 A.M. BANCROFT COPY CENTER 2440 BANCROFT WAY

MISS L.L. EIGAR

Reprinted below are excerpts from letters by a Miss Laura Levga Eigar, originally published in pamphlet form by the Dialectical Immaterialism Press of Baltimore, in 1989.

International Court of Justice
Peace Palace
2517 KJ The Hague
Netherlands

Honorable Judge of World Domestic Court:

Please add this letter as an addition to my letter of March 31, 1989 mailed to you on Reg. No. R 584-725-591, April 3, 1989 from Baltimore Main Post Office by Miss L. L. Eigar.

a. Ears, called here pillow cases, total removal and finalized with vanilla, plugs removed by Arab Eel, April 19, 1989.

b. Heart Pond removed for third time in life on April 18, 1989 with strings, marbles and bulger.

c. Colon, April 21, 1989, total again for second time in life; father, son and holy ghost (liquid, strings and marbles) removed, applied vanilla heavy to tea and honey taken previous months (20 lbs.).

d. Manhood, April 21, 1989, removed after corals and crust taken off from bottom-vanilla extract (pure) and verbaled rot slim.

e. My bibb lettuce on womb being removed by lizards after intake of vanilla for a full month, very strong odor.

f. Iron poison long disc removed from heart March 31, 1989, has given me no basic problems (a squirrel) and bromozeltzer created an awfully lot of hard candy sticks for my wild squirrels, pets, to pull out, which they have from heart and it sounds like a new motor (tea and honey prior intake for 9 mos.) Remaining poison tributaries removed by my error some two days later? Also, two iron poison ponds on bottom hips verbaled out, April 26, 1989.

g. My neck in back on shoulders and nape cleared until it blew into chest cavity. I'm after broken health all these years with split back from rib cage and all the help of man, etc.

h. Fist in eye from Uncle Sam, April 16, 1989, broke my cheek bone and created massive bruised flesh with liver iron showing until today May 4, 1989? Had a picture taken for claim and for some reason a hard lump still remains on cheek bone — bruise turned yellow.

i. CUP of LIFE and Pond on NOSTRADAMUS, April 24, 1989, removed strings, marbles and bulger as usual.

j. Ink removed through top of head again this year for summer months, April 29, 1989.

k. Bear Claws (4) removed May 2, 1989 from back with clearance through Island Volcano with bear and white bull seal roars. This was removed during 1956 to same point for Presidential Potentials and Ex's alum, (5 cups), also 1980.

l. Neck, throat cleared after a full months effort with vanilla and verbaling. Ratcoon pulled out all hards created by bromozeltzer with my wild squirrels. Removing hard balls on center throat tubes at this time.

m. Head brain and all a total clearance at this time.

n. All Old Age removed from spine and acid burns eaten out by ratcoon at base and several up the spinal column, he is very thoro more so than my squirrels.

o. Broken health tube in right leg removed when hard plug was taken out, also chains on throat, bars on back Bitter Sweet and tubes on ribs. Maybe now I can find energy to complete all expected of me by the US State Dept. Washington, D.C.

SECOND ENTRY May 8, 1989

Hopefully, this will be enough for me to gain my five (5) cloned babies of August 1985, from Delaware State Hospital, Head Authority, for my pattern of life, since a house will be required and my ten acres for food will be allotted as stated by legal law, Honorable Judge Henry Shaw, of Delaware County Delaware, OHIO. My claim on the Ten (10) acres took place in 1944 at Harlem High School, Center Village, Ohio, by authority Mr. DeLong principal and Mrs. Elward Caldwell, of Westerville, OHIO, my English teacher for taxes to cover school expenses. I graduated from Westerville, OHIO, in Class 1949.

p. Removed large plug from back of right shoulder Gland to generate their function, also, bottom plug.

Would appreciate your interest for my return to Copenhagen, Denmark, where I have one of my working career checks going into Andelsbanken to be waiting on me when I arrive by plane. Will send a 40′ container to PORT MAN-

"Hopefully, this will be enough for me to gain my five (5) cloned babies of August 1985 from Delaware State Hospital."

AGER's OFC. where ship Maersk Line, enters for legal hold and security just as my Passports and VISA's are arranged for and received.

Shall be typing Supreme Court Report for Industrial Act Ledger removal and collection of values created such as my new Ford Van in navy blue from Baptist Church Parsonage, Cleveland, Ohio, created in late 1980 with doctors paperwork for authority, my car is on a HOLD ledger and I require it at this time seriously. Would your office be able to gain the car Van ahead of time?

"NO LONGER CAN EAT DRIED BEANS, May 2, 1989."

q. My efforts to be thoro has caused me to drink 4 oz. of Pure VANILLA.

r. Egyptian Collar-crystallized with bromozeltzer and verbally removed into chest for closing tissue again, May 6, 1989.

s. BULGERS on Bitter Sweet back and "T" cross (back), and diareary Iceland "Ice Cream Cones" total removal on second attempt, May 5, 1989.

t. Removed BULGERS from "Manhood" for final, May 8, 1989, third and final removal in my life time.

u. NO LONGER CAN EAT DRIED BEANS, May 2, 1989.

Cordially,

Miss Laura Levga Eigar (Miss B. L. Seeley)

Copies:

1. Dir. Geo. P. Schultz, US, State Department
2. Judge, Richard B. Metcalf Probate Court, Columbus, OHIO
3. United Nations Center, Wash., D.C. 20006
4. President Ronald R. REAGAN, USA
5. Judge, Henry Shaw, Delaware County Court House, Delaware, OHIO

communists, schools(s), god(s) National Debt BRAINWASHED

1983 JULY 5 6:00 P.M. (ABOUT...1-U.n.o.-(UNITED nature's organization INFO. WIRE.(PAGE 1).
WHEN WORLD nEW$meddA$, "WON'T TELL YOU THE REAL TRUTH(S)", DON'T BUY THEM & THEIR IDEOLOGY($
)..WITH A NEW NON WORLD NETWORK TV/Radio WORLD TALK SHOWS, WE CAN "BACK UP" WORLD POPULAT-
IONS SO WE CAN FEED ALL WORLD STARVING AND HOUSE THEM TOO...BACKING UP ALL WORLD WRONGS...

(((WORLD ADVERTISE ALL THESE PAGES NOW...)))

LEARN THE RIGHT IDEOLOGY. NATURE'S LAWS.

OBSERVATION /EXPERIMENT NO. 1

AT BIRTH A BABY AVERAGES '6' POUNDS-AT AGE 20 THIS PERSON'S WIEGHT IS '100' + POUNDS OF WATER! MULTIPLIED BY '5 BILLION PEOPLE' ADD UP TO '500 BILLION POUNDS OF WATER'! MATALIK SAYS 'GROWING WATER BY US' OR THIS PHENOMINON CREATE OUR 'NATURAL CATASTROPHIES -LIKE: 'RECORD' WORLD DROUGHTS, EARTHQUAKES & VOLCANOS-(CAUSED BY WATER BOILING UNDER OUR EARTH.), HOT & COLD TEMPURTURES, WINDS. FLOODS CAUSED BY RECORD MAKING OF WATER PUMPS, RAIN MAKING-(STEALING OTHER CONTINENTS, STATES, ETC. RAINS.) CULVERTS, ETC. MATALIK SAYS OVER POPULATION TAKES OUR WORLD WATER SUPPLY. THIS CONFLICTS WITH ALL IDEOLOGIES THAT PEOPLE GROW WATER OR ARE MOSTLY WATER.

Facsimile of a flyer, circa mid-1980s.

HOUSE ON THE ROCK

I can't fathom how the House on the Rock could have been built. It's like when scientists attempt to describe the relative distance between an atom's nucleus and its electrons — the scale is simply not human.

I FIRST HEARD ABOUT HOUSE ON THE ROCK when an acquaintance named Max returned from Madison, Wisconsin. He'd visited the popular roadside attraction on the advice of friends, who assured him that the long drive to Spring Green, 50 miles west of Madison, would be well rewarded. When he described the trip to me, however, Max didn't seem at all sure it was worth the long drive — or the steep admission price. His memory of the trip provoked only weariness.

"There's no escape from the one-way self-guided tour.[1] It's claustrophobic and exhausting. There's so much stuff that there's no way you can take it all in," Max sighed.

He went on to give House on the Rock — simultaneously — a fantastic and a terrible review, which tipped me off that it was something I definitely had to see. Nonetheless, I hadn't a clue as to what it was all about.

Several years later, I visited House on the Rock on my way west, and came to understand what Max had been talking about; as I made my way through the tour, I realized House on the Rock had to be experienced to be believed — although even after I experienced it, I didn't believe it; its very existence was impossible.

When I think about the scale of House on the Rock, aided by a glossy souvenir book and postcards, I can't fathom how it could have been built. It's like when scientists attempt to describe the size of the Universe, or the relative distance between an atom's nucleus and its electrons; the scale is simply not human. Like the pyramids of Egypt or Stonehenge, one is tempted to say it must have been built by extraterrestrials. **Alex Jordan Jr.,** the genius behind House on the Rock, must have been a giant from an alien world, posing as a human.

Despite its colossal size, many elderly people spend the entire day there, seemingly relaxed and happy. I, on the other hand, was overwhelmed and tired after only two hours. My feet hurt, and I wanted it to be over; I spent the last hour of the tour walking as fast as I possibly could. I felt like I was trapped in Wonderland, and wanted out.

The driveway leading to House on the Rock could be seen as a warning to the timid to turn back. The long road is flanked by dozens of giant casks that suggest an escape from Planet of the Onions. We arrived promptly at 9 a.m., the official opening time, but the driveway was already crowded with vans and cars from almost every midwestern state, as well as many from the east, south, west and Canada. We stood in line and braced ourselves for the inevitable.

I glanced at the tour map and saw that "House on the Rock" was more than just "House on the Rock." The house itself, indeed built on a rock, was only one of 29 attractions! Other structures, linked by long walkways, constituted most of the tour. I was beginning to get the idea this might be too much, even for me.

We began the tour, dutifully following signs that told us which direction to go (indispensable amid the many corridors). I soon realized, after ooh-ing and ahh-ing over an impressive mechanical orchestra, that we had 23 more exhibits ahead of us. I began to feel slightly disoriented, mildly fearful, and didn't know why.

The house, "an architectural marvel" built on 60-foot Deer Shelter Rock, 450 feet above the Wyoming Valley, is #7 on the tour. Jordan, the builder, had visited the rock in his youth; it was a favorite spot for picnics, and later, for "a whole gallon of Tom Collins." When Jordan began work on the house in the early 40s, he didn't even know who owned the land he was building on, but in 1953, he leased the rock for $7.50 a year. In 1956, his father bought the entire 240 acre farm for $12,000.

When he began building, Jordan was joined by helpers and friends, who carried all building materials up by hand; this was the first of many tasks fit for giants. (There were no blueprints, only a miniature model.) In all,

1. The tour has been changed to alleviate this problem; it is now divided, with three different entrance points.

they moved 5,000 tons of limestone and 5,000 tons of mortar, and planted 55,000 trees and 55,000 shrubs. Eventually they installed a lift.

In 1959, after more than 15 years of labor, the house appeared to be finished, but to Jordan it was only "half-done." The house was a bizarre sight for people driving by, and soon the "goddamn Sunday gawkers" started coming around, asking for tours. The next summer, in order to discourage the tourists, Jordan began charging them 50 cents, but the plan backfired. He took in $15 the first day, and "drank real scotch that night."

What the gawkers saw that first summer day in 1960[2] was a unique "Japanese House" replete with "man-sized" fireplaces, hi-fi, an electric oven built into rocks, a bell gallery (minus the bells), and a waterfall decorated with changing colored lights on the patio. The House is the ultimate bachelor pad, though Alex Jordan — a life-long bachelor — never lived there full-time. He did, however, have all-night parties there. Its low ceilings give it a cave-like feeling even though its 14 rooms are 60 feet up. Jordan's biographer notes that "since Alex always appreciated and enjoyed a good fireplace, he built five of them in the original House alone." This was before he decided to build a colossal "world's largest" fireplace in one of the later additions. He just couldn't stop building. By 1962, he'd completed a five-room addition, including the "world's largest" wind chimes. At this point there was no more rock to build on and "the only place to go [was] out into space." It was time to build the Infinity Room.

The original rooms are impressive, luxurious and unique, but far and away the star attraction is the Infinity Room, a man-made mystery spot and bridge to nowhere. Jordan conceived of the Infinity Room in the 40s and produced a design in 1962. When he showed it to his associates, he couldn't convince them it was possible. But 23 years later they were proved wrong; the Infinity Room opened to the public in 1985. Originally, it was to be "cantilevered from the living room out across the island rock observation platform and then 75 feet beyond." The completed room actually extends 218 feet. As you walk along the "infinite" corridor, peering through the 3,264 windows at the valley below, you become subject to an optical illusion, but perhaps, also to mild apprehension. The narrowing room looks as though it goes on forever; if you keep walking to the end, you might discover that you are standing — with 20 other adults — at the point of a slim bough, over a steep cliff. You might just then become a little concerned and dash as fast as you can out of the room to the next attraction, as I did.

The pyramid of circus elephants, accompanied by 50 mannequins dressed in exotic costumes.

The house is an architectural marvel, but the rest of the tour is a relentless excess of marvels. It's fun to see an animated orchestra or a collection of antique dolls or carousel horses. But is it still fun after the 40th animated orchestra, 100th horse and 500th doll? Is it possible to appreciate the world's largest cannon or the world's most complete collection of Bauer and Coble lamps? And what if this amalgamation of "largest" collections were surrounded by dinosaur-sized animated sculptures, 20,000 blinking lights and authentic life-sized replicas of 19th century shops? What do you look at first? How can anyone appreciate it all? What in the blazes are they trying to do to my brain?

Between the moments of disbelief, however, are moments of pure wonder. Some of the excesses of House on the Rock are delightful; its most delightful, for me, are the "greatest collection in the world" of music machines and pipe organs. These mechanical orchestras, organs and music boxes, found throughout the tour, are operated by special House on the Rock tokens. I don't know how many of these automatic orchestras there are, but there are many more than one would think could exist in the entire world — if one were to think of them in the first place. The life-sized orchestras are made up of sometimes 100 mechanical musicians with real instruments, including pianos, harps, cymbals, drums — the works. Each plays one or two songs, usually popular orchestral works such as The Nutcracker Suite or Strauss' Blue Danube. "The Blue Room" contains the world's only mechanically operated symphony orchestra. For those who can't appreciate

2. Some people had already seen parts of the house, beginning in the early 40s. It wasn't officially open to the public until 1960.

classical, there's the Peacock Organ, a "91-key Mortier with percussion, horn and accordion accompaniment" which "features music with a Latin beat, especially the Tango."

The House on the Rock

Each music machine plays in its own maniacal frenzy, amid splendor, blinking lights or gaudy props. "The Blue Room" is authentically furnished with rococo mirrors, chandelier and candelabra; "The Mikado" is surrounded by "Oriental Opulence"; "The Blue Danube" is a simulation of Strauss' "azure and gold" Vienna.

This animated collection contains authentic replicas and new designs, as well as real antiques. Such machines were popular in 19th century Europe, in public gathering places such as hotel lobbies and saloons. Though it appears to the viewer that the instruments are really being played, this is in part, an illusion. Some of the instruments — xylophones, accordions and bells — actually do play, but the strings and woodwinds do not. The house technicians quoted in Jordan's biography point out that "the whole thing is pneumatically done. There are relays, there is a paper roll that drives through a tracker bar, all controlled by vacuum. Each instrument is played with air on a pneumatic system, exactly like that of a player piano." Recently computers were added to control the machines. All the technology is so well-hidden that it in no way hinders the wonder of it all.

Alex Jordan himself designed some of the machines. The ever-popular "Mikado" is a good illustration of his obsession with "The Mysterious Orient." Rather than real Asian music, it plays "Dance Macabre" and "Ritual Fire Dance." "Two life-size Oriental figures, made of papier mâché, are highly animated. One plays an elaborate flute and his cheeks actually puff in and out. The other plays a large kettle drum, and as they both play, their bright eyes scan the room, eyebrows raised, and mustaches bob up and down."

Each machine, no matter how corny, summoned up my long-dormant "childlike sense of wonder." After about 20, however, I didn't think any more could excite me that day. But that was before I experienced the largest carousel in the world.

This attraction would be enough wonder for one day. The souvenir book boasts, "it has taken our artisans more than a decade to plan, construct, and hand-finish the 269 imaginative interpretations of real and mythical creatures that are arranged as many as seven abreast on the deck. It is 80 feet in diameter and 35 feet high — with more than 20 thousand lights illuminating the extraordinary concept. ..." The extraordinary concept is real enough, weighing in at 35 tons, with an estimated value somewhere around $4.5 million.

It is not only the biggest, but possibly the most maniacal carousel in the world. Unfortunately (or fortunately) no living creature is ever allowed to ride this ever-rotating automaton. After the initial shock, you gaze at what are supposed to be carousel horses, and realize that they are not horses at all, but mythical beasts: horse-bunnies, mermaids, centaurs, rooster-maidens, sea unicorns, zebras, a bulldog, frogs, boars, walruses. The carousel is trimmed at the top with 18 "hand-crafted" peacocks.

Such is the carousel itself; but true to the theme of "excess," the carousel isn't the only wonder in the carousel room. Mounted on the ceiling and walls are a collection of Jordan's nearly 1,000 antique carousel horses, arranged in a "stampede." The area behind the carousel is lined with 1,740 feet of mirror. Perhaps strangest of all are the mannequin/angels propped everywhere above, looking somewhat frowzy for angels. Perhaps Jordan bought out a collection of department store mannequins, then crudely clothed them in white sheets and nailed on wings. Along with the wings, their mannequin breasts peek out from behind the white costume which barely covers them.

As we left the Carousel Room, I was sure its unbridled excess was the climactic grand finale of House on the Rock. I didn't realize that there was more ahead: the Circus Room, the Cannon Building, and most curious of all: the Organ Building, Alex Jordan's personal favorite.

The visitor is guided to The Organ Building, originally called "The Inferno Room," through a devil's head, and on through the "Devil's Throat." This is probably the kookiest room in the whole place. It's called "The Organ Room," and as you might expect, it contains the three largest theater organ consoles in the world, not to mention a 45-foot high "Perpetual Motion Clock." The arrangement of all this is less than conventional: "catwalks ingeniously guide you past, through and over astonishing arrangements of customized diesel and hydraulic pumps, heroic sculpture, gigantic clockwork, engaging little shops, a mixed bag of objets d'art — and the component instrumentation of a magnificent organ trio of unparalleled versatility." Another observer noted, "the room is crammed with huge copper vats and bronze fittings that seem like they should join together somewhere, pieces of old and unidentifiable electrical equipment, curved iron walkways and spiral staircases, many inaccessible; that lead nowhere. ... organ pipes are everywhere." Nestled between all this machinery is a collection of huge beer steins as well as a giant propeller that "once helped drive a rare whaleback freighter."

Getting tired yet? Well, you haven't even heard about the Heritage of the Sea Building, with its 200 foot sea creature (longer than the Statue of Liberty is tall) fighting an octopus, over 200 "museum sized" model ships, an enormous collection of scrimshaw and the contents of an entire maritime museum. Or the Circus Building's world's largest collection of miniature circuses comprised of over 1 million pieces, as well as "the most complete collection of Baranger Motions," which, if you didn't already know, are animated jewelry displays. And — oh, yes — the Cannon Building, combining the world's largest cannon, animated doll carousels and a sculpture of the "four horsemen of the apocalypse."

If there is a message in all this material madness, it may well be "too much is never enough." House on the Rock contains probably the largest collection of "largest collections" in the world. Here are some: the largest collection of Bauer and Coble lamps (similar to Tiffany), including the only Bauer and Coble "Mushroom Lamp" in existence; the world's largest fireplace; the world's largest wind chimes; the world's largest carousel; the world's largest organ console; the world's largest cannon; the world's largest collection of miniature circuses; "one of the most complete" collections of Fredric Remington bronzes; "perhaps the grandest" collection of amaryllis in the world; a crown jewel replica collection; an armor collection; immense doll collections; a carousel horse collection.

House on the Rock contains, probably, the largest collection of "largest collections" in the world.

What about Alex Jordan? Was he mad? Independently wealthy? Did he have a deprived childhood? Jordan's official (though sketchy) biography provides answers to most of these questions.

Alex Jordan Jr. (1914-1989) acknowledged that his own theme was excess. He once told the house's sculptor, "all my life it has been the same. If I was going to have a drink, it wasn't going to be just one. If I was down to three packs of cigarettes, I was panicked and had to go into town for seven or eight more. There's never been enough. My whole life I've never been able to get enough of anything." He subscribed to 38 magazines, including, his favorite, *the Pumper,* a trade journal of the sewage disposal industry. For the most part, however, his excessive tendencies seem to have been channelled entirely into the building and embellishing of House on the Rock, as well as furnishing it with grand collections. He himself lived relatively simply, staying in home territory to work on the House. Since he abhorred travel, he bought the immense collections, for the most part, by phone.

Perhaps Jordan's introduction to excess was the Catholic Church, via his devout mother. Church doctrine never really sunk in, though church decor apparently did. His introduction to building was via his father, an architect, whose greatest achievement was a fancy rooming house at the University of Wisconsin called Villa Maria. Aside from the fact that Alex Jr. was artistic and "good with his hands," he had a fairly normal childhood and youth, was handsome and well-built and even played on his high school football team.

Alex Jordan, beautiful dreamer

For some reason, southern Wisconsin was a hotbed of innovative building design around this time. If you visit the area you will no doubt notice and possibly visit the several Frank Lloyd Wright houses just up the road from House on the Rock. Alex Sr. was desperate to show off his Villa Maria plans to the great architect. Finally, Jordan was granted an audience; Wright, known to be arrogant, looked at the plans and said, "I wouldn't hire you to design a cheese case for me, or a chicken coop." Instead of crushing his architectural zeal, the experience stoked it. Alex Sr. planned his revenge, a "Japanese House" that would blow even Frank Lloyd Wright's socks off. House on the Rock, though designed and built by his son, achieved Alex Sr.'s plan for revenge. He is probably gloating — from his grave — since it is far more popular than any of the Wright homes nearby.

Like other artistic souls, Alex Jr. tried his hand at various career paths, and none quite fit. He tried pre-med but dropped out after witnessing an operation. He drove a cab for a while. With a friend, he embarked upon several somewhat shady entrepreneurial schemes: using an infrared camera, they'd take pictures of peoples' houses, and then try to sell them for $2 each to the owners; they developed a solution — made of cement dissolved in water — to stop runs in ladies' stockings, making $50 a day during the Depression. None of these enterprises lasted long.

Jordan never married his life-long companion, Jennie Olson, whom he met in the 30s. He shared his poetry with her, passionate verse — not about love, but about his dream house. In his magnum opus[3] he sings of shelves, books, records and a hi-fi cabinet. His personal ecstasy is — not Jennie — but a bronze statue of an old Hindu, Ali Baba jugs, "Pewter and bronze and hammered brass, old carved wood and gleaming glass, statues and weird candlesticks, aladdin lamps with magic wicks ..." He dreams — not of marriage — but that "one long thin room will hang in space." Just about everything he wrote in the long poem became real, even the absurd room hanging in space.

3. Jordan's poem was based on the poem "What Was Its Name?" written by Don Blanding.

Alex Jordan remained obscure, even after his creation became well-known; that was how he wanted it. He turned away all publicity, including a spot on the *Dick Cavett Show*. He once remarked, "anonymity is my greatest commodity." When *Ripley's Believe It Or Not* television show did a segment on the house, Jordan was nowhere to be found. Probably, he was nearby, incognito, watching the reactions of the House's visitors, as he liked to do. If someone thought they recognized him, he would claim to be the plumber or the electrician.

Alex Jordan Jr. died in 1989, a year after he had finally sold the House on the Rock enterprise, by that time a multi-million dollar corporation with half a million visitors per year. He left over $1 million to his most valued employees. Its current owner continues to carry out Jordan's many future plans for the House, and business is better than ever.

House on the Rock represents madness backed by business success. Every cent that Jordan earned through admissions was reinvested in House on the Rock. One can only speculate on what Jordan's creations would have been like without money, but I suspect the question is meaningless. Jordan would have earned the money one way or another; his dreams depended on it. Since his dreams were purely material, he may be one of the few people who could actually make them come true.

Thanks to Paula J. Phillips, Public Relations/Marketing Director of House on the Rock, for clarifications and corrections.

JAMES HAMPTON'S THRONE

ON A RECENT TRIP TO WASHINGTON, D.C., I visited the National Museum of American Art, hoping to see an exhibit that had astounded me 14 years before. Just inside the entryway to the small museum was a wide corridor, with exhibits on either side. On the right hung a painting with two or three smoothly applied colors arranged like swatches in a hardware store paint display. Occasionally someone would stop to look at this testament to Artistic Progress for a moment or two, but usually that space was empty. On the other side of the corridor stood *The Throne of the Third Heaven of the Nations Millenium General Assembly*. This was the exhibit I'd come for, and I wasn't disappointed. It was as majestically strange as I'd remembered it.

There were none of those minimalist empty spaces in front of the Throne, and sometimes the handful of curious on-lookers grew into a crowd. Its creator had somehow transformed discarded materials — old wooden furniture, foil wrappers from store displays, bottles and cigarette boxes, light bulbs, cardboard, insulation board, desk blotters and transparent plastic sheets — into a glistening byzantine palace. Atop the central object — literally a throne — were the words, "FEAR NOT."

The man who created the Throne, **James Hampton** (1909-1964), was a small, quiet, bespectacled black man who lived and died in complete obscurity. He would be surprised to learn that his work is installed in a National Art Museum rather than a church; he considered himself a saint or messiah, not an artist. Throughout his life Hampton was visited by God and His angels, and he built the Throne at their prompting.

That Hampton's work was saved at all after his death is nothing short of a miracle. Since 1950, Hampton had been renting an unheated garage in a Washington, D.C. slum; this was where he built and housed the Throne, which by his death in 1964, consisted of 180 "glittering objects" arranged symmetrically around the central throne. When Hampton's

sister arrived in Washington to reclaim his body, she saw the Throne for the first time. However impressed she may have been, she wasn't inclined to preserve her dead brother's creation; she didn't have the money. Fortunately, the owner of the garage saved Hampton's work from imminent destruction. He contacted a reporter who wrote an article, alerting the National Collection of Fine Arts to its existence.

Possibly Hampton intended the Throne to be occupied by Jesus when He returned.

Hampton moved to Washington from rural South Carolina while still a teenager, and worked as a janitor for the General Services Administration for most of his adult life. His father had been an itinerant preacher and gospel singer, and Hampton — who died of cancer the age of 54 — was not able to fulfill his dream of becoming a preacher after retirement. Hampton was a loner, and his true calling was the solitary construction of a religious monument, the Throne.

According to Hampton, the design of the Throne was directed by heavenly beings, including Moses, the Virgin Mary and God Himself, who frequently visited the talented janitor. Hampton's notebooks contain records of some of the visitations, which began well before he rented the garage in 1950. One passage reads, "This is true that the great Moses the giver of the tenth commandment appeared in Washington, D.C. April 11, 1931." Another entry describes a visitation that coincided with the Pope's proclamation of the Assumption of the Virgin as Church Dogma: "This design is proof of the Virgin Mary descending into Heaven, November 2, 1950. It is also spoken of by Pope Pius XII."

In addition to supervising work on the Throne, God taught Hampton an intriguing script. A small notebook was found filled with the script; at the bottom of each page, is written, in English, "Revelation," and the author is given as "Saint James." The same script was also found on the objects surrounding the Throne, usually preceded by an English word or phrase, possibly a translation.

On one object, Hampton wrote, "the word millenium means 'the return of Christ and a part of the Kingdom of God on earth.'" Many other objects were labeled with references to the Book of Revelation, chapters 20 and 21, which describe the Resurrection, the Judgment, the New Heaven and the New Earth. We can only speculate, but possibly Hampton intended the Throne to be occupied by Jesus when He returned.

To add weight to this interpretation, the museum curators have found suggestive parallels between the Book of Revelation and Hampton's Throne: In his vision, John had seen God seated on a throne of silver and gold surrounded by a multitude of angels; Hampton's glittering throne of gold and silver foil is itself surrounded by winged objects which clearly suggest angels. Furthermore, God instructed John to record his vision of the Second Coming of Christ in a little book in a cryptic language; Hampton filled a little book with a cryptic language, possibly a record of his own vision.

In addition to the many references to Revelation and the Millenium, the Throne also pays homage to **A. J. Tyler,** a local black minister, very popular until his death in 1936. Portions of the Throne are labeled "Tyler Baptist Church"; Hampton's notebook states that the mysterious "Saint James" is pastor of the "Tyler Baptist Church."

Hampton didn't belong to a formal congregation, but did approach nearby churches to suggest they might install the Throne. Hampton told few people about his project, however; when he did try to publicize it by contacting a local newspaper, he was ridiculed.

Now reporters and art critics alike heap praises on Hampton and the Throne. In 1976, Robert Hughes wrote in *Time* magazine that Hampton's Throne "may well be the finest work of visionary religious art produced by an American."

Hampton probably wouldn't have had much use for public acclaim anyway; he was sustained by his vision. But Hampton created the Throne to share his vision with others. Found on his bulletin board were the words, "Where There Is No Vision The People Perish." James Hampton was more than a mystic. He was a healer.

PART V

OUTTAKES

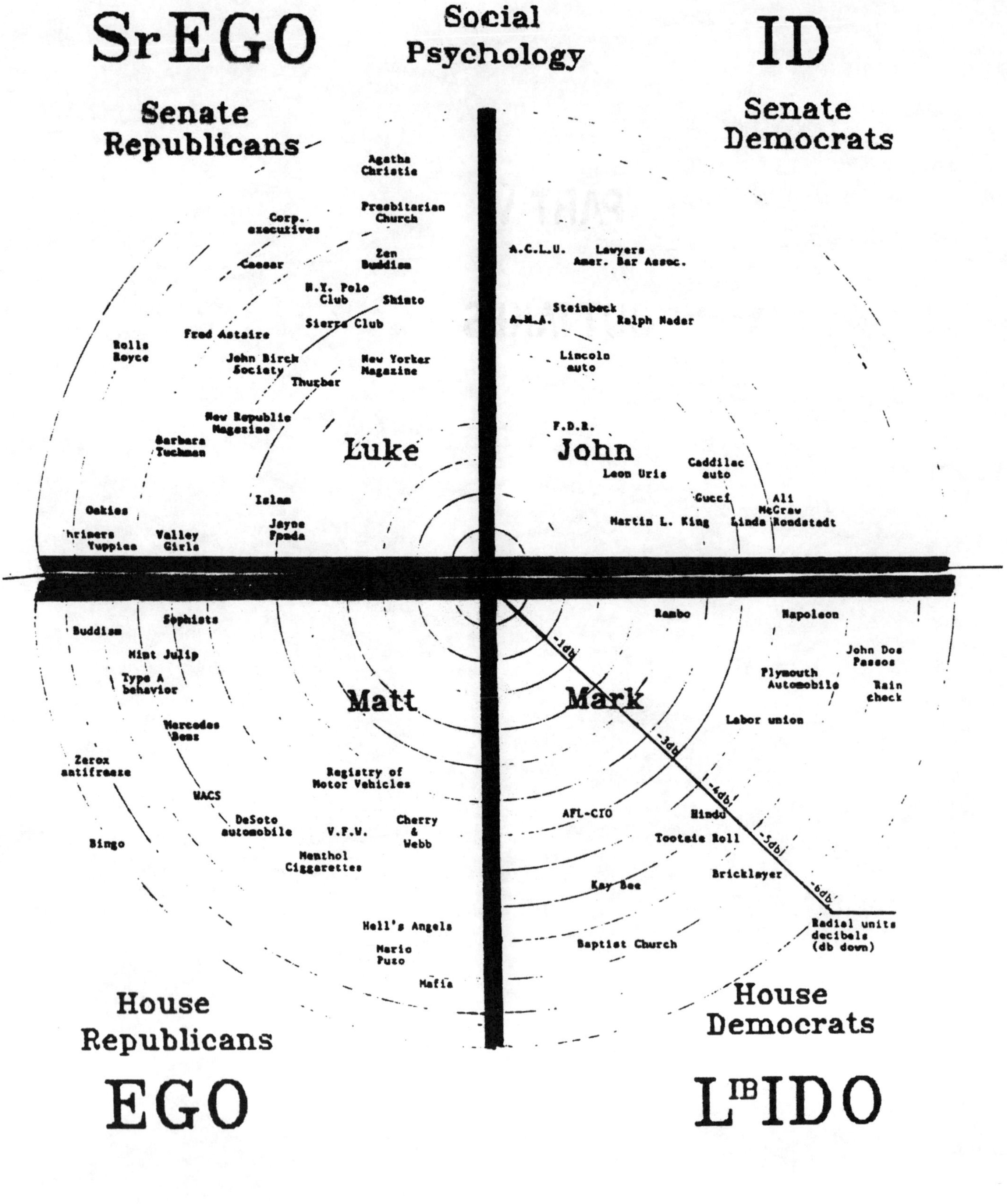
SrEGO
Social Psychology
ID
Senate Republicans
Senate Democrats
Agatha Christie
Presbitarian Church
Corp. executives
Zen Buddism
Caesar
N.Y. Polo Club
Shinto
Sierra Club
Fred Astaire
Rolls Royce
John Birch Society
Thurber
New Yorker Magazine
New Republic Magazine
Barbara Tuchman
Luke
Islam
Okies
Valley Girls
Yuppies
Jayne Fonda
A.C.L.U.
Lawyers Amer. Bar Assoc.
Steinbeck
A.M.A.
Ralph Nader
Lincoln auto
F.D.R.
John
Leon Uris
Caddilac auto
Gucci
Ali McGraw
Martin L. King
Linda Rondstadt
Buddism
Sophists
Mint Julip
Type A behavior
Matt
Mercedes Benz
Zerox antifreeze
WACS
Registry of Motor Vehicles
DeSoto automobile
V.F.W.
Cherry & Webb
Bingo
Menthol Ciggarettes
Hell's Angels
Mario Puzo
Mafia
Rambo
Napoleon
John Dos Passos
Plymouth Automobile
Rain check
Mark
Labor union
-1db
-3db
-4db
-5db
-6db
AFL-CIO
Hindu
Tootsie Roll
Bricklayer
Kay Bee
Baptist Church
Radial units decibels (db down)
House Republicans
House Democrats
EGO
LIBIDO

GEORGE HAMMOND:
THE ORIGIN OF THE CROSS

AFTER STUDYING EINSTEIN'S GENERAL Theory of Relativity for two years as a doctoral candidate in physics, George Hammond admits that he never did "understand a word of it." Twenty years later, Hammond applied that same General Theory of Relativity to life, and attained something far more satisfying than a PhD. He found the "scientific proof of God."

Hammond's treatise, *The Origin of the Cross* (published in 1986), is the culmination of five years of "nearly full time and continuous research" into psychology, physiology, zoology and theology, as well as a deep probing of the Congressional Quarterly. Contained in the treatise is the scientific theory which Hammond believes will revolutionize psychology, neurology, theology and political science; application of the theory could alter the course of human history.

Hammond's hypothesis is that just about everything—human anatomy, the brain, psychology, theology and government—follows the structure of the Cartesian Coordinate System.[1] Hammond's observation that all these seemingly disparate phenomena have the same four-way structure yields fantastic results:

> [T]he Bicameral/Two-Party [political] system is the macroscopic manifestation of the Cartesian structure of psychology . . . the Cross of Christianity is obviously the symbolic representation of the Cartesian Structure of the human mind . . . the Four Gospels of the New Testament are seen to be exactly the historical representations of the four personalities of the Structural Model of Personality in psychology. This theory not only provides a proof of the Bicameral/Two-Party system, it provides a scientific proof of Christianity.[2]

In his fervor to prove his theory, Hammond combines conventional logic and the results of scientific studies with his own lingering schizophrenic trains of thought; in addition to the classical forms of argument he relies heavily on arguments based on appearances and the sounds of words. Hammond's analysis of Freud's "Personality Diagram" is a good example of this:

> . . . the author [Hammond] has shown how the Freudian diagram becomes the Cartesian diagram. What Freud has called Repressed, the author interprets for these purposes, as the "Oppressed," the Libido, (the vast poverty stricken sector of the world, the lower left; Africa, Asia, India, etc., etc.) The small bubble labeled pcpt.-cns. (perceptual-conscious) the author takes to be an eye. On the other side of the diagram is a symmetric open space without an eye. Freud has drawn a "one eyed" diagram. The author interprets this as the fact that he discovered what has only recently been discovered by modern research, that the right brain is predominantly visual. If we complete Freud's diagram by adding the left eye, we have a face and it is the face of a man. The unconscious mind is now seen to lie in the middle, the deepest part of the brain.[3]

The result of this kind of logic is a theory that begins as a model for social psychology, but ends up showing that the DNA molecule contains Heaven and that General Relativity is the mathematical proof of God.

Years before beginning his research, Hammond had left the university and attempted to hold a job in applied physics; instead, he gave up on physics and ended up exploring "the off color side of life," and "bohemian existence to the limit." After some ten years of "sex and drugs and rock 'n' roll," Hammond made one last attempt to resurrect his failed career; he sent out 100 resumés but didn't get even one reply. Hammond subsequently returned to his home town, where he "sank further and further into schizophrenia" and poverty. When Hammond was first committed to the local mental hospital, it was

Hammond made one last attempt to resurrect his failed career; he sent out 100 resumes but didn't get even one reply.

1. Named for René Descartes, its inventor; this is the x-axis and the y-axis from high school algebra.
2. *The Origin of the Cross*, p. 1.

The four center cells form the mollusk's "quadrapartite" brain. Hammond was astounded to learn that "this structure . . . is probably the closest known thing to the scientific origin of the Cross of Christianity!!"

merely "for observation," but two years later he'd been hospitalized three times and was living on both medication and welfare.

It was around this time that Hammond came upon his theory—not as an instantaneous revelation—but gradually:

> This theory came about as a practical matter as a way of identifying which groups of people were antagonistic towards me, which groups were indifferent and which groups were friendly. Just on the grounds of first impressions. For instance if I were a cab driver in a military town, I might find that WAVES were more familiar than WACS, or Corporals liked me more than Sergeants. After a while, of this continued observation and negotiation with people, the thing began to appear as a simple "angle" or geometry. There were basically people above me in class and people below me in class and each class seemed to be divided in half, bad and good. The bads were against me and the goods were for me, up or down. As time progressed I realized that it wasn't bad and good, it was some kind of basic difference. The whole thing was a nearly visible, "X". It was some kind of an up, a down, a left and a right. I seemed to be more in the upper left, and the people that really didn't like me were lower right! I soon came to realize that the left and the right were the political left and the political right, the Democrats and the Republicans. Lower class Republicans definitely don't like me. Upper class Republicans are kind of stand offish but mainly indifferent. Lower class Democrats are friendly but basically indifferent. Upper class Democrats are "my people." [4]

Hammond had heard of Julian Jaynes' Bicameral Mind theory before, but hadn't been interested. Now, he "suddenly grabbed Jaynes' book like it was the answer to my problem." He knew now that "the left and the right was the Bicameral Mind! Between the well known 'class struggle' and the Bicameral Mind, I had found out what 'X' was!"[5] Hammond conjectured that the "left" and the "right" in politics actually correspond to the left and right brains, and, analogously, the Senate and the House correspond to the "upper" and "lower" brain, forming a Bicameral/2-Party political system, or BI/2P for short.

Every day for three months, Hammond rode his bicycle 10 miles to the library, and spent eight hours going over the *Congressional Quarterly* to confirm his hypothesis. He was trying to plot congressional voting on a cartesian graph, but collapsed in the library and was taken to a hospital, a result of overwork and skipping meals. Hammond wisely went on to other matters and, instead of confirming his theory, he expanded it to include Freud's four "personalities," The Four Gospels of the New Testament and the "Four Estates."[6] The resulting correspondences are in the table below.

Hammond wasn't satisfied with mere analysis; he wanted hard evidence for this four-way structure. Proceeding "with baited breath, to the anatomy archives to find out if this could be possible," the budding scientist discovered, among other confirmations of his theory, the so-called "Molluscan Cross," a four-way structure formed at the 128-cell stage in the development of a mollusk. The four center cells form the mollusk's "quadrapartite" brain. Hammond was astounded to learn that "this structure . . . is probably the closest known thing to the scientific origin of the Cross of Christianity!!"[7] Furthermore, he found that "Lo and behold, it turns out that the entire human body is based on Cartesian geometry! From the egg to the adult, the whole thing is Cartesian!"[8]

Hammond points out that the two-way theory of the brain hasn't yielded results anywhere near as amazing as this. In contrast, the four-way theory is what would be termed a "fundamental result," with unexpected consequences:

Quadrant	Freud	Legislature	Gospel	Estate
Upper Right	SuperEgo	Senate Republicans	Luke	Nobility
Upper Left	ID	Senate Democrats	John	Clergy
Lower Right	Ego	House Republicans	Matthew	Military
Lower Left	Libido	House Democrats	Mark	Peasants

3. Ibid., p. 31.
4. Ibid., p. 4.
5. Ibid.
6. Traditionally, the third estate was the "commons" or bourgeoisie, and the fourth estate was the press.
7. *The Origin of the Cross*, p. 8.
8. Ibid., p. 36.

> The first result of the Cartesian theory, is to predict that there is a scientific basis to the Cross of Christianity—startling, spectacular, unexpected! The Cartesian theory proves that the BI/2P system is the only theoretically correct form of government—a scientific proof! . . . Even more intriguing the Cartesian theory says that the legendary Four Gospels of the Bible are the entire scientific theory of Personality structure in psychology. Overwhelming and spectacular results! This theory, it appears, has all the expected earmarks of a fundamental breakthrough.[9]

Armed with a fundamental breakthrough, Hammond is now free to speculate on such "mysteries" as why Social Class is on the vertical axis while Political Party is horizontal. Social Class, he reasons, is simply a result of "height differential" between the upper and lower class; it's a documented fact that the average height in the U.S. Senate is 3.5 inches higher than the norm; and so, by default, Political Party is horizontal. Furthermore, Hammond "would be willing to bet" that a high proportion of Democrats are left-handed; therefore, the BI/2P system is simply "the tall the short the right and the left."

But, ultimately, the positions of the two axes are caused by even more fundamental forces: the vertical influence is gravity, while the horizontal influence is the earth's rotation. And, since the left-right orientation of the earth's rotation is reversed in the Northern and Southern hemispheres, the "rights" originate in the north, while the "lefts" originate in the south. "The BI/2P System then, is the result of terrestrial influences acting on the Cartesian geometry of the human body."[10]

There are other influences as well, first and foremost the basic human desire to raise the standard of living. This drive, Hammond asserts, is actually what Freud called the Libido. Hammond then, rather than consulting a dictionary, applies the psychoanalytical method of free association to analyze the meaning of "Libido":

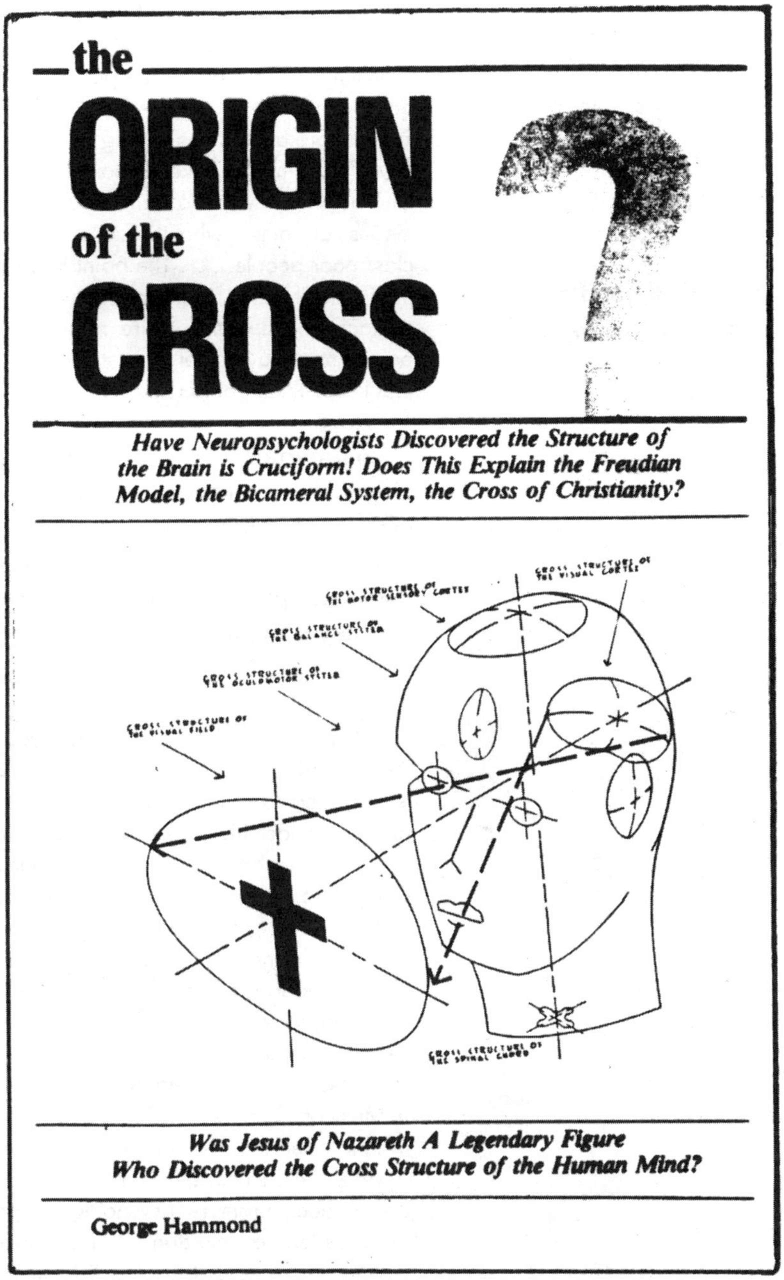

the
ORIGIN
of the
CROSS
Have Neuropsychologists Discovered the Structure of the Brain is Cruciform! Does This Explain the Freudian Model, the Bicameral System, the Cross of Christianity?
Was Jesus of Nazareth A Legendary Figure Who Discovered the Cross Structure of the Human Mind?
George Hammond

9. Ibid., p. 39.
10. Ibid., p. 41.

"I'd like to get to the bottom of who started putting chili on the american hot dog, the guy must be related to the Tylenol killer."

Now if [the Libido is the desire to raise the standard of living] why, one wonders, did Freud come up with the name "Libido" for it? Now I don't believe in looking words up in the dictionary, I think you can tell what every word means just by the sound of it and I'm wondering why he named it the Libido. My interpretation is this, Libido sounds like liberal maybe even limbo. Now liberals are poor people, anybody with money sure isn't a liberal. Furthermore any names ending in o are usually lower class names, like limbo which is some kind of African voodoo dance. So what Libido means, or rather, who they are, is the lower class poor people. . . . The point that I'm making is this, if there is a central motivation in psychology and it is the desire to survive, these people must have a lot of it, it's the only thing that keeps them going. . . .[11]

Continuing on the same theme, Hammond points out that the upper classes sometimes use symbols of the third world, such as Oriental Rugs, to facilitate psychological development; but they shouldn't get carried away with this:

Just saying something like "do you know there are 900 million people starving in China" is supposed to reorient your mind to the "big picture." In fact this is probably where the word Orient comes from. Titles like "Murder on the Orient Express" convey the same message. It doesn't have to be the Orient however. The British constantly rave about India. Even the Beatles had to go to India and pick up a Guru and learn to play the Sitar. Upper middle class people cover their houses with Oriental rugs for instance. Wearing Hawaiian shirts or sporting a Mexican Sombrero will also make you an instant celebrity. The point is, it does help develop the unconscious mind, it gives you status, it does promote psychological development, as long as you don't do it abusively, like putting chili on a hot dog, which must be the most disgusting thing I've ever seen in my life. I'd like to get to the bottom of who started putting chili on the american hot dog, the guy must be related to the Tylenol killer.[12]

For the purposes of Hammond's grand theory, he calls this aspect of Libido the "Albedo," using it to complete the scientific proof of Christianity. To do this, Hammond explains The Trinity, as well as a host of other three-way systems on the Control Theory concepts of Input, Output and Feedback in the table below.

To Hammond, the most important application of Control Theory however, is to Human Progress: Input is the Genetic Code; Output is Human Development; and Feedback is "the law of nature, physics, society, etc." Hammond maintains that when our physical and psychological development finally catches up with our genetic code (in about 5000 years), we will have reached the Kingdom of God. Thus, according to an equation in control theory,[13] as the standard of living approaches infinity, psychological and physical development approaches 100%, or the Kingdom of God. Furthermore, it is "intuitively obvious to even a casual observer that an 'infinite standard of living' is possible."[14] Therefore Hammond has achieved no less than a *scientific* proof that The Kingdom of God is possible.

Hammond uses Control Theory to prove that The Kingdom of God is possible, but he needs no less than the General Theory of Relativity to prove that God actually exists, here and now.

Again, Hammond relies heavily on association, making much of the correspondence between the gravity of physics and the metaphorical gravity of human behavior. Some people are "light on their feet," while others are depressed and "heavy." This psychological *feeling* of gravity is actually due to physical gravity; those who feel gravity less, are those who have a higher degree of physical and psychological development, i.e. whose bodies and minds are closer to the genetic code. Furthermore, those developed people perceive time differently and even age

Control Theory	**Freud**	**Government**	**Trinity**	**Consciousness**
Input	Superego	Executive	Father	Unconscious mind
Output	Ego	Legislative	Son	Conscious mind
Feedback	Id	Judiciary	Holy Ghost	Albedo

11. Ibid., pp. 44–45.
12. Ibid., p. 45.
13. G=A/1+A, where G is the "Gain" and A is the "Amplification" of the system. Hammond never explains the exact relationship between G and A, and Input, Output or Feedback.
14. *The Origin of the Cross*, p. 50.

more slowly than, say, someone who is depressed. This, Hammond points out, is identical to the "Twins Paradox" of Relativity.[15]

. . . Now the fundamental result of relativity is that clocks moving at different speeds, run at different rates. . . . Muons for instance are known to have a lifetime of two microsecs but when observed traveling with a velocity near the speed of light they live for 50 or 60 microsecs. In the human body it is reasonable to believe that there is some kind of fundamental information flow that is perhaps a code, modulating a carrier that is traveling near the speed of light. If the speed of the carrier slows down or speeds up for any reason, it could cause the "clock," the information code, to slow down or speed up. . . . Now it is known that there is a "velocity" time dilation as well as a "gravitational" time dilation and they are identical, so that when this carrier wave slows down it feels like an increase in gravity also. . . .

Now this application of relativity to life, is not as far off and sketchy as we think it is. In fact it is my thesis that its time has come. The scientific proof of God is here, it has arrived, it is at hand. I am convinced that within a matter of months, a few years at the most, it will be confirmed to within a "reasonable scientific certainty," as they say in scientific circles. . . .

I am pretty convinced that Heaven resides in the DNA molecule, in other words, the DNA molecule and the genetic code, already have Eternal Life, and it achieved this the day that it discovered replication (creation). Now the human body is being "created" in the image of the DNA molecule, this is a scientific fact. Now if we are being created in the image of God, the DNA molecule must be God, roughly speaking. Why doesn't the body have Eternal Life? Because it isn't fully developed in accordance with the DNA blueprint, it is only catching up with this blueprint. . . .[16]

Hammond's discussion is beginning to look like the ravings of a college math student on LSD, especially, his final observation that the input is the Universe, the output is Life, and the feedback is God. He discovers from this that despite evidence to the contrary, humanity has a bright future:

In a few decades or less we can assume that the Three Branches of Government and the Bicameral/Two-Party system will be generally accepted as the basic form of government in all nations. An identity with the Trinity and the Cross in religion. The United Nations will probably manifest this form also. An enormous stabilization of world politics will ensue. Drastic (up to 50%, I have heard) cuts will be made in nuclear arsenals. A program of military build-down, in inverse proportion to the standard of living will become the new long range military philosophy.

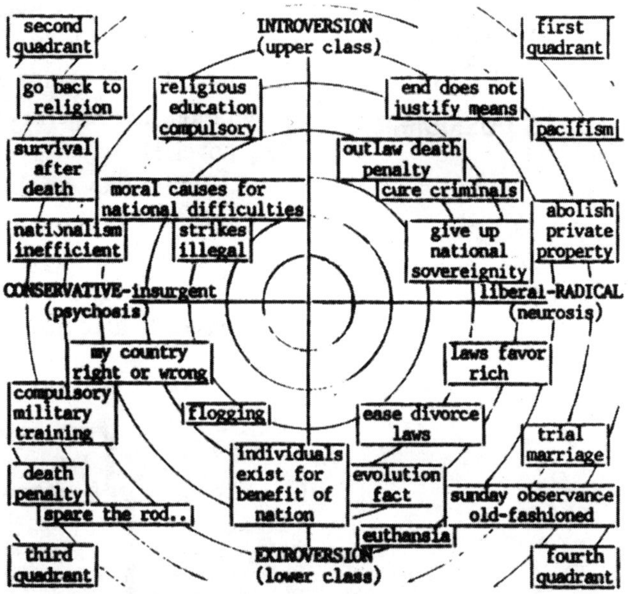

fig. 11 Eysenck's Two-Factor Model (schematic)

. . . The scientific theory of psychology and theology will unify all governments all cultures all languages and all religions. They are all simply embellishments of the same simple structure, the Cross. . . . The unity of mankind is achieved in the scientifically proven form of universal government. . . .

A universal language can be expected to be achieved within 500 to a thousand years and poverty eliminated before that. Genetic control of all diseases and illnesses within 1000 to 2000 years. Within 3000 years the aging process will no longer be considered a problem. By the year 6,000 food clothing and shelter will be as free as the air we breathe. By the year 7,000 every living person will be God.[17]

Though Hammond's wild leaps from control theory and physics into mysticism are not liable to convince any physicists, his observations and correspondences are thought-provoking. We tend to take the structures of our institutions (such as the legislature), our social classes and our symbols (such as the cross) for granted, and seldom ask if they might be otherwise. Hammond does ask interesting questions even though he does seem to know the answers prior to conducting any research. And some of his observations are in line with the observations of others.

15. The Twins Paradox predicts that if one twin were to travel in a rocket close to the speed of light for, say, 20 years, when he came back, the twin who remained on Earth would have aged more quickly than the traveling twin.
16. *The Origin of the Cross*, pp. 55–56.
17. Ibid., p. 65.

His identification of the cross as a basic symbol—though Hammond doesn't seem to know this—is in agreement with the psychological observations of Jung. Jung also identified *four* psychological "functions": feeling, thinking, sensation and intuition. Furthermore, Hammond's application of abstruse scientific fields like control theory, to anything and everything, may not yield any hard scientific data, but it does make one think. Clearly, without such conjectures and wild hypotheses, there would be no exploration, no experiments and no new discoveries.

Hammond has achieved no less than a scientific proof that The Kingdom of God is possible.

While they might not be important to science, Hammond's "discoveries" are all-important to Hammond. In fact, as he reports in *The Origin of the Cross*, they basically give meaning and value to a life which, until he made them, was awash in depression and failure. While struggling with severe personal problems, Hammond was able to forge a meaningful connection between God, Society, and his own psyche; for this, he deserves our admiration.

Bibliography

Hammond, George. *The Origin of the Cross.* Hyannis, MA: Hammond Psychology Publishing, 1988.

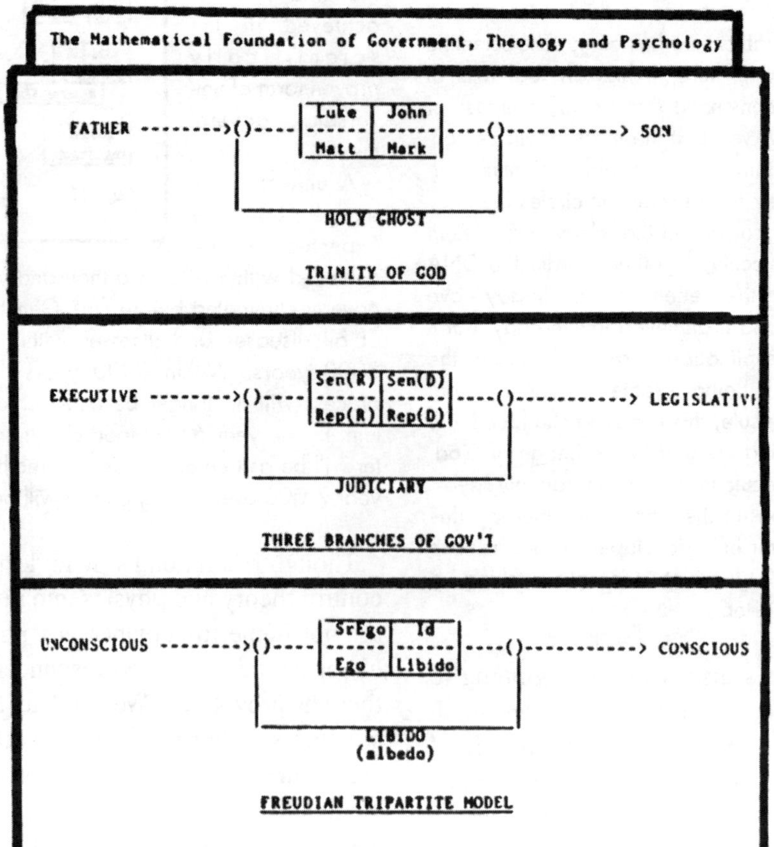

[The Freudian Model]

fig. 18 **Schematic diagram of the relation of the Trinary Model of Behaviorism and the Cartesian Model of Personality Structure- in Theology, Government and Psychology.**

MAXINE SUTTON PETERS
QUEEN OF PEACE

May 22, 1973

The Honorable Richard M. Nixon
President
The United States of America
Washington, D.C.

Dear Mr. Nixon:

This is the fourth time I have been thrown into St. Elizabeths Hospital because of my attempts to see you regarding the fact that I have not been credited for my work. That you used my Foundation's work as well as took the credit for my World Peace Strategy without the decency of saying thank you.

I am now thoroughly convinced that you don't intend to credit me because you represent the white power structure which is the real white racist lie, the United States of America. Therefore, I deem it necessary to express myself in this letter as I see fit.

I am convinced beyond a shadow of a doubt that the Whiteman is the devil and everything he stands for is a lie. His bureaucratic constituents are all neurotic because they too are advocates of his lie. It is no wonder they are retarded.

"It is now possible to control an area the size of California by the flick of a switch."

You and others knew before I did that I was the Brown Baby, the human robot secretly used as a sacrifice since birth, 33 years of my life, to test the truth of the Holy Bible and the Islamic religion (the Holy Koran) practiced in the United States.

Now that I have been brought out of the hypnosis I have been under the past 33 years, I wish to say that I am shocked to no end that the United States of America could stoop to such a low degrading act as to purposely engineer a persons life secretly against him to see how much pain he can endure, then program him under hypnosis with the answers to the study.

I happen to be the blood line Great Grand Daughter of Frederick Douglas and the Great Great Grand Daughter of King Kamalmal of the Hawaiian Islands. I received the key to Hawaii from my people when the USA programmed me there in February 1970. Also, I am the Grand Secretary of the Eastern Stars for the State of Florida. As the Queen of Peace, I am the highest ranking military commander in the world.

During this revolution I am declaring this nation a state of emergency under marshal law. The United States of America has secretly programmed its people and the world on computer by use of a laser beam which is wireless harnessed energy. Electrical Stimulation of the Brain (ESB). It is now possible to control an area the size of California by the flick of a switch. If this monster decided to use it vindictively to kill all the people it could do this too. The TRUTH is that the United States of America is witchcraft and voo doo by machine, meant to do harm.

I witnessed the area of Anacostia as far over as D.C. General Hospital immobilized in broad day light. The whole area looked like a ghost town. Not a soul was in sight except a few cars which I assumed was Secret Service. This was all a part of the Eastern Star Initiation, pure insanity.

In San Antonio, Texas, I witnessed true witchcraft, voo doo and hypnotic warfare, I was the victim. I had to use every wit imaginable to survive. I realize now that I was not suppose to return alive. The TRUTH again is that man can be instantly killed by the glance of the eyes and certain words used in different voice ranges.

It is frightening to know the TRUTH about what is happening to the people and they are unaware. If I had died then so would humanity because no one would have known what hit them, these things have been done to them secretly. I try not think about the danger we are in because it is my responsibility now to lead the people to safety. I was not given a choice in the beginning, I was chosen. This whole madness is just as much shock to me as it is the nation. It caught me totally by surprise.

"Your stubbornness is jeopardizing the lives of the people. Instead of you making this situation any easier for me, you have added to my suffering by having me locked up in St. Elizabeths Hospital, trying your damnedest to have me permanently committed."

I realize what a great responsibility I have been given, the weight of the world on my shoulders. It has been just God and me alone and the prayers of the people who are aware of my plight.

I charge the United States of America with practicing genocide on the human race. Some of these atrocities are secretly programming humans by computer towards their destruction, as I have mentioned; secretly using humans in illegal research studies designed for death; keeping slavery secret during modern times by creating test tube babies of all races and programming them on innocent unsuspecting females, creating the breakdown in family structure; agressing nations through war under the pretense of alerts (namely Vietnam) e.g. October 1963, Department of the Army Staff Study, Operation Big Lift engineered by the administration and all lies to the people up to this date of 397 years.

In lieu of the aforementioned facts, I found it necessary to claim my Asian-Black blood and call this revolution. You received my telegram on February 7, 1973, claiming the Nation of Islam. In behalf of my flag which is red, black and green, representing the blood lines of the World, (ABO) I reclaim this land the *Nation of Islam* for the people.

Now, I ask you Mr. Nixon, how you intend to restore the faith of the indians and the black people of this world in the United States of America. Your stubbornness is jeopardizing the lives of the people. Instead of you making this situation any easier for me, you have added to my suffering by having me locked up in St. Elizabeths Hospital, trying your damnedest to have me permanently committed. You have had full knowledge of me since January 12, 1973, when I personally hand carried you a three hour tape which I recorded on the TRUTH. You are also aware of the fact that I am only receiving a mere $61.00 per week unemployment while going through this hell and you would have the unmitigated gall of causing this to be cut off.

I will close by saying that this is a hell of a price to pay for my freedom and the freedom of the people. Further, it is painful to know that my father, a kindly subtle gentleman and of royal blood, was beaten to a pulp for 68 years of his life, so poor that he had to work two jobs all of my life to survive. Not only this, but the fact that he is retired after 29 years of Government service only receiving a meager $280.00 per month that he and my mother must exist on when he is the natural heir to a throne that the USA literally stole from him.

I am asking you to resign or be impeached, your seat rightfully belongs to me.

Sincerely,

Maxine Sutton Peters
AMARALAKEEM
Queen of Peace
(TRUTH)
GOD

RUTH LEEDY
HOLLOW EARTH ACTIVIST

To Ruth Leedy whether or not the earth is hollow isn't an exercise in armchair geography, it's a matter of life and death for the entire human race. Leedy believes, not only that the earth is hollow, but also that it is about to undergo a cataclysm caused by a reverse in the magnetic poles-engineered by UFO forces inside the earth-and that this knowledge is being covered up by the scientific community. To support these allegations, Leedy doesn't depend on revelations from God or channeled messages from the Space Brothers. No, Ruth Leedy is more sophisticated than that. She bases her arguments on hard, scientific data: information and photos culled from popular books such as *The Jupiter Effect*, periodicals such as *Scientific American* and works by Isaac Asimov, as well as more technical sources.

Describing herself as a "trained journalist," Leedy has been persistently doing research and printing a newsletter on a small scale for "many years," building "the case in a way that [is] both logical and supported by the facts." She is very careful, and proud of the fact that she doesn't "drag in irrelevant material about cave dwellers and subterranean passageways," instead focusing "on the *large* abyss within the planet, and what will happen when that abyss, with polar openings, reforms itself during a shift in the axis . . ."[1]

Possessing an unusual cognizance of her own fringe status, Ms. Leedy acknowledges that the ideas that she promotes are not likely to be accepted by the scientific community. She is also able to look critically not only at the "crackpot" literature from which she borrows ideas, but also at her own beliefs:

> . . . I can look at the writings of Velikovsky, Raymond Bernard and Marshall Gardner and see elements of the crackpot in what they've written. There will be unsubstantiated statements, or allegations that cannot be proven one way or the other, logical non sequiturs and various kinds of errors. And yet each of them has at some time or another said something that struck me as brilliant and valuable. It is up to the reader to wade through the murky waters of crackpot literature, if he or she dares to do so, and try to separate the useless and dangerous ideas from those that could have some value. Many of us are afraid to try this—afraid our minds will be contaminated in the process. I admit I had this fear as I first set out to read Raymond Bernard's book *The Hollow Earth*. And it did take me a while to sort out what he had said, so that for a while I may have accepted some ideas or arguments that later seemed foolish to me. . . .[2]

Though her arguments are rational, she admits that her inspiration is from prophecy, which by itself proves nothing:

> . . . One reason I've stuck with this is that I've seen clear indications in the prophecies of Christ, Nostradamus and Edgar Cayce, and in various religious myths that when a cataclysm is described, the hollow earth concept is included. The light that appears in the clouds when the heavens shift or when the poles shift (which is the same thing) is the light of the earth's central sun shining through newly created polar openings. An axis in northern Europe, for example, causes polar openings to be formed by centrifugal force in that region, while the present openings would be filled in. Cayce specifically said there would be upheavals in the Arctic and Antarctic immediately prior to the shifting of the poles.
>
> . . . I have tried to document everything I've said from scientific sources. The prophecy, however, tends to inspire me even though I know it doesn't prove anything. It tells me where to look for the truth, and time and time again I have found it there.[3]

Ruth Leedy finds truth in prophecy, but her intended audience finds truth in hard, scientific data. Like many UFO investigators, Leedy is not a scientist, and doesn't

1. Ruth Leedy, personal letter, 8/19/91.
2. Ruth Leedy, personal letter, 3/10/93.
3. Ibid.

The New Abyss

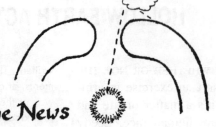

Hollow Earth End-Time News

No. 2 Pub. by Ruth A. Leedy, RD 3 Box 240-B, Dover, DE 19901 July-Aug. 1991

ASTOUNDING PROOF THAT MARS IS HOLLOW

Sun Angle Proves Polar Cap Lighted From Inside Planet

Book Shows Mt. Olympus Near Equator, Gives Maps And Grid Needed to Figure Sun Angle on Side of Mars

Many books show photographs of Mars with a polar cap that is unbelievably bright. The Aug. 4, 1969 photo by Mariner 7 is among the most dramatic of these.

For nine years I have labored to prove that the polar cap in the Aug. 4 photo must be lighted from within the planet. But until now I had no convincing way of determining the exact latitude the sun was striking.

This information is provided in Space Science and Astronomy, edited by Thornton Page and Lou Williams Page. We find the Aug. 4 photo on p. 193, with these words:

"Nix Olympica (later renamed 'Olympus Mons') is the white circle 3/4 in. toward upper left from center."

Now this is a valuable clue. In fact, the planet has been tilted so that Olympus Mons is at a 45 degree angle from the center point, so that when you go 3/4 inch toward upper left (45 degrees) you will find Olympus Mons exactly there.

There was no such tilting of the picture as seen in Patrick Moore's Guide to Mars. There the south pole was at the bottom of the picture.

What does this tell us? It gives us a way of finding the equator and also the exact angle at which the sun is striking the side of the planet.

What is the latitude of Olympus Mons on the planet Mars? From maps on pp. 189 and 199 and an accompanying table we learn that it is located at 21 degrees latitude, 132 degrees longitude.

Turning to a large version of the photograph as shown in Patrick Moore's Guide to Mars, we now find the white circle in the lower middle portion of the picture. How can we proceed to find the equator, and the angle of the sun's light on the side of the planet?

Since the planet is tilted forward,

Long Distance Earth Photos Show Lighted Polar Cap

FIG. 73. Mars from Mariner 7 at 293,200 mi. distance, on Aug. 4, 1969, at 10:28 UT with longitude 115° centered. Nix Olympica (later renamed "Olympus Mons") is the white circle ¾ in. toward upper left from center. Bright south-polar cap at bottom. (JPL-NASA photo.)

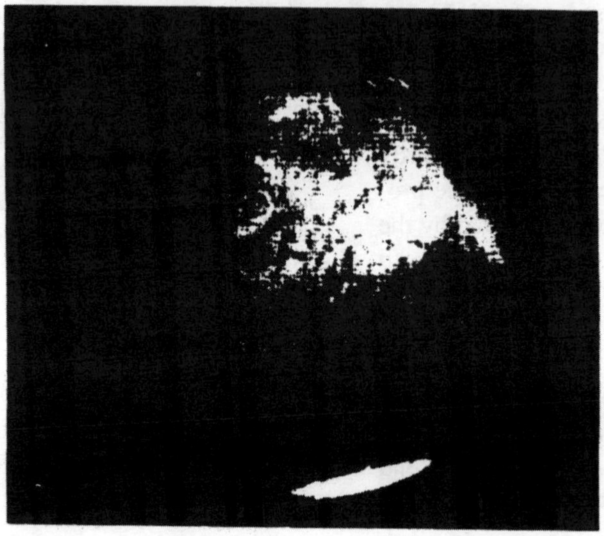

Also: Polar Shift Summary

actually conduct any scientific experiments of her own. The only data she has access to appears in the popular scientific press, amounting to photographs and "hints" from scientists and their representatives.

Leedy's favorite illustrations are ultraviolet photos of the Earth, as seen from Apollo 16. They show light at the poles which look a lot like polar openings illuminated by a central sun—to someone who wants to see them. The official explanation for the light is the *aurora borealis*. Leedy's rebuttal to this is that in time exposure photographs such as these, "the aurora should look even more blurry and indistinct since it is caused by high speed particles striking the atmosphere." In fact, these pictures, available to anyone who wishes to see them, "show just what a polar opening should look like with the central planetary sun shining through it."[4]

Leedy seems to be aware that in themselves, these pictures, which are so "illuminating" to her, probably don't convince the natural skeptic, such as myself. All she can really hope for, is to plant seeds of doubt in peoples' minds, so that they might do a little digging themselves. She provides her readers with a photo of Mars which, at first, had even me wondering.

Taken from Mariner 7 in 1969, this photo shows a very distinct bright polar "cap" on Mars. This bright cap is ostensibly due to large areas of polar ice, which reflect light very well. But, as Leedy points out, to reflect light, the ice must have light shining onto it, and the only possible light source is the sun. But in this photo, it doesn't look as if the sun is shining from an angle which could illuminate the cap. "Looking as if" isn't good enough for Leedy, however; for years she had been laboring to prove that the sun in the photo is shining from an angle that couldn't illuminate the cap; she finally achieved this, with help from an Astronomy text with a map of Mars. She actually calculated the angle from which the sun was shining, based on the lit up areas on the rest of the planet in the photo, and, sure enough, says Leedy, at that angle, the polar region should remain dark. Leedy concludes that the reason that the "cap" is illuminated is because it's not really an ice cap at all, but a polar opening with Mars' central sun shining through.[5]

Leedy might have been able to avoid all of her many years of work, if she had only realized that Mars has an atmosphere. The gases surrounding the planet are thick enough to refract the sunlight, and to thus illuminate the ice cap.[6] She might also have asked a few more questions about the photo before reaching her conclusion, but one suspects that Ms. Leedy is not seeking answers, because she knows them already.

Because she was able to extract such a calculation from an astronomy text—the very text which contained the Mars photo, as well as the Earth photos—Leedy concludes that the authors of the book know that the Earth and Mars are hollow, but are not at liberty to impart this information to the public. So they are providing clues for observant readers, such as Ms. Leedy, to figure it out for themselves.

Scientists provide more than just clues on the subject of magnetic pole reversal as well as a host of other possible catastrophes. In one issue of her newsletter, Leedy cites a number of sources which discuss the observed weakening of the magnetic field and that this may eventually cause a magnetic pole reversal. The scientists in question usually forecast such events millennia in the future. But Leedy's analysis of the statements by Asimov, Kenneth A. Hoffman, and others shows that the catastrophe could occur during the next few decades:

> Isaac Asimov included the field reversal in his book *A Choice of Catastrophes*. He said that if present rates of decline were to continue, the field would die out completely by the year 4000. . . .
>
> Hoffman . . . said that at the present rate of decline the field would vanish completely in 1500 years, not 2000 as Asimov had written . . .
>
> Hoffman stated that physics provides two processes that could account for the weakening of the field—flux diffusions which acts slowly,

Leedy concludes that the reason that the "cap" is illuminated is because it's not really an ice cap at all, but a polar opening with Mars' central sun shining through.

4. Ruth Leedy, personal letter, 8/19/91.
5. *The New Abyss: Hollow Earth End-Time News #2*, July/August '91.
6. Thanks to Walter Minkel for pointing this out.

The UFO forces, it seems, are deadly serious about keeping the impending cataclysm, as well as the hollow earth, secret.

and frozen-in flux which acts quickly. He wrote:

". . . Based on observations of the present-day field, frozen-in flux appears to dominate short-term changes- changes that occur over a period of a few decades." . . .

. . . [T]here could be an increase in the magnetic field's rate of decline. . . . Though it may cause a gradual heat increase to begin with, it can lead to dramatic increases farther down the line. . . .[7]

The fact that scientists and writers such as Asimov say a catastrophe *may happen*, is enough evidence for Leedy to conclude that it *will happen*, and soon. The unanswered questions—"SCIENCE CANNOT EXPLAIN HOW RADIOACTIVITY BUILDUP FAILS TO CAUSE COMPLETE MELTING IN MANTLE" and "SCIENCE CANNOT EXPLAIN WHAT HOLDS AXIS STEADY AS ROTATION SPEED CHANGES"—leave an explanatory vacuum, which isn't left empty for long:

> This analysis of polar shifting shows it as a gradual, predictable process, necessary to the cooling of radioactive materials in the mantle.
>
> . . . Walter Sullivan states (p. 93):
>
> "Over the past 2500 years the total field of the earth has weakened by about 50 percent. This may be a prelude to a new reversal within a few centuries."
>
> If the field was declining in the time of Christ, and he was in touch with UFO experts who could predict a field reversal, then we can understand how he could predict a cataclysm for a future generation.[8]

That future generation is us. Leedy goes on:

> Jesus evidently thought we needed to be notified that a cataclysm was coming. How could he know that future scientists would not tell us? Perhaps because he knew UFO forces would apply pressure to keep them silent. Perhaps he knew the UFO forces quite well, since the seemingly magical powers he displayed were similar to those shown by UFOs today. . . .[9]

Beginning her line of argument with quotes from scientists and Isaac Asimov, and using quotes from speculative books such as *The Jupiter Effect* along the way, Leedy typically ends up with quotes from prophecy, abandoning all previous efforts to stick with the evidence. She doesn't seem to realize that all the evidence in the world isn't going to convince scientists of anything if it's pieced together with speculation and prophecy.

When the experts comment on catastrophe, even man-made cataclysms such as overpopulation or global warming, Leedy interprets these speculations as veiled comments about the pole shift. Asimov apparently leads the pack in "hollow earth figures of speech." When he is speculating about space travelers "hollowing out the asteroids," or living in the "inside world" of a spaceship, he is really hinting about the hollow earth. Leedy the muckraker observes: ". . . in Sept. 1980 Asimov was quoted in *The Mother Earth News* as predicting the end of civilization as we know it by the year 2010. He also spoke of 'hollowing out the mini-planets' (asteroids) and compared our planet to the hull of a spaceship. Many other hints of hollow earth and cataclysm have come from him."[10]

Knowing that people might be more inclined to believe Isaac Asimov than Ruth Leedy, Leedy tried to publicize Asimov's veiled warnings, but the plan backfired:

> In early April 1992 I did a mailing to over 100 newspapers and members of Congress in which the headline "Guarded Warnings: Asimov" appeared on the front page of my newsletter about a coming polar shift. Several days later Asimov's death was reported. Natural causes were cited, but it seemed his death could have been timed to prevent his responding to the allegations I had made.[11]

The UFO forces, it seems, are deadly serious about keeping the impending cataclysm, as well as the hollow earth, secret. The reason they don't want us to know is that we have something that they want:

> If we knew the earth is hollow, we would know that the solar wind must be defining the axis and that therefore a new axis will come

7. *The New Abyss: Hollow Earth End-Time News #2.*
8. Ibid.
9. Ibid.
10. Ibid.
11. Ruth Leedy, "Civilization to Die: Asimov."

about when the solar wind begins striking the new magnetic poles that will form in the coming decades. We would understand that a new axis would mean a violent reshaping of polar openings—a cataclysm.

If we knew that, we would understand the need to prepare—to relocate large populations in lands that will vanish or be covered with ice. We would take steps to save our society.

. . . The polar openings will begin reforming, throwing dust and ocean water into the air and setting off seismic activity worldwide. Panic will set in, sparking wars for safe territory.

UFOs will descend, offering rescue to the righteous (This promise is commonly found in UFO prophecies of world disaster.) They will have their harvest of blood and hormones and whatever they need to help sustain their existence beyond the paltry life span that nature has to offer.[12]

The whole story may be even worse than that. Leedy goes on to speculate that not only will the UFO forces "reap a harvest of human blood under the guise of grand rescue mission," but that they have actually engineered the pole shift for this purpose. True to form, Leedy backs up her speculations with quotes from "experts."

. . . What could be more diabolical, more utterly evil, than to take hold of the very axis of the earth and shake it and thus shake and shatter the lives of countless humans and other living things? Of course no one could literally shake the axis. But in the grandeur of their self-imagined greatness they could aspire to do the next best thing. They could arrange for natural forces to shift the axis ahead of the scheduled time. . . .

. . . The earth, like any smaller nuclear reactor, can be made to heat up more quickly by raising the temperature of the radioactive materials. This heat increase accelerates the destruction of the magnetic field to the point where new magnetic poles will arise in reversed position, redirecting the solar wind to two new target points and thus shifting the axis.

. . . [An article in *Scientific American*, 5/88] pinpoints certain "hot spots" in the southern hemisphere where small, reversed fields are already in existence, growing stronger and moving southward. An expert is cited as believing this "is the process that eventually reverses the earth's field."

And if UFO forces knew of these hot spots which triggered a field reversal, could they not take steps to step up heat production in those spots?

In fact, if this were possible, and could guarantee a rich harvest for their society, might it not become for them a social and political necessity? To us it is a diabolical scheme. To them it is just a necessary expedient, a fact of life. . . .[13]

To Leedy and her co-publisher M.L. Lawrence, the UFO forces' elaborate schemes to obtain blood and hormones takes many forms. In addition to their plot to cause a global catastrophe (as if we needed help in this department!) they are also attempting to control individuals through electronic devices implanted near their brains, accomplishing this via UFO abductions, phony child "finder" programs, and even through the "programming" of yuppies:

There is a new breed of human species wandering the surface of this planet. They are not strange looking entities, but have all the normal limbs and internal organs humans have had for eons. They are people between the ages of 28 and 38 more commonly known as yuppies, or as I call them, "Programmed People." This may sound amusing at first, but it is a very serious subject, as you will soon learn.

This generation developed with computers dominating every facet of their childhood, from simple hand held computer games to computer dating. Computers also dominate their adult lives with the use of home computers to balance checkbooks to computers that regulate the stock market. . . . As far as yuppies are concerned, "If it is not in the computer, it does not exist." This is a very dangerous way of thinking.

Anyone who is dependent upon computer programming to run their life is an easy candidate to be themselves programmed. . . .

. . . In 1988 there was a TV commercial about implanted electronic chips that would interact directly with the brain. On Jan. 19, 1990 a plan was announced on national news to implant children and pets for the sake of a national "finder" program. This is an excellent scare tactic to pressure parents into believing that implanting their children will ensure a safe return should they become missing. Keep in mind that parents of young children are in the 28 to 38 age bracket and everything involving electronics is acceptable to them. The children... are completely unaware that someday, probably in the very near future, they will be

"Anyone who is dependent upon computer programming to run their life is an easy candidate to be themselves programmed. . . ."

12. "UFOs Fear Our Knowledge," *The New Abyss: Hollow Earth End-Time News #5*, 2/3/92.
13. "ENGINEERING AN AXIS CHANGE," Ibid.

"We feel the public is entitled to know the relationship between the magnetic field and the axis NOW . . . We want these facts stated plainly and fully so that every citizen knows how the axis and magnetic poles are related, and how a process now under way could shift the location of both. . . ."

contacted via "implants that interact with their brain" to perform some hideous task or to surrender to a so-called higher intelligence.

All people who have been abducted by the occupants of . . . UFOs, have had electronic devices implanted somewhere in their body, usually near the brain. The reason for this is to find and control them at some later date for whatever purpose the abductors deem necessary. . . .[14]

Even though our enemies are powerful enough to ruin our lives and our world without our even knowing about it, Ruth Leedy sees hope for mankind, which is why she persists in her crusade:

. . . If society as a whole were to see a polar shift coming and this were publicly admitted by the experts, I think you would see many preparations undertaken. Coastal peoples would be relocated inland. Homes would be reinforced. Food would be stockpiled. Trees would be planted to hold the topsoil.[15]

In addition to the newsletter, Leedy now also circulates something called the "Polar Shift Manifesto," demanding a "clear public examination" of the magnetic reversal, the principles of the earth's rotation and how the rotation would be affected by changes in the magnetic field:

We feel the public is entitled to know the relationship between the magnetic field and the axis NOW. . . We want these facts stated plainly and fully so that every citizen knows how the axis and magnetic poles are related, and how a process now under way could shift the location of both. . . .

Leedy suggests that concerned citizens collect signatures on the document and then send it to their senators and congressmen. Though it's probably not possible to thwart the cataclysm itself, we can probably save ourselves through an all-out nationwide effort, coupled with a hollow earth/pole shift educational campaign.

Leedy may be on to something; we always respond more quickly to an enemy or a natural disaster than to destruction brought on by our own stupidity. Be that as it may, no one is likely to take her one-woman campaign very seriously. But this doesn't stop Ruth Leedy, who has Edgar Cayce, Nostradamus and Jesus Christ on her side, and maybe even Isaac Asimov.

14. "Have You Been Implanted?: The Programming of America" by M.L. Lawrence, Ibid.
15. Personal letter, 3/10/93.

MYSTERY WRITERS

PART I: BOSTON

MY FIRST FEW YEARS IN BOSTON WERE greatly enhanced by the efforts of someone we came to know as the "Mystery Writer." There were those who claimed to have seen him while in the act of writing his messages-on traffic signal boxes, lamp-post bases, boarded-up storefronts and plywood construction barriers—but these reports were not consistent. Some said he was a small, dark, Italian-looking man, and others said he was tall and blond. Up until the time we noticed that there were no new messages, the identity of the Boston Mystery Writer remained a secret.

The first issue of *Kooks Magazine* featured a report on the Boston Mystery Writer, by Nenslo, who had devotedly recorded all of the messages he possibly could, either in a little notebook, or by photograph. I too, began to record the messages and soon found myself taking special excursions into parts of the city that were likely to contain new ones. After several years, I considered the process of finding new messages while watching the old ones either fade away or disappear altogether, to be an inherent part of living in Boston. When I began to notice that there hadn't been any new messages for six months or so, I reluctantly concluded that our beloved Mystery Writer had gone away. Sadly, I realized that he had either been institutionalized, was very ill, or had died.

In his report, Nenslo had expressed a special feeling for the Mystery Writer's messages, which to most, were just plain baffling:

> . . . These messages, written in black or green magic marker, reveal unexpected perception of connections between apparently unrelated events and objects. The Boston police, The District Attorney, public health and various universities form a strange web, warped and altered by world events and the private experiences of the writer. The style is naggingly familiar, like the dedicatedly declaratory style of Dr. Bronner and All-One-God-Faith, or Brainbeau's World War Two Jeep Accident Head Injury. The writer has a message and is compelled to transmit it; yet the message itself never seems to make it through. We are left with a sense of a vast form of which but a few small tentacles creep into the light.
>
> I have seen for myself that people do stop in the street to read the messages, and wander off baffled and occasionally stunned. The Mystery Writer's true gift is a new and strange type of confusion which reflects the puzzling complexity and inter-relatedness of our world.
>
> After reading and recording so many of these declarations, however, I have begun to feel the forces moving behind daily events. I have come to comprehend the pattern of these utterances and can unhesitatingly state that they are all true. I present them now in the hope that you, too, will join me in this perception.

After Nenslo's report appeared in *Kooks #1*, I included a special feature in subsequent issues of *Kooks*, entitled "Mystery Corner," which was simply a record of the latest messages from the Mystery Writer. Below, I've reprinted what I consider to be the most interesting among all the messages:

BOSTON UNIVERSITY IS PROBing THIS PAPER'S SOURCES OF NEWSPRINT

PERSONS WITH AN ARGENTINA INCOME USE OLD SOUTH CHURCH TO WASTE THE TIME OF JEWISH BLACK-SMITH BANKERS.

LIVING QUARTERS is a home THE QUARTER-MASTER SUPERVISES THE SHIP'S WHEELHOUSE A QUARTER TO NINE is either a light 0845 or a dark 2045 p.m.

120 LANDLORD'S BEEN A PAP SMEAR TROUBLEMAKER SINCE 1974.

RUSSIANS WHO SPEAK FLUENT AMERICAN ENGLISH ALSO SPEAK FLUENT CHICAGO POLISH. THOSE RUSSIANS ARE DOING INDUSTRIAL ESPIONAGE IN THE USA

WATER WAS FLOWING IN THE FOUNTAINS OF ZURICH, SWITZERLAND DURING THE WINTER OF 1968 TO REMOVE DISEASES FROM FAUCET WATER.

BOSTON UNIVERSITY IS NOT FOR MY PONY! FROG POOL; MY ANCESTORS DIDN'T POISON A SINGLE FLY!

POLSKA PRINTED TWO POSTAGE STAMP COPYs OF MOTHERHOOD BY Stanislaw Wyspianski. HE ALSO DID STAINED GLASS ART. MOST OF HIS BRIEF LIFE WAS LIVED NEAR KRAKOW, POLSKA. WYSPIANSKI WROTE DRAMA ABOUT MARRIAGE BEFORE HE LOST AN ARM.

QUINCY BRANCH OF THE BAY BANK GAVE INTEREST & A QUICK LIST OF BOSTON SECURITY GUARDS "FRIENDLY" TO HIS M.O.

THE CRIMINAL FROM LOST RECORDS & FROM NEW HAMPSHIRE PAYS KNOWN STREET CRIMINALS TO FOLLOW & TO PHYSICALLY ASSAULT CONSUMERS OF APPLESAUCE

DISTRICT ATTORNEY REFUSED TO PROSECUTE IN 1968; ASSAULTED AT KENMORE 24 APRIL 1988 WITH A BLOW TO THE RIGHT SIDE OF MY HEAD COUPLED WITH A RACIAL INFERENCE AGAINST ASIANS.

IF YOU PAINT THIS WRITING OVER; DUPONT ON ALBANY STREET WILL SUFFER PHYSICAL DAMAGE FROM 1988 CRUSADER KNIGHTS M.O.

IN A HANDWRITTEN LETTER, ABRAHAM LINCOLN WROTE; "YOU WAS RIGHT; I WAS WRONG."

BOSTON UNIVERSITY GRADUATES HAVE A WALLPAPER DIPLOMA. KNOWLEDGE IS NOT PROOF OF SIN OR VIRTUE.

ALL BOARDING PLYWOOD MUST HAVE A HEALTH KNOT HOLE

? WHERE AND WHEN WERE THE THREE REQUIRED WEDING BANNS FOR THE AUGUST MARRIAGE OF John Dukakis PUBLISHED? SON OF MICHAEL AND KITTY DUKAKIS WHO GOVERN MASSACHUSETTS

BOSTON EDISON GETS ITS SUBTOTAL FOR DOWNTOWN CROSSING FROM THE ABOVE GENERAL ELECTRIC "AND LEAD US NOT INTO TEMPTATION" [Written under a tiny electric meter.—Ed.]

THE SAINT PETERs OF CHRISTIANITY GIVE LARGE AMOUNTS OF DATA TO MARSH CHAPEL WHICH DOES NOT HAVE A NEED TO KNOW ABOUT ANY OTHER BUILDING. MARSH CHAPEL IS SITUATED, IN A HIGH SECURITY AREA OF BOSTON UNIVERSITY, WITH EXPERTISE GREATER THAN THAT AVAILABLE TO THE PRESIDENT OF THE UNITED STATES. THE SECURITY OF BOSTON UNIVERSITY FEEDS ITS DATA TO EUGENISTS, BOTH SIDES OF ANY BIGOTRY, STATIC MISERY, CHANGEFOR THE SAKE OF BROKERAGE, FOREIGN ASSASSINS, ET CETERA. EXCURSION FARES ARE BETTER FOR PUBLIC HEALTH THAN SHUTTLE BUSES.

CARITAS IS RESEARCHING OLD CHURCH FIRES TO GET GUILT MONEY.

THE RUSSIANS SLOWLY & SECRETLY GAVE THE CITIZENS OF BAYONNE, NEW JERSEY VARIOUS PHYSICAL DISABILITYS WITHOUT BENEFITS.

PARIS, FRANCE BUILT THE MEXICO CITY SUBWAY

OLD SAFES ARE AN AIR-HAMMER JOB

NIEMAN-MARCUS OF TEXAS TELLS POLICE TO TREAT ITS JEWELS AS INGOTS. CURRENTLY, NIEMAN-MARCUS IS SHIPPING JEWELS IN ANTIQUE WOOD FURNITURE.

NORTHEASTERN UNIVERSITY MADE DUNKIN DONUTS BAIT FOR TUNNEL RATS. A PUBLIC HEALTH HAZARD WAS CAUSED BY THE POISON: THE TUNNEL RATS DIED ANYWHERE. SPRING TRAPS DON'T LESSEN PUBLIC HEALTH.

BEFORE THE INVENTION OF SAFETY FILM, ASBESTOS WAS HEAVILY USED TO PREVENT THEATRE FIRES. UNITED STATES MARSHALL HAS PET CAREER CRIMINALS LOOSE ON THE STREETS

U.S.P. LOWERED STANDARDS YEARS AGO; e g. WEAK GELATIN.

198seven
CITY (BOSTON) HOSPITAL HIDDEN SECURITY FOUND A FELLOW WITH A HEAD INJURY (RIGHT SIDE) AND SENT HIM TO A CLINIC WITH LESS THAN $200 A WEEK DECISION; PUT HIS BLOOD ON PAPER; DID NOT GET BED REST.

TOO MANY PISTOLS NEAR NEW WORLD BANK; SUMMER ST.

MASSACHUSETTS DOES NOT HAVE A POOR-HOUSE. MASSACHUSETTS HAS TOO MANY EMPLOYEES FROM DORCHESTER WORKING IN STATE AGENCYs.

ALSO DONE IN ITALY IN 1968 METRO POLICE GET REVENGE BY TELLING THIEFS YOU HAVE HEROIN IN YOUR "bags."

TAR DUST RELEASES DORMANT MICROBES WHICH MAY OR MAY NOT MAKE YOU SICK. AVOID 1988 WOODEN HOUSE CROWDS.

TO WASTE POLICE WORK, WHEELOCK COLLEGE INDUCES A PATERNITY CHARGE.

PRIVATELY OWNED UNIVERSITY HOSPITAL IS HEAVILY SUBSIDIZED BY THE UNITED STATES GOVERNMENT CYBORG RESEARCH & BLOOD RESEARCH.

Too near St.Patrick's
Taught single women to mingle only with cake-in-the-box bachelors

SEAGRAMS WHISKEY STUDIED THE EFFECT OF ALCOHOL ON BANK CHECKS
Federigo da Montefeltro, DUKE OF URBINO, lost an eye in a tournament. Piero della Francesca painted his profile.

MOST OF THE INVESTMENTS OF MASSACHUSETTS GENERAL HOSPITAL ARE IN ROUTE 128 ELECTRONICS WHICH ARE REPRESENTED IN BOSTON BY DIGITAL ELECTRONICS. NUTRITION WAS THE SALES AGENT. HOSPITAL GIVES FREE GUARD SERVICES TO FOOD TRUCKS

DON'T EAT LUNCH
ONLY YOU PERSONALLY
AVOID OFFICE CROWDS.

SEATTLE PEPPERMINT TEA
HAS JEWELRY STORE TENANTS.

FORMER PRESIDENT JIMMY CARTER CAUSED POLAND VS. CHICAGO TO DO HIS PERSONAL PREJUDICE.

MILK WITH VEGETABLE OIL SUBSTITUTED FOR MILK FAT.

SHE SELLS STOLEN ANTIQUE BOOKS IN EUROPE TO PHONY STUDENTS

JAMAICAN CANDLES ARE MADE FROM AN EXON REFINERY BY-PRODUCT.

'QUAKERS TOLD THE STONE QUARRY THAT IT COULDN'T GROW OLIVES'

FOR YEARS, TRIPLE-DECKERS SPEND IN ANY CITY OTHER THAN BOSTON.

TRIPLE-DECKERS DID THE MOST DAMAGE TO YOUR ATMOSPHERE.

SQUIRRELS EAT SUICIDE BIRDS

AMERICAN EXPRESS, BOSTON EMPLOYEES CASH PAY CHECKS FOR CHANNEL 7 T.V. STOCK

KING'S CHAPEL FOLLOWS VICTIMS; KINGS CHAPEL IS PUTTING stale SUGAR IN YOUR COFFEE. HERSHEY CANDY FORMERLY SOLD SUGAR TO MASSACHUSETTS COFFEE HOUSES

PEOPLE WHO PAY THEIVES GET THE SAME JAIL TERMS AS THE CAUGHT

A POLITICAL AGITATOR, WORKING FOR EMERSON COLLEGE, LIVES IN THE TOWN-SHIP OF NEWTON

South end has telephones U.S.A. EMPLOYEES HAVE FORMED cells OF INSUBORDINATION: OVERPAID GOVERNMENT EMPLOYEES GIVING PART OF THEIR CHECKS TO SECRET SATELLITE

PINKERTONS ARE NOT INVOLVED WITH 1989 CLASS RINGS. THE TRAIN & CHURCHES HIRE PINKERTONS FIRED BY POLICE & PSYCHIATRY. A RESIDENT OF CAMBRIDGE AND SUPPORTER OF THE SACKLER MUSEUM WAS FOLLOWED BY WHICH URGES beggars in the queen's palace. translation from the Italian

PART II: CHICAGO

Tom Gengler, a correspondent in Chicago, having no previous knowledge of the Boston Mystery Writer, reported on a similar phenomenon in Chicago:

> This summer I spent a couple days photographing the plentiful odd literature on downtown Chicago lampposts. My favorites are the work of an unknown thinker who posts sheets covered with short enigmatic phrases concerning the UN and one General Manda. Manda is "older than Methusela," "oldest human: 500 to 10000 years old years," "Elected to UN jobs on 40 UN resolutions," 'Speaker 1492 to 2010 etc etc etc," and apparently he's responsible for the Manda Act and multiparty elections. These small posters have been proliferating steadily for a few years at least... Other pieces herald "assembly line surgery old into young" or "cross breed meat animals fish-fowl bones-bone rubber aluminum wood steel etc sleep De tox." A unique example claims that,

The UN still Has the problem of the Notzi Mafia War criminals gangs that attempted to Massacre Wipe out the UN General assembly security Council & etc etc they were tried sentenced to Death on UN resolutions / 1925 to 1945 they did the same to the US Supreme Court: the White House: etc etc etc (.)

LEO BARTSCH
UFOS ARE GOD'S ANGELS

Leo Bartsch, "the one and only most outspoken UFO researcher in all southwestern Oregon since 1959" doesn't get along very well with preachers; they wish he'd just stop talking about UFOs. Nor does he get along very well with UFO enthusiasts; they wish he'd just stop talking about the Bible. Neither preachers nor the UFO crowd will accept, as Bartsch keeps telling them, that the Bible is "the best book on UFO," and that UFOs are angels sent by God to expose "false religion."

Bartsch, a resident of Coos Bay, Oregon since the forties, began his devotion to UFO research in 1959, but the story of his one-man crusade begins three years earlier, at the death-bed of his first wife. "When she died I was holding her head in my left arm," Bartsch recounts. "And it felt like something just crawled in that arm. Afterwards, I had to go to the doctor. The hand had the shakes and it was like the blood didn't want to go into that arm." Part of his arm became numb, and its movements were out of his control; despite doctors' attempts to heal it, the arm only got worse.[1]

During the next few years, despite his sick arm, Bartsch remarried and continued his career as a real estate agent. But on September 27, 1959, Bartsch suddenly became a man with a mission. At 3 a.m. of that day, Bartsch awoke, and, though he saw nothing and heard nothing, he somehow "just knew" that a UFO was near, and told his (second) wife that "something out of the universe just went low over this roof." Though his wife felt nothing, Bartsch "became weightless for almost a minute," and his "arm became normal instantly." Bartsch realized that his wife thought he was drinking or having a nightmare, so he told her to be sure to look at the clock and remember the time; he knew somehow that his story would be backed up with a report in the next day's newspaper.

Sure enough, the next morning a Coos Bay newspaper reported that a woman and her two young sons in nearby Empire had reported seeing a brightly colored object passing low over the ground; they saw their object at exactly the same time that Bartsch became weightless. There was another report in Redmond, Oregon, shortly before, which also fit the description of the Empire sighting.[2]

Before this incident, Bartsch had been busy with his career, and hadn't paid the slightest attention to flying saucers. But now, after being "exorcised by a UFO," Bartsch began gathering information and attending UFO research meetings. But his most burning questions weren't answered until 1962, when he began to "look for spiritual help."

> For some unknown reason I looked up and silently said, "Oh, God, who are Thou?" Then suddenly my entire left arm that had been healed back in 1959 felt like a sparkling electric contact, yet wonderful!
>
> Then suddenly I heard these words, "How did you like your answer?"[3]

Bartsch began studying the Bible which convinced him that UFOs are electric living creatures sent by God to fulfill prophecy. Assuming that the clergy would be interested in such information, Bartsch wrote letters to over 100 churches, but received only three replies: one minister told Bartsch that he had a warped mind, another telephoned to ask what UFOs were, and the third arrived in person, expecting to meet "the most demon-possessed man on earth." Bartsch continued to entertain the representatives of organized religion at his home, but soon realized that they were incapable of understanding the truth about UFOs.

1. "UFO crusader flies high on his theories: Leo Bartsch on a mission" by Mike Thoele, *The Register-Guard*, Eugene, OR, 4/18/88.
2. Ibid.; "Are U.F.O.'s Supernatural?" by Malcolm L. Koch, *WEEKLY*, Bandon, OR, 2/18/77; "I WAS EXORCISED BY A UFO" by Beauregard Briggs, *National News Extra*,9/15/74.
3. "I WAS EXORCISED BY A UFO."

I had a Baptist minister and a Pentecostal in my home on time to talk to me about my UFO stuff. They got to arguing so much they weren't even talking to me. Then there was a knock on the door and it was a Seventh-day Adventist. Pretty soon all of them got into one big hell of an argument. I never had such a wonderful time as I did listening to the three of them cut each other up.[4]

Besides a good laugh, the clergy provided Bartsch with the last piece to his UFO puzzle: The reason God was sending UFOs to earth was to expose organized religion as "false religion," in preparation for the Last Days. Bartsch was now ready to go public with his earth-shattering message.

Bartsch began a letter writing campaign which included newspapers, government officials, celebrities and his fellow UFO researchers; he corresponded with J. Allen Hynek for years; he also received a very positive, personal reply from Shirley MacLaine. But the response from the mainstream UFO crowd was disappointing:

I kept saying, 'Let's start with the word supernatural and everything would fall into place.' Figure it out. You can't shoot 'em down. You can't capture 'em. They've got to be supernatural.

But all those other people wanted to talk about our space brothers. They wanted to talk about ships from Mars and Venus—cigar-shaped ones and round ones and small ones and big ones. They'd talk about everything but the supernatural. They want 'em to be made out of nuts and bolts and iron. If that was true, the junkyards would be full of 'em by now.[5]

Bartsch continued to hold court in a special room he'd set aside for UFO discussions, which doubled as world headquarters of the "UFO NEWS." When the flying saucer fans arrived he'd show them a UFO episode of the TV program "You Asked For It," to break the ice. But inevitably, they would try to explain UFOs scientifically. As soon as Bartsch would bring out his Bible, they'd leave.[6]

But Bartsch held his ground, and continued to search for converts elsewhere. During the 70s, he blanketed the U.S. with letters and flyers, one state at a time.

THE MISSION OF THE UFO

UFO **SATAN IN THE PULPIT EXPOSED BY THE UFO** UFO

It took a UFO encounter of the 4th kind to give me a jolt and a revelation on how Satan deceives the whole world right from the pulpit (Rev. 12:9).

Now notice, "God" said, Come out of "Her" my people, or come out of this Great Whore, the mother of harlots, and the harlots are our conflicting religions or religious confusion, which becomes the Great Babylon religion that deceives all nations (Rev. Chapters 17–18). And Satan can be in the pulpit as a minister of righteousness, or as an apostle of Christ (II Cor. 11:13–15).

Which are the false Christs and false prophets that sincerely believe they are the true servant of Jesus Christ, and they will show great signs and wonders that will deceive the very elect, unless the days be shortened, or none shall be saved (Matt. 7:22 and 24:21–24).

And this is also called the Mark of the Beast, the world's greatest religious deception on earth who will perform miracles that will deceive all religions, both great and small, rich or poor, bond or free (Rev. 13:16 and 19:20).

So the mission of the UFO are here to seal the hundred and forty-four thousand (Rev. 7:3).

Before the very elect are deceived, then the UFO will pour out the seven last plagues which will cause great tribulations like never before since the beginning of the world.

Inspired by a UFO encounter that revealed the inner man (II Cor. 4:16–18), and the real mission of the UFO.

As a retired business man, this will be my last works on earth. (267–2524) 744 So. 4th, Coos Bay, Ore. 97420.

4. "UFO crusader flies high on his theories: Leo Bartsch on a mission."
5. Ibid.
6. "Are U.F.O.'s Supernatural?"

He also began placing large ads in the Coos Bay World, with headings such as, "UFO FROM GOD OR SATAN?":

My UFO encounter back in 1959 did reveal the answer to this. Yet as a business man, the last thing I wanted was a confrontation with conflicting religions. But when some religions teach that UFO are satanic—this caused me to become very outspoken about the real mission of the UFO, and soon found myself judged and condemned, right from the pulpit, where you cannot speak in your own defence, where brainwashing is legal and this mass hypnosis has become a billion dollar business, that will not allow reproof for correction. So let us find out why all the religious leaders ordered Jesus put to death (Matt. 27:1) and why a religion (NOT UFO) deceives the whole world (Rev. 18:23).

We know a serpent has a forked tongue, and satan was called "that old serpent which decieveth the whole world (Rev. 12:9). . . . And now, these serpents and devils transform into ministers of righteousness and false apostles of Christ (2 Cor. 11:13-15). . . .

But this will be exposed by a flying object 15x30 feet (Zech. 5:1-4) and the flying objects of God are many. So to cover this up, these blind guides try to hypnotize their captivated audience into BELIEVING only the occult world contact UFO, or that satan has a counterfeit for everything God has, to have you believe that UFO are satanic. But the "ONLY" satanic UFO comes out of the mouth of those who speaketh with forked tongue, because they hope and pray they are not from God.

Inspired by a UFO encounter that revealed the inner man (2 Cor. 4:16-18).

Leo Bartsch (non-sectarian) [7]

Only recently, after Whitley Streiber and others have suggested that their experiences with alien creatures belong to the supernatural, rather than the physical realm, has the UFO community even considered the possibility that UFOs could be something other than "brothers from another planet." Bartsch, it seems, is ahead of his time, despite his reliance on the Bible for information. His insistence that UFOs are "Electric Living Creatures," is at least as plausible as the standard idea that UFOs are little ETs in spaceships, who just happen to defy all known laws of physical reality.

The UFO can disappear right before your eyes; and they do pulsate and glow in all colors of the rainbow, and are consistent in causing electro magnetic effects all over the world. But first let us compare the electric eel, which scientists now call "Living Lightning," and can recharge itself instantly. So these UFO could be supernatural living creatures which can recharge themselves instantly. But where do they come from? When we know where our mysterious eternal energy, called electricity, comes from, we will know where these UFO come from. . . .

Lightning proceeded from the throne (Rev. 4:5), and lightning is electric; and God's throne is like wheels of fire that issue a firey stream (Dan. 7:9-10); And the face of angels have the appearance of lightning (Matt. 28:3), and they ascend in a flame of fire (Judges 13:20).

Perhaps we could understand all this better if we knew more about a certain living creature whose body is like beryl, and his face is as the appearance of lightning, and his eyes as lamps of fire (Dan. 10:6); or a living creature which comes with a rainbow on his head and his face as it were the sun and his feet as pillars of fire (Rev. 10:1). Yes, a living creature which may look like a fireball, rocket, meteorite, or a UFO glowing in all colors of the rainbow. . . .[8]

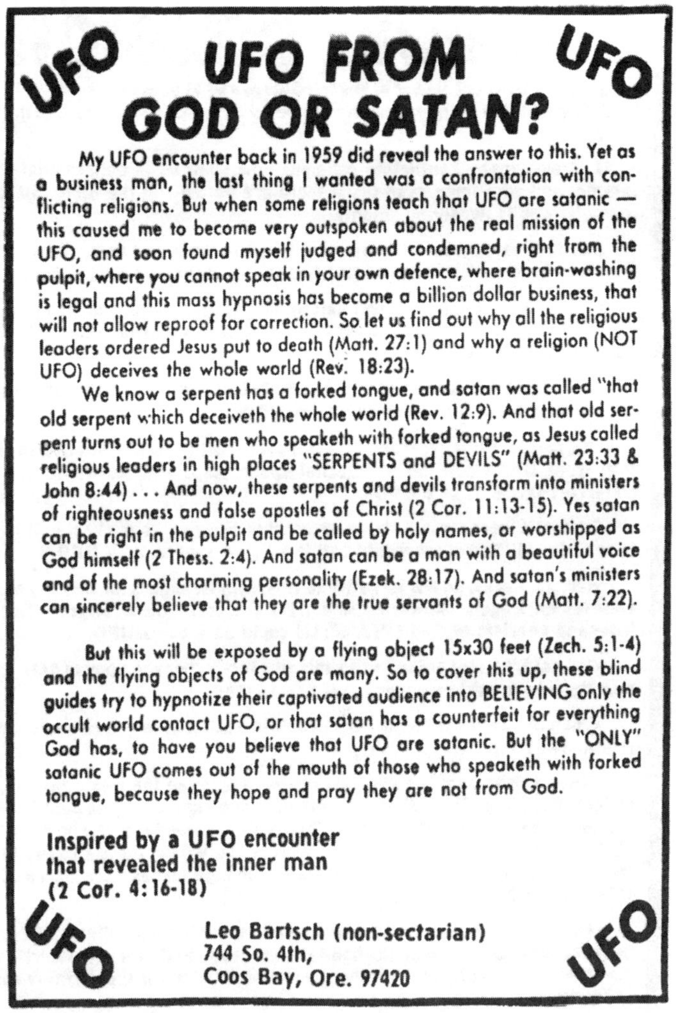

UFO FROM GOD OR SATAN?

My UFO encounter back in 1959 did reveal the answer to this. Yet as a business man, the last thing I wanted was a confrontation with conflicting religions. But when some religions teach that UFO are satanic — this caused me to become very outspoken about the real mission of the UFO, and soon found myself judged and condemned, right from the pulpit, where you cannot speak in your own defence, where brain-washing is legal and this mass hypnosis has become a billion dollar business, that will not allow reproof for correction. So let us find out why all the religious leaders ordered Jesus put to death (Matt. 27:1) and why a religion (NOT UFO) deceives the whole world (Rev. 18:23).

We know a serpent has a forked tongue, and satan was called "that old serpent which deceiveth the whole world (Rev. 12:9). And that old serpent turns out to be men who speaketh with forked tongue, as Jesus called religious leaders in high places "SERPENTS and DEVILS" (Matt. 23:33 & John 8:44) . . . And now, these serpents and devils transform into ministers of righteousness and false apostles of Christ (2 Cor. 11:13-15). Yes satan can be right in the pulpit and be called by holy names, or worshipped as God himself (2 Thess. 2:4). And satan can be a man with a beautiful voice and of the most charming personality (Ezek. 28:17). And satan's ministers can sincerely believe that they are the true servants of God (Matt. 7:22).

But this will be exposed by a flying object 15x30 feet (Zech. 5:1-4) and the flying objects of God are many. So to cover this up, these blind guides try to hypnotize their captivated audience into BELIEVING only the occult world contact UFO, or that satan has a counterfeit for everything God has, to have you believe that UFO are satanic. But the "ONLY" satanic UFO comes out of the mouth of those who speaketh with forked tongue, because they hope and pray they are not from God.

Inspired by a UFO encounter that revealed the inner man (2 Cor. 4:16-18)

Leo Bartsch (non-sectarian)
744 So. 4th,
Coos Bay, Ore. 97420

. . . And now electricity is like an angel to man when man transformed electricity into man's messengers to send, or teleport, his words and image almost instantly all over the world by radio or TV. Even man was transported from one place to another instantly in Biblical times (Acts 8:39-40). Angels did act in

7. "The World," *Coos Bay*, OR, 11/11/83.
8. "UFO Electric Living Creatures" by Leo Bartsch.

various capacities as guardians, messengers, and did transport.

Now UFOs seem to travel the same way, as does electricity send or receive; and electricity is a visible fire or invisible things as are angels. We may entertain angels unaware, Heb. 13:2. . . .

. . . The Great Northeast Blackout of Nov. 9, 1965 that could not happen (but did) which took even the Government electrical commission a week to decide the whole Northeast of USA and 30 million people were blacked out by one little relay switch. Well, they had to give some answer or admit UFO. . . . If God should remove all electricity from this earth even man's brain cells would blackout as it is known they also register electricity. . . .

Ezekiel's wheel sounds like a living dynamo which he called the wheel with-in a wheel a living creature that did light up like lightning and was like a whirlwind. Ezekiel spoke with the Spirit of God in him, or God spoke through him as man does through radio or TV except God's way is perfect and limitless; so when Ezekiel said it was a living creature, that is just what it was! So is live electricity; so are UFO; and if you are earthbound or grounded don't touch a live wire to find out unless you are positive. . . .[9]

It's been nearly 35 years since Bartsch's UFO encounter, and still, nobody has produced a crashed saucer or an extraterrestrial, alive or dead. UFO researchers may finally begin to look at alternatives to the "ET hypothesis," [10] but they will probably never give any credit to Leo Bartsch, for saying that UFOs are supernatural before anyone else did.

UFO **UFO WILL** UFO

EXPOSE RELIGION

It took a UFO encounter of the third kind, and 25 years of research to understand why "All the religious leaders ordered Jesus Christ put to Death." (Matt. 27:1).

And why many conflicting religions now want us to believe that UFO are satanic, and why some even insist there are no UFO in the Bible. So judge for yourself, who is deceiving whom?

Isa. 60:8 says, Who are these that fly as a cloud and as doves to their windows? So here we have an unidentified flying object, or a UFO in the Bible.

Matt. 2:9 says, the star went before them until it came and stood over where the child (Christ) was. Now if we saw a star moving around like this today we would call it a UFO.

Zech. 5:1 & 2 tells of a flying roll 15 by 30 feet. Now if we saw a flying roll 15' x 30', we would call it a flying saucer or UFO.

In Ezek. 30:9 it is recorded "messengers shall go forth from God in ships." A ship from God would be a Celestial space ship, and we would call it "extraterrestrial, E.T. or a UFO.

Ezekiel's wheel was a flying object that looked like a wheel within a wheel (Ezek. Ch. 1). Today we would call it a flying saucer, or a UFO.

Heb. 13:2 says, be not forgetful to entertain strangers for thereby some have entertained Angels unawares. And UFO are certainly strangers. The twenty-thousand chariots of God (Psa. 68:17) could be today's UFO.

God said, he (not satan) will show wonders in heaven above (Acts 2:19), and now the whole world wonders about these UFO.

When the Lord went before the people in a pillar of fire they would not believe (Num. 14:11-14).

When Elisha saw the chariots of fire, and even the pilots therein, he was ridiculed (2 Kings 2:11-23). And I was ridiculed right from the pulpit, where you cannot speak in your own defence. This made me wonder just who is that old serpent called Satan, the devil, that deceives the whole world? (Rev. 12:9), and found that Jesus called ... religious leaders in high places "Serpents and Devils" (Matt. 23:33 & John 8:44).

And the whole world will be deceived by conflicting religions (Rev. 18:23), because they have become the habitation of devils and every foul spirit (verse 2). And this is just the tip of the iceberg on how the UFO will expose these conflicting religions.

(More to come)

UFO **Inspired by a UFO encounter that revealed the inner man (2 Cor. 4:16-18)**

Leo Bartsch (non-sectarian) 744 So. 4th, Coos Bay, Ore. 97420 UFO

9. "Flying Saucers, Electricity and the Bible" by Leo Bartsch.
10. The ET Hypothesis states that UFOs are the direct result of real, physical, extraterrestrial beings.

JULLIAN SWIG

CATCH 22 IS THE SCAM WHAT AM (excerpts)

BRIEF RECITAL OF PERSONAL HISTORY ESTABLISHING INJURIES CONTEXT FOR BANK OF AMERICA TORTS OF FALSE IMPRISONMENT, ET AL.

Following High School I attended Diablo Valley Jr. College in Concord, CA but could not interest myself in scholastic ambition. I took part time work at Payless Paint Centers, an expanding chain of retail paint stores in Walnut Creek. I functioned as a sales clerk, stock clerk and sign letterer. I soon dropped out of Diablo Valley College. After three years at Payless I moved to Berkeley where I took evening work with the Post Office, and during the days developed a truck based sign lettering service for gas stations and retailers. I dropped the Post Office when I was able to go full time on sign painting. I shared my grandparents' East Bay home which had a garage and basement suitable for sign manufacture.

When my grandfather died in 1976 I was provided $7,000 inheritance with which I purchased equipment and took and renovated an Albany, CA industrial garage. By virtue of talent, reputation and circumstances I should have blazed ahead into middle class security and rewarding involvement in the creative challenges of my work. My skills and knowledge of my craft were coming to fruition. There was steady demand for my work.

Nonetheless at that time I was given good cause to become extremely concerned when I found that state courts on repeated occasions refused to protect claims against encroachments upon my commercial rights. I became the victim of a capricious suit against me for $100,000. That lawsuit was based on the mere fact that I had plead in small claims court against my adversaries (a service station-car wash) for contract breach (refusal to pay for sign labor). The technical abuses practiced against me in that litigation were so extraordinary that I was left to feel that my enterprise would be vulnerable prey to any thugs or aggressors who might from time to time find themselves in favor with the judicial powers.

The car wash as well as several other indicators of abuse of judicial office directly experienced by me in other matters caused me to feel a real sense of alarm. Conditions of stress were escalated in my life. My rights were not seriously regarded by the courts and my most cherished possession, the right to pursue the vocation of my choice, was being squandered by evident instances of power brokering and political favor.

It seemed imperiative to me that I generate public cognition of the situation. I researched the Constitution and used my skills as a publicist to project visibility of my plight. I believed that such a thing as public indignation existed and could be rallied to my support. (I was oblivious to covert schadenfreude in my fellow Californians.)

By virtue of my outspokenness and civil disobedience gestures, criminal charges were brought against me. My exposition of judicial abuses was interpreted as "threatening public officials," a felony offense. I experienced pre-trial jailing for five months along with the manipulations of court assigned attorneys who wanted to avoid the risk of advocating the controversial constitutional issue I had alleged. I was required to await trial in jail in spite of strong O.R. recommendations from my community. Assigned counsel avoided contact with me while I was in jail.

The jailing caused me to lose rental of sign shop premises. The identity void this created in my life was intense. I still could think in no other terms than those of projecting public visibility. I found myself rebuffed in efforts to project my message on public access radio or T.V. In turn I focused on street demonstrating. I felt that a technique of whimsy could soften and allow for more receptivity for my message. I fashioned an unknown comic paper head sack for myself and demonstrated with a sign against KGO in San Francisco. I stressed the idea that there is no free speech in a culture where privately owned media dominates audience access. I consumed cartridge charged nitrous oxide balloons

CATCH 22 IS THE SCAM WHAT AM

THE IMMUTABLE CATCH 22 STATUS OF JULLIAN SWIG

By group neglect to secure me protection of my individual rights Californians have created in my person an anything-goes-man within their midst. While they would welcome me, the living exponent of their neglect (fully unshackled from their restraint), expelled from the realm of their awareness, this they could now do only as outlaws operating outside the constitution themselves, or as a gang collectively or by representatives operating under color of law (not under sanction of law).

I have no intention of making myself inconspicuous.

There is no undoing the fruits of public neglect. My legal status as an untouchable is irreversible save as I may choose to enter into a voluntary settlement with the government.

THE CONSTITUTION MAKES IT SO.

REFUSALS TO PROTECT RIGHTS

As a prerequisite to understanding this matter one must accept as fact that the State of California has substantially and conclusively refused me protection of rights.

It is not incumbent upon me to render to anyone palpable proofs that this is so. Immutable common law and procedural law requires the fact be accepted. Challenges and offers of proof on this subject were made in three separate legal forums. Prosecutors for the state never responded to their official duty to deny, repudiate or disprove my declarations and offers of proof. Proof of state refusals to protect my rights has been concluded in law under the common law tradition of acquiescence and default.

A district attorney's sly silences do not profess the people's clean hands.

CATCH 22

Catch 22 is not a scam. It is a cumulative-collective product of the intellectual and moral refuge which is bureaucracy, which is a scam. Catch 22 is case law fountainhead of California Constitutional definition:

> *These great rights are founded in the law of nature, but nature has provided no Courts in which contested claims can be litigated or admitted rights can be enforced. Hence arises one of the necessities of a Government, which is instituted for the very purpose of protecting and securing these natural rights, as is declared by Sec. 2 of Art. 1. The Government owes the duty of protection to the people in the enjoyment of their rights, and the people owe the correlative duty of obedience and support to the Government. The one is dependent upon the other.* **The Government cannot justly claim obedience when it refuses protection.** *The citizen cannot demand protection without he renders the equivalent of obedience and support.*
>
> *Cohen vs. Wright*, 22 C 293 (1863)

The whole of the *Cohen vs. Wright* text speaks a plain language and is a refreshing contrast to the philosophical confusion of the relativists and of the hordes of 20th century trendy intellectuals.

The State of California refused Jullian Swig protection of his rights. Jullian Swig proved that to be a fact and cited *Cohen vs. Wright* as explication of a constitutional primary, i.e., of the sine qua non of jurisdiction per se. Jurisdiction is the major premise in any circumstance of law.

I trust the reader to be knowledgeable of the science of arithmetic.

NOTICE AND A WARNING

The purpose of this publication is warning and notice to all California government functionaries, employees and agents:

I. I will be paying no taxes and yielding no support to the state of California or to any California local government. local government.

II. I will pay no parking fees or citation fines in any California jurisdiction. Red flags and curbs are carte blanche to Catch 22.

III. Any attempts to assert forced compliance to or penalties for or trials for any alleged violations of any state or local codes will result in the filing and service of a Federal Civil Rights action against any involved arresting officer and his superior, prosecuting attorneys or bureaucrats, municipal corporations or townships or any ranking officials who neglect to announce and enforce a hands off Jullian Swig policy in their hierarchies . . . or it may result in other reprisals I may deem appropriate.

Anyone arresting Jullian Swig under alias or identity unknown circumstances must release him as soon as he or she is informed of and can confirm his identity.

All Precinct Captains. Put Jullian Swig on the "Most Unwanted List," dig? Go tell it to the computer.

All government functionaries, employees and agents are directed to take notice of all the documentation appearing in and made reference to in:

JULLIAN SWIG vs. STATE OF CA et al. C-82-1529-WTS
United States District Court, Northern District San Francisco
(Watch this also for upcoming damages award. If jurists don't learn of the immutable common law in law school they must pay tuition in the school of life.)

DRUGS

In the name of sanity and economic common sense I offer support of my status to any principled, market based import and distribution of cocaine, marijuana, hashish or LSD.

THERE'S MORE

The complete Catch 22 papers and history are available by sending $11 check or money order per copy to:

Jullian Swig
P.O. Box 1122
Berkeley, CA 94701-1122

 E.B.E. 11/19/82

through the mouth of the paper head sack to enhance the comic effect and to make my demonstration chore more interesting.

One morning (Nov. 5, 1979) before intending to drive to S.F. I stopped for pocket cash where I had a checking account at the main branch of the Bank of America in Berkeley. I saw the bank was unusually crowded. I decided to wear the head sack into the bank. When I was in the bank over 10 minutes the floor manager requested I remove the sack. I did so, but only to reveal my features. The floor manager demanded that I keep the sack off. I objected. The bank called the police.

After the police arrived and confirmed what should have been obvious, that I carried no weapon, the bank insisted that I be arrested. Twenty four hours later I was released from confinement from Berkeley jail as the charges against me had been dropped. During that 24 hours however my mind was beset with the spectre of jail and a system which could again manipulate me for its own purposes and where my rights would not be represented.

Perhaps most painful to me was the invisibility of my plight. I was not the member of a society or a class against whom the practice of bias or prejudice is openly acknowledged. Protection for commercial transactions necessary to business life had been denied to me, but my peers were apathetic, and contemporary society was not ready to acknowledge that any exceptions to the myth of equal opportunity could exist for a middle class white male.

The utter invisibility of my situation and the continuing evasions and denial of facts by officials were deeply unsettling to me. Why should a public service institution such as a bank insist that I maintain an outward symbol of normality? Things were not normal. My demeanor in the bank had not been pushy or vulgar, it had simply been unique. Moreover I was not a half wit kook who had singled the bank itself out as a target for all social woes. The bank had not been the object of my criticism.

A few hours after release from jail I returned to the bank with the paper head sack and a tape recorder. This was the same bank my father's business had patronized since it opened its doors, the same bank from which I had taken and repaid my first and second commercial loans. It was also the bank my great grandfather had notorized for A.P. Gianinni in 1904. I again on the bank's request willingly removed the paper head sack to reveal my features, and the bank again insisted that I keep it off. I refused and the bank insisted on closing out my account over my objections. The police had again been called to remove me though I had done nothing to make their assistance necessary.

As I had been disenchanted on the prospects of obtaining civil justice in Pro Per and had never been able to afford or trust a lawyer it wasn't until almost a year later that I filed suit against the Bank of America. My pleading survived demurrer and significant discovery was accomplished by interrogatories. . . .

My litigious behavior and nurturing of the case from Nov. 1980 til 1982 was I think in itself indicative of the mental injuries I sustained. I plead a very large award and fantasized that the case could be parlayed into a landmark for free speech law.

Mental distress I have read is often characterized by over-intellectualization and a striving to find significance for one's suffering. I was excessively over intellectualizing following Nov. 5, 1979. The bank's conduct underscored in me the idea that my social worth had been permanently devalued and that I would be civilly helpless whenever economic superiors might choose to abuse me. . . .

My psychiatrist is prepared to attest to the upset and suffering I underwent. His testimony can be complimented by self tape recordings I have made since Nov. 1979, by possible testimony of personal acquaintances and evaluations of professional expert witnesses. . . .

I invite attorneys to consider entry into this case on champerty. I caution you to beware of first impressions or a rush to understand. I am not the usual plaintiff. I am ready to bring my tape, myself, and my materials around. When the hurdle of acceptance has been surmounted you'll find me an easy client to work with. . . .

Cordially,

Jullian Swig

Update by Jullian Swig:

. . . **In 1990 U.C. Campus Police** (operating off the UC Campus) committed theft and retention of my means to a livelihood, my 1986 Toyota van for which I am the first and only owner, and for which I am the undisputed owner at law, and for which I fully pre-paid its original purchase through a dealer in 1986, and for which I have never thereafter or since caused or permitted any compromise to my clear absolute ownership of the property.

Knowing me to be the owner, UC Police afforded not one iota of due process and they specifically refused statutory duty upon my demand to be taken before a magistrate. I brought a civil rights and conversion suit against them in the US District Court in S.F. . . .

U.S. Magistrates have evaded and are evading the clear and simple merits of my claim. It appears they have committed treason and a violation of their oaths to defend and support the U.S. Constitution.

Judicial misrepresentation of facts it unavoidably appears were set up in deliberate avoidance of duty. **This has affected not only sanction for the theft of my van, but AGAINST ALL FREE CITIZENS** it throws out the welcome mat for unrestrained police confiscation of private property—no warrant, no due process required! . . .

Remaining to me is only the prospect of a **dark horse** (obscure) **appeal to the US Supreme Court.**

The tribal drums of modern society, the media, would cause people to believe that matters of this nature do not exist. . . .

Being that the 4th estate, *the print and the electronic press*, appear to me to engage in selective disclosure, and of non-presentation of matters of this nature, I claim for myself sanction of right and the right to private journalism. Note that I claim only that it appears to me the court has acted in these manners, **I draw no conclusions for you, but I do verify all facts presented**. . . .

EUGENE KREPLEY

SAVAGE TREATMENT

DEAR SIR MR. A. WHITNEY ELLSWORTH

I hope you can please use your influence to help me with a savage treatment, that has destroyed my whole life of sixty three years. I can not manage this myself, I only get deeper into trouble every day, if you can not see some way to help me, I gess my whole life, will be lost to this horrible treatment.

My problem is this. I have been buged all of my life by those machine they bug people with. I do not even know the name of the machines. I think they or called personality transmitters, though I am not sure. The people who operate the machines, tell me they or called communication machines.

Every thing about these machines is keep a secret where I am concerned. There address there name, and the owner, who I gess must be some goverment department.

Forty one years ago two women started talking to me who run, these PT machines, eighteen to twenty four hours a day. Allways the same two women, I can indemnify them by there voices. How these two women have managed this talking is more then I can understand. Going forty one years with out a vacation, or a single day of rest I just can not explain. How I have lived through this cruel unusual treatment I do not know. It has left me a failure a depressed man. A skid row man.

The machine women have never tried to be decent with me, when this all started it begain, in the most violent manner you can image. I was actually drove insane, turned into a mad wild man, by those cruel unruly machine women. They had me arrested then commited to a insane asylum, Mayview State Hospital Pittsburgh PA. The way those two women operate there machines, and talk, I think they or the people who should have been committed to a insane asylum not me.

I was in the insane asylum about three weeks before I know what had been done to me. Then the two machine women begain talking to me in a logical manner, not in a good way, just in a way I could comprehend. Untill this day this mad talking, has not stopped for one day. I bet it cost the tax payers no less then one million dollars, just to destroy the life of a poor working man me. I have never been told why I have to be a victim, suffer this crazy treatment. I was in the asylum from 1936 till 1945.

In the insane asylum I was treated in the most terrible way, For Nine years, I was brainwashed so much by the PT machine women, I appeared a deafmute. This made it impossible for me to have myself discharged from the asylum, I appeared so withdrawn. I was forced by the machine to work in the institution kitchen, twelve hours a day, for nine long years, with a cent of pay, or a day of rest. Just think about those two mad machine women sit in there machines, for nine long years, making my life so tragic. I once even managed to run away from the asylum, but that only lasted five days, the two machine women had me arrested by the police then returned to the asylum. I do not have the words that can tell you how brutal, I was treated in the asylum, only that it was disastrous a living death.

I will go so far as to say I was treated as barbarously and vulgarly as the people in the Nazi concentration camps. Except in one way I managed to live through it all.

Since I was discharged from the asylum in 1945 the machine women have not stopped this treatment, for one day. They have squandered there life and my life I think with this useless torture.

When I was in the asylum I was told by the two machine women how, they destroyed my life in the twenty three years before my commitment. This letter must come to a end some time, it would take a book to tell you all, of the crimes these machine people have used on me.

So here is a simple list with out details, PT machine rape mant thousand times, school drop out, no chance to vote, or be married, fights with my family and other people, stealing, bad health from PT machine radiation, mistakes at work that cost money made me look like a fool, brainwashing that caused me to be a failure, I hope that is enough to make you with to help me.

The two machine women keep telling me that all I have to do to escape this torture, is find a job with themselves, then they turn around and make it so difficult, for me to have a job runing PT machines, that I could never find a job with themselves. Between there brainwashing and secrecy it makes it impossible, for me to find a job with them. I dont think the machine would give me a job they just say that because it seems so decent. They only to use there PT machines on me, but the worst of all is they do there work in such a terrible brutal way.

I have asked many people and many organization to help me, all have refused, the machine try to tell me they wont help me because I dont give them money. I would pay them if they would send me a bill. You must not forget I am writing about goverment departments, I would think to offer these people money, seems like graft. I just dont understand.

Lawyers refuse to help me because I dont have the address of the PT machines, and Doctors tell me they take care of people not machines. I think the truth is I am only a poor man and no body cares about how much I suffer.

I was moved to Pittsburgh 45 years ago by these PT machines people, from the state of Florida, when I was 15 years old, I have never been told why I was moved. I only know how cruel I have been treated by PT machines in both Florida and Pennsylvania. This all has made my life so tired I need your help so much. The machine women make it so difficult for me to write, I hope you will excuse my mistakes. I think the PT machine people or trying to keep there crazy work a secret. Allso the machine people have tried to make me become a skid row man, but I have refused, and manage to work.

Thank you Sincerley
Eugene Krepley

Ps I decided to send you this letter because your paper The New York Review Of Books is so interested in society so wisely

Just think one million dollars was spent squander to brainwash and torture me for 66 years tax payers money soem of your moeny this all caused me to become row man a complete failure

Those PT machine people claim I work with them I think this is not true I have never worked with those mad insane cruel savage croked cowardly yellow ingroant silly PT machine people this treatment is forced on me every single second I cant escape this cruel treatment my self I need help . . .

TRUTH MISSIONARIES'
CHAPTER OF POSITIVE ACCORD

WHILE CHRISTIAN FUNDAMENTALISTS ARE BUSY using the Bible to prove that sex for fun is forbidden by God, Truth Missionaries' Chapter of Positive Accord (TMC+A) are using that very same Bible to prove that God is actually having sex up in heaven and enjoying it. TMC+A members biblically and scientifically "prove" the physicality and active sexuality of God, as well as Goddess, the feminine aspect of the Deity, for whom they have developed an entire system of theology. They reverently address this entity by the name "Goddess," as opposed to "The Goddess," because She's no flimsy pagan idol, but a powerful force who literally initiated Jesus to Godhood:

> TMC+A is REAL NEW AGE (or beyond it) RELIGION! Our religion in NOT a rehash of ancient superstitions and hallucinations. It is NOT pseudospiritualist fantasy of intelligence functioning without physicalness, but nonphysical ideativeness correlated with the Natural physical factors of intelligence, functioning united together, YES, we recognize and worship a GODDESS, but SHE is NOT the flimsy 'spirit' of pagan mythology. Rather, She is GODDESS with ALMIGHTY Energy from SuperNatural PHYSICAL TRUTHS, scientifically evidenced and Biblically PROVEN! . . . Her sex activity enabled Jesus' conception and ascension and more! Her Holy Energy preserved Jesus' corpse from decay and resurrected him. Our Biblical proofs also show why Jesus was NOT God until She initiated with acts bringing Divine equality, including sex. And these proofs also tell why She and the original male Person, Who are God are each Co-Savior with Jesus. We do not resort to ignorance and hypocrisy. Our literature is consistent with current science and Biblical facts.

TMC+A was founded by Arch Bishop Lynn Johnson, D.D.D. Th., and incorporated as an Illinois non-profit organization in 1973. Since that time, TMC+A has been nationally advertising its proofs and disproofs and "NONE of them have ever been refuted." It has attracted kindred souls from all over the U.S. and Canada, if the branches listed in the newsletter are any indication. And, despite its inclusion of "absolute proofs," TMC+A in practice emphasizes democracy and cooperation. The literature, written originally by Johnson, is not adhered to as dogma; instead it is under constant scrutiny for consistency and Truth, revised during meetings by consensus vote.

The strange appellation "Truth Missionaries' Chapter of Positive Accord" refers to the members, called "Truth Missionaries," who are dedicated to avoiding hypocrisy "by efforts for the positive consistency or 'positive accord' of our behavior with our own principles."

If, after reading the literature, you feel yourself to be in positive accord with it, it is only a matter of time before you will be able to earn the ecclesiastical degrees Doctor of Divinity and Doctor of Theology. And if there's a vacancy, you can even apply to become a member of the hierarchy, and perhaps become, Bishop, Arch Bishop, Co-Bishop, Prelate(ss), Arch Prelate(ss), Co-Prelate(ss), Fore Prelate(ss), Vice Prelate(ss), Dean, Co-Dean or Arch Dean.

TMC+A literature, called "tracts" are available free at TMC+A meetings, or for a nominal fee by mail, as a kind of correspondence course in Divinity. These her-etical reading lessons seem to be 10th generation xeroxes of manuscripts that were badly typed to begin with; add to this the fact that they are packed densely with theological and technical information, and you realize that earning your D. Th. or D.D. might not be so easy after all.

The tracts are combined into a 3-part "book" consisting of three essays which "Biblically PROVES the reality and sexuality of the Goddess, and disproves celibacy of Jesus Christ (which some allege), as well as some other proofs, disproofs, and information, which should interest you." This includes very technical information on brain research, physics and mathematics.

The authors are careful to distinguish between their "absolute" and "non-absolute" proofs. "Some of our proofs are absolute or very nearly so," they claim. "In our absolute and our near-absolute proofs and disproofs, whenever there is any assumption, the counter-assumption is also considered as another case, so that it covers ALL possible conditions." Such rigor is admirable, though it's easy to see that there is at least one TMC+A belief that they have failed to identify as an assumption: that the Judeo-Christian Bible is true.

"We are children of God, not borne merely from a human father; nor an exclusively male Almighty Father."

Though TMC+A constantly revises its proofs and disproofs, its beliefs are stable, as summed up in the general information sheet:

> Most of our literature is devoted to theology about the real Goddess. Biblically, She is the female of two original persons, Who are God. Much later, She resurrected Jesus Christ with Her special Divine Energy ('Holy Spirit'). After doing this, She initiated Jesus for ascension to Godhood (Although born human, Jesus had the Divine hereditary Components. These were inactive, and Jesus was not God before being initiated). She also enabled Jesus' conception. Virgin Mary gave Jesus a distinctive, but human birth and later he died a human death in a way some other humans died. God preserved Jesus' corpse from decay during death. Then the Goddess (not Mary) gave Jesus birth again by resurrection. There is no marriage in Heaven, but there is LOVE. Sex is mainly for the expression of love. Both Yahweh and Jesus are the Goddess' Consorts. Persons, Who are God, are both physical and spiritual (sexual parts are not merely ornamental). . . .

The Table of Contents for the TMC+A three-part book could be used a guide to TMC+A theology: "Jesus' Sex Activity Before His Godhood," "Anthro-pomorphic Sensuosity of God (including Goddess)," "EXPLODING MYTHS of NONPHYSICAL MIND & EMOTIONS," "CHEMICAL TRANSFER of INTELLECT & ETERNAL LIFE," "WHY GODDESS', NOT MARY's, SEX DREW GOD's SPERM for SON," "BIBLICAL SUBREPTION by ANCIENT CHAUVINISTS," "TRANSCENDENCE to IDEAL FLESH RENEWAL" and "WHY the MYTH, REINCARNATION, IS FALSE."

The basis for this strange combination of Christianity, Scientific Materialism and Feminism can be found in main tract #91, "GODDESS' REALITY & HER MISSION" which begins the TMC+A lesson course:

> . . . The *REAL Goddess* isn't derived from the fantasy of any mythical pagan goddess conceptions. She is Sovereign as any Lord God (Yahweh and Jesus Christ, Both Her Divine Consorts), SHE Being Their *Divine Mistress*. . . .
>
> We are children of God, not borne merely from a human father; nor an exclusively male Almighty Father. Fathers can sire, but do not bear children, the child borne within and born from the mother. As led by the Spirit of God, *Holy and Feminine*, we find the Way of the very essence of love that mothers all living, thus borne children of God.
>
> Her Personality, all of God's feminine character, is denied by impersonal Pantheistic theology, and by masculine-only monotheistic and polytheistic religions. She is Goddess, slandered by feeble, limited capacity pagan and Neo-pagan goddess concepts, some of which are mentioned in the Bible (Ashtoreth, Diana, etc.) and are limiting feminine splendor in a most profane way, tarnishing Her true magnificence.
>
> The Goddess is included as Creator (God), and is an ACTIVE Member of Divinity, a Giver of life and love, with sexuality intended for action, if appropriate (including Special Divine Techniques and all other worthy techniques from foreplay, through Divine coitus, to after-play-originating and continuing as desired with Yahweh, many, ever many countless times for Their pleasure, but only once for issuance of the Genetic Factor for His son, and also with His very son as *Divine Initiatrix*, after Her Holy Spirit gave the human son of God birth again, resurrecting his corpse). She effectuated inactive nature of Jesus' Divine Heritage in an initiation process involving the most dynamic Divine sexual acts to EQUAL EVERYTHING with Yahweh and Herself, as well as knowledge, stamina, etc. where Jesus was less than God. She is not fantasy, nor ornament, but purely real, and is the Person to whom the Holy Ghost refers in the "Father, Son and Holy Ghost" Trinity. In modern society "Spirit" has replaced "Ghost", but that is what She has been in most "Christian" minds. A patriarchal rulership of the past exterminated awareness of the Goddess reality, forbearing only remnants of Her, much like a "ghost". God's Will Be Done (Her Will, too).

TMC+A members are unequivocal about their disdain for pagan and Neo-pagan practices and beliefs. They maintain that it is one of the most famous of pagans, Plato, and his successors, the neo-Platonists, who are largely to blame for the anti-female and anti-sexual attitudes of Western Religion today. Platonists and neo-Platonists are guilty of promoting the "ghost in the machine" mind/body split concept of human consciousness, which TMC+A rejects. Instead, TMC+A accepts modern scientific materialism, viewing all consciousness, emotion and mind as the product of physical processes:

> NOW, preponderant scientific evidence shows intelligence, emotions and consciousness are *physical ELECTRO-CHEMICAL PROCESSES* . . .
>
> Nerve signals *inducing emotions* are modified by expectations, purposes and past experiences with *glands and muscles.* Any LOVE *requires* and basically *IS* EMOTION! Every atom is made of moving particles of energy. And every living cell is a *radial center* of *bioplasmic (psychic) energy.* This is proven with Kirlian photography. This energy and/or brain's own radio waves may be used in telepathy, telegnosis, telekinesis, acupuncture, and dowsing. Various instruments *physically* find, focus, measure, amplify, and sometimes use this energy, especially that radiating from *living human flesh,* thus revealing it as another *physical* form. . . .

TMC+A's mating of scientific materialism with belief in the Bible yields not only physical deities but also physical immortality for humans:

> The Biblical fact of chemical transmission of knowledge and eternal life is now evidenced by facts from scientific experiments, which support these prospects, and even prove chemical transfer of intellect and chemical retardation of some aging. . . . FOREVER PHYSICAL is a theology of uncaused effectuation of physical Divinity in this Nature of reality, and of UNcaused SuperNatural origin of physical Divinity (God), CO-Primary with original TRUTH. . . .

Though it members believe in the physicality of the Deity and the divinity of the physical, TMC+A is not a "free love" religion. It adheres to Yahweh's sexual prejudices, asserting that ". . .Yahweh (the Father) is *NOT* homosexual, and does *NOT* masturbate, because of reasons of *CONSISTENCY of His Will*. . . ." Yahweh is a REAL MAN, and like all other real men, he has sperm:

> Jesus was a male, not a female. ALL human males have an unpaired "Y" chromosome, which Mary, a female could not supply. In Nature, there is parthenogenesis, or offspring (children, progeny) from virgin females of various species, including some laboratory mammals, but such *offspring are always female.* Biblically, Jesus is the only begotten son of God. "Begotten" very definitely refers to *genetic* and indeed *sexual procreation.* . . . So God *BEGAT* Jesus, NOT by adoption, NOT by breath (as Adam), NOT by design (as angels), but by some process involving sex. That is, the Biblical "Holy Ghost" was then a form of Holy Energy permeated by God's Holy Sperm *(H genes)*, Which God sent to impregnate Mary with Jesus. . . . Human reproduction occurs *only when each parent supplies 1/2 of the chromosomes* (scientific fact). So, Yahweh must have produced the *male genetic portion* directly for Jesus' sex designation. ...

The fact that human females cannot supply the Y chromosome, combined with the fact that Mary, a virgin, supposedly gave birth to Jesus, could also prove that Jesus was not male, but female. No doubt we could take our pick of theologies, feminist or otherwise, "proved" via the simultaneous acceptance of "current science" and "Biblical facts."

Science and religion may soon be reunited, if the proliferation of new theologies, such as TMC+A, is any indication. The first small steps to this reunification have usually meant incorporating scientific results or the scientific method into a non-materialist, spiritually-oriented belief system; this would include both the "Bible Scientists," who use the scientific method selectively to back up their interpretation of the Bible, and also, those New Age philosophers who use scientific results selectively to back up their belief in, say, Taoism. TMC+A does the opposite, embracing the scientific materialist philosophy that everybody else is rejecting, and incorporating the Bible into it, rather than vice versa. For this reason, I suspect that TMC+A is a 20th century fluke, which will probably go the way of state communism, lobotomy, and other materialist solutions to spiritual problems.

"Every atom is made of moving particles of energy. And every living cell is a radial center of bioplasmic (psychic) energy. This is proven with Kirlian photography."

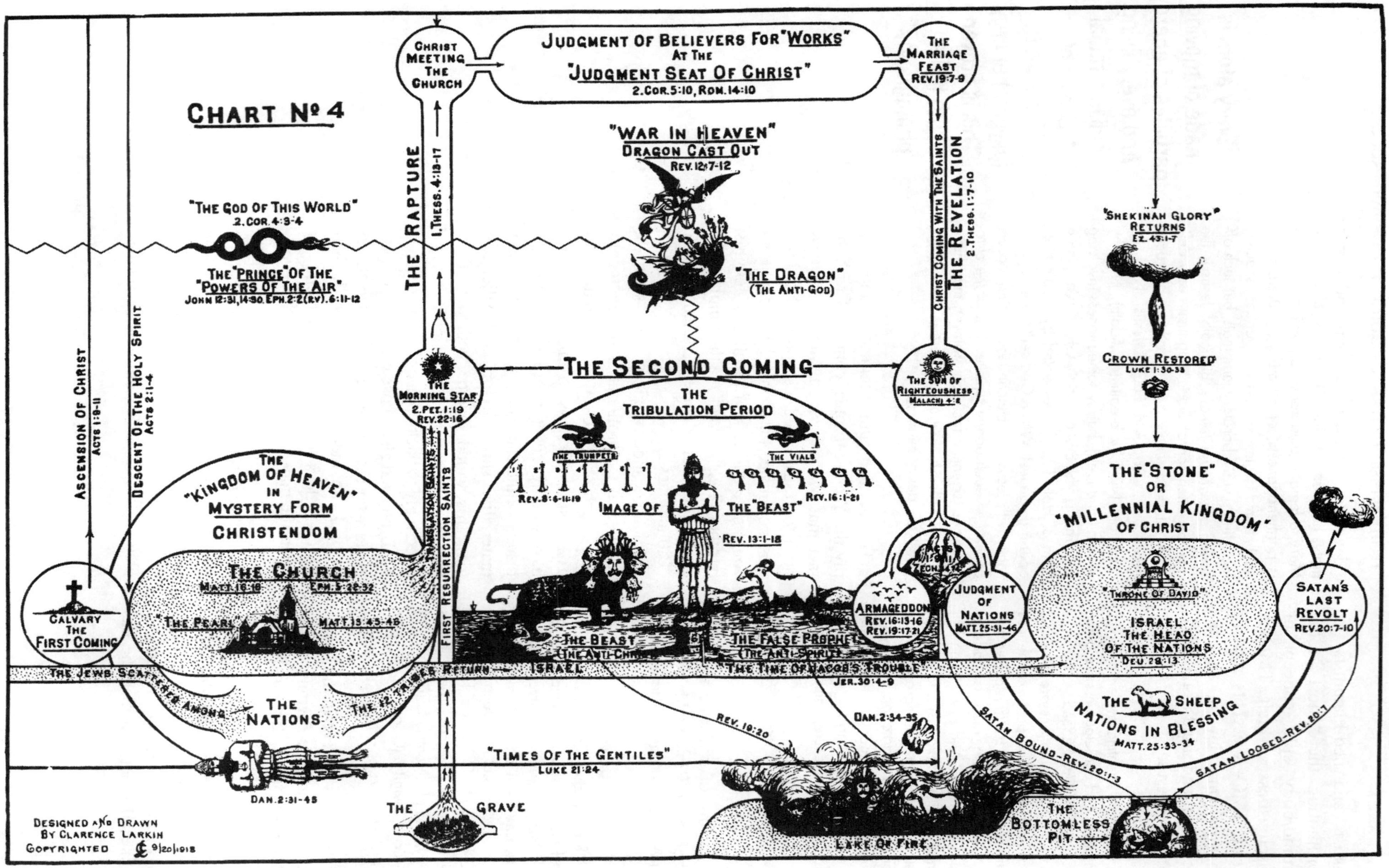
Chart № 4
Christ Meeting The Church
Judgment Of Believers For "Works" At The "Judgment Seat Of Christ"
2. Cor. 5:10, Rom. 14:10
The Marriage Feast
Rev. 19:7-9
"War In Heaven"
Dragon Cast Out
Rev. 12:7-12
"The God Of This World"
2. Cor. 4:3-4
The "Prince" Of The "Powers Of The Air"
John 12:31, 14:30, Eph. 2:2 (RV), 6:11-12
"The Dragon" (The Anti-God)
The Rapture
1. Thess. 4:13-17
Christ Coming With The Saints
The Revelation
2. Thess. 1:7-10
"Shekinah Glory" Returns
Ez. 43:1-7
Crown Restored
Luke 1:30-33
Ascension Of Christ
Acts 1:9-11
Descent Of The Holy Spirit
Acts 2:1-4
The Second Coming
The Morning Star
2. Pet. 1:19
Rev. 22:16
The Sun Of Righteousness
Malachi 4:2
The Tribulation Period
The Trumpets
Rev. 8:6-11:19
The Vials
Rev. 16:1-21
Image Of The "Beast"
Rev. 13:1-18
The "Kingdom Of Heaven" In Mystery Form
Christendom
The Church
Matt. 16:18
Eph. 5:32-32
"The Pearl"
Matt. 13:45-46
Translation Saints
First Resurrection Saints
The Beast (The Anti-Christ)
The False Prophet (The Anti-Spirit)
Armageddon
Rev. 16:13-16
Rev. 19:17-21
Judgment Of Nations
Matt. 25:31-46
The "Stone" Or "Millennial Kingdom" Of Christ
"Throne Of David"
Israel The Head Of The Nations
Deu. 28:13
Satan's Last Revolt
Rev. 20:7-10
Calvary The First Coming
The Jews Scattered Among The Nations
The 12 Tribes Return
Israel
The Time Of Jacob's Trouble
Jer. 30:4-9
The Sheep Nations In Blessing
Matt. 25:33-34
Rev. 19:20
Dan. 2:34-35
Satan Bound-Rev. 20:1-3
Satan Loosed-Rev. 20:7
"Times Of The Gentiles"
Luke 21:24
Dan. 2:31-45
The Grave
The Bottomless Pit
Lake Of Fire
Designed and Drawn By Clarence Larkin
Copyrighted 9/20/1918

EDGAR C. WHISENANT: THE WORLD WILL END IN 1988 ON BORROWED TIME (excerpts)

THE BIBLE'S MYSTERIES UNRAVELLED

The major prophecies of all the Old and New Testament prophets have now been put together. Each prophecy verifies all other prophecies. All verses in the book of Revelation now have the dates of occurrence assigned by scripture. We now know which seven years will be the Tribulation. Every major event of the Tribulation is known, as well as the dates on which these events will occur. We know the exact day that the Millennium begins and ends, as well as the dates of the events in between. These events were never restricted from our knowledge, but only the day and hour of our Lord's return for the Church, and that event was limited only to the day and hour, and not the week, month or year.

. . . God used the dates of the last three Feasts in the years 1988 through 1995 to begin and end the counts of days given in the Old and New Testament books of Ezekiel, Daniel and Revelation. The lunar dates of the last three Feasts of Israel, which begins and ends the counts of days given in Ezekiel, Daniel and Revelation, will only fit 1988 through 1995. At no other time in history or the future will these Bible counts fit. **This is unfakeable and undeniable proof that the 70th week of Daniel**, called the Seven-Year Tribulation, starts in 1988. . . .

THE LAST GENERATIONS

. . . The last wicked generation, who would not repent of their sins and accept Jesus as their Messiah, started May 14, 1948, the day Israel became a nation. It will end 40 years later on the Day of Atonement, Sept. 21, 1988, Yom Kippur, 1988. . . .

ROSH-HASH-ANA 1988 IS THE KEY

If Rosh-Hash-Ana, 1988 is the date of the Rapture of the Church, the dates of the remaining end-time events can now be found. The Rapture will occur sometime during the period of Rosh-Hash-Ana, between sunset, Sept. 11 and sunset, Sept. 13. The next Feast is ten days later, Day of Atonement, Sept. 21. This day Antichrist will sign the Peace Pact with Israel to start the 70th week of Daniel, also known as the Tribulation.

Five days later, Feast of Tabernacles, Sept. 26, the two witnesses will arrive to seal the 144,000 Jewish Christian missionaries. . . .

At midweek of the 70th week of Daniel, or 3 1/2 years into the Seven-Year Tribulation, March 12, 1992, Jesus takes legal possession of the earth from Satan. (Rev. 11:15). He does not take physical possession until Armageddon, Oct. 4, 1995, when He physically returns to earth. . . .

ED WHISENANT COMMENTS

. . . Man can now know every event of the end-time to the very second except for the day and hour of the Rapture. That is the only mystery in the whole thing. Isn't that just like God. He said day and hour. He didn't say week, month and year. You don't add to God's word, you don't subtract from God's word. . . . I've never seen anything so beautifully fit together before in my life. And it just seemed to flood in. All the possibilities and ramifications. We could know everything at the end of the thousand years. God never had any secrets from His prophets. He told them all this. I'll bet there are a lot of mysteries in those old prophets that'll now come to light (Amos 3:7).

He would not have put it together if His time had not been right. Five years before it was gonna happen. These dates, the last three Feasts of Israel, on the lunar cycle from '88 to '95, would have meant nothing to anybody, including me, if I had not had the 886 end-time Bible prophecies at my fingertips with all the references. . . .

I spent a few months copying everything. I mailed it to at least 50 preachers at one time. I went to great effort. All my money went to that. Because I thought they could understand. Man, I must have been the laughing stock of the continent, in their opinion. "This guy is a real cuckoo." It wasn't decently typed up. It was drawn, a lot of it, with pencil and paper, research notes in the roughest form. I was so thrilled to get it out, saying, "Look, our Lord's coming back! Praise God, jump up and down, tell the people! Don't just sit there any more!"

I've since mailed out over 700 copies to everybody I thought loved God's word. I've spent well over $20,000 of my own money over the last five years trying to tell the world.

We now know all the events of the 70th week of Daniel, three world wars, three Raptures, three judgments and all the events of the Millennium and their dates. Now we'll just sit down in front of the evening news and watch the events unfold. . . .

88 REASONS why the RAPTURE will be in 1988 (excerpts)
A Summary
88 REASONS WHY ROSH-HASH-ANA 1988 MUST BE THE TIME OF THE CHURCH'S RAPTURE

You only need one good solid reason why 1988 will be the church's Rapture. Here are 88 plus reasons why Rosh-Hash-Ana 1988 is the year of the church's Rapture for you to pick one from.

REASON #1

It is evident that, in the mind of most Christians today, Matt. 24:36 is believed to prohibit anyone from being able to see the day of our Lord's return approaching. Matt. 24:36 states that "No one knows about that day or hour, not even the angels in heaven, nor the Son, but only the Father." In looking at this statement, you can easily see that it is impossible to know the exact day and hour of the Lord Jesus' return.

If Jesus arrives at one particular instant of time, there are 24 time zones around the world, and each time zone has multitudes of Christians in it. How are you going to identify that particular instant in each time zone on earth? Also there are always two days existing on earth at the same time; only at the exact second that the earth passes through the international date line does only one day exist on all the earth. . . . So you can see the problem in trying to tell all the Christians covering the earth at any one instant of time the exact day or hour of our Lord's return.

However, this does not preclude or prevent the faithful from knowing the year, the month, and the week of the Lord's return.

REASON #8

The Jewish people recognize the significance of the 40 years from 1948 to 1988.

Rabbi Meir Kahane, the rabbi who wants to throw out all Arabs in Israel, is acutely aware of the 40-year grace period given by God starting in 1948. . . .

REASON #12

I Thess. 5:3 says, "while they (the world) are saying peace and safety! Then shall destruction come upon them suddenly like birth pangs upon a woman with child; and none shall escape." Jer. 6:9-15 says, "peace, peace, they say when there is no peace."

This was the last prophecy that needed to be fulfilled before the Rapture takes place. When this peace (and safety) movement is worldwide, then shall destruction come upon them suddenly and none shall escape. This peace movement had reached the capacity of 200,000 to 300,000 in Europe in 1986, and "Hands Across America" brought the United States into the movement.

On 1 July 1987, the New Age Movement had a rally for peace in every capital of the world.

So when all the world cries for peace and safety, destruction will come on them suddenly (World War III, World War IV, and World War V at Armageddon), and none shall escape.

This is the first time in history that all capitals of the world have cried out in unison for peace.

REASON #27

The total of 2,520 years is 36 generations of 70 years each (from Daniel's prophecy of the 70 weeks) to 1988. 602 B.C. - 70 = 532 + 1988 = 2520 ÷ 70 = 36 generations to Rosh-Hash-Ana 1988. The time of the Gentiles given in Lev. 26:18 is given at 7 x 360 = 2520 years.

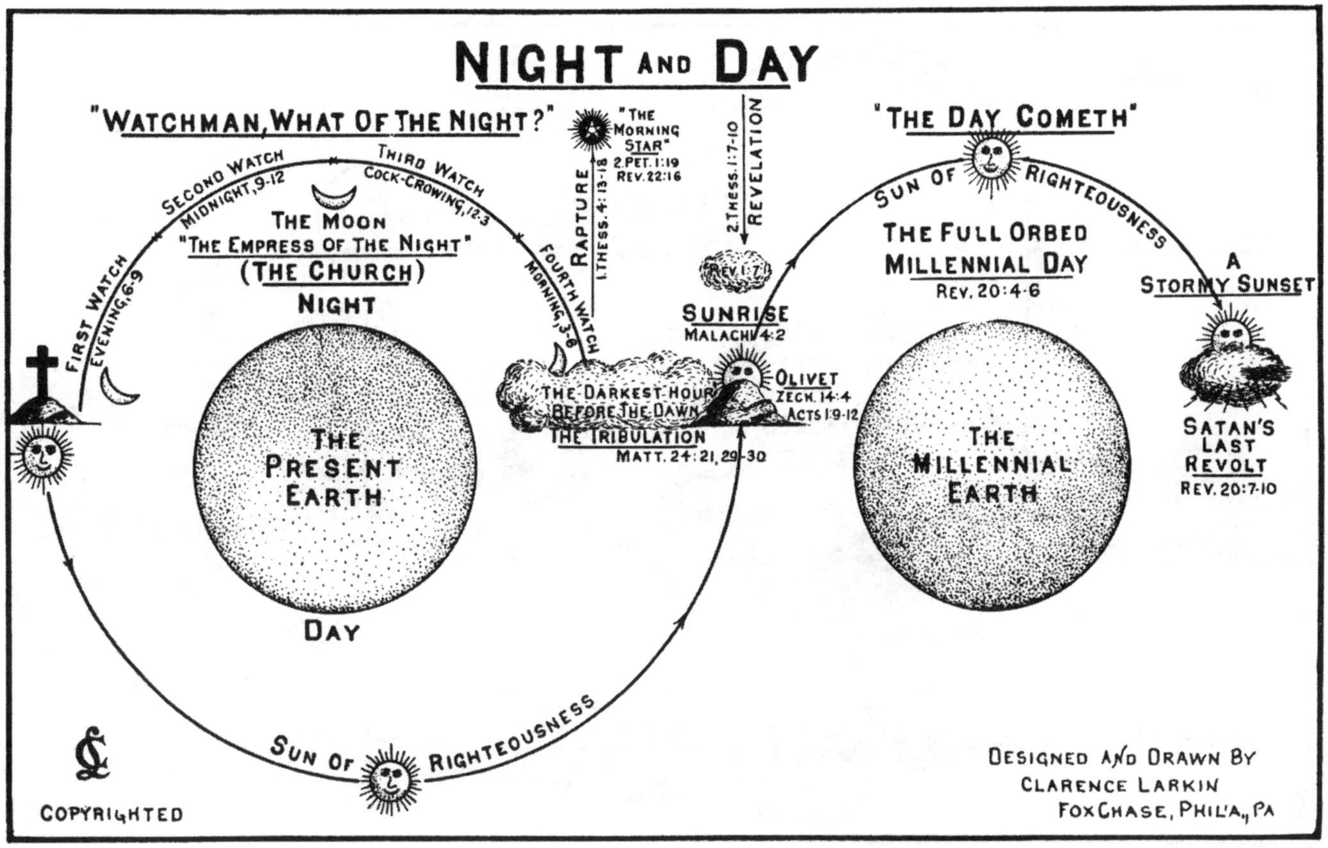

REASON #59 (NON-BIBLICAL)

The New Age Movement (which are Satan worshippers) are looking for their "New David" which is Satan in 1991-1992. If the 70th week of Daniel began in the fall of 1988, then 1992 would be the time the idol would be set up for the Abomination of Desolation, and Satan would start his 3-1/2 year rule, with Armageddon being in the end in 1995.

End-time events are now coming together so rapidly that they boggle the mind in thinking about them.

A MESSAGE TO THE UNITED STATES

Once you are conceived (and I did not say born), you are going to live forever. The only question is where: heaven or hell? That is all decided in this lifetime. . . .

I find several hundred references to the United States in the Old Testament alone. This may seem high, but I know there are many of them. . . .

Nuclear Winter will last five years in the northern third (60 degrees) of the earth (which covers the United States) from statements made by Carl Sagan on Nuclear Winter, plus additional statements made in the Bible. We also know the whole continent will be as dark as midnight 24 hours a day for this entire five-year period, with temperatures never rising above zero fahrenheit. Mass starvation and unburied bodies will result. The Department of Defense expects the destruction to be so complete that you can walk from Little Rock to Dallas over ashes only. All food will be gone; all water will be radioactive, except for underground water. . . .

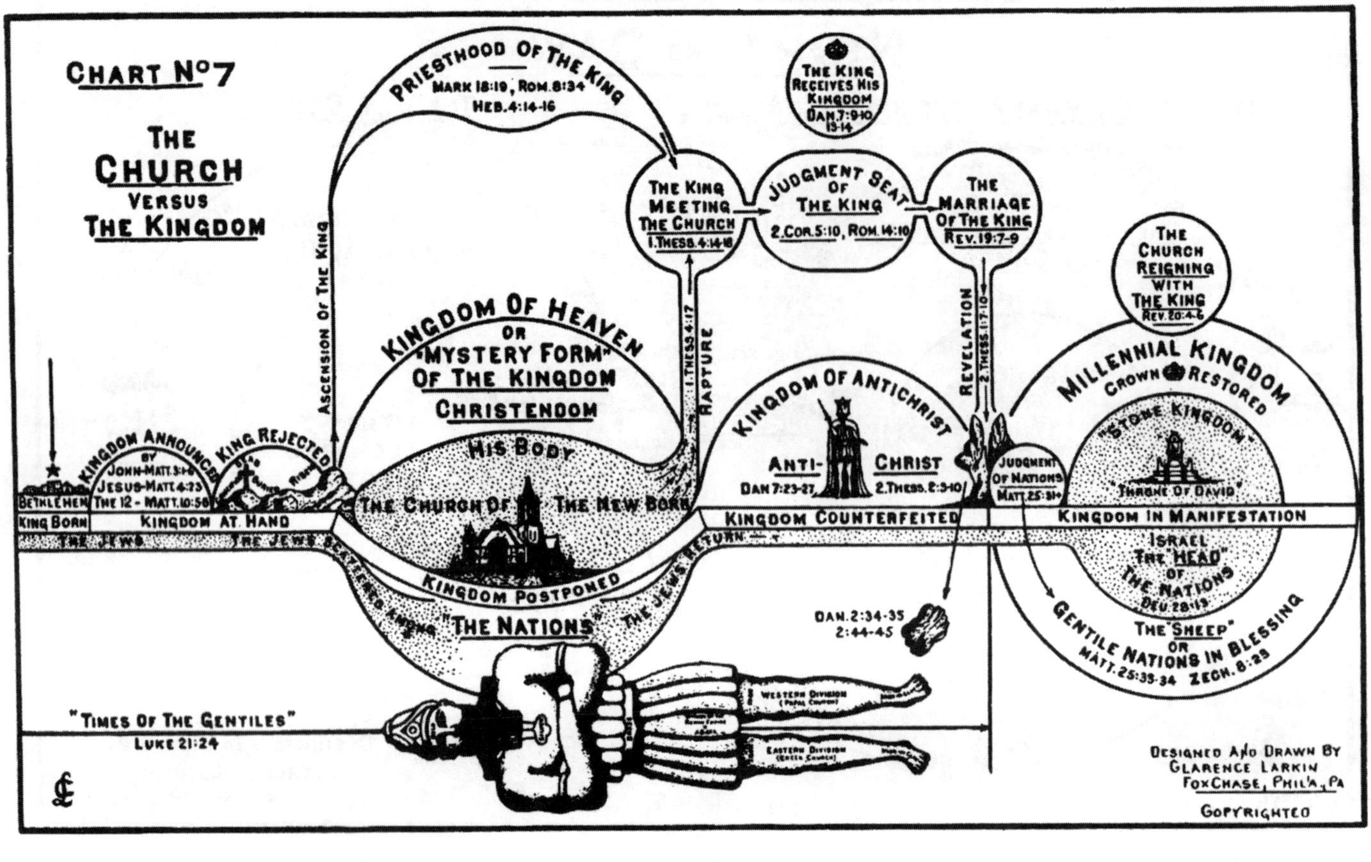

KOREAN CHRISTIANS
RAPTURE IN 1992

IN NOVEMBER, 1991, THE *BOSTON HERALD* carried an ad headlined, "RAPTURE IN 1992, Jesus is coming on the air," paid for by an organization called "Mission for the Coming Days." This Korean group had also been spotted in downtown Boston, preaching THE END and passing out literature.

The *Boston Herald* ad read:

> In near future, many who have waited eagerly for Jesus and lived holy and faithful lives will instantly be changed into holy bodies and raised up to meet the Lord in the air. Such a wonderful event is called "rapture." There will be quite a confusion in the world after rapture looking for a large number of disappeared people. However, raptured holy brides of Jesus will rejoice seven years of Wedding Feast while the whole world, including left behind lukewarm Christians, will enter Great Tribulation where most of them will be killed. God's righteous beloved children will be delivered, but unrepentant ones will face His Judgement and perish.
>
> European Economic Community (E.E.C.) or United Europe will be this ten-nation confederacy, and the antichrist will appear upon its unification in 1992. He will establish seven years of peace treaty with Israel, but will break it after three and a half years. He will put a stop to their sacrifice and grain offering and force them to worship him. Those who do not worship will be martyred. (Dan. 9:27)

Later in 1992, after moving to Portland, Oregon, I was surprised to see a full-page ad (on the following page) in the city's daily, the Oregonian. Obviously, the group had placed ads all over the country, and probably, all over the world. The ad, an elaboration of the first one, ominously warned unbelievers that the rapture would occur on October 28, 1992. There was still just a little time left to repent.

When October 28 arrived, I became apprehensive-not because I expected the world to end-but because I was concerned for those who did. Shortly after, I attempted to contact the Mission For the Coming Days at their Salem, Oregon post office box. As expected, my letter was returned, unopened, stamped, "RETURN TO SENDER, NO FORWARDING ORDER ON FILE." Perhaps the faithful had vanished into thin air. I heard nothing of them until picking up *Fortean Times #66* months later.

According to *Fortean Times*, Mission for the Coming Days, based in Sydney, Australia and led by Pastor Chang Hun Jo, was not the only group involved in the rapture prediction. In Korea, Pastor Lee Jang Lim of the Tami Missionary Church had amassed one million believers and Ha Bang-ik of the Davera Mission Church also had a healthy following. Pastor Lee was arrested in late September, 1992 on charges of illegally converting some of the £2 million in donations he'd received into American dollars. The police also discovered £230,000 in bonds, which were due to mature in 1995; this would have been 3 years into the Great Tribulation, when money was supposed to have been worthless.

Neither Pastor Jo of the Mission for the Coming Days—who was affiliated with the fraudulent Pastor Lee—nor his followers were deterred by these revelations. There were at least four "doomsday related suicides" in the various groups during 1992, a horrific testament to the depth of their faith.

As of 1993 nothing more has been heard from the groups. It will be worthwhile, however, to observe the post-"rapture" evolution of the faithful. The sects may eventually come up with a new rapture date, though this is unlikely; in past cases of failed prophecy, new predictions were made almost immediately upon the heels of the original date. It is more likely that they will develop a new theology—as the Millerites did when they became Seventh-Day Adventists—or that they will disappear altogether, returning home not to their savior's arms, but penniless, to Korea.

IGNORE INNER SELVES

at your own peril. They know all the tricks to throw tantrums, get their own way, waste your time, your money, & your energy. Don't get left out! Be boss—not as a dictator, but as a loving friend. Release your tremendous inner powers. Order "Don't be afraid of your mind." Guaranty enclosed. Send $2.
CALVIN COTTAM, Dept. IF
1017 ARLINGTON, LOS ANGELES 19, CALIF.

PSYCHOZICS, "THE well-guarded secret of the BOMBARDING THOUGHT." For worthy purposes only. $3.00. Adults. Satisfaction or refund.—Clarion, Box 1769-Z7, Chicago, Ill. 60690

HOW TO THINK TO LIVE FOREVER. $1.00.—P.O. Box 4603, Dallas 6, Texas.

YOU can become a SUPERMAN! This state is the birthright of all men and women. No mirage, but proven fact. The world is crying out for true Bearers of the Light. For details write to: American Secretary, Brotherhood of the Illuminati, 3035 First Ave. South, St. Petersburg 12, Florida.

SUPERET LIGHT is coming. Your key to this knowledge is found in these books. Star of the Future; Miracle Woman's Secret; Human Atoms Power; World Aura Discovery; Ancient Canyon; Atoms Aura Reveals Secrets; Key to Success; Superet Light; Important: Heal Thyself with Superet Light. These nine books are available at $1.00 each, ppd. Write: Superet, Box 488, Jamacia 31, N. Y.

"HUMAN is MYSTERY"

50-year inquiry probes deepest phenomena, reports thoughtform (TF) experiments, tests and controls; human cells, atom, instruments, photography, biomagnetic disease immersion, etc. Condensed. Illustrated. Authorities. Endorsed. Only 25 cents. EDUCATIONAL THOUGHT FOUNDATION, Box 1155, St. Augustine, Fla. 32084.

The GOLDEN THOUGHTFORMER

LIVE that simple ORDER in thought producing all "Miracles" . . . TF or Think Fast Thoughtforming (since you are a Thoughtform). Easily self-taught, and think-walk-ride through stone and steel. TF Manual of Thoughtforming, Thoughtreading, Thoughtlearning, Thoughtfeeling, etc. $2.00. (30 years research.)
SENSITRON SYSTEM
Box 1126 (F), St. Augustine, Florida

RELIGIOUS FAITH DESTROYS YOU. Read the books of William Hallgarth, "Strange Research" ($1.00) and "I Shall Teach Thee Terrible Things" ($1.00).—P.O. Box 225, Belmar, N. J.

CHOOSE THE UNFORBIDDEN — An Introduction to Astro-Eugenics—reveals: Everything you need to know about choosing your mate and planning your family. Send $3.00—L. Donee. P.O. Box 5802, San Diego, California 92105

"SANITARY GERMS" Book, $2.50. "INTERLUDE" Sheet Music-Words, 35c. —Dr. Emil F. Tiesen, Freeman, S. Dak.

EARTH AXIS SHIFT

Coming soon. Know HOW, WHY, WHEN. Oceans overrun lands destroying life, property. Scientifically, mathematically, geologically extrapolated. Latest 1968 edition, $1.00 postpaid.
EMIL SEPIC
2510 Harrison Avenue, Eureka, Calif. 95501

BOTTOMLESS PIT, entrance to Hell beyond South Pole at Rainbow City. Entrance for flying saucers driven by fallen angels (gods). Revelation 20 and occult research.

ANGLO-SAXON RELIGION. For literature write: Anglo-Saxon, Box 681, The Dalles, OR 97058

WILL YOU BE ALIVE IN 1975?

When will the world strife end? Will there be one more world war? In what year shall we witness the advent of permanent peace on earth? Here is an astounding book that tells how the Masters have been foretelling the future through one man for the past 30 years. He has been predicting political trends, business cycles, natural and man-made catastrophies, rise and fall of important men, wars, revolutions, and new inventions, since 1930 and his forecasts have been unbelievably correct. Statesmen, financiers, diplomats, corporation heads, and thousands of lesser folk, have been amazed by the accuracy with which he pinpoints future happenings and the time when they will occur.

All authorities on world affairs are agreed on one thing — that we live in a period of danger to all humanity. Never was there a time when a knowledge of the future would be of such value to you. These forecasts may save you many, many times their cost. This book may show you what line of business to go into for greatest profit. It may show you how to increase your life span by many years. We stand at the doorway of a new kingdom where each of us can be a king in his own right. Will you be ready to enter?

In order to reach the greatest number of people, the price of the book WILL YOU BE ALIVE IN 1975?, has been kept so low that anyone can afford it — only $2.00. You may send remittance or order book on our free examination plan and return book if you are not delighted by it. If you decide to keep it, send us $2.00 plus 25c bookkeeping charges, within two weeks.

OUR GUARANTEE: So amazingly accurate are these predictions that we are willing to make you a proposition: IF ANY ONE of the forecasts in this book do not come true in the years ahead, then return the book at any time within the next five years for full refund of your $2.00.

But act at once. This edition will not last long. Mail your order NOW — before you miss these important forecasts. Mail your order to: THE BOOK OF DESTINY, 26-B So. Highland Ave., Ossining, N.Y. 10562.

OCCULT POLICE

EXCITEMENT
ADVENTURE
PSYCHIC DEVELOPMENT
Join
OCCULT POLICE
FOR BOOKLET SEND $1 TO
BOX 1574, KEY WEST, FL. 33040

THE JAREDITE ADVOCATE, a monthly publication, (1 year—$3.00) is dedicated to the exposure of the WATCHERS, the race created by Lucifer, which has controlled earth for 8,000 years. Control the A.M.A., plotted the death of Lincoln, J.F.K. Infiltrated into U.S. High Courts, State Department. Attempting to destroy U.S. through Communism. Are the "Beast" of Revelation. For free copy of the JAREDITE ADVOCATE, write Sons of Jared, Box 29026, Los Angeles, Calif. 90029

THE SUN RISES—A remarkable book! Taken clairvoyantly from the Akashic Record. An authentic account of the beginning of the world's first and greatest civilization—The Continent of Mu. 442 pages — clothbound, $3.00.—Lemurian Fellowship, Ramona 4, Calif.

READ "PSYCHO IMAGE" and obtain an outlook upon the mind-body relationship that may change your life. Send $2.00 to P.O. Box 1073, Provo, Utah.

WHY DO MOST PEOPLE

in the world avoid shaking hands? Just custom? Are "primitives" more aware of lurking harm? Are we spiritual barbarians? Can you pick up "invisible" ills, vibrations, troubles, pains? Don't lose your energy! Order "The psychic dangers of shaking hands & how to protect yourself." Guaranty enclosed. Send just $2 now.
CALVIN COTTAM, Dept. OF
1017 ARLINGTON, LOS ANGELES 19, CALIF.

MAD AT GOD? Discover why. Free leaflet. — Allis Murray, Saltville, VA 24370

BIBLE ERRORS? Many! Send for FREE references concerning contradictions, inconsistencies and violations against proven scientific laws.—Frank Battle, Box 647-L Dover, N.J.

MAGNETIC IS LIFE! Magnetism is death! Live law of Nature's Magnet. Be happier, healthier, live longer. Order "Nature's Law for People," $10.00.—Nature Publications, 800 Sunset, Manhattan, Kansas 66502

ORDER BOOKLET "The Key To All That Is." The best dollar you ever spent.—Kepner, Box 2623, San Diego, Calif.

RESURRECTED Billions will farm ocean bottoms when seas removed by coming whirlwind! Free. Write: Harvest-SD, Jefferson City, Mo. 65101.

BREAKTHROUGH!

Religions are no longer mysterious. Everything explainable as being human nature. Read at no risk: **THE RELIGIOUS PSYCHOLOGY OF THE HUMAN RACE.**
$1.00 ppd. One year guarantee.
Saburo Katamoto, Dept. F
P.O. Box 24184, Seattle, WA 98124

TRANSLATED DREAM of Baal Mystic, 25c.—Ideograph Inst., Box 2301, Norman, Okla.

SECRET OF THE 144,000 Virgins, 10c. — Leonard Austin's Physicalism, De Sota, Iowa. 50069.

WORLD-WIDE CHASTISEMENT WARNINGS
Limited copies. $2.00 each.
FORSMARK
5865 Brierhaven, Memphis, Tenn. 38138

EARTH FLAT, fact not theory original Egyptian astrologers knew. Subscribe to FLAT EARTH NEWS. Years subscription and membership $5.00. PROOF.—International Flat Earth Research Society, Box 2533, Lancaster, CA 93534

"SECRET: The Gizeh Pyramids," by T. N. Tastmona; 144pp., 11x14 inches, big type, 96 ilustrations; 2nd ed. $25.00, 3rd ed. $15.00, same content. No metaphysics. Basic discoveries that revolutionize science of Egyptology and Jewish/Christian "theology." Tastmona **theorem**: Old and New Testaments are **hoaxes** by Egyptian atheists. Tastmona **fact**: YHVH (Jehovah) is IHUH Egyptian **heliocentric** formula; Peter is Peteh-ur a comet meteor stone. Remit to: The Thothmona Book Co., Dept. F, 520 Fifth Avenue, New York 36, N.Y.

"THE MIRACLE OF THE MAGNITUDES." This exciting new book on causes of physical phenomena, hot off the press. An amazing new scientific theory of unification of natural laws and theories. Embraces just what the title implies. Beautifully bound 6 x 8½ volume published by the author. First edition of limited publication. Its simplicity will be appreciated. Scientific throughout. Postpaid anywhere, $3.75 per copy, check or money order. Mail orders to: Miracle of the Magnitudes, 6802 S.E. Overland St., Portland, Oreg. 97222

THE THEORY OF UNIVERSAL EXPANSION presents, perhaps the most important single idea of this century. $2.00 — James Carter, Box 831, Avalon, CA 90704

BIBLIOGRAPHY

I HAVE USED THE FOLLOWING BOOKS AND periodicals over the years for my general research. The list is by no means exhaustive. For example, I didn't include the myriad "'zines" dealing with "fringe" topics that have come out in the past several years, only 'zines I myself have used for source material.

Books and articles pertaining to specific chapters follow the general bibliography.

GENERAL

Cohn, Norman. *The Pursuit of the Millennium.* New York: Oxford University Press, 1957.

Cohn, Norman. *Warrant for Genocide.* Chico, CA: Scholars Press, 1981.

Curran, Douglas. *In Advance of the Landing: Folk Concepts of Outer Space.* Abbeville Press, 1985.

Evans, Dr. Christopher. *Cults of Unreason.* New York: Farrar, Straus & Giroux, 1974.

Festinger, Riecken and Schachter. *When Prophecy Fails.* New York: Harper & Row, 1956.

Gardner, Martin. *Fads and Fallacies in the Name of Science.* New York: Dover Publications, 1952, 1957.

Jastrow, Joseph. *Error and Eccentricity in Human Belief.* New York: Dover Publications, 1935. (Formerly titled *Wish and Wisdom, Episodes in the Vagaries of Belief.*)

Kafton-Minkel, Walter. *Subterranean Worlds.* Port Townsend, WA: Loompanics, 1989.

Mackay, Charles. *Extraordinary Popular Delusions and the Madness of Crowds.* New York: The Noonday Press, 1932.

Melton, J. Gordon. *Encyclopedia of American Religions.* Wilmington, NC: McGrath Publishing Company, 1978.

Melton, J. Gordon. *Encyclopedic Handbook of Cults in America.* Garland Reference Library of Social Science V. 213, 1986.

Michell, John. *Eccentric Lives and Peculiar Notions.* Secaucus, NJ: Citadel Press, 1984.

Parfrey, Adam, ed. *Apocalypse Culture.* Portland: Feral House, 1990.

Rubinsky, Yuri & Wiseman, Ian. *A History of the End of the World.* New York: Quill, 1982.

Schultz, Ted, ed. *The Fringes of Reason.* New York: Harmony Books, 1989.

Stang, Rev. Ivan. *High Weirdness by Mail.* New York: Simon & Schuster, 1988.

Vallee, Jacques. *Messengers of Deception: UFO Contacts and Cults.* Berkeley, CA: And/Or Press, 1979.

Vallee, Jacques. *Revelations: Alien Contact and Human Deception.* New York: Ballantine Books, 1991.

Catalogs

Adventures Unlimited (PO Box 22, Stelle, IL 60919)

Loompanics Unlimited (PO Box 1197, Port Townsend, WA 98368)

Magazines

Critique (Bob Banner, ed., Santa Rosa, CA., defunct).

Fate (PO Box 64383, St. Paul, MN 55164-0383).

Fortean Times (20 Paul St., Frome, Somerset BA11 1DX, UK).

Skeptical Inquirer (PO Box 229, Buffalo, NY 14215-0229).

Strange (PO Box 2246, Rockville, MD 20847).

UFO (PO Box 1053, Sunland, CA 91041)

'Zines

Factsheet Five (R. Seth Friedman, ed. PO Box 170099, San Francisco, CA 94117).

Off The Deep End (Tim Cridland, ed. PO Box 85874, Seattle, WA 98145).

Would You Believe? (Armand Laprade, ed. HC 80, Box 156, Marshall, AR 72650)

PART I

RELIGION

As Sayyid Al Immam Issa Al Haadi Al Mahdi (Isa Muhammad). *Leviathan 666.* Brooklyn, NY: The Original Tents of Kedar, 1971, 1990.

As Sayyid Al Immam Issa Al Haadi Al Mahdi (Isa Muhammad). *The Paleman.* Brooklyn, NY: The Original Tents of Kedar, 1975, 1990.

Barrettt, Leonard E. Sr. *The Rastafarians.* Boston: Beacon Press, 1977, 1988.

Burridge, Kenelm. *New Heaven, New Earth.* Oxford & New York: Basil Blackwell, Ltd., 1969.

Cohen, Daniel. *Waiting for the Apocalypse.* Buffalo, NY: Prometheus Books, 1983.

Eliade, Mircea. *The Myth of the Eternal Return or, Cosmos and History.* Princeton, NJ: Princeton University Press, 1954.

Greenstone, Julius. *The Messiah Idea in Jewish History.* Philadelphia: Jewish Publication Society of America, 1906.

Haddad, Yvonne Yazbeck and Smith, Jane Idleman. *Mission to America: Five Islamic Sectarian Communities in North America.* Gainesville, FL: University Press of Florida, 1993.

"Jail for Mr. Jeffers Via His Golden Chariot," *The American Weekly,* 6/3/45.

Jacobs, Virginia Lee. *Roots of Rastafari.* San Diego: Avant Books, 1985.

Lincoln, C. Eric. *The Black Muslims in America.* Revised edition, Boston: Beacon Press, 1961, 1973.

Lounds, Morris, Jr. *Israel's Black Hebrews: Black Americans in Search of Identity.* Washington, DC: University Press of America, 1981.

Malcolm X, with the assistance of Alex Haley. The Autobiography of Malcolm X. New York: Grove Press, 1964.

Marsh, Clifton E. *From Black Muslims to Muslims: The Transition from Separatism to Islam,* 1930-1980. Metuchen, NJ & London: The Scarecrow Press, 1984.

Muhammad, Elijah. *How to Eat to Live.* Bronx, NY: Sabazz Publications, 1967.

Muhammad, Elijah, *Message to the Blackman in America.* Chicago: Muhammad's Temple No. 2, 1965.

Prince-A-Cuba, "Black Gods of the Inner City," *Gnosis* #25, 1992.

Rex, Möbius. *Prophecy: A History of the Future.* Berkeley, CA: Rex Research, 1986.

Roy, Ralph Lord. *Apostles of Discord.* Boston: Beacon Press, 1953.

Saxon, Wm. Norman. *The Mask of Edom.* Merrimac, MA: Destiny Publishers, 1985.

Smith, Worth. Miracle of the Ages — The Great Pyramid. Holyoke, MA: The Elizabeth Towne Co., Inc., 1934.

Thrupp, Sylvia, ed. *Millennial Dreams in Action.* The Hague: Mouton, 1962.

Weber, Timothy P. *Living in the Shadow of the Second Coming: American Premillennialism, 1875-1982.* Chicago & London: The University of Chicago Press, 1983, 1987.

Welsh, Melinda. "Sacramento's Army of God," *Sacramento News & Review,* 5/4/89.

Wilson, Peter Lamborn, Scandal: Essays in Islamic Heresy. Brooklyn, NY: Autonomedia, 1988.

Wilson, Peter Lamborn. "Shoot-Out at the Circle 7 Koran: Noble Drew Ali and the Moorish Science Temple," *Gnosis* #12, 1989.

Worsley, Peter. *The Trumpet Shall Sound: A Study of "Cargo" Cults in Melanesia.* New York: Schocken Books, 1968.

PART II

SCIENCE

Anti-Gravity Articles #1 (Infolio A12-AG1). Jean, NV: Rex Research.

Browning, Iben & Winkless, Nels. *Robots on Your Doorstep.* Portland, OR: Robotics Press, 1978.

Browning, Iben. *Climate and the Affairs of Men.* Burlington, VT: Fraser Publishing, 1975, 1987.

Browning, Iben & Evelyn Garriss. *Past and Future History: A Planner's Guide.* Burlington, VT: Fraser Publishing, 1981.

Carmer, Carl. Dark *Trees to the Wind: A Cycle of York State Years.* New York: William Sloane Associates, 1949.

Childress, David Hatcher, ed. *The Anti-Gravity Handbook.* Stelle, IL: Adventures Unlimited Press, 1985.

Cridland, Tim. Unpublished interview with Amanda Fielding, 7/27/93, London.

"Dutch Student Bores Hole in his Head to Prove Theory of Added Brain Activity," *Beyond,* Nov. 1969, Vol. 2, No. 15, pp. 69-71.

Ehret, Prof. Arnold. *Prof. Arnold Ehret's Mucusless Diet Healing System.* Beaumont, CA: Ehret Literature Publishing Company, 1922, 1977.

Ehret, Prof. Arnold. *Rational Fasting.* Beaumont, CA: Ehret Literature Publishing Company, 1975.

Fielding, Amanda. "Blood and Consciousness." New York: Glucocracy, 1978. (Published for the exhibition "Trepanation for the National Health" at PS1, New York.)

Hassel, William F., PhD. "Future Physics and Anti-Gravity," MUFON Symposium Proceedings. Seguin, TX: MUFON, 1977.

Hollingshead, Michael. *The Man Who Turned on the World.* New York: Abelard-Schuman Limited, 1973.

Huges, Bart & Mellen, Joe, a dialogue in *The Transatlantic Review,* Number 23, Winter 1966-7, London.

Koresh. *The Cellular Cosmogony.* Estero, FL: The Koreshan Unity, 1921.

Rainard, Robert Lynn. *In the Name of Humanity: The Koreshan Unity.* Unpublished Master's Thesis, University of South Florida, 1974.

Royce, Damian and Zolot, Jason. *Did God Destroy the Dinosaurs?* 1992.

Schadewald, Robert. "Some Like It Flat: A Brief History of the Flat Earth Movement," *The Fringes of Reason* (edited by Ted Schultz). New York: Harmony Books, 1989.

Schadewald, Robert. "The Earth was Flat in Zion," *Fate,* May 1989.

Seike, Shinichi. *The Principles of Ultra Relativity.* Uwajima City, Japan: Gravity Research Laboratory, 1969, 1978.

Wave Theory of Gravitation (INFOLIO S7-SEE). Jean, NV: Rex Research.

PART III

METAPHYSICS

Barker, Gray. *Men In Black: The Secret Terror Among Us.* Jane Lew, WV: New Age Press, 1982.

Brown, Anthony Cave. *A Bodyguard of Lies.* New York: Bantam, 1976.

Doreal, M. *Adam and the Pre-Adamites.* Castle Rock, CO: Brotherhood of the White Temple.

Doreal, M. *Armageddon Plan for Safety.* Castle Rock, CO: Brotherhood of the White Temple.

Doreal, M. *Mysteries of Mt. Shasta.* Castle Rock, CO: Brotherhood of the White Temple.

Doreal, M. *Mystery of the Moon.* Castle Rock, CO: Brotherhood of the White Temple.

Doreal, M. *Polar Paradise.* Castle Rock, CO: Brotherhood of the White Temple.

Doreal, M. *The Inner Earth.* Castle Rock, CO: Brotherhood of the White Temple.

Doreal, M. *The Ten Lost Tribes of Israel.* Castle Rock, CO: Brotherhood of the White Temple.

The Hierarchical Minds. A Pictorial Tour of Unarius. El Cajon, CA: Unarius Educational Foundation, 1982.

Immortality Unveiled. Ft. Lauderdale, FL: World Ionization Institute, 1985.

Kueshana, Eklal. *The Ultimate Frontier.* Stelle, Illinois: The Stelle Group, 1963.

McClure, Kevin. "The UFO Cults," *Phenomenon: Forty Years of Flying Saucers.* John Spencer and Hilary Evans, Eds. New York: Avon Books, 1989.

Marranzino, Pasquale. "Denver Mystic is Constructing Atomic Armageddon Refuge," *Rocky Mountain News,* 8/30/46.

Mehle, Michael. "Mountain Village Fights Cult Image," *Rocky Mountain News,* 10/14/90.

Noone, Richard W. *5/5/2000 ICE: THE ULTIMATE DISASTER.* New York: Harmony Books, 1982.

Norman, Ruth, et. al. *The Masters Speak: Vol. 8, Part 1.* El Cajon, CA: The Unarius Science of Life, 1975.

White, John. *Pole Shift.* New York: Doubleday, 1980.

Zuckerman, Leo. "Science Fantasy Hailed as Best Fiction," *Rocky Mountain News,* 6/2/55.

Part IV

Politics

Crabtree, Ray. *View of Life and Things.* New York: Crabtree & Co., 1974.

Farrell, V.L.A., compiler. *LAWSON: From Bootblack to Emancipator.* Detroit, MI: Humanity Benefactor Foundation, 1934.

Lawson, Alfred. *Creation.* Melvindale, MI: Humanity Publishing Company, 1931.

Lawson, Alfred. *Direct Credits for Everybody.* Melvindale, MI: Humanity Publishing Company, 1931, 1945.

Lawson, Alfred. *Lawsonomy, Vol. I, God's Physical Manifestation.* Melvindale, MI: Humanity Publishing, 1922, 1923, 1931, 1935.

Lawson, Alfred. *Manlife.* Melvindale, MI: Humanity Benefactor Foundation, 1923.

Russell, Woody, ed. *National Hobby News,* (PO Box 612, New Philadelphia, Ohio, 44663).

"Tale of a Plot to Rid Earth of Humankind," *San Francisco Examiner,* 4/14/91.

Trebay, Guy. "Urban Underdevelopment." *Village Voice,* 3/13/90.

Part V

Conspiracy

Constable, Trevor James. *The Cosmic Pulse of Life.* Tustin, CA: Merlin Press, 1976.

Constable, Trevor James. "UFOs Are Living Creatures," *UFO Report,* Fall, 1975.

Constable, Trevor James. "Ahrimanic Control of the Earth," *Critique* #28.

Cooper, Vicki. "The UFO Fascists," *UFO,* Vol. 7, No. 4, 1992.

Cooper, William. *Behold a Pale Horse.* Sedona, AZ: Light Technology Publishing, 1991.

Bane, Bernard M. *The Bane in Kennedy's Existence.* Boston: BMB Publishing Company, 1967.

Bane, Bernard M. *The Grand Model of Mind.* Boston: Forum Publishing Company, 1962.

Cox, Norma. *The Holyland Above and Below.* Marshall, AR: Secrets, 1987.

Ecker, Don. "The Whistleblowers — Part 1: Focus on Bill Cooper," *UFO,* Vol. 5, No 4., 1990.

Trachtenberg, Joshua. *The Devil and the Jews.* Philadelphia: The Jewish Publication Society of America, 1943.

Part VI

Enigmas

The Dream Lives On... The House on the Rock. House on the Rock Executive Staff, ND.

Laffoley, Paul. "Elements of the Time Machine: Homage to H.G. Wells," *Journal of the US Psychotronics Association,* Summer, 1990.

Laffoley, Paul. *The Phenomenology of Revelation.* New York: Kent Fine Art, 1989.

Moe, Doug. *Alex Jordan: Architect of his Own Dream.* Spring Green, WI: House of Wyoming Valley, Inc., ND.

Steiger, Brad. *Gods of Aquarius: UFOs and the Transformation of Man.* New York: Harcourt Brace Jovanovich, 1976.

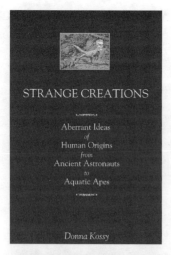

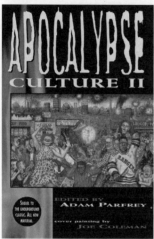